MOS and Special-Purpose Bipolar Integrated Circuits and R-F Power Transistor Circuit Design

TEXAS INSTRUMENTS ELECTRONICS SERIES

Applications Laboratory Staff of Texas Instruments Incorporated ■ DIGITAL INTEGRATED CIRCUITS AND OPERATIONAL-AMPLIFIER AND OPTO-ELECTRONIC CIRCUIT DESIGN

Applications Laboratory Staff of Texas Instruments Incorporated ■ ELECTRONIC POWER CONTROL AND DIGITAL TECHNIQUES

Applications Laboratory Staff of Texas Instruments Incorporated ■ MOS AND SPECIAL-PURPOSE BIPOLAR INTEGRATED CIRCUITS AND R-F POWER TRANSISTOR CIRCUIT DESIGN

Carr and Mize ■ MOS/LSI DESIGN AND APPLICATION

Crawford ■ MOSFET IN CIRCUIT DESIGN

Delhom ■ DESIGN AND APPLICATION OF TRANSISTOR SWITCHING CIRCUITS

The Engineering Staff of Texas Instruments Incorporated ■ CIRCUIT DESIGN FOR AUDIO, AM/FM, AND TV

The Engineering Staff of Texas Instruments Incorporated ■ SOLID-STATE COMMUNICATIONS

The Engineering Staff of Texas Instruments Incorporated ■ TRANSISTOR CIRCUIT DESIGN

The IC Applications Staff of Texas Instruments Incorporated ■ DESIGNING WITH TTL INTEGRATED CIRCUITS

Hibberd ■ INTEGRATED CIRCUITS

Hibberd ■ SOLID-STATE ELECTRONICS

Kane and Larrabee ■ CHARACTERIZATION OF SEMICONDUCTOR MATERIALS

Luecke, Mize, and Carr ■ SEMICONDUCTOR MEMORY DESIGN AND APPLICATION

Runyan ■ SEMICONDUCTOR MEASUREMENTS AND INSTRUMENTATION

Runyan ■ SILICON SEMICONDUCTOR TECHNOLOGY

Sevin ■ FIELD-EFFECT TRANSISTORS

MOS and Special-Purpose Bipolar Integrated Circuits and R-F Power Transistor Circuit Design

Edited by
BRYAN NORRIS

Manager, Applications Laboratory
Texas Instruments Limited

McGRAW-HILL BOOK COMPANY

New York St. Louis San Francisco Auckland Bogotá
Düsseldorf Johannesburg London Madrid Mexico
Montreal New Delhi Panama Paris São Paulo
Singapore Sydney Tokyo Toronto

Library of Congress Cataloging in Publication Data
Main entry under title:

MOS and special-purpose bipolar integrated circuits and
R-F power transistor circuit design.

(Texas Instruments electronics series)
Includes bibliographical references and index.
1. Integrated circuits. 2. Metal oxide semiconductors. 3. Field-effect transistors. I. Norris, Bryan.
TK7874.M18 621.3815'3'042 76-41175
ISBN 0-07-063751-2

1234567890 HDBP 785432109876

Contents

SECTION 1. MOS INTEGRATED CIRCUITS

SECTION 2. SPECIAL PURPOSE BIPOLAR INTEGRATED CIRCUITS

SECTION 3. FIELD EFFECT TRANSISTORS

SECTION 4. RADIO FREQUENCY POWER APPLICATIONS

Preface

The aim of this book is to provide up to date information on a broad range of semiconductors, and to give straightforward examples of how the devices may be used in practice. All the chapters have therefore been written by practising professional engineers with these aims in view.

The chapters in this book on Circuit Design cover a wide range of semiconductor devices and I have grouped them into broad device-type sections. These are MOS Integrated Circuits, Special Purpose Bipolar Integrated Circuits, Field Effect Transistors and Radio Frequency Power Transistors. The first chapter of each section is of an introductory nature.

In the first section on MOS I.C.s the Applications Chapters cover what are, in my opinion, the most important areas: Memory, Terminals, Computational and Interconnecting or Interfacing with other devices.

A wide range of special bipolar integrated circuits exists today but only a small number of their applications can be described. However, the spectrum is covered from circuits which are mainly digital with linear peripherals, such as Line Drivers and Receivers and Read-Only Memories, to completely linear circuits, such as the Double Balanced Mixer and the Audio Power Amplifier.

The major areas in which the FET is used, i.e. R.F. applications, high impedance and switching or 'chopping' circuits, are described in specific chapters of the third section.

Finally, the chapters of the fourth section explain the use of power transistors in tuned and single-sideband amplifiers and as frequency multipliers.

I should like to thank all the authors – for without their efforts this book would obviously not exist – and in particular, my colleague, David Bonham, for his help in tying up the loose ends.

BRYAN NORRIS

Applications Manager
Texas Instruments Limited

SECTION 1.

MOS INTEGRATED CIRCUITS

I PROCESS TECHNOLOGIES

by
Howard Cook

To understand why metal-oxide-silicon, MOS, technologies are used for the manufacture of digital integrated circuits to the extent that they are today, it is necessary to examine the basic device and manufacturing processes which are used in its implementation. As opposed to bipolar processes which use the conventional pnp or npn bipolar transistors as the basic circuit elements, MOS processes rely on the field effect transistor (FET) principles.

BASIC CONSTRUCTION

Figure 1 shows the basic construction of a p channel MOS FET and its schematic symbol. The n type substrate has two p type diffusions in its surface which form the Source and Drain of the device. A thin layer of silicon dioxide covers the area of the n type substrate between the Source and Drain diffusion. An aluminium electrode is deposited on the surface of this oxide layer and forms the Gate electrode. With no bias voltage applied between the gate electrode and n type substrate, there is no conduction path between the two p type diffusions. However, if a negative bias is applied to the gate electrode, the field beneath the electrode may be sufficient to cause the n type substrate material in this area to invert and become p type, thus forming a conduction channel between the two p type diffusions[1]. The applied gate voltage at which this conduction channel just begins to form is called the 'threshold voltage' of the device. In this case, since the conduction channel is formed by the n type material inverting to p type, this is called a p channel device.

Most of the advantages of this type of device arise from two main features. The first of these features is the very high input impedance and isolation between source and drain. This allows the driver device to fan out to many similar devices in a circuit, since no input dc current is drawn, and also, to isolate charge on capacitive nodes of a circuit, giving rise to a data storage facility. This can be used to construct dynamic circuits, where the power supply to the circuit is disconnected for the majority of the time to reduce power dissipation. Another feature of the MOSFET is that it exhibits bilateral symmetry. The same device may be used to both charge or discharge the subsequent node in the circuit, thus reducing the number of devices necessary to implement many functions. A further advantage of MOS devices is the much lower number of process steps required to fabricate an active element compared with bipolar processing. Although the basic model

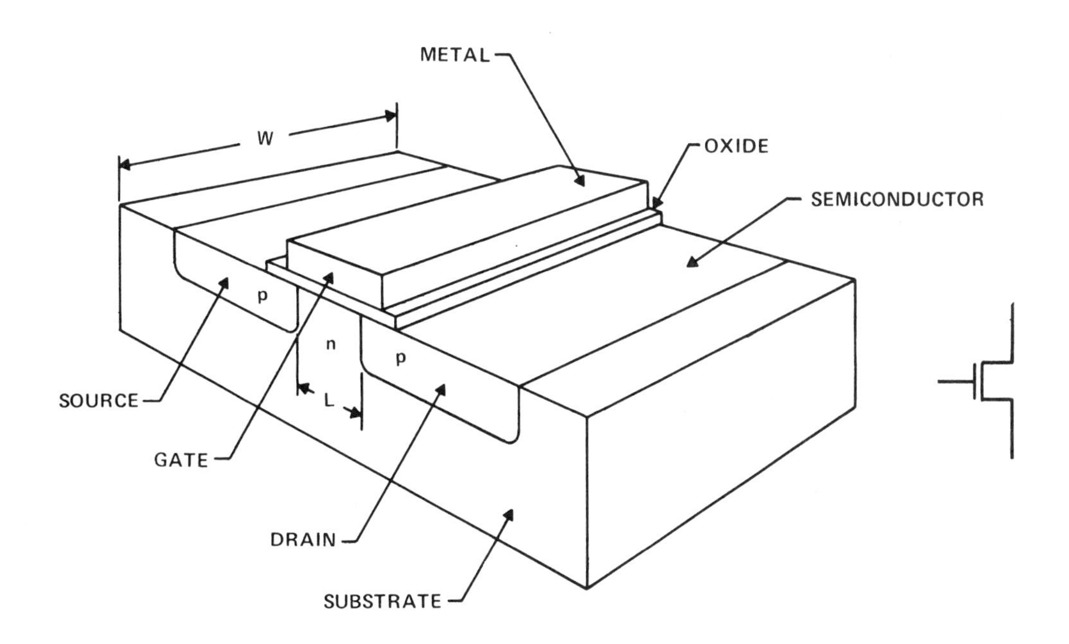

FIGURE 1. Basic Construction and Schematic Symbol

shown in Figure 1 is somewhat idealised, it does resemble the most simple of the current processing techniques, i.e. the standard thick oxide process.

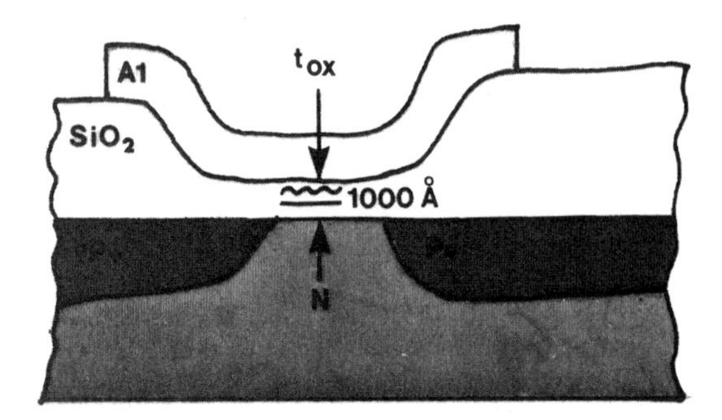

FIGURE 2. Standard Thick Oxide MOS Process

STANDARD THICK OXIDE PROCESS

In practice, the diffusion areas and metal depositions cannot be controlled to the extent suggested by the drawing in Figure 1 and the more irregular appearance shown in Figure 2 is nearer to the actual shapes of these areas. It can be seen that there is considerable overlap between the gate metal electrode and the source and drain diffusions. This gives rise to appreciable capacitances between these electrodes as well as from the electrodes to the substrate. A second feature of this simple device is that threshold voltage is too high, ≏ 4V, for the device to be directly compatible with TTL.

As already stated, the threshold voltage of an FET is the applied gate bias at which the conduction channel just forms. If this device is to be driven from a common saturated transistor logic family, such as T.T.L., then it is necessary for the threshold voltage of the FET to be similar to the voltage switching levels of the logic family. For operation with T.T.L. this should be in the region of 2·2V. If the threshold voltage is not directly compatible with the logic family, then it becomes necessary to interface either passively or actively, between the logic system and the MOS system, as described in Chapter V.

The threshold voltage can be derived from the expression:

$$V_T = \Phi_{MS} - \frac{Q_s}{C_{ox}} + 2.\phi_f - \frac{Q_b}{C_{ox}}$$

where

V_T = Threshold voltage
Φ_{MS} = Work function metal – silicon
Q_s = Charge per unit surface area at silicon-oxide interface
C_{ox} = Gate capacitance corresponding to oxide over channel area
ϕ_f = Fermi potential
Q_b = Bulk charge/unit area associated with channel depletion region

It can be seen that a significant factor in this expression is the capacitance C_{ox} and increasing this gives rise to a lower value of threshold voltage V_T. The value of capacitance C_{ox} is given by

$$C_{ox} = \frac{\epsilon_o \times \epsilon_{ox}}{t_{ox}}$$

where

t_{ox} = Gate oxide thickness
ϵ_{ox} = Relative permittivity of oxide
ϵ_o = Permittivity of free space (constant)

Hence the capacitance of the gate region can be increased by reducing the thickness of the gate oxide layer, or by changing the insulating material in the gate region from oxide to another material with higher relative permittivity. Reducing the oxide thickness can cause problems in production yields and repeatability, but using a higher permittivity material is feasible, and this method gives rise to the Nitride MOS process.

NITRIDE PROCESS

Figure 3 shows the construction of a device using this process. The oxide layer in the gate region has been reduced in thickness compared with the standard thick oxide process, but a layer of Silicon Nitride, Si_3N_4, has been added making the total thickness of the gate insulator t_{ox}. This is normally the same value as t_{ox} for the thick oxide process but the permittivity of the gate insulator is increased by the use of the nitride layer, which has a higher value of ϵ than the oxide. This arrangement gives rise to a lower threshold voltage and the device can be made TTL compatible by using a negative voltage rail in the order of −12V. It is not possible to entirely replace the oxide layer with nitride due to effects at the nitride – substrate interface causing variations in V_T. The stability of the threshold voltage is one factor which limits the extent to which this process technique may be applied, although it does have an extra advantage, in that the nitride layer acts as a good surface protection against contamination.

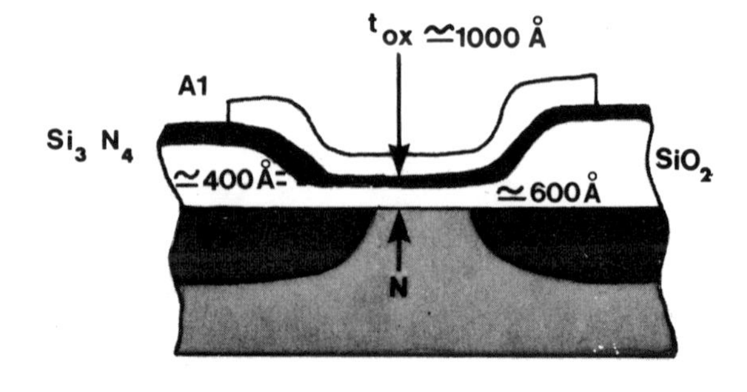

FIGURE 3. Nitride MOS Process

Table 1

STANDARD THICK OXIDE MOS PROCESS	
ADVANTAGES	DISADVANTAGES
● SIMPLE PROCESS ● LOW COST ● WELL PROVEN AND UNDERSTOOD ● RELIABILITY ESTABLISHED ● INDUSTRY STANDARD–WIDE SECOND SOURCING	● NON-TTL COMPATIBLE ($V_T = -4{\cdot}0V$) ● +12, – 12V POWER RAIL NEEDED FOR TTL COMPATIBILITY ● POOR SPEED POWER PERFORMANCE
NITRIDE MOS PROCESS	
ADVANTAGES	DISADVANTAGES
● SIMPLE PROCESS ● TTL COMPATIBILITY ($V_T = -2$ to $-2.5V$) ● LOW COST/HIGH YIELD ● IMPROVED DENSITY	● THRESHOLD STABILITY ● POOR SPEED/POWER PERFORMANCE ● –12V RAIL NEEDED IN TTL SYSTEM

Table 1 shows a comparison of the advantages and disadvantages of these two processes. They are both simple processes using few steps in production and capable of giving high production yields. This gives rise to low cost, and good reliability. Both processes suffer from a poor speed power performance figure, due to the relatively high values of inter-electrode (gate-source, gate-drain, and source-drain) capacitances.

A method of improving the speed/power performance by reducing inter-electrode capacitance is by using an ion implantation technique to achieve the doping of the source and drain areas of the chip. Ions of the dopant material are accelerated to high velocity and directed at the surface of the chip. By adjusting the accelerating voltage, the energy of the ion beam can be controlled, and thus the depth of penetration of the ions into the surface of the silicon can also be controlled. Thin layers of silicon oxide will be transparent to the ion beam, but thick oxide areas will stop the ions from being absorbed. Figure 4 shows how this may be used to accurately define the edges of the source and drain diffusions by using the gate metal electrode to mask the gate oxide area from the ion beam. The thin oxide layer at the sides of the gate electrode allows the beam to penetrate to the surface of the substrate and form the edges of the p diffusions. This gives rise to a much smaller overlap between the gate and the source and drain. The ion beam can also be used to modify the doping of the substrate surface in the conduction channel, thus modifying the threshold voltage of the device. Using this method, the threshold voltage can be made as small as required, and, in fact, can be made zero, or even positive. This latter condition would mean that the device would be normally 'on' and would only turn 'off' at a positive value of gate bias. Such devices are useful as Depletion Mode load devices in place of conventional Enhancement Mode load devices which operate in the usual way, (negative V_T).

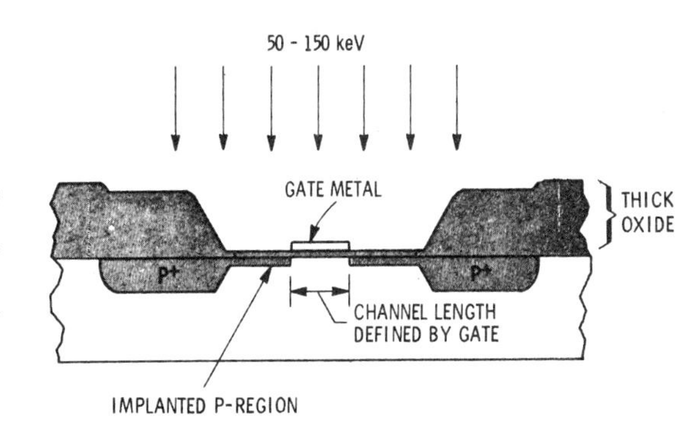

FIGURE 4. Ion Implant Process

Figure 5 shows two inverters, one using a conventional enhancement load device, and the other using a depletion mode load. The graph shows the characteristics of these devices. It can be seen that the depletion mode device is always 'on' for negative V_{DS} and acts as a current source, supplying constant drain current.

SILICON GATE PROCESS

Another method used to accurately define the gate-source and gate-drain geometries is the Silicon Gate process. In this construction the gate electrode is made of polycrystalline silicon buried in silicon oxide, as shown in

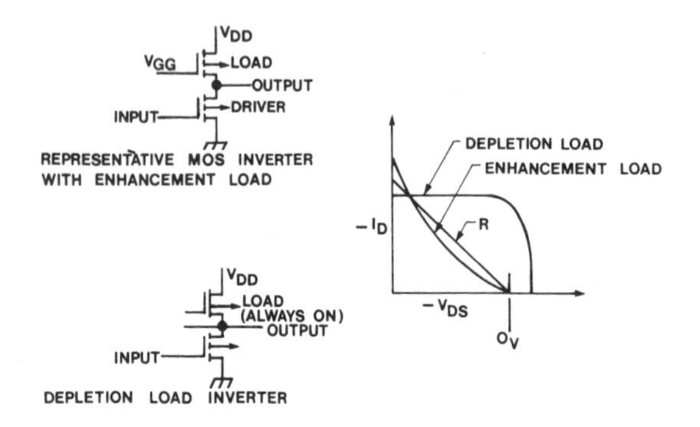

FIGURE 5. Load Devices and Load Lines

Figure 6. This has two main advantages. The first is that the polycrystalline silicon gate electrode may be used as a mask for the source and drain diffusions, thus making the correct alignment of gate, source and drain automatic. This gives rise to good manufacturing yields and lower inter-electrode capacitances. The second major advantage is that the polycrystalline silicon has a lower work function Φ_{MS} = 0·6V, than aluminium, giving rise to a lower threshold voltage. Devices made using this process may be directly TTL compatible, and are capable of a much better speed-power performance than the processes previously described.

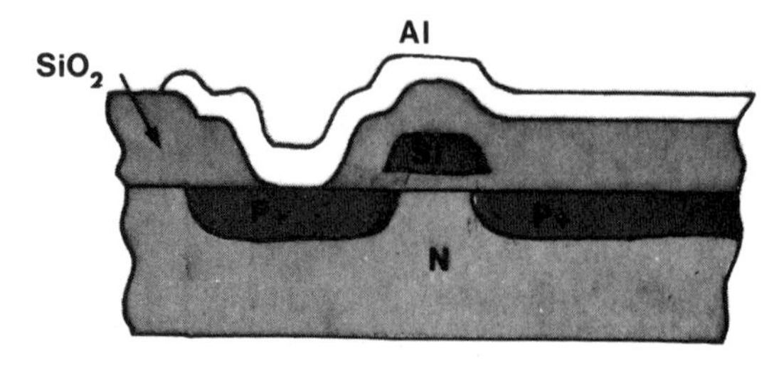

FIGURE 6. P Channel Silicon Gate

Table 2 shows a comparison of the silicon gate process with ion implant processes.

An additional advantage of the silicon gate process is the provision of another level of interconnection between devices on the same chip. As well as having a metal interconnection pattern on the surface, and the p+ diffusions under the surface, there is now the polycrystalline silicon conductor material buried in the oxide, which may be used for interconnecting.

All the examples discussed so far have used an 'n' type substrate inverting to a 'p' type conduction channel under the influence of negative gate bias, thus forming p channel devices. There is a major advantage in using the opposite type of construction, i.e. using a p substrate material with n+ diffusions into it. This relies on a conduction channel being formed by the p substrate material inverting to n type under the influence of a positive applied gate bias. In a n channel device, the majority carriers in the

Table 2

ION IMPLANT PROCESS	
ADVANTAGES	DISADVANTAGES
● SIMPLE PROCESS ● ESTABLISHED METAL GATE PROCESS ● HIGH YIELD (CONTROLLABLE V_T) ● GOOD SPEED/POWER PERFORMANCE ● TTL COMPATIBILITY POSSIBLE ● IMPROVED PACKING DENSITY POSSIBLE ● DEPLETION LOADS POSSIBLE	● ONLY 2 LEVELS INTERCONNECT (Si GATE =2½)
SILICON GATE PROCESS (P–CHANNEL)	
ADVANTAGES	DISADVANTAGES
● TTL COMPATIBILITY 2½ LEVEL INTERCONNECT CAPABILITY ● HIGHER DENSITY THAN METAL GATE ● BETTER SPEED/POWER THAN NITRIDE (SELF ALIGNED GATE)	● CONSIDERABLY MORE COMPLEX THAN METAL GATE ● HIGH PROCESS COST

Table 3

N–CHANNEL SILICON GATE	
ADVANTAGES	DISADVANTAGES
• EXCELLENT SPEED/POWER PERFORMANCE	• MORE COMPLEX PROCESS THAN METAL GATE
• 2½ LEVEL INTERCONNECT	• LOW FIELD THRESHOLD
• HIGHER PACKING DENSITY THAN P-CHANNEL Si GATE OR METAL GATE	
• TTL COMPATIBLE	
• SINGLE RAIL (5V) OPERATION POSSIBLE (DEPLETION LOADS)	

channel are electrons, which have a higher mobility than holes, giving rise to a much better speed/power performance. The advantages and disadvantages of this process are shown in Table 3.

So far, various methods of fabricating MOSFETS have been described with some of the basic parameters highlighted to justify the existence of all these processes to non-process engineers. There are other factors which are also important, such as the transconductance (g_m) which is defined [2] as

$$g_m = \frac{\partial I_D}{\partial V_G}\Big|_{V_D}$$

If the g_m per unit area is higher for a given process, then if all other conditions are equal, the device will operate at a faster speed. Alternatively, the size of the device can be reduced, without losing performance.

An expression from which g_m may be derived is:-

$$g_m = \frac{\mu.\epsilon_o.\epsilon_{ox}.W}{t_{ox}.L} \times (V_G - V_T)$$

where W and L are the device dimensions shown in Figure 1. From this expression it can be seen that with the nitride process, for example, where C_{ox} is increased, then the g_m of the device is increased.

COMPLEMENTARY MOS PROCESS

The MOS designer has available all these different processing techniques from which to choose the most suitable for the particular application. If the completed MOS device is not going to be used with any other type of logic family, then there is no need to strive to make the device, for example, TTL compatible. There is, however, another design technique which is gaining acceptance as being a major technology in MOS integrated circuit design. This is not so much a new process, but the concept of using both n channel and p channel devices in complementary pair configuration on the same chip, forming the basis of the Complementary MOS process. Figure 8 shows an n channel and a p channel FET both on the same n type substrate. To implement the n channel device (the right-hand FET) it is necessary to first diffuse a 'tub' of p type material, which not only takes up considerable chip area, but also substantially increases the number of process steps required. The major advantage of this complementary circuit design technique is that very low power dissipation may be achieved for a given function. The two devices in Figure 8 are shown in the schematic diagram, on the right-hand side, connected as an inverter. The gates are connected together, and hence when a logic 'high' level is applied to the gate, the n channel device will turn 'on' and the p channel device will turn 'off'. When a logic 'low' is applied at the input, the opposite will occur. Thus at no time is there a path for dc current to flow through the circuit. The only current that does flow is a transient during the change over time from 'high' to 'low' or 'low' to 'high' state. This gives rise to very low power dissipation at low operating frequencies, which is very useful for battery operated equipment, etc. However, as the frequency of operation increases, the power dissipation due to the current transient at changeover becomes more significant, and at approximately 2 MHz, the dissipation is equal to that of Schottky Low Power TTL (Series 74LS). This is shown in Figure 9.

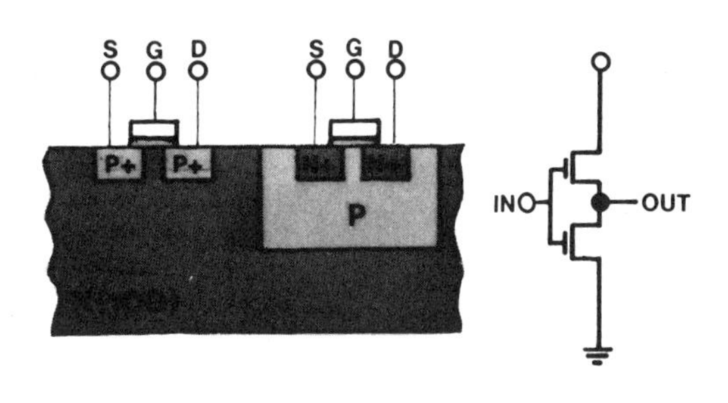

FIGURE 8. Basic Complementary MOS Construction

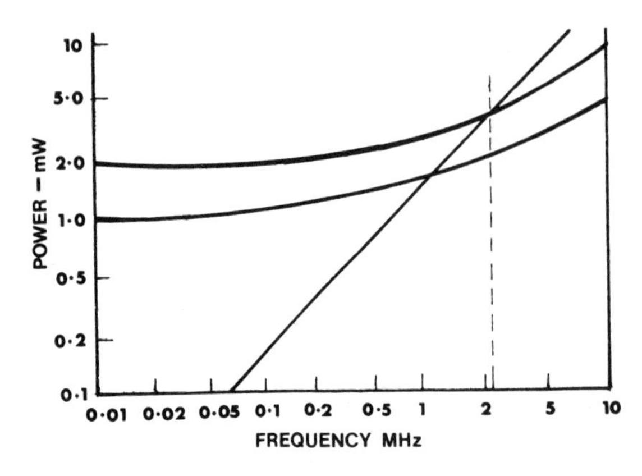

FIGURE 9. Comparison of CMOS and Bipolar Power Consumption with Operating Frequency

A summary of the salient features of all these processes is shown in the comparison chart of Table 4. As the process complexity increases down the table, so the process economy decreases. However, improvements in manufacturing techniques tend to keep pace with the increasing process complexity, and make these more sophisticated processes a viable proposition.

CHARGE COUPLED DEVICES

There is a new concept in MOS circuit design which does not use the FET as the basic element. Instead it relies on charge being driven from one stage of the circuit to the next stage by the electric field under a pattern of conductors on the surface of the device. By using multiphase clocks, the charge on one stage may be stepped through successive stages, giving rise to a very simple shift register structure. This is the principle of operation of Charge Coupled Devices (CCD).

Figure 10 shows a cross section through a CCD structure. The metal electrodes are connected to the three phases (ϕ_1, ϕ_2, ϕ_3,) of the system clock as shown. The bias applied to electrodes 1, 4, 7, etc. by clock ϕ_1, causes a 'well' in the depletion layer in the surface of the silicon substrate. Similarly, phases ϕ_2 and ϕ_3 cause 'wells' under

Table 4. Process Comparison

	SPEED POWER RATIO	PROCESS ECONOMY	TTL COMPATIBILITY	PACKING DENSITY	SPECIAL FEATURES
STANDARD THICK OXIDE		●●●●		●	
NITRIDE	●	●●●	●●	●	
ION IMPLANT	●●	●●●	●●●	●●	
SILICON GATE (P–CH)	●●	●●	●●	●●●	
SILICON GATE (N–CH)	●●●	●●	●●●	●●●●	HIGH SPEED–RAMs
COMPLEMENTARY	●●●●		●●●●		ULTRA LOW POWER

THE MORE ●● THE BETTER

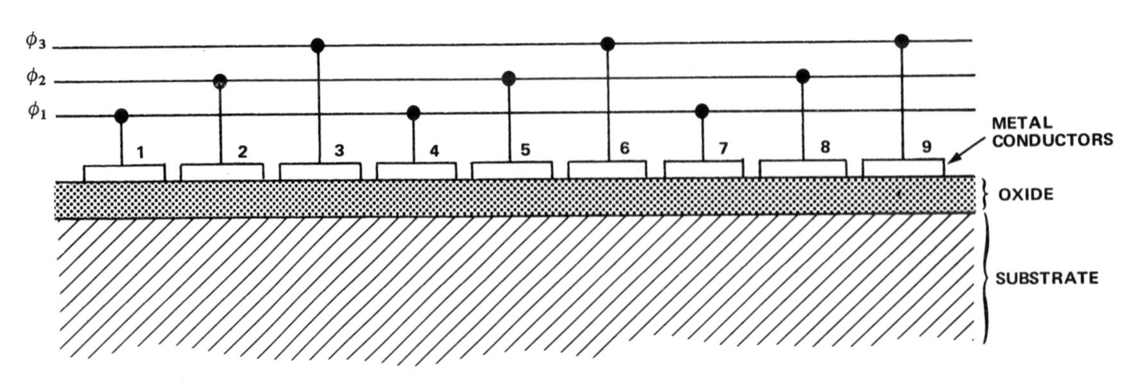

FIGURE 10. Cross Section Through CCD Structure

electrodes 2, 5, 8 etc. and 3, 6, 9 etc. As illustrated in Figure 11, a charge of minority carriers is injected into the depletion region at the beginning of the device (represented by - - -) and is propagated along the device by the action shown. In Figure 11(a), charge has been injected into the potential wells under the electrodes. In Figure 11(b), a larger bias has been applied to the ϕ_2 electrodes, causing a deeper potential 'well' under them. The stored charge then moves towards the deeper 'well'. Figure 11(c) shows that the ϕ_1 bias has been removed, and the charge remains isolated in the ϕ_2 'wells'. By applying a suitable sequence of potentials to the electrodes, the charge can be propagated along the full length of the device.

The stored charge constitutes the signal, and since, in theory, the full charge is transferred from stage to stage, operation can be digital or analogue. Hence this technology is suitable for digital shift registers, and analogue delay lines. Another field of application is for light image sensing, since light falling on the chip will modify the charge stored at each node according to the light intensity at that point. The construction geometry of these devices is extremely simple and gives rise to very high packing density of storage nodes. This, coupled with the small number of process steps required, makes CCD potentially a very low cost process, and the first devices using this technology are just beginning to appear.

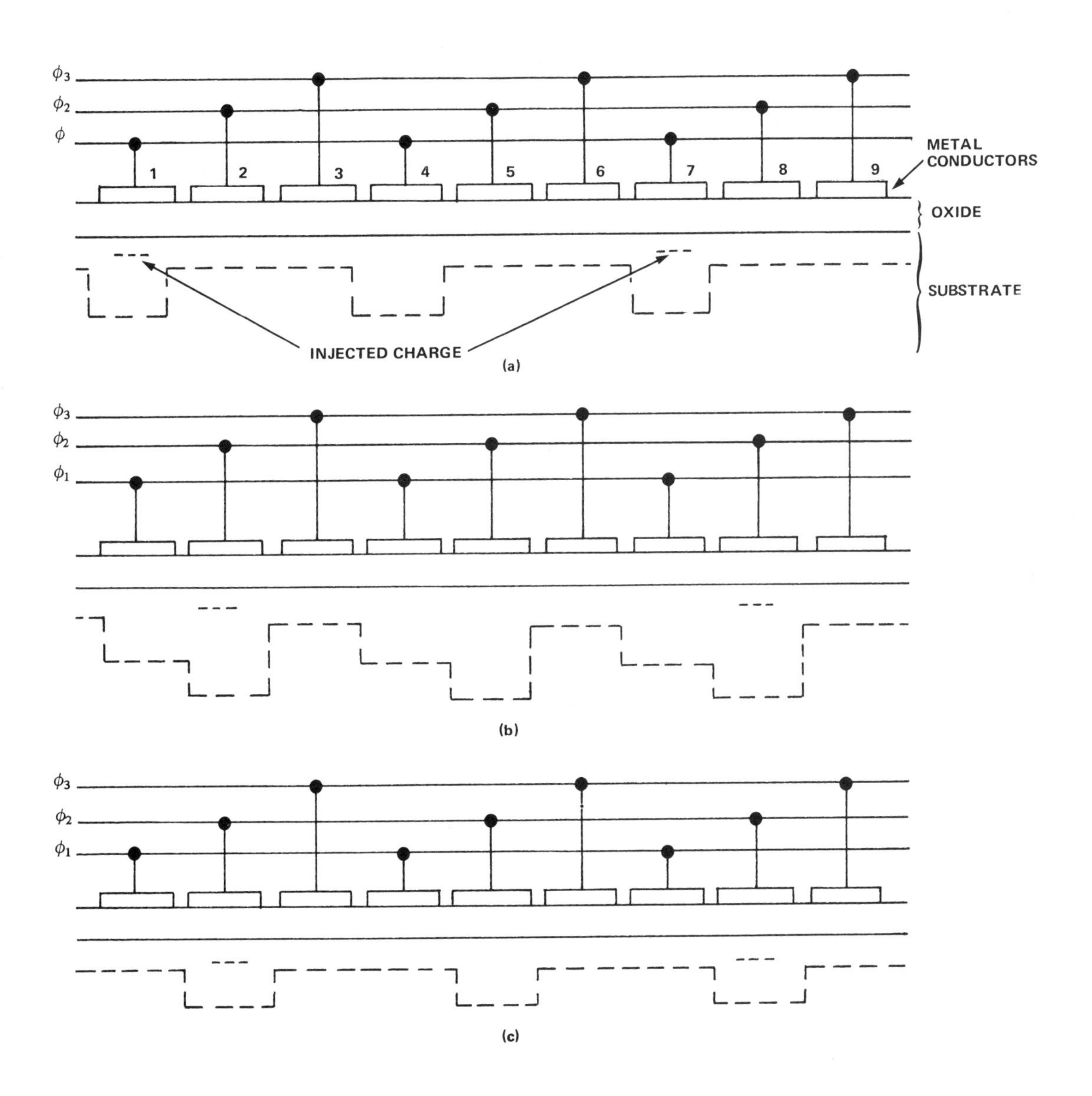

FIGURE 11. CCD Operation

REFERENCES

1. The Engineering Staff of A.M.I., *M.O.S. Integrated Circuits,* Van Nostrand, 1972.

2. Robert H. Crawford, *MOSFET in Circuit Design,* Texas Instruments Electronic Series, McGraw Hill, 1967.

II MOS IN TERMINALS

The functions performed by terminals are data processing operations such as entry, buffering, transmission/reception and the display of the digital data. MOS/LSI is particularly well suited for these functions.

Figure 1 shows a block diagram of a typical terminal system.

Relative to data processing times, the communications link varies from very slow to slow. Teletype grade lines are generally used for asynchronous transmissions and are limited to about 120 characters per second. Voice grade lines are used for synchronous data transmission and are good for about 600 characters per second. Wideband lease lines are available for up to 1200 characters per second. The modem on the end of the communication line prepares the data for transmission down a serial data channel.

RECEIVER/TRANSMITTER

Serial data from the line is accepted and translated to parallel data for use in the terminal. For transmission, the parallel data is converted to serial.

A device or subsystem, which is designed to perform these functions, is known as a Universal Asynchronous Receiver Transmitter (UART). An example of such a subsystem made using MOS technology is the TMS 6011 JC/NC UART.

Figure 2 shows a functional block diagram of the TMS 6011 JC/NC. The receiver section of this device will accept serial data from the transmission line and convert it to parallel data. The serial word will have start, data and stop bits. Parity may be generated and verified. The receiver section will validate the received data transmission by checking the proper parity, start and stop bits and convert the data to parallel. The transmitter section will accept parallel data, convert it to serial form and generate the start, parity, and stop bits. Receiver and transmitter sections are separate and the device can operate in full duplex mode.

To allow maximum flexibility of operation, the unit has also been designed as a fully programmable circuit. The device can operate either in full duplex (simultaneous transmission and reception) or in half duplex (alternate transmission and reception). The data word may be externally selected to be 5, 6, 7, or 8 bits long. The baud rate is externally selected by the clock frequency, which can vary between 0 and 160 Hz. The parity, which is generated in the transmit mode and verified in the receive mode, can be selected as either odd or even. It is also possible to disable the parity bit by inhibiting the parity generation and verifi-

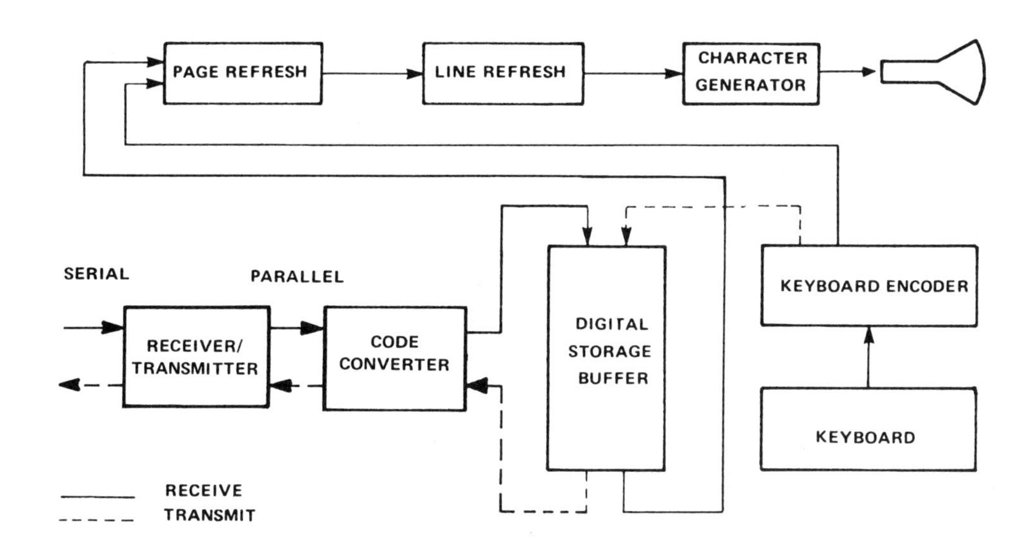

FIGURE 1. Block Diagram of a Typical Terminal System

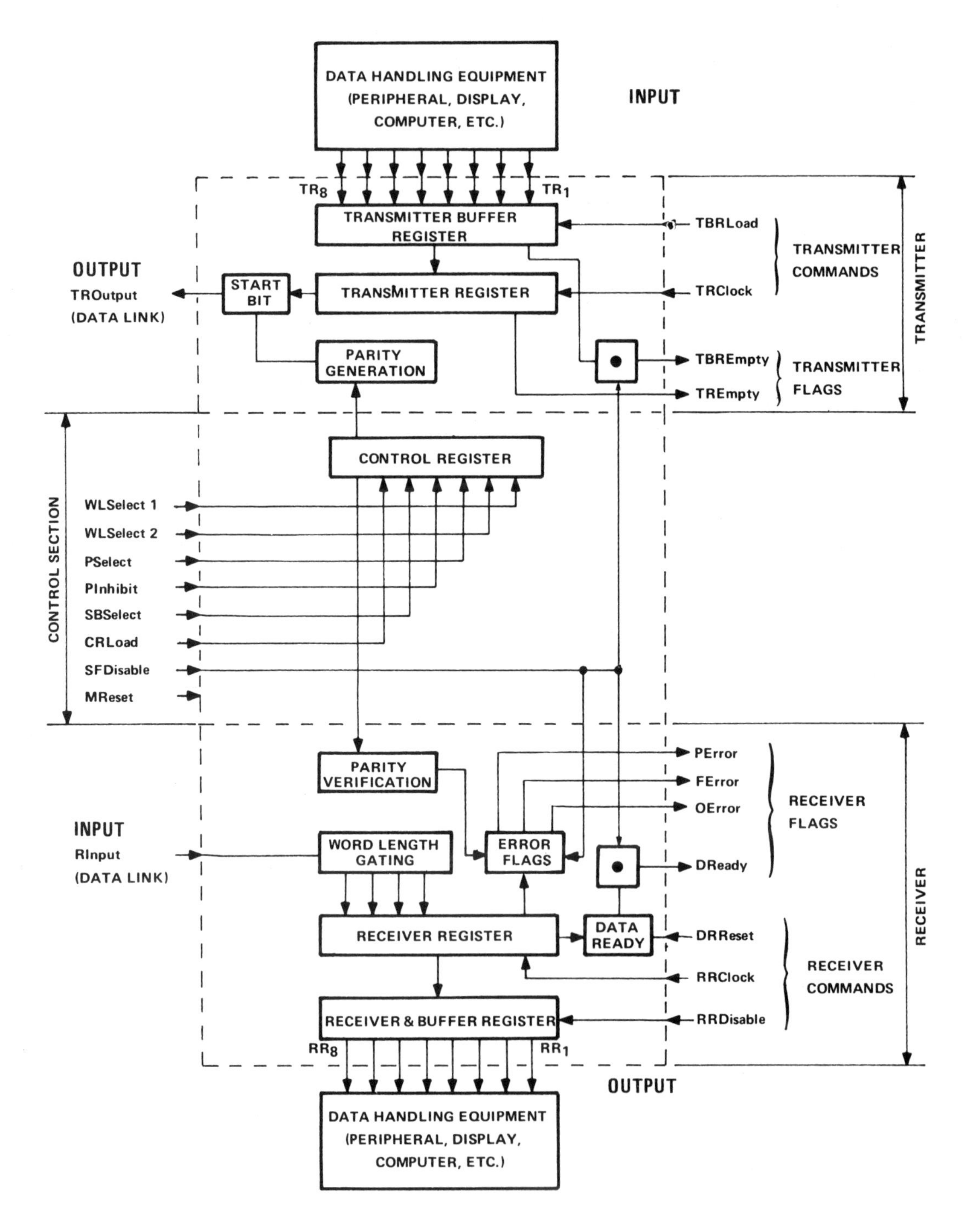

FIGURE 2. Functional Block Diagram of TMS 6011 JC/NC

cation. The stop bit can be selected as either a single- or double-bit stop. Static logic is used to maximize flexibility of operation and to simplify the task of the user. The data holding registers are static and will hold a data word until it is replaced by another word.

To allow for a wide range of possible configurations, triple-state push-pull buffers have been selected on all outputs except serial transmission and TREmpty flag. They allow the wire-OR configuration.

The subsystem can be used in a wide range of data handling equipment such as Modems, peripherals, printers, data displays, and minicomputers. By taking full advantage of the latest circuit design and processing techniques it has been possible to implement the entire transmit, receive, and format function necessary for digital data communication, in a single package, avoiding the cumbersome circuitry previously necessary.

P-channel enhancement-mode low-threshold technology permits the use of standard power supplies (+5 V, −12 V) as well as direct TTL/DTL interface. No external components are needed.

The operation of this device can be best understood by visualizing the subsystem as three separate sections: 1) transmitter, 2) receiver, and 3) common control. The transmitter and receiver sections are independent while the control section directs both receive and transmit.

Transmitter Section

The transmitter section will accept data in parallel form, serialize it, format it, and transmit it in serial form. Parallel input data is received on the transmitter buffer register data inputs TR1 through TR8. Serial output data is transmitted on the TROutput terminal. Input data is stored in the transmitter buffer register. A logic 'low' on the TBRLoad command terminal will load a character in the transmitter buffer register. If words of less than 8 bits are used, only the least significant bits are accepted. The character is justified into the least significant bit, TR1.

The data is transferred to the transmitter register when TBRLoad terminal goes from 'low' to 'high'. The loading of the transmitter register is delayed if the transmitter section is presently transmitting data. In this case the loading of the transmitter register is delayed until the transmission has been performed.

Data is transmitted in serial form on the TROutput terminal. The data is clocked out by TRClock. The clock rate is 16 times faster than the data rate. The data format is as follows: start bit, data, parity bit, stop bits (1 or 2). Start bits, parity bits, and stop bits are generated by the subsystem. When no data is transmitted the output TROutput sits at a logic 'high'. The start of the transmission is defined as the transition of TROutput from a logic high to a logic 'low'

Two flags are provided. A logic 'high' on the TBREmpty flag indicates that a word has been transferred to the transmitter register and that the transmitter buffer register is now ready to accept a new word. A logic 'high' on the TREmpty flag indicates that the transmitter section has completed the transmission of a complete word including stop bits. The TREmpty flag will sit at a logic 'high' until the start of transmission of a new word. Both transmitter buffer register and transmitter registers are static and will perform dc storage of data.

Receiver Section

The data is received in serial form on the receiver input RInput. The data is presented in parallel form on the eight data outputs RR1 through RR8. RInput is the data input terminal. The data from RInput enters the receiver register at a point determined by the character length, the parity, and the number of stop bits. RInput must be maintained high when no data is being received. The data is clocked through the RR clock. The clock rate is 16 times faster than the data rate. Data is transferred from the receiver register to the receiver buffer register and appears on the 8 RR outputs. The MOS output buffers used for the eight RR terminals are triple-state push-pull output buffers which permit the wire-OR configuration through use of the RRDisable terminal. When a logic 'high' is applied to RRDisable, the RR outputs are floating. If the word length is less than 8 bits, the most significant bits will be at a logic 'low'. The output word is right justified. RR1 is the least significant bit and RR8 is the most significant bit.

A logic 'low' applied to the DRReset terminal resets the DReady output to a logic 'low'. Several flags are provided in the receiver section. There are three error flags (parity error, framing error and overrun error) and a data-ready flag. All status flags may be disabled through a logic high on the SFDisable terminal.

A logic 'high' on the PError terminal indicates an error in parity. A logic 'high' on the OError terminal indicates an overrun. An overrun occurs when the previous word was not read, i.e., when the DReady line was not reset before the present data was transferred to the data receive holding register. A logic 'high' on the DReady terminal indicates that a word has been received, stored in the receiver buffer register and that the data is available on outputs RR1 through RR8. The DReady terminal can be reset through the DRReset terminal.

Common Control Section

The common control section directs both the receiver and the transmitter sections. The initialization of the subsystem is performed through the MReset terminal. The Master Reset is strobed to a logic 'high' after power turn-on to reset all registers and to reset the serial output line to a logic 'high'. All status flags (parity error, framing error, overrun error, data ready, transmitter buffer register) are disabled when the SEDisable is at a logic 'high'. When disabled, the status flags float. (3 state buffers in 3rd state). The number of bits per word is controlled by the WLSelect 1 and WLSelect 2 lines. The word length may be 5, 6, 7, or 8 bits.

The selection is as follows:

WORD LENGTH	WLS1	WLS2
5	Low	Low
6	Low	High
7	High	Low
8	High	High

The parity to be checked by the receiver and generated by the transmitter is determined by the PSelect line. A logic 'high' on the PSelect line selects even parity and a logic 'low' selects odd parity. The parity will not be checked or generated if a logic 'high' is applied to PInhibit; in this case the stop bit or bits will immediately follow the data bit. When a logic 'high' is applied to PInhibit, the PError status flag is brought to a logic 'low', indicating a no-parity error because parity is disregarded in this mode. To select either one or two stop bits, the SBSelect terminal is used. A logic 'high' on this terminal will result in two stop bits while a logic 'low' will produce only one. To load the control bits (WLSelect 1, WLSelect 2, PSelect, PInhibit, SBSelect) a logic 'high' is applied to the CRClock terminal. This terminal may be strobed or hardwired to a logic 'high'.

CODE CONVERTERS

A terminal system is designed to operate with one code, USASCII for example. For it to use information from sources using other than USASCII code, Selectric for example, a code converter must be included in the terminal system.

Codes are used to transfer information over data links between such equipment as peripherals, terminals, and computers.

A code word is a binary word that represents either an alphanumeric character or a command.

For instance:

The letter A is represented by 1000001	in USASCII code
The command DEL (delete) is represented by 1111111	in USASCII code

Depending on the code used, the size of the alphabet (characters and commands) may vary between 64 and 256. The number of bits in a common alphanumeric code word may vary between 6 and 8.

Many different codes are commonly used in data processing equipment. Equipment is built for a specific code and for that code only. To build a system from several pieces of data processing gear using different codes, it is necessary to convert codes.

MOS ROMs are ideally suited for code conversion. The code to be translated is fed at the input of the ROM and the output of the ROM represents the translated input code.

The most popular ROM size for code converter applications is the 2048-bit organized as 256 words x 8 bits. A ROM this size will handle all the usual codes for data transmission. (The most cumbersome code is the EBCDIC with room for 256 characters of 8 bits.) Because most codes use a 7-bit word and a 128-character alphabet, it is often possible to make a 2048-bit ROM, organized as 256 words of 8 bits, work both ways and not only translate code A into code B but also, upon command, translate B into A.

Codes and Their Definitions

An almost endless variety of codes exists for data transmission. This causes a problem because users have difficulty in agreeing on a code, and when they do they often modify it slightly for their own purposes. Some of the most popular codes are:

Hollerith: Hollerith is used on punched cards. It is a 12-bit code with a very large alphabet (256 characters and commands). This is the code used on the 80-column punched cards as shown in Figure 3. A normal card punch machine will only punch 64 characters. Because of these limitations, the Hollerith code is not generally used for data transmission.

BCD Code (Binary Coded Decimal): BCD is a very simple code with 64 characters of 6 bits. This is the code used with the new SYSTEM 3 IBM punched cards (96 columns, 6 bits/column).

EBCDIC (Extended Binary-Coded-Decimal Interchange Code): EBCDIC is a widely-used code with room for 256 characters of 8 bits as shown in Figure 4.

USASCII (USA Standard Code for Information Interchange): USASCII is the only code on which seems to agree with everybody throughout the world. The code uses 128 characters, 7 bits per character. Often, users are not interested in the full 128 characters and need only the 64 characters subset boxed within the table in Figure 5. In this case, only 6 bits per character are needed, and either b7 or b6 may be dropped.

The international version of USASCII is called ISO. The 7-bit ISO is almost identical to the USASCII, except that certain characters may be replaced by national characters (£ instead of $ for instance). The 6-bit ISO is obtained by dropping b_6.

Selectric Line Code: Because IBM Selectric Typewriters are commonly used as terminals, several Selectric codes are being used. The most common is the IBM Correspondence Selectric Line Code. It is a 7-digit 128-character code. A certain amount of logic is necessary to go from Selectric Line Code to Selectric Bail Code shown in Figure 6.

Baudot Code: A very simple 32-character 5-bit code, the Baudot is used mainly in teletype equipment, illustrated in Figure 7.

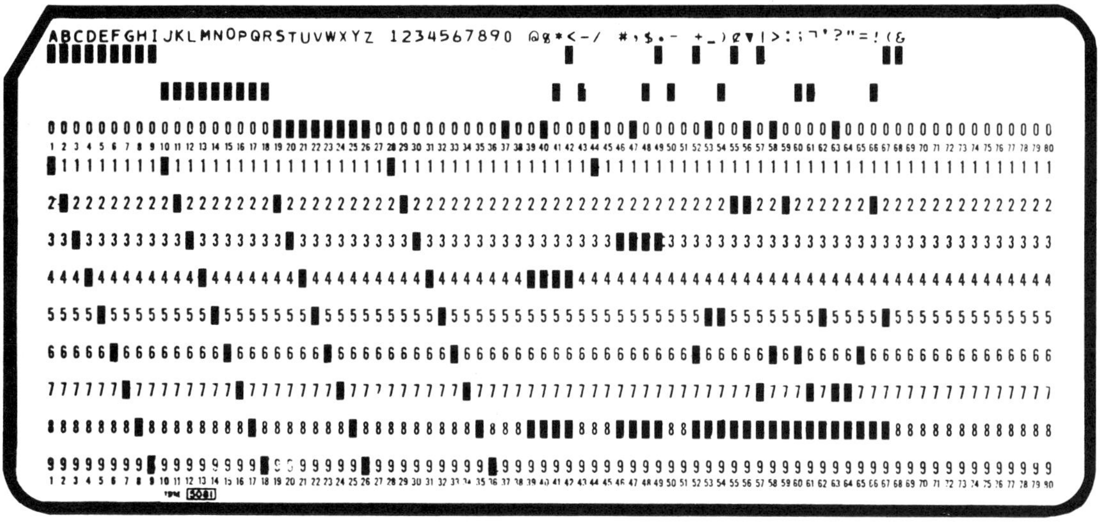

FIGURE 3. *Card with Hollerith Code*

b7 → b6 → b5 → Bits					0 0 0	0 0 1	0 1 0	0 1 1	1 0 0	1 0 1	1 1 0	1 1 1
b4 ↓	b3 ↓	b2 ↓	b1 ↓	Column → Row ↓	0	1	2	3	4	5	6	7
0	0	0	0	0	NUL	DLE	SP	0	@	P		p
0	0	0	1	1	SOH	DC1	!	1	A	Q	a	q
0	0	1	0	2	STX	DC2	"	2	B	R	b	r
0	0	1	1	3	ETX	DC3	#	3	C	S	c	s
0	1	0	0	4	EOT	DC4	$	4	D	T	d	t
0	1	0	1	5	ENQ	NAK	%	5	E	U	e	u
0	1	1	0	6	ACK	SYN	&	7	F	V	f	v
0	1	1	1	7	BEL	ETB	'	7	G	W	g	w
1	0	0	0	8	BS	CAN	(	8	H	X	h	x
1	0	0	1	9	HT	EM	)	9	I	Y	i	y
1	0	1	0	10	LF	SUB	*	:	J	Z	j	z
1	0	1	1	11	VT	ESC	+	;	K	[	k	{
1	1	0	0	12	FF	FS	,	<	L	\	l	¦
1	1	0	1	13	CR	GS	–	=	M	]	m	}
1	1	1	0	14	SO	RS	.	>	N	∧	n	~
1	1	1	1	15	SI	US	/	?	O	—	o	DEL

FIGURE 5. *USA Standard Code for Information Interchange (USASCII)*

b4	b5	b6	b7	Bits b0 b1 b2 b3 →	0000	0001	0010	0011	0100	0101	0110	0111	1000	1001	1010	1011	1100	1101	1110	1111
↓	↓	↓	↓	Row ↓ / Column →	0	1	2	3	4	5	6	7	8	9	10	11	12	13	14	15
0	0	0	0	0	NUL	DLE	DS		SP	&										0
0	0	0	1	1	SOH	DC1	SOS						a	j			A	J		1
0	0	1	0	2	STX	DC2	FS	SYN					b	k	s		B	K	S	2
0	0	1	1	3	ETX	TM							c	l	t		C	L	T	3
0	1	0	0	4	PF	RES	BYP	PN					d	m	u		D	M	U	4
0	1	0	1	5	HT	NL	LF	RS					e	n	v		E	N	V	5
0	1	1	0	6	LC	BS	EOB	UC					f	o	w		F	O	W	6
0	1	1	1	7	DL	IL	PRE	EOT					g	p	x		G	P	X	7
1	0	0	0	8		CAN							h	q	y		H	Q	Y	8
1	0	0	1	9		EM							i	r	z		I	R	Z	9
1	0	1	0	10	SMM	CC	SM		¢	!		:								
1	0	1	1	11	VT				.	$	,	#								
1	1	0	0	12	FF	IFS		DC4	<	*	%	@								
1	1	0	1	13	CR	IGS	ENQ	NAK	(	)	—	'								
1	1	1	0	14	SO	IRS	ACK		+	;	>	=								
1	1	1	1	15	SI	IUS	BEL	SUB	|	—	?	"								

FIGURE 4. Extended Binary-Coded-Decimal Interchange Code (EBCDIC)

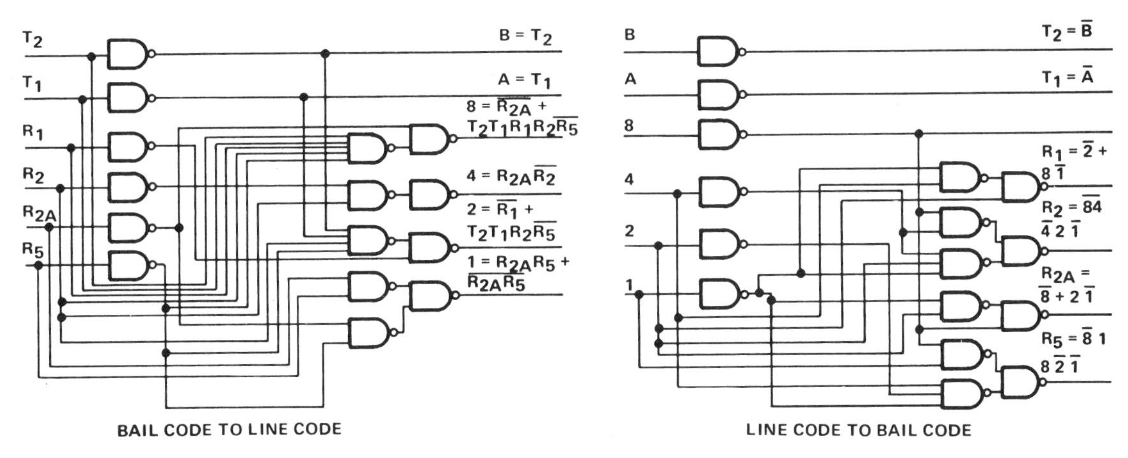

FIGURE 6. Conversion Necessary to go from Selectric Line Code to Selectric Bail Code and Vice-Versa.

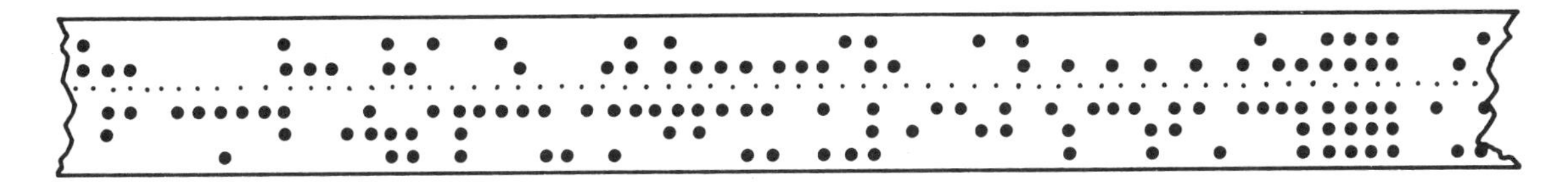

FIGURE 7. Example of Baudot Code

Other common codes include: IBM System 360 8-bit code, Honeywell 64 characters, GE 64 characters, UNIVAC 64 characters, Burroughs 64 characters, and IBM 47 characters.

Practical Implementation

The ROMs are very adaptable to code conversion and can be programmed for this application. Because of the wide variations within a code family, in each case a truth table of the codes to be converted is needed before the device can be implemented.

The particular device is determined by the number of codes, the number of characters in a code, and the number of bits in a code-word, e.g. TMS 4103 JC/NC ROM has 5 codes, 64 characters and 7 bits.

DIGITAL STORAGE BUFFERS (DSBs)

It is often necessary to buffer information between the transmission line and a terminal. The rate of data transmission sometimes may be different from the rate of display. Such a function may be accomplished through storage registers but in this case the data is not always available at the output. A good solution for this problem is the use of an organized digital storage buffer also called Silo Buffer.

An example of such a device is the TMS 4024 JC/NC whose functional block diagram is shown in Figure 8. This is a first-in first-out digital storage buffer that will store up to 64 nine-bit words. The major components of the device include a 9 x 64 dynamic random access memory (RAM), three shift counters, and comparison and control logic. A RAM-type organization results in zero ripple-through time. Data written at the input when the register is empty is immediately available on the output. The input and output are completely independent of each other. Input and output timing can be dependent on the clock timing (synchronous mode) or can be operated independently (asynchronous mode). The dynamic RAM requires two-phase continuous clocking at a specified minimum frequency. The clocks can be driven directly from TTL logic. Again low-threshold, thick-oxide, MOS p-channel enhancement-mode technology is employed to allow interfacing with TTL/DTL circuits without external components.

The device will process data at any desired rate from dc to one-half the continuous clock frequency. At a nominal 500 kHz clock rate the maximum data rate is 250 kHz. Data is processed in parallel format, word by word. Write and read commands are used to enter and dump data. Data entry and dump may be either synchronous or asynchronous (in relation to the clock). Asynchronous operation is limited to data rates of less than one-third of the clock frequency. A positive-going edge on the read or write line is recognised as a command. It must occur while $\phi1$ is 'high' for synchronous operation. A write command causes the data present on the input to be transferred into the buffer. Data-in must be true for the periods during which $\phi2$ is 'low'. For asynchronous operation the Data-in must be true for two periods after the write command is given, because the write command may be given at any time in relation to the clock. If both the read and write lines are brought to a logic 'high', the device is disabled and the data

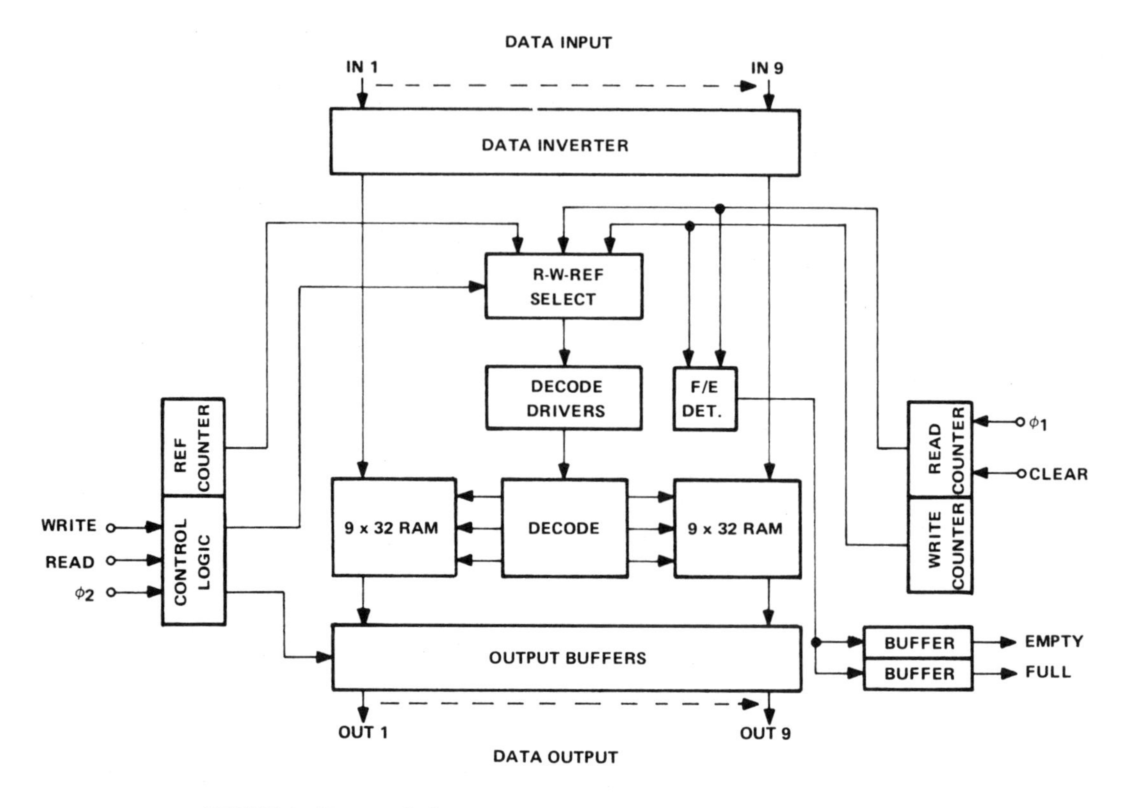

FIGURE 8. Functional Block Diagram of TMS 4024 JC/NC Digital Storage Buffer

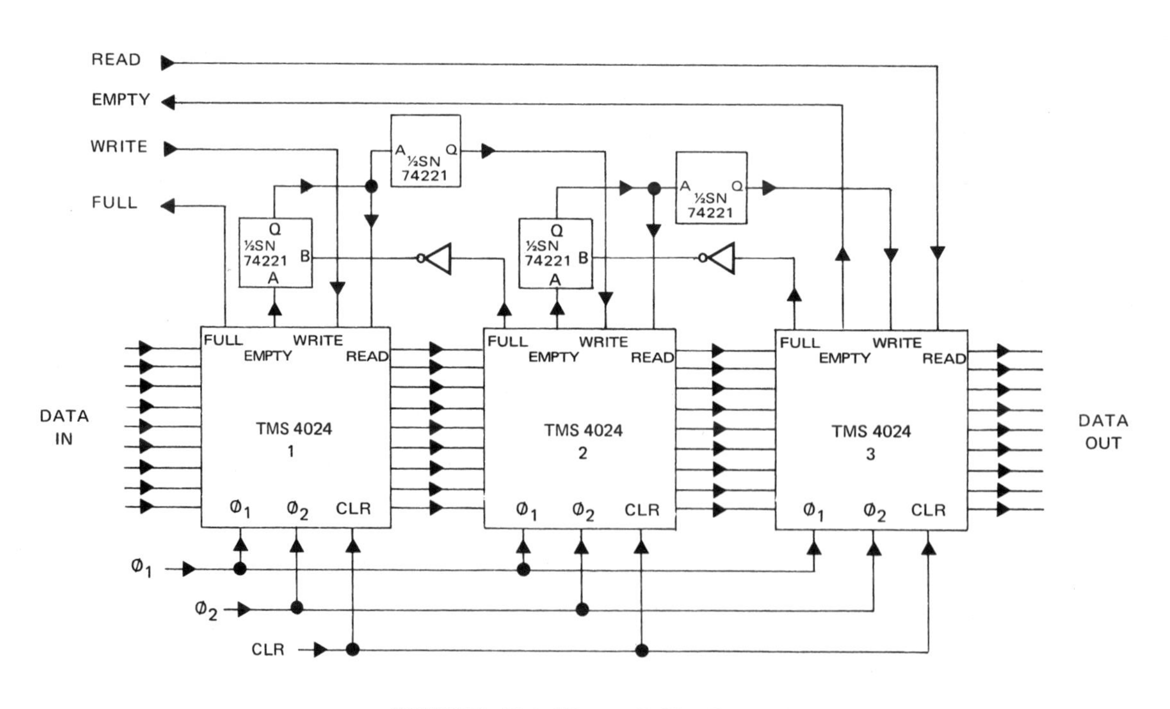

FIGURE 9. Digital Storage Buffers Cascaded

outputs are floating. The data present in the register is conserved while the chip is disabled. A Clear command is provided to clear all contents of the digital storage buffer. When the Clear line is brought to a logic 'high', it invalidates all other commands. Completion of a Clear operation is detected by a logic 'high' on the 'Empty' status output. Status outputs (Empty and Full) are provided to indicate the state of the register and avoid invalid operation. A logic 'high' on the Full status output invalidates Write commands and a logic 'high' on the Empty status output invalidates Read commands.

It can be 'cascaded' to form multiples of 64 words (x 9 bits) by using the arrangement as shown in Figure 9. Here the Empty output of device 1 is connected to the A input of the first monostable. The Full output of device 2 is inverted and connected to the B input of the monostable as an inhibit function. The Q output of the monostable is connected to the Read input of device 1 and the Write mono. of device 2. This may be repeated for as many stages as required. The example shown is of three stages giving 192 words of 9 bits. Assuming the sequence begins with a clear command, all Empty flags will be 'high' and Read 'low'. The first Data word is written into device 1 by taking its Write input to a logic '1' level, for a maximum of one clock period. The Empty output of device 1 goes to a logic '0' and triggers the first monostable, to give a pulse of approximately one clock period. This causes the data to be read out of device 1 and written into device 2. In this way the data 'ripples' through all the devices, and is eventually stored in the last device. When the last device is full, the Full output changes to a logic '1' level. This puts a logic '0' on the B input to the monostable of the previous stage, thus inhibiting any further data transfer into the last device until some data is read out of it. The Full output will then return to logic '0'. It should be realised that it takes several clock cycles for data to ripple through all the devices from the time it is entered into the first device, until it is available at the output of the last device. The number of clock cycles obviously depends upon the number of stages.

To expand the memory in parallel, the simple arrangement shown in Figure 10 can be used to extend the number of bits.

CHARACTER GENERATORS

MOS ROMs offer an extremely versatile approach to character generation which can be used advantageously in terminal systems.

They are programmed during manufacture to store data which may be read out on command to create the image of letters, numerals, and symbols in some sort of display system such as a cathode-ray-tube (CRT), array of lamps, or matrix-type printer. Each device can store more than 2000 bits of data (enough for 64 characters in one device) and includes addressing and decoding circuitry. The MOS circuitry is static rather than dynamic. No clocking is required.

Speed performance of static MOS ROMs is adequate for both low-speed applications and high-speed CRT data displays. Their small size and low power consumption in addition to their low cost make them attractive replacements for existing character generators in many display systems.

Fundamentals

Tube-type character generators take various forms. Some like the *monoscope* consist of an electron gun, electrostatic deflection plates, and a target on which the characters are formed. In a character generator of this type,

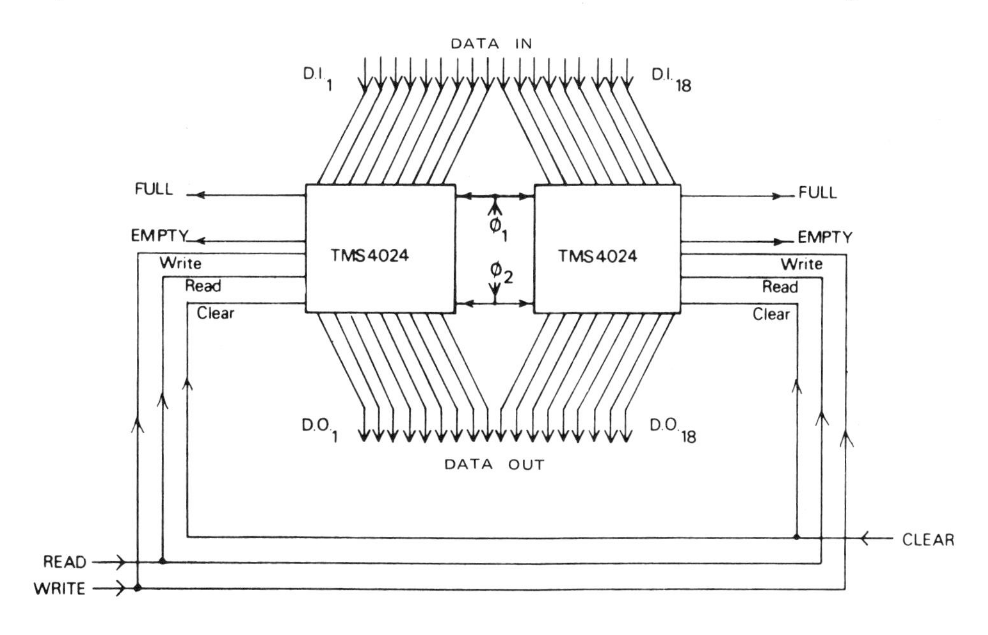

FIGURE 10. Digital Storage Buffers Paralleled

an incoming digital code specifying the character to be displayed is first converted to deflection voltages. The electron beam is deflected accordingly to the appropriate target location which contains a metallized image of the desired character. This beam then scans the target in synchronism with the beam in a cathode-ray tube (CRT) display. Secondary emission from the metal image provides a video signal for the CRT, reproducing the character on its face.

In some CRT displays the character generation is performed within the CRT itself. In this case, a thin metal *stencil* with character shapes etched through is used to extrude the beam to the desired character shape. After leaving the gun, the beam is deflected to a character location on the stencil, passes through the stencil, and is converged to the tube axis. It is then deflected again, this time to a position on the CRT face, where the shaped beam causes the selected character to appear.

With these tube-type character generators, the digital code specifying a character must first be converted to positional information before character selection can be achieved. On the other hand, digital character generators use a more direct approach than the tube type. Digital types generally consist of a read-only memory (ROM) in which a given input code produces a digital output describing a character specified by the user. This digital output is then converted into a visual image as described below. The use of ROMs for character generation eliminates the need for bulky tubes or special-purpose CRTs. They can also be used in non-CRT applications such as billboard displays and matrix type printers.

Practical Implementation

There are many different output code schemes that might be designed into an ROM character generator. However, the dot matrix output format is perhaps the easiest to visualize and use. Consider a 5 X 7 dot matrix used to present the letter A as shown in Figure 11. If each of the dot positions is a lamp, then the dots in the letter A are *on* lamps, while the others are *off*. The *on* lamps correspond to logical '1' outputs of an ROM with a 35-bit output word, while the *off* states correspond to a logical '0' output. In CRT displays, the same logical two-state output can be used to blank and unblank the beam. A sequential output from an ROM is generally more desirable than 35 parallel outputs because video information can be supplied as the beam is moving.

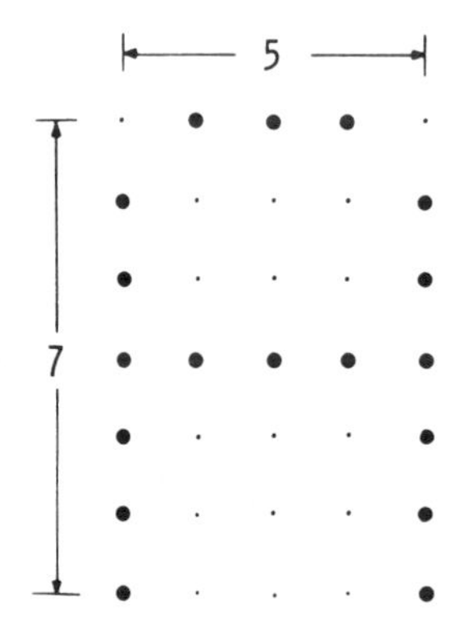

FIGURE 11. Letter "A" in 5 X 7 Dot Matrix

In order to use a ROM to generate a variety of characters a large ROM is necessary. For most display applications 32 characters is a bare minimum. A 64 character alphabet corresponds to a wider range of applications. Certain data display applications will necessitate as many as 96 or even 128 characters. The size of the dot matrix used depends on the definition needed for the display. Most human factor experts agree on the fact that a 7 X 5 character font presents enough definition for most applications while a 7 X 9 character font is much more eye pleasing. A 7 X 9 font permits, for instance, a good representation of complex characters such as the money sign and the ampersand. The total number of bits needed is as follows:

32 characters 7 X 5	1120 bits
64 characters 7 X 5	2240 bits
128 characters 7 X 5	4480 bits
64 characters 7 X 9	4480 bits
128 characters 7 X 9	8960 bits

It would be costly and awkward to implement such a large number of bits through diode or classical bipolar logic. Core memories require special drive and sense circuits and are difficult to modify for different customer character requirements. Therefore in recent years, a viable alternative, especially as far as character generation is concerned, has been ROMs. The cost per bit is low, and likely to decrease further, and there are also savings in weight, size and power consumption.

Two examples of ROMs suitable for character generation are the TMS 2501 JC/NC with a row output format, and the TMS 4103 JC/NC with a column output.

Both these devices have been designed with a static logic source which permits the simplest system design and eliminates the need for the special clocking circuits required by dynamic MOS configuration.

The TMS 2501 JC/NC series allow the user to display one out of 64 characters on a 7 x 5 matrix. Rather than having all outputs available simultaneously only one row of the dot matrix is available at a time. By addressing the 3 row select lines as shown in Figure 12 the corresponding row is displayed on the output. The direct character font of the TMS 2501 is represented in Figure 13.

The 3 bit row address input is internally decoded in 8 row select inputs. Only 7 of them will be used for most display applications. Such a 'row output' device will find its application in raster scan displays (TV monitor type displays).

The TMS 4103 JC/NC device has been designed for use in CRT and billboard displays.

Rather than having all outputs available simultaneously, only one column of the dot matrix is available at a time. By driving one of the five column-select inputs shown

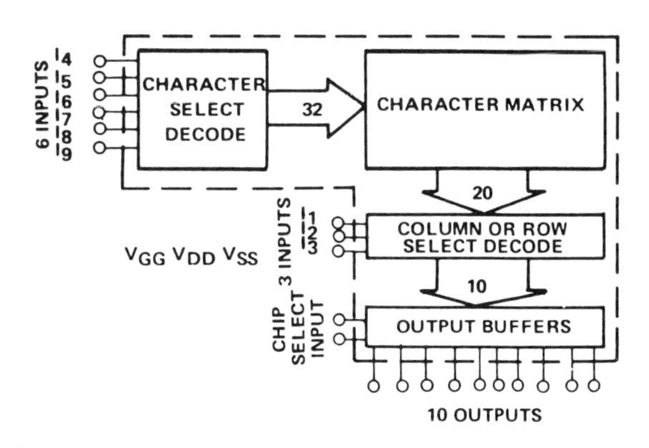

FIGURE 12. Functional Block Diagram of TMS 2501 JC/NC ROM

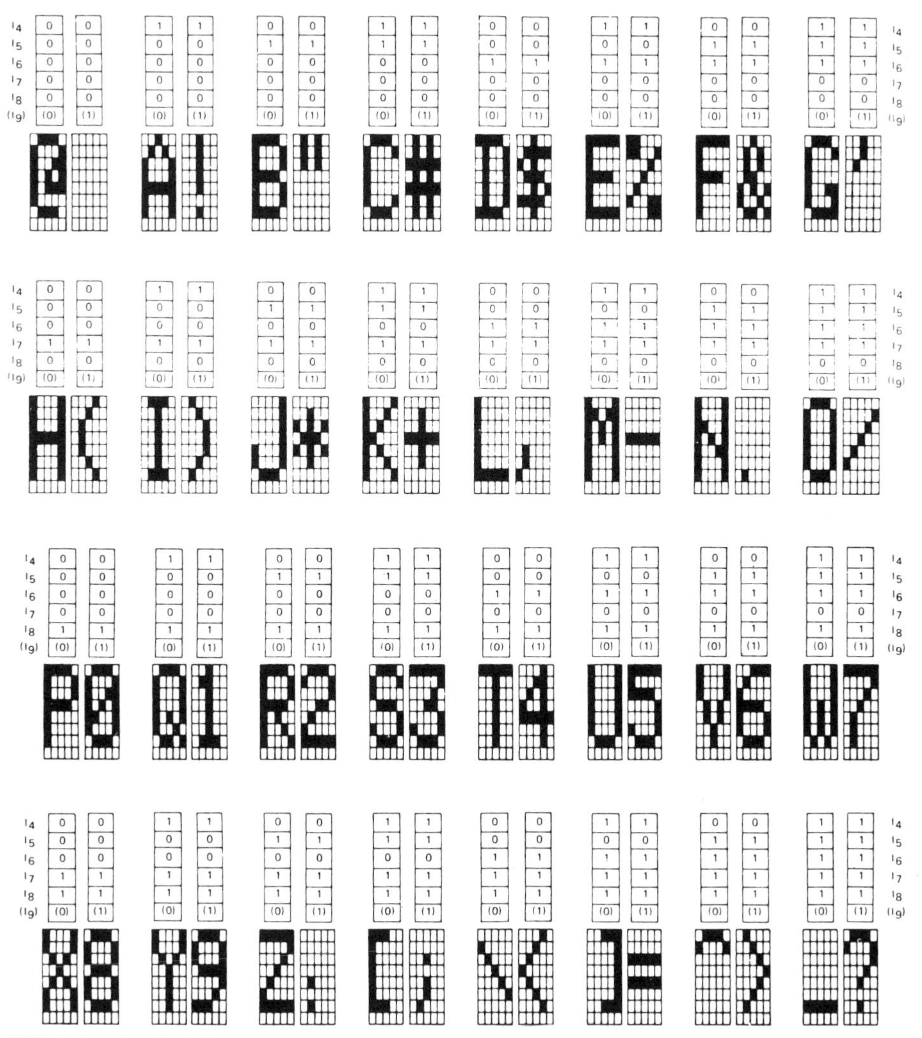

FIGURE 13. TMS 2501 JC/NC Character Font

in Figure 14, the corresponding column is made available at the output. Thus this character generator accepts USASCII input coding and provides 64 standard characters in a 5 x 7 dot array, and an entire character can be obtained in less than 1.5 μs.

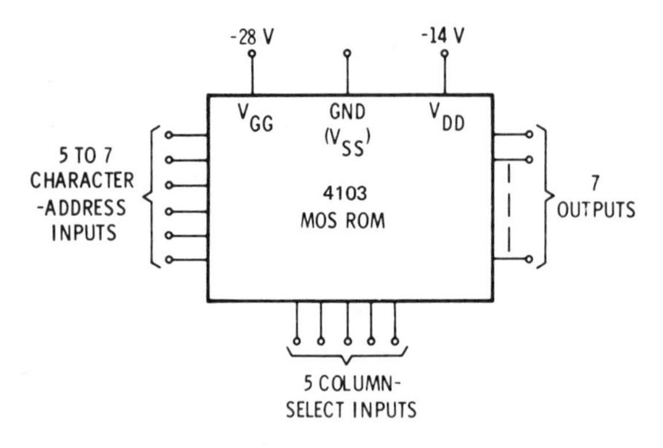

FIGURE 14. Pin Functions of MOS ROM TMS 4103

The memory matrix of the' 4103 device consists of 2240 P-channel MOS devices arranged in a 32 X 70 array. As shown in Figure 15, the 32 horizontal lines drive the MOSFET gates, while their drains are connected to one of the 70 output lines. Every device has its source grounded. When one of the 32 gate lines is driven negative, those devices which have their gate connected are turned on, pulling down the voltage of the corresponding output line. Whether a gate is connected or not is determined by mask programming, with a connected gate corresponding to a dot in the output format.

The block diagram in Figure 15 shows the interconnection of all circuits in an ROM of the TMS 4103 type: the decoder, memory array, and output selection circuits. In order to arrange the 64 characters with a 5 X 7 matrix, two characters are encoded on each of the 32 gate lines. Five of the six bits (or six of seven) in the input code are used to drive the decoder, with the sixth bit, as shown in Figure 15, connected to the output buffer to choose between the two characters.

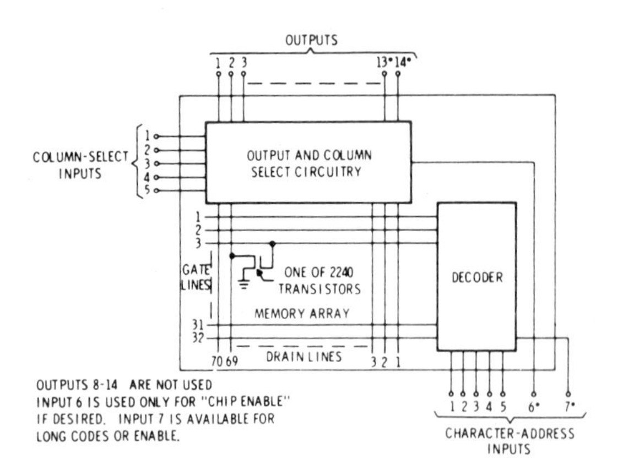

FIGURE 15. Functional Diagram of all Circuits within an MOS ROM of the TMS 4103

Programming of the MOS ROMs is done at the second-oxide-removal processing stage. Unused transistors have a layer of thick oxide over their gate regions (Figure 16). The other masks used during the process are the same for all the devices in one series. Fully computerised methods are used to cut the second-oxide removal mask ensuring fast turnaround time and completely eliminating code errors. A picture of the TMS4103 chip is shown in Figure 34 at the end of the chapter. The thin oxide, thick oxide, and metal are different shades of gray. The decoding, buffer and memory matrix sections are on the right, top and centre respectively, and the programmed areas can be seen in the memory matrix.

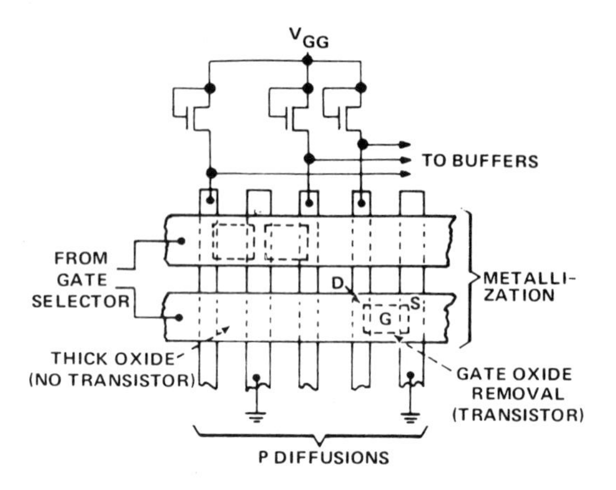

FIGURE 16. An MOS Transistor can be Either Constructed or Omitted by Growing Either a Thin-Gate Oxide or a Thick-Gate Oxide

Power Supply Requirements: Two power supplies are required, V_{DD} and V_{GG}. The TMS 2501 JC, NC uses a V_{DD} of -5 V and a V_{GG} of -17 V. In most systems the designer will want to translate all power supplies up by 5 V and the following voltage V_{SS} +5V, V_{DD} = 0 V, V_{GG} = -12 V. This will permit a TTL device interface. The typical power dissipation of this device at 50°C is 280 mW. V_{DD} and V_{GG}, are nominally -14 V and -28 V for the' 4103 device. No current is drawn from the -28 V V_{GG} supply, since it is internally connected only to MOS gates. About 25 mA is drawn typically by the memory array from the -14 V V_{DD} supply at 20°C ambient temperature, resulting in a 350-mW power dissipation. Additional power is dissipated in the output buffer devices, depending on the external output conditions. In most cases the designer will translate all power supplies by 14 V, and use V_{SS} = +14 V, V_{DD} = 0 V, V_{GG} = -14 V as power supplies. This will also simplify TTL interface.

Address and Select Inputs: The TMS 2501 JC/NC type uses an exhaustive decoder (6 inputs in 64 x 8 x 5 organisation). It uses a 3 input address for the row (or column) select.

All of these inputs are connected to MOS gates. Each input is protected by a field-plate zener diode against gate damage due to static charge accumulation. Because onlv gates are being driven, the inputs appear capacitive and require no current other than the small leakage current associated with the protective zener.

The nominal logic voltage on the inputs are the following:

Logic High V_{SS}
Logic Low V_{DD}

This leads to the following input definition:

TMS 4103 — Power supply +14 to −14

	MIN	NOM	MAX
High = 0	+11 V	+14	14.3
Low = 1		0	3 V

TMS 2501 — Power supply +5 to −12

	MIN	NOM	MAX
High = 1	3.5	5	5.3
Low = 0		0	3 V

Output Characteristics: The TMS 2501 JC/NC features a triple-state push-pull output buffer connected between V_{SS} and V_{DD}. This will permit direct TTL capability. The fan-out of the TMS 2501 buffer is 2 TTL gates.

The' 4103 type character generators have a single transistor with an open drain at the output which can be returned to a negative voltage through external circuitry. A schematic showing a portion of the relevant internal MOS circuitry for this type appears in Figure 17. When a dot is to occur, the output device is turned on, pulling the drain toward ground. Otherwise, the device remains *off.*

As in a discrete MOSFET, the drain current of the output buffer is affected by its drain-to-source voltage V_{DS} and gate-to-source voltage V_{GS}. The value of V_{DS} is dependent on the external circuitry being driven, whereas V_{GS} is determined internally.

Speed Performance: The output current of an MOS character generator does not change instantaneously after a new input is applied. A delay occurs which is dependent on the following factors: the character program within the memory; whether a character-address, row-address or column-select input is changed; the characters involved if character address is altered; the direction of output change-*on* to *off* to *on.*

A primary source of delay is the charging of the gate lines in the memory array. The more gates connected or the more dots programmed in the character, the larger the capacitance and the longer the time required to charge the line. Position of the character storage area in the matrix

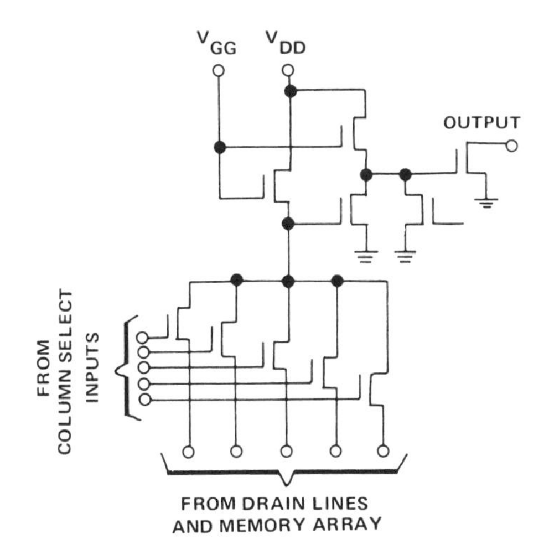

FIGURE 17. Portion of Output Circuitry

also affects delay due to the distributed-RC nature of the diffused drain lines.

Response to a character-address change involves the longest delays. Beginning with an output initially *off,* if a column or row is selected and an input code is applied that will result in the output turning *on,* the resulting output current has the appearance in Figure 18(a). If the output is initially *on* and being turned *off,* Figure 18(b) is applicable.

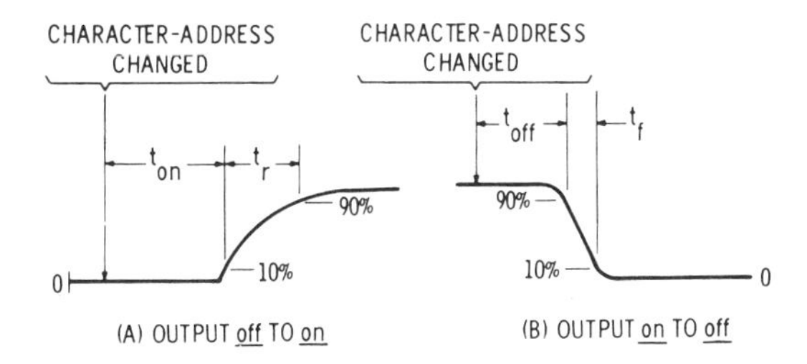

FIGURE 18. Voltage Response of an MOS ROM Output When Switched by a Character-Address Change

For a given character, t_{on} is always greater than t_{off} because the output resistance of the decoder is greater when charging a gate line than when discharging it. Because these delay times are dependent on the particular character format desired by a customer, no definite values can be assigned to t_{on} and t_{off} for all memories.

Within a given memory, both t_{on} and t_{off} can vary, depending on the character chosen. Variations from 200 ns to 350 ns for t_{on} and from 60 ns to 160 ns for t_{off} are possible.

Turn-on and turn-off delays also exist when a column is enabled or disabled with a character-address input already applied. Both of these delays are typically less than 100 ns for the' 4103 device.

The current rise time at an output is always greater than the fall time. Rise times can be as long as 200 ns while fall times are generally less than 100 ns.

The discussion of the speed is not only theoretical. There are many cases when the system design makes a maximum access time mandatory. When a plain TV monitor (625 lines) is used, the image is regenerated 25 times per second. If the desirable 80 characters per line of text is to be used a character must be obtained every 625 ns.

At 400 ns over this temperature range the TMS 2501 has speed to spare. The access times of the two character generators are as follows:

	TMS 2501	TMS 4103
Character	400 ns	700 ns
Row (column) select	300 ns	300 ns

Input and Output Interfacing: The TMS 2501 JC/NC interfaces directly to TTL, DTL as seen in Figure 19. All inputs, outputs, chip select and column select lines are directly TTL compatible without external components.

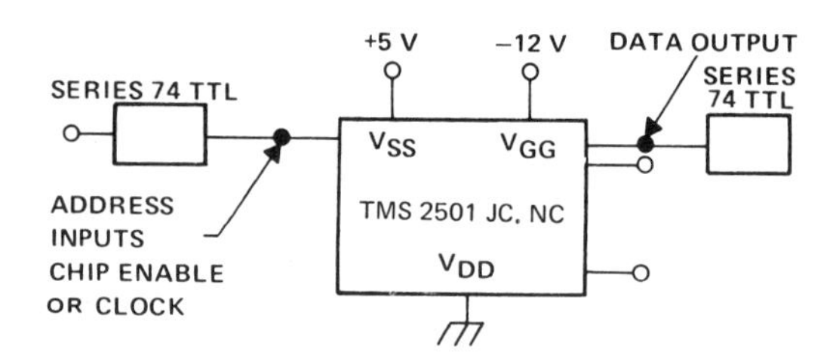

FIGURE 19. Interfacing TMS 2501 JC/NC With Series 74 TTL

As far as the TMS 4103 type of device is concerned interfacing is most easily achieved when the ground of the MOS device is brought above the TTL ground as shown in the example given in Figure 20. In this configuration the character-address, row-address and column-select voltages do not have to swing below ground. Consequently, TTL open-collector gates or MSI decoders can be used at the character-address, row-address and column-select inputs. The SN7416 open collector TTL gates are ideal for this purpose. Discrete npn transistors may also be used with their bases driven by a TTL output; the 2N3014 or its plastic version the 2N4420 is recommended for this application.

While either the open-collector gates or npn drivers could be used at the column-select inputs, an MSI decoder such as the SN7445 may be more convenient since only one output at a time needs to be enabled. The value of load resistance R should be about 2 kΩ for high-speed operation. It may be increased at lower speeds to lessen current drain.

Output interface circuitry must convert the current output of the character generator to a voltage swing capable

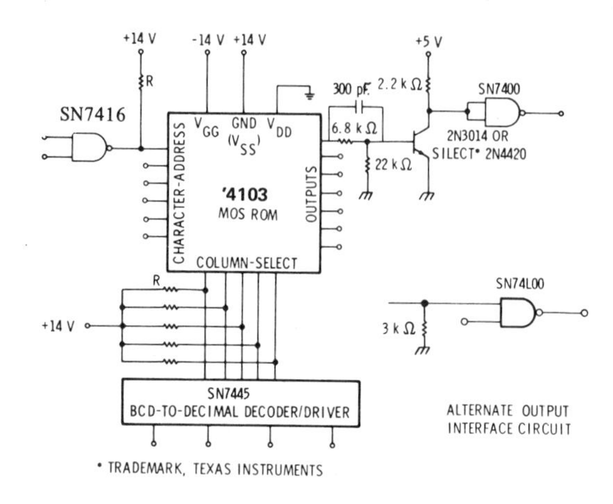

FIGURE 20. Interfacing a '4103 MOS ROM with 54/74 TTL

of driving a 54/74 TTL input. It should not respond to the maximum leakage current for an *off* output, but must respond to the minimum current for an *on* output.

A simple circuit which meets these requirements for the '4103 type is the npn transistor inverter shown at an MOS ROM output in Figure 20. The 22kΩ base resistance assures that the transistor will not be turned on with an ROM output leakage current and transistor leakage current (I_{CBO}) of 20 μA. A 2.2-kΩ load resistance assures that a good logical 0 appears at the TTL input when the ROM output current is *on*. A 6.8-kΩ resistance has been added in series with the MOS output to limit power dissipation in the memory, while the 300pF capacitor maintains switching speeds. As an alternative, use of low-power 54/74 TTL for the output interface circuitry only requires a 3-kΩ resistor to ground, to convert the character generator output current into acceptable logic voltages.

In some applications not every output needs a separate interface circuit. The system in Figure 26 which is discussed in the next section, requires only one interface circuit for seven outputs.

DISPLAY SYSTEMS

Matrix

A moving billboard display could be arranged as shown in Figure 21. The seven character-generator outputs each drive one lamp in the far right column. Each pattern entered at the right is shifted to the left by other logic circuits in synchronism with the changes of column-select inputs. After five shifts the entire character is visible. All column-select inputs are then disabled so that spaces can be entered in the light matrix between characters.

A column-output character generator can also be used to obtain printed characters. The seven outputs can be connected to a column of seven light-emitting diodes arranged over a strip of moving, light-sensitive paper or film. Movement of the paper provides the spacing between columns as the column-select inputs are sequenced.

CRT Screen

The logic block diagram of a system for displaying a single character on a CRT is shown in Figure 22. Two

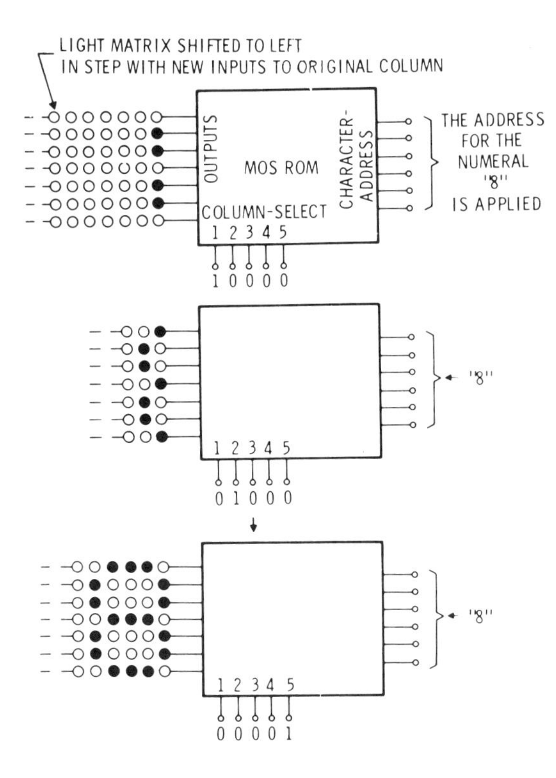

FIGURE 21. Functional Diagram of a Moving Billboard Display Using One MOS ROM for Character Generation

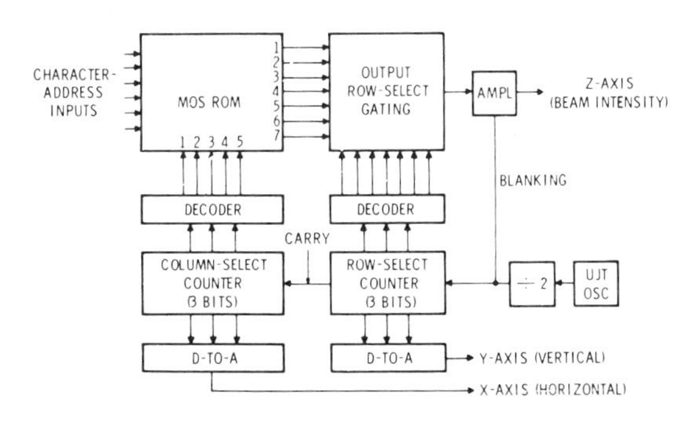

FIGURE 22. Functional Diagram of Circuitry for Projecting One Character on a CRT Using an MOS ROM

counters are involved; one sequences through the seven outputs of an MOS character generator while the other selects a column. A digital-to-analog converter connected to each counter provides a staircase waveform for vertical or horizontal deflection. The scanning sequence is shown in Figure 23. It begins at the bottom-left dot position of

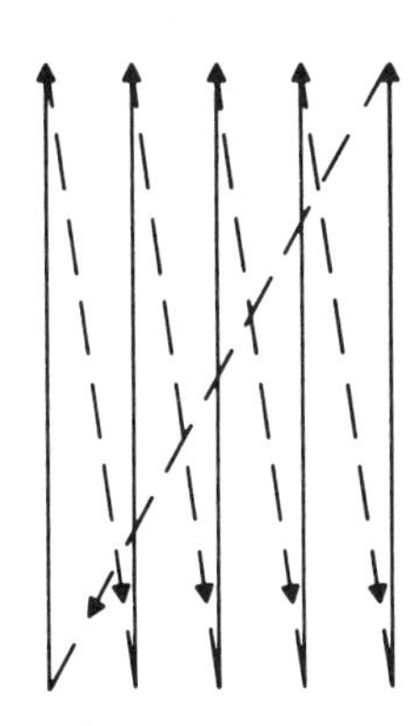

FIGURE 23. Scan Pattern for Single Character CRT Display Generated by an MOS ROM

the 5 X 7 dot matrix and ends at the top-right position before retrace. At the end of each vertical column scan, the row-select counter resets and advances the column-select counter to the next column position. An entire scan over the 35 dot positions must be repeated rapidly enough so that flicker of the display is not apparent. A rate of 60 Hz is generally considered adequate for all standard CRT phosphors and brightness levels.

Waveforms showing the relationship between the deflection signals, Z-axis output, and counter conditions are shown in Figure 24 for the first two columns of the number "8". The Z-axis output is always low while the

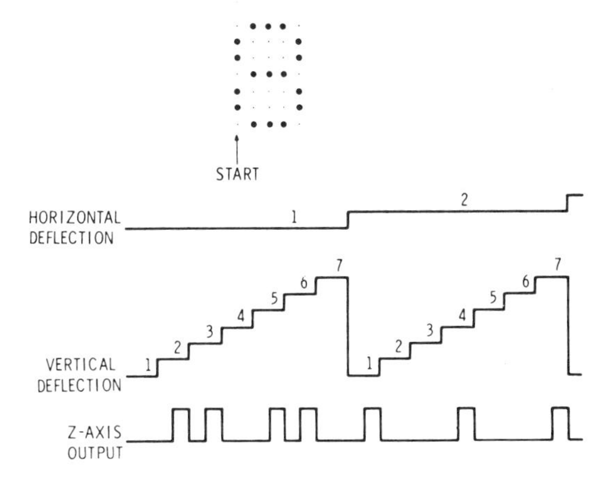

FIGURE 24. Deflection and Z-Axis Signals for Single-Character CRT Display as in Figure 13.

beam is being stepped between dot positions and remains low for a portion of the dwell time at a dot position. This blanking allows the display system to be used with an ordinary laboratory oscilloscope having an ac-coupled

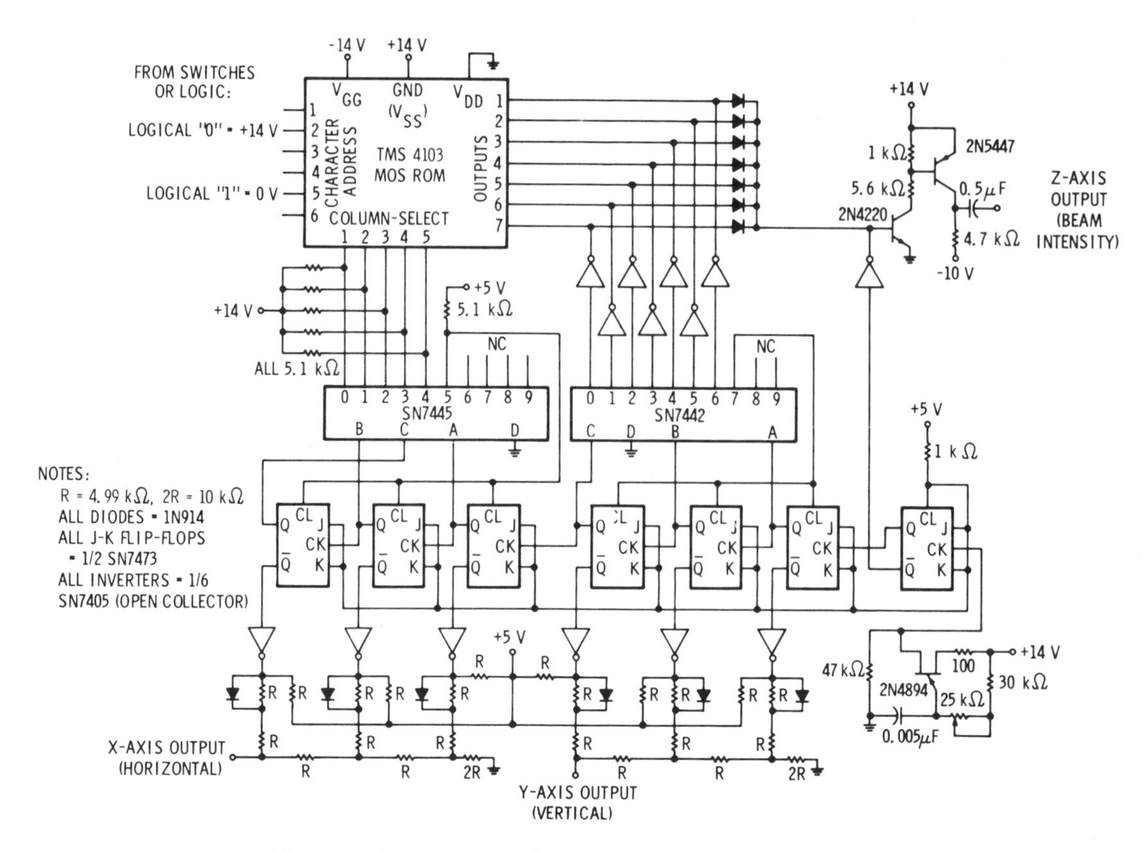

FIGURE 25. Complete Circuit for Single Character CRT Display System

Z-axis input. It also eliminates all potentially visible retrace lines. Without blanking, the output would not fall when stepping between *on* dots. The beam would stay turned on between steps, creating dc restoration problems with an ac-coupled Z-axis.

The single-character display system just described is implemented in Figure 25 using TTL for the counters. decoder, and D-to-A conversion. A UJT oscillator running at 4.2 kHz is first divided by two to produce the blanking signal for the Z-axis amplifier. As the blanking signal is applied, the row-select binary counter is clocked. The resultant count is converted to an analog voltage by a 3-bit D-to-A converter consisting of three open-collector TTL inverters and a modified binary ladder network, causing a vertical movement of the beam. When the row-select decoder senses the eighth state of the binary counter, it resets this counter and clocks the column-select counter. An identical D-to-A converter provides the horizontal deflection signal.

The decoder, a SN7445N, used for the column-select counter, interfaces directly with the MOS character generator, using load resistors. The decoder outputs have a 30-V breakdown potential and can sink up to 80 mA.

The decoder for the row-select counter drives open-collector TTL inverters which together with the diode array allow only one output from the character generator to drive

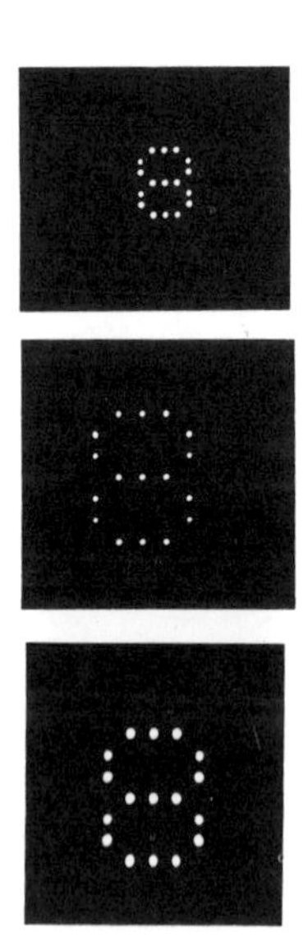

FIGURE 26. Scope Photos of Numeral "8" Obtained Using an Oscilloscope (and the Circuit of Figure 25) Different sizes and appearances result from adjusting oscilloscope gain, focus and astigmation controls

the output amplifier. This simple arrangement eliminates the need for separate interface circuits on each output and can be used at high speeds as well as the speeds encountered in this system.

In Figure 26 is shown a photograph of the number '8' obtained with this system and an ordinary oscilloscope having decoupled X and Y inputs and an a.c. coupled Z input. Size and aspect ratio of the character can be adjusted by the gain controls on the scope, and dot size can be varied with the focus and astigmation controls.

The extension of the single-character display system just discussed to a system capable of displaying one entire line of characters is relatively straightforward. The column-select decoder must first be modified so that spaces can be inserted between characters. Two column widths are sufficient, and are easily obtained without extensive modification as shown in Figure 27. All columns are disabled for the first two counts of the column-select counter so that no Z-output can occur during this time. (The spacing delay may be used to address a new character in the ROM.) A character-address counter is advanced when the column-select counter resets. The binary outputs of this counter drive a D-to-A converter with as many output voltage steps as there are characters, each step having a height equal to

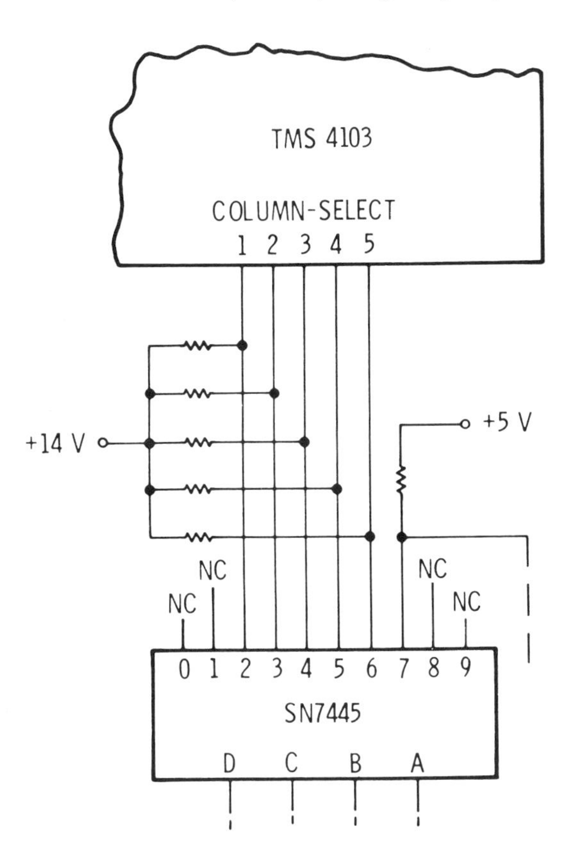

FIGURE 27. Modification to Column-Select Decoder in Figure 25 for Character Spacing

seven column-select steps. Summing of the column-select and character-select D-to-A converter outputs results in the total horizontal deflection signal.

A new character input is applied to the MOS character generator each time the character-address counter advances. This may be achieved by clocking MOS shift registers containing the character codes of the characters to be displayed at each reset of the column-select counter.

As the number of characters on a line becomes large, the horizontal deflection voltage approaches a sawtooth waveform. In practice, a sawtooth can actually be used, eliminating the need for two D-to-A converters. A linear ramp generator which is reset when the character-address counter resets, provides a suitable horizontal signal if a slight tilt to the characters is permissible.

By adding still another counter, several lines of characters can be displayed. This line-address counter is advanced when the character-address counter resets. A D-to-A converter provides a staircase waveform with as many steps as there are lines. This staircase waveform is summed with the staircase waveform from the row-select converter to provide the total vertical deflection signal. The basic organization of this system is apparent from the above.

TV Raster Scan

Most CRT displays presently being built use raster scan. This is a TV type of sweep. A raster type CRT is very similar to a TV monitor. As a matter of fact, some manufacturers actually use TV monitors for their displays. The CRT beam is swept in a raster of lines by applying a synchronized voltage range to the X and Y deflection circuits.

The image is formed by modulating the beam intensity with a video signal at appropriate times during the raster sweeps.

Typical commercial TV video is essentially an analog signal. There are many shades of gray between pure white and jet black. For a display, we can simplify the video and use only two levels of intensity – black and white. Thus, the video signal can be fed into the CRT as a series of 0s and 1s and the image can be made up of a series of dots and blanks that are interpreted as lines, characters, etc.

Advantages:

- Economical hardware (TV)
- Simple deflection circuits
- Simple digital logic
- Economical refresh
- Constant flicker rate independent of information

Disadvantages:

- Use of light pen is difficult
- Need storage even for blank areas of the screen
- If data is not alphanumeric, data preparation is cumbersome

The most common character fonts for raster scan CRT displays employ 5 X 7 or 7 X 9 matrices.

In a CRT display, only one dot of a character can be presented at a time. For this reason, video information to blank and unblank the beam must be completely serial. Therefore any parallel outputs of a character generator must be sequentially inspected.

In a raster-scanned display like that in conventional television the CRT beam moves vertically after a complete horizontal sweep. Control of the beam to obtain the scanning pattern in Figure 23 for each character is not readily available. It therefore becomes desirable when using a dot-matrix MOS character generator to display only a portion of a character at a time, rather than scan over a complete character before going on to the next one.

One row from each character in a line of characters can be presented during one horizontal sweep as shown in Figure 28. A total of seven sweeps is required to display a character with 5 X 7 dot matrix. Since conventional TV displays use interlaced scanning, alternate rows must be displayed in each field, i.e. rows 1, 3, 5, and 7 in one field and rows 2, 4, and 6 in the other.

The character generator output for this kind of display should consist of five parallel outputs chosen on a row-selectable basis. Speed requirements prevent a column-

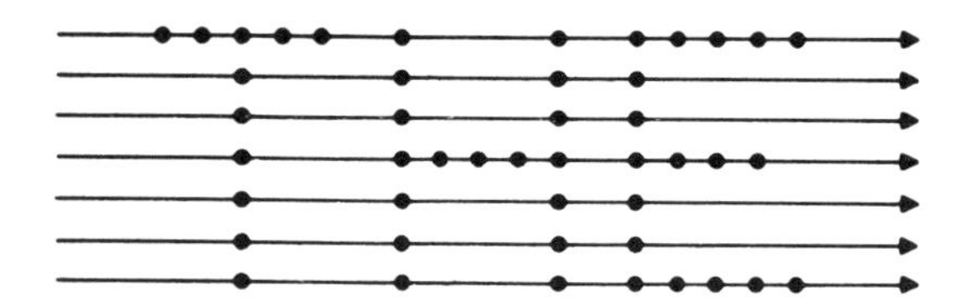

FIGURE 28. Raster Scanning of Dot Matrix Characters as in a Television Picture Tube

selectable output, such as provided by the '4103 type MOS ROMs, from being used effectively. For this reason the 2500 type of row-selectable device was developed.

TV character displays are popular because of the inexpensive monitors available. Additional logic costs above those required for a simpler X-Y display system must be considered along with other system requirements before a decision is made on the scan technique and monitors to be employed.

CRT 'Stroked'

A CRT character display can be obtained by generating a sequence of vectors or strokes on the CRT to describe a desired character. Instead of using a dot matrix to represent the character, the image is formed from a series of connected lines. Control of these lines comes from information stored in several '4103 type MOS ROMs used together. Consider an 8 position X-Y stroke representation of the character 'A' as shown in Figure 29. The initial point of operation is at the coordinate X = O, Y = O. The first stroke (1) goes to X = 1, Y = 1 with Z = 0; therefore, the CRT beam would move diagonally to the new position with the beam off. The second stroke (2) moves the beam

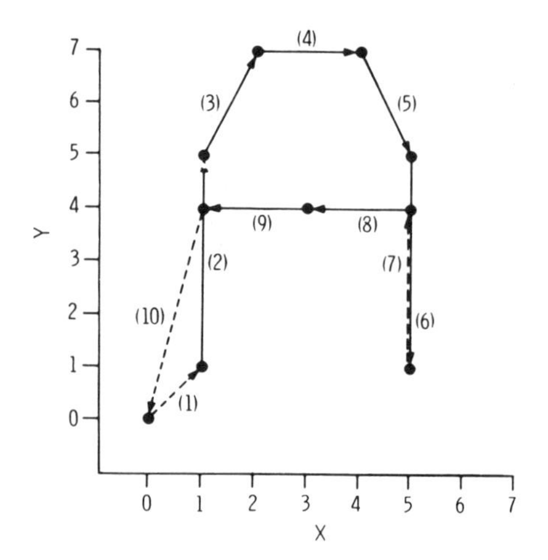

FIGURE 29. Letter "A" in 8 Position, 10 Stroke Matrix

from its last position (X = 1, Y = 1) to the next position X = 1, Y = 5 with the beam on, thus drawing a vertical line on the CRT four units high as the beam moves. The strokes continue to describe the character until completed, with the last stroke returning the beam to the initial position. A block diagram of a display system using this technique is shown in Figure 30. Note that of the seven outputs from the '4103 type MOS ROMs, three outputs are used to

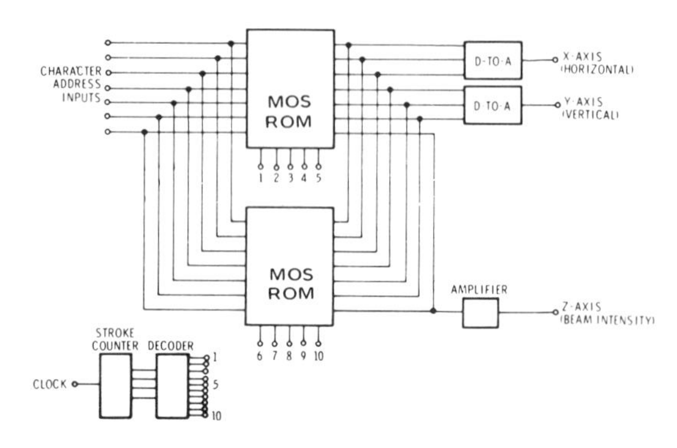

FIGURE 30. Functional Diagram of Circuitry for Projecting One Character on a CRT Using Stroke Generation

designate the Y coordinate and one output controls the CRT beam intensity. By using more MOS ROMs, the number of strokes per character can be increased resulting in a displayed character with finer resolution.

A somewhat different approach greatly increases the resolution of the displayed character. Instead of generating the absolute coordinates X and Y at each stroke time, as shown in the system of Figure 30, only the changes in coordinate locations need be generated at each stroke time.

The seven outputs from the 4103 type MOS ROMs would be coded to represent the X axis by 3 outputs (sign and 4 lengths), the Y axis by 3 outputs (sign and 4 lengths) and the Z axis by one output (beam blanked or unblanked). The character begins at an initial position on the CRT. During the first stroke time the CRT beam can move in any direction in increments of 0, 1, 2, or 3 units with the beam blanked or unblanked. During the second stroke time the beam can again move in any direction in 0, 1, 2, or 3 unit lengths with the beam *on* or *off*. The initial position of the beam for the second stroke time is the final position of the beam at the end of the first stroke time. Implementation of the above requires some means of holding the D-to-A output voltage at the end of a stroke time, and then summing this voltage with the change in voltage required during the next stroke period. A second method of implementation would be to use two 3-bit registers to store the absolute coordinates of X and Y and two 3-bit adders that would add the change in locations from the MOS ROM outputs to the location held in the registers, arriving at the new location in absolute coordinates. To maintain the CRT line at the same brightness, the beam intensity can be modulated by observing the unit lengths the beam must move during one stroke time and controlling the Z-axis voltage correspondingly. By using more MOS ROMs of the '4103 type, displays having 10, 15, or perhaps 20 strokes per character can be obtained.

KEYBOARD ENCODER

MOS keyboard encoders provide many advantages compared to bipolar circuits and therefore, are becoming used more and more. MOS provides greater system simplicity. One reason for this is that because of the high level of integration achieved through MOS/LSI, an entire keyboard encoder can be implemented on one single package – direct contrast to the numerous discrete devices and/or integrated circuits used with bipolar techniques. Because it employs fewer components MOS/LSI allows considerable savings in hardware in addition to the simpler, more reliable design.

Furthermore, more cost savings arise from MOS encoders through the savings in related costs, such as printed circuit boards, labour and testing – all again directly related to fewer components. With MOS keyboard encoders, all codes can be changed easily through one mask artwork change. A fixed printed circuit board design can be used. It does not have to be changed when the codes are changed.

Higher degrees of system performance can be achieved. With MOS keyboard encoders, two and N-key rollover are obtained easily. Data-ready terminals, storage flip-flops and other elements can be easily incorporated in the design. In addition, the code words associated to 1 key in the different modes need not be related.

Basic Functions

Activation: Generally, a key controls a simple switch which is open when the key is at rest and closed when the key is depressed. A common variation is a reed switch controlled by a magnet mechanically attached to the moving part of the key.

In addition to switches there are other ways to detect the depression of a key. The depression can change the capacitance of a capacitor, the ohmic resistance of a resistor or the inductance of a winding. Hall effect (semiconductor) devices also may be used for the activation of a key.

Number: The number of isolated outputs per key varies. Generally, there is only one output per key. But some coding schemes necessitate two, attained by implementing two switches per key or by using two diodes at the output of the switch.

The number of keys in a keyboard varies depending upon the equipment in which the keyboard is used. MOS techniques are applicable to any number of keys. It is believed, however, that MOS techniques are of special interest for numbers of keys between 32 and 128. This is an area in which the considerable cost savings gained by MOS techniques compared to bipolar techniques are most evident. It must be remembered that the total of 128 keys is not a limit imposed by MOS techniques – it is the practical limit of the size of keyboards.

Key Bounce: When a mechanical switch is closed, the contacts do not come to rest immediately. There is a definite "key bounce." Frequency of this contact bounce and the settling time vary according to the characteristics of the switch itself. The encoder must consider this key bounce phenomenon to avoid spurious encoded outputs. Well-designed keyboard encoders provide ways of adjusting for key bounce.

Data Ready Terminal: For indication that the contacts have settled and that the bounce has ceased, an output terminal should be included in the encoder design. A logical signal on this terminal indicates that the output data is valid.

Mode: Depression of a key may result in more than one output word. In many keyboards, for example, depression of the same key generates an upper-case or a lower-case letter (and the corresponding codes at the output of the keyboard encoder). The number of words generated by the depression of a single key is defined as the number of modes. Shift keys (also called mode select keys) are used to determine which mode corresponds to the depression of a key. Most keyboards employed in computer equipment use two, three, or even four modes. Most keyboards used in calculator equipment, however, use only one mode.

It must be noted that an MOS keyboard encoder places no restriction on code words associated with the different modes on any given key. There may be no relation whatever between these coded outputs because MOS keyboard encoders use read-only memory techniques. It is comparatively easy to implement a multimode keyboard encoder with bipolar techniques as long as the words associated with the different modes for any given key differ by only one or two bits. If such is not the case (which is very common with keyboards used in terminal equipment) the amount of logic needed with bipolar techniques becomes very cumbersome.

Simultaneous Key Depression: It is common for a keyboard operator to depress two or more keys simultaneously. Obviously, this can cause problems with the generation of an output signal. Most keyboards do not include a mechanical key interlock which prevents the depression of more than one key at a time. Therefore, some type of electronic "lockout" or "rollover" must be a necessary part of a keyboard encoder to ensure that only one output – the proper output – is generated despite the fact that two or more keys were depressed simultaneously.

N-Key Lockout: One way of overcoming the problem of output determination when two or more keys are depressed together is known as N-key Lockout. Such a circuit is a part of certain keyboard encoders.

If this is designed as a part of the circuit, when two or more keys are depressed at the same time, within the settling period of the contacts or the sampling period of the keyboard encoder, the keyboard encoder will not generate any data output. When one key is depressed, the keyboard encoder generates the proper output. But when a second key is depressed while the first one is also depressed, the keyboard encoder does not generate any output as long as the first key is not released. When the first key is released, the output corresponding to the second key is generated. Thus, if N keys are depressed simultaneously no output will be generated until all keys are released except one.

N-Key Rollover: Another way of overcoming the problem of simultaneous key depression is N-key rollover. In an N-key rollover system, when a key is depressed the corresponding output is generated. If the first key remains depressed while a second key is depressed, the output corresponding to the second key is generated. When a third key is depressed while the two first keys (or one of them) are still depressed, the output corresponding to the third key is generated. In an extreme case, all of the keyboard keys except one may be depressed. When the last key is depressed, the corresponding output is generated.

N-key rollover, which has been shown increases typing speed considerably, is commonly found on electric typewriters. Because most typists are accustomed to electric typewriters, it is extremely desirable to include these same features on keyboards used for terminals.

Generally, it may be assumed that N-key lockout is sufficient when a visual indication CRT screen, paper printout, and other methods corresponds to the depression of a key. N-key rollover, while desirable in all instances, is absolutely necessary when no visual indications corresponding to the depression of a key are provided.

Fairly difficult and complicated to attain with bipolar techniques, N-key rollover is, however, relatively easy to implement with MOS techniques.

Output Wire ORing: A system may include more than one keyboard. Or if a very large number of keys are desired, it may be necessary to use several encoders for one keyboard. The design of the encoder output circuits must be such that the corresponding outputs of several encoders may be directly tied together and that the resulting output be the logic sum of the connected output. In an MOS keyboard encoder, this can be achieved by using single-ended buffers or special enable logic.

Output Latches: It is often desirable to keep the output word corresponding to a key available on the outputs of the keyboard encoder until the next key is depressed. To accomplish this, latches must be provided in the encoder. The MOS encoders discussed later detail how this is accomplished with MOS techniques.

Static Keyboard Encoders

Static MOS keyboard encoders make use of static ROM techniques. Except for the key bounce circuits and the output latches, an MOS static keyboard encoder essentially consists of a large MOS read-only memory with as many outputs as there are bits in the desired output code.

As shown in Figure 31 a possible implementation would be to assign one key to each read-only memory input. This is not desirable because:

1) The number of input terminals would become much too large (the largest package commonly used in MOS has 40 pins while most keyboards have from 40 to 90 keys). This would force the utilization of several ROMs in a wire-ORed configuration.

2) If an off-the-shelf ROM were to be used, the number of bits would become ludicrous. In a normal ROM the n inputs are decoded in 2^n terms. If a custom ROM were to be used, it would, of course, be possible to forego the decoder and to access directly the read-only memory matrix. This is possible since only one switch could be closed at a time.

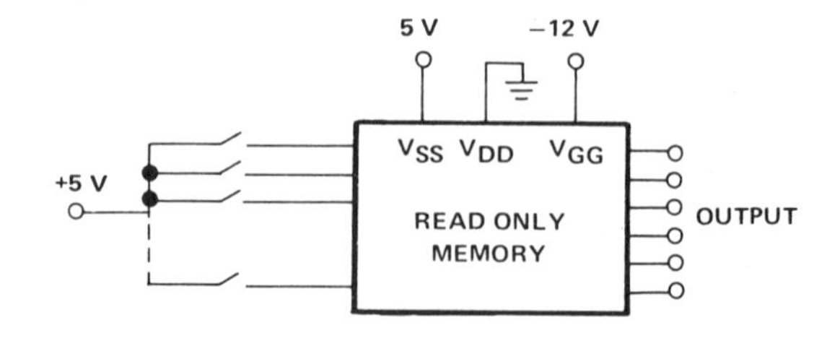

FIGURE 31. Assigning One Key to Each ROM Input is not Desirable

Static keyboard encoders automatically provide N-key lockout. The decoder section of the ROM is programmed to accept only input words which consist of specific patterns of logic "1" and logic "0". No other combinations will be accepted by the decoder, nor result in an output.

N-key rollover may be obtained easily with a static keyboard encoder if the switches are wired to produce a voltage pulse instead of a voltage level upon closure. The width of the voltage pulse must be at least equal to the access time of the ROM.

Static keyboard encoders do not necessitate clock. They are simple to use and N-key rollover is easily obtained. Their only drawback is that two diodes per key are necessary when one-contact switches are used. However, computer-type diodes are inexpensive and can often be mounted in the reed-switch housing, taking the place of the wire going to the upper part of the reed, as shown in Figure 32.

Dynamic Keyboard Encoder

Scanning techniques are commonly employed when bipolar logic elements are used to implement keyboard encoders. The same techniques are applicable to MOS keyboard encoders.

Basically, a dynamic keyboard encoder consists of these five elements:

1) A binary counter.
2) A decoder driven by the most significant bits of the counter (slow count).
3) A multiplexer driven by the least significant bits of the counter (fast count).
4) A one shot fed by the output of the multiplexer.
5) A ROM for mode select and code conversion.

The key switches are used as cross points in a matrix, the lines of which are the outputs of the decoder, and the columns of which are the inputs to the multiplexer. All of the columns of the matrix are scanned for each step of the decoder. Such a system is shown in Figure 33.

A key closure results in logic '1' at the output of the multiplexer and the output is used to stop the counter. The output of the counter, when stopped, is the ROM input address. A '1' on the output of the one-shot signifies that the data is valid (data ready).

The MOS scanning keyboard encoders used in such systems offer many advantages compared to their bipolar counterparts:

1) The high level of integration allows the designer to implement the entire circuit in one package instead of several packages.
2) The ROM section of the MOS keyboard encoder can be expanded to store several unrelated modes/key.
3) Codes can be modified by a single-level artwork change on the MOS device instead of a printed circuit board change.
4) A clock generator can be incorporated on the chip easily.
5) Two-key rollover is inherent to the scanning approach. N-key rollover may be obtained simply through shift-register techniques in the MOS scanning approach, and this circuitry can be incorporated on the chip.

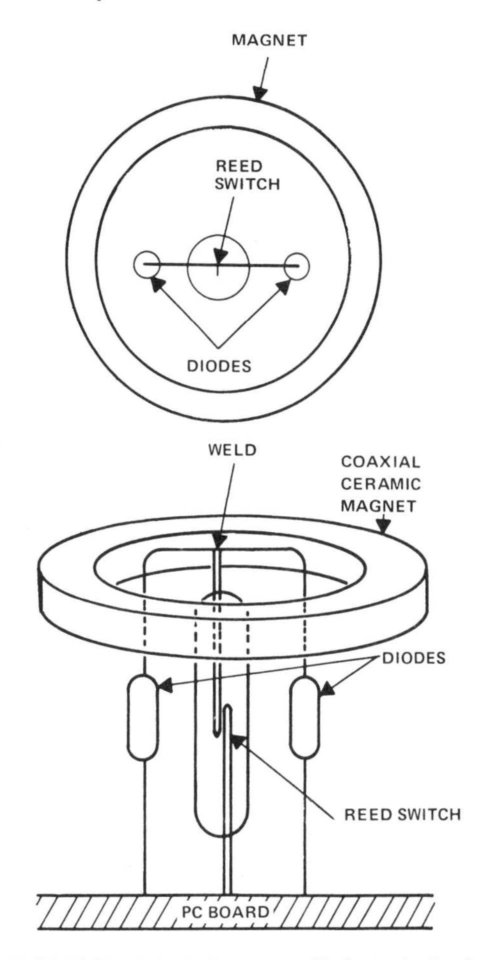

FIGURE 32. Method of Mounting Diodes in the Reed-Switch Housing When One-Contact Switches Are Used

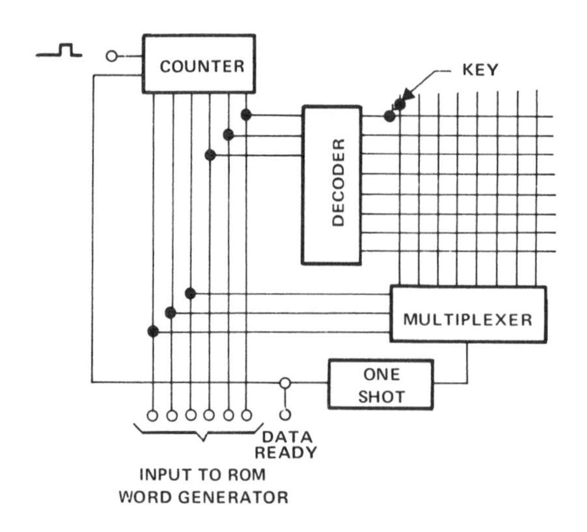

FIGURE 33. Block Diagram of a Typical Dynamic Keyboard Encoder

FIGURE 34. Photograph of a TMS 4103.

III THE RANDOM ACCESS MEMORY

by
Howard Cook

The semiconductor memory element has already made an enormous impact on the industrial electronics industry. This is partly due to its higher performance than core memories, and lower cost than high performance magnetic systems such as plated wire. It is also due to its greater convenience of use. No mechanical or physical knowledge is required to build a system using a semiconductor memory device, unlike magnetic systems which require considerable specialised knowledge. These factors combined with the low cost are important factors in the growing interest in memory devices in non-computer applications and it is likely that memory devices similar to those described in this chapter will be used in consumer electrical apparatus. For example, in the T.V. set information transmitted during the frame synch. period, could be stored and then displayed at the touch of a button.

The first major assault by the semiconductor industry on the virtual monopoly of magnetics in memory systems was the introduction of 1024 bit p-channel Random Access Memory (RAM) devices at the beginning of this decade. The first of these to be introduced was the '1103, and despite some undesirable characteristics which required special care in the use of the device, demand for it rapidly increased throughout the industry and many memory system manufacturers were soon committed to designs using the '1103. Later devices, such as the TMS 4062/3 (AMS 6002), offered better performance and fewer problems in use.

The advantages of the later generation of devices were sufficient to influence some systems manufacturers, but the majority felt that they should persevere with the '1103, since so much had been spent on system development with this device, until something happened which would offer a significant cost advantage over the '1103 and warrant new system designs.

The next logical step in semiconductor memory development after 1024 bits is 4096 bits of storage per device. To be able to produce devices of this capacity economically called for a change in technology, and the n-channel silicon gate process was therefore developed commercially. This process combines the advantages of the silicon gate technique, i.e. smaller device geometry and easier interconnect, with those of n-channel processing. In the n-channel Field Effect Transistor, FET, the majority carriers are electrons, which have a greater mobility than the hole carriers in a p-channel device. This results in a better speed-power combination for the device, as discussed in Chapter I.

The RAM is not only an essential unit in any high performance memory system, but is also becoming a useful function in modern logic circuit design. By definition the RAM is a data storage element in which the access time to the stored data is identical for all storage locations. This differs from a recirculating store, for example, where the access time to any particular stored bit depends upon the position of that bit at the moment of accessing.

The usual approach to manufacturing a RAM storage element is to use some form of two dimensional matrix of storage cells, whether these cells are ferrite cores, plated wire elements, or semiconductor circuit. Owing to the regular pattern of the matrix and interconnections, a large number of the latter type, i.e. the semiconductor circuits, may be fabricated in a small area on a silicon chip, and the improvements in semiconductor processing techniques have enabled devices with up to 4096 (64^2) storage cells to be manufactured. Examples of two MOS RAMs are the TMS 4063 1024 bit device (commonly abbreviated to 1k bit) and the TMS4030 4096 bit (4k) memory.

DEVICE DESCRIPTIONS

1k Bit RAM

The TMS 4063 is a high performance MOS RAM organised as 1024 words by one bit. An access time of 150ns is attainable, and a cycle time of 290ns. It only requires two clock signals without any overlap, which considerably simplifies the design of the control circuit.

The '4063 differs from the earlier 4062 only in that the 'clock' and 'chip select' inputs to the device are internally connected to a common pin, thus allowing the TMS 4063 to be packaged in an 18 pin dual-in-line (D.I.L.) pack.

The basic cell uses four transistors with unique support circuitry which gives rise to high performance yet low power dissipation. The low input capacitance simplifies the design of driver circuits necessary to interface with transistor-transistor logic (TTL). The differential outputs are capable of being wire-OR'ed to facilitate memory expansion. In this case each memory is controlled separately by the Chip Select/Clock input.

The reading of information stored within the memory is non-destructive, but since the device is dynamic, it is necessary to periodically refresh the stored information.

4k Bit RAM

The TMS 4030 is a 4096 word x 1 bit dynamic RAM fabricated using n-channel silicon gate processing. Its 300ns maximum access time and 470ns maximum cycle times make it ideally suitable for large memory applications. Its inputs and output, except for the single clock, are directly compatible with Diode Transistor Logic (DTL), TTL and all similar logic families. This enables a considerable cost saving in peripheral interface devices to be made, quite apart from the fact that the memory device itself sells at a lower cost/bit than any 1k memory device. The device incorporates internal registers for the Address inputs and the Chip Select input to simplify the input timing requirements. It can be seen from the timing diagrams on the data sheet that the many 'don't care' conditions make it extremely simple to operate the TMS 4030.

The power dissipated during operation at maximum speed is approximately 0.1 mW/bit, and the power during standby (i.e. Chip Enable at logic 'low') is approximately 2mW. To obtain these low power requirements, it has been necessary to employ dynamic circuitry techniques in the design of this device, and hence Refresh cycles are necessary in most applications to maintain the integrity of the stored data. The requirement for Refreshing the data is that all 64 combinations of address $A_0 - A_5$ must be exercised within the stated Refresh period. (2ms at 70°C). The power supplies required to operate the memory are V_{DD} = 12V, V_{BB} = −3V, V_{CC} = 5V, and V_{SS} connected to 0V. The +5V supply is obviously compatible with the logic supply of the remainder of the system, and the −3V substrate bias supply has to sink only a very small current. This supply may be economically generated within the memory system to save using an external supply.

The Storage Cell

The first MOS memories developed used static type storage cells as shown in Figure 1a. These are similar in operation to bipolar memory devices being made up of cross coupled bistables. These cells are then arranged in a matrix, and the selection of one X address and one Y address uniquely selects one cell. The differential outputs of the cells are connected to the Read lines. To read the contents of a cell, it is necessary to detect the polarity of the differential current flowing in these lines. The contents of these static cells remain unchanged until new information is written in. In such cells one transistor is always conducting, which gives rise to a certain power dissipation – an important consideration. To reduce power consumption, the dynamic type of cell was introduced (see Figure 1b). In this cell the transistors making up the bistable are connected to the power rail via two more transistors which are controlled by the clock signal.

When the clock signal is at the V_{DD} supply, this cell operates as a static cell, but when the clock signal is at V_{SS}, the cell is disconnected from the V_{DD} supply and does not conduct current through either transistor. The information is stored on the parasitic capacitors associated with the gate of each transistor which controls the state of the bistable when the clock returns to V_{DD}. The power consumption is thus reduced, but since the charge leaks away from the gate capacitances, it is necessary to periodically refresh the information simply by pulsing the clock line to V_{DD} and allowing the current which then flows through the cell to reinforce the charge on these capacitors. The TMS 4063 uses a dynamic cell such as this (Figure 2).

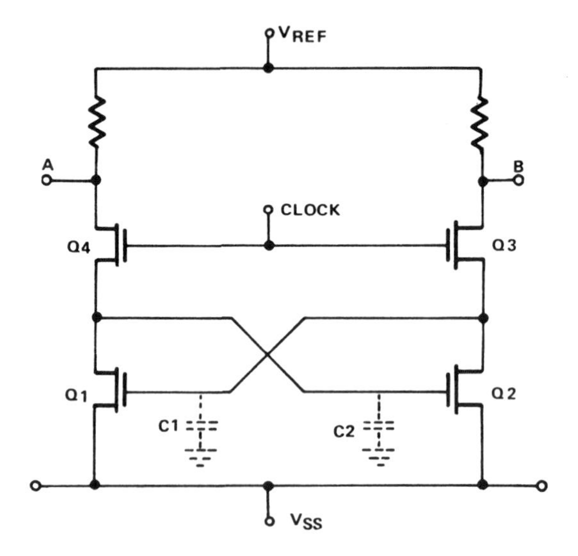

FIGURE 2. Memory Cell of the TMS4062/3

a) STATIC FOUR-TRANSISTOR CELL

b) DYNAMIC FOUR-TRANSISTOR CELL

VDD

CLOCK

φ

BIT LINE 1

BIT LINE 2

READ WRITE LINES

VSS

FIGURE 1. Cell Arrangements

The transistors Q1 and Q2 form the bistable and transistors Q3 and Q4 connect the bi-stable to V_{REF}. The capacitors C1 and C2 are the parasitic gate capacitors of Q1 and Q2. To write information into this cell either point A or point B is forced to V_{SS} by means of external circuitry, thus deciding the state of the bistable. To read the information stored in the cell, it is necessary to detect the current which flows from either point A or point B to V_{REF} when the cell is addressed. These functions may be performed by discrete circuitry or by means of an integrated circuit i.e. the SN75370, a device specially designed for this purpose, and described in Chapter IV.

Organisation of the 1k Device

The memory cells are arranged in a matrix of 32 rows by 32 columns. The ten addresses (A_0 to A_9) are divided up such that the first five (A_0 to A_4) select the rows and the last five (A_5 to A_9) select the columns, via the row and column decoders (see Figures 3 and 4).

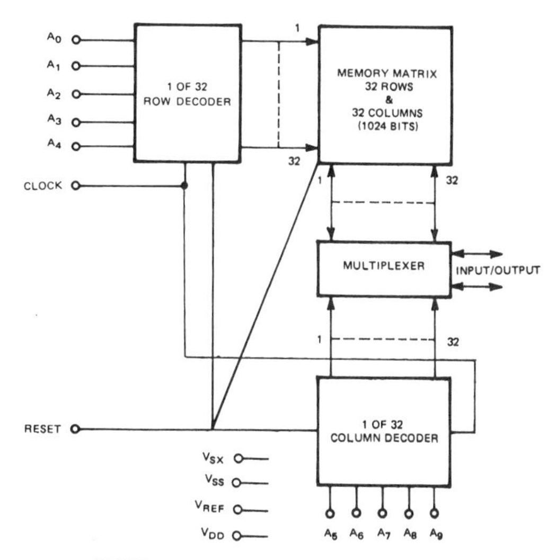

FIGURE 3. TMS 4063 Block Diagram

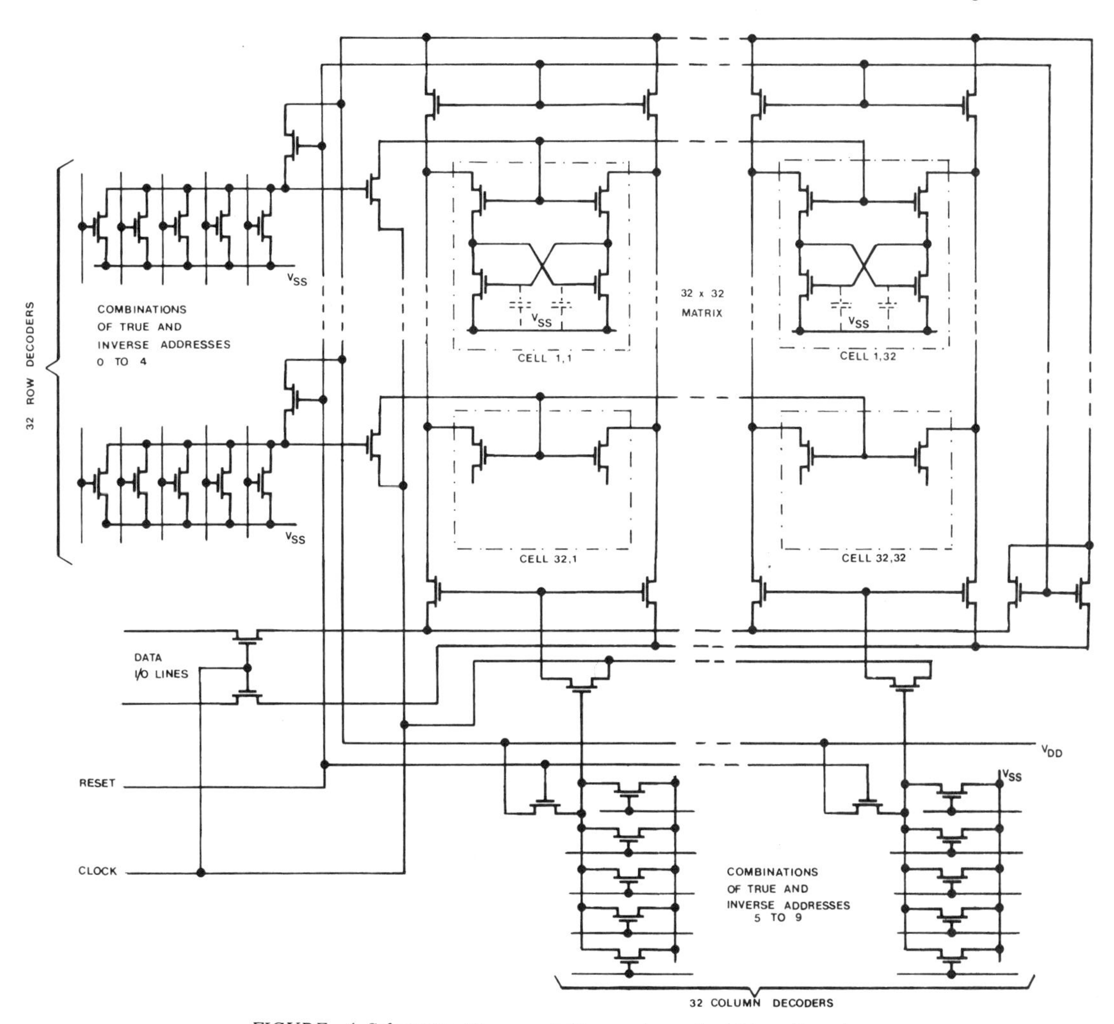

FIGURE 4. Schematic Diagram of Storage Array & Address Decoders

The clock signal drives all 32 cells in the selected row, and also, at the same time, connects the selected column of 32 cells to the internal data highway which appears externally as the Input/Output (I/O) lines. The Reset input precharges all the internal lines before a cycle, and also drives the row and column decoders. The 32 cells, in the row selected by the decode of address A_0 to A_4, are refreshed by the clock signal. When the clock is at V_{DD}, one transistor of each of these cells is held 'on' by the charge on the gate capacitors, and the current, flowing through this device, reinforces this charge. The 32 rows have to be addressed for refreshing at least once during the stated refreshing period (2ms).

Organisation of the 4k Device

The heart of the 4k RAM is a bit cell containing a transistor and a storage capacitor. The 4096 bits are organized in a matrix of 64 rows by 64 columns as can be seen on the photograph of the device, Figure 5. The rows are selected by decoding the addresses A_0 through A_5 while the columns are selected by decoding the addresses on pins A_6 through A_{11} (see Figure 6). In the middle of the memory matrix, there are two rows of dummy cells with a differential sense amplifier between them. There are 64 such sense amplifiers, one per column, with a dummy cell on either side. This arrangement is shown in Figure 7 for a single column.

When the chip-enable clock is low, the potentials on both halves of the column inputs to the sense amplifiers are equalized by the internal clock ϕ. During the same time, an intermediate voltage is directly written into the dummy cell capacitors by the precharge voltage generator. This intermediate voltage is halfway between a high level and a low level that would be stored in a bit location.

When the chip-enable clock goes high, the addresses are gated into the circuit. The row address decode then selects one row of 64 bits and also selects the opposite dummy row, such that the selected row and the dummy row are on opposite sides of the differential amplifiers. During a read operation, the bit-storage capacitors on the selected row share their charge with the parasitic capacitance on their half of the respective column. On the other half of the columns, the dummy bit storage capacitors share their respective charges. This charge sharing then produces a corresponding voltage change on the column. Since the voltage change produced by the bit capacitors is either lower or higher than the voltage change produced by dummy-bit capacitors, a voltage differential is set up across the two inputs to the sense amplifier. The sense amplifier is then enabled by the internally generated ϕ_{DS} clock and causes the sense amplifier (which is basically a pair of cross-coupled inverters) to latch. If one side of the sense amplifier latches high, the other side latches low and vice versa. This restores the voltage readout from the bit-storage capacitors on the selected row, in effect refreshing the 64 bits in a manner similar to the read/restore performed with core memories. The column decode address then gates one of the 64 columns through to the output buffer.

During a write operation, the column decode address selects the column to be tied into the date-in line. During ϕ_{DS} the sense amplifier on the selected column latches as dictated by data-in and the new data is then written into the cell selected by the row decode address. The other cells on this row go through a refresh cycle only.

FIGURE 5. Photograph of TMS4030 RAM.

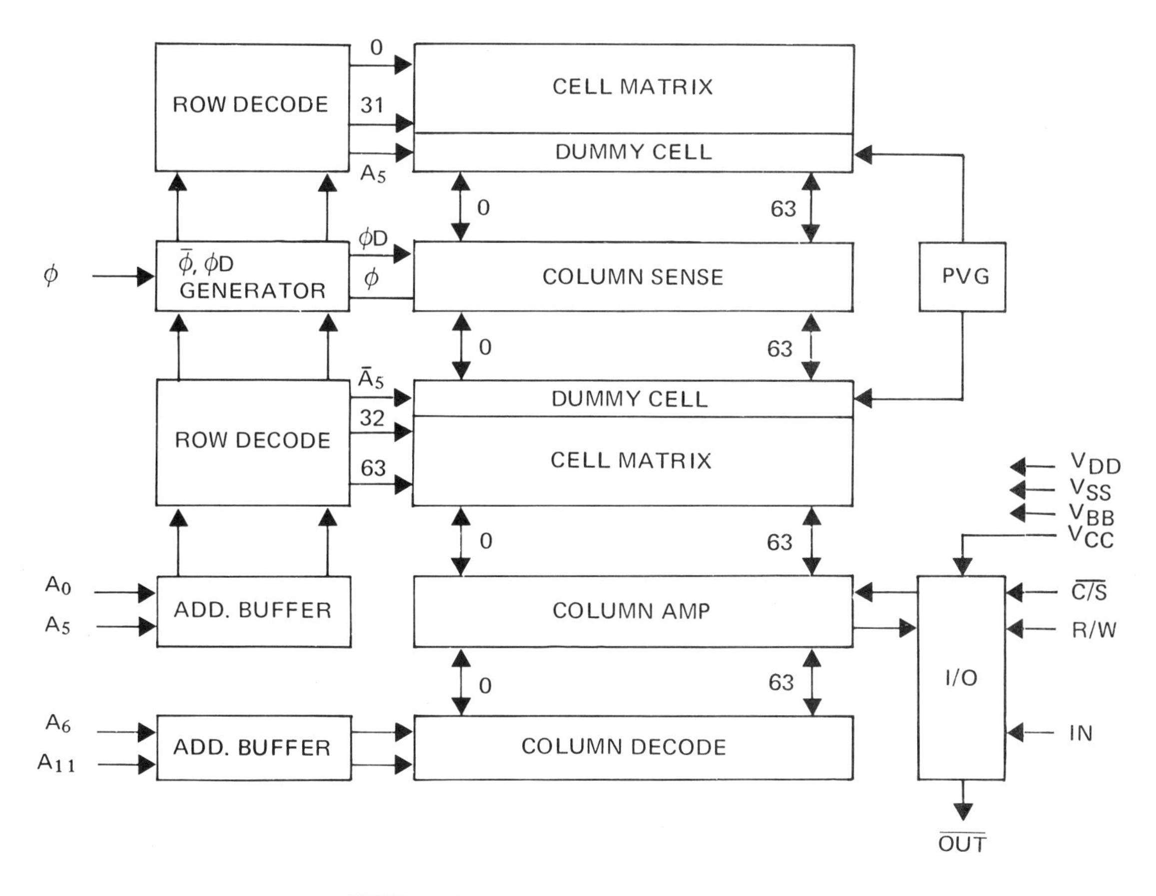

FIGURE 6. Functional Block Diagram of 4k RAM.

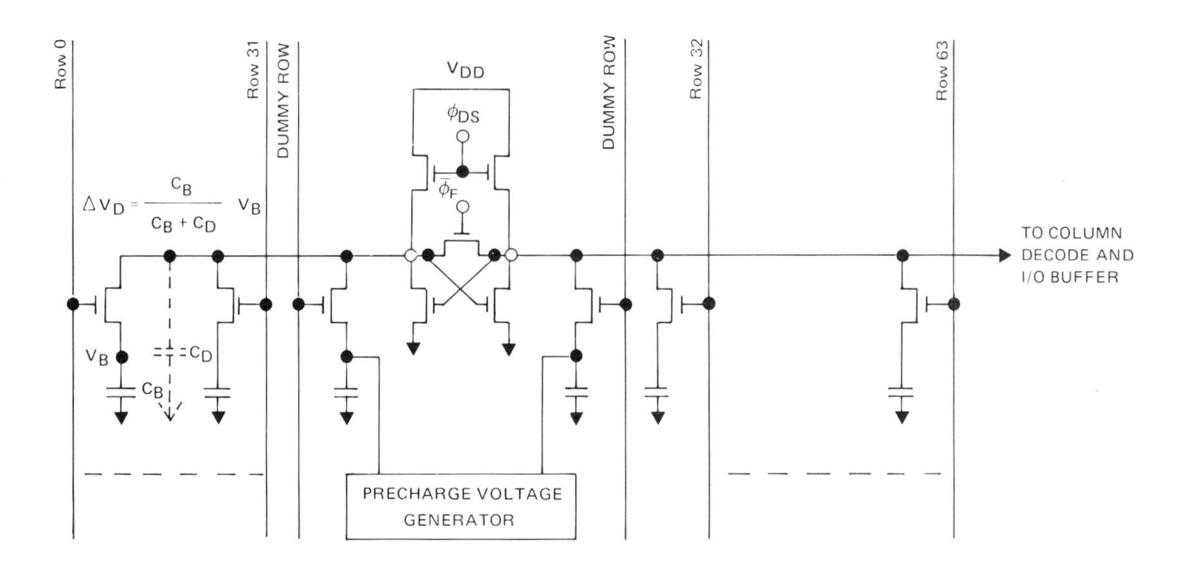

FIGURE 7. Sense Circuit For Single Column of 4k RAM.

OPERATION OF 1k RAM

The connections to the device may be grouped as follows:

(i) Address: The ten address inputs select a particular cell.
(ii) Clock Signals: (Clock and Reset). These two signals control the operation of the device.
(iii) I/O Lines: These two lines are used in reading and writing of information out of and into the device.
(iv) Power Rails: The four power connections are:

V_{SX} (Substrate Bias)	+22.5V
V_{SS} (Source)	+20V
V_{REF} (Reference)	+ 7V
V_{DD} (Drain)	0V

These power rails must be decoupled close to the memory with Tantalum and Ceramic capacitors to keep voltage movement to a minimum. The OV should be supplied as a ground plane or as tracking of generous proportions on the printed circuit board.

The V_{SS} supply rail has to supply current to the TMS 4063s whereas the V_{DD} and V_{REF} rails have to sink current. The standby power of the device is in the order of 2 mW. During this time all the address and Clock inputs are at V_{SS}. When run at maximum speed, the power consumption is in the order of 120mW.

Inputs

The Reset: causes all the internal connections and the output lines to be pre-charged after each Read, Write or Refresh cycle. It also disconnects the cells from external signals. In this state the address input capacitance is very low, making it easy to change the address information. The duration of the Reset period may be reduced by driving the Reset input more negative than V_{DD}.

The Addresses: may be divided into two groups, X and Y. The first five addresses, inputs A_0 to A_4, drive the rows of the matrix, and the second group, inputs A_5 to A_9 drives the columns. Each of these groups is decoded to select one from 32 rows or columns. The Addresses must be set up during the Reset period. Only one cell will be addressed when the Clock is driven to V_{DD}. There is necessarily a delay t_{DD} between Reset going to V_{SS} and Clock going to V_{DD} for the row and column decoders to be discharged (see data sheet).

The Clock: drives one row of 32 cells determined by the row decoder. During the Clock period, all these 32 cells have their information refreshed. It connects the points A and B (see Figure 2) of each cell in the selected column to the I/O lines of the device. The Clock input must be present for all cycles.

Input Capacitance: The inputs to the MOS device are essentially capacitive. It is, therefore, necessary to use circuits capable of driving capacitive loads. Table 1 shows the value of these capacitances. These circuits have to be capable of driving a large number of inputs for large memory arrays. When calculating the total capacitance, it is necessary to also consider the capacitance of the printed circuit wiring.

Table 1 Input Capacitance
$V_{in} = V_{SS}$

	CHARACTERISTICS	VALUE typ.	pF max.
C_{AD}	Input Capacitance, Address	2.5	3.5
C_R	Input Capacitance, Reset	30.0	40.0
C_C	Input Capacitance, Clock	30.0	36.0
$C_{I/O}$	Capacitance, I/O (not selected)	2.5	3.5

All necessary interface circuits are discussed fully in Chapter V.

Cycles

Read: The information of the cell selected by the addresses A_0 to A_9 appears on the I/O lines, a short delay (t_{CD}) after the negative transition of Clock.

Refresh: This is necessary to maintain the information stored in the cells as described earlier. The refreshing of the 1024 bits of the memory, requires 32 cycles within the 2ms Refresh period, to select every row at least once. If more than one memory device is connected together to increase the capacity, all the devices may be refreshed simultaneously, thus still only requiring 32 cycles. The Refresh cycle is the same as a Read cycle, but it is necessary to hold the I/O lines to V_{REF} via a low impedance to prevent movement of these lines corrupting stored data. If the 32 rows of the matrix are selected during the Read cycles, within the 2ms period, then additional refreshing is not necessary.

Write: This is the same as a Read cycle except that one of the I/O lines has to be forced to V_{SS} during the Clock period.

OPERATION OF 4k RAM

The areas which are worthy of consideration for exploiting the advantages of the TMS 4030 are:-

Input/output techniques.
Refreshing techniques.
Generating V_{BB}.

The refreshing techniques are discussed in the control section of this chapter.

Input/Output Techniques

The Address, Chip Select, Read/Write, and Data inputs to the TMS 4030 are similar in nature, being approximately 5pF input capacitance, and requiring input levels as shown in Figure 8. Although the upper threshold is 2.2V the inputs may be taken as high as V_{DD} if required.

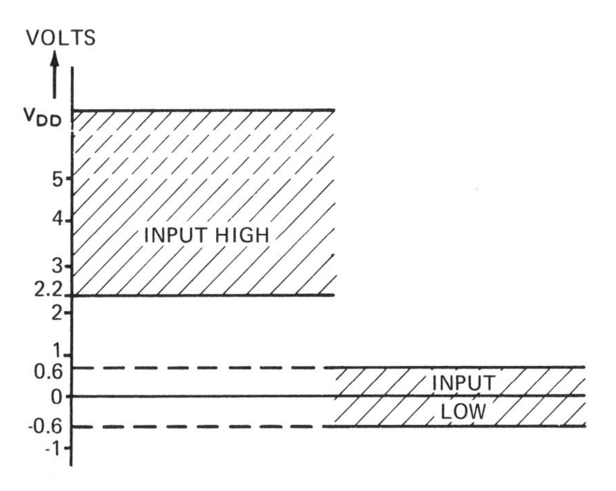

FIGURE 8. Input Voltage Levels (Except CE)

These voltage levels are obviously compatible with TTL, DTL etc. However, although a small number of inputs may be driven from a standard TTL gate, when a large number of inputs are connected in parallel the capacitive load becomes too great to be driven by normal TTL devices without additional components.

Figure 9 shows the normal limiting conditions. In (a) a logic gate with active pull-up is used to charge the capacitive load. The active pull-up (totem pole) resembles a constant current source, and hence the output voltage rises linearly with time. The rate of rise, and hence the time(t) to reach $V_{out(max)}$ depends on the current that the logic gate can source from its output.

In (b) an open collector gate with a pull-up resistor to 5V is used for the same function. The output voltage now rises exponentially, with a time constant $R_C.C_L$. As with any exponential, the output will reach 95% of its maximum in 3 time constants, i.e. $t=3.R_C.C_L$. However if the pull-up resistor is to V_{DD}, the output voltage will achieve 2.2V in a much shorter time. The third example, (c), shows the case of a logic gate discharging a capacitive load. It is necessary to use a series resistor, R_S, to limit the current out of the capacitor into the output of the gate. Without this resistor, the initial peak current would exceed the maximum sink capability of the device, and damage could occur. Once again the voltage waveform is exponential, and the time for the output to fall to within 5% of the minimum voltage is $t=3.R_S.C_L$.

One practical method of driving the capacitive load is to use a logic gate with an output stage capable of sourcing and sinking high currents. Two such devices are the SN74128 dual 4 input positive NAND and the SN74S140 quad 2 input positive NOR line drivers. These devices have an output capability of approximately ±50mA, and hence require a 100Ω resistor in series with each output. They will drive a 100pF load with edge speeds of <30ns, as shown in Figure 10.

The advantage of using these devices is that they combine the necessary drive capability with a choice of logic function and their static power dissipation is low. For driving much larger capacitive loads, it is necessary to resort to more conventional techniques, e.g. the SN75361 MOS driver device as described in Chapter V. Finally, if economy is more important than power dissipation, then the MOS inputs may be driven from a standard open collector buffer device (e.g. a SN7416, SN7417, SN7438 etc.) with series output resistor, and collector pull-up resistor to V_{DD} as described above.

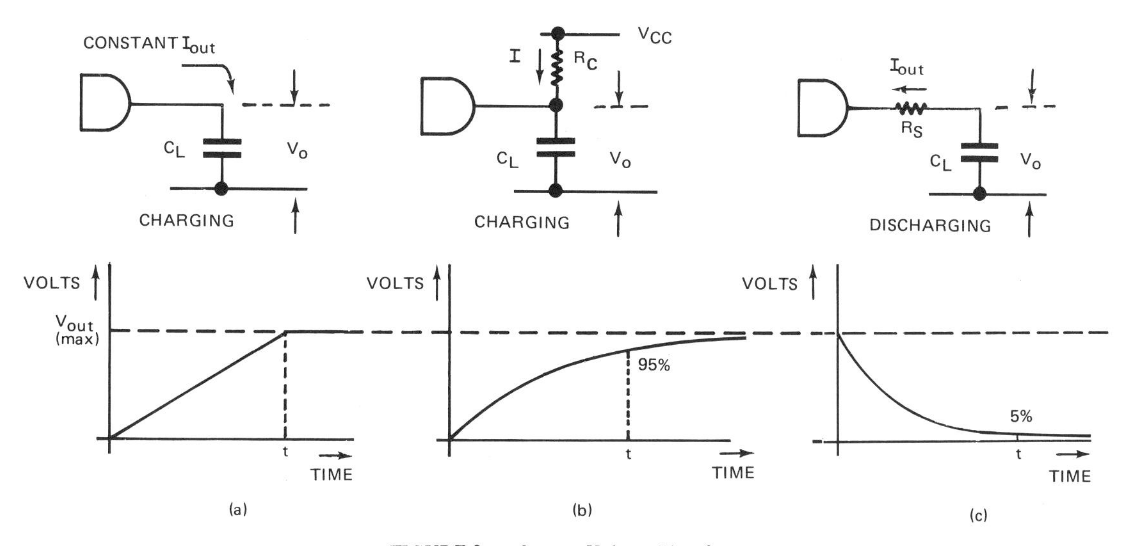

FIGURE 9. Output Voltage Waveforms

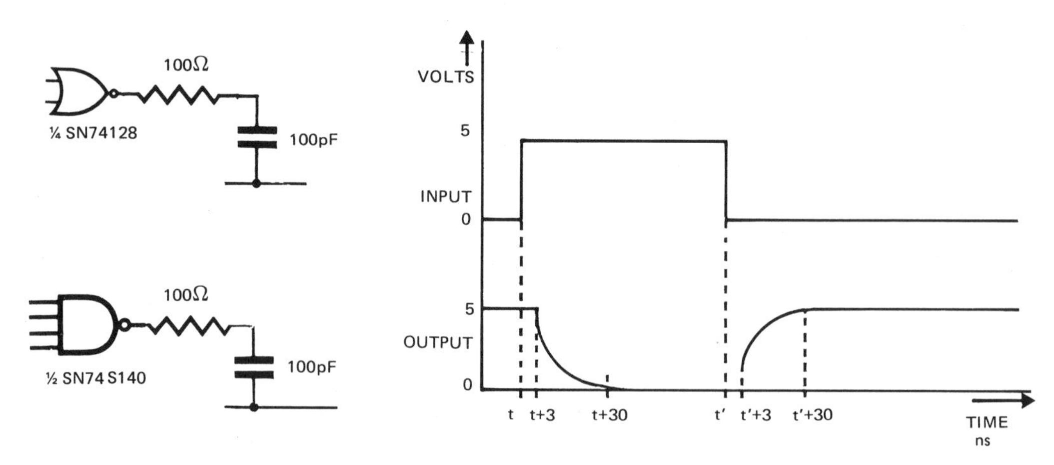

FIGURE 10. Using 50Ω Drivers

The Chip Enable input requiring a 12V swing, is easily driven from the SN75361 or SN75363 devices specifically designed for this purpose.

The Data Output of the TMS 4030 is capable of driving two standard TTL inputs. (i.e. I_{out} = −3.2mA). However, if speed is the ultimate criterion, then the capacitance connected to the Data Output should be kept to a minimum, since the current available from the output is relatively low. Hence wiring (printed circuit or otherwise) should be kept as short as possible, and driving one TTL input will give rise to faster edge speeds than when driving two. Although wire –'OR' ing several memory outputs together is normal practice to expand the number of words per bit, it should be remembered that this does add capacitance to the output line, and hence slow down its edge speeds.

Generating V_{BB}

By generating V_{BB} (−3V) within the system, the requirement for an additional power supply is removed. This supply is particularly suitable for generation since the current requirement is extremely low, even in very large systems (100μA max/TMS 4030).

The circuit shown in Figure 11 will generate a stable voltage rail of −3.1V, capable of sinking 10mA. This corresponds to the I_{BB} current of 100 TMS 4030s. The clock inputs are derived from the Refresh clock in the system, and the values shown in Figure 6 will be satisfactory for operation from a 500Hz 1:1 mark-space ratio clock.

EXPANDING THE MEMORY

It is normal for more than one RAM to be connected together to give greater than 1k words, and/or greater than 1 bit word length: e.g.

1 x TMS 4063	1k words x 1 bit
n x TMS 4063	nk words x 1 bit
m x TMS 4063	1k words x m bit
m.n.x TMS 4063	nk words x m bit

Similarly, more than one card of nk words by m bits may be connected together to further increase system capacity.

Bit Expansion

The size of the TMS4063 is 1024 words of 1 bit. To increase the system size to 1024 words by N bits, N TMS 4063 devices are connected with all their address and clock inputs paralleled, and each pair of I/O lines connected to ½ SN75370 (or other bit drive/sense circuits). Thus when an address is selected, one bit in each memory device is activa-

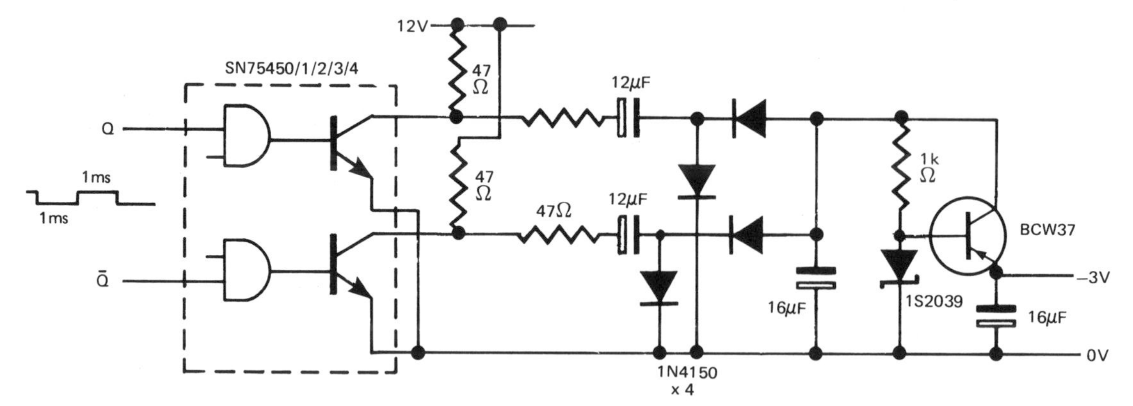

FIGURE 11. −3V Generator Circuit

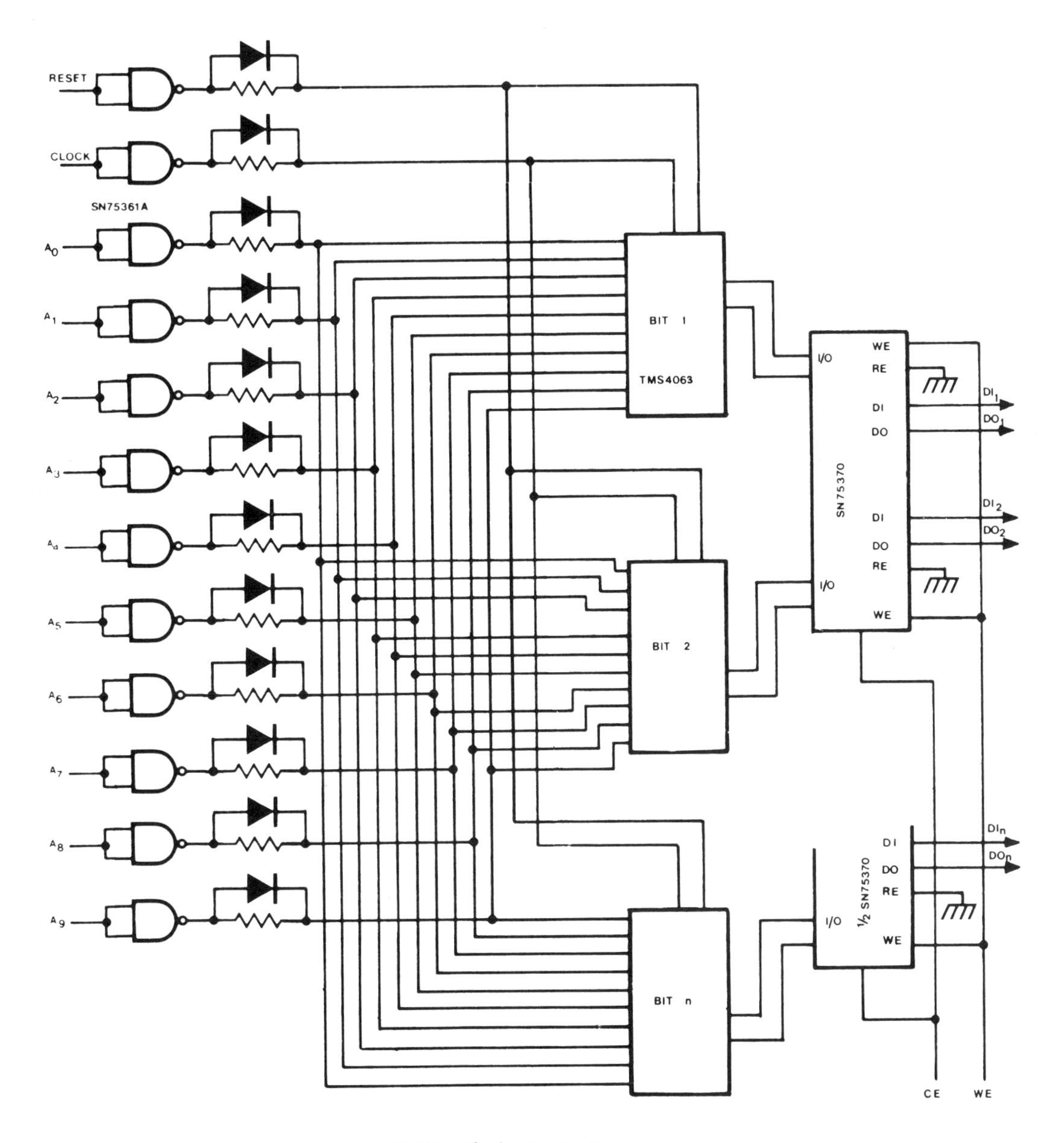

FIGURE 12. 1k x N. Bit Organisation

ted, forming an N bit word. This organisation is shown in Figure 12.

There is a practical limit to the maximum number of devices which may be connected together. This is due to the capacitive load of the TMS 4063 inputs on the clock and address drivers. Depending on the required speed of operation, these circuits are only capable of driving a certain maximum capacitance. To further increase the word length however, it is permissible to parallel up the clock and address inputs of several planes of N bits, at TTL level. To refresh M cards of N bits still only requires 32 cycles, since cycling addresses A_0 to A_4 selects every bit in the memory.

Word Expansion

The differential output lines of the TMS4063 and the corresponding drive/sense lines of the SN75370 are designed to allow more than one TMS 4063 to be wire-OR'ed into it. The capacitance of the I/O lines of a non-selected TMS 4063 is 3.0pF, and each ½ x SN75370 is capable of driving 60pF. When deciding how many 4063s to wire–OR together, it is necessary to also consider the capacitance of the printed wiring, etc. on the printed circuit board (P.C.B.). Since the output (DO) of the SN75370 is three-state, the outputs of several such devices may also be wire-OR'ed together, to further increase the number of words.

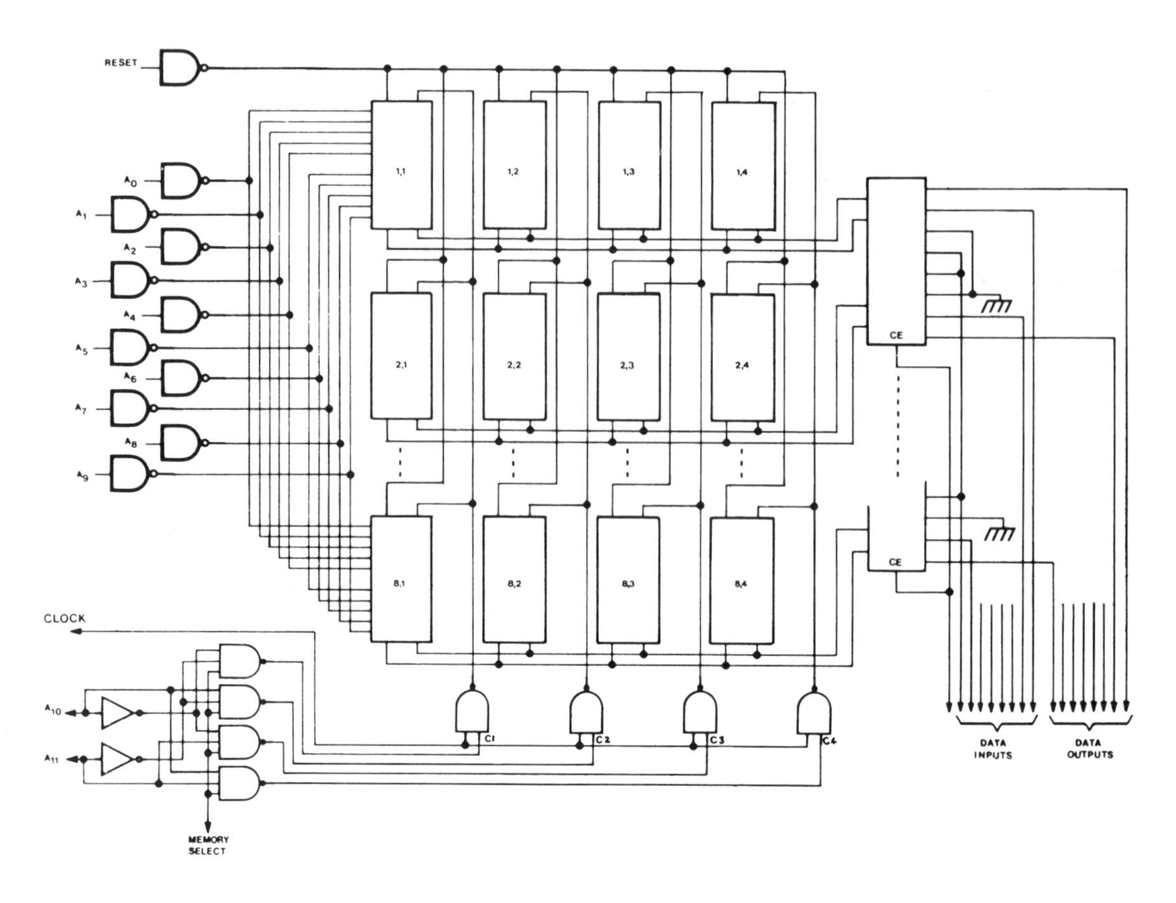

FIGURE 13. 4k Word x 8 Bit Memory Organisation

4k Word x 8 Bit System

Figure 13 shows the schematic diagram for such a system, which could be assembled on a modest sized P.C.B.

The TMS 4063 packages are arranged as an 8 x 4 matrix with the 10 address inputs of all the devices connected to a common 10 drivers. The I/O lines of each of the four devices in each row are wire 'OR'ed together into the I/O inputs of half an SN75370, giving 4096 words x 8 bits. The Reset inputs are all commoned, and driven from a single driver. The Clock inputs are used to select the particular row of 1024 words x 8 bits to be accessed at any instant, and hence have to be selected by decoding two more addresses, A_{10} A_{11}. The 3-input NAND gates used in this decode also have one input of all four gates connected to a Memory Select point which has to be at a logical '1' before any row can be selected.

As described, this system is designed for optimum cost rather than power dissipation. To reduce the power dissipation the Reset should also be controlled by the decoded addresses, as is Clock and the Memory Select. Provision should be made for Memory Select to inhibit the address drivers such that when Memory Select is a '0' (not selected) all the address and clock inputs of the memory devices are 'high', this being in the 'low' stand-by power state. If this is done, then the Memory Select must be driven to a '1' whenever a Refresh cycle is required, as well as for normal cycles. Also, during Refresh, the clock inputs, controlled by the decode A_{10} and A_{11}, must all be enabled, otherwise a greater number of Refresh cycles, including A_{10} and A_{11}, must be performed.

A single memory module, such as this, may be used as a small system with the necessary control circuitry, or else it may be used as part of a large system, with many such modules to give greater number of words and/or greater word length. However, the control circuitry required to support stored data in either case is identical.

CONTROL CIRCUITS FOR 1k RAM

The control circuitry for a memory system using 1k RAM type devices has to serve several functions.

(a) To generate the timing of the various clock pulses, address strobe, Read and Write strobes, and Memory Select (if applicable).

(b) To generate the Refresh addresses, and multiplex these with the addresses from the 'outside world.'

(c) To either generate Refresh cycle requests from an internal clock and process these to initiate Refresh cycles at sufficient frequency to support data, or else to process Refresh cycle requests generated by the computer, or other external source. In each case, the Refresh activity may be either synchronous or asynchronous with the normal memory operation, and the control circuitry must ensure that the Refresh cycle does not clash with a normal cycle in the asynchronous case. (Assuming that this situation does not arise in the synchronous case.)

(d) To decode higher order addresses which are used to select memory modules in large systems using the Memory Select inputs of the modules.

(e) To take care of normal cycle control and interlock and generate necessary output 'flags' required by the processor.

The design of the control circuit is influenced by several factors:

(i) Required Access time
(ii) Required Cycle time
(iii) and (iv) Power dissipation and cost. (Priority depending on individual requirement.)

It may well be that the Access time and Cycle time are not important, in which case the power and cost considerations predominate.

Synchronous System

It is more usual for cycle times in the range of .5 to 1μs to be required and the first circuit is designed around this performance. It is suitable for a synchronous system where the controlling clock is supplied from the processor to the memory.

The basis of the timing generation circuit in this first example is an 8 bit serial-in/parallel-out TTL shift register SN74164. This is connected as shown in Figure 14. The data input is initially a '1' and the first clock pulse moves this '1' into the first stage, whereby it appears on output A. This output is inverted and used to change the state of the data input latch to a 'O'. Subsequent clock pulses move the stored '1' through the shift register until it appears on the output connected to the 'clear' monostable the SN74121. The $\overline{Q}$ output of this monostable resets the data input latch and clears the shift register. Figure 15 shows this action.

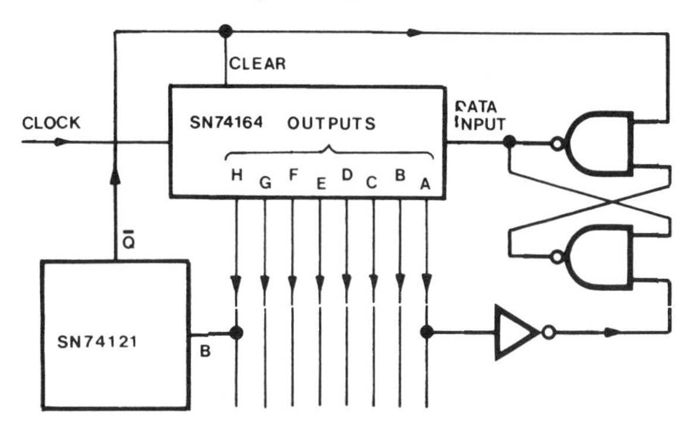

FIGURE 14. Basic Timing Generation

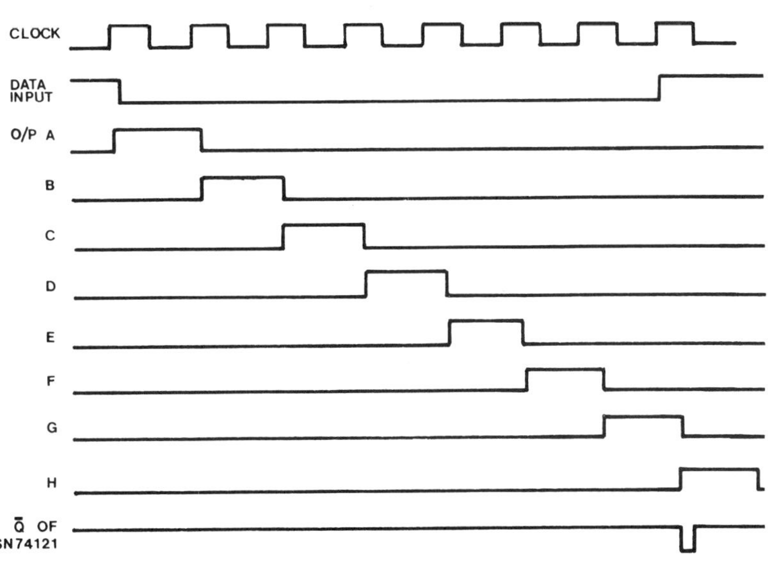

FIGURE 15. Sequence of Timing Circuit

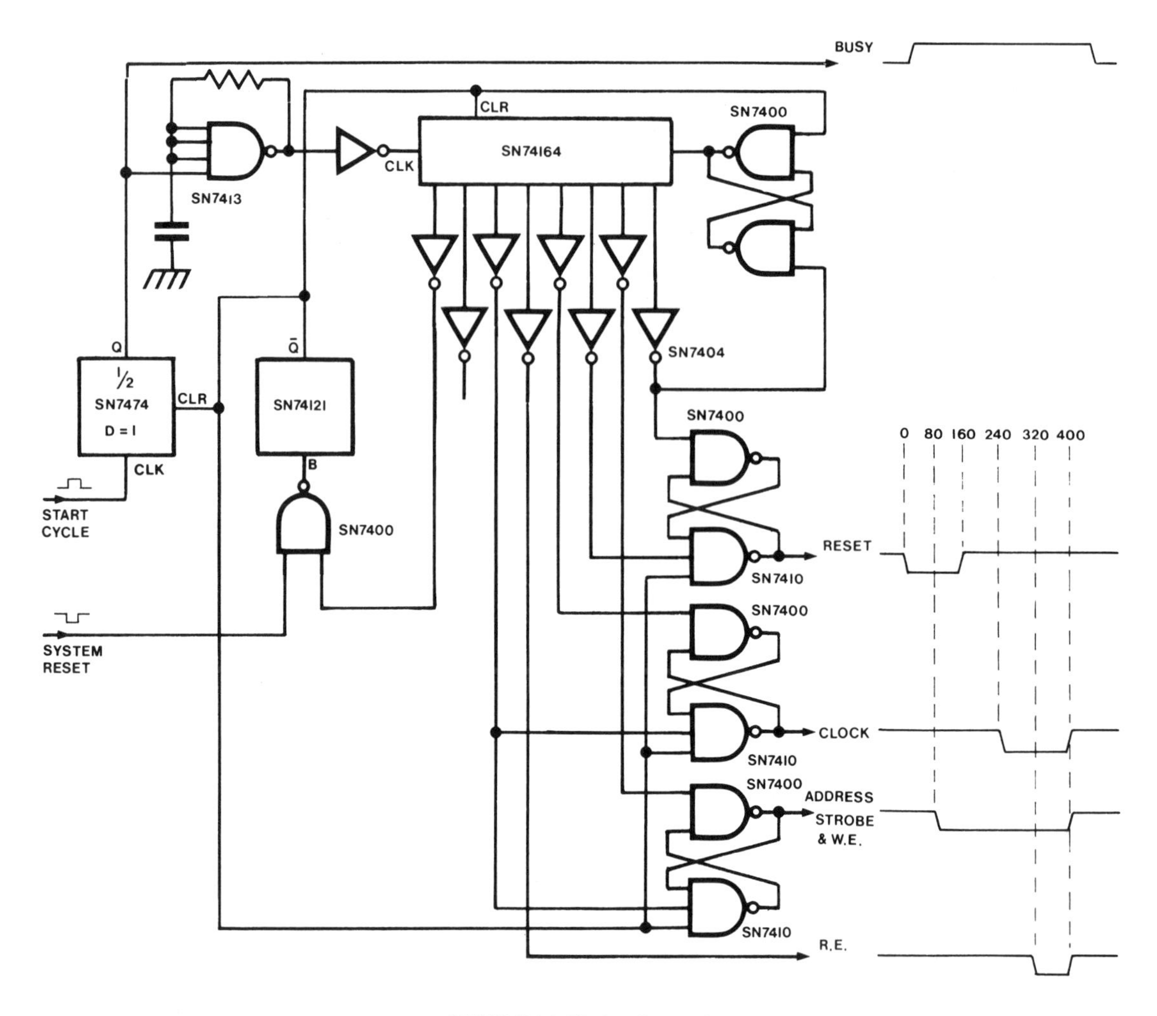

FIGURE 16. Timing Generation

In this mode the shift register is acting as a delay line, and combinations of the outputs may be used to generate the required pulse timings. The input clock to the shift register can be generated by a Schmitt gate with CR feedback, which is gated with the cycle control signal. If the clock period is 80ns a reasonable timing diagram may be obtained. This is shown in Figure 16.

One of the advantages of this system is that the timing of all the outputs is controlled by only one factor, i.e. the Schmitt oscillator. Under normal circumstances the frequency variation of this oscillator when the 5V logic supply is varied ±0.5V does not affect the system reliability, since the waveform timing is generous compared to the minimum values laid down in the device specification. However, if better frequency stability was required, a two-transistor multivibrator could be used, instead of the Schmitt oscillator.

To generate the refresh addresses, the input clock from the processor, etc. must be counted, to give an output which, in turn, will clock the refresh address counter at the correct rate. This is shown in Figure 17. The input clock to the address counter (an SN7493) is also used as the least significant output, and hence has to be 1:1 mark-space ratio.

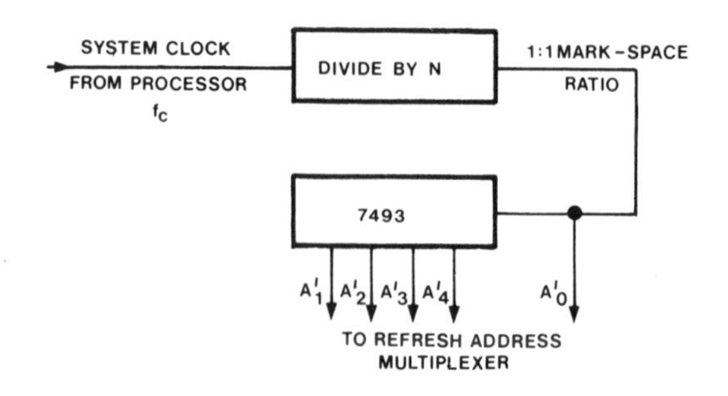

FIGURE 17. Refresh Address Generation

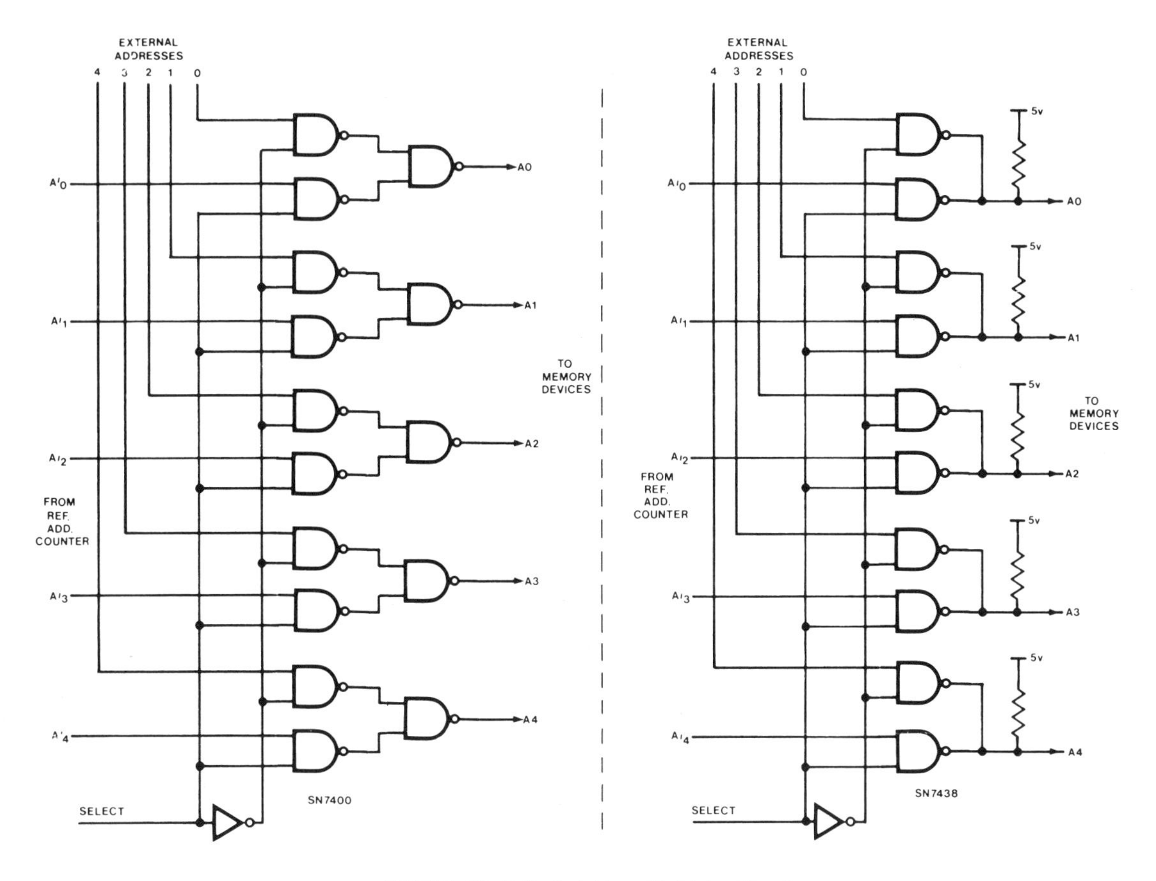

FIGURE 18. Refresh Address Multiplex Circuits

IF REFRESH PERIOD = 2ms

TIME BETWEEN REFRESH CYCLES = $2 \times 10^{-3}/32 = 62.5\,\mu s$

fAo' LEAST SIGNIFICANT ADDRESS FREQUENCY = $1/2 \times 62.5 \times 10^{-6} = 8$ kHz.

HENCE N (DIVISION FACTOR) = $f\ /8 \times 10^{3}$

These five addresses A_0 to A_4 then have to be multiplexed with the operational addresses from the 'outside world'.

The two most economical solutions for the address multiplexing are shown in Figure 18, although another alternative is to use two SN74157 quad 2 line to 1 line multiplexers. The latter takes up less physical space, but has a higher component cost. Figure 18 (a) shows the multiplex function made up from 15 NAND gates, and Figure 18 (b) shows an open collector NAND solution, requiring 10 gates and 5 resistors. The latter solution is particularly suited to driving the addresses through back-plane wiring, etc. in multi-board systems.

The one remaining function for the control logic is to process the Cycle Initiate and Read/Write signals and to co-ordinate the normal cycle and Refresh cycle functions. With a synchronous system it is fairly straightforward to make the normal cycle and Refresh cycles mutually exclusive. The easiest way of doing this is to use the Refresh cycle pulse to inhibit the normal cycle initiate pulse, thus giving total priority to the Refresh. Having arranged for this to be the case, then a very simple circuit, such as shown in Figure 19, is all that is needed.

The SN74123 monostables give a pulse output at each edge of the A_0 Refresh address waveform. These outputs are 'OR'ed into a latch which stores the fact that the cycle, initiated by its output, is a Refresh cycle, and it remains set until the end of the Refresh cycle. The outputs of this latch are used to control the Refresh address multiplexer, and the Read and Write Enable outputs which must be inhibited during Refresh. The latch output is also 'OR'ed into another latch along with the normal cycle initiate, since these two signals never occur together, and this forms the 'Busy' latch, also remaining set until the end of the cycle. The Busy signal may sometimes need to be inhibited during Refresh, and this may be accomplished using the output of the Refresh latch.

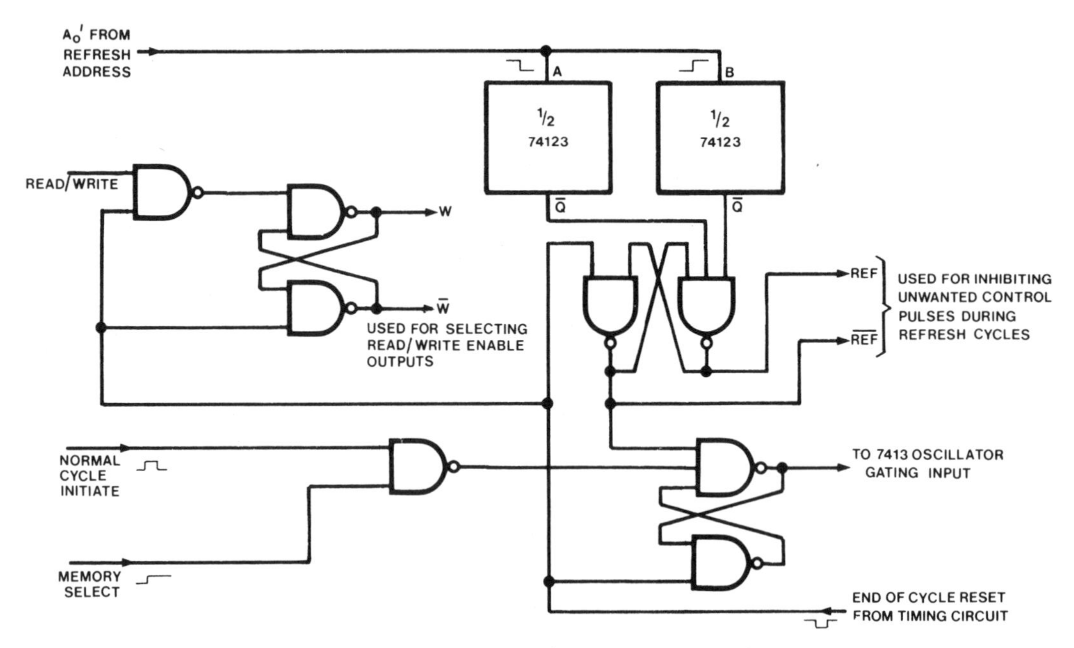

FIGURE 19. Refresh/Normal Cycle Control.

Figure 20 shows the complete control system using these circuits. Any extra output pulses that may be required can be generated in a similar manner to those shown, such as Data Available, etc.

There are many ways of generating the system timing pulses, e.g. L.C. delay line, monostables, shift register (as described), latches with time constants, etc. each of which may have its particular merits in terms of timing accuracy, thermal stability, power rail variation immunity, cost or other aspect. One of these alternatives is shown in Figure 21 using D-type latches, Schmitt trigger gates, and CR time constant circuits.

During standby, the capacitors C1 and C3 are charged to 3.3V. The capacitor C2 is discharged. The output of the Schmitt trigger network N2 is 'low' and N4 is 'high'. At the positive transition of the cycle request, the output Q of N1 is 'low'. The combination R1 and C1 is discharged. When V1 = 0.8V, the output of Schmitt trigger N2 changes the state of latch N3. The output $\overline{Q}$ of N4 which is initially at 'O', goes to a '1'. The latch N1 is reset to '1' by the preset input, and components R2 C2 are charged.

When V2 = 1.6V, all the inputs of N4 are 'high' and the outputs goes to '0'. Capacitor C3 which was initially charged to V3 = 3.3V discharges through resistor R3

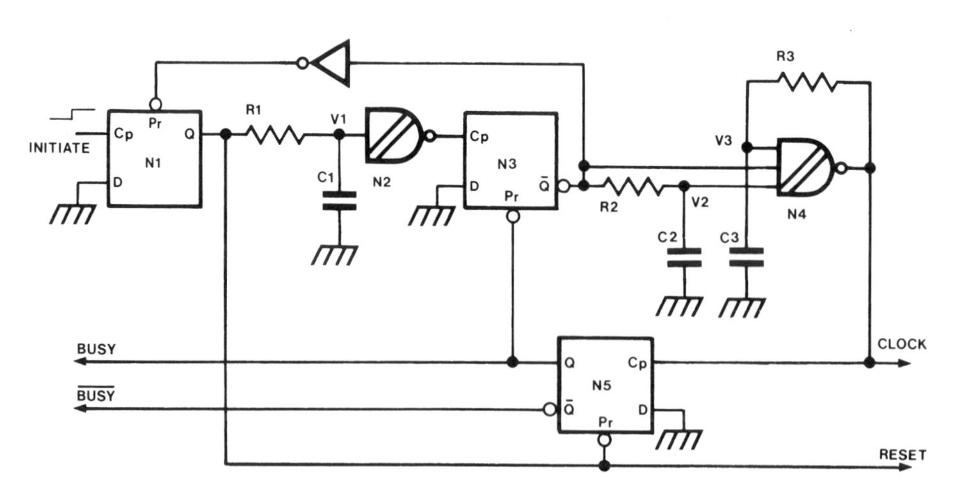

FIGURE 21. Alternative Timing Generation

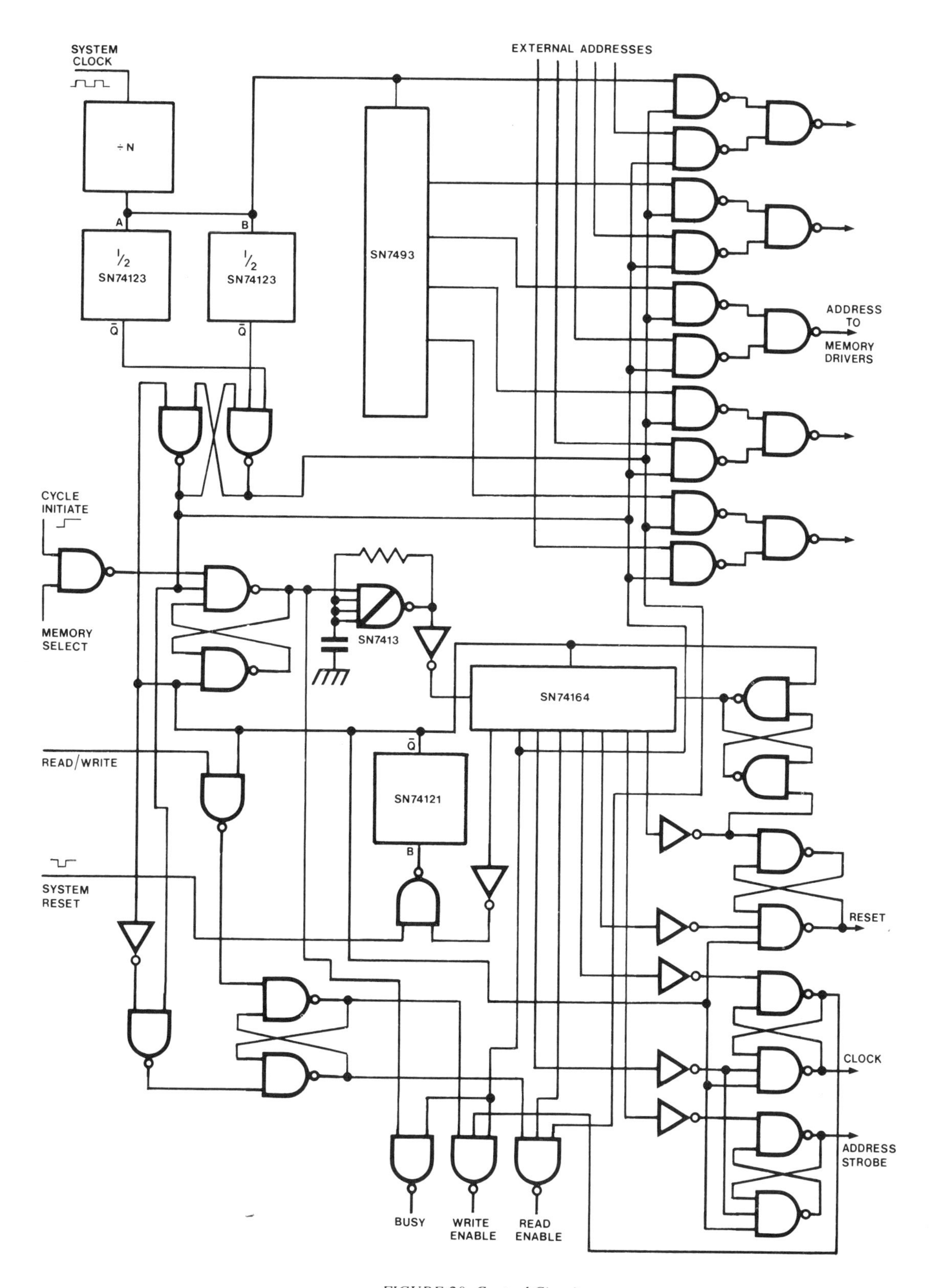

FIGURE 20. Control Circuit

towards OV. When V3 = 0.8V, the positive edge of N4 drives the latch N5 which resets the latch N3 to $\overline{Q} = 0$ by the preset input. This $\overline{Q}$ output immediately turns off the Schmitt N4 which ensures that it cannot oscillate. The latch N5 will be reset to Q3 = '1' at the beginning of the next cycle.

The length of the reset signal is determined by components R1 and C1, and by the propagation times of Schmitt N2, latches N1 and N3, and the invertor. The length of the decode delay t_{DD} is determined by components R2 and C2 and by the propagation time of the Schmitt N4. The length of the clock pulse is determined by components R3 and C3 and the propagation delay of Schmitt N4.

The output Q of latch N5 is high throughout the duration of the cycle. This may be used to indicate that the memory is busy.

The temperature stability of these different times depends mainly upon the capacitors. It is necessary to use high stability capacitors, e.g. poly-carbonate, or mica.

Asynchronous Systems

In an asynchronous system, the cycle request from the processor, and the Refresh activity of the memory are totally independent. Hence there has to be provision to store the normal cycle request if it occurs while a Refresh cycle is in progress, and similarly to store the Refresh cycle request (internally generated) if it occurs during a normal cycle. The problem then arises of priority when a normal cycle request and a Refresh cycle request occur at the same instant. Priority has to be given to one or the other, and the lower significance request has to be stored until the end of the ensuing cycle, and then acted upon.

Apart from this requirement, the control system is the same as the synchronous systems described previously, with respect to timing generation, address multiplexing, etc. Figure 22 shows a block diagram for the system. The latches A and B store the initiate signals, and are reset appropriately, i.e. when a normal cycle ends, the normal cycle latch B is reset, and not the Refresh latch A (and vice versa).

CONTROL CIRCUITS FOR 4k RAM

Refreshing Techniques

The TMS 4030 requires 64 Refresh cycles within the 2ms minimum refresh period (70°). However, there are several ways in which they may be implemented, and each has its own advantages. The most simple case is when the normal system activity causes Read or Write cycles to be performed on the 64 combinations of A_0 to A_5 without any additional cycles, within the 2ms. This situation does arise when the device is being used in a serial mode (as a shift register).

Another method is possible if the system is not required to operate at the maximum speed of the TMS 4030. A Refresh cycle can be performed at the end of every normal cycle, thus effectively doubling the cycle time of the device. A counter supplies the addresses A_0–A_5 in sequence, during the Refresh cycles. However, this relies on there being at least 64 memory cycle requests during the 2ms. The advantage of this system is that the memory is never 'Not Available' due to Refresh, but simply appears to the processor to have a cycle time of approximately 1μs.

One of the most common systems is to have an oscillator in the memory, generating a pulse every 1/64th of the Refresh period. This Refresh Clock is either sent out to the Processor (or whatever else is controlling the

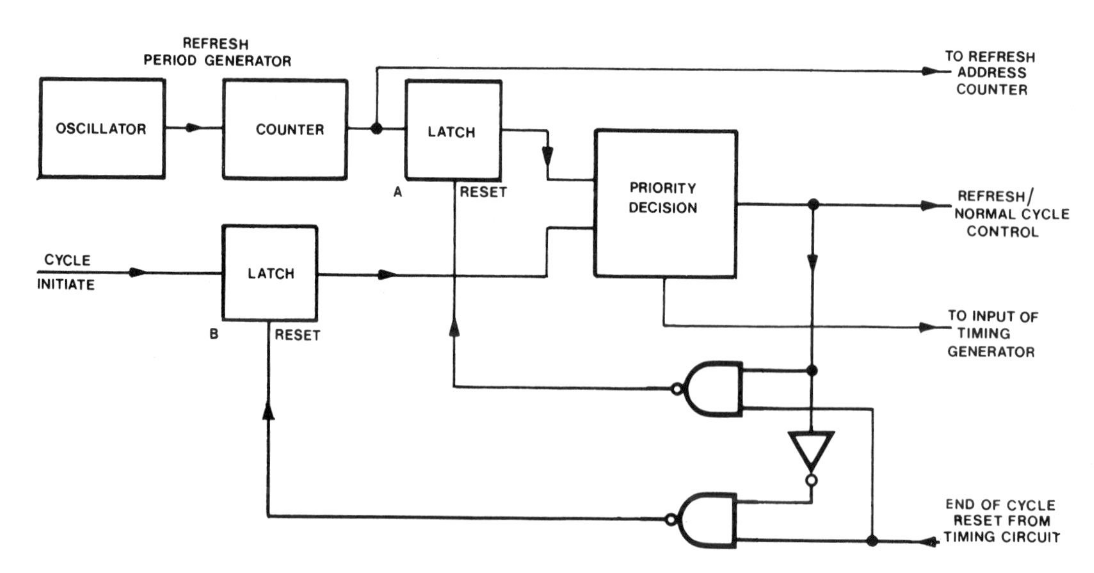

FIGURE 22. Asynchronous Control Circuit

memory) to indicate that the next cycle must be a Refresh cycle, or, alternatively, it initiates control circuitry within the memory system to override any subsequent cycle requests, and to perform a Refresh cycle immediately the cycle in progress (if any) is completed. In the first case (synchronous) the processor organises the Refresh cycle, and hence 'knows' that the memory is 'Not Available'. In the second case, (asynchronous), since the Refresh activity is all carried out within the memory system, the only evidence of this to the Processor is an apparently long cycle now and then. The worst case would be when the memory receives a cycle request immediately after a Refresh cycle has commenced, and the Processor has to wait for the Refresh cycle to finish and then for the normal cycle to be executed.

To make use of the low power standby condition possible with the TMS 4030, another possibility is to arrange for the 64 Refresh cycles to take place consecutively in a burst lasting approximately 32μs. The advantage of this system is that the entire control logic of the memory (including the Refresh address counter), with the exception of a 2ms clock, may be disconnected from the 5V supply for the remainder of the time (i.e. 2ms – 32μs = 1.968ms). This is especially useful where the memory is being operated with a standby battery power supply, and quiescent power dissipation must be kept to an absolute minimum.

These arrangements are shown diagramatically in Figure 23.

If the time taken by Refresh activity is an embarrassment to the processor, it may be reduced by several methods. The dynamic memory device requires refreshing because charge leaks away from the capacitors on which it has been stored. This leakage is the normal semiconductor thermal leakage effect, and is very much a function of temperature. Although the Refresh period is stated as 2ms at 70°C, an approximate law may be applied, which states that the leakage doubles for every 10°C rise in temperature. Using this law allows two things. First, the device may be operated at temperatures above 70°C by increasing the Refresh rate accordingly (e.g. 1ms at 80°C). The second possibility is to reduce the percentage of time for which the memory is 'Not Available' due to Refresh at lower temperatures. To obtain reliable operation over a wide temperature range, without performing more Refresh cycles than necessary, it is possible to add a temperature dependent component in the Refresh Clock circuit such that the oscillator frequency follows this approximate law.

Some applications may dictate that the interruptions due to Refresh be kept to an absolute minimum. If this is important enough to justify a fairly large increase in the amount of logic necessary to control the Refresh activity, then a memory function can be included in this logic. This is to record the fact that a particular memory address combination has been accessed within the Refresh period, and if this is the case, then the Refresh cycle on that address combination is omitted for that Refresh period. A block diagram for such a system is shown in Figure 24.

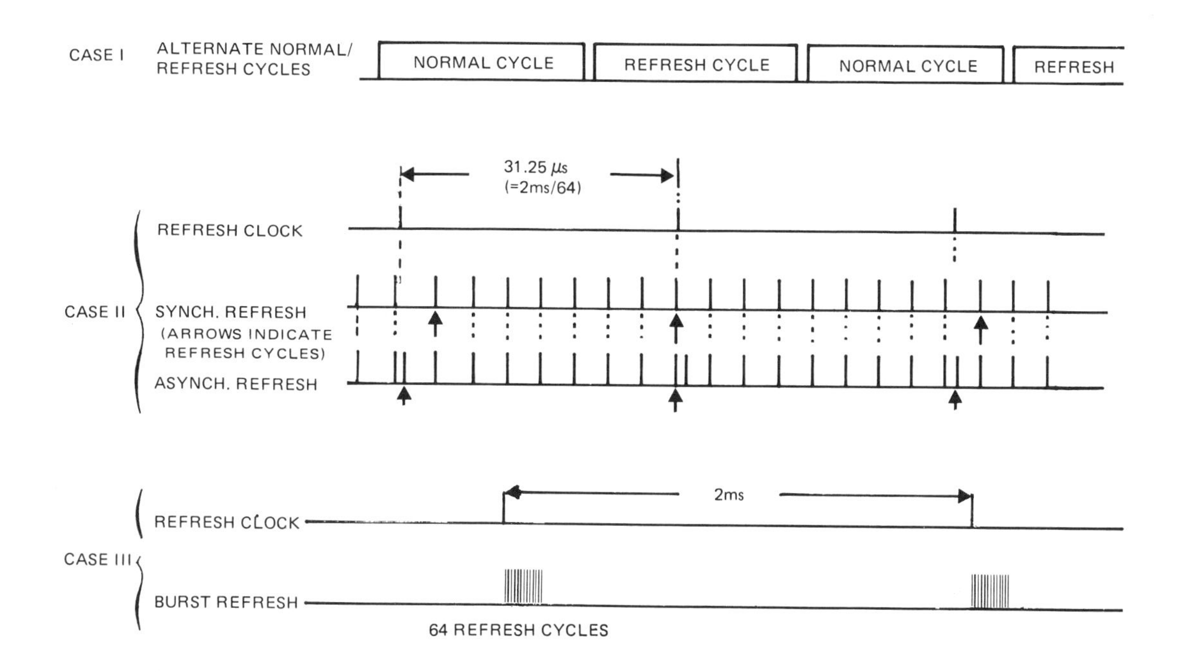

FIGURE 23. Various Refresh Organisations

The blocks shown in heavy outline are common to the majority of memory systems. The other blocks perform the Refresh cycle minimisation. Each time a normal cycle takes place, the relevant combination of addresses $A_0 - A_5$ is also applied to the 64 bit memory, and a '0' written into that location. Whenever the Refresh clock calls for a Refresh Cycle, and generates a new Refresh address via the address counter, this address is also applied to the 64 bit memory. The content of this location is read out, and if it is a '0', the Refresh cycle is prevented from taking place, and a '1' is written back into the memory. In this way, the Refresh cycles are only allowed to take place on the addresses which have not been accessed (read or write) within the Refresh period.

APPLICATIONS

MOS RAM devices are suitable for a wide range of applications. As previously stated, they are capable of high speed operation using relatively simple support circuitry and system timing, and also have the advantages of a very low power stand-by mode, when the dissipation is less than 2mW.

In certain applications, every address of the memory may be accessed within the Refresh period of 2ms. When this is the case, additional Refresh cycles are not necessary. Such an application is generating the characters for a CRT display for a data terminal. Another application where this condition may be met is using the R.A.M. as a recirculating shift register replacement. Here the memory address inputs are connected to the outputs of a 10 or 12 bit counter, the input of which is continuously clocked. A recirculating shift register may be considered as a loop of data moving past a stationary point, whereas the R.A.M. used in this application is represented by a point moving round a stationary loop of data. This is effectively the same thing. The advantage is that very large 'shift registers' may be constructed in this manner, using more than one RAM., and only when the number of addresses is so large that the address counter cycle time becomes longer than the Refresh period, does external Refresh circuitry become necessary.

This idea may be modified such that the address counter is not continuously clocked, but instead is clocked by the advent of data to be written in. Hence data appearing at random time intervals from some source may be stored sequentially in the memory and read out again in sequence at a later stage. This application would require external Refresh cycle generation.

For mainframe applications using the 1k RAM, it may be necessary to discard the low power dissipation between cycles in favour of the 150ns access time. However unused memory cards may be disabled on the basis of the most likely address to be next accessed is the one most recently accessed, which is the basic assumption used in shuffling data in a cache memory. Hence a large proportion of the memory can be in the low power state, whilst the average access time can approach the 150ns.

For applications requiring non-volatile data storage, batteries may be employed at moderate cost. It then only becomes necessary to sense power supply failure (which has been done for many generations of core memories to ensure correct power supply shut-down sequence for data retention) and switch in the stand-by batteries, at the same time inhibiting all memory activity so that all devices are in the low power state.

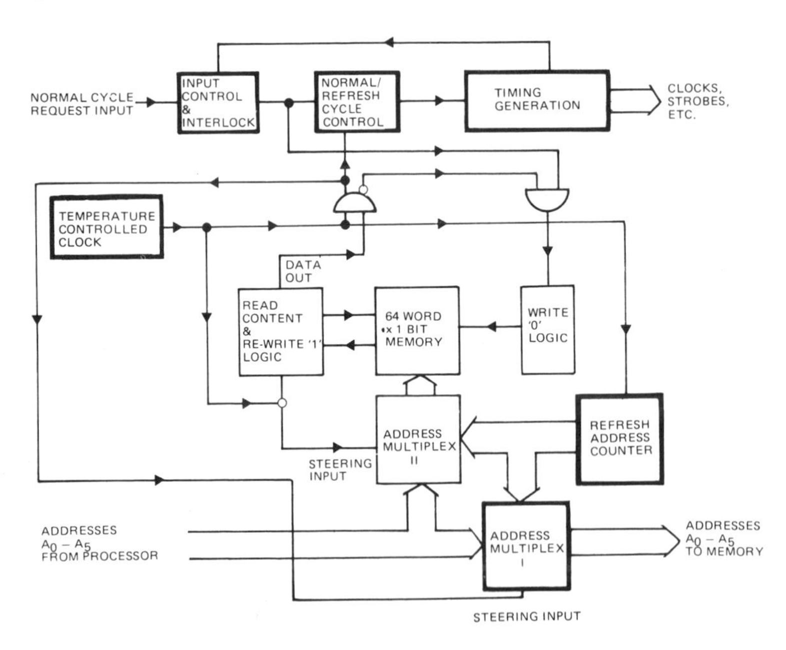

FIGURE 24. A Sophisticated Refresh Control Circuit for a 4096 Word Memory

IV ARITHMETIC PROCESSOR

by
Bob Parsons

Another major area where LSI MOS devices have made a contribution is in the computational field, the best example being the rapid development and abundance of pocket calculators. The actual devices used for these are specific and generally only supplied to the calculator manufacturer. Also they are not easily adapted to other applications as they have, for example, keyboard entry and de-bounce routines which limit the rate of data inputs, and the output data is coded for a particular type of display, i.e. it is not a normal arithmetic code, e.g. BCD or Binary. However, an MOS computational device is made especially for a wide range of general arithmetic processing, i.e. the TMS0117NC, and this chapter describes this device and its applications in order to illustrate an MOS computational product and its utilization. This digital block is designed to process numerical data in BCD format, and performs the most commonly required arithmetic operations. Numbers of up to ten digits can be processed in under 100 milliseconds. Even when only partially utilized, it gives a considerable cost saving when compared with more conventional arithmetic techniques. Its applications include automatic control systems, 'on-line' data analysis, digital correlators, weighing machines, and computing counters/frequency meters. The device requires a minimal amount of external control logic, and solutions to complex problems may be obtained by using it as a 'mini' central processor unit (CPU) in conjunction with bipolar integrated circuit Programmable Read Only Memories (PROMs) as the microprogram stores, as described both in this chapter and Chapter VII.

The various functions that a processor will perform may be classified into three types – arithmetic, register, and internal control ('housekeeping'). Register and simple arithmetic operations, such as data interchange and add/subtract 1, require a minimal amount of internal microprograms and are rapidly executed. More complex arithmetic operations, such as multiplication and division, use a considerable portion of the program space and take proportionately longer to execute. The time taken to carry out 'housekeeping instructions,' e.g. reset after error flag, is variable, being dependent on the state of the internal program.

INTERNAL ORGANISATION

As shown in Figure 1, internally a typical processor consists of a 3520 bit ROM for microprogram storage and control; a 182 bit 5 register dynamic Random Access Memory (RAM) 3 of which are used for data and two for flag storage, a decimal Arithmetic Logic Unit (ALU), control timing and output decoders.

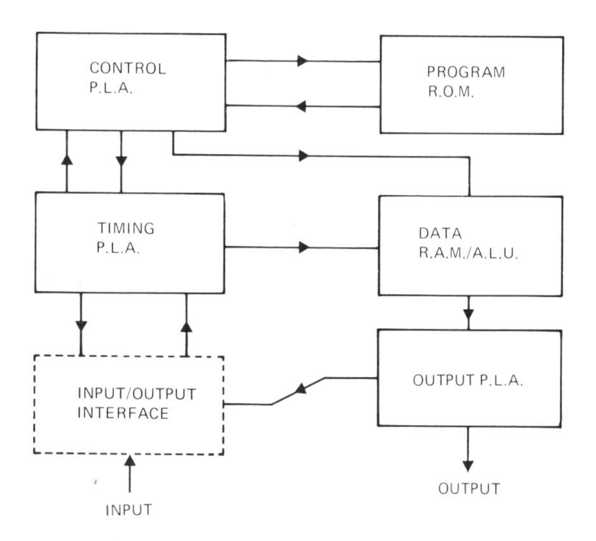

FIGURE 1. Internal Organisation of TMS0117

By using ROMs for program internal storage and 'programmable logic arrays' (PLAs), a very flexible device can be produced. By changing a single mask the microprogram can be modified to carry out operations such as $x^{1/2}$, $x^{-1/2}$, $(x^2 + y^2)^{1/2}$ etc.

DATA INPUT/OUTPUT AND CONTROL FUNCTIONS

The device's inputs, outputs and control terminals are shown in Figure 2.

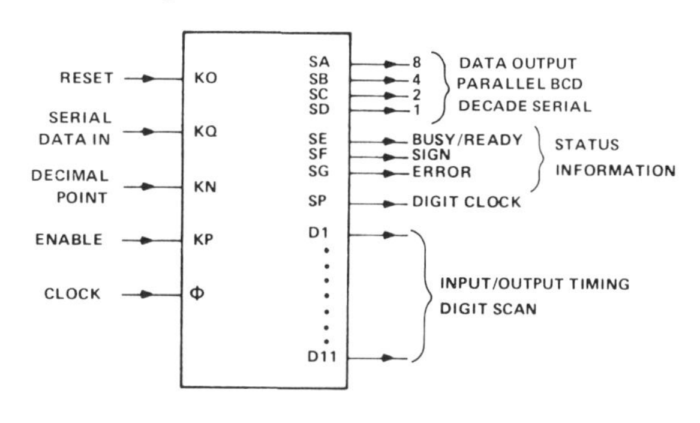

FIGURE 2. TMS0117 Inputs, Outputs and Control Terminals

Table 1. Input Coding

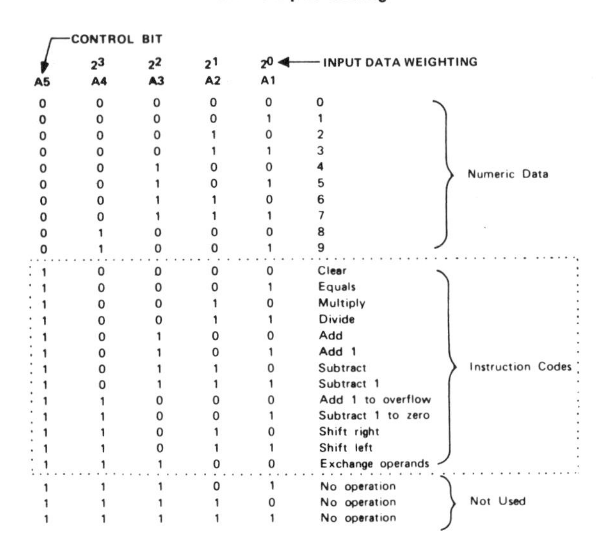

A5 (CONTROL BIT)	A4 (2^3)	A3 (2^2)	A2 (2^1)	A1 (2^0) ← INPUT DATA WEIGHTING		
0	0	0	0	0	0	Numeric Data
0	0	0	0	1	1	
0	0	0	1	0	2	
0	0	0	1	1	3	
0	0	1	0	0	4	
0	0	1	0	1	5	
0	0	1	1	0	6	
0	0	1	1	1	7	
0	1	0	0	0	8	
0	1	0	0	1	9	
1	0	0	0	0	Clear	Instruction Codes
1	0	0	0	1	Equals	
1	0	0	1	0	Multiply	
1	0	0	1	1	Divide	
1	0	1	0	0	Add	
1	0	1	0	1	Add 1	
1	0	1	1	0	Subtract	
1	0	1	1	1	Subtract 1	
1	1	0	0	0	Add 1 to overflow	
1	1	0	0	1	Subtract 1 to zero	
1	1	0	1	0	Shift right	
1	1	0	1	1	Shift left	
1	1	1	0	0	Exchange operands	
1	1	1	0	1	No operation	Not Used
1	1	1	1	0	No operation	
1	1	1	1	1	No operation	

Table 2. Numeric Coding

	SA	SB	SC	SD	SE	SF	SG	DIGIT
DATA	0	0	0	0	0	0	0	0
	0	0	0	1	0	0	0	1
	0	0	1	0	0	0	0	2
	0	0	1	1	0	0	0	3
	0	1	0	0	0	0	0	4
	0	1	0	1	0	0	0	5
	0	1	1	0	0	0	0	6
	0	1	1	1	0	0	0	7
	1	0	0	0	0	0	0	8
	1	0	0	1	0	0	0	9

NOTE: Data is extracted from MSD (D10) first to LSD (D1) last.

Data Input

There are two types of data input, both of which are entered on the KQ terminal i.e. numerical data, operational commands. The serial data input line requires its information in the form of a serial five-bit word. Four bits are used as a data/instruction code and the fifth bit as a control. The control determines whether the four-bit code is interpreted as data or as an instruction. This input coding is shown in Table 1.

In order to reduce the number of package pins required for data entry, the five-bit code is serialized. The processor generates sequential digit strobes, D1 to D11, that enable the input data to be serialized. A gate implementation of the entry logic and a simplified timing diagram are shown in Figure 3.

The data entries are controlled by the enable input, as described under Interfacing. Numeric entries are limited to ten digits. Any zeros that are required to fill the unused most-significant-digit positions preceding number entry ('leading zeros') need not be entered; but if, from a systems point of view, it is necessary to enter them, they will be ignored by the processor. Data are entered most-significant-digit first.

Data Output

There are two types of data output – numeric and status.

Numeric Data: is presented as digit serial/bit parallel, Binary Coded Decimal (BCD) during digit times D10 (MSD) to D1 (LSD) on outputs SA to SD (see Table 2). This serial information repeats after 11 digit times, i.e. once every digit cycle. Outputs D1 to D10 can be used to strobe an external display or indicate the beginning and end of the output data word. An output digit clock is provided on output SP to enable the user to clock output data into an external register. The digit clock timing is arranged such

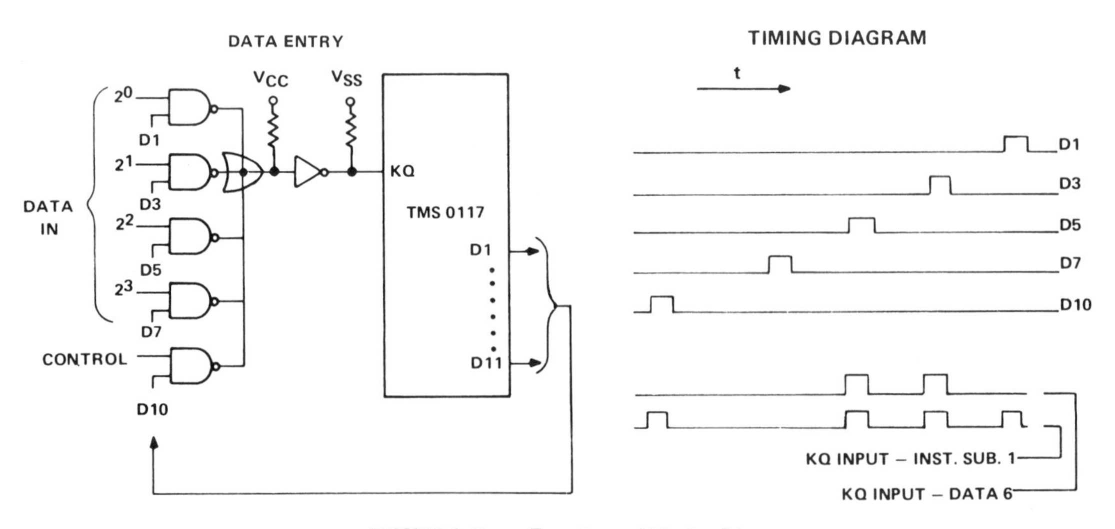

FIGURE 3. Entry Function and Timing Diagram

that output data is valid on either edge of the digit clock. Similarly digit strobes D1 to D11 also inset the data outputs.

Status Information: i.e. the internal state of the processor (housekeeping), is available on outputs SE to SG during D11 time. Output D11 may be used to clock outputs SE to SG into an external register. The status coding is shown in Table 3.

Table 3. Status Coding

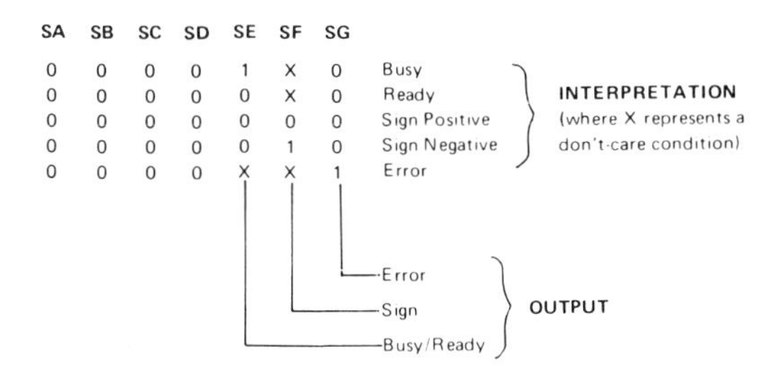

SA	SB	SC	SD	SE	SF	SG		
0	0	0	0	1	X	0	Busy	INTERPRETATION (where X represents a don't-care condition)
0	0	0	0	0	X	0	Ready	
0	0	0	0	0	0	0	Sign Positive	
0	0	0	0	0	1	0	Sign Negative	
0	0	0	0	X	X	1	Error	

During D11 time, outputs SA to SD are zero. Output SG indicates an error, such as numeric overflow or an invalid operation. Status outputs have the following priorities.

1) Error output SG invalidates all other numeric and status outputs. If an error indication occurs, the processor enters a locked state and must be reset by the KO input.
2) Busy/ready output SE invalidates numeric and sign data, unless it indicates that the processor is ready to accept new data or instructions, i.e. only when there is no error and the ready signal is present are the sign and numeric outputs valid.

An example of the data output timing is shown in Figure 4. As shown, the serial output data represents –0190654003. The numeric and sign outputs are valid since the processor indicates that it is READY and there is no ERROR during D11 time.

Decimal Point (DP)

The processor operates in fixed-point mode on input and output. The point is not interposed between input digits, i.e., there is no input or output data code representing DP. DP is, in fact, implied by the digit time at which input KN is taken to a logic High. Decimal-point format is shown in Table 4.

KN may be taken to a logic High by means of a fixed link with the required digit output D1 to D10. If the position is to be determined by means of logic inputs, then open collector gates can be used to determine the KN-digit

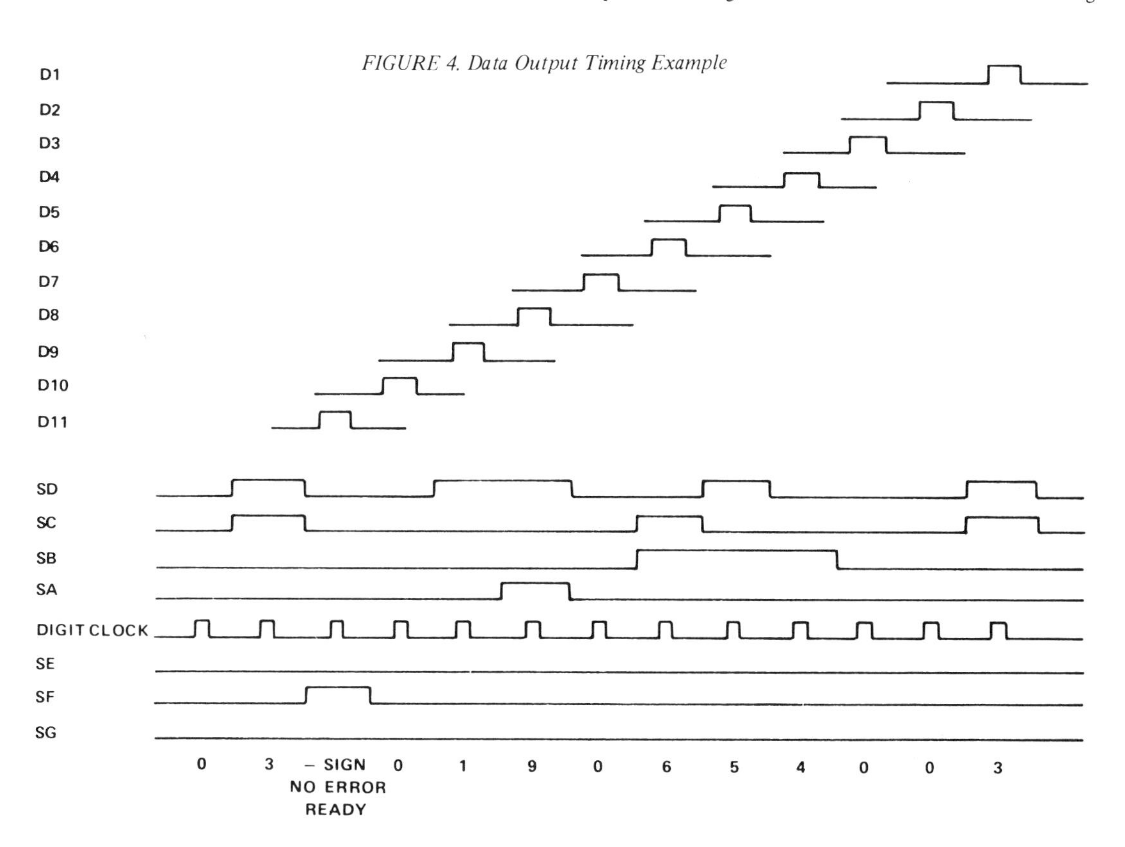

FIGURE 4. Data Output Timing Example

Table 4. Decimal Point Format

DEC. PT POSITION	OUTPUT REGISTER (MSD ↓ … LSD ↓)		
0	X X X X X X X X X X •	D10	Digit time at which KN = V_{SS}
9	X • X X X X X X X X X	D9	
8	X X • X X X X X X X X	D8	
7	X X X • X X X X X X X	D7	
6	X X X X • X X X X X X	D6	
5	X X X X X • X X X X X	D5	
4	X X X X X X • X X X X	D4	
3	X X X X X X X • X X X	D3	
2	X X X X X X X X • X X	D2	
1	X X X X X X X X X • X	D1	

connection in a manner similar to data entry.

The decimal point is not entered in the normal flow of entering numbers but is set for any calculation by the KN to digit line link. This link does not affect an addition or subtraction problem, but it does affect multiplication and division. The decimal is not stored internally; therefore, erronerous answers will result if the connection is changed while performing a series of calculations. To prevent errors, RESET or CLEAR the chip after changing the decimal point position.

Timing and Operating Sequence

The timing of the data entry and control is determined by the enable input in conjunction with the status outputs. It is best expressed in 'digit times', i.e. the time between leading edges of successive digit pulses, and 'digit cycles', i.e. the time between leading edges of successive D1 pulses.

To initiate a data entry cycle, the enable input KP is taken to a logic High (V_{SS}). After a variable delay, the status outputs will indicate that the processor is in the BUSY mode. Data entry will be possible during the READY mode only. The device will ignore inputs when performing an operation. The entry cycle will last 14 to 23 digit times, depending on which digit is 'on' when the enable connects to V_{SS}. Enable must be released within 5 digit times from BUSY signal unless the special mode of operation is desired. (In the special mode the enable is kept High throughout the operation). Data inputs are changed each time the processor goes from the READY to the BUSY state until the entire sequence is completed. This speeds up data input since the processor may be ready internally to accept new data, but, because of the multiplexed output, the READY output cannot be given until D11 time. Since data entry and some operations, such as Add 1, Shift Right, etc., are short, the BUSY time will only be 1 to 3 digit cycles.

Data and instructions are entered in the same order as with a +, –, = type of keyboard. In addition to chain operations, e.g. z x b x c =, there is an 'implied constant' mode. The processor retains the last operator and number

Table 5. Examples

	Entry	Display	Comments
1)	100	100	Display entry
	–	100	Stored as instruction
	3	3	Display entry
	=	97	Executes previous instruction
	=	94	Constant mode, instruction is sub 3, executes and displays
	–	94	Stored as instruction
	50	50	Display entry
	=	44	Executes previous instruction
	=	–6	Constant mode instruction is sub 50
	=	–56	Constant mode instruction is sub 50
2)	100	100	Display entry
	–	100	Stored as instruction
	3	3	Display entry
	+	97	Causes previous instruction to be carried out and stores current instruction.
	10	10	Display entry
	+	107	Previous instruction carried out and stores current instruction
	3	3	Display entry
	–	110	Executes previous instruction and stores current instruction
	99	99	Display entry
	–	11	Executes previous instruction and stores current instruction
	12	12	Display entry
	=	–1	Executes previous instruction and displays result
3)	–	0	Stored as sign/instruction
	5	5	Display entry
	X	–5	Enters instruction and interprets – as sign and displays
	3	3	Display entry
	=	–15	Executes previous instruction and displays result
4)	–	0	Stored as sign/instruction
	5	5	Display entry
	X	–5	Enters instruction and interprets – as sign and displays
	–	–0	Enters sign and displays
	5	–5	Enters data and displays with associated sign
	=	25	Executes previous instruction and displays result
5)	100	100	Display entry
	+	100	Enters add instruction
	–	200	Enters sub instruction and executes previous instruction
	3	3	Display entry
	=	197	Executes previous instruction and displays result
6)	100	100	Display entry
	–	100	Enters sub instruction
	–	0	Enters sub instruction and executes previous instruction
	5	5	Display entry
	=	–5	Executes previous instruction and displays result

DATA INPUT AND DIGIT LINES

*Decimal point – one switch and only one switch permanently closed.

FIGURE 5. Data Input and Digit Lines

entry before an 'Equal' operation, as a constant.

The + and – code is interpreted as a sign after a Multiply or Divide operation, and as an operation at any other time. Successive Equal operations cause multiple executions of the previously stored instructions and the associated data, i.e. constant mode operation. Various examples of sequential operations are shown in Table 5.

Table 6. Time Required to Complete Functions

FUNCTION	TIME
Number entry, single digit	5.2 ms maximum
Operation instruction entry	6.9 ms maximum
Shift left or right	1.72 ms
Increment or decrement	3.4 ms
Exchange operands	5.2 ms
Add, subtract	8.6 ms
Multiplication	70 ms (worst-case numeric inputs)
Division	80 ms (worst-case numeric inputs)
Digit cycle time	1.72 ms
Digit time	156 μs

Table 6 shows the time required to complete the functions indicated for a nominal 250-kHz clock rate.

INTERFACING

Input

As previously explained, input data is serialised by means of the digit strobes. This is shown diagramatically in Figure 5, c.f. Figure 3, where this is implemented with logic gates.

The data input lines are KN, KO, KP and KQ. The 'boxes' represent a logical or direct switch connection between the digit lines D1 to D11 and K inputs. The K inputs will interpret as a logic 'High' a voltage that lies between the substrate supply voltage V_{SS} and $V_{SS} - 1.5$V, and as logic 'Low' a voltage between the gate supply voltage V_{GG} and drain supply voltage V_{DD} +1.2 V. The simplest input interface may be a TTL open-collector gate with a pull-up resistor to V_{SS}. (Figure 6)

INPUT INTERFACE

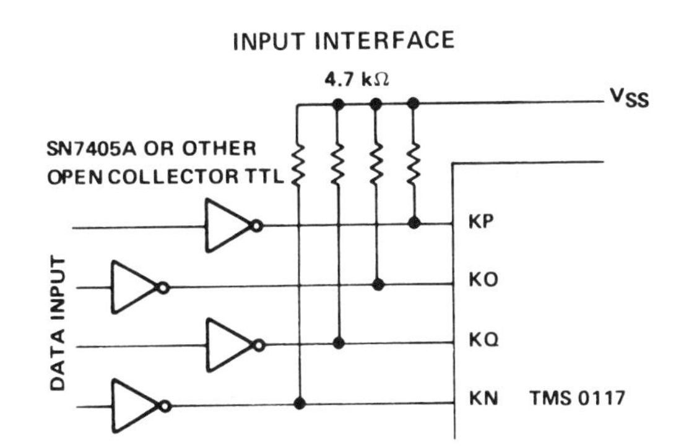

FIGURE 6. Input Interface Circuit

OUTPUT INTERFACE

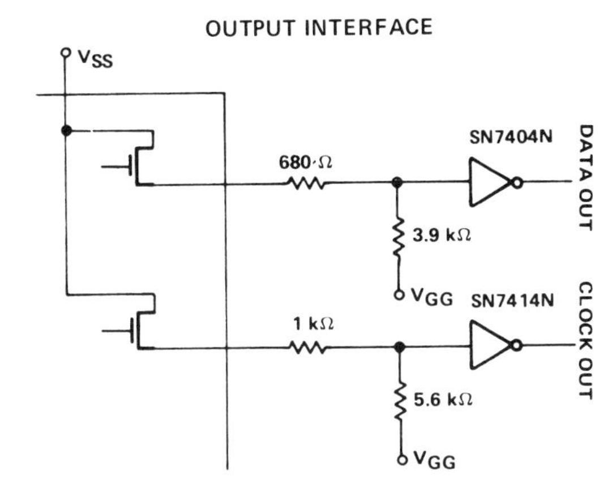

FIGURE 7. Output Interface Circuit

All data and control inputs have an internal pull-up resistor to V_{SS}. The load presented to an external driver is the internal resistor (30 kΩ) and the capacitance of the gate clamp protection diode.

Output

All outputs, D1 to D11, data and status are open-drain buffers. These output buffers have a typical channel resistance $r_{DS(on)}$ of 250 Ω and can supply in excess of 5 mA from V_{SS}. An economical output interface compatible with TTL is shown in Figure 7.

Any output, e.g. digit clock, that is required to drive a TTL clock input should be interfaced with a Schmitt trigger, such as the SN7414N integrated circuit. The Schmitt trigger is required because the fall time of the open-drain output is of the order of 150 nanoseconds and is not directly compatible with edge-triggered TTL inputs.

PRACTICAL APPLICATIONS

A Subsystem

The peripheral circuits required to operate a TMS0117NC are shown in Figure 8. These provide: TTL compatibility on data input and output, a visual display of the contents of the output register and the necessary control logic. The circuit operation is as follows:–

Clock Generation: Transistors Q1 and Q2 form a self-starting single-phase clock generator with a pulse repetition rate of 250 kHz. The required output voltage swing is from V_{SS} to V_{GG}. The clock input of the TMS0117 has an internal buffer with a typical capacitance of 10 pF, thus allowing component economy in the design of the clock generator.

Data Input: As previously stated the data input is classified as control and numeric. The class is determined by the select input of a 4-pole 2-way multiplexer N1 whose outputs are serialized by means of the digit strobes and open collector gates N2 to N5. The serial data is interfaced to the input KQ by an open collector buffer N7 with a pull-up resistor to the substrate supply V_{SS}. The fifth data bit, i.e. the one that tells the processor if the other four inputs are data or an instruction, is serialized by gate N6 and digit strobe D10.

Data Output: Data output consists of status and numeric information. Status information is obtainable only during D11 time from outputs SE, SF and SG. The D11 output clocks these into a 3-bit staticizer N8 to N10. A Schmitt trigger N18 ensures edge speed and loading compatibility between the D11 output and the clock input of the staticizer. Status outputs are then displayed by visible-light-emitting diodes (VLEDs) operated from the staticizer outputs.

Numeric information is available from outputs SA to SD during times D1 to D10 in serial BCD form. By using digit strobes as digit enables for the display it is possible to produce an economical dynamic display using any multi-digit common cathode 7 segment monolithic device. The serial BCD output is converted to seven-segment code by the decoder N11. This then drives the segment drivers N12 and N13. The displays which have a common cathode for each digit, are enabled by digit drivers N14 and N15, which have been designed for direct compatibility with the TMS0117 digit outputs. The peak segment current of 40mA is defined by 56-Ω resistors in series with the segment drivers.

Overall Operation: The data control line to multiplexer N1 is set up by an external input which tells the processor to accept numerical or control data. A single clock edge (start) transfers a logic Low to the output of latch N16. This takes the enable input KP of the processor to a logic High, instructing it to carry out a data entry cycle. A short time after enabling, the status output from latch N8 (BUSY) also goes to a logic High, indicating that the processor is entering data. This output resets and holds the Q output of N16 to a logic High, ensuring that the enable input is removed from the processor as soon as it is BUSY. Thus, further enable commands are prevented from being entered during this time. As soon as the status outputs indicate that the processor is READY, the reset to bistable circuit N16 is released allowing further enable commands.

Programmable BCD Calculator

In order to economise on package count the system has been arranged to operate with 8 decade numbers.

Programming: So that the calculator may be easily programmed, the program language is constructed with a minimum number of commands. The program format consists of an 8 bit word,

A8 A7 A6 A5 A4 A3 A2 A1

The first three bits A8, A7 and A6 determine the type of instruction, the five remaining bits specify the Instruction, Memory Address, or an Input/Output Command. An exception is the Branch Command determined by A7 and A8, where the remaining 6 bits specify the Branch Address. Table 7 shows the basic instructions.

Mathematical Operations (000): These are defined by instructions with the following format:–

A8	A7	A6	A5	A4	A3	A2	A1
0	0	0	X	X	X	X	X

mathematical operation — type of mathematical operation

Bit A5 is not used. Bits A1 to A4 define the particular mathematical operation. The actual operations for the various codes of A1 to A4 are given in the dotted box section of Table 1.

Table 7. Basic Instructions

Instruction Number	A8	A7	A6	
C0	0	0	0	Mathematical operation
C1	0	0	1	Read (input)
C2	0	1	0	Write (output)
C3	0	1	1	Stop
C4, C5	1	0	X	'Jump' if sign +
C6, C7	1	1	X	'Jump' if sign –

Memory Operations, Input/Output (001 and 010): Memory commands control the interchange of data between the calculator and the random access memory. The instruction 001XXXXX transfers data from the memory location addressed by XXXXX (A1–A5) into the calculator. Similarly the instruction 010XXXXX causes output data from the calculator to be stored in the memory location addressed by XXXXX. The bits A1 to A5 can address the first 32 memory locations. Data storage may be classified into 3 types.

a) Temporary storage for results of partial calculations.

b) Constant storage such as π, ϵ etc.

c) Input/Output data. Each of the 32 memory locations could be used as an input/output store through which data could be transferred to and from the calculator.

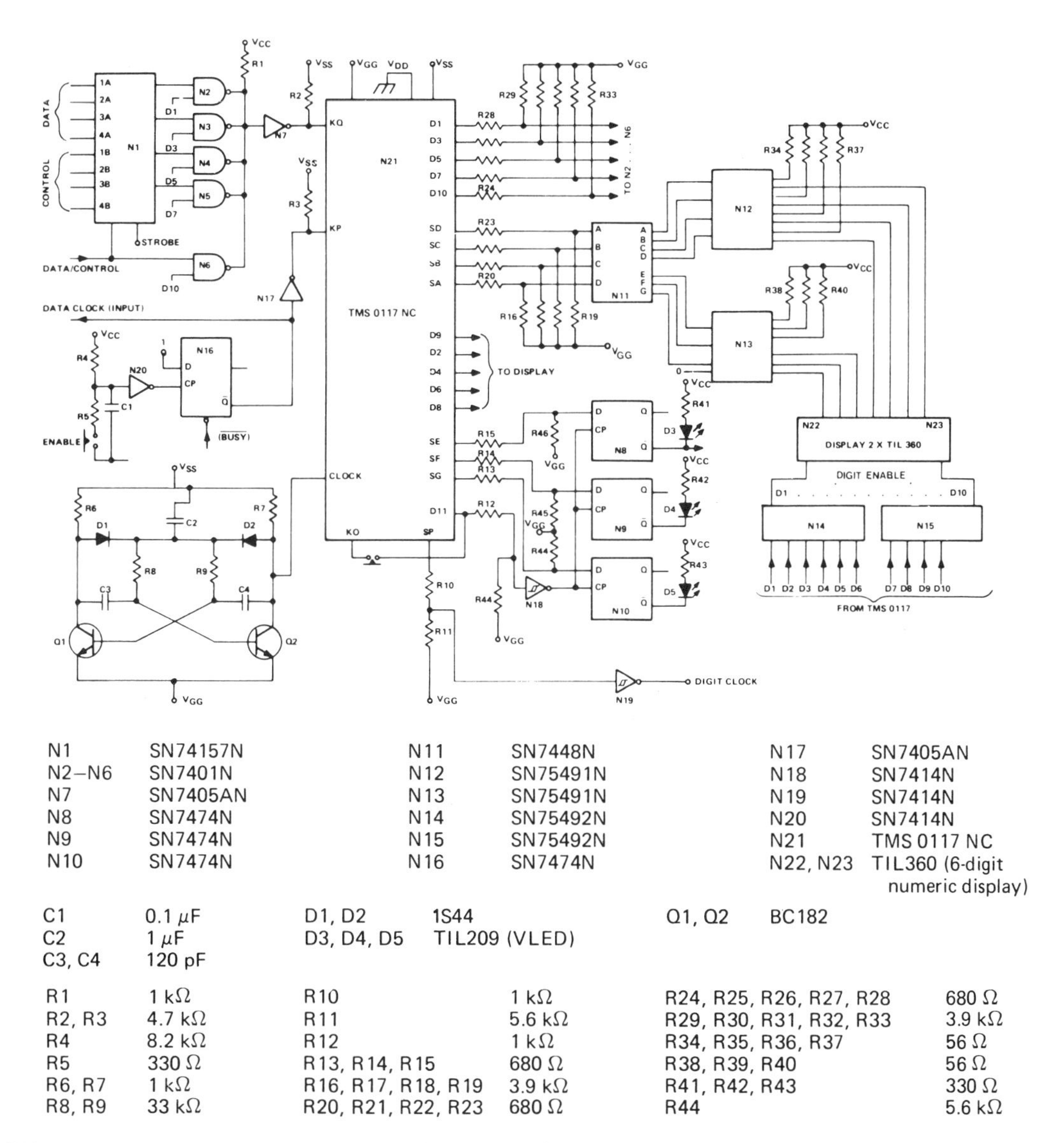

N1	SN74157N	N11	SN7448N
N2–N6	SN7401N	N12	SN75491N
N7	SN7405AN	N13	SN75491N
N8	SN7474N	N14	SN75492N
N9	SN7474N	N15	SN75492N
N10	SN7474N	N16	SN7474N
N17	SN7405AN	N18	SN7414N
N19	SN7414N	N20	SN7414N
N21	TMS 0117 NC	N22, N23	TIL360 (6-digit numeric display)

C1	0.1 μF	D1, D2	1S44	Q1, Q2	BC182
C2	1 μF	D3, D4, D5	TIL209 (VLED)		
C3, C4	120 pF				

R1	1 kΩ	R10	1 kΩ	R24, R25, R26, R27, R28	680 Ω
R2, R3	4.7 kΩ	R11	5.6 kΩ	R29, R30, R31, R32, R33	3.9 kΩ
R4	8.2 kΩ	R12	1 kΩ	R34, R35, R36, R37	56 Ω
R5	330 Ω	R13, R14, R15	680 Ω	R38, R39, R40	56 Ω
R6, R7	1 kΩ	R16, R17, R18, R19	3.9 kΩ	R41, R42, R43	330 Ω
R8, R9	33 kΩ	R20, R21, R22, R23	680 Ω	R44	5.6 kΩ

NOTE: Many of the integrated circuits contain multiple elements; the total number of packages is considerably lower than the number of device designations.

FIGURE 8. TMS0117 as a Subsystem

Stop Instruction (011): When this instruction is carried out the calculator will stop until an external start signal is applied. This instruction is employed, for example, when the calculator is used with automatic test equipment or in machine tool applications, in order to synchronise the calculator with external equipment.

Branch Instructions (10 and 11): This form of instruction is used when 'decisions' i.e. non sequential programming, are to be made, e.g. a particular address contains the instruction (10101000). If the result of the previous calculation is positive, a 'branch' is made to the instruction at address location (101000) and this instruction carried out. If the sign is not positive it continues as normal.

With 6 bits of program address it is possible to address 64 instructions. If the required program contains more than 64 instructions (e.g. 256) it is possible to accommodate these additional instructions by indirect addressing. The program can be divided into groups of 64 instructions and, by placing a Branch Instruction in the most significant bits of an address, it is possible to address from group to group:–

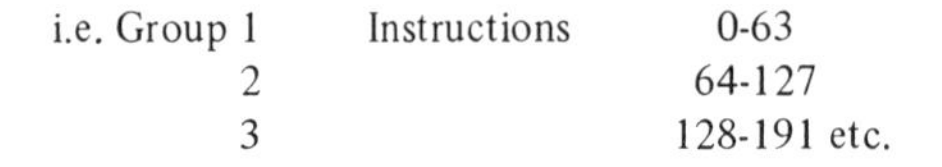

i.e. Group 1	Instructions	0-63
2		64-127
3		128-191 etc.

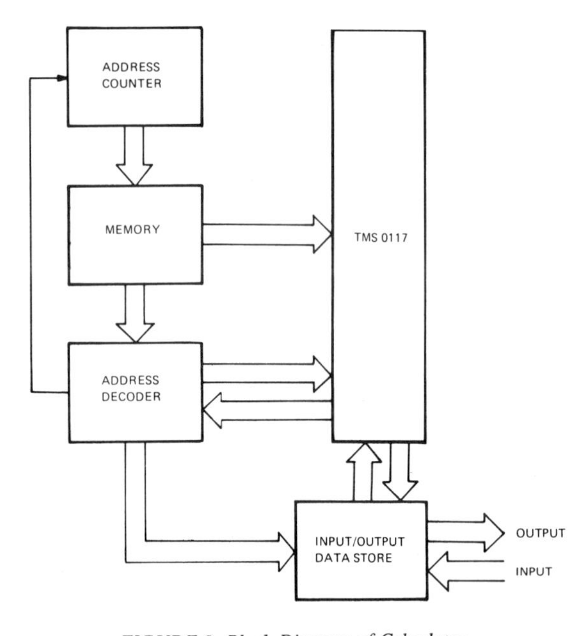

FIGURE 9. Block Diagram of Calculator

Circuit Description: The block diagram of the Programmable BCD calculator is shown in Figure 9. A programme address counter is used to ensure that the programme steps are carried out in the correct order. After the execution of each programme step, the counter is incremented by one. The output from the address counter addresses the memory containing the programmed instructions that are to be carried out. These programmed instructions are then decoded by an instruction decoder which controls the address counter when a branch instruction occurs and synchronizes the calculator with the memory and input/output logic.

In the logic circuit of Figure 10, the two 4-bit synchronous counters, N3 and N4, form the programme address counter. Their outputs feed the address inputs of the two memories, N1 and N2, which contain the stored programme. In the circuit shown, SN74188A, user programmable, read only memorys (PROMs) have been used. However, this type of memory should only be used when a 'permanent' programme is required. For programme flexibility a random access memory (RAM) such as the SN7489 or SN74200 may be used. The number of programme steps can, of course, be increased beyond 256 by adding additional memories and address counters. The outputs A1 to A8 of the instruction ROM are divided into two groups as explained previously. Outputs A1 to A5 define a particular operation, add, multiply etc., and A6 to A8 a 'basic' instruction such as perform a mathematical operation, read input data etc. At all other times outputs A1 to A5 specify an address. Bits A6 to A8 are decoded into 1-out-of-8 lines by decoder N5 to form the control lines C0 to C7. Instructions C2 (write data into output store), C4/5 and C6/7 (branch instructions) are completed within one digit cycle time and the programme counter is incremented at the next D11 pulse. The time taken to carry out instructions C0 and C1 (Mathematical operation/read input data) is variable and is determined by the time taken for the calculator to complete its internal micro programmes. The programme counter moves on to the next instruction when the status output of the device changes from busy to ready. If a 'stop' instruction C3 is decoded, the processor will only step to the next instruction when an 'External Start' signal is applied. A branch instruction is handled as follows:- When such an instruction is detected by decoder N5, the output from gate N9B or N9C changes to a logical '1'. This together with the sign input enables gate N8B (AND-OR invert) causing its output to change to a logical '0', thus enabling the synchronous load input of the programme counters N3 and N4. When clocked, these will not increment by one, but will be loaded with the data present on lines A1 to A6; which is the branch address of the next programme step. Although there are six address bits they may only be used by indirect addressing as explained earlier. The most significant outputs (bits 7 and 8) of the 8 bit address counter are reloaded during a branch instruction so that these remain unchanged. When the 'Step Programme/Continue' switch is in the 'Step Programme' position, the processor will stop after it has completed each instruction. It may be restarted by means of the External Start or the Increment input.

The input/output control logic, shown in Figure 11, forms part of the instruction decoder. The decoded instruction C2 (write output data in RAM) obtained from the instruction decoder, enables the memory address encoder N27. The inputs of this encoder are obtained from the calculator digit strobe outputs, so that, when encoded,

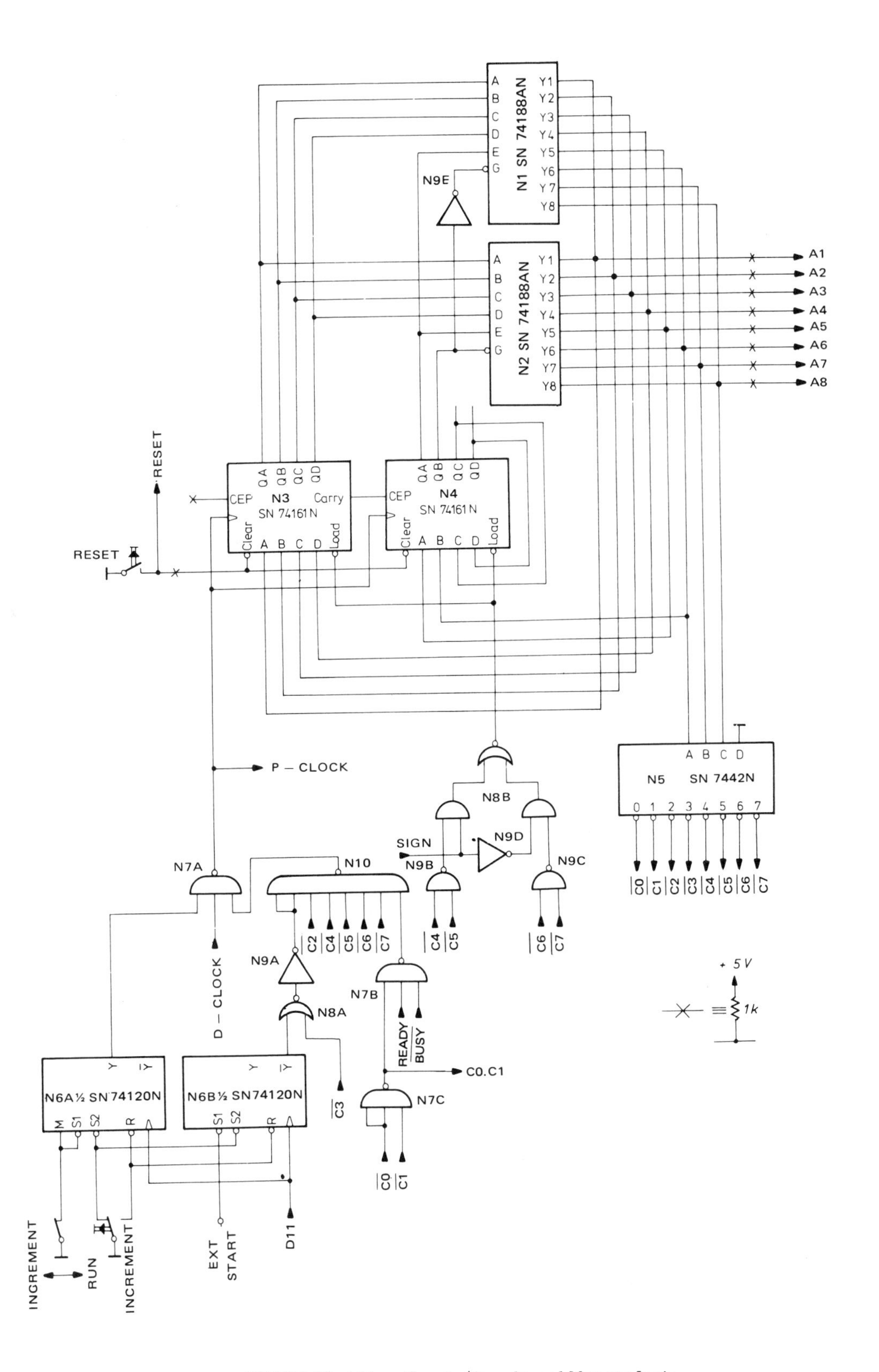

FIGURE 10. Address Counter/Decoder and Memory Logic

these define the address locations in which the output data from the processor is to be written. During a 'read input' instruction, the address inputs A, B and C to the memory are obtained from counter N28 via the multiplexer N26. The read address counter N28 increments by one after each decade has been entered. After the complete number (8 decades) has been entered the Q_D output of N28 changes to a logical '1', producing a 'ready' output. This enables the instruction counter and decoder, allowing the processor to continue. When an 'Instruction Input' C0 is decoded, the synchronous load input of counter N28 is taken to a logical '0'. After the processor has completed an instruction entry cycle, a Reset-clock (R-clock) is produced (derived from the Digit-clock (D-clock) and the busy/ready output of the processor, clocking the counter N28. This causes the data (0001) present on its load inputs to be transferred to its Q outputs and the Q_D output to change to a logical '1', again indicating 'entry complete' and allowing the processor to continue.

The random access data memory, shown in Figure 12, is addressed by the A1 to A5 outputs of the programme stores N1 and N2. These 5 bits can address a total of 32 locations. Associated with the store is a parallel data input and output channel. The data words are organised as 8 decade numbers. Each RAM is able to store two such words, i.e. 64 bits. Input data, which is in parallel form,

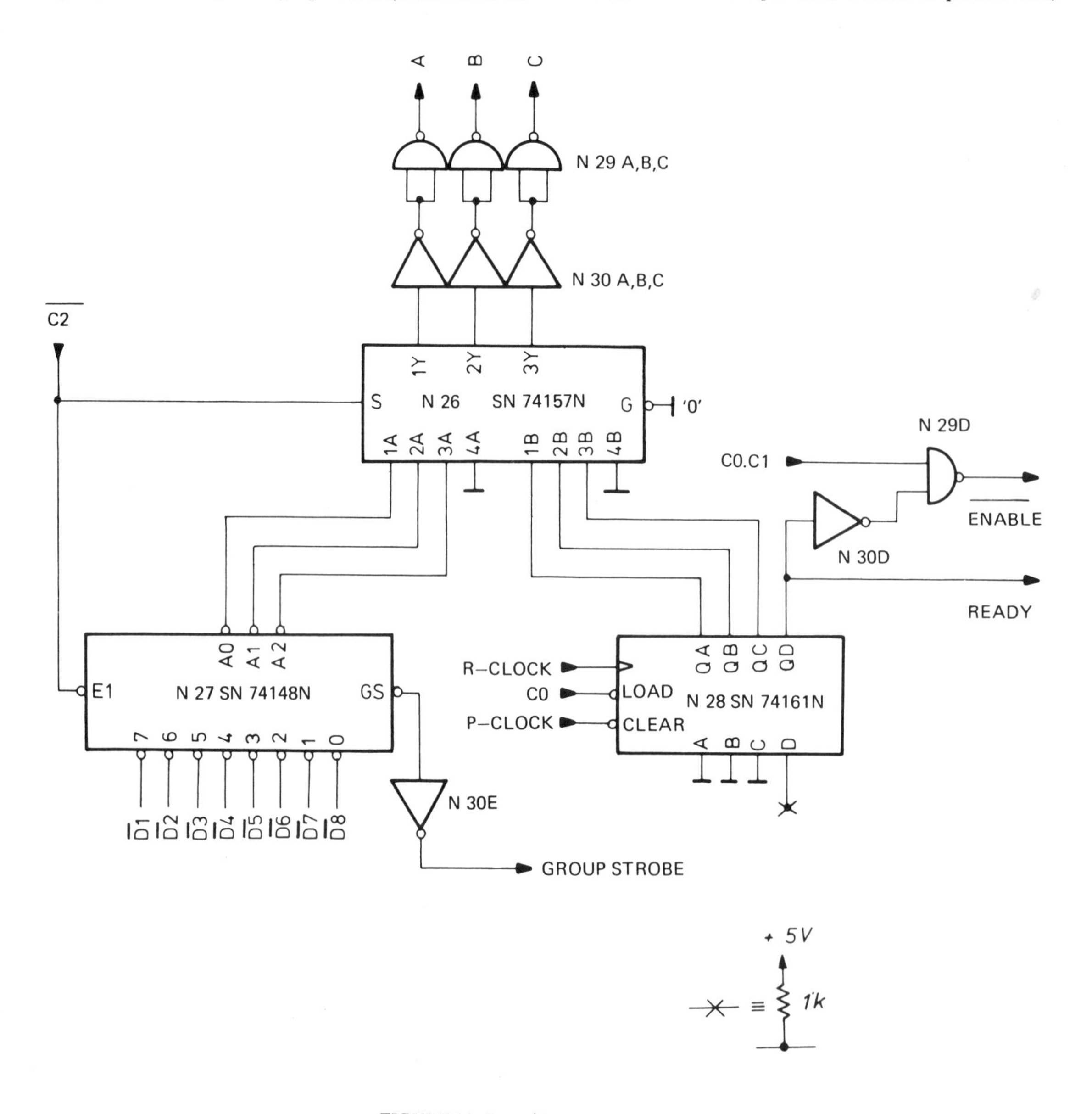

FIGURE 11. Input/Output Control Logic

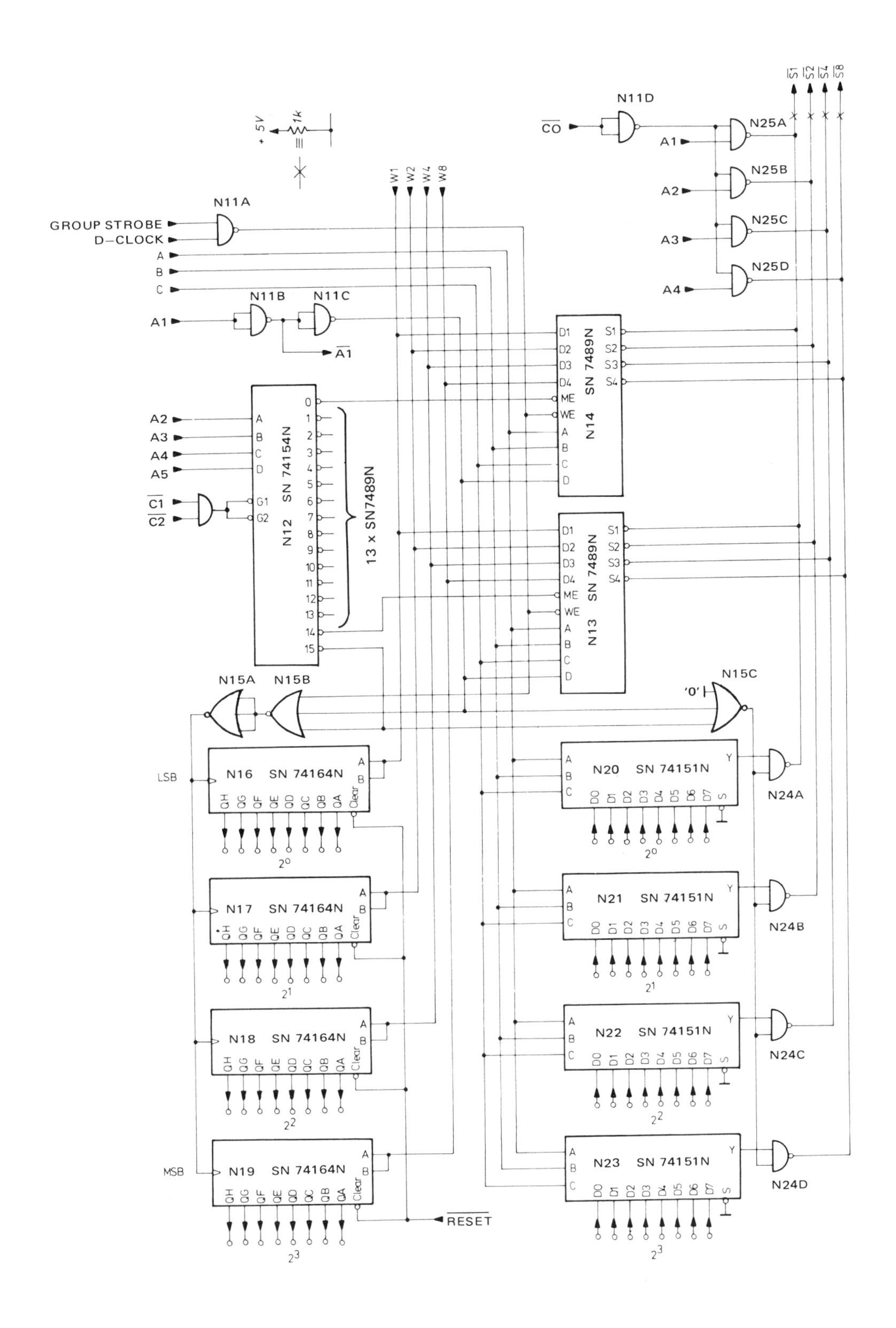

FIGURE 12. Input/Output Data Memory

is converted to decade serial, by means of multiplexers N20 to N23. The output of each multiplexer is 'wire ORed' with its corresponding output from the RAM before being transferred into the arithmetic unit. Data for the arithmetic unit may therefore be derived from an external source or from the RAM store by controlling the logic states of inputs C1 and C2 or C0. Serial output data from the arithmetic unit is converted into parallel form by means of 8 bit shift registers N16 to N19. In the system shown only two SN7489 RAMs have been used, this number may of course be increased to suit a particular application. In many instances it is economical to replace some of the RAM storage by ROM storage in order to hold numerical and conversion factors, constants such as ϵ, π, cms./ins, etc.

The arithmetic functions of the BCD calculator are all performed by a TMS0117 processor, as shown in Figure 13. A master 250 kHz clock is generated by a Schmitt trigger oscillator, N31A, followed by a buffer, N32A, and interface transistor, VT1. The clock waveform generated is symmetrical about the supply V_{DD} with an amplitude of ± 7.2V. Output timing is determined by the 'busy/ready', D11 and D-clock outputs. Bistable network N38 produces a logical '1' at its Q output for the time that the processor is busy. Pulse synchroniser N39 produces an R-clock every time the processor status outputs change from 'busy' to 'ready' and the R-clock also increments the memory address counter after each data entry. Two types of overflow are produced: one when the magnitude of a numerical calculation exceeds ten digits, (overflow 1); the other when the result of an operation exceeds 8 digits, (overflow 2). The latter signal is produced by 'ANDing' the segment H(SH) 'dipstick' output with the D9 output.

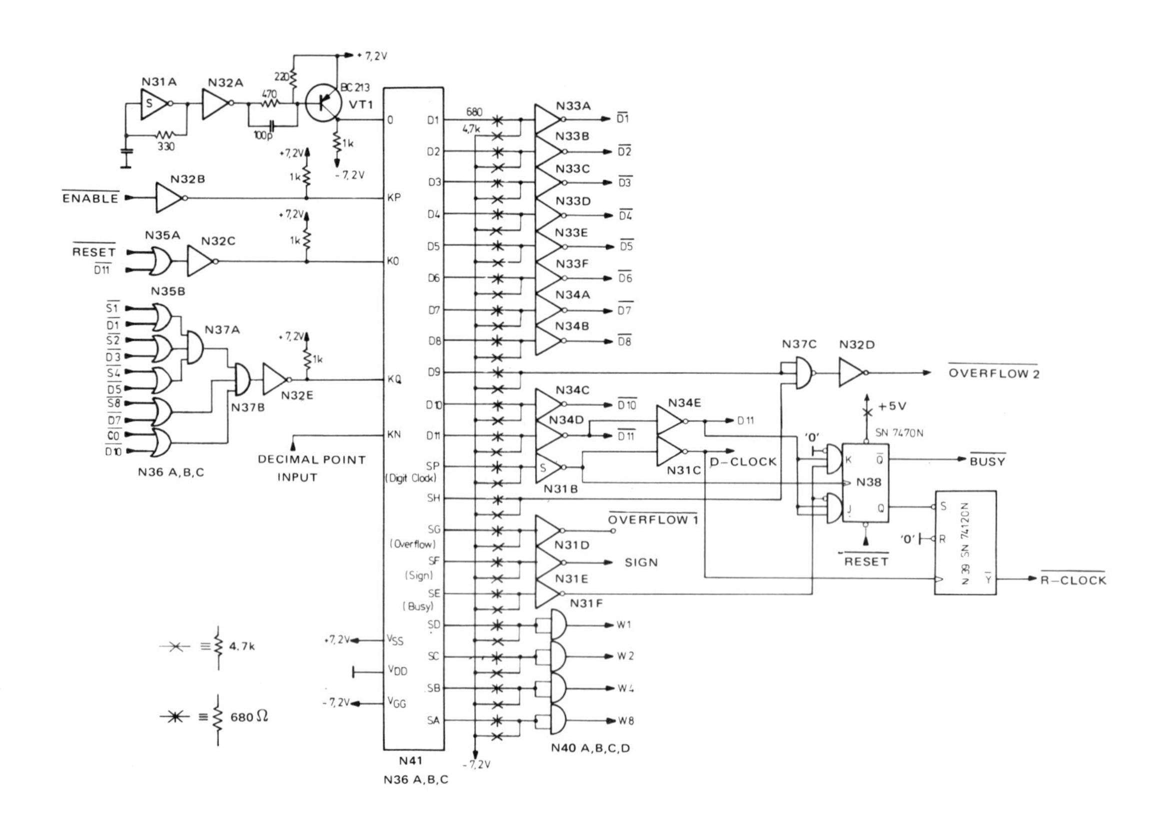

FIGURE 13. Arithmetic Unit

V INTERFACING MOS DEVICES

by
Howard Cook

In terms of speed, cost and packing density, MOS devices are suitable for many functions. Typical of these are memories and shift registers. However, the MOS inputs and outputs are frequently not directly compatible with bipolar logic, e.g. TTL, and the necessary interface circuitry must be carefully designed if cost and speed advantages of the MOS device are to be conserved.

REQUIREMENTS

Clock Drivers

P-channel MOS devices usually require input signals (e.g. clocks and addresses) with voltage swings in the order of 20V peak to peak. These may or may not use 0V as the upper or lower level. If 0V is the lower level, then there are some integrated circuits designed specifically for this function. However, if this is not the case, discrete circuits or hybrid circuits have to be used.

MOS inputs have a very high D.C. impedance and thus only present a capacitive load to any driving circuits. This capacitive load may vary from 2pF for the inputs to some devices, to 40pF for others (e.g. TMS 4063 Reset input, 40pF max.) It is frequently required to drive the inputs of many devices in parallel, and the load on any one driving circuit may be several hundreds of pico Farads.

Since the 'on' impedance of a MOSFET is closely related to its gate potential, the tolerances on the upper or lower levels of the input waveforms to the MOS devices are normally quite tightly specified for operation of the device at maximum speed. This imposes additional requirements on the driver circuits in terms of the 'sit' levels of the output waveforms.

Very often, the propagation delays through the driver circuit, and the output rise and/or fall times contribute directly to the access time of the memory, or the limit on the maximum clocking rate of a shift register. These are further factors to be taken into account. It is also important to consider the two other major factors, power dissipation and cost. With clock drivers it is normal for the quiescent output condition to be one level, and to pulse to the other level during operation. This differs from some address driver applications, where it may be necessary for the output to remain in either state for long periods of time. In this latter case, power dissipation must be kept to a minimum for both output states, if it is, as usual, an important consideration in the system design.

The cost of a driver circuit made up of discrete components is probably 50% component cost, and 50% assembly, printed circuit board (P.C.B.) area etc. Hence the cost is closely related to the number of components. The cost of a totally integrated driver circuit is nearer 90% component cost, and 10% assembly, P.C.B. area, etc.

The power dissipation is worth discussing in greater detail, since it is relevant regardless of the type of driver circuit used. The power dissipated in a driving circuit is made up of three components:

(1) As a result of driving charge into and out of the capacitive load.

(2) By the driver circuit elements when the output is static at both high and low levels.

(3) By the driver circuit elements when the output changes state, with no output load connected.

In case (1) the dissipation in the driver output devices can be expressed as

$$P1 = \tfrac{1}{2}CV^2 . 2 . f$$

where C = load capacitance
V = Voltage transition
f = cycle frequency.

as $\frac{1}{2}CV^2$ is the energy change in the capacitor when the voltage across it is changed by V. In any one cycle this change occurs twice (assuming only one output pulse per cycle), once at each pulse edge. The rate of change of energy is then $\frac{1}{2}CV^2 . 2 . f$.

For case (2) the powers can be represented as:

P_{OH} = Static power when output is 'high'.
P_{OL} = Static power when output is 'low'.

When the device is switching, the static power will be made up of a fraction of both of these, according to duty cycle. If the ratio of 'output high' time to 'output low' time is N:1 then:

$$P2 = P_{OH} \cdot N/(N+1) + P_{OL} \cdot 1/(N+1) = (N . P_{OH} + P_{OL})/(N+1)$$

In the third case, the power dissipation is a constant at any one frequency, defined by the driver circuit components. In circuits employing a 'totem pole' type of output stage, this dissipation can become very significant at high frequencies, due to the high current surge through the totem pole devices when they are both instantaneously 'on' during changeover of the output state. If this dissipation is labelled P_{CO} then the total power dissipated in the driver, driving a load C_L at frequency f through voltage V is given by

$$P_{tot} = P1 + P2 + P3 = C_L.V^2.f + (N.P_{OH} + P_{OL})/(N + 1) + P_{CO}$$

A graph of these components of the total power dissipation may be drawn for some typical totem pole output driver circuit, as shown in Figure 1.

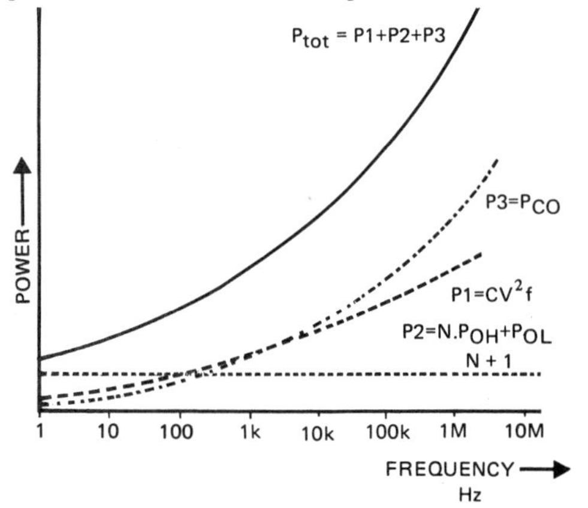

FIGURE 1. Typical Power Dissipation Curves.

The total power dissipated in the circuit has to be less than the rated maximum dissipation if the device is an I.C.

Discrete Circuits: The most basic circuit is simply a common emitter inverter, as shown in Figure 2. The output

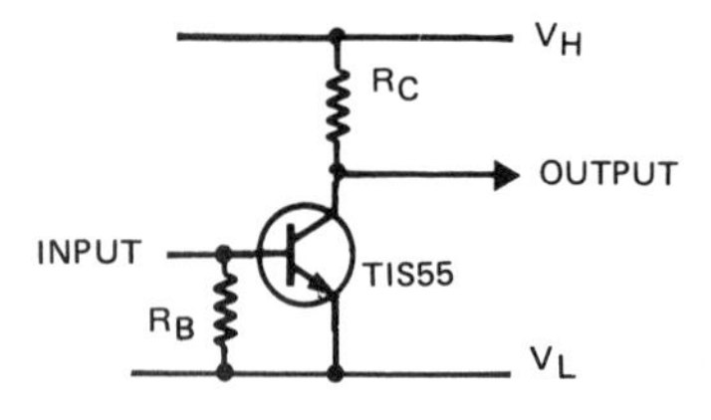

FIGURE 2. Common Emitter Inverter.

rise time is controlled by the collector resistor R_C. Resistor R_B is necessary to draw charge out of the base to ensure a positive turn 'off' action when the input base drive is removed. For fast operation a good switching transistor should be used, with short storage time, low $V_{CE(sat)}$, and an acceptable h_{FE}. (normally 10 or greater). The power dissipation when the output is 'high' (P_{OH}) is zero, and P_{OL} is made up of the $I_C{}^2.R_C$ dissipated in resistor R_C and the $V_{BE}/R_B{}^2$ of the base resistor. The dynamic power due to the load P1 is shared between the collector resistor and the transistor, whilst the power at changeover is probably not significant at reasonable edge speeds and frequency (i.e. if rise and fall times are small compared with cycle time).

This circuit can drive small capacitive loads, but has the disadvantages that the rising output edge is exponential (defined by R_C and C_L) and that resistor R_C dissipates power continuously in the V_{OL} state. This imposes a practical limit on the minimum value resistor which can be used to achieve a short time constant for the rising exponential.

Both of these problems may be reduced by adding an emitter follower gain stage which uses an extra transistor and diode (and resistor–explained later.) This circuit, Figure 3, will give similar output rise times with a much

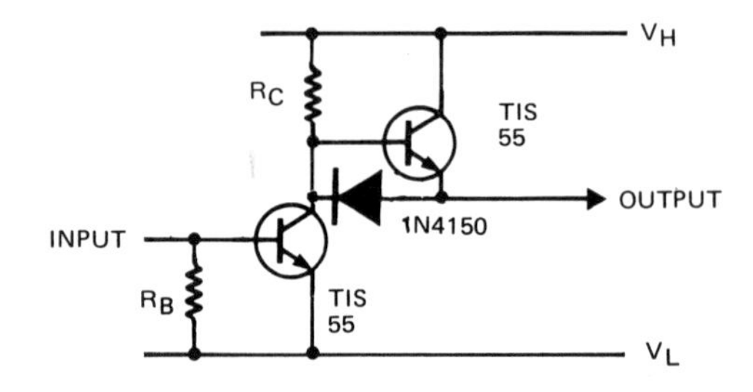

FIGURE 3. Improved Basic Inverter Circuit.

larger value of resistor R_C, thus reducing power dissipation and the continuous current requirement of the first transistor. The disadvantages are that the output low level is now one $V_{CE(sat)}$ plus the diode forward voltage V_F above V_L, and the output high voltage is one V_{BE} below V_H. However, this is normally acceptable.

Obviously, this circuit can also be used to give fast rise times, by using a lower value of R_C. If this is the case, a small value resistor (≏22Ω) will almost certainly be needed in series with the output. This increases the damping of the circuit formed by the capacitive load and the wiring (printed or otherwise) which is predominantly inductive, so that ringing and overshooting are controlled.

To further increase the load driving capability; i.e. to be able to drive the same load with faster edges, or to drive a larger load with the same edge speeds, a complimentary pnp-npn booster stage can be added to the output, as shown in Figure 4. Once again, these two devices have an effect on the output levels.

V_{OH} is now $V_H - 2V_{BE}$ and

$V_{OL} = V_{CE(sat)} + V_F + V_{BE} + V_L$

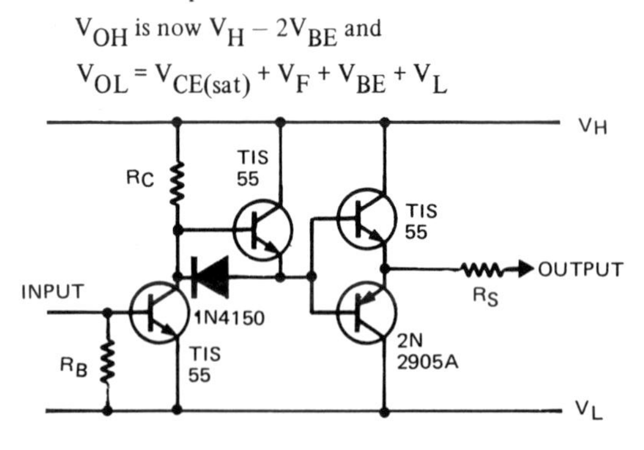

FIGURE 4. Inverter with Booster Output.

However, as before this is usually acceptable. The series resistor R_S is now certainly necessary, due to the low impedance of the output stage, and the faster switching speeds which will probably be used.

All these circuits so far are designed so that they dissipate zero power in the V_{OH} state. If it should be necessary to dissipate zero power in the V_{OL} state, a pnp version can be used, Figure 5. The main disadvantage of this

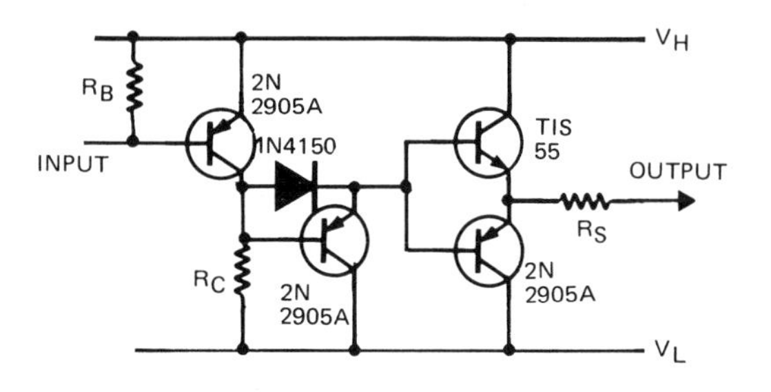

FIGURE 5. Pnp Version of Driver Circuit.

circuit is the lack of good fast pnp transistors capable of withstanding the necessary voltage. The method of driving the input of these circuits once again depends upon the specific application.

If V_L is OV then the input may be driven directly from the output of an open collector TTL gate, as shown in Figure 6. When this is the case, the base turn 'off' resistor is

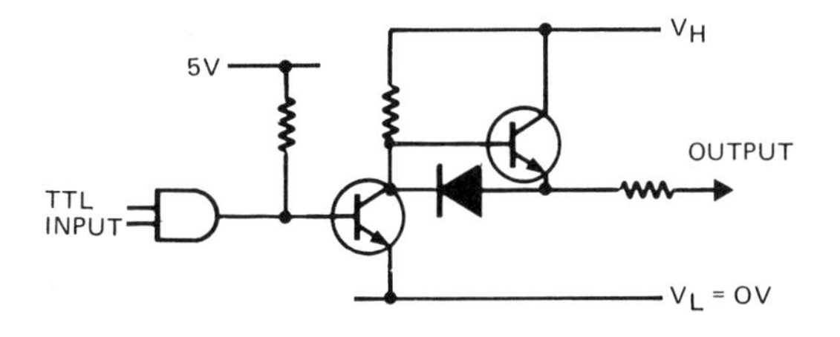

FIGURE 6. Driving from Open Collector TTL.

omitted, since the V_{OL} of the TTL gate is 0·4V max., which is low enough to turn the transistor 'off' quickly, and hold it 'off'. However, it is necessary for the TTL gate to be situated in close proximity to the transistor it is driving. This, with a good current return path from the transistor emitter to the TTL device ground connection, maintains reasonable switching speeds and noise immunity. If this is not possible, and long printed circuit tracks or wiring are involved, then it is necessary to drive from a device such as the SN74S140 which is capable of sourcing 40mA from its output, as shown in Figure 7. A series resistor is used to define the current out of the TTL gate, and this may be shunted by a small, low inductance capacitor to speed up the turn 'on' time. A base turn 'off' resistor is now necessary.

These methods are suitable for any duty cycle of operation. However, for duty cycles up to about 80%, capacitor coupling may be used. The TTL gate is open collector, Figure 8. The diode is necessary to recover the

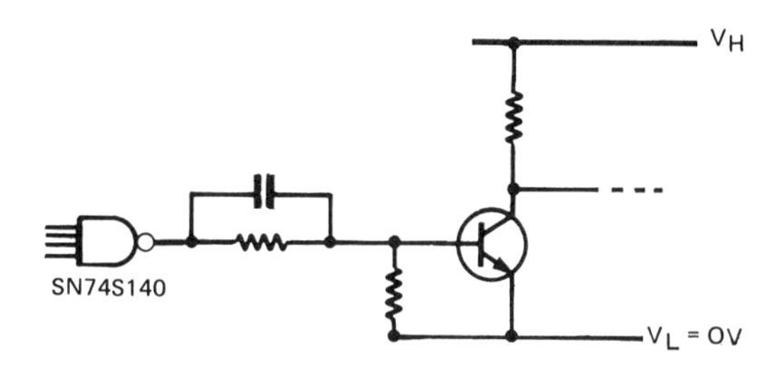

FIGURE 7. Driving from Remote TTL Source.

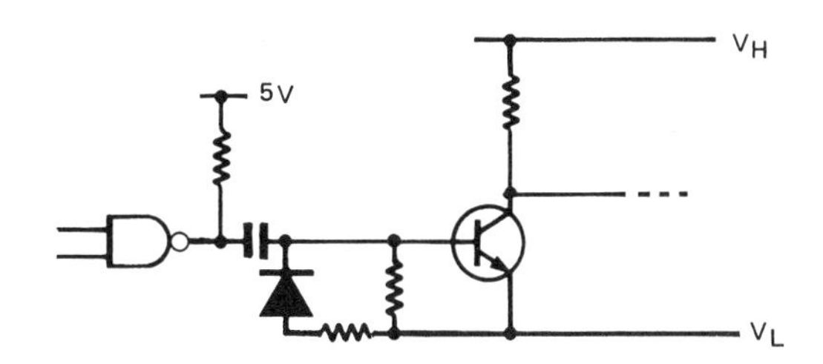

FIGURE 8. Capacitor Coupling.

coupling capacitor when the TTL gate output goes 'low' again, the resistor in series with the diode limiting the peak current through the capacitor into the gate output. This circuit has the advantage that V_L does not have to be 0V. If this is the case and 100% duty cycle is required then some other form of level shift circuit must be employed, Figure 9. The pnp transistor, used in unity gain common base

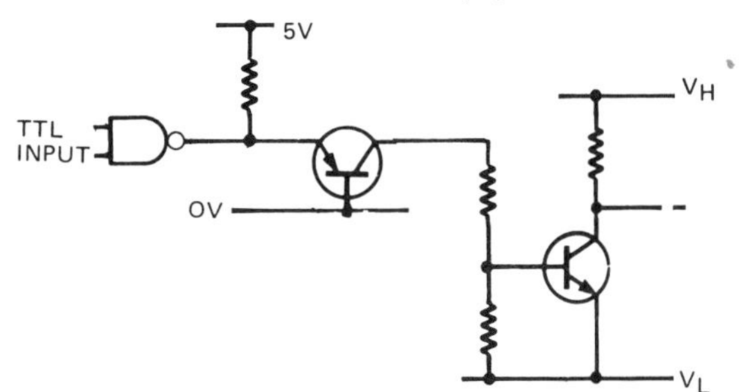

FIGURE 9. Pnp Level Shifting.

mode, acts as a level shifter. To reduce the power dissipated in this transistor, there is a resistor in series with its collector to decrease the voltage across the pnp when it is conducting.

Integrated, or Partially Integrated Circuits: The simplest of these, providing that V_L = 0V, is to use an open collector TTL gate, with suitable output voltage and current characteristics, e.g. SN7406 Hex inverter, Figure 10. Once again, the output characteristics of this circuit can be improved by adding extra components, as for the discrete circuits described earlier. Instead of using normal TTL open collector devices, the SN75450B family of peripheral driver devices shown in Figure 11 are very suitable, having high output sink current capability, and being available in a full range of functions.

Using these circuits, the required logic function may be achieved for the overall driver circuit, as shown in Figure 12. Once again, these circuits are only suitable for

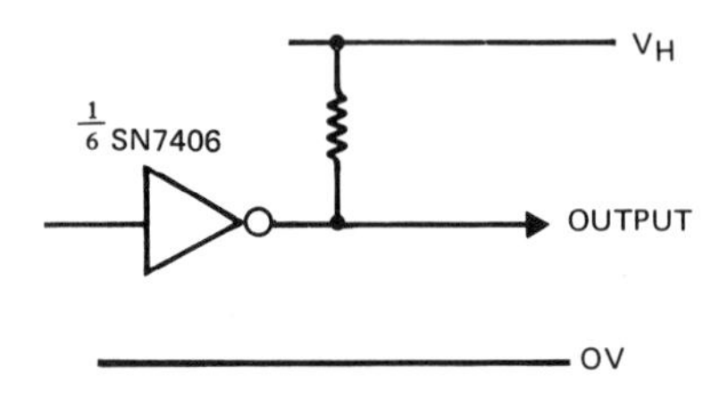

FIGURE 10. Simple Integrated Driver.

applications where V_L = 0V. If this is not the case, then capacitor coupling has to be used as before. However, for the majority of memory driver applications, it is usual for V_L to be 0V, and there are two fully integrated driver devices which may be used. For driving very large capacitive loads made up of a number of smaller capacitances, it is possible to have one booster circuit associated with each part of the load, and to drive all the boosters from one integrated circuit. This also has the effect of reducing the capacitance due to the printed circuit board layout, since each booster may be situated close to the load that it is driving, as illustrated in Figure 13.

The SN75361AP is a device which is especially suitable for MOS driving. As shown in Figure 14 it is a bipolar circuit consisting of two 2-input NAND gates, with one input of each gate being commoned and the other input free. Inputs 1 and 2 are single TTL loads (1.6mA) and the input S, is the equivalent of two TTL loads. The device requires two power supplies, V_{CC} = 5V, V_{SS} = V_{SS} of MOS, and 0V. The outputs are of the high current 'Totem Pole' form with current limiting protection. The device is capable of operating with V_{SS} in the range 4.75V to 24V. The SN75361AP is capable of driving up to 1000pF, at speeds suitable for MOS memory clock inputs. The Totem Pole outputs are protected against overshoots by clamping diodes. The standby power consumption (outputs high) is in the order of 10mW. Since the load driven by this device

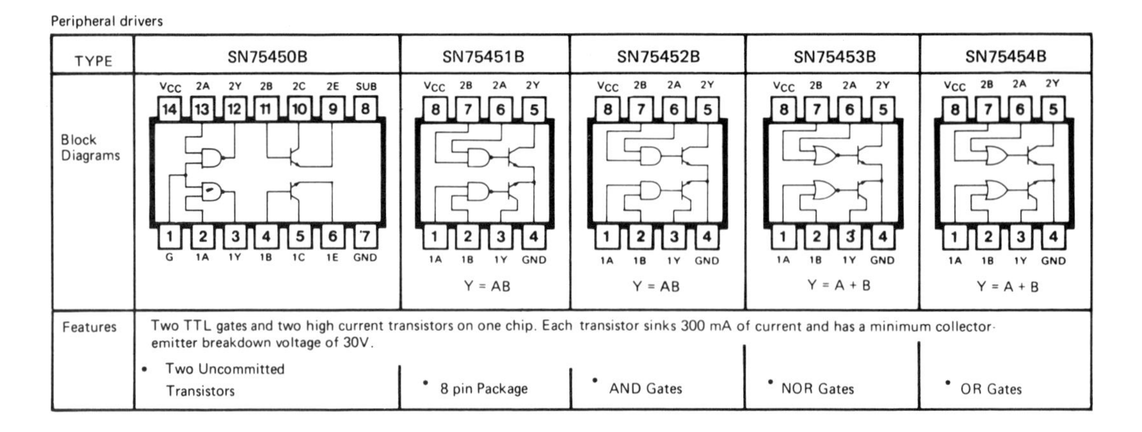

Peripheral drivers

TYPE	SN75450B	SN75451B	SN75452B	SN75453B	SN75454B
Block Diagrams	V_{CC} 2A 2Y 2B 2C 2E SUB (14 13 12 11 10 9 8); G 1A 1Y 1B 1C 1E GND (1 2 3 4 5 6 7)	V_{CC} 2B 2A 2Y (8 7 6 5); 1A 1B 1Y GND (1 2 3 4); Y = AB	V_{CC} 2B 2A 2Y (8 7 6 5); 1A 1B 1Y GND (1 2 3 4); Y = AB	V_{CC} 2B 2A 2Y (8 7 6 5); 1A 1B 1Y GND (1 2 3 4); Y = A + B	V_{CC} 2B 2A 2Y (8 7 6 5); 1A 1B 1Y GND (1 2 3 4); Y = A + B
Features	Two TTL gates and two high current transistors on one chip. Each transistor sinks 300 mA of current and has a minimum collector-emitter breakdown voltage of 30V.				
	• Two Uncommitted Transistors	• 8 pin Package	• AND Gates	• NOR Gates	• OR Gates

FIGURE 11. SN75450B Family

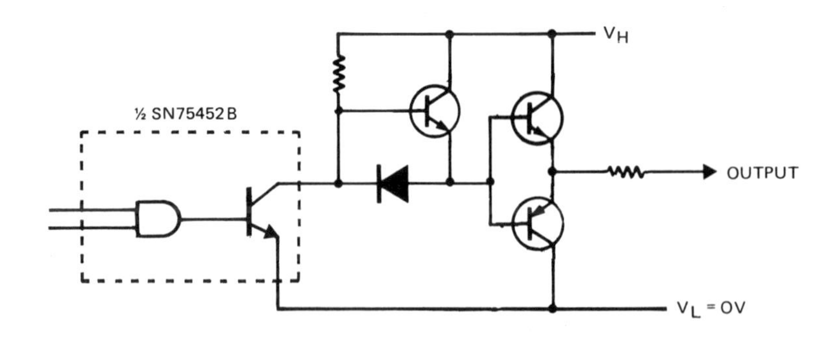

FIGURE 12. Inverting Driver Circuit (NAND).

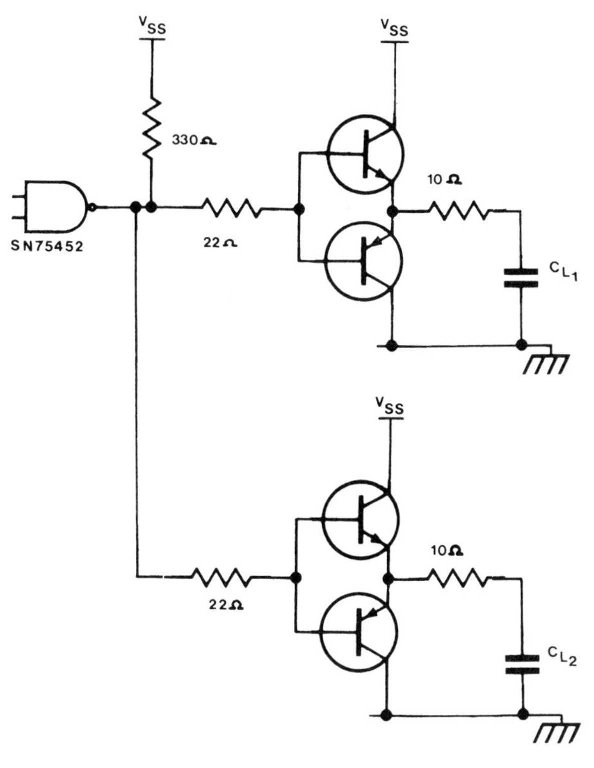

FIGURE 13. Driving More than One 'Booster' Stage

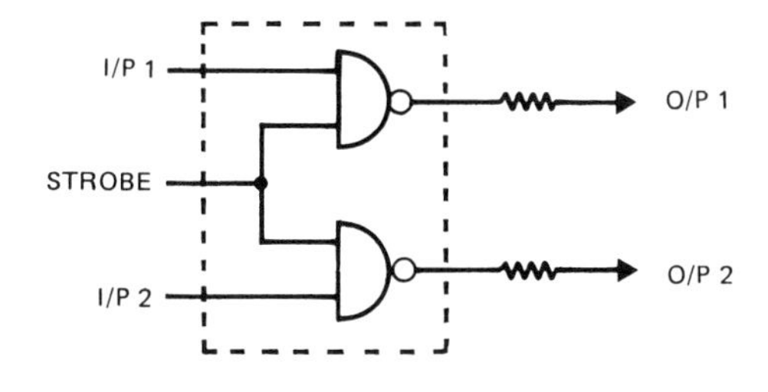

FIGURE 14. SN75361AP

consists mainly of a lumped capacitance at the end of an inductive line with very little resistance, fast switching of the device output causes serious ringing. To reduce the Q of this reactive load circuit, it is necessary to use a small resistor in series with the driver output. However, this resistor causes a degradation in switching speed and a compromise must be arrived at, whereby the ringing is reduced to acceptable levels, without slowing the edge speeds excessively. To speed up the rise time, it is possible to shunt this resistor with a fast diode (e.g. 1N4150). Using such a circuit, and with the series resistor of 10Ω, the propagation time t_{pHL} is about 26ns and t_{pLH} is around 32ns, with a load of 400pF. (The propagation times are made up of the delay through the device and the output rise or fall times). The load of 400pF is equivalent to 160 address inputs, or 14 Reset or Clock inputs of the TMS 4063.

The second fully integrated device is the SN75365 (Figure 15), which is a quad two-input NAND device. This has an extra power supply input V_{BB}. It may be operated with this connected to the V_{SS} input, or when used to drive '1103 type' memory devices, may be connected to the V_{BB} supply of the 1103. Once again, resistors in series with the outputs are required. The data and performance of this device are shown in its data sheet.

Data Inputs/Outputs

The data input and output levels of most MOS shift registers and Read Only Memories (ROMs) are either directly TTL compatible, or only require the addition of a 'pull-up' or 'pull-down' resistor to interface with a TTL logic gate. However, with Random Access Memories (RAMs), in order to achieve high operating speeds, the data inputs and outputs are often MOS levels, i.e. high voltage swings for data inputs, and low current levels for data outputs. Two examples of this are the '1103 type' devices, and the TMS 4063.

In the case of the'1103, the data input is similar in all respects to a clock input, with a capacitance of approximately 7 pF. The drivers suitable for clock driving are also suitable for driving these inputs. The data output is in the form of a current (500μA min. for output high) which must be sensed, and converted to a TTL voltage. The most effective way of performing this function is to use the SN75107, 108, 207, 208 devices, depending upon required function and speed, as illustrated in Figure 16.

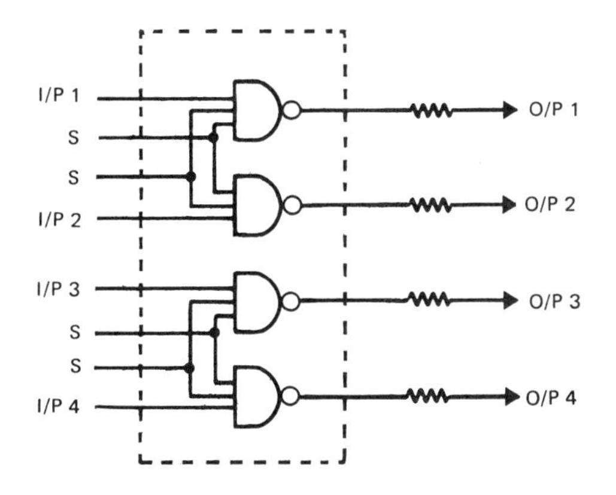

FIGURE 15. SN75365

These devices are dual circuits, each half comprising of a differential amplifier stage, and a TTL gate. To make full use of the differential amplifier, it is advisable to run a dummy data line all the way from the memory device, alongside the actual data line, and connect the dummy line to the non-inventing input. Thus, any common mode noise picked up in these data lines, from switching clocks etc., is rejected by the differential amplifier. It is necessary to provide a current path to V_{DD} for the sense signal at the

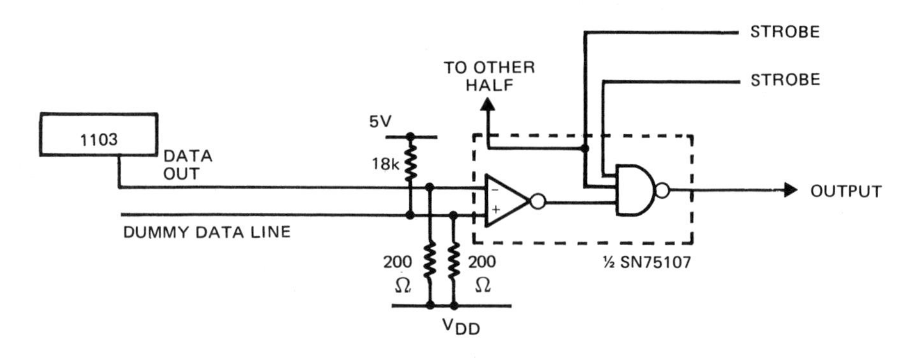

FIGURE 16. Data Sensing of 1103

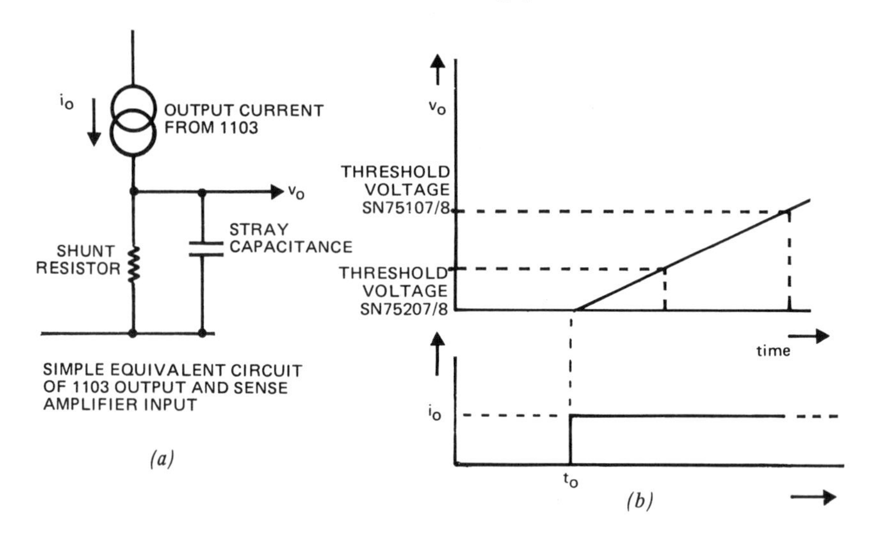

FIGURE 17. Effect of Input Threshold Voltage

amplifier input, via a resistor, to develop a voltage excursion to switch the amplifier. In the case of the SN75107 and 108 (open collector o/p version of the '107) the input threshold is 25 mV. If very fast speeds are required, then the SN75207 and '208 allow faster operation, since their input threshold is guaranteed 10mV max. This means that the output current from the 1103 which is charging up the stray capacitance on the data line, as well as developing a potential difference across the input resistor of the sense amplifier, has to charge these stray capacitances to a lower potential. It can achieve this in a shorter time. This is easily understood by reference to Figure 17.

It is also possible to sense the output of the '1103 device using a low power TTL gate, and a resistor to ground, as shown in Figure 18. This is essentially a low cost solution, and is only suitable for applications where high speed is not required.

The TMS 4063 requires specialised circuitry for both the data input and output functions. This memory device has a pair of differential data lines which are used for both writing and reading of data. Figure 19 shows how discrete

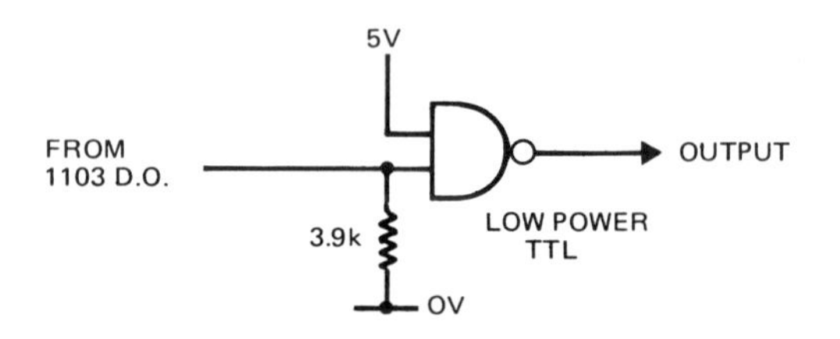

FIGURE 18. Simple Sensing Circuit.

transistors may be used with an integrated circuit comparator to perform these functions. A differential amplifier, of the SN72720 type, and a zener diode, such as 1N5230B (in series with a 270Ω resistor for level conversion), are used.

The SN72720, a dual device with separate outputs, is ideal, and has a response time of about 15ns to the ramp input presented to it in this application. A similar device is the SN72820, which has an extra gain stage, and is slightly quicker in operation. There is also a version of this available with output strobes, called the SN72514, which is very

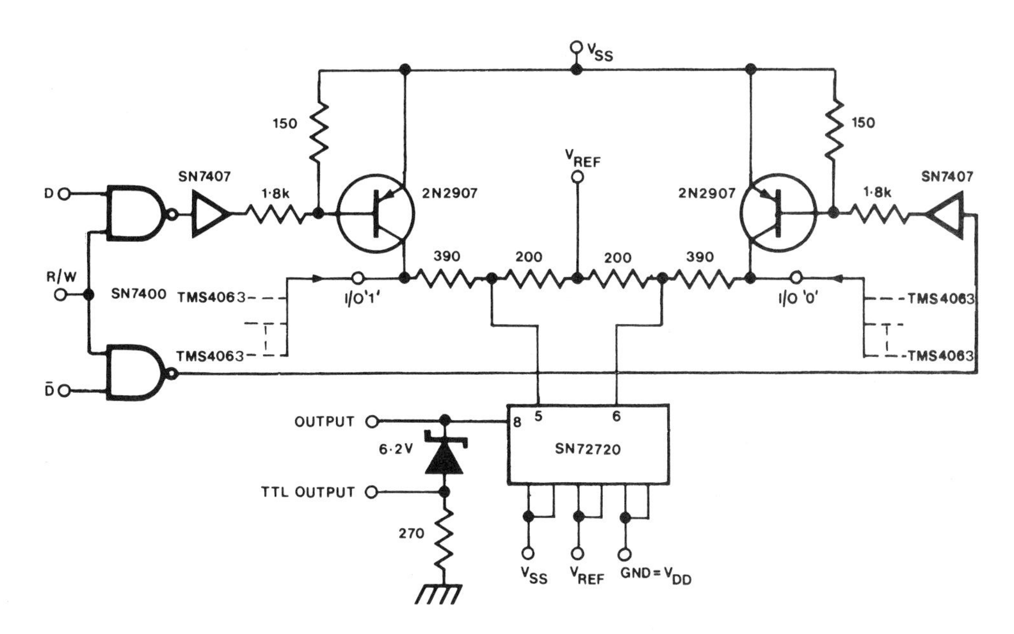

FIGURE 19. Discrete Read/Write Circuit

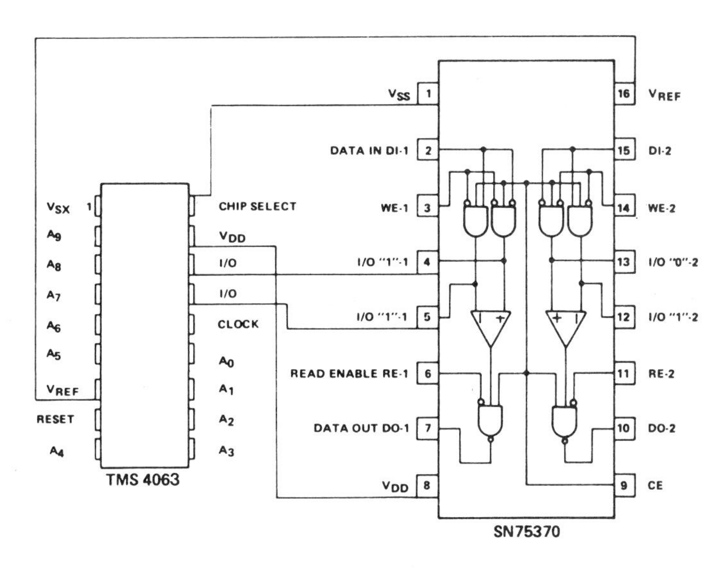

FIGURE 20. Connecting the SN75370 to the TMS4063

useful in applications where an additional strobe gate after the comparator is undesirable. All these devices have an absolute maximum differential input voltage of ±5V which must not be exceeded during the Write cycles, and a protective resistor network is necessary on the inputs. If the device is operated between the V_{SS} and V_{DD} power rails, the 'O' level output will be about 7V. Hence a Zener diode and resistor are necessary on the output to convert to TTL level.

This Read/Write circuit is obviously quite complex, uses many components, takes up much space, and dissipates considerable power. In a large multi-digit memory, all these factors are undesirable. The alternative solution is to use the SN75370 which is a device specifically designed for this application as shown in Figure 20. This requires no external components, and is a dual device, performing the complete Write-drive Read-sense functions for two memory word bits. For operation it requires two control signals as well as Chip Enable. i.e. Write Enable and Read Enable. The timing diagram, Figure 21, shows the operation of these inputs. The delay from Read Enable going 'low', to the Data Output being valid (t_{RED} = Read Enable Delay) is typically

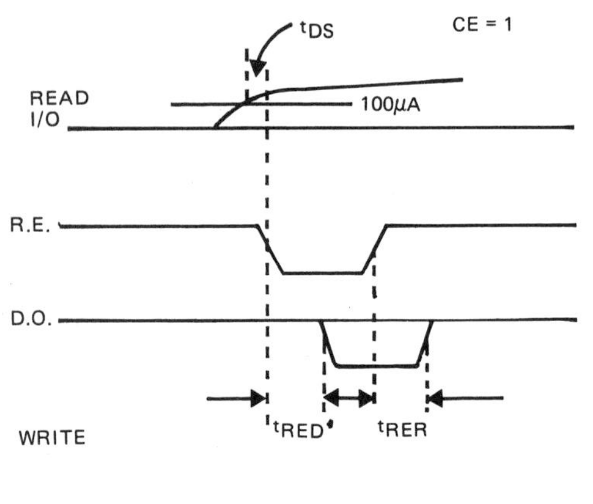

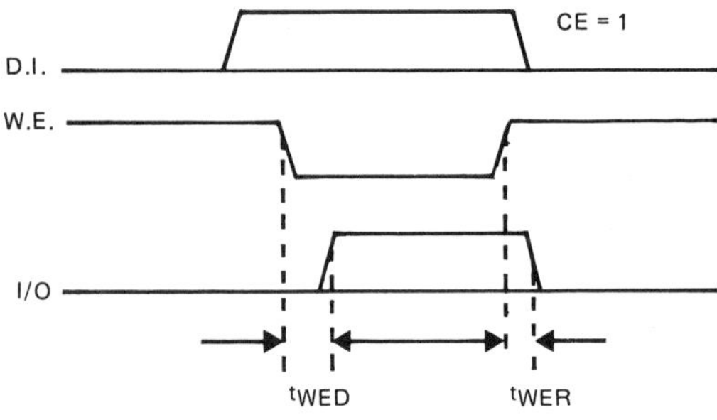

FIGURE 21. Timing Diagram

15ns. It is necessary for the data on the I/O lines to be present for a period previous to this, (t_{DS} = Data Set-up) of approximately 10ns., owing to the propagation time through the sense amplifier of the device. When Read Enable returns 'high', there is a delay (t_{RER} = Read Enable Recovery) before the valid Data Output ends of typically 15ns.

WORKED EXAMPLES

This section describes the steps involved, when designing a system for a specific application, to optimise some of the circuits previously mentioned.

Consider a 4k word x 16 bit modular high speed system where the Access time is the all-important factor. If the memory element used is the TMS4063 1024 bit R.A.M. as described in Chapter III, the following figures may be immediately derived from its data sheet:–

'Reset' input capacitance (1 device) = 30pF typ., 40pF max.
∴ 16 'Reset' inputs in parallel = 640pF max.
(Note that when calculating the load, or any other value associated with driver circuits, etc. provision must always be made for reliable operation under 'worst-case' conditions, hence in this case the maximum figure of 40pF is used for the 'Reset' input.)

'Clock' input capacitance (1 device) = 30pF typ., 36pF max.
16 'Clock' inputs in parallel = 576pF max.

'Address' input capacitance (1 device) = 2.5pF typ., 3.5pF max.
64 'Address' inputs in parallel = 224pF max.

The requirements for the 'Reset' driver and 'Clock' driver circuits are similar in terms of load, but differ in terms of quiescent output polarity. To achieve a fast Access time, the 'Reset' input to the TMS4063s must remain low between cycles, and the cycle commences with 'Reset' going high. The 'Clock' inputs are high during this time and go 'low' for a minimum of 100ns, at least 60ns after Reset has gone 'high'. At the end of the 100ns min Clock period both 'Clock' and 'Reset' return to their original state, as shown in Figure 22.

The driver circuit shown in Figure 23 will operate with a 570pF load and an output cycle as shown in Figure 24. This is suitable for the 'Clock' inputs of a TMS 4063 memory array. With capacitor C_L = 570pF, to obtain rise and fall times of 20ns or less:

$$C_L R_S < 20 \cdot 10^{-9}/3$$

$$\text{i.e. } R_S = 10\Omega$$

Transistors VT3 and VT4 are both operating as emitter followers. For VT3 the npn device, a BLY33 VHF transistor is eminently suitable, and the 2N2905A is suitable for VT4. Transistor VT2 is also an emitter follower with $I_{C(max)}$ of ≏100mA, for which a BFR39 can be used. Transistor VT1 is the only saturating switch, and the TIS55 is a good low cost device. Resistor R_C has to supply the base current to VT2, and pull up the collector of VT1.

∴ $I_{B(max)}$ for VT3 and VT4 $= I_{out(max)}/10$
$= 100\text{mA}$

The h_{FE} of a BFR39 @ I_C = 100mA and V_{CE} = 20V
= 25 min.

Hence, the base current = 100/25
= 4mA.

The base input capacitance of VT2 ≏ 60pF
and the collector capacitance of VT1 ≏ 10pF

Therefore, if the rise time is to be 20ns and neglecting base current to transistor VT2:

$$\text{Time constant } CR_C = 20 \cdot 10^{-9}/3$$
$$\text{or } R_C = 20 \cdot 10^{-9}/3 \cdot 70 \cdot 10^{-12}$$
$$= 94\Omega$$

Neglecting the capacitance at this point, the value of resistor R_C necessary to supply I_B (= 4mA) into transistor VT2 is:

$$(20 - V_{CE(sat)} - V_{BE} - V_F)/4 \cdot 10^{-3}$$

$$= 18/4 \cdot 10^{-3}$$
$$= 4{\cdot}5\text{k}\Omega$$

Hence, taking both requirements into account:

$$R_C = 94 \cdot 4{\cdot}5 \cdot 10^3/(94 + 4{\cdot}5 \cdot 10^3)$$

$$= 92\Omega - \text{use } 82\Omega$$

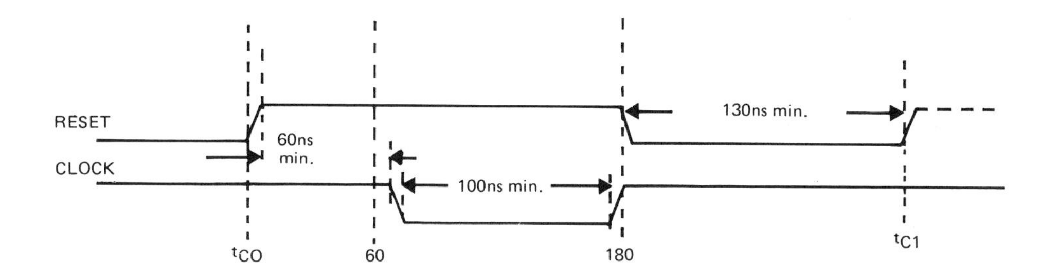

FIGURE 22. Clock & Reset Timing Requirements

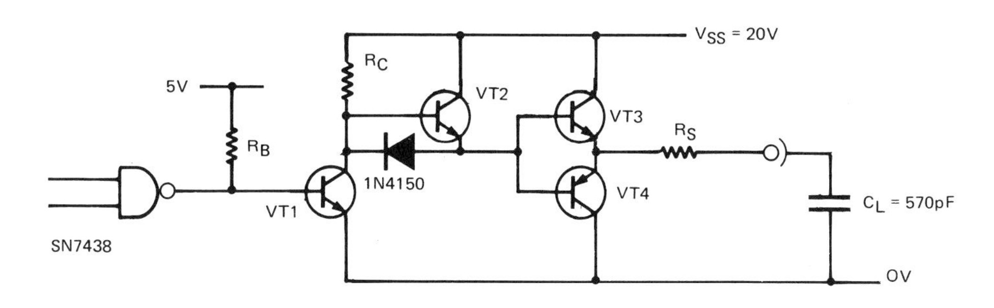

FIGURE 23. Clock Input Driver Circuit

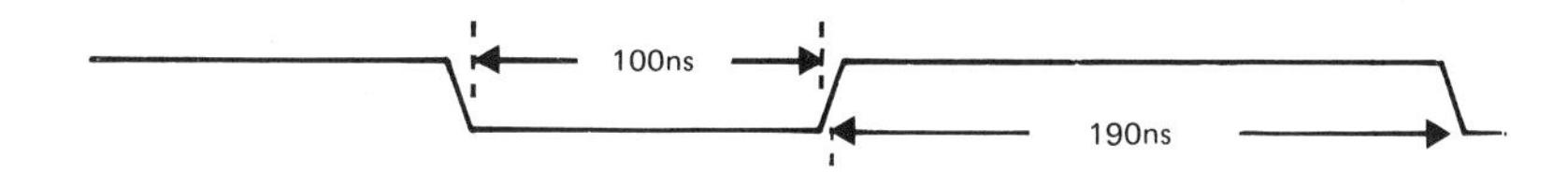

FIGURE 24. Output Duty Cycle Waveform

With $R_C = 82\Omega$

I_C for VT1 $= (20 - V_{CE(sat)})/82$
$= 240mA$

At this collector current:

$h_{FE} = 15$ min.
$\therefore I_B = 240/15$
$= 16mA$
$R_B = (5 - V_{BE})/16 \cdot 10^{-3})$
$= 220\Omega$

The TTL output has to sink $(5 - V_{out})/R_B$ (= 21mA.)

Hence the SN7438 or similar open collector buffer output device must be used.

With an output 'high' level of 19V and an output 'low' level of 0·8V the times for this circuit are:

t_{pd} ('1' to '0') = 24ns
t_{pd} ('0' to '1') = 16ns
t_r = 24ns
and t_f = 26ns

The components of power dissipation are:

P1 (due to capitive load) $= C.V^2.f$
$= 570 \cdot 10^{-12} \cdot 350 \cdot 3{\cdot}5 \cdot 10^6$
$= 698$ mW

This is dissipated mainly in the two output transistors and the output series resistor.

P2 (due to circuit elements in static conditions)

$$= P_{OL} \cdot t_{OL}/t_{cycle} + P_{OH} \cdot t_{OH}/t_{cycle}$$

With the output 'high', the only dissipation is in the output of the TTL gate and its 'pull-up' resistor.

i.e. in TTL gate $I_{out} \cdot V_{out}$ $= 21 \cdot 10^{-3} \cdot 0{\cdot}4$
$= 84mW$

in 'pull-up' resistor $I^2 R_B$ $= (21 \cdot 10^{-3})^2 \cdot 220$
$= 97mW$

$\therefore P_{OH(tot)}$ $= 181mW$

With the output 'low'; resistor R_C will dissipate:

$(20 - 0{\cdot}5)^2 / 82 = 4{\cdot}63W$

Transistor VT1 will dissipate:

$I_B \cdot V_{BE} + I_C \cdot V_{CE(sat)}$

$= 3{\cdot}5 \, . \, 1{\cdot}5/220 \quad + 19{\cdot}5 \, . \, 0{\cdot}5/82$
$= 0{\cdot}024 \quad + 0{\cdot}119$
$= 143\text{mW}$

$\therefore \quad P_{OL(tot)} = 4{\cdot}77 \text{ W}$

and $P2 = 4{\cdot}77 \, . \, 100/290 \quad + 0{\cdot}18 \, . \, 190/290$
$= 1{\cdot}64 \quad + 0{\cdot}11$

$\therefore \quad P1 + P2 = 2{\cdot}45 \text{ W}$

P3 (Power dissipation due to the switching losses in the circuit) is insignificant (i.e. <10mW)

A similar procedure is employed to design the opposite polarity for the reset input.

The address driver requirement is not so stringent. Consider the timing diagram shown in Figure 25. If the addresses were to be driven high during the non-valid periods, then only a fast fall time is required, and a very slow rise time (<130ns) can be used. A peripheral driver device (SN75450B series) with a pull-up resistor on the output, as shown in Figure 26, would be suitable for this application.

For a 4k word x 16 bit system, this circuit would have to drive 64 address inputs. From the TMS4063 data sheet, the maximum address input capacitance is 3pF. Hence the driver load is 3 x 64 = 192pF = C_L. The time constant of the output waveform is $C_L R_C$ which must be $< \frac{1}{3}$ x 130ns if the output voltage is to achieve 95 per cent of V_{SS} within 130ns.

$\therefore \quad C_L R_C = 43{\cdot}3 \, . \, 10^{-9}$

$R_C = 43{\cdot}3 \, . \, 10^{-9} \, . \, 1 \, . \, 10^{-12}/192$

$= 220\Omega$

The resistor R_S is required in series with the output to limit the maximum current out of the load capacitance into the driver output to 300mA or less.

$R_S = V_{SS}/0{\cdot}3$

$= 68\Omega$

This should give an output fall time of:

$3C_L R_S = 3 \, . \, 192 \, . \, 10^{-12} \, . \, 68$
$= 39\text{ns}$

The actual performance figures were:

t_{pd} ('0' to '1') = 41ns

t_{pd} ('1' to '0') = 19ns

t_r = 70ns

and t_f = 24ns

If a faster fall time is required, a transistor and diode may be added to the output, as shown in Figure 27.
Resistor R_C is still 220Ω.
Resistor R_E has to limit the current through the 2N2905A to ≏ 600mA.

$\therefore \quad R_E = 20/0{\cdot}6$
$= 33\Omega$

The output fall time is now:

$3 \, . \, 192 \, . \, 10^{-12} \, . \, 33$
$= 19\text{ns}$

The actual performance figures were:

t_{pd} ('0' to '1') = 35ns

t_{pd} ('1' to '0') = 20ns

t_r = 65ns

t_f = 17ns

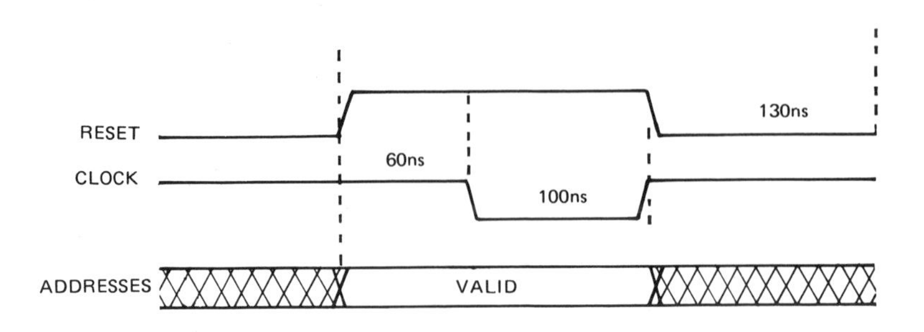

FIGURE 25. Address Timing Diagram.

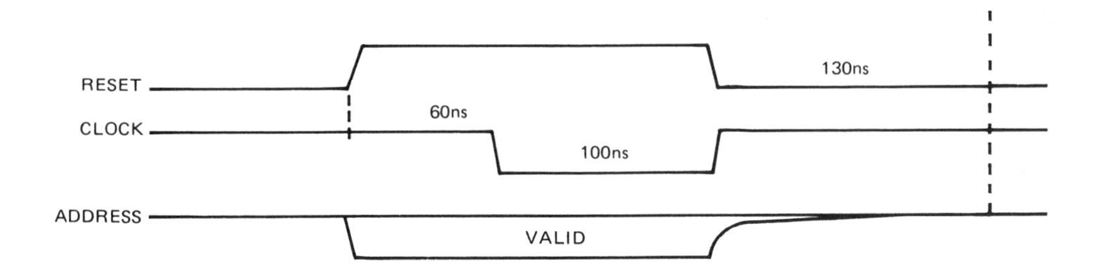

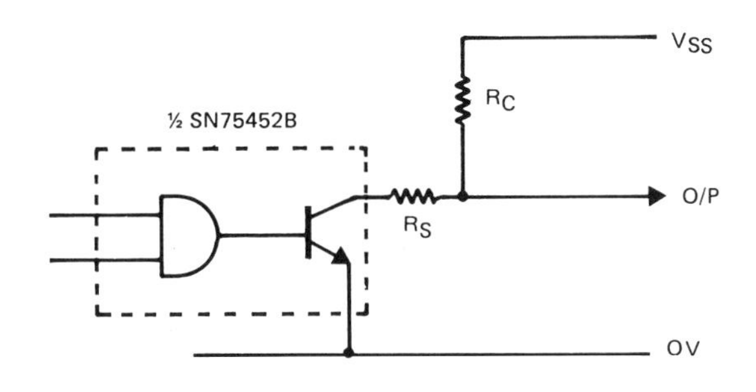

FIGURE 26. Simple Address Driver and Output Waveform

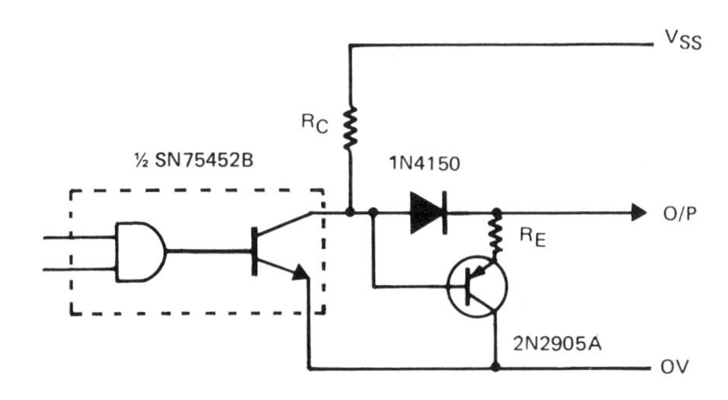

FIGURE 27. Faster Address Driver.

CONCLUSION

Interfacing between TTL systems and MOS devices has often been a problem to potential MOS users. There is no mystique involved in designing suitable circuits, as has been shown. It is always a case of deciding on the required factors in order of importance, and then designing the circuit to achieve the best compromise of all the design criteria. With discrete component circuits, the cost is directly proportional to the number of components involved, the final cost being made up of component cost, assembly time, test time, printed circuit board space, reject contingency, etc. These cost factors should be taken into account when comparing the cost of a discrete component circuit with that of an integrated device.

New MOS devices appear regularly, and many later generation devices are TTL compatible at inputs and outputs. However, very high speed devices will probably be using high level inputs for some time, and will require the use of similar interface circuits to those described.

It is emphasised that the best results from a circuit can only be obtained if the circuit is designed for the specific application. Although a circuit from a report of another system may appear to 'work,' the chances are that it is not optimum for its new application in terms of cost, speed, power dissipation, etc. Such optimum performance has to be designed.

SECTION 2.

SPECIAL PURPOSE BIPOLAR INTEGRATED CIRCUITS

VI LINE DRIVERS AND RECEIVERS

by
Dale Pippenger and Richard Mann

A number of the I.C. devices mentioned in the previous chapter can be used as line drivers or receivers, e.g. the SN75450B series are particularly suited for simple line driving. This is because the noise margins of most logic circuits are adequate for the transmission of digital data over a distance of a few inches. The transmission of error-free data over longer lines in noisy environments, however, requires the use of special transmission-line drivers and receivers and the careful selection of a suitable transmission line. This requirement is especially critical when data transmission is between computer consoles or between a computer and remotely located peripheral equipment. Therefore a series of integrated-circuit line drivers and receivers has been developed which can interface between DTL or TTL circuits and long lines for clean, free data transmissions e.g. Table 1 lists these devices and the transmission system for which they have been especially designed. This chapter contains information which is intended to help systems design engineers by covering circuit operation, circuit characteristics, and applications. Typical results using different types and lengths of lines are also provided.

DATA TRANSMISSION

A study of the problem of data transmission indicates that the use of a terminated transmission line is desirable from a performance standpoint, since signal reflections are eliminated, allowing high-speed data transmission. A balanced or two-wire system is often used because in such a system, noise is primarily common-mode and can be rejected by a differential-input line receiver with adequate common-mode rejection properties.

Depending on the length of the transmission line, the costs of the line and of its installation can be influencing factors in the selection of the line. For short transmission lines, the use of relatively expensive shielded coaxial cable may be acceptable. For longer lines, however, the use of less expensive flat or twisted-pair cable is desirable. To further decrease the cost of a transmission system, a 'party-line' system may be employed in which several line drivers and receivers share a common transmission line.

A high-speed driver/receiver system designed for long transmission lines is almost universally applicable since it can also be used to advantage with shorter lines or lower data-transmission speeds. The following characteristics are desirable for such a system:

1) High-speed data transmission (⩾10 MHz).
2) Use of popular supply voltages.
3) Compatibility with popular logic.
4) High sensitivity (<50 mV) at receiver input.
5) Receiver speed insensitive to overdrive.
6) High receiver input impedances.
7) High common-mode rejection at the receiver input.

Table 1 Basic Data Transmission Categories

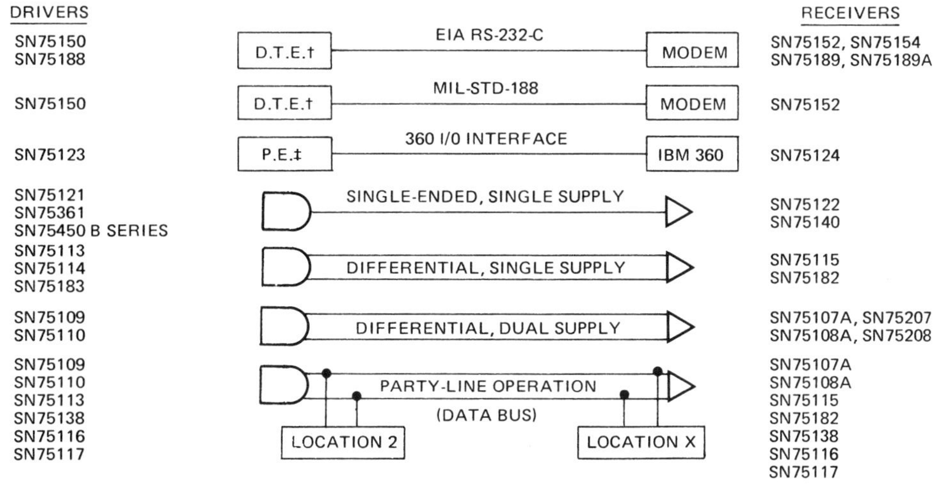

† Data terminal equipment.
‡ Peripheral equipment.

8) Strobe capability for receiver.
9) Driver capable of driving low-impedance terminated lines.
10) *Inhibit* capability for driver, with high output impedance in inhibit mode.

A system satisfying these requirements is shown in the functional diagram of Figure 1. A balanced, twisted-pair transmission line is terminated at each extreme end in its characteristic impedance. The line terminations also bias both lines at a nominal positive level of a few hundred millivolts. The driver is composed of a stage that converts input logic levels to voltage levels that control a current switch. The current switch unbalances the voltage on the transmission lines, resulting in a voltage difference at the receiver input.

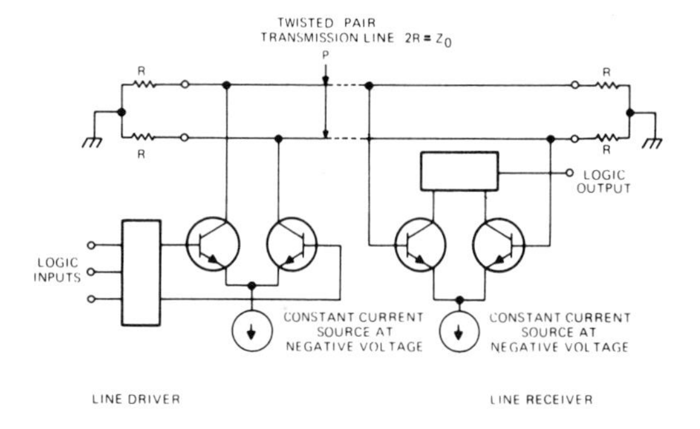

FIGURE 1. Functional Diagram of a Basic High-Speed Transmission System

The input stage of the receiver is a differential-input stage that exhibits high rejection of common-mode input signals. An intermediate stage converts the polarity of the line signal to the desired logic levels at the receiver output. It should be noted that the driver output is not affected by the common-mode signals induced on the line, thereby insuring error-free transmission and recovery of data.

An important feature of the system of Figure 1 is that provisions can be made for removing the driver output current from both lines, as indicated in Figure 2. In this *inhibit* mode, another driver may be used to transmit data over the line. A strobe or gate provision on the receivers allows any driver to communicate with any or all enabled receivers while other drivers are inhibited and other receivers are strobed off. Line receivers and drivers may be connected anywhere along the line. It should be noted that line terminations are required only at the extreme ends of the lines as the output and input impedances of transmitters and receivers are high compared to the line impedance. A single transmission line can therefore service several computer or peripheral equipment consoles.

The concepts described above are implemented by e.g. the SN55107 series. These circuits are designed for compatibility with popular TTL (transistor-transistor logic) integrated circuits and for use with balanced terminated transmission lines.

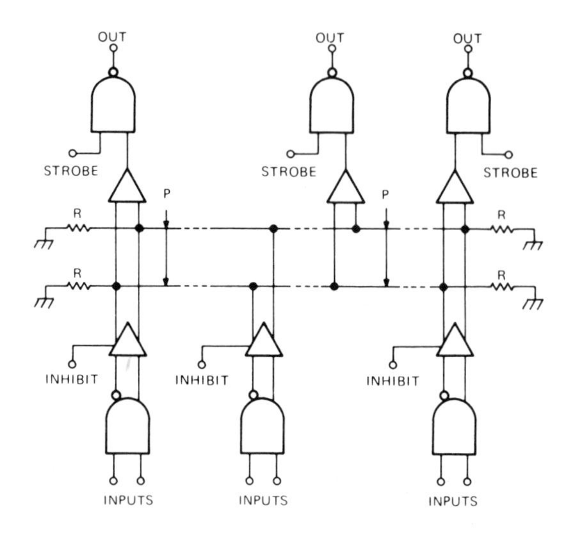

FIGURE 2. Expansion of the Basic System to 'Party Line' Operation

TRANSMISSION LINES

Types of Lines

Many types of wire and cable are used to interconnect logic systems. Plain insulated wire or loose shielded wire are sometimes used, but not in long line interconnections due to the indeterminate value of their line impedance. Coaxial cables used are typically of the 50-Ω and 75-Ω variety. There are special types of coaxial cables with lower or higher impedances, but seldom are impedances ever over 200 Ω.

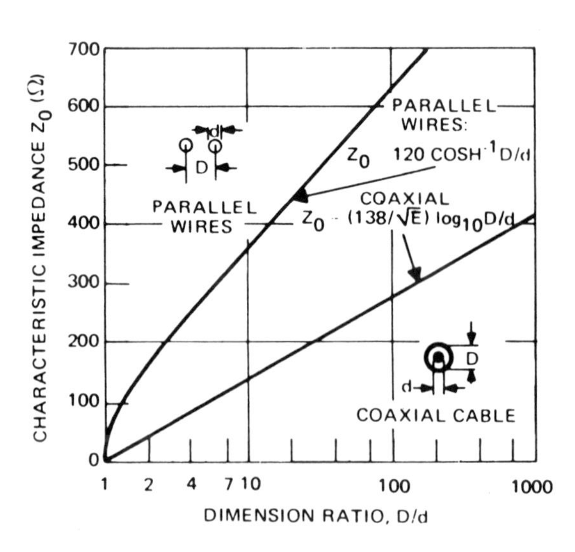

FIGURE 3. Characteristic Impedances of Parallel and Coaxial Lines as Functions of Dimension Ratio

Twisted pair lines normally have an impedance of 100 Ω to 200 Ω which may vary under special conditions e.g. ingress of moisture. The chart in Figure 3 shows that for any given cable size a twisted-pair line has considerably greater impedance than a coaxial line.

The impedance of any unknown line may easily be determined with an RX meter—the line impedance Z is computed from the measured short-circuit impedance Z_{sc} and the open circuit impedance Z_{oc} thus: $Z = (Z_{sc} Z_{oc})^{1/2}$.

Normally the line impedance is considerably smaller than the driver output or receiver input impedances. This is very desirable since connecting several drivers and receivers to one line does not affect the line impedance, so that critical mismatch is avoided.

Signal Degradation

In long lines the transmitted signal experiences two types of degradation: frequency-insensitive and frequency-sensitive. Frequency-insensitive degradation is primarily the attenuation due to line resistance. The resistance of the wire is insensitive to frequency except at very high frequencies where skin effect becomes evident.

Figure 4 shows the resistive attenuation for different line length and resistivity. The signal swing is set by the driver output current and the line impedance. It may be approximated as $I_{out}\ R_T/2 = I_{out}\ Z_0/4$, where R_T is the value of the line-terminating resistors and Z_0 is the line impedance.

By using e.g. the SN55/75109 driver (I_{out}=6 mA) and a twisted pair line with an impedance of 100 Ω and an attenuation factor of 0.01 Ω/ft, it can be seen from Figure 4 that data may be transmitted (theoretically) over line lengths of several thousand feet before line resistance effects degrade signal amplitude to an unusable level.

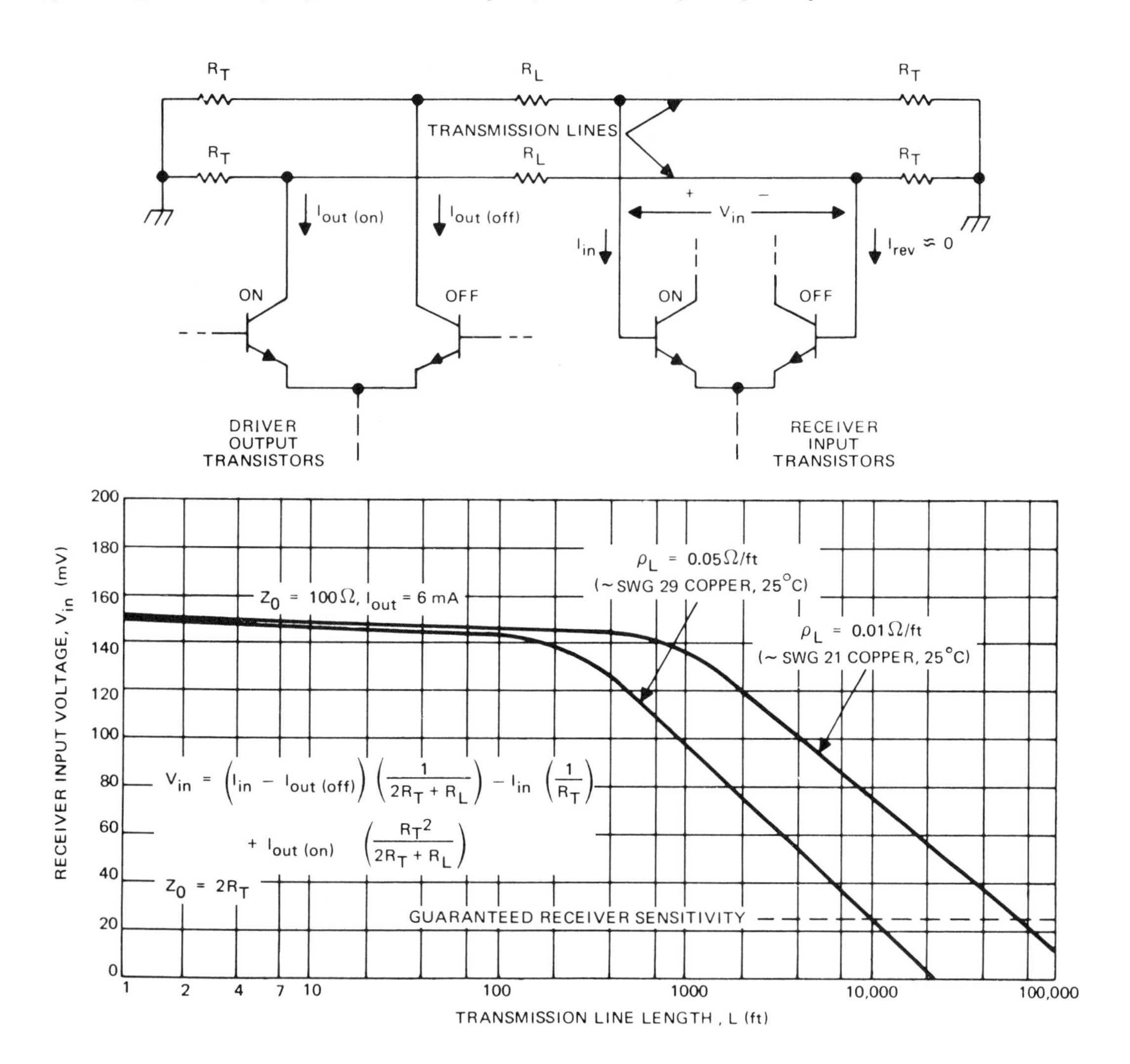

FIGURE 4. Resistive Attentuation With Length of Typical Transmission Lines

The other category of signal degradation, frequency-sensitive type, is related to the capacitive characteristics of the line. As an example, Figure 5 shows the attenuation of

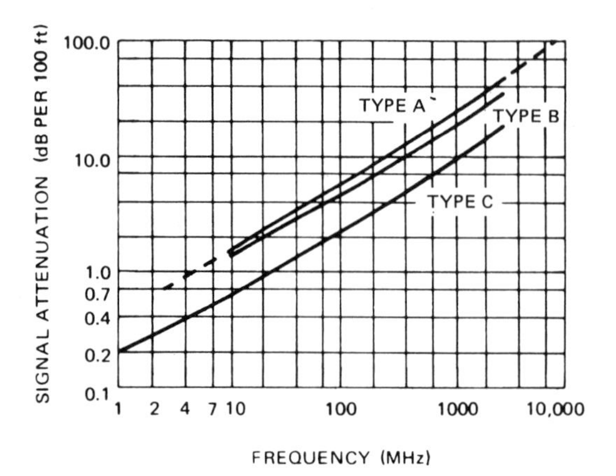

FIGURE 5 Attenuation With Signal Frequency in Typical Coaxial Cables

various coaxial lines with respect to frequency of operation. For instance, type B coaxial cable has an attenuation of about 17 dB per 100 feet of length at 1 MHz.

The attenuation of a twisted pair of flat wires is a little more difficult to determine due to its sensitivity to different physical characteristics and environmental conditions. A typical example of the frequency-sensitive attenuation of twisted pair lines is given in Figure 6.

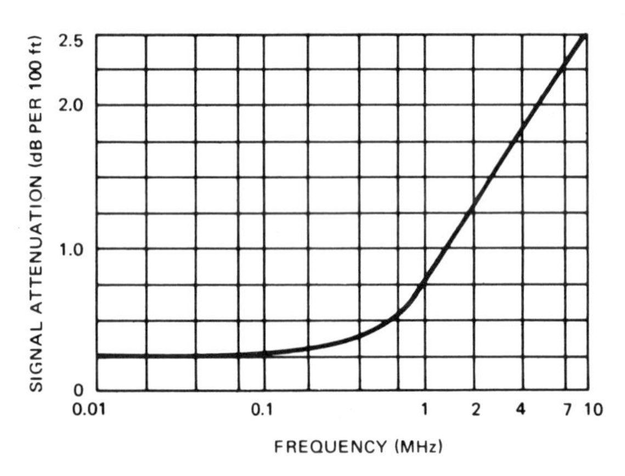

FIGURE 6. Signal Attenuation With Frequency in Twisted-Pair Transmission Line (SWG Solid Wire 23 With 0.060-in Plastic Cover, (Twisted 4.5 Times Per Foot)

Most receivers are designed to detect differential signals as small as 25 mV. The maximum decibels of attenuation A_{max} that can be tolerated may be computed thus: $A_{max}=20 \log_e V_{diff}-28$, Where V_{diff} is the signal swing at the driver output, expressed in millivolts. As an example, in the case of a line driven by a signal of 0.5 V amplitude, the maximum attenuation is 20 $\log_e$ 500−28=26 dB. From Figure 5 type A coaxial cable has about 1.5 dB attenuation per 100 feet at 10 MHz. The maximum permissible length of coaxial in this example is about 1700 feet. For operation at 1 MHz, type A cable has 0.4 dB/100 ft, and the maximum length is about 6500 ft.

When a twisted pair is used, the characteristics of the line need to be known. In a laboratory experiment, a pair of SWG 23 plastic insulated wires were twisted about 4.5 times per foot of length. Figure 6 shows the attenuation per 100 feet at different frequencies. This information may be used to determine the maximum length that could be driven in this particular case.

RELEVANT DEVICE CHARACTERISTICS

Receivers

A receiver circuit should have a typical propagation delay of say 15 ns, to make it ideal for use in high-speed systems. The receiver delay should be almost completely insensitive to overdrive voltages of 10 mV or greater. Such a circuit would respond to input signals with repetition rates as high as 20 MHz.

Input Sensitivity: The input sensitivity is defined as the differential d.c. voltage required at the inputs of the receiver to force the output to the logic gate threshold voltage level, and is typically 3 mV. This feature is particularly important when data is transmitted down a long line and the pulse is deteriorated due to line effects. A receiver with this sensitivity also finds many other applications such as comparators, sense amplifiers, level detectors, etc.

Common-mode Voltage Range: The common-mode voltage range or CMVR is defined as that voltage applied simultaneously to both input terminals which, if exceeded, does not allow normal operation of the receiver. The recommended operating CMVR is ±3V, making it useful in all but the noisiest environments. In extremely noisy environments, common-mode voltage can easily reach ±10 V to ± 15V if some precautions are not taken to reduce ground and power supply noise, as well as crosstalk problems. When the receiver must operate in such conditions, input attenuators should be used to decrease the system common-mode noise to a tolerable level at the receiver inputs. Differential noise is also reduced by the same ratio.

These attenuators are often intentionally omitted from IC receiver input terminals so the designer may select resistors which will be compatible with his particular application or environment. Furthermore, the use of attenuators adversely affects the input sensitivity, the propagation time, the power dissipation, and in some cases the input impedance (depending on the selected resistor values), therefore reducing the versatility of the receiver.

The ability of a receiver to operate with a ± 15-V common-mode voltage at the inputs can be checked using the circuit shown in Figure 7. Dividers with three different

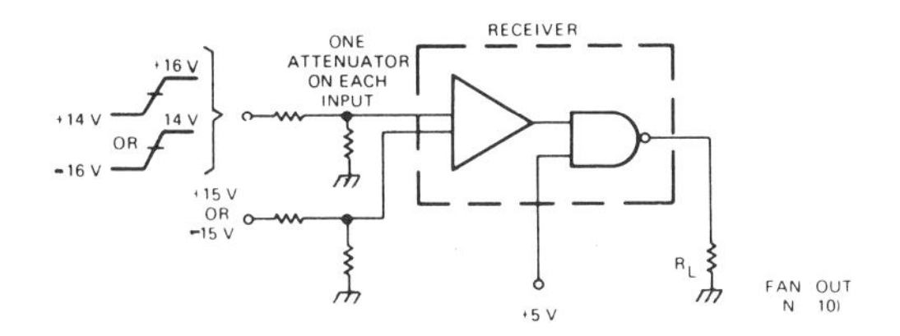

FIGURE 7. Common-Mode Circuit for Testing Input Attenuators

values presenting a 5-to-1 ratio may be used so as to operate the differential inputs under ± 3 V common-mode voltage. Careful matching of the two attenuators is needed so as to balance the overdrive at the input stage. Examples of the resistances which could be used are:–

Attenuator 1:	2 kΩ to 0.5 kΩ
Attenuator 2:	6 kΩ to 1.5 kΩ
Attenuator 3:	12 kΩ to 3.0 kΩ

Input Termination Resistors: To prevent reflections; the transmission line should be terminated in its characteristic impedance. Matched termination resistances normally in the range of 25Ω to 200Ω are required not only to terminate the transmission line in a desired impedance, but also to provide a necessary d-c path for the receiver input bias. Careful matching of the resistor pairs should be observed or the effective common-mode rejection ratio will be reduced. An important point here is that the stray capacities associated with the load resistors should also be balanced with respect to ground by careful layout.

The input circuit of the receivers should meet the requirements for low input currents (30 μA typical) and high input impedance for low loading on the lines; important considerations for 'party-line' applications.

Reference Voltage: A differential receiver can be used as a single-ended line receiver or comparator by referencing one input as shown in Figure 8. The operating

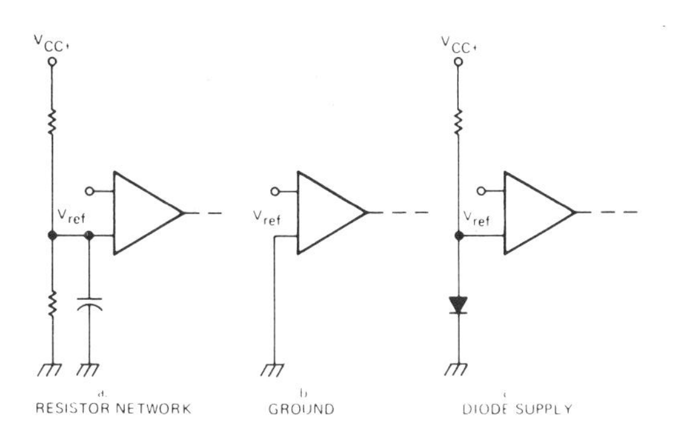

FIGURE 8. Some Methods of Referencing Receiver Inputs

threshold voltage level is established by (and is approximately equal to) the applied reference input voltage, V_{ref}, selected within the operating range.

A simple method of generating the reference voltage is the use of a resistor voltage divider from either the positive V_{CC+} or negative V_{CC-} voltage supplies as in Figure 8a. The reference can also be obtained by a diode (Figure 8c) or a reference supply or just ground (Figure 8b). The bias current required at the referenced input is low (typically 30 μA). Therefore, voltage dividers of this type may normally be operated with very low current requirements and may be used also to supply a number of paralleled reference inputs.

In noisy environments, the use of a filter capacitor may be recommended as indicated in Figure 8a.

Drivers

As stated previously, for reliable operation with less than optimum conditions, drivers should be primarily designed to drive balanced terminated transmission systems which virtually eliminate the adverse effects of line capacitance. These circuits should have low propagation delay (about 10 ns) for high-speed operation.

Input: Drivers should also accept TTL input levels and convert them into an output current suitable for supplying to the transmission line.

Output: An output current of, say, 10 mA allows very long balanced lines to be driven at normal line impedances of 50 to 200 Ω. The resulting low-level differential signals minimize power dissipation. The most positive level at the bases of the driver output transistors should allow at least –3V of noise induced on the lines before saturation of the driver output occurs. The high collector-emitter breakdown of the driver output transistors should allow up to +10V of induced noise before transistor breakdown occurs.

PRACTICAL DEVICES

Receivers

The functional block diagram of a typical family of dual line receivers is shown in Figure 9. The logic of the two devices in the series is the same, but the SN55/75107A has a standard TTL *totem-pole* output, while the SN55/75108A has an open-collector output allowing wired-OR operation. Both the drivers and receivers have two functions per package which can be used independently of each other.

The receivers are designed to work with power supplies of +5 V and –5 V so that only one extra supply is needed when used with TTL or similar logic. The circuit consists of a differential input stage which is coupled to another differential amplifier by a pair of emitter followers so that a high common-mode rejection ratio (CMRR) is obtained. A second emitter follower couples the amplifier stage to one input on a standard TTL multi-emitter stage. The two other inputs on this stage are used to provide a gate function for each individual receiver and a common strobe for both receivers. The conditions for a logical '0' at the receiver output are that both the gate and strobe inputs are high and the differential input is ⩾25 mV with the positive input being the most negative. Conversely a logical '1' output occurs when the positive input is more positive by a value ⩾ 25 mV. The SN55/75107A and SN55/75108A will both sink 16 mA at 0.4 V in the low state and the SN55/75107A will source 0.4 mA at 2.4 V in the high state. The SN55/75108A collector leakage is less than 250 μA in the logical '1' condition.

Due to the design of the balanced input stages of the receivers they will handle a common-mode signal of at least ±3 V without false operation. The common-mode capability can be increased further by tapping down the line terminating resistors. This will decrease the differential sensitivity pro rata. However, in most cases the differential input will considerably exceed the minimum required.

Drivers

The line drivers SN55/75109/110A have a circuit arrangement as shown in Figure 10. As with the receivers the power supplies are ±5 V. Each driver in the package consists of a TTL compatible input stage followed by a differential stage, driving a current-mode output stage so that a constant current is switched into either side of the line pair, according to the state of the input. The current to the other side is zero and the driver looks like an open circuit. This current mode of operation allows any value of load resistance to be connected across the line. This is important in a party-line system where a driver may be at the terminating end of a line as well as at the sending end. The driver output current is 6 mA for the SN55/75109 and 12 mA for the SN55/75110.

Another feature important for party-line operation is the inhibit input-gate which allows either driver-output stage to be turned off completely regardless of the data

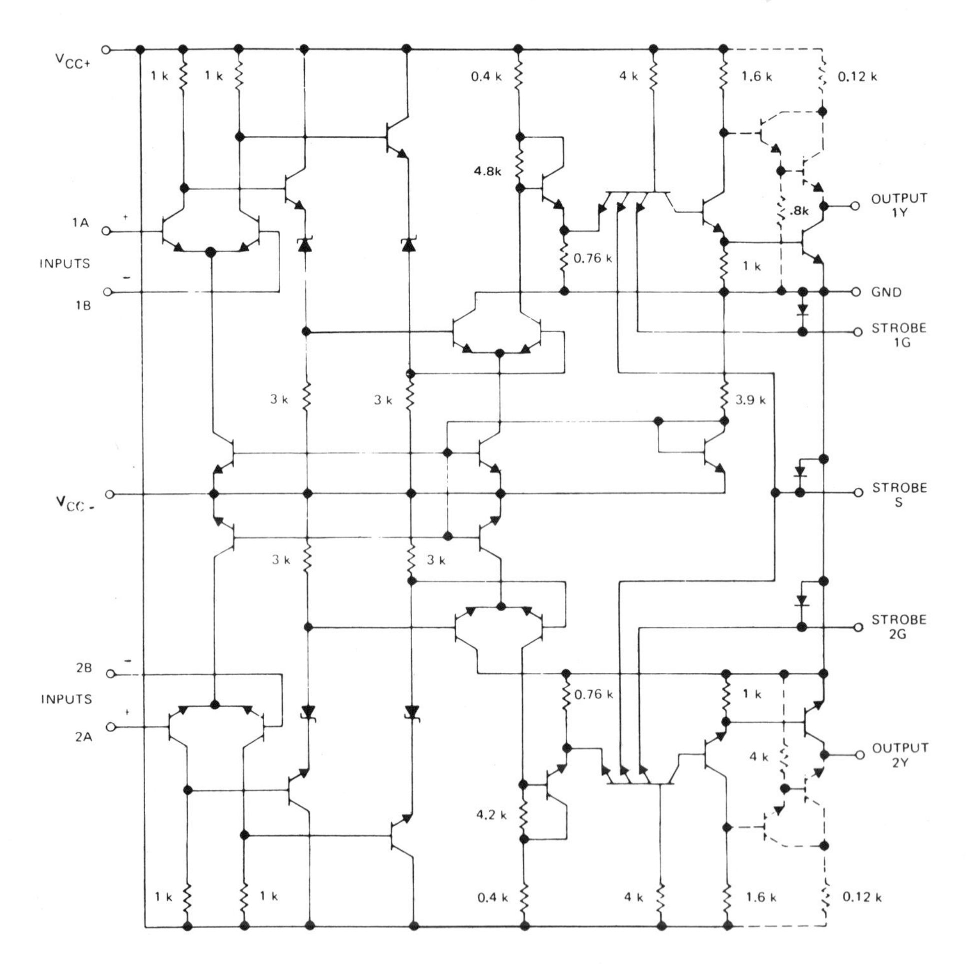

FIGURE 9. Schematic Circuit of SN55/75107A and SN55/75108A Dual Line Receivers

input. There is also a common inhibit input which allows both drivers to be turned off simultaneously. For an output stage to operate, both the individual and the common inhibitor inputs must be at a logical '1'. In the off condition the output current is less than 30 μA so that a large number of drivers can be used on a line without causing significant loading. The receivers and drivers can both withstand a common-mode line voltage of ± 3 V without running into breakdown or saturation.

General Considerations

In any application of devices such as, for example, the SN55107 series, there are two important precautions to be observed. First, when only one driver in a package is used, the outputs of the other driver must either be tied to ground or inhibited, or excessive power dissipation may result. Second, when only one receiver in a package is being used, at least one of the differential inputs of the other receiver should be terminated at some voltage between +3 V and −3 V, preferably at ground. Failure to do so causes improper operation of the unit being used because of common-bias circuitry for the current sources of the two receivers.

There are some other equally basic but less critical recommendations about unused driver gate inputs. Where these inputs are left open-circuited, the propagation delay to a logical '0' is increased by about one nanosecond per input. In high-speed systems this could be a significant factor. For faster switching times, unused gate inputs can be tied to a positive voltage source of 2.4 V to 5.5 V. The positive supply voltage V_{CC+} may be used if it is regulated to 5.5 V maximum. This disposition greatly reduces the distributed capacitance associated with the emitter, bond wire, and package lead of the input transistor. It also

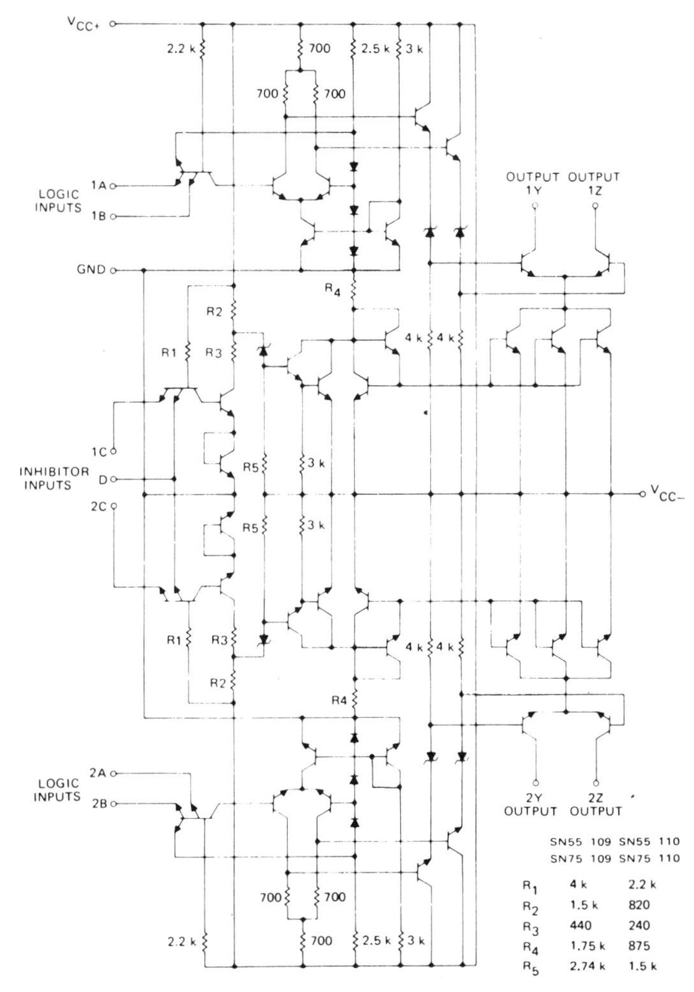

	SN55 109 SN75 109	SN55 110 SN75 110
R_1	4 k	2.2 k
R_2	1.5 k	820
R_3	440	240
R_4	1.75 k	875
R_5	2.74 k	1.5 k

NOTES: 1. COMPONENT VALUES SHOWN ARE NOMINAL.
2. RESISTANCE VALUES ARE IN OHMS.

FIGURE 10. Schematic Diagram for SN55/75109 and SN55/75110 Dual Line Drivers

insures that no additional degradation occurs in the propagation delay times. The best solution is to join unused inputs to a used input on the same gate. This method provides the fastest switching speeds since the stray capacitances are driven by the preceding gate. This method also provides protection against excessive supply surges since the 54/74 TTL outputs at a logical '1' are typically 3.5 V and are current-limited.

The unused gate inputs may be tied to V_{CC} through a resistor. The value of the resistor should not be less than 1 kΩ or the supply voltages transients could damage the inputs. The upper limit is determined by the voltage drop caused by logical '1' input currents and by the minimum supply voltage.

SYSTEM APPLICATIONS

Unbalanced or Single Line (Ended) Systems

Line driver and receiver I.C.s may be used in unbalanced or single line systems whose basic format is as shown in Figure 11. Although this arrangement does not

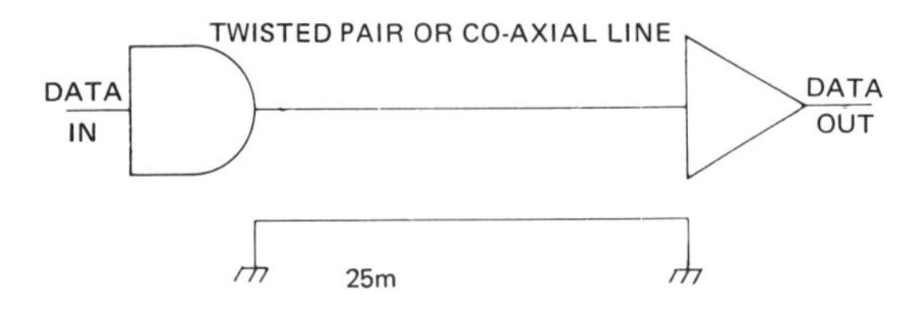

FIGURE 11. Simple Single Line System

offer the same performance as balanced systems for long lines, it is adequate for very short lines where environmental noise is not severe. As mentioned at the beginning of this chapter, a number of standard TTL devices can be used for this mode of operation. Devices which are much more suitable, however, are the high output current SN55/75450B dual peripheral driver series, as described in the previous chapter, or, especially, the devices designed for this purpose such as the SN55/75121 and '122, the '123 and '124, the '138, the SN75150 and '152, and the '188 and '189.

Figure 12 shows one of them being applied in a circuit with a ½ SN75152 as the receiver. Such a system will drive 1000 feet of co-axial cable up to a frequency of 500kHz. Additional features of this particular circuit are the 'OR' capability of the driver and the adjustable noise immunity of the receiver. The fact that three voltages are necessary, however, could be inconvenient. If an SN75450B driver, say, is used in conjunction with a receiver such as the (dual) SN75140 or (triple) SN55/75122, the system will operate from a single 5V supply. An extension of the single line system to include party line operation is shown in Figure 13, where the SN55/75122 receiver is coupled with its partner line circuit the (dual) SN55/75121 driver.

Differential line drivers and receivers may also be used in a single line system, if their greater sensitivity is required. In such systems, the receiver threshold level is established by applying a d-c reference voltage to one receiver input terminal and supplying the transmission line signal to the remaining input. The reference voltage should be optimized so that signal swing is symmetrical with respect to it for maximum noise margin. It can be provided either by a separate voltage source or a voltage divider from one of the available supplies.

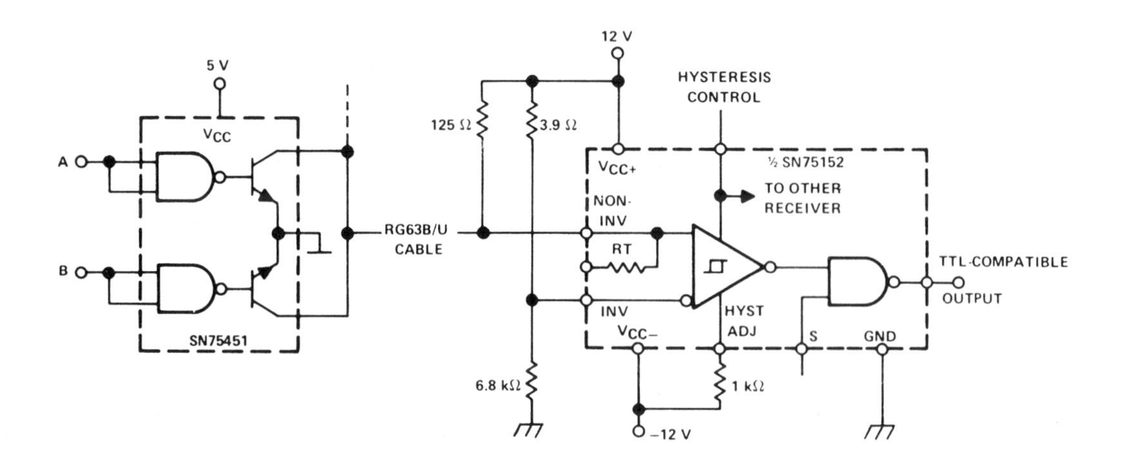

FIGURE 12. Single Line System using a Dual Peripheral Devices as a Driver

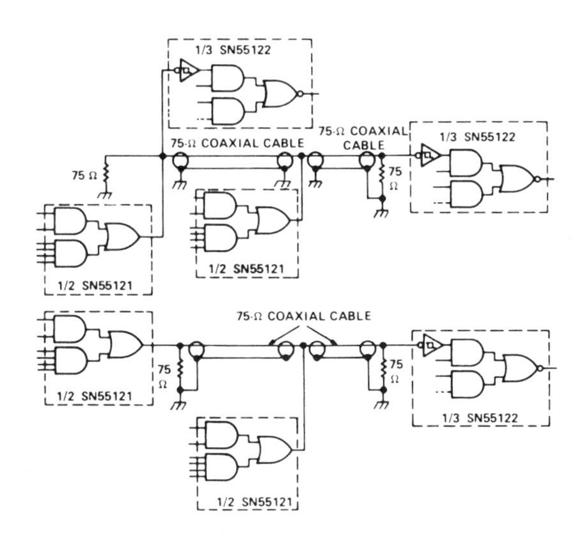

FIGURE 13. Single Line System with Party Line Operation

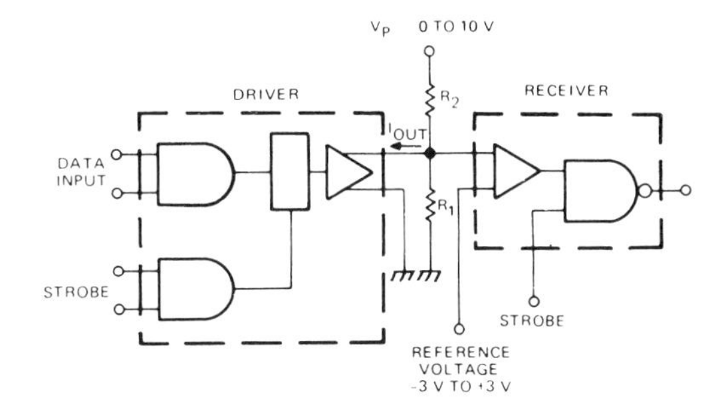

FIGURE 14. A Typical Single-Line Transmission Method Using Differential Devices

A single-ended output from a driver is used in single-wire systems as shown in Figure 14. A coaxial line is preferred, to minimize noise and crosstalk problems. For large signals swings, devices with a high output current are recommended. The unused driver output terminal should be tied to ground as shown in Figure 14. The voltage at the output of the driver is then given by $V_{out} = (V_P - R2\ I_{out})(R1)/(R1 + R2)$, where I_{out} is the given output sinking current. The values of R1 and R2 affect the amplitude of the pulse and its position with respect to ground.

One-Channel Balanced Transmission:

As discussed earlier many line circuits are designed for use in high-speed data transmission systems that utilize balanced, terminated transmission media such as twisted pair lines. Such a system operates in the balanced mode, so that any noise induced on one line is also induced in the other. The noise appears as common-mode at the differential receiver input terminals, where it is rejected. The ground connection between the line driver and line receiver is not part of the signal circuit, so that system performance is not affected by circulating ground currents and ground noise.

The special output circuit of drivers allows terminated transmission lines to be driven at normal line impedances. High-speed operation of a system is ensured since line reflections are virtually eliminated when terminated lines are used. Crosstalk is minimized because of the low signal amplitude, low line impedances, and because the total current in a line pair remains constant.

A basic balanced transmission system of the type given in Figure 1,but using SN55107 series devices is shown in Figure 15. The SN75207 and '208 dual sense amplifiers have a tighter input sensitivity than the SN55/75107A and '108A. (It was this fact that allowed them to operate at higher frequencies as MOS memory sense amplifiers in the previous chapter.). Therefore when used as receivers in the differential system of Figure 15 a longer transmission line length is possible. Data is transmitted on the twisted-pair

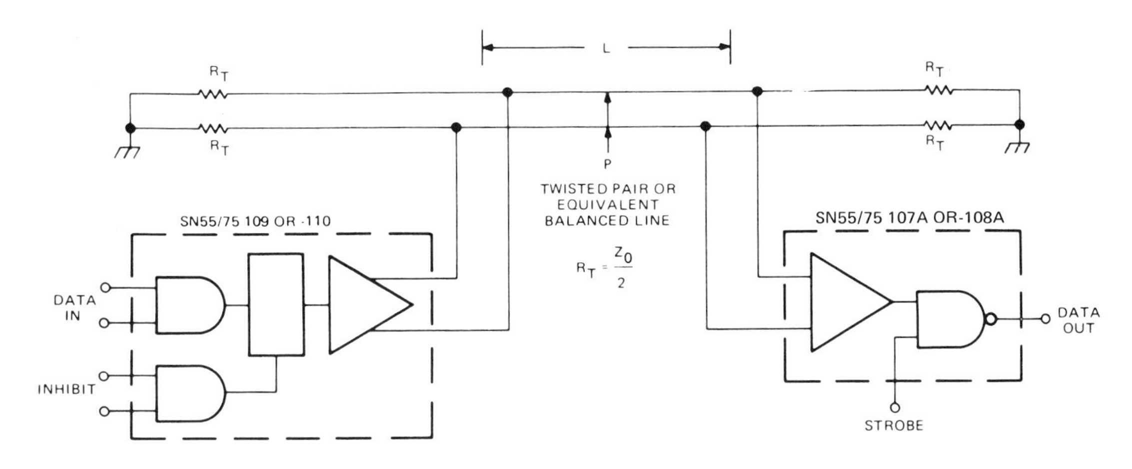

FIGURE 15. Use of SN55107 Series Devices in a Typical Single-Driver, Single-Receiver Transmission System

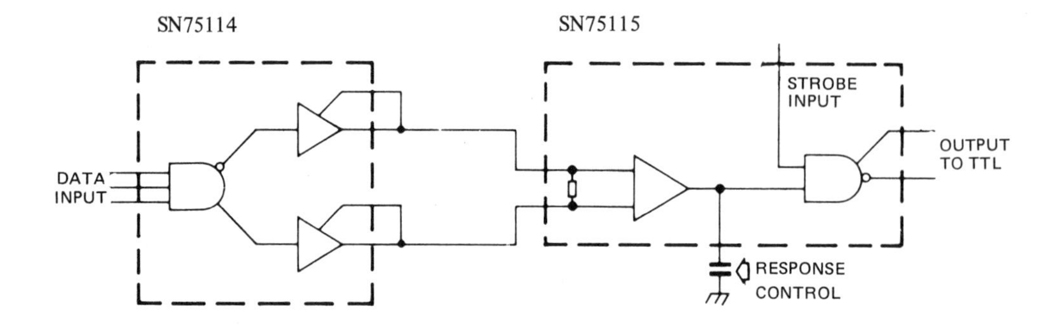

FIGURE 16. Typical Single Supply Differential System

line by unbalancing the line voltages by means of the driver output current. Line termination resistors, labeled R_T, are required only at the extreme ends of the line. For short lines, termination resistors only at the receiver end may prove adequate. Signal phasing depends on the driver output and receiver input polarities on the line.

Again the necessity of using two voltage supplies with the SN55/75107 series of devices might be inconvenient, so Figure 16 shows a system which employs the SN55/75114 and '115 pair of devices which operate from a single supply.

Party-Line Balanced Systems:

The need to communicate between many receivers and line drivers using one line per channel could require large amounts of wire and consequently increase the installation costs. For example, in transmitting and receiving information from the cockpit of an airplane to some remote area in the tail of the plane, the wire required for a multi-channel system might well weigh more than all of the equipment involved. Thus a method for sharing a single transmission line by several drivers and receivers is desirable.

The strobe feature of receivers and the inhibit feature of line drivers such as the SN55107 series allows them to be used in party-line (also called 'data-bus') applications. Examples are shown in Figures 17, 18 and 19. In each of these systems, an enabled driver transmits data to all enabled receivers on the line while other drivers and receivers are disabled. Data can therefore be time-multiplexed on the transmission line. The party-line system thus offers maximum performance at minimum cost for those applications in which it is usable.

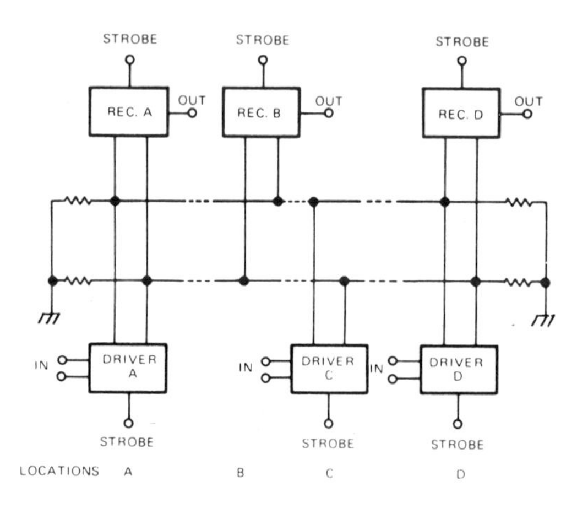

FIGURE 17. Simple Party Line System with Driving and Receiving Stations Scattered Along the Line

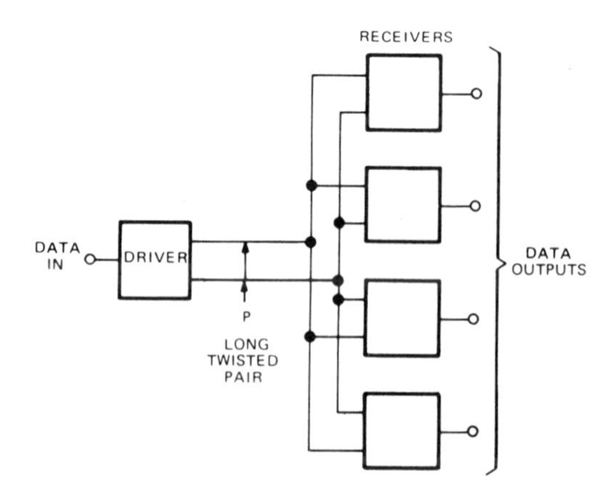

FIGURE 18. Party-Line Concept of One Driver Transmitting to One of Many Receivers

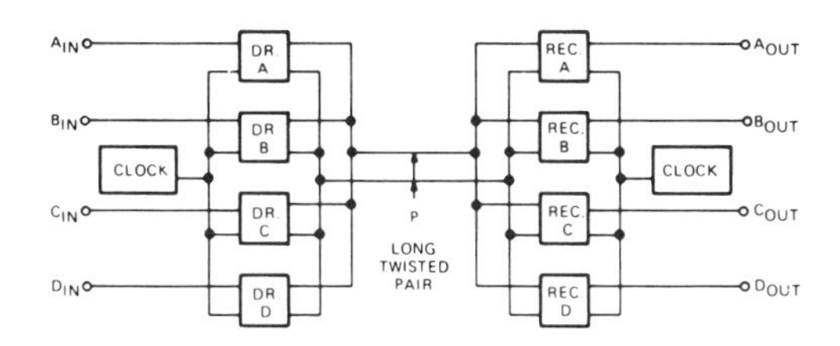

FIGURE 19. Conceptual Diagram of Four Transmission Channels Sharing the Same Party Line

Addressing System: this application is intended to illustrate the principles involved in party line transmission. Although built and tested satisfactorily, a specific requirement would probably require several modifications to function correctly in the desired mode. However,the application described demonstrates the ability of line drivers and receivers to transmit data on a party line with consistent accuracy. The circuit techniques may be applied to any party line system where remote addressing and address recognition is required.

The block diagram of a two-station system is shown in Figure 20. The operation is as follows: The two stations, A and B, each have a wired-in address code which corresponds to the other station. When driver A starts to transmit, the address code is clocked serially into a pulse generator. The latter encodes a logical '0' as a pulse with a 2:1 mark/space ratio, and a logical '1' as a pulse with a 1:2 mark/space ratio. Driver B is inhibited during this time. When all eight bits of the code have been transmitted driver A is itself inhibited. The code will have been received by receivers A and B and the pulse width detected so that eight corresponding logic levels are serially shifted into a memory with parallel outputs. The eight outputs are compared with a wired address code and in this case comparator B will recognize its own address. When this happens driver B is enabled and pulse generator B is triggered so that it transmits a code which is recognized by comparator A. This process will stop when one false bit of data is transmitted. There is no need for the station-clock generators to be synchronized as long as the frequency is within the range of the pulse-width discriminators. In a practical system the address code would probably be followed by further data which would be allowed to reach the station output only if the address code was appropriate.

A logic diagram is shown in Figure 21.A 4 MHz signal clocks flip-flop N1A whose Q1 output drives the rest of the circuit. The clock is gated via the clear input to the flip-flop so that the clock can be started in the correct phase.

Networks N2A and N2B form a three state counter with the following truth table:

Clock Pulse	Q2	Q3
0/3	0	0
1	1	0
2	1	1

By selecting either Q2 or Q3, pulses can be obtained with either 1:2 or 2:1 mark/space ratios of a pulse repetition frequency (p.r.f.) of 4/(2X3) MHz. The selection is performed by gates N3A, N3B and N3C and controlled by the D_O output of shift register N8.

At the end of each pulse there is a negative edge at output Q2 which is used to clock the divide-by-8 section of an SN7493N 4-bit counter. This also clocks the shift registers N8 and N9 via gates N6A and N6B so that the next bit of the address code appears at D_O on N8. After eight code pulses there is a negative edge at the D_O output of the counter N4, which clocks flip-flop N1B. This in turn, clears flip-flop N1A, resets the counter and inhibits the line driver. The action of the pulse generator is now inhibited until network N1B is cleared. The data pulses are continuously detected by all the receivers in the system. The leading edge of each pulse is positive at the output of the receivers. This edge triggers the monostable N10, whose pulse width is approximately half way between that of a '0' pulse and that of a '1' pulse (in this case 1.250 μs). When the pulse generator is inhibited gate N6C is enabled by output Q4 so that the negative trailing edges of the data pulses will clock the shift registers. The level of the serial data input S_{in}, on register N9, is controlled by the monostable output. For a narrow pulse the clock edge will occur while the serial input is high putting a logical '1' into the register. Conversely, a wide pulse puts in a logical '0'. If a condition arises where the outputs of the registers from left to right are 01100101 then the output of gate N7 falls to '0'. This clears flip-flop N1B and changes the mode of the shift registers so that parallel data will be clocked in when the clock input receives a negative edge. This comes from the Q1 output. A new address code (10110100) is now

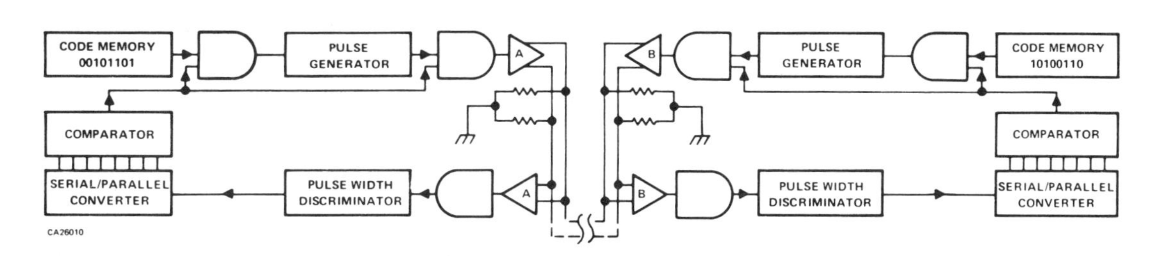

FIGURE 20. A Block Diagram of a Two Station System

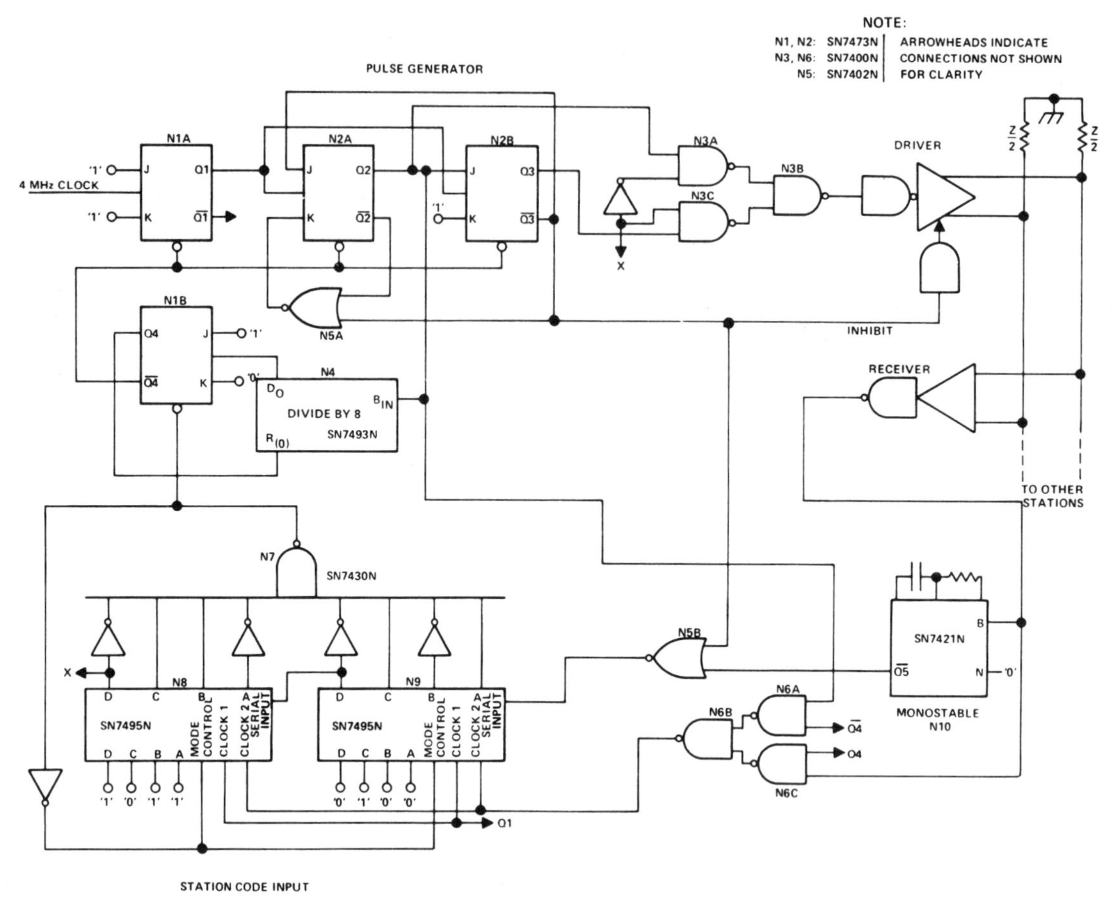

FIGURE 21. Logic Diagram of an Address Code Generator and Detector in a Two-Station System

clocked into the shift registers resetting the output of N7 to a '1' and the mode control to the shift condition. The outputs of flip-flop N1B disable gates N5B and N6C so that the shift registers are isolated from the receiver and are clocked only by the pulse generator output Q2

The oscillogram, in Figure 22 shows the input to line driver A (10110100) and the corresponding output from receiver B. In this case, the master-clock speed has been increased to approximately 17 MHz giving a pulse repetition frequency of 2.8 MHz. The two stations were linked by 100 yards of *bell-flex* having a characteristic impedance of 120 Ω. The two waveforms are identical in content but there is a delay of 500 ns due to the propagation time of the cable. The propagation delay of the driver and receiver alone is 16 ns. The oscillogram, in Figure 23 shows the differential and common-mode line voltages at the input of receiver B measured under the same working conditions as Figure 22. The time base has been slowed down to show both codes. The signal from driver A has been degraded by the cable but is still ample to drive the receiver. Each pair of codes is followed by a space equal to twice the cable delay since the codes must travel from B to A and back again before a signal reappears at receiver B. The common-mode waveform demonstrates an interesting effect which is

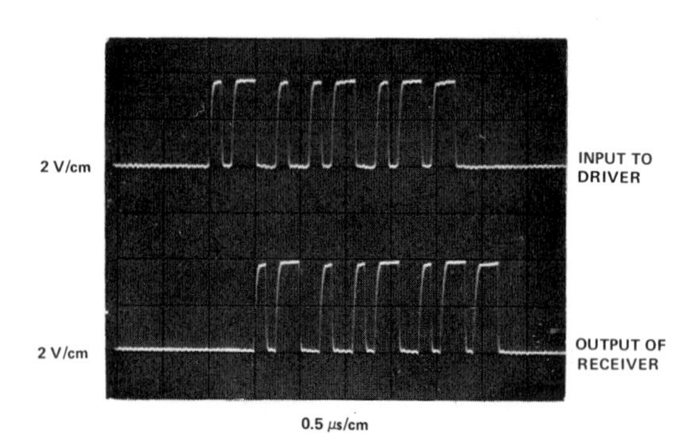

FIGURE 22. Oscillogram Showing the Input to Line Driver A (10110100) and the Corresponding Output from Receiver B

due to the inductance of the cable. Although the cable has a fairly constant characteristic impedance between conductors, the impedance between conductors and ground is far from constant unless the cable is balanced and shielded. In practice, the common-mode impedance of the cable appears inductive and therefore when the current changes direction from station to station, regardless of the conductor in which it flows, there will be an exponential common-mode

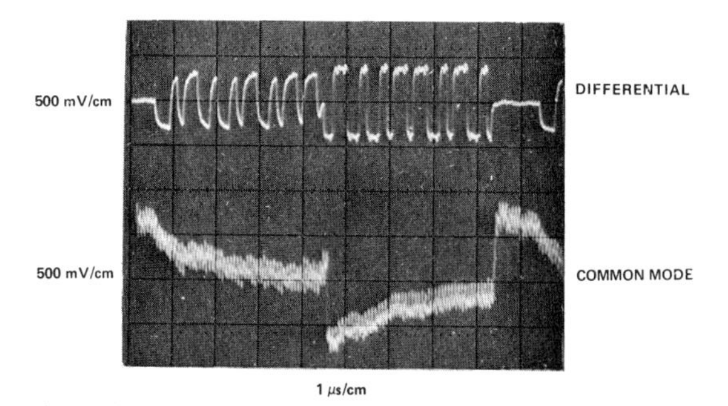

FIGURE 23. Oscillogram Showing the Differential and Common-Mode Line Voltages Measured at the Input of Receiver B, Under the Same Conditions as Figure 22.

COMMON MODE VOLTAGE ± 3 V AT 1 MHz

2 V/cm V_A

2 V/cm V_B

5 V/cm V_O

500 ns/cm

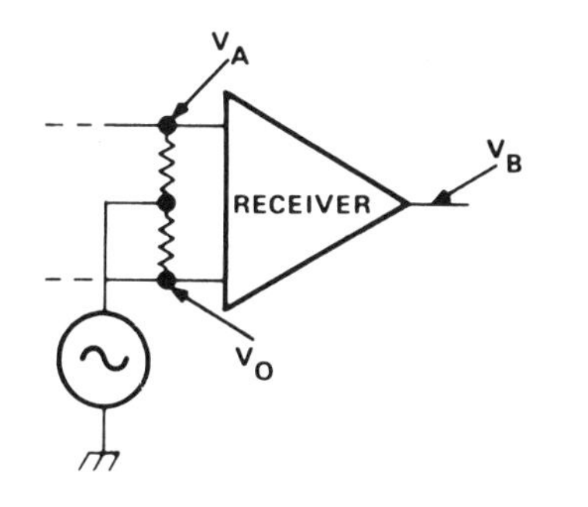

FIGURE 24. Oscillogram Demonstrating the Common-Mode Rejection Capability of the Receivers

voltage spike. This spike depends on the driver current and the time-constant of the cable and terminating resistors. This common-mode signal will normally be within the handling capacity of the receivers, but a method of reducing it is shown later. The common-mode rejection of the receivers is shown in Figure 24 in which a 3 V peak-to-peak 1 MHz signal is produced at the receiver inputs by varying the ground potential seen by the junction of the terminating resistors. Although the differential signal is apparently swamped, the correct code still appears at the output of the receiver. The common-mode signal has no effect on the driver, because, when the line is terminated at each end, the ground potential of the receiver will be halved at the driver, due to the divider network formed by the load resistors (see Figure 25).

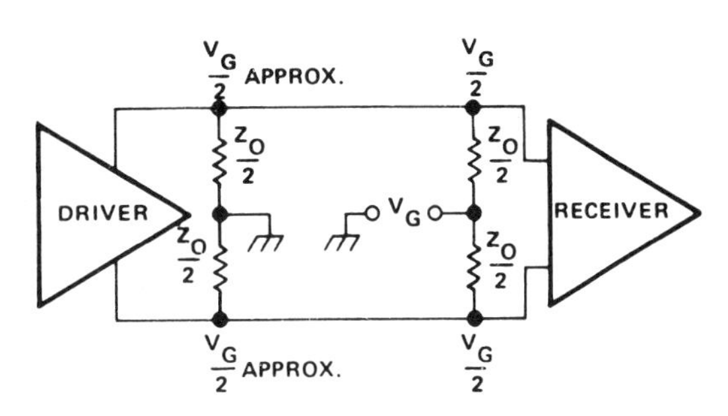

FIGURE 25. Circuit Showing How Common-Mode Signals Have no Effect on the Driver Because the Ground Potential of the Receiver is Halved at the Driver Due to the Divider Network

Combined Data and Clock Transmission

The system just described does not have a clock reference common to all stations but relies on the pulse generator frequency staying within the range of the pulse-width detector. If it is necessary to transmit data and the corresponding clock signal down a single line – pair then the inhibit condition of the line drivers can be used to produce the three current states required. The circuit is shown in Figure 26 and the corresponding input and output waveforms in Figure 27. This circuit uses only half of a driver package, a complete receiver package and an SN7400N quad 2-input NAND gate.

The input data is fed to the A terminal on the driver, and the clock or synchronization signal is fed to the inhibit A terminal. This means that when the clock is high, one line or the other will carry the signal current depending on the state of input A1. When the clock is low, neither line conducts, and the receiver outputs are determined by the bias resistors R1 and R2, which ensure that the receiver outputs are high when the driver is inhibited. The clock pulses are recovered by gate G1 which looks for a logical'0'at either of the receiver outputs. The data signal is restored by a simple latch, G2 and G3. This gives a Non

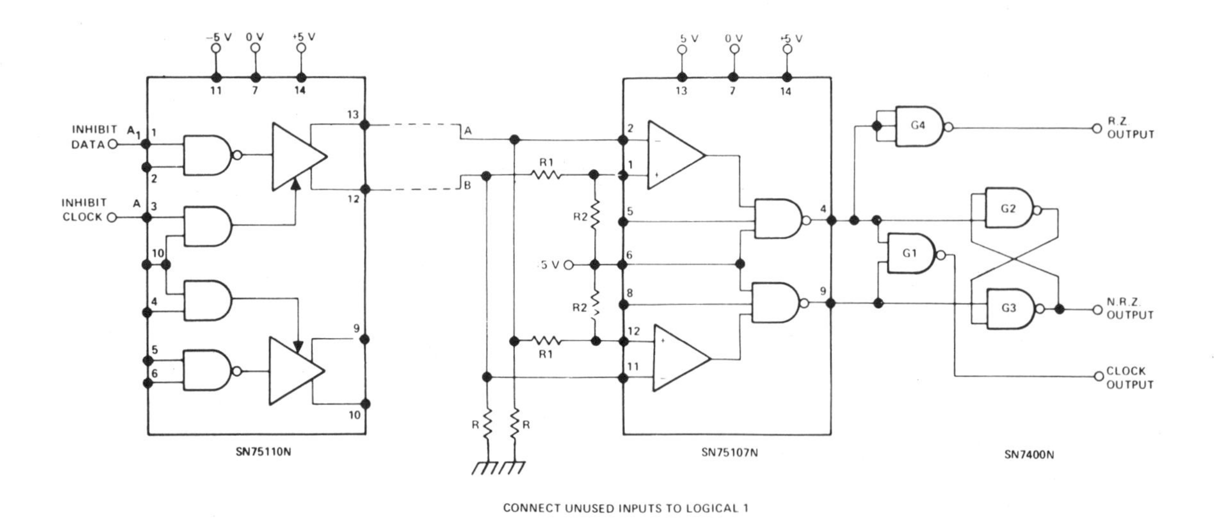

FIGURE 26. Data and Clock Transmission Down a Bifilar Line

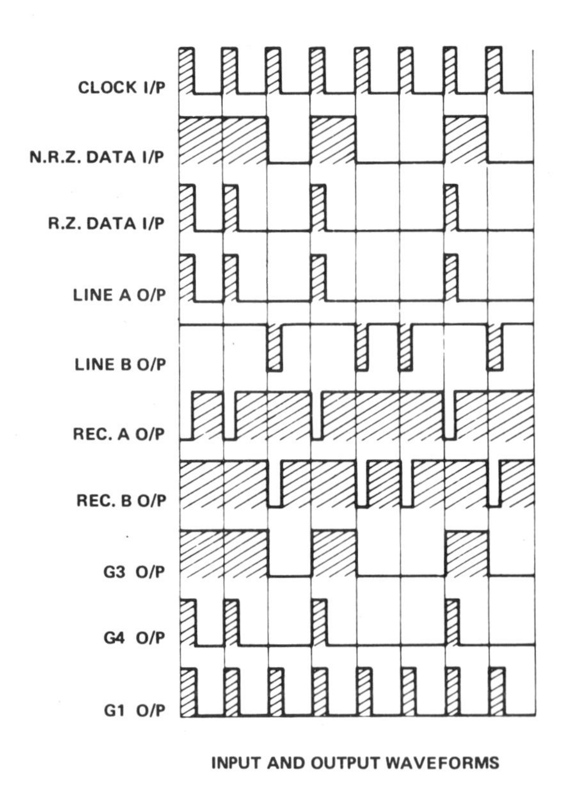

FIGURE 27. Input and Output Waveforms for the System Shown in Figure 26.

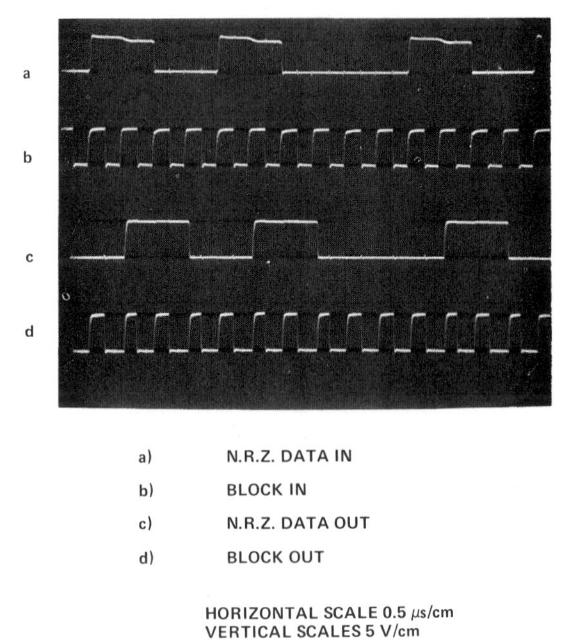

a) N.R.Z. DATA IN

b) BLOCK IN

c) N.R.Z. DATA OUT

d) BLOCK OUT

HORIZONTAL SCALE 0.5 μs/cm
VERTICAL SCALES 5 V/cm

FIGURE 28. Oscillogram Showing the Inputs and Outputs of the System in Figure 26.

Return to Zero (NRZ) signal. If a Return to Zero (RZ) signal is required this comes from gate G4.

Each of the load resistors R, equals half the line impedance Z_0. The line is loaded at one end only, since data is transmitted in only one direction. If Z_0 is fairly low (about 100Ω) a 12mA driver SN75110N may be required. R1 and R2 are about 47 Ω and 1 kΩ respectively. This assumes that the full common-mode noise range is required and that the receiver sensitivities are at their minimum. It is not always possible to design a system which will meet these worst case conditions for all practical values of line impedance and attenuation. However, receiver sensitivity is usually well above the minimum and the noise immunity can often be relaxed, allowing a workable system to be achieved. The oscillogram, Figure 28 shows the inputs and outputs of a system as described above. The clock rate is approximately 3 MHz and the transmission line is again 100 yards of flat twin *bell-flex*.

Reduction of Common-Mode Voltage Spike

As stated earlier, any change in the sum of the currents flowing in the two halves of a bifilar line, either in magnitude or direction, will tend to produce an exponential voltage spike due to the common-mode inductance of the line. This is illustrated in Figure 29 in which a 12 mA driver is alternately switched on and inhibited. The inductance between the line pair and ground is 4.75mH and this gives a maximum spike of 300mV with a fall time of 165μs. The rise and fall times will be affected mainly by the line inductance, the mutual inductance between lines and the terminating resistors. It is unlikely that this spike will be of a magnitude that seriously affects the operation of the circuit. However, if it is essential to reduce the spike, the following approaches may be used to keep the total driver-current constant even when the data section is inhibited.

An ideal solution would involve a separate positive current source as shown in Figure 30. With this system the base drivers to the extra transistor, Q1 and Q2 are arranged so that Q1 would source a current equal to the collector current of transistor Q4; and transistors Q2 and Q3 would both be *off*. For a change of data input level, the conducting and non-conducting pairs reverse and when the IC line driver is inhibited, transistors Q1 and Q2 are both *off*. This arrangement ensures a zero net current in the line-pair at all times but requires rather elaborate circuitry and a lot of discrete components.

A simpler solution is shown in Figure 31. Here the second driver in a package is used to provide a current sink whenever the first driver, which is used for data transmission, is inhibited. The two resistors R and R′ are equalized so that the differential current in the line is zero when the first driver is inhibited. Wiring to the inverter should be as short as possible to minimize the propagation delay between the inhibit functions. By this means the current from a driver station will be constant except during the brief change-over period. Resistors R and R′ impose an extra loading on the line. However, they are about 500 Ω each for a 12 mA driver and 1 kΩ each for 6 mA driver, or approximately 10 or 20 times the resistance of Z_0. Figure 32 shows the results of this method applied under the conditions indicated in Figure 29. The width of the voltage spike has been reduced from 165 μs to 15 ns. This allows the amplitude to be reduced by a capacitive filter without seriously affecting the data transmission rate.

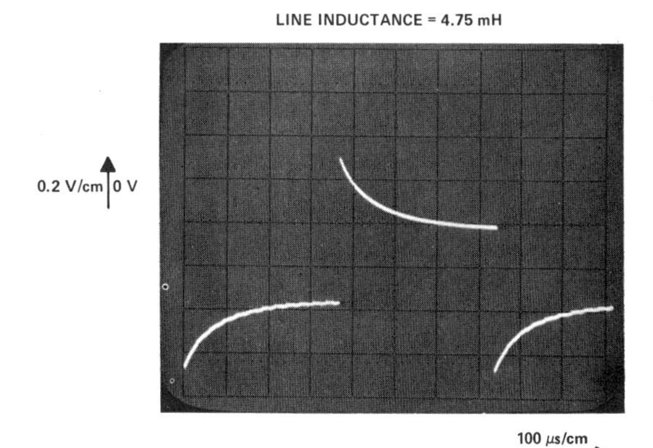

FIGURE 29. Oscillogram Showing Voltage Spike Caused by Common-Mode Inductance of Bifilar Line when a 12 mA Driver is Alternatively Switched on and Inhibited

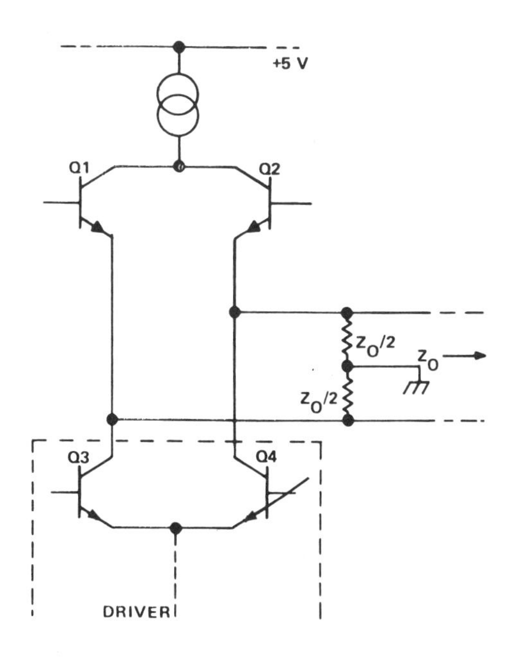

FIGURE 30. Separate Positive Current Source that May Be Used to Ensure that the Total Current From a Driver is Constant Even When the Data Section is Inhibited

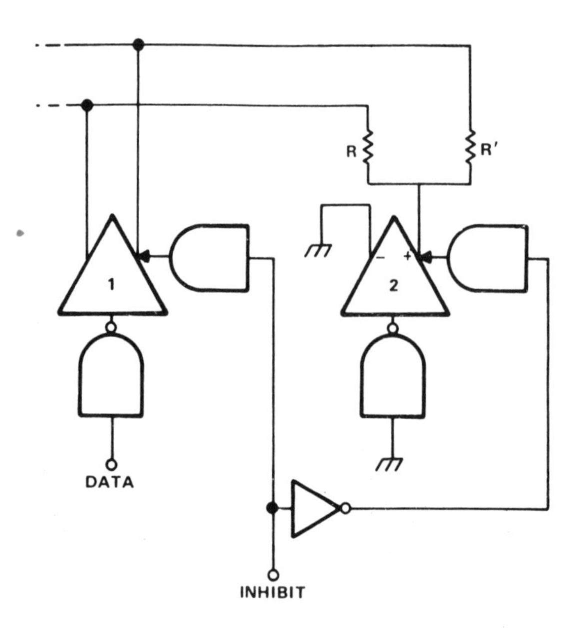

FIGURE 31. Circuit Showing the Second Driver in Package Being Used as a Current Sink when the First Driver is Inhibited

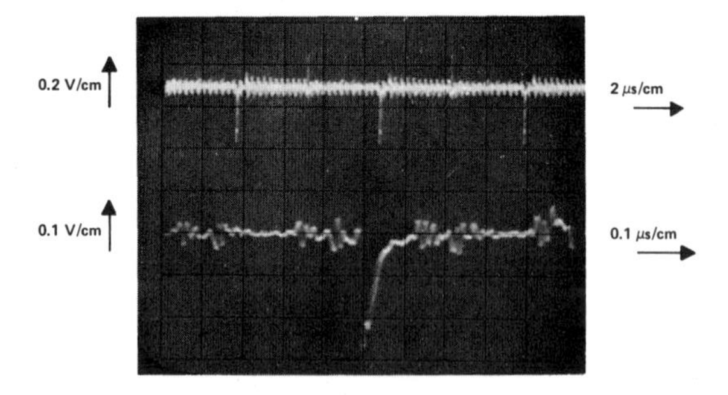

FIGURE 32. Oscillogram Showing the Effect of Using the Circuit in Figure 31. Compare to Figure 29 obtained under the same conditions

VII (PROGRAMMABLE) READ-ONLY MEMORIES

by Bob Parsons
and Jean-Marie Krausener

Since their introduction in the late 1960s, fixed program semiconductor memories have established themselves as one of the most versatile integrated circuit functions available to designers. They offer a unique combination of flexibility, performance and low cost in a highly usable form. Their applications range from micro program storage, code conversion and generation (as discussed with MOS devices in Chapter II), to the production of analogue waveforms. Recently, the progress achieved in bipolar large scale integration technology has allowed the creation of Read-Only Memories (ROMs) with a high capacity and very short access times. These memories are fixed content and are either mask or fusible link programmable. There are, of course, other methods of producing Programmable Read Only Memories (PROMs) e.g. MNOS charge injection devices. All the applications given in this chapter are applicable to these alternative forms of PROM.

As an introduction, the characteristics and organisations of a simple, low capacity ROM/PROM will be described. The organisation and applications of more complex devices will be discussed later.

DESCRIPTION OF THE SN7488 I.C.

The SN7488* I.C. is a mask programmed 256 bit read-only memory organised as 32 words of 8 bits each. An average access time of 35 nanoseconds, and TTL inputs and outputs, provide a good system flexibility. The user programmable version of this device is the SN74188A. The memory is organised as 32 words of 8 bits each, and includes essentially (as shown in Figure 1):

– a 5 bit address decoder
– a 256 bit memory
and 8 output buffers.

The memory is addressed in binary notation by 5 inputs A, B, C, D, E. Also provided is a memory enable input G, which must be at a logical 'zero' for the memory to be addressed. When G is at a logical 'one' all outputs are read as logical 'ones'. When the Enable input is a logical 'zero' and an address is applied to the 5 inputs, one of the 32 gates is enabled taking one of the 32 horizontal rows to a '1' level. Depending on the word which is programmed at this address the vertical lines to the eight output buffers are

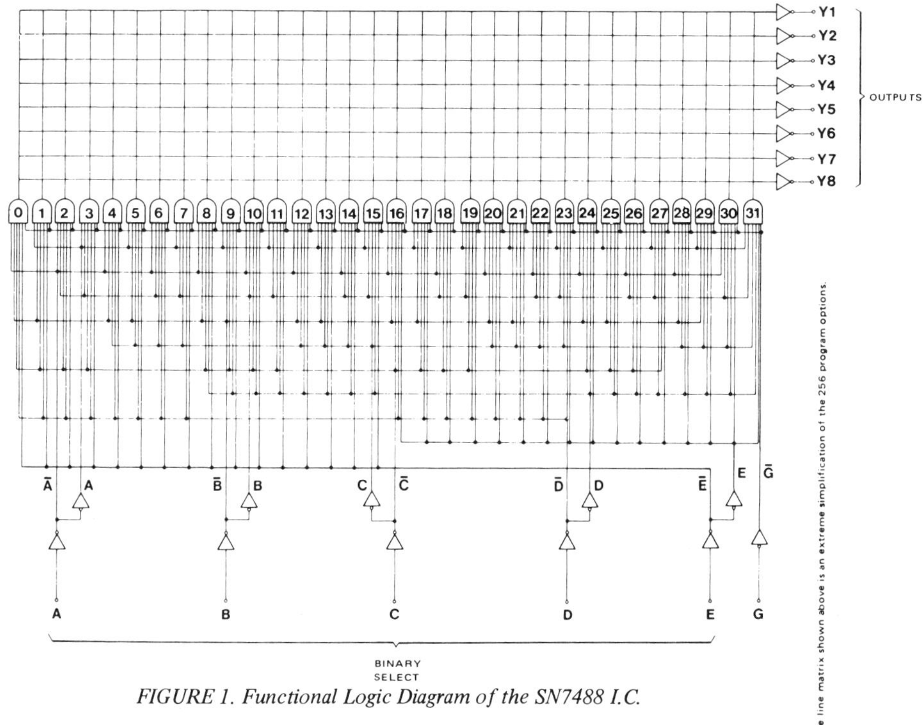

FIGURE 1. Functional Logic Diagram of the SN7488 I.C.

* *The SN7488 is now designated SN7488A*

connected to the decoded row or are open circuit. Those vertical lines which are connected are pulled up to a logical '1' and the word programmed at this address is thus transferred to the 8 output buffers.

ORGANISATION OF ROMs

Increasing the length of words

When words of more than 8 bits (number of bits in a word) are to be stored it is necessary to parallel several ROMs as shown in Figure 2. Each word is placed in the various memories in the following way:–

– bits from 1 to 8 are located in the first memory.

– bits from 9 to 16 in the second.

– bits from 17 to 24, in the third, etc.

The different parts of a word are located at the same address on each device. Figure 2 shows a memory containing 32 words of 32 bits, which requires 4 paralleled SN7488 memories.

Applications requiring an odd number of bits, or less than whole multiples of the number of outputs, can be implemented with a smaller memory and a data selector as illustrated in Figure 3. The arrangement shown will provide one more bit to the word length. Simplicity of design is characterized by the fact that the address of the additional bit is derived directly from the existing address register. Other selectors can be implemented which provide 2 additional bits.

Increasing the memory capacity

ROMs containing more than 32 words, while keeping a length of 8 bits, need a decoder acting on the Enable inputs. Thus memories are alternately interrogated and the corresponding outputs are connected in 'Wired-OR' configuration, as shown in Figure 4, which illustrates a 512

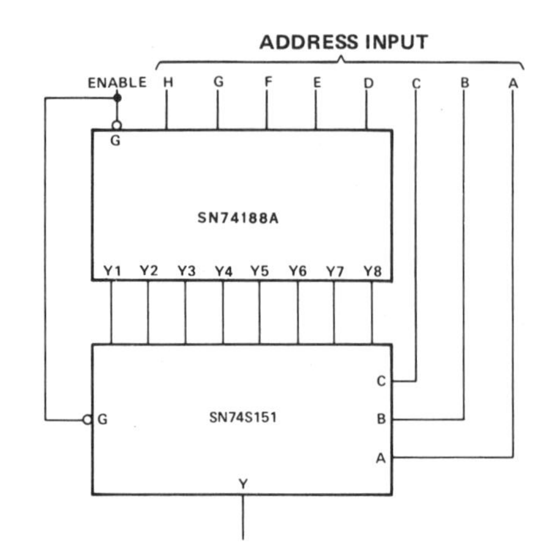

FIGURE 3. Modifying Number of Bits in a Word

word 8 bit ROM. This ROM is addressed by 9 bits, A, B, C, D, E, F, G, H and I; I being the most and A the least significant. The first 32 words of 8 bits are located in the memory on the left, which acts when the '0' output of the SN74154 is decoded (F.G.H.I = 0000). The following 32 words are located in the second memory enabled by an output '1' from the decoder (F.G.H.I = 1000), and so on, such that each of the 32 groups is situated in a SN7488 memory controlled by one of the decoder outputs. Note that as the 16 memories are jointly addressed a buffer is required, e.g. an SN7440 device to drive the address inputs A to E.

Simultaneously increasing the capacity and the word length

High capacity memories with words of more than 8 bits are obtained by combining both principles described previously. For example, if a 16 bit 256 word ROM is

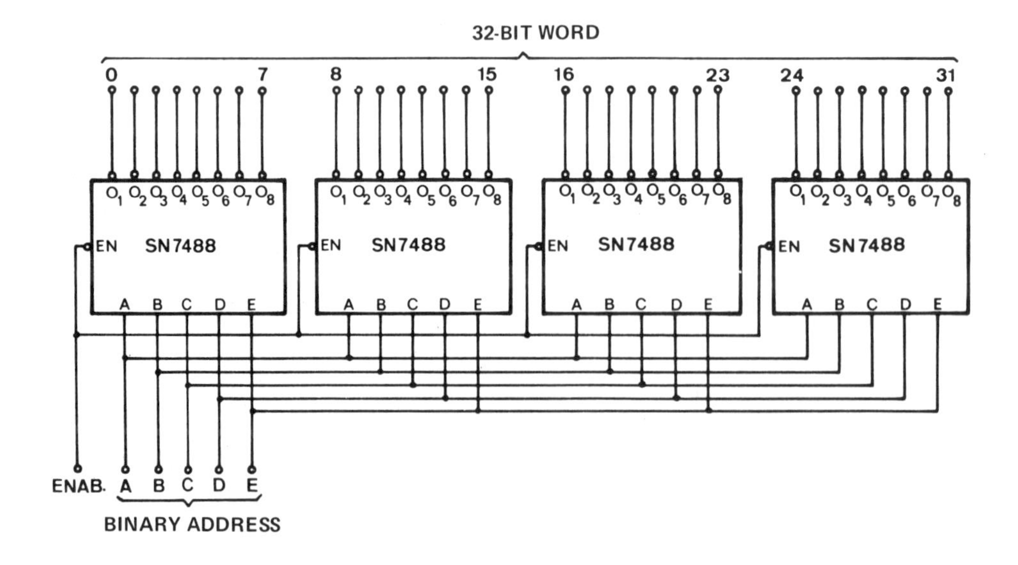

FIGURE 2. ROMs in Parallel

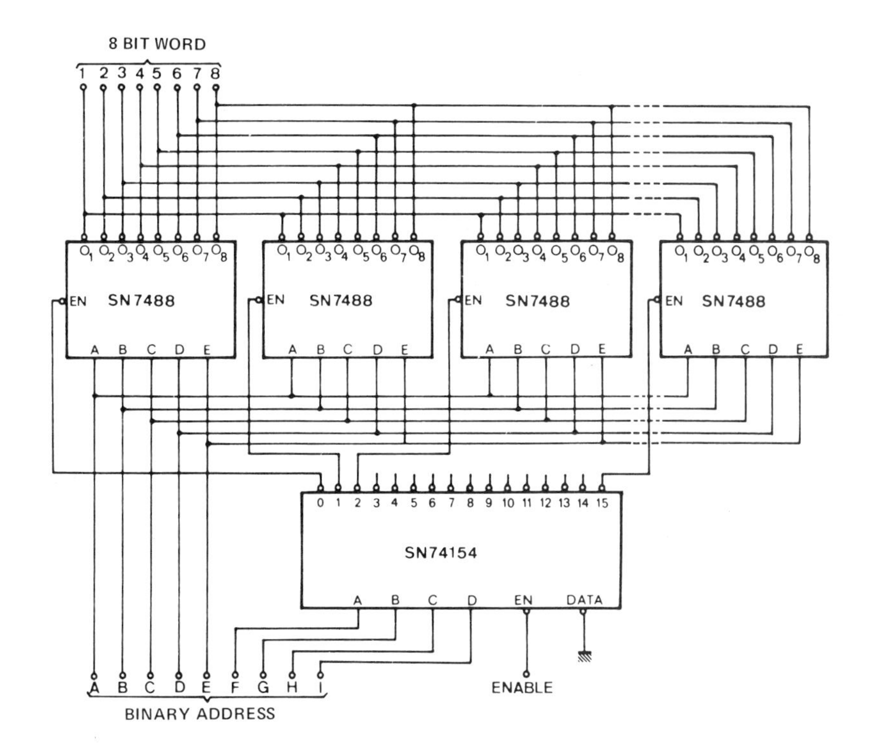

FIGURE 4. Increasing the Memory Capacity

required a circuit similar to that shown in Figure 5 is used. In order to obtain 16 bit-words, it is necessary to use two groups of SN7488 memories, with paralleled outputs. Each group has 8 x SN7488 devices to form the 256 word memory. The first 32 words are included in the M1 memory, M1.1 containing the first 8 and M1.2 the last 8 bits. Words 32 to 63 are placed in the memories M2, etc. To address this memory requires 8 bits. The first 5 in order of increasing weight, A, B, C, D, E, simultaneously address all the memories. The last 3, F, G, H, act on the inputs of a decoder SN7442. The '0' output connected to the ENABLE inputs controls the two memories M.1.1 and M.1.2, the '1 output' the M2 memories, and so on, until finally 'output 7' controls the M8 memories.

Part of a very much larger memory system, such as may be used for complex character generation, is shown in Figure 6. As illustrated, one-fourth of a 65k-bit memory, organized as 4096 words of 16 bits, is implemented with an x, y, z decode pattern requiring only a single SN74S139 to complete the memory enable and a resultant address. Word capacity is increased to 4096 due to the fact that 16 sets of outputs are connected to the data output bus lines. The 16-bit word length is achieved by paralleling the outputs as described previously.

This 65k-bit memory is implemented with only 65 packages: 64 SN74S287s and an SN74S139. (The 'S287 is a user programmable ROM of 1024 bits arranged as 256 words of 4 bits). Intermediate buffer/drivers are not re-

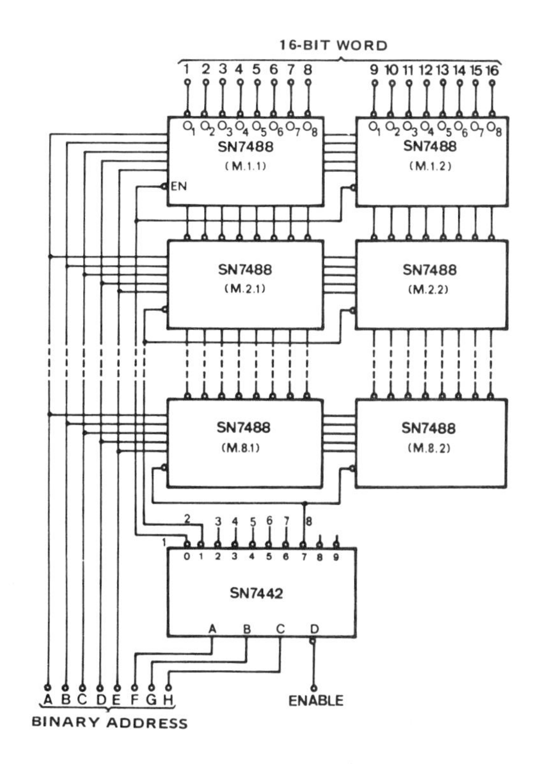

FIGURE 5. Increasing Both Capacity and Word Length

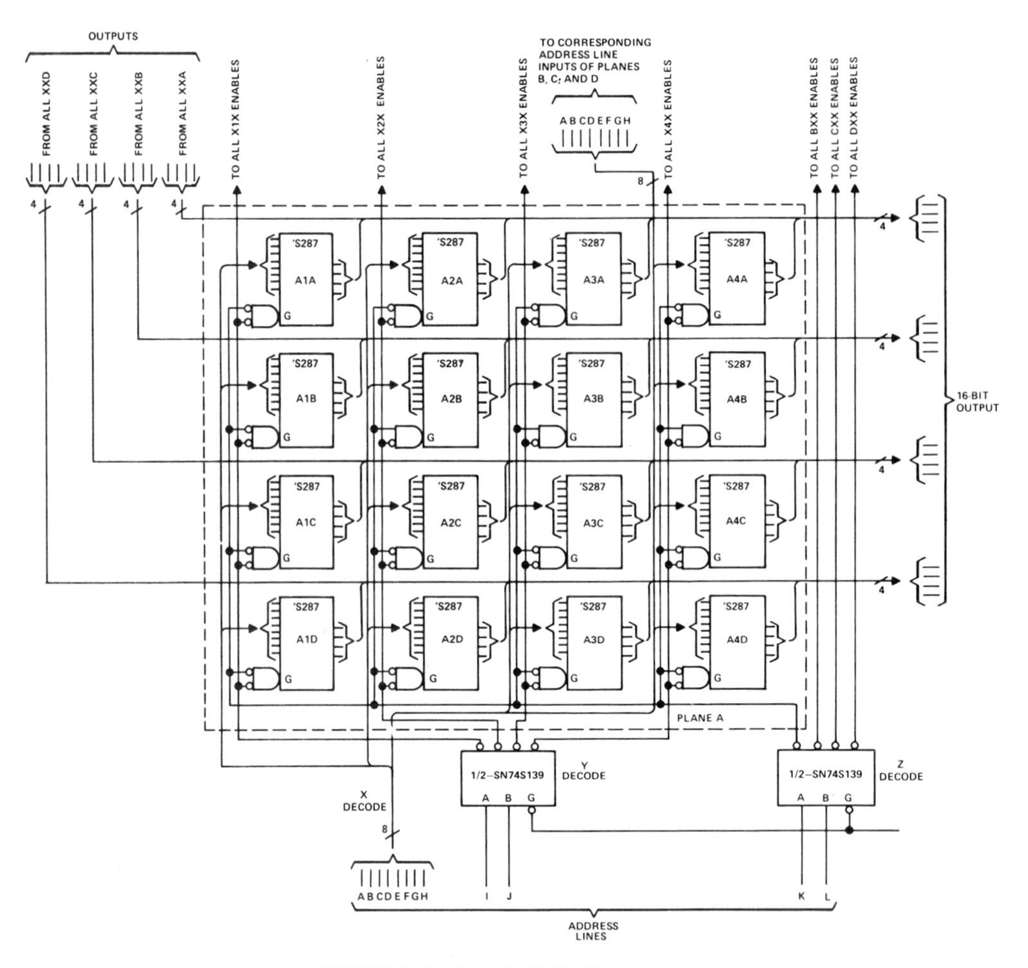

FIGURE 6. Section of 65k Bit Memory Array

quired between the 2 to 4 line decoder and the enable inputs as all are low-current p-n-p inputs. The total loading on each 'S139 output is 4mA sink and 400 μA drive current. Each of the respective 64 address inputs are connected common (i.e. all A s, all B s, etc.) and their loading is only 16mA sink and 1.6mA drive current.

Memories with words of less than 8 bits

Sometimes memories with words of less than 8 bits are needed, for example, 4, 2 or 1 bit. By using 2, 4 or 8 input multiplexers, these memories can be obtained:

ROM Organized as 128 Words of 4 Bits. This 512 bit memory requires two SN7488 devices as illustrated in Figure 7. 128 words are addressed from 7 bits A, B, C, D, E, F and G; A being the least significant bit and G the most significant. In such an arrangement the words are placed in a memory in the manner shown in Table 1. The output selection is made with SN7451 AND-OR-INVERT gates.

ROM Organized as 128 Words of 2 Bits. In this memory, as illustrated in Figure 8 the output selection is obtained by a dual 4 input multiplexer SN74153. 7 bits, A,

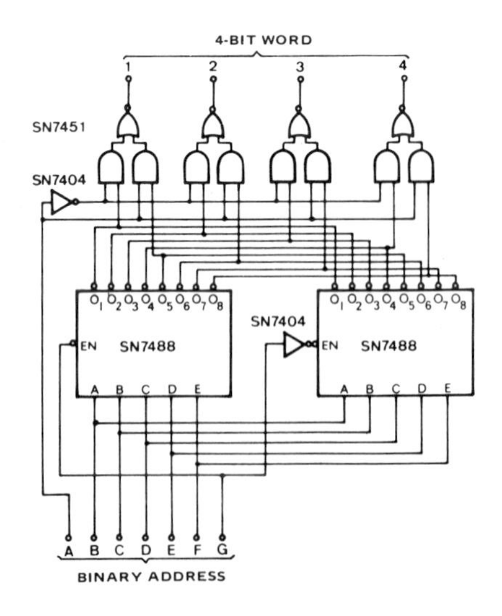

FIGURE 7. ROM Organized as 128 Words of 4 Bits

TABLE 1

ADDRESS	MEMORY 1		MEMORY 2	
	AG 00	10	AG 01	11
B C D E F	$O_1O_2O_3O_4$	$O_5O_6O_7O_8$	$O_1O_2O_3O_4$	$O_5O_6O_7O_8$
0 0 0 0 0	WORD 1	WORD 2	WORD 65	WORD 66
1 0 0 0 0	WORD 3	WORD 4	WORD 69	WORD 68
. . . . . .	. . . . .	. . . . .	. . . . . .	. . . . . .
1 1 1 1 1	WORD 63	WORD 64	WORD 127	WORD 128

B, C, D, E, F and G are addressed; G being the most significant bit. The two bits of low weight, A and B, determine the group of two addressed outputs. The organization of such a memory is shown in Table 3.

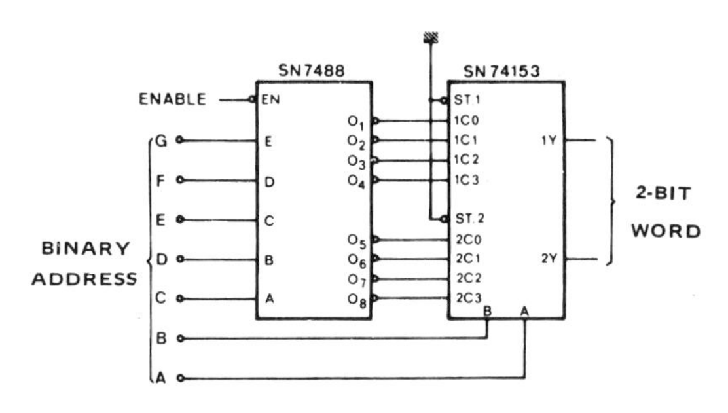

FIGURE 8. ROM Organized as 128 Words of 2 Bits

TABLE 2

ADDRESS	AB=00	AB=10	AB=01	AB=11
C D E F G	O_1 O_5	O_2 O_6	O_3 O_7	O_4 O_8
0 0 0 0 0	WORD 1	WORD 2	WORD 3	WORD 4
1 0 0 0 0	WORD 5	WORD 6	WORD 7	WORD 8
..	..	..	..	..
1 1 1 1 1	WORD125	WORD126	WORD127	WORD128

ROM Organized as 256 Words of 1 Bit Each. In such an application, e.g. where the purpose is to obtain a function of 8 variables, A, B, C, D, E, F, G, H; H being the most significant bit. The choice of the output is made by using an 8 input multiplexer SN74151, addressed by the lowest variables A, B and C (Figure 9). The 256 words of 1 bit each are selected in the following way; the first eight in the first line are addressed by D, E, F, G, H = 00000 and the following eight words in the second line by 10000, etc.

RANDOM LOGIC FUNCTION GENERATORS[1]

A ROM or a PROM is essentially a store giving access to a location upon application of a specified address. It is, therefore, possible to use any ROM or PROM for the generation of logical functions. As an example the SN7488A or SN74188A memory can produce on its 8

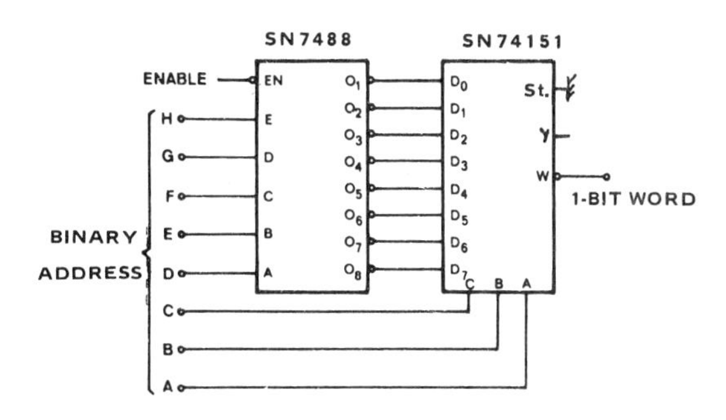

FIGURE 9. ROM Organized as 256 Words of 1 Bit Each

outputs, 8 Boolean functions each of 5 variables. For a specific combination of input variables A, B, C, D, E there is a certain value of function F. The input combination addresses one eight-bit position in the memory, and the desired value of function F is stored at this location. The other possible combinations of the five input variables are stored at the remaining 31 locations. For example, the 8 following fuctions are to be realized.

$F1 = A \oplus B \oplus C \oplus D \oplus E$

$F2 = AB + C\overline{D}E + \overline{A}CD$

$F3 = ABC + \overline{E}$

$F4 = (\overline{A} + B)(\overline{C} + \overline{D})$

$F5 = \overline{A}BCDE + ABCD\overline{E}$

$F6 = A\overline{B}E + BC + B\overline{D}E + \overline{B}D$

$F7 = \overline{A}BCDE + A\overline{B}CDE + AB\overline{C}DE + ABC\overline{D}E + ABCD\overline{E}$

F8 = maj (A, B, C, D, E) [e.g. more than 2 out of 5]

Such functions as these are typical of those which would be required to control the JK inputs of a complex counter. The counter may be, for example, counting in the sequence required to produce a calendar clock.

Table 3 shows how the positive logic functions can be located in the memory. Figure 10 illustrates the equivalent random logic circuits needed to generate three of these functions (i.e. F2, F3 & F7). The method presented here is expandable to functions of more than 5 binary variables, and it is possible to generate simultaneously more than 8 functions by using the various patterns of expanded ROM or PROM bit capacity.

MICRO PROGRAMME STORE

ROMs and PROMs are ideally suited to storing control instructions and numerical constants for use with a digital processor. An arrangement, such as shown in Figure 11, can be used to generate trigonometric functions, or process sequential data such as that obtained from a weighbridge or navigational system. As described in detail in Chapter IV the TMS0117NC is a ten digit MOS 'number cruncher', which requires a five bit instruction code. As explained four of these bits can either be data (binary coded decimal) or an instruction. The fifth bit determines

TABLE 3

WORD	INPUTS						OUTPUTS							
	BINARY SELECT					ENABLE								
	E	D	C	B	A	G	F8	F7	F6	F5	F4	F3	F2	F1
0	L	L	L	L	L	L	L	L	L	L	H	H	L	L
1	L	L	L	L	H	L	L	L	L	L	L	H	L	H
2	L	L	L	H	L	L	L	L	L	L	H	H	L	H
3	L	L	L	H	H	L	L	L	L	L	H	H	H	L
4	L	L	H	L	L	L	L	L	L	L	H	H	L	H
5	L	L	H	L	H	L	L	L	L	L	L	H	L	L
6	L	L	H	H	L	L	L	L	H	L	H	H	L	L
7	L	L	H	H	H	L	H	L	H	L	H	H	H	H
8	L	H	L	L	L	L	L	L	H	L	H	H	L	H
9	L	H	L	L	H	L	L	L	H	L	L	H	L	L
10	L	H	L	H	L	L	L	L	L	L	H	H	L	L
11	L	H	L	H	H	L	H	L	L	L	H	H	H	H
12	L	H	H	L	L	L	L	L	H	L	L	H	H	L
13	L	H	H	L	H	L	H	L	H	L	L	H	L	H
14	L	H	H	H	L	L	H	L	H	L	L	H	H	H
15	L	H	H	H	H	L	H	H	H	H	L	H	H	L
16	H	L	L	L	L	L	L	L	L	L	H	L	L	H
17	H	L	L	L	H	L	L	L	H	L	L	L	L	L
18	H	L	L	H	L	L	L	L	H	L	H	L	L	L
19	H	L	L	H	H	L	H	L	H	L	H	L	H	H
20	H	L	H	L	L	L	L	L	L	L	H	L	H	L
21	H	L	H	L	H	L	H	L	H	L	L	L	H	H
22	H	L	H	H	L	L	H	L	H	L	H	L	H	H
23	H	L	H	H	H	L	H	H	H	L	H	H	H	L
24	H	H	L	L	L	L	L	L	H	L	H	L	L	L
25	H	H	L	L	H	L	H	L	H	L	L	L	L	H
26	H	H	L	H	L	L	H	L	L	L	H	L	L	H
27	H	H	L	H	H	L	H	H	H	L	H	L	H	L
28	H	H	H	L	L	L	H	L	H	L	L	L	H	H
29	H	H	H	L	H	L	H	H	H	L	L	L	L	L
30	H	H	H	H	L	L	H	H	H	H	L	L	H	L
31	H	H	H	H	H	L	H	L	H	L	L	H	H	H
ALL	X	X	X	X	X	H	H	H	H	H	H	H	H	H

H = high level, L = low level, X = irrelevant

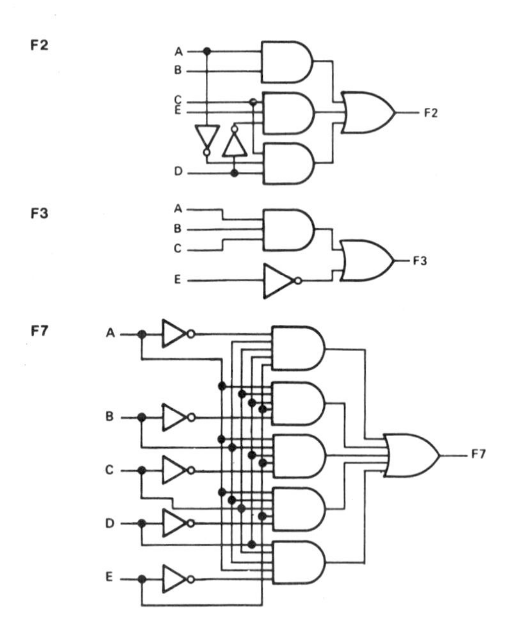

FIGURE 10. Some Equivalent Random Logic Circuits

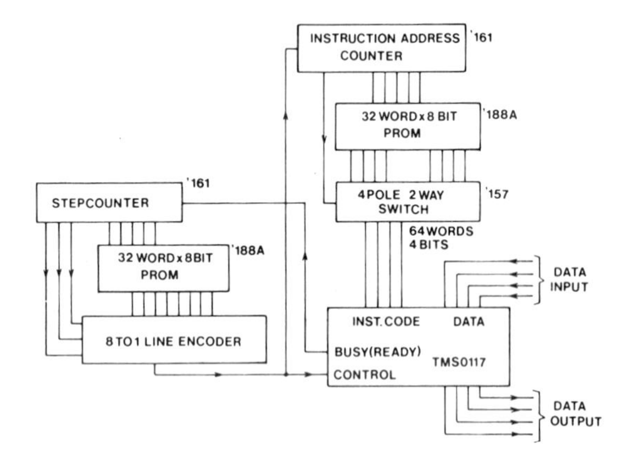

FIGURE 11. Microprogramme Store

whether the other four bits are to be interpreted as an instruction or as numeric data. In order to define the operating sequence, it is necessary to know which operations are to be 'number entry' and which are to be arithmetic instructions. This is defined by the single control bit obtained from a '188A PROM organised as 32 words of 8 bits. The required organisation is 256 words of 1 bit. The conversion is achieved by using an 'LS152 eight-to-one line demultiplexer to sequentially select the eight outputs of the PROM. The selection inputs of the multiplexer are driven from the last three bits of the 'LS161 control counter. The instruction codes are stored in a separate '188A PROM, the address to this being incremented by the 'LS161 instruction address counter, every time the output from the control PROM changes from a 'data entry' to an 'instruction' command. The instruction PROM is organised as 32 words by 8 bits, and has its output reorganised as 64 words of 4 bits by means of a '157 quad two line to one line demultiplexer.

CODE CONVERTERS

The use of ROMs as code converters was discussed in Chapter II using MOS devices. Further examples of code conversion are explained here. However, apart from the brief segment describing a conventional 'shift and add' technique for comparison purposes, they all use bipolar ROMs/PROMs which are particularly suited for small specialized systems.

Parallel Operation

A typical example of a specialized code conversion is one which converts Morse code into ASCII. Use of a PROM, e.g. the SN74188A, is necessary to allow the special programme required to be written into the memory. The system is shown in Figure 12. The Morse dots and dashes are sorted in a format generator into logical 'ones' and 'zeros'. To overcome the problem that not all Morse characters are of equal length, they are loaded into a shift register, with each character preceded by a fixed filler code. The combined character output, (Morse and the remainder of the filler code) from the shift register is transferred into a buffer store whose parallel data outputs address PROMs. These are interconnected such that their organisation gives 64 words of 8 bits. Each memory is programmed to convert the Morse/filler code into ASCII code. There is sufficient storage available for the system to handle code groups as well as alpha numeric characters. The ASCII output code addresses a large ROM operating as a character generator, e.g. the TMS4103 as described in Chapter II.

Arithmetic Operation

Shift and Add Technique: The conventional method[2] for performing binary to BCD conversions has been the shift and add technique. This is a form of binary to BCD

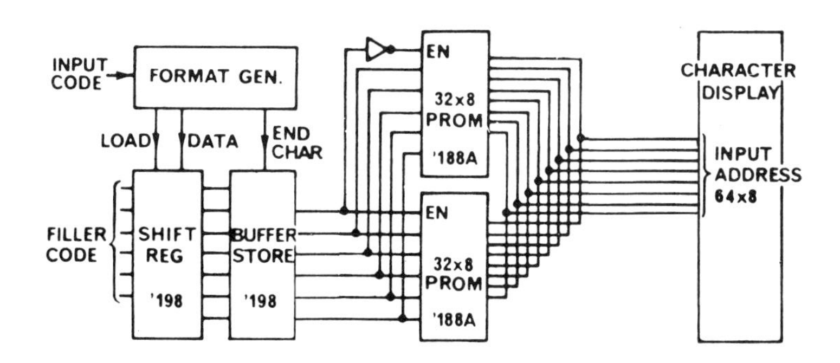

FIGURE 12. Code Conversion Using PROMs from Morse to ASCII

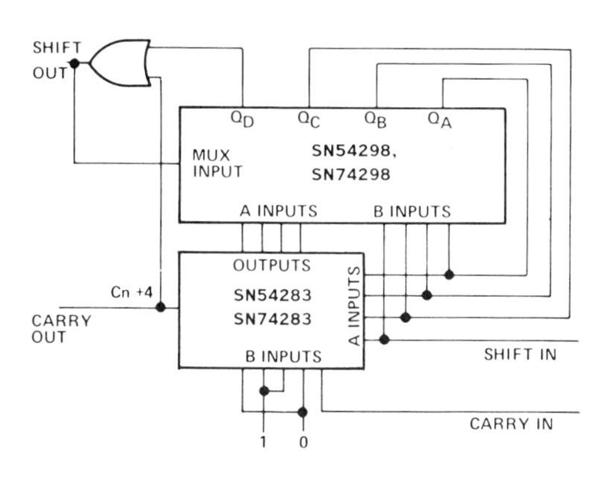

FIGURE 13. Typical 'Shift & Add' Digit Conversion

conversion in which 4-bit bytes are shifted through a 'correction' process. As they are shifted through, the presence of a number greater than 9 (1001) is detected, and 6 (0110) is added as a 'correction' to the developing number. Adding 6 to any 4 bit binary number which is not a valid BCD number 'corrects' the binary number to the equivalent BCD number. The primary drawback of the 'shift and add' technique is that it is relatively slow when large numbers are involved. For example, 10 ones (binary 1023) is to be converted into 1 0000 0010 0011 (BCD 1023). 10 shifts are required, and each of the last 7 shifts may involve corrections. Each correction can generate a carry to the next higher digit only; so, a simple ripple adder may be used with little loss of speed. This operation can be implemented with the SN74298, SN7432, and SN74283, as shown in Figure 13. An obvious method of increasing the conversion speed and to reduce the control logic is to utilize ROMs/PROMs.

Using ROMs/PROMs: An example of a 7 bit BCD code converter is illustrated in Figure 14. The 7 input bits correspond to 128 different decimal positions (0 to 127). Note that the hundred digit is '0' if the input binary number is less than 100 and '1' if the input binary number is between 100 and 127. Therefore, it is not necessary to store this digit in a memory, a simple decoder for numbers greater than 100 is sufficient. This has been done with a SN74H52 by decoding the hundred in the following way:–

$F = 2^6 . 2^5 . (2^4 + 2^3 + 2^2)$

The units correspond to the memory outputs O_5, O_6, O_7, O_8 and the tens to the outputs of O_1, O_2, O_3, O_4. The first 32 numbers (corresponding to the numbers between 0 and 31) are stored in memory 1, on the right part of the circuit shown in Figure 14, activated by the condition $2^6 . 2^7$ applied on the "ENABLE" input. Numbers 32 to 63 are situated in memory 2, numbers 64 to 95, in memory 3; and numbers 96 to 127 in memory 4. Each of these memories is made active by placing on the "ENABLE" input the following:–

Memory 2 $\overline{\text{ENABLE 2}} = 2^6 . 2^5$
Memory 3 ENABLE 3 $= 2^6 . 2^5$
Memory 4 ENABLE 4 $= 2^6 . 2^5$

The system shown can be extended to BCD code converters of more than 7 bits by adding blocks of memories for units and tens above 128, and if needed, storing in the memory the hundreds.

Binary to BCD and BCD to Binary code conversions are such a common requirement that specific ROMs have been produced to carry out these conversions i.e. the SN54/74184/5A. These devices, their operation and applications, are discussed fully in a chapter of the preceding volume[3].

SEQUENCE GENERATORS

Sequence generators may be used as counters, sequencing through a code that is dependent upon externally applied inputs. During the operation of a sequencer each step performed is dependent on the result of previous operations. Such generators are ideally suited for controlling industrial processes. An example of a simple sequencer is given below.

The study of a sequential system should be made by using a flow diagram. Such a diagram is given in Figure 15. This has 16 states with two external variables M and N which should never be simultaneously at a logical '1'. Also, M and N are at a logical '1' only during the transition time between the decision period and the following state. As an example, it is assumed that 4 output variables are to be generated at each of the 16 states. In such an application, a ROM is useful because each of the 16 states can be coded by 4 internal variables. The state which exists at a particular moment addresses the memory which in turn indicates, at the output, the address of the following state (Table 4). When the sequence is interrupted, as for example in state 4, coded ABCD=0100, with E = 0 (where E stands for M + N); state ⑤, coded 0101 is obtained if E = 0, that is M = 0; and state ⑬ coded 1101, if E = 1, that is M = 1.

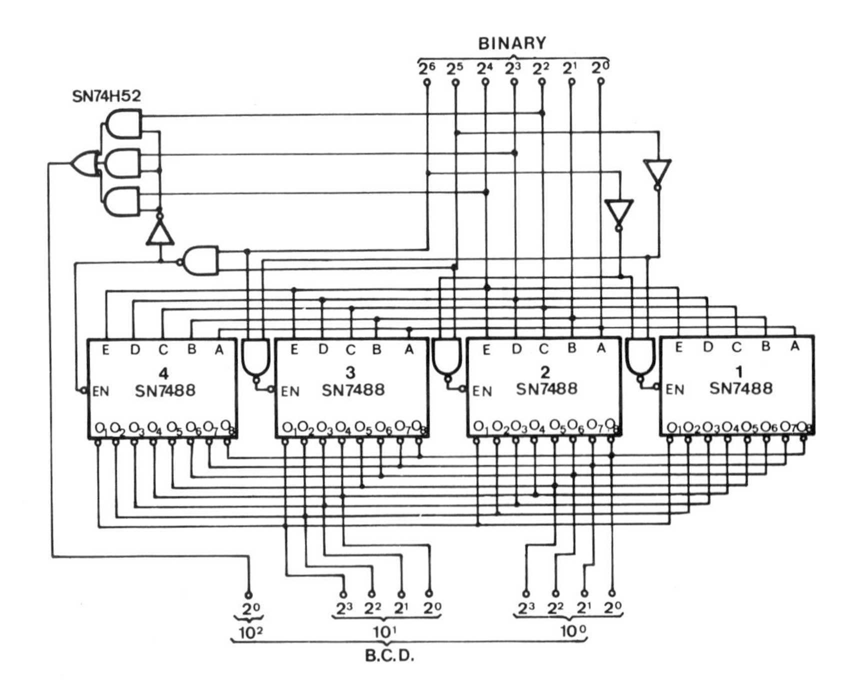

FIGURE 14. 7 Bit BCD Code Converter Using ROMs

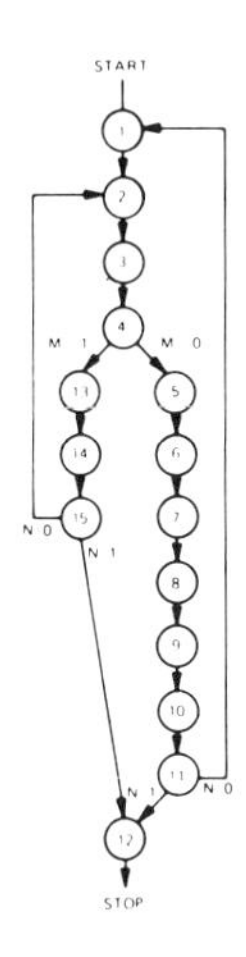

FIGURE 15. Flow Diagram

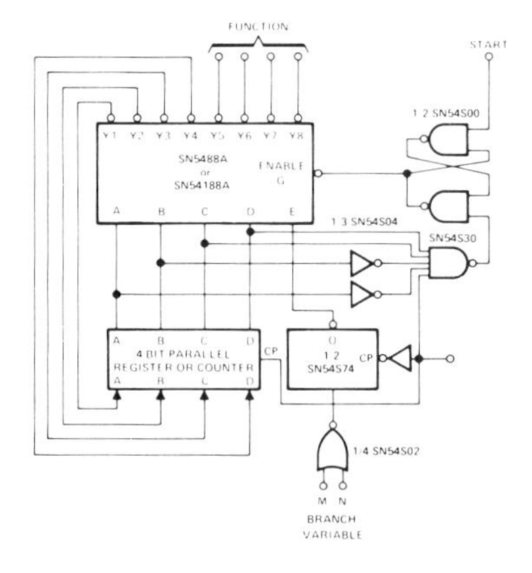

FIGURE 16. Synchronous Sequential Generator

A synchronous sequential generator can be constructed as shown in Figure 16, with a 5-bit register (an SN7495 and an SN7474) to hold the address between two clock pulses. When state 12 is reached, i.e. A B C D = 0011, this position is decoded, and as the next clock pulse goes to a logical '1' the cross-coupled NAND gate RS latch (½ SN7400) is cleared, applying a logical '1' on the ENABLE and setting all the outputs at '1'. The system is then at the STOP position. This method can be used instead of the sequential approach to a system using for example, the HUFFMAN[4] method, which is always long and tedious. It is sufficient to implement a code for each of the stable states and to memorize the various states by using the given example as a model. Therefore, it is useful, in each case, to adapt the organization of the memory to the number of output bits to be generated. In some cases it is possible to use the output variables as state variables, if the latter are different at each state. In this case, the memory will be considerably simplified.

Table 4.

EQUIVALENT STATES	WORD	INPUTS						OUTPUTS							
		BINARY SELECT					ENABLE	NEXT STATE				FUNCTION†			
		A	B	C	D	E	G	Y1	Y2	Y3	Y4	Y5	Y6	Y7	Y8
(15)→(2)	0	L	L	L	L	L	L	L	H	L	L				
(1)	1	H	L	L	L	L	L	L	H	L	L				
(2)	2	L	H	L	L	L	L	H	H	L	L				
(3)	3	H	H	L	L	L	L	L	L	H	L				
(4)→(5)	4	L	L	H	L	L	L	H	L	H	L				
(5)	5	H	L	H	L	L	L	L	H	H	L				
(6)	6	L	H	H	L	L	L	H	H	H	L				
(7)	7	H	H	H	L	L	L	L	L	L	H				
(8)	8	L	L	L	H	L	L	H	L	L	H				
(9)	9	H	L	L	H	L	L	L	H	L	H				
(10)	10	L	H	L	H	L	L	H	H	L	H				
(11)→(1)	11	H	H	L	H	L	L	H	L	L	L				
(12)→STOP	12	L	L	H	H	L	L	H	H	H	H				
(13)	13	H	L	H	H	L	L	L	H	H	H				
(14)	14	L	H	H	H	L	L	L	L	L	L				
START	15	H	H	H	H	L	L	H	L	L	L				
(15)→(12)	16	L	L	L	L	H	L	L	L	H	H				
	17	H	L	L	L	H	L	X	X	X	X				
	18	L	H	L	L	H	L	X	X	X	X				
	19	H	H	L	L	H	L	X	X	X	X				
(4)→(13)	20	L	L	H	L	H	L	H	L	H	H				
	21	H	L	H	L	H	L	X	X	X	X				
	22	L	H	H	L	H	L	X	X	X	X				
	23	H	H	H	L	H	L	X	X	X	X				
	24	L	L	L	H	H	L	X	X	X	X				
	25	H	L	L	H	H	L	X	X	X	X				
	26	L	H	L	H	H	L	X	X	X	X				
(11)→(12)	27	H	H	L	H	H	L	L	L	H	H				
	28	L	L	H	H	H	L	X	X	X	X				
	29	H	L	H	H	H	L	X	X	X	X				
	30	L	H	H	H	H	L	X	X	X	X				
	31	H	H	H	H	H	L	X	X	X	X				
	ALL	X	X	X	X	X	H	H	H	H	H	H	H	H	H

H = high level, L = low level, X = irrelevant
†Programmed to supply the functions and/or operand as required.

ARITHMETIC OPERATIONS

Binary Multiplication

Common yet comparatively slow operations in, for example, computers are multiplication and division. As described in detail in another chapter of the preceding volume, Wallace tree adders and ROMs acting as look-up tables can be used for fast multiplication[5]. As can be seen, however, from the circuit diagram of a 16 x 16 bit multiplier, a large number of devices are required. A considerable reduction can be effected by forming the Wallace tree adders with ROMs. By using low power Schottky fabrication techniques the required bit density necessary to produce these devices can be achieved. Further reduction can be obtained by incorporating the two 4 x 4 bit multiplier ROMs in a single device e.g. the SN74S274 as shown in Figure 17. This device can be arranged to provide the basic building block for an n-bit-by-n-bit multiplier as the necessary subproducts are available for accumulation in a SN74S275 7-bit-slice Wallace tree. This is effectively a 7 input adder followed by a 3 input adder. The functional equivalent is shown in Figure 18 and can be used in three ways:

(i) With the simulated 3 bit adder for minimum package count.

(ii) With the SN74H183 for high speed additions as shown in Figure 19.

(iii) It can also be cascaded to handle larger number of bits/slice.

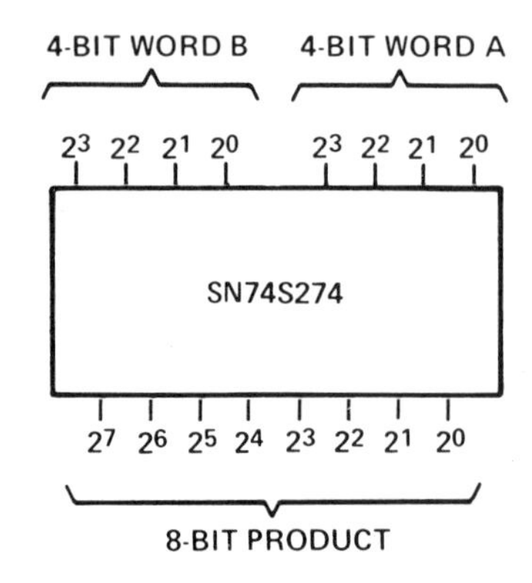

FIGURE 17. 4 Bit by 4 Bit Parallel Multiplier

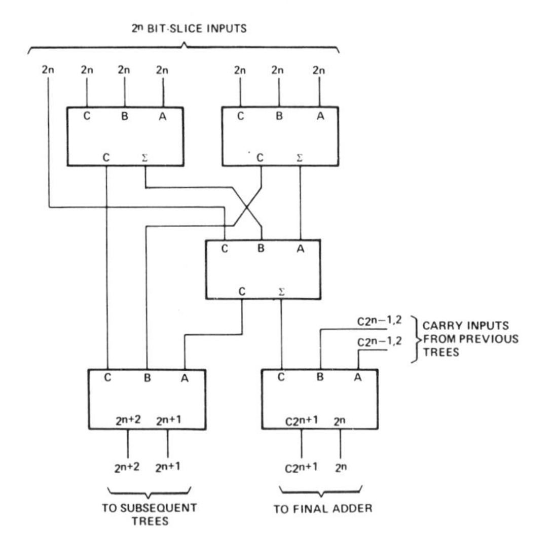

FIGURE 18. SN74S275 Cascadable 7 Bit Slice Wallace Tree

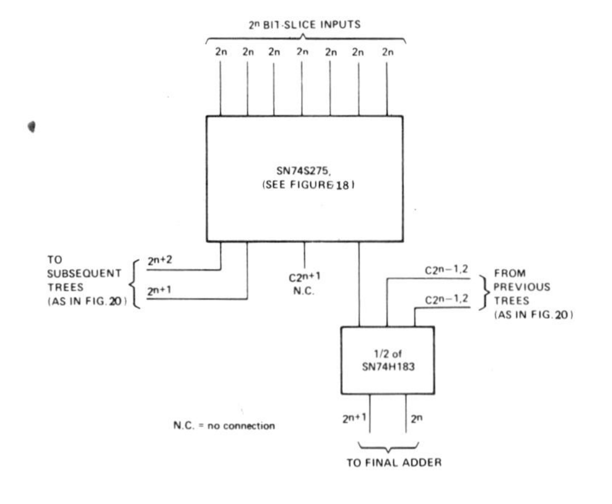

FIGURE 19. High Speed 7 Bit Slice Wallace Tree

The SN74S274 and SN74S275 can be used to implement up to a 16 x 16 multiplier (with or without the simulated 3 input adder) in only one main level (taking the 3-to-2 bit addition as a minor level). Figure 20 is an example of a 16-by-16 multiplier which can be implemented with bit-slice accumulation as illustrated in Figures 18 and 19. Table 5 gives an indication of the speed performance of a system, such as shown in Figure 20, comparing two different package arrangements.

Table 5

TYPE NO.	REDUCE PKG. COUNT (PACKAGES)	REDUCE MULT. TIME (PACKAGES)
SN 74S274 s	16	16
SN 74S275 s	16	16
SN 74H183 s	6½	14
SN74283 s	6½	1
SN 74S181 s		6
SN 74S182 s		2
TOTAL PACKAGES	45	55
16 X 16 MULTIPLY TIME	180 ns typ.	106 ns typ.

Binary Division and Square Rooting

Many computing systems use add/subtract and shift algorithms to perform division and square rooting by restoring or non-restoring methods. An iterative method for performing division and square rooting is described here. Both procedures require the use of a very high speed simultaneous multiplier such as that previously described. A small amount of additional logic will convert this system into a divider or square rooter as shown in Figures 21 and 23. As stated, division is carried out by an iterative method. If the dividend is denoted by A and the divisor by B then the first step is to make an approximation Q_1 to the quotient Q. This first approximation is then multiplied by the divisor B. The result should be, if the initial choice of the value of Q_1 was correct, equal to the dividend A. The product Q_1 B is then compared with the dividend. The result of this comparison indicates whether the value of the quotient chosen was too large or small, and therefore the direction of the adjustment that must be made in order to approach the correct value. A system based on this principle is shown in Figure 21.

The high speed multiplier uses 'S274 ROM look up tables in conjunction with 'S275 Wallace tree adders and 'S181 arithmetic logic units (ALUs). The quotient register comprises 'S174 and 'S175 D type storage latches. High speed comparison of the product Q_nB with the dividend is carried out by cascaded 'S85 four bit comparators as shown in Figure 22.

The iterative process begins with a one being inserted into the most significant bit location of the quotient register. Comparison of the dividend with the product formed by multiplying the contents of the

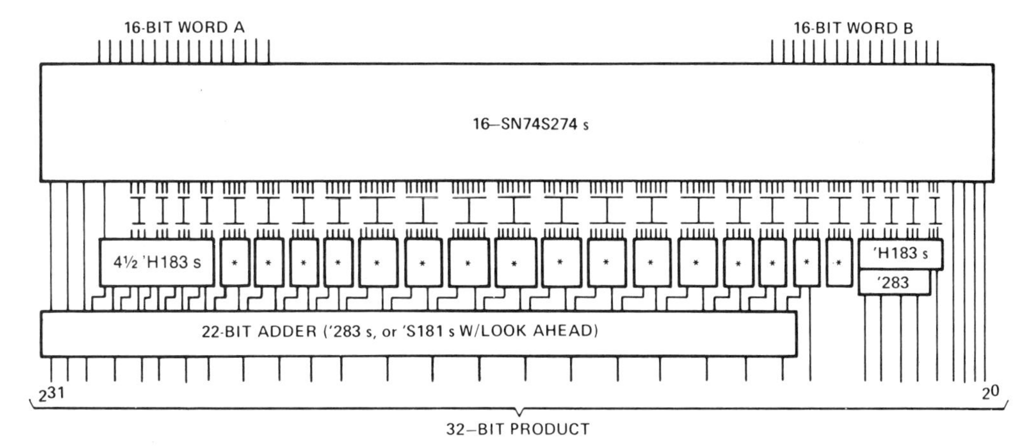

* Each of these boxes represents a 7-bit-slice Wallace tree as shown in either Figure 18 or Figure 19

FIGURE 20. 16 Bit by 16 Bit Parallel Multiplier

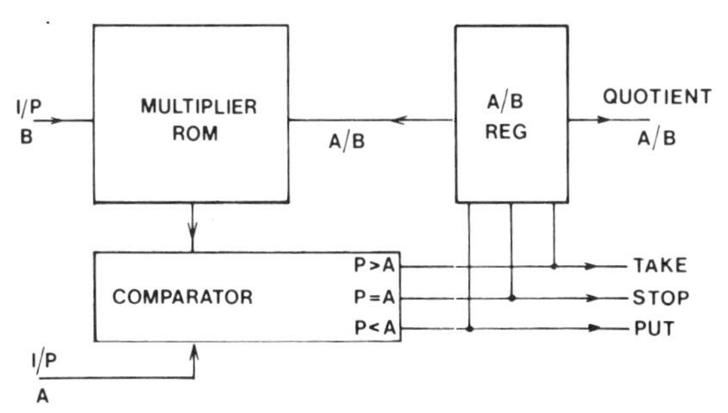

FIGURE 21. High Speed Divider Block Diagram

quotient register by the divisor can give three results:–

(i) If the product is equal to the dividend then the quotient is too small. A one is inserted into the next least significant bit and the most significant bit allowed to remain.

(ii) If the product is greater than the dividend the quotient is too large. The one is removed from the most significant bit location and is inserted into the next least significant bit location.

(iii) The above processes are continued until all positions of the quotient register have been inspected or the 'divide stop' condition is reached.

This method will allow the quotient of two 14 bit binary numbers to be formed in under 2 microseconds.

Binary square rooting may be carried out in a manner that is almost identical to that used for division. The system block diagram is shown in Figure 23. As in the divider example, a one is placed in the most significant digit position of the output register in which x will be formed. The contents of this register is the initial value of x. This is then squared by the high speed multiplier and the result compared with the input x. The system operation is now similar to that of the divider previously described.

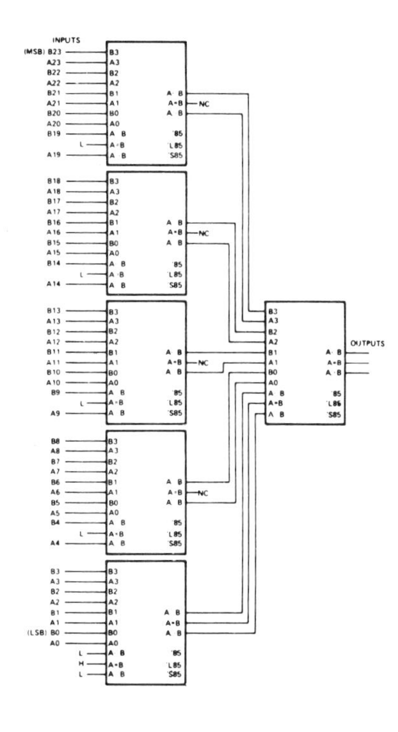

FIGURE 22. High Speed Comparison using 4 bit Comparators

ANALOGUE APPLICATIONS

Up to the present time analogue applications have been almost entirely the domain of linear circuits. The availability of large capacity ROMs now means that digital techniques may be applied to solving complex analogue problems. As examples of this further use of ROMs/PROMs two applications are described, analogue transfer function and trigonometric function generation.

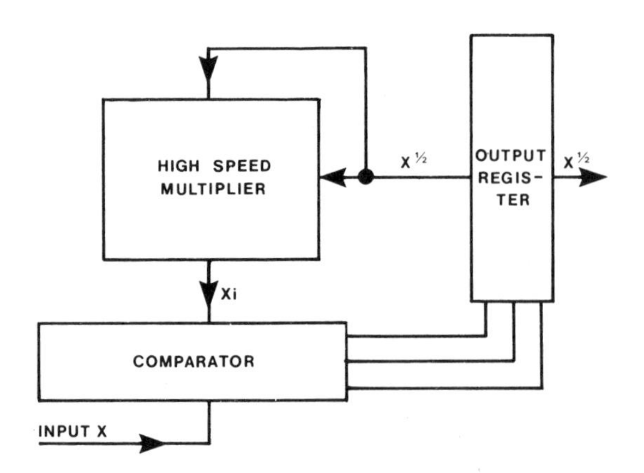

FIGURE 23. Binary Square Rooter

Analogue Transfer Function Generation

An application which, to date, has been a difficult operation is that of analogue transfer function generation e.g. an industrial process employing a non-linear transducer would probably require the transducer output to be linearised in order to control the operation. Figure 24 shows, for example, a curve, y=f(x) which needs to be produced in order to linearise the transducer output. The method of achieving this is, first of all, to divide the function up into straight line sections, as shown in the insert, in a similar manner to the method used when generating functions with analogue techniques. However, using these, one is probably limited to, say, twenty sections on the curve, where as with a digital technique several thousand sections could be used depending on the accuracy required.

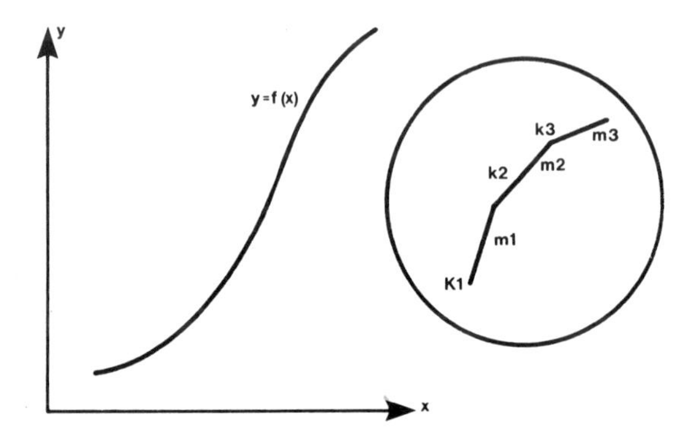

FIGURE 24. Example of Function to be Reproduced

Figure 25 gives the block diagram of a function generator using linear interpolation. The analog x input goes through an Analog to Digital Converter (ADC) whose output addresses two ROMs, e.g. the 32 words x 8 bits SN7488s or the 256 words x 4 bits '187s, if a fixed function is required. (Alternatively PROMs such as the 32 words x 8 bits '188A, the 64 words x 8 bits '186, the 256 words x 4 bits 3 state 'S287 or the 256 words x 4 bits 'S387 could be used If an easy modification of the function is required then RAMs such as the 1024 words x 1 bit TMS4063, the 4096 words x 1 bit TMS 4030 or the 256 words x 1 bit SN74200 should be employed). In the system shown the gradient of each section of the curve is stored in the first ROM. The second ROM contains the constant value, k, which determines the starting point of a section. The outputs from both the memories are converted to an analog voltage by means of Digital to Analog Converters (DACs). The output from the gradient DAC is then multiplied by the x input in an analog multiplier whose output is therefore the mx term of y=mx+c, the equation of a straight line adjoining two adjacent turning points. The constant term, c, defining the beginning of each section is then added to the mx term by means of an analog adder. The output of the adder is therefore y, where y=mx+c, which defines the output function over each section. Although two ROMs are shown, it is, in fact, not necessary to use both, as the gradient can be obtained simply by subtracting k1 from k2 etc.

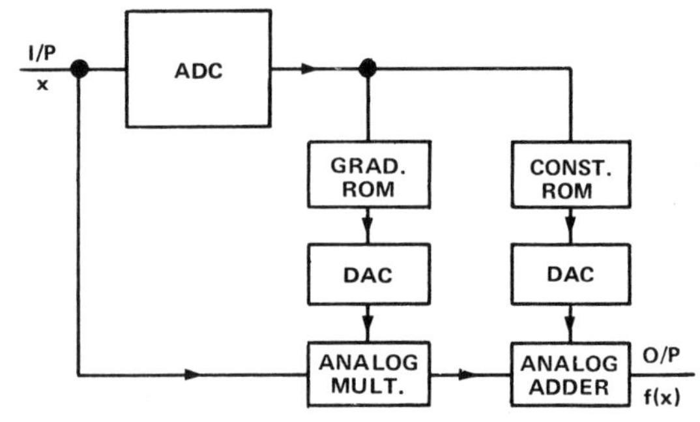

FIGURE 25. Transfer Function Generator

Trigonometric Function Generation

The system to be described may be used to generate a time varying function f (t) or a static function f (x) if y is single valued over the range of interest. Specific values of the required function are stored in a PROM. Intermediate values are obtained by interpolation. Most methods of interpolation require either additional arithmetic elements or another ROM containing a difference table. The system shown in Figure 26 linearly interpolates between f (x) values stored in the ROM by means of a time averaging technique. In order to average between two stored values of y to give the correct value of y at X+ΔX the two y values are alternately switched into a low pass filter. The ratio of the times that each value is switched into the filter is directly proportional to the magnitude of ΔX. The output of the filter is therefore a time averaged signal, equal to the value of Y at X+ΔX.

With reference to Figures 26 and 27 the system operation is as follows. The bit address to the SN74186 PROM is obtained from a 6 bit binary adder, the inputs of which are derived either from an external address input (X)

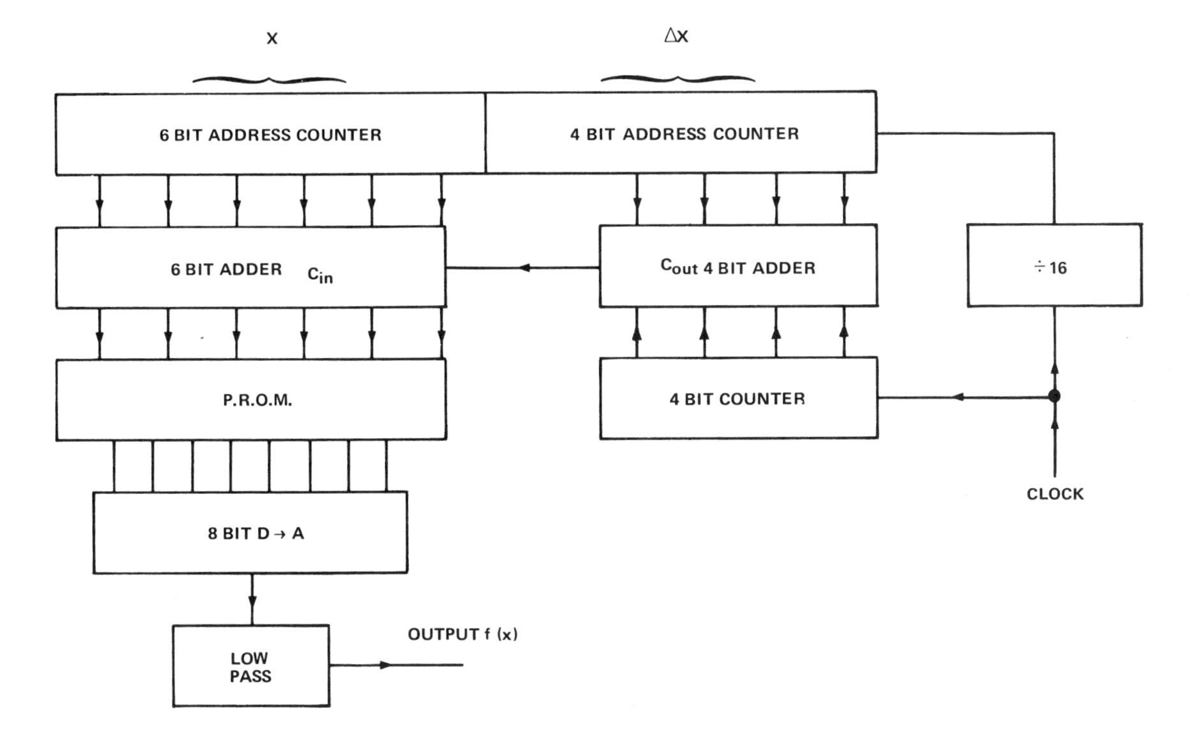

FIGURE 26. System Block Diagram

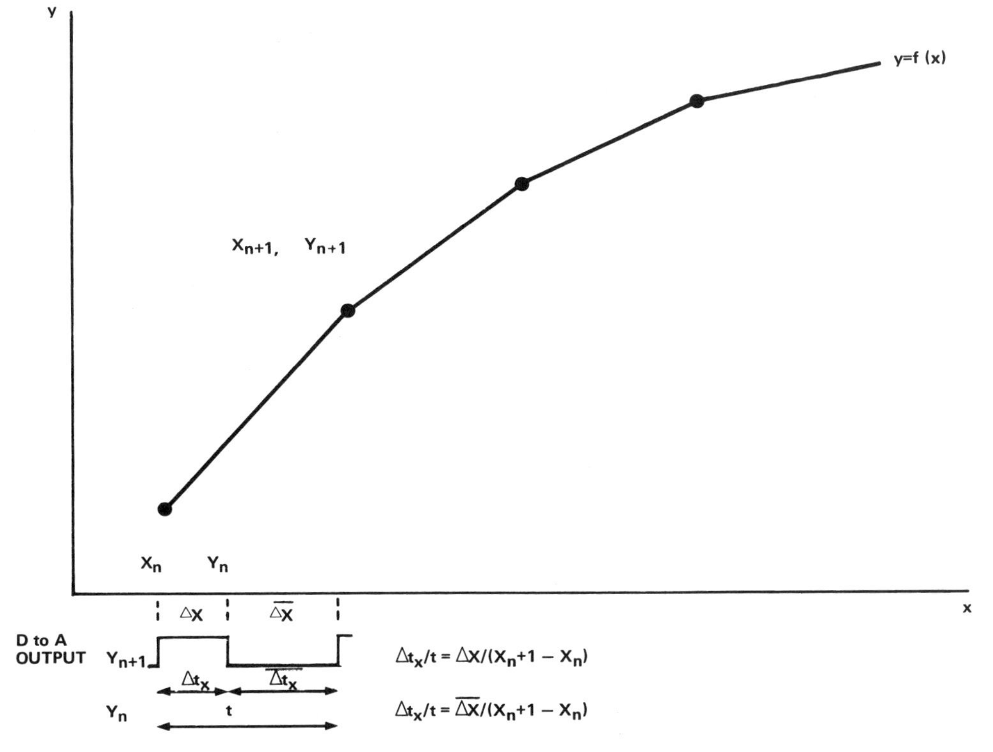

FIGURE 27. Graphical Representation of System Operation

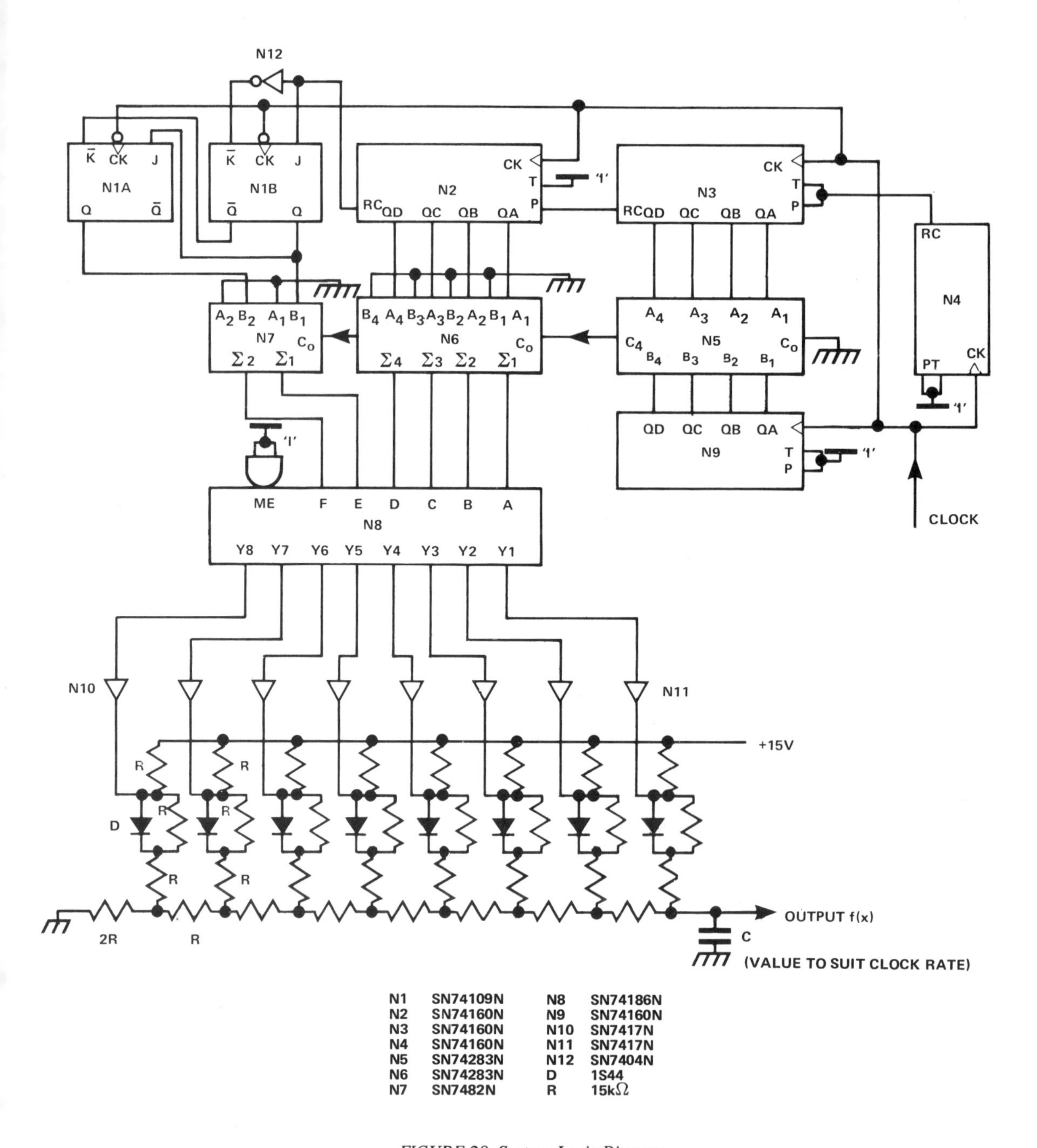

FIGURE 28. System Logic Diagram

or a 6 bit counter. The carry input C_{in} to this adder is derived from the 4 bit interpolation adder. When C_{in} is at a logical '0' the adder outputs represent X_n and when at a logical '1' they represent X_{n+1}. The time that C_n is at a logical '1' is determined by the carry output of the 4 bit interpolation adder. The interpolation adder is fed from two sources, the ΔX input (part of the address counter) and the output of a continuously incrementing counter. If the 4 bit address counter contains zero then no carry output is produced during a cycle of the incrementing counter, and the 6 bit address to the PROM addresses Xn. If however ΔX was 2 for example, a carry would be produced from the interpolation adder for 2/16 of the cycle time of the incrementing counter. The output from the PROM would be the average $2/16X_{n+1}$ and $14/16X_n$. The averaging circuit may be a simple CR filter utilising the output impedance of the digital to analog converter as the resistive component. The complete circuit diagram of the system is shown in Figure 28.

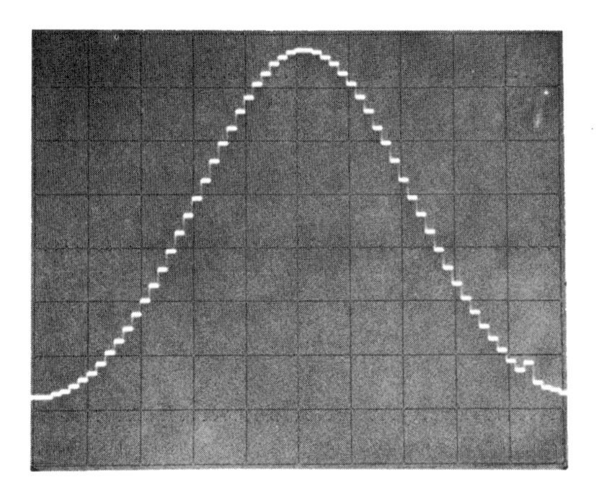

Sin^3 (x) No Interpolation

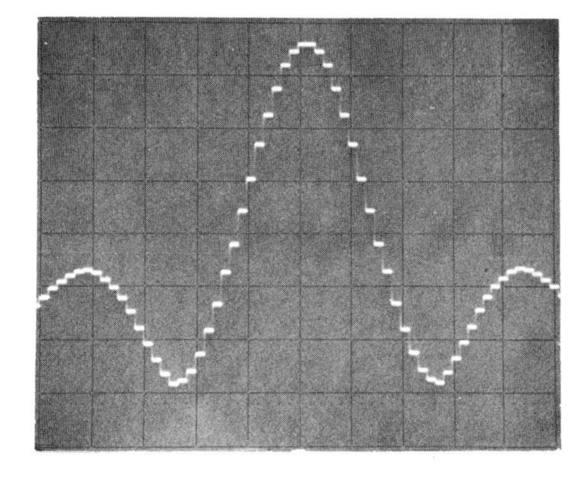

(Sin x)/x No Interpolation

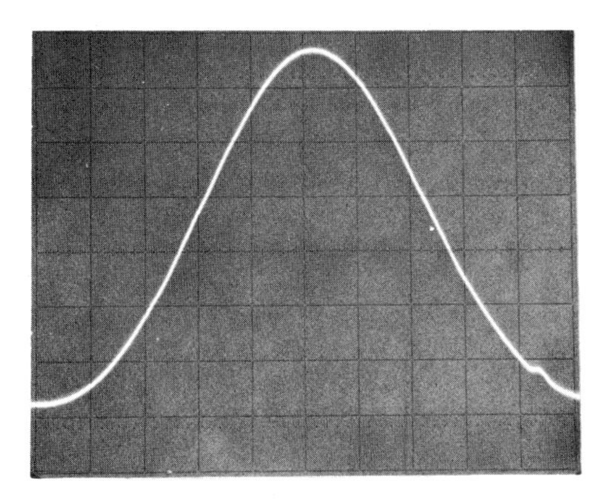

Sin^3 (x) Interpolation and Smoothing

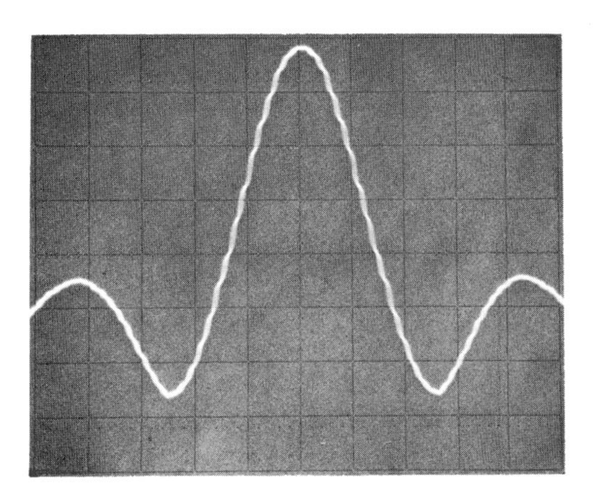

(Sin x)/x with Interpolation

Figure 29 illustrates the type of result that may be obtained using this method of generation.

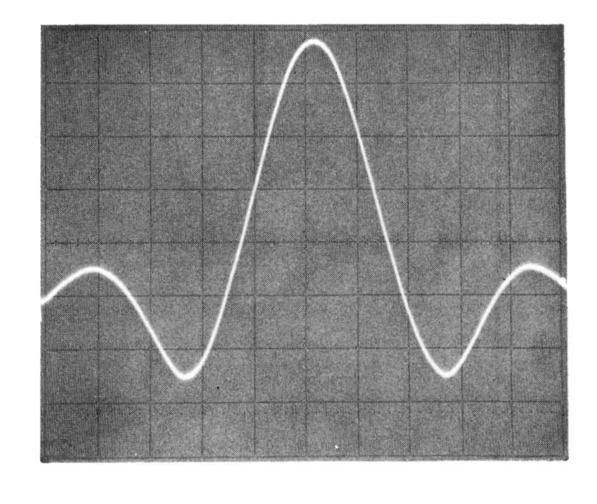

(Sin x)/x with Interpolation and Smoothing

FIGURE 29. Illustrations of some Functions Generated

REFERENCES

1. B. L. Norris Editor, *Semiconductor Circuit Design, Vol. II,* Texas Instruments Limited pp. 83-88, April 1973.
2. J. F. Couleur *I.R.E. Transactions on Electronic Computers,* Dec. 1958, Volume EC7, No. 4, pp. 313-316.
3. B. L. Norris Editor, *Semiconductor Circuit Design Vol. II* Texas Instruments Limited, Chapter XI pp. 101-112, April 1973.
4. D. A. Huffman, *Synthesis of Sequential Switching Circuits,* J. Franklin Inst. Volume 257 No.3 pp. 161-190, No. 4, pp. 275-303, March, April 1954.
5. B. L. Norris Editor, *Semiconductor Circuit Design Vol. II,* Texas Instruments Limited, Chapter XII, pp. 113-120, April 1973.

VIII A ZERO CROSSING DETECTOR AND PULSE GENERATOR

by
Jurek Budek

In more recent years, industry has shown itself increasingly ready to accept power control by solid state devices. Many innovations have been introduced in the field of switching and controlling power, e.g., optically coupled triacs with zero voltage switching and gallium arsenide diode light source devices[1]. Furthermore, voltage input phase control for triacs and thyristors, used in conjunction with burst firing techniques for transformer and inductive loads,[2] enlarge considerably the area in which semiconductors can be used beneficially.

The advantages offered by solid state switching are obvious. Mechanical contactors and relays, having moving parts, are subject to wear and tear and require periodic maintenance. In addition to the cost of the maintenance, the inconvenience caused by the interruption of work, especially in nonattended stations, is another factor to be considered. A triac, used as a semiconductor switch, has features which overcome these difficulties and is ideally suited for frequent operation. It must be remembered, however, that by using a solid state contactor, complete isolation is not possible. In fact, a triac inserts into the circuit a very high impedance when in the ' off ' position, and for complete electrical isolation, an ' off ' load switch is recommended.

Thyristors and triacs, used in a phase control mode, produce considerable radio frequency interference (RFI) due to the step change in current, and the suppression methods become more difficult and expensive as the load increases. In domestic appliances, particularly, the RFI is acute and must be suppressed according to BS 800.

Electric heaters, and other loads with a long time constant, may be controlled by passing through them a selected number of full or half cycles. The current then will be in phase with the voltage and since the switching takes place at the point where the voltage crosses zero, there will be no problem of RFI. Such control is called burst firing or zero voltage switching. Burst firing is not suitable for lamp dimming (at 50/60 Hz) due to the flicker, or for motor speed control, or with transformer loads unless certain steps, which will be explained later, are taken.

The SN72440 zero voltage switching IC is a combination of a threshold detector and a zero-crossing trigger, i.e., it allows a triac (or thyristor) to be triggered when the ac input signal crosses through zero volts.In this manner, the load utilizes the full-cycle supply voltage as opposed to the partial cycle typical to phase control power circuits.

CIRCUIT DESCRIPTION

Besides the zero-voltage detector and differential amplifier, the circuit includes a sawtooth generator, an output section, resistors which may be used as a voltage divider for the reference side of the resistance bridge, and the active elements of a sawtooth generator. An external sensor suitable for the application and an external potentiometer form the input side of the resistance bridge.

The SN72440 can be used either as an on-off control with or without hysteresis, or as a proportional control with the use of the internal sawtooth generator. Although its principal application is in temperature control, other uses include photosensitive control, voltage level sensor, ac lamp flasher, small relay driver, or a miniature lamp driver.

The inhibit function (pin 5) prevents any output pulses from occurring when the applied voltage at the inhibit input is typically 1 V or greater.

The circuit shown in Figure 1 provides on-off temperature control. Electrolytic capacitor C1, maintains the dc operating voltage; the voltage developed across it is approximately 12 V due to the arrangement of the two zener diodes, D5 and D6, and the diode D7. The voltage between pins 1 and 4 will fluctuate with the frequency of the firing of triac since the energy to fire a triac comes from capacitor C1. In this circuit configuration, the thermistor used must have a negative temperature coefficient. During most of the ac cycle, transistor Q1 is turned on by the current flow through either D1, Q1 and D4 or D2, Q1 and D3 depending on the polarity of the ac voltage between pins 1 and 3. The collector current of Q1 turns on Q6. With Q6 on, base-drive to transistors Q7 and Q8 is inhibited, resulting in no output pulses to fire the triac. When the ac voltage crosses zero, Q1 and Q6 are turned off, enabling Q7 and Q8 to turn on. The current then will flow from the positive side of capacitor C1 through MT1 and then the gate of the triac to pin 10 and, via transistor Q8, back to the negative of the capacitor C1, thus firing the triac. Each output pulse at every zero-crossing point is either inhibited or permitted by the action of the differential amplifier and resistance bridge circuit. The differential amplifier consists of transistors Q2, Q3, Q4, and Q5 and the resistance bridge consisting externally of the 8-kΩ thermistor and a 10-kΩ potentiometer and internally two 10-kΩ resistors joined together by linking pins 8 and 9. As the controlled temperature begins to rise, the positive voltage applied to pin 13 increases. The differential amplifier acts to lower the potential of the base of transistor Q1 enough to allow it to stay on for the complete cycle, thus inhibiting the output pulses. Similarly, when the temperature falls, Q1 is allowed to turn off during zero-voltage crossing points and permits passage of the output pulses. The width of the output pulses at pin 10 can be varied within certain limits. Increasing the value of external resistor R20 will increase

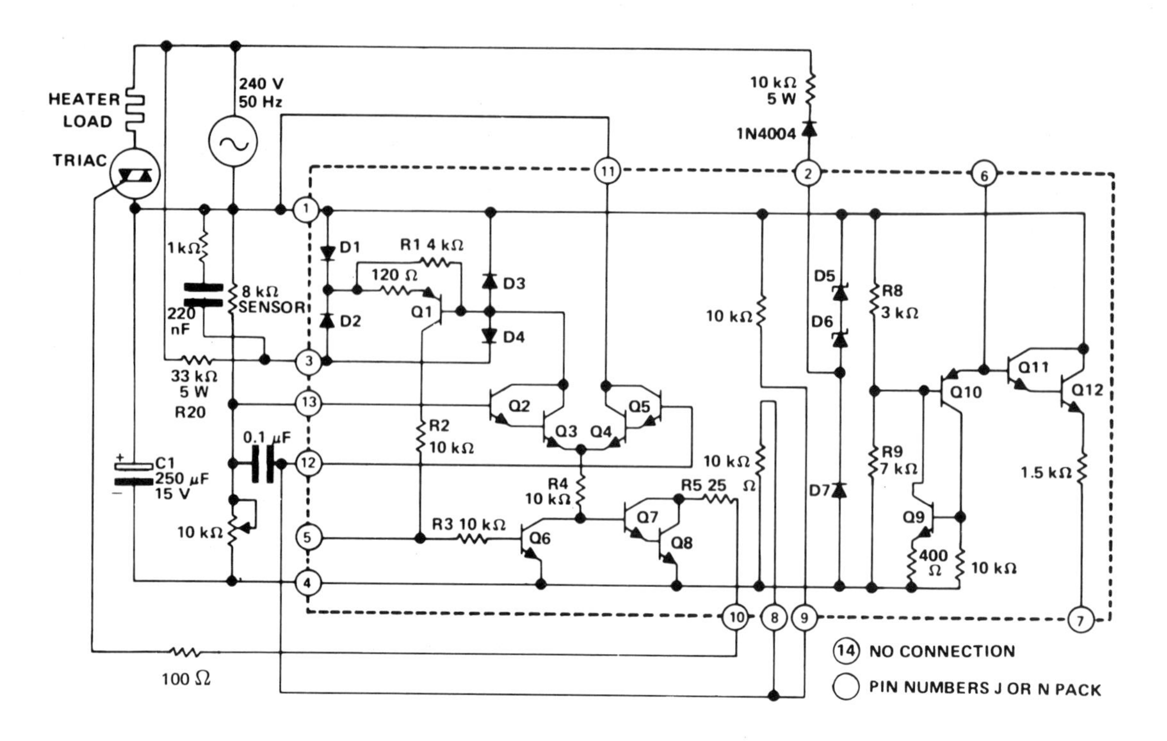

FIGURE 1. On-Off Temperature Controller using SN72440

the width of the pulses. Typically the pulses are 100 μs with a 33-kΩ resistor, and approximately 250 μs with an 82-kΩ resistor.

It is possible that with only the basic circuit components already mentioned, a ' half waving ' of the triac could occur, i.e., the triac will conduct in one direction only. This happens when the 'latching' current, which is different in the direction from MT1 to MT2 than from MT2 to MT1, has not been reached before the triggering pulses disappear. This ' latching-in' current is a function of the instantaneous voltage applied to the main terminals of the triac at the same time as the gate pulses. By shifting the trigger pulses, a higher voltage can, in effect, appear at the main terminal of the triac. This is implemented in the circuit, as shown in Figure 1, by connecting a delay circuit between pins 1 and 3 consisting of a 0.22-μF capacitor in series with a 1-kΩ resistor.

The circuit shown in Figure 2 provides proportional control of a heating system. The circuit is basically the same as Figure 1, with the exception of the sawtooth generator being included in the overall system.

Transistors Q9 and Q10 are connected as a thyristor in order to discharge the external capacitor C2 very quickly. The values shown in the Figure 2 give a sawtooth time constant of approximately 1.5 s, i.e., between 10 to 75 times the line voltage period. Although this time constant can be changed by varying either the external capacitor C2 or the external resistor, it is preferable to vary the capacitor because too small a resistor value will cause transistors Q9 and Q10 to stay on continuously.

Figure 3 shows the effect of the sawtooth voltage at pin 13 on the output pulses. At the start of the sawtooth waveform, the base of transistor Q1 is high and output pulses occur at pin 10. When the sawtooth voltage reaches a certain voltage value or above, the Q1 transistor will turn ' on, ' inhibiting pulses at pin 10. Variation in thermistor resistance, caused by the change in temperature, moves the sawtooth up and down and thus varies the number of pulses which appear at pin 10.

TRANSFORMER AND INDUCTIVE LOADS

When a transformer is switched ' on ' at peak voltage, assuming a demagnetized core, EMF must be immediately established opposing the applied voltage. The flux required must have a maximum rate of change, i.e., will start to increase from zero. These conditions are precisely the same as normal operation conditions, where the magnetizing current lags the voltage by 90°, (i.e., a steady state condition), hence there are no current transients. Assuming that a voltage of zero value is applied to the transformer throughout the first half period, the voltage is positive and subsequently the EMF negative, such that the flux for the first half-cycle must continuously increase. It begins at zero and reaches double its normal peak at the end of the first half-cycle. The magnetizing current required to produce twice the normal flux density may be several times greater

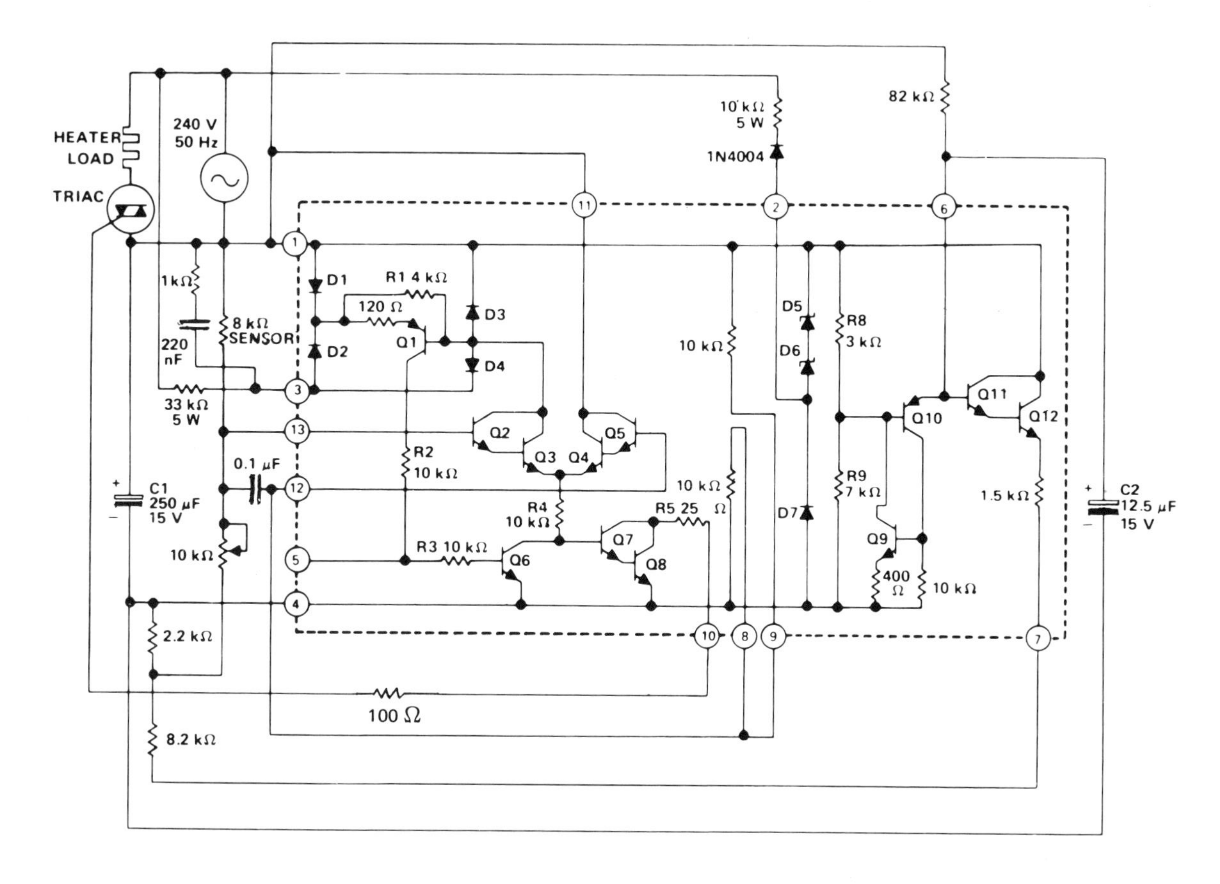

FIGURE 2. Proportional Control for a Heating System

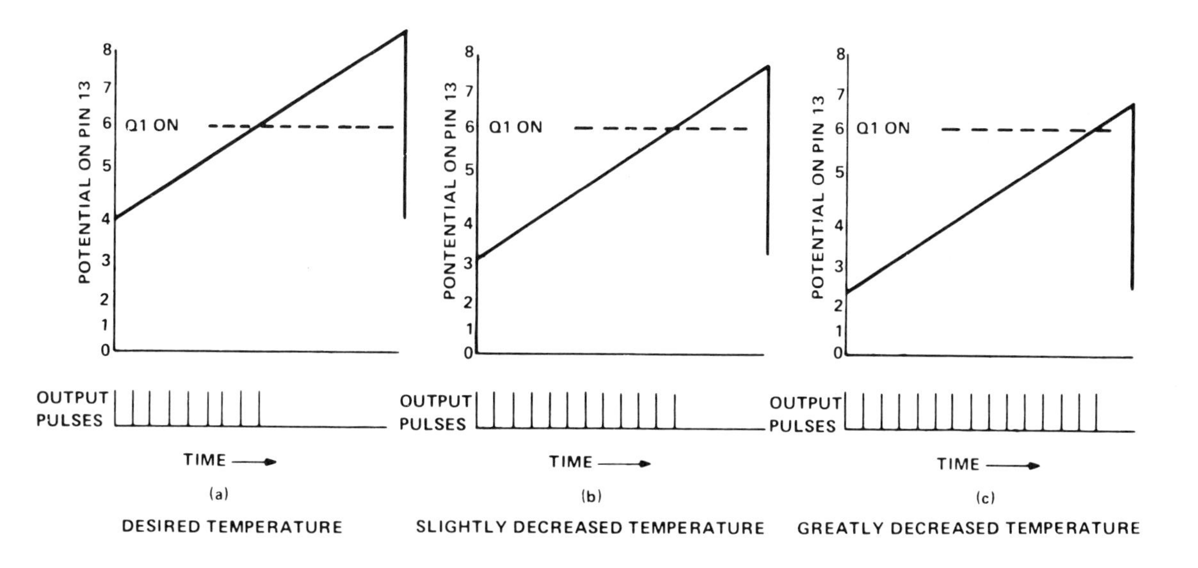

FIGURE 3. Effect of Sawtooth Voltage on Output Pulses

than the full load current. The severity of inrush current will depend on the point on the sine wave at which the switch has been closed.

Consequently, the application of zero-voltage switching IC to transformer control presents certain problems. First, the SN72440 device controls the switching in half cycles and not in full cycles. Therefore the trains of half sine wave pulses in the burst firing mode may be asymmetrical, i.e., they may contain more positive than negative pulses, which will magnetize the transformer core in one direction and aggravate subsequent switching conditions. Second, since the current lags the voltage in inductive loads, the pulses must be extended, otherwise 'latching' current can never be reached.

Manual Control

Figure 4 shows a burst firing, manual control for transformer loads. Basically, it uses the zero-voltage pulse generator SN72440 with pulses advanced to lead the supply voltage by 60° by means of a 0.1-µF capacitor in series with a 1-kΩ resistor connected between pin 3 and the line. In order to make the differential amplifier less sensitive, and thus suitable for manual control, 5.6-kΩ resistors were added between pins 12 and 4, and 13 and 4, and the external thermistor replaced by a 10-kΩ resistor. Connecting a 0.022-µF capacitor between pin 3 and 5 inhibits every second pulse, thus generating one pulse every full cycle. For isolation purposes, the output from pin 10 is applied to the SN7413 Schmitt trigger IC via a pulse transformer.

The Schmitt trigger is used to improve the system noise immunity, as well as to decrease the rise time of the pulses which are applied to the SN74122 retriggerable monostable IC. By adding external timing components, i.e., a 2.2-µF capacitor between pins 13 and 11 and a 33-kΩ resistor between pin 13 and the positive rail, the output from the monostable will maintain the positive extended pulse as long as the input pulses are applied every 20 ms. Its output, pin 8, is then connected to the gate of the triac via two 2N3708 transistors connected as a Darlington pair.

By varying the 5-kΩ potentiometer connected to pin 13 of the SN72440, burst firing control can be achieved. Figure 5 shows some of the oscillograms of the primary current of a transformer with an 0.8 power factor load and illustrates that a wide range of control has been achieved, from one cycle to continuous control. The first pulse of the current is always less than steady state and the number of positive and negative pulses is equal.

Automatic Control

For automatic temperature control of the transformer load, the manual operation circuit of Figure 4 must have some modifications made to it, i.e. the 10kΩ resistor is replaced by an 8-kΩ negative coefficient thermistor, a 10-kΩ potentiometer takes the place of the 5-kΩ potenti-

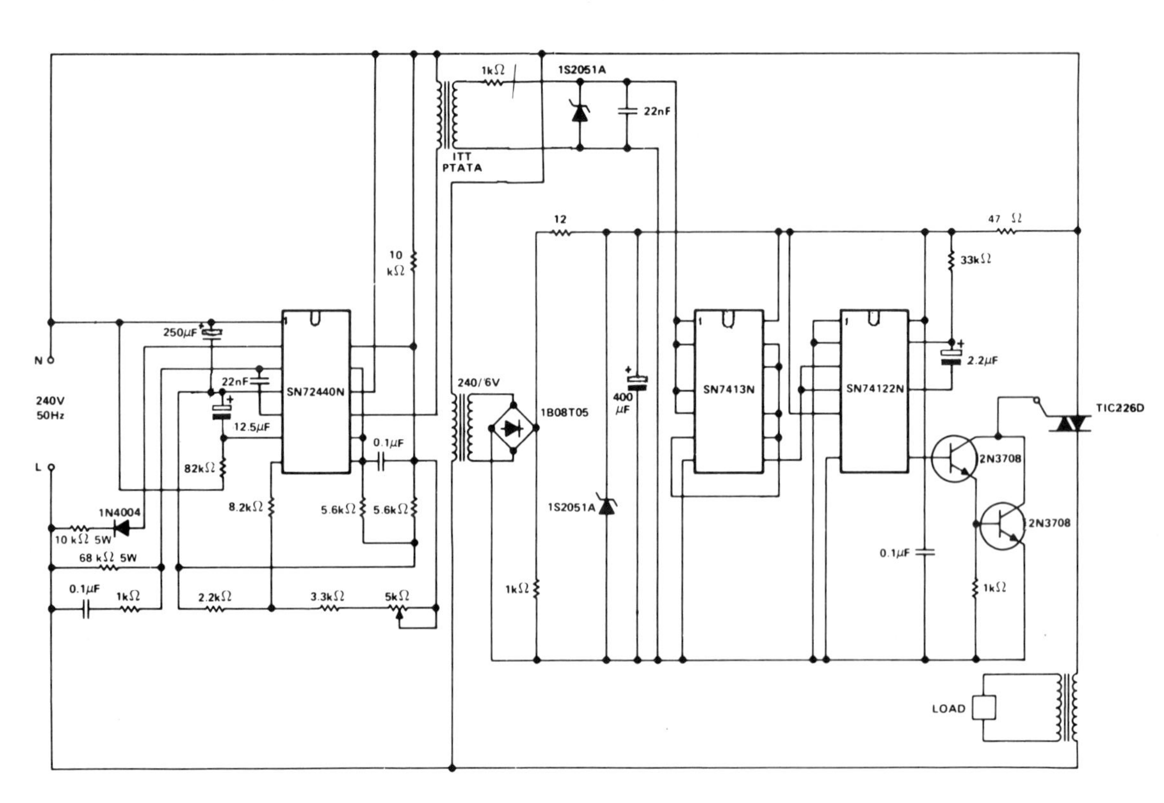

FIGURE 4. Burst Firing for Transformer Loads

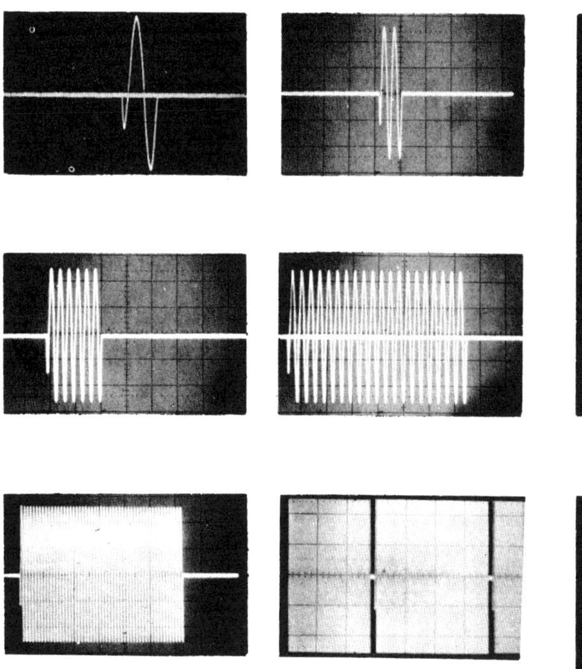

FIGURE 5. Oscillograms Illustrating the Control Range

ometer and 3.3-kΩ resistor in series, and the two 5.6-kΩ resistors are removed.

Figure 6 shows some of the oscillograms taken on the primary side of a transformer with 0.8 power factor inductive load. Figure 6(a) gives the switching point of the mains supply, triggering pulses advanced approximately 60°. Figure 6(b) shows the transformer primary voltage and current lagging it by 30°. Figure 6(c) gives primary volts and current simultaneously when switched on. In order to maintain a continuous pulse from the retriggerable monostable IC, the output pulsewidth, t_W, must be longer than 20 ms, i.e., the time interval of the input pulses.

The pulses, however, must not be too long, otherwise asymmetrical operation will take place. The pulses must be with the limits:

$$20 \text{ ms} < t_W < 20 \text{ ms} + (\alpha + \phi)$$

where pulsewidth, t_W, $\simeq 0.32\, R_{ext} C_{ext} (1 + 0.7/R_{ext})$ ns (from data sheet)

R_{ext} is in kΩ

C_{ext} in pF

α is advancement of the pulses in ms

ϕ is the lagging angle between current and voltage in ms.

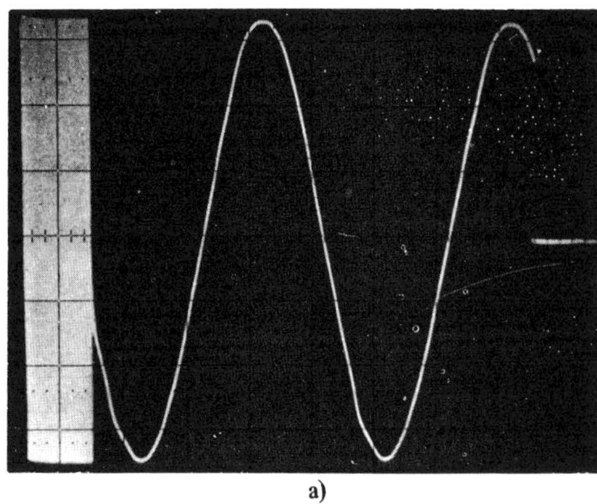

a)

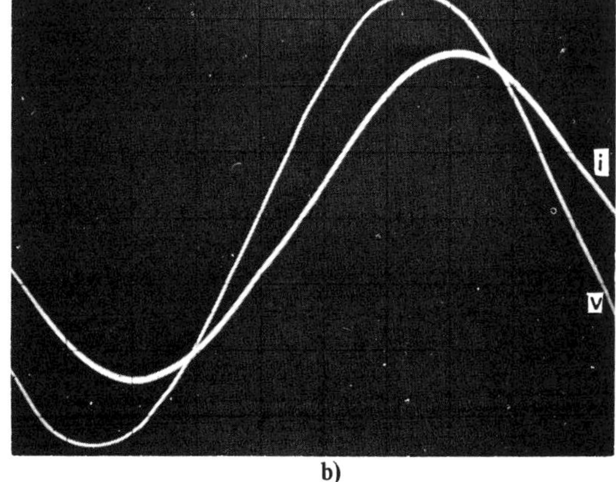

b)

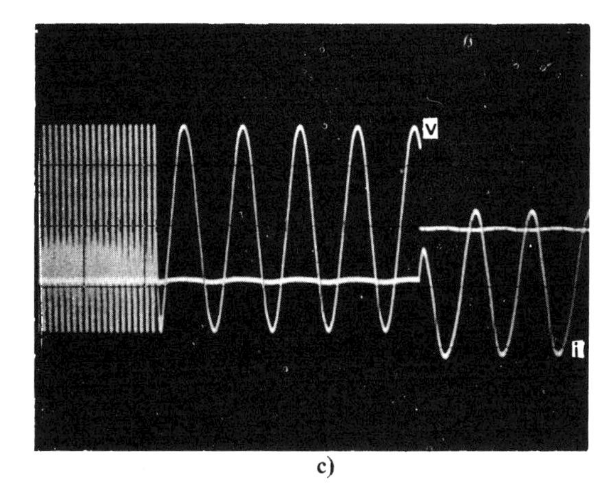

c)

FIGURE 6. Oscillograms Illustrating Voltage and Current Waveforms

REFERENCES

1. B. L. Norris Editor, *Semiconductor Circuit Design,* Vol. 1. Texas Instruments Ltd. pp. 17-18, April 1972.
2. B. L. Norris Editor, *Semiconductor Circuit Design,* Vol. I, Texas Instruments Ltd. pp. 26-28, April 1972.

IX A DOUBLE BALANCED MIXER

The process of mixing two signals of two different frequencies to obtain a third signal is a widely used function in all types of communication system. With the widespread use of the single side-band suppressed carrier, (SSB), type of transmission the demand for circuits to perform this function is increasing. In a SSB system the frequency conversion process must be accomplished by a mixing or heterodyning action, rather than the frequency multiplying process which would result in a loss of the original modulating signal plus increased unwanted distortion products. In many respects the processes of modulation, mixing and detection are basically the same; their requirements and circuit analysis are very similar. They operate on the basic principle in which two signals of different frequencies f_o and f_s are applied to either one or two input ports. The output signal is a complex function best expressed by a power series such as:–

$$E_{out} = a_0 + a_1 \cdot V_{in} + a_2 \cdot V^2{}_{in} + a_3 \cdot V^3{}_{in} + a_4 . V^4{}_{in} \quad \ldots\ldots. (1)$$

The series and its expansion is covered in detail in Chapter XII.

A mathematical expansion of this expression involving the two input signals of frequency f_o and f_s will show the following products in the output:

f_o, f_s

$f_o \pm f_s$

$2f_o \pm f_s, f_o \pm 2f_s$

$3f_o \pm f_s, f_o \pm 3f_s$

$4f_o \pm f_s, f_o \pm 4f_s$ and so on.

The order of the product $nf_o \pm mf_s$ is defined as the sum of n + m. Generally, the strongest components are the lower order products. As such, only these are considered to be of importance. Since the desired output is either the sum or difference frequency $f_o \pm f_s$, all undesired components should be eliminated.

The attenuation of these undesired components is a major problem in the design of mixers and modulators. Often, mixer and modulator circuits are followed by filters or tuned circuits which attenuate those frequency components outside the desired pass band range. This method of attenuation is adequate for attenuation of high order products and other components outside the desired pass band. However, some of the odd order intermodulation products fall inside or very close to the desired pass band. Their attenuation is primarily a function of the mixer itself.

Balanced modulator mixer circuits have the advantage of suppressing one of the input signals, usually the carrier, and also cancellation of harmonics of the same by applying two signals equal and opposite in phase to each other at the output. In the double balanced mixer, this is extended to include both input terminals. The degree of attenuation is dependent upon the balance of the two output signals. If both signals are equal and opposite in phase, maximum cancellation occurs. Balance can be achieved by matching components. Since this is impractical when using discrete components one or more adjustment controls, such as variable capacitors or resistors, can be used to offset the balance due to mismatch in components.

Although discrete component matching is impractical, component matching can be achieved by using integrated circuit techniques. A balanced modulator/mixer circuit is ideally suited to integrated circuit design since its power and voltage requirements are not high and no tuned circuits are necessary for obtaining the desired balance. A monolithic integrated circuit that has been developed to perform as a double balanced modulator or mixer will, in general, require no controls to achieve balance. Such an integrated circuit could be produced with seven matched transistors and resistors as shown in Figure 1, i.e. the SN56/76514.

CIRCUIT DESCRIPTION

Since component matching is achieved with integrated circuit techniques, a high degree of cancellation of undesired frequency components in the output signal is obtained. The device has three inputs and two separate outputs available. Other points in the circuit are brought out for a.c. bypassing and power supply connections. The circuit offers a definite size advantage over discrete component systems. No external adjustments are necessary to meet most of the required attenuation and isolation specifications. The device consists of two cross-coupled differential amplifiers, the tails of which are driven by a third differential pair. Transistors VT1 and VT2 form a differential pair for one input signal whilst transistors VT5 and VT6 form a single ended input stage for the other signal. The device operates as a double balanced system in that both signal inputs are balanced out and appear greatly attenuated at the outputs. The collectors of VT1 to VT4 form the output connections where signals are available in push-pull or single ended form.

D.C. Characteristics

The circuit may operate from a single supply or two separate supplies. Maximum supply voltage is 15V (single ended) with a typical operating range of 10 to 12V. The bases of transistors VT1/4 and VT2/3 form the differential connections for one input signal. If single ended operation is required, the unused bases should be bypassed to ground by a capacitor, the size of which depends upon the frequency of operation. The base of transistor VT6 is decoupled for both balanced and single ended operation. A.c. coupling should be used to both inputs and outputs to prevent d.c. unbalance in the circuit. Particular care is required when operating a device at low frequencies as the coupling capacitors will usually be of the electrolytic type and leakage in the input capacitors will degrade the balance in the circuit. This still applies if the signal inputs operate around earth potential. A.c. coupling is still required but leakage problems will be minimised.

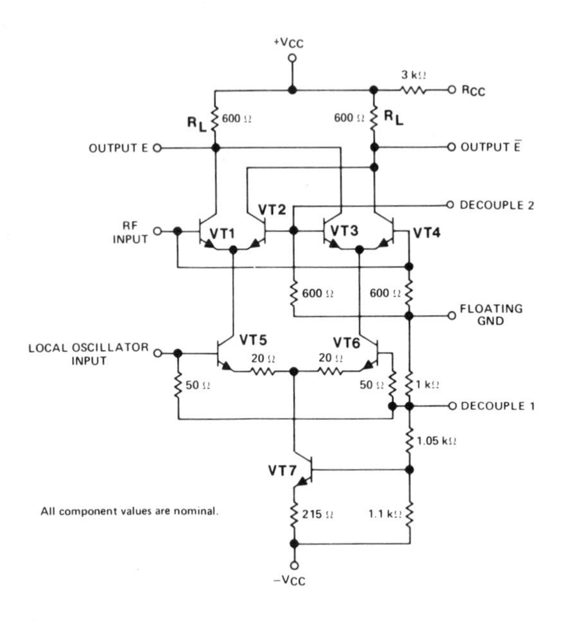

FIGURE 1. Internal Circuit Diagram of the SN 56/76514 Double Balanced Mixer

A.C. Characteristics

The device was designed to present a low impedance at the inputs. This is nominally 50 Ω for the signal and 600 Ω for the oscillator inputs for the circuit of Figure 1. Table 1 shows the variation of the real part of the single-ended input impedance with frequency.

Table 1

Frequency	Local Oscillator Input	RF Input or Decouple 2
MHz	Ω	Ω
5	63	530
10	62	450
50	68	360
100	80	290

The output impedance of the mixer is dependent upon the operating frequency and the collector load resistor, R_L. A 600 Ω resistor is supplied on the chip. This value can be reduced by externally connecting a resistor in parallel from the + V_{CC} supply to collector. The relationship between the load resistor R_L and frequency of operation can be seen from the following equation:–

$f_{max} = 1/2.\pi.R_L.C_m$

where C_m is the input miller effect capacity and is given by:

$C_m = C_{BE} \cdot R_L/R_E$

The circuit of Figure 1 will operate satisfactorily up to 150 MHz. Depending upon the required signal isolation and conversion gain it may be used at higher frequencies. Conversion gain is a function of the oscillator voltage level as related to the desired output signal. A large oscillator voltage will give good conversion gain but the odd order intermodulation products will be higher. A low oscillator voltage results in poor conversion gain, poor noise figure and therefore relatively higher feedthrough ratio. The derivation of the transfer characteristic of the device shows the output, V_o, to be:–

$V_o = -600\,(0.018)\,e_2 \tanh(38.e_1/2)$

for the on-chip loads of 600 Ω, where e_1 is the RF input voltage and e_2 is the oscillator input voltage.

APPLICATIONS

Mixer

One obvious use of the device is as a mixer, where a carrier f_o is mixed with a signal f_s. The desired outputs are $f_o \pm f_s$. However, as a result of the deficiencies in the mixing process other outputs are produced. Generally, the higher the order of the intermodulation product, the lower the amplitude.

The curves given in Figures 2, 3 and 4 illustrate the performance of the SN56/76514 double balanced mixer as a frequency converter using the input frequencies of 1 MHz and 10 MHz. These measurements were made with a filter in the 1 MHz input. This improves the level of harmonic distortion present at the input to better than 90dB down on the wanted sideband. This was necessary to give accurate results for the intermodulation product measurements. Figures 2 and 3 are graphs plotted relative to mean sideband levels. A large number of results have been included because it is not easy to characterise a device such as a mixer, which operates over a wide range of input frequencies and levels. It can also be seen that the user must make a compromise between the levels of intermodulation products at the output and feed-through from the input that he can tolerate. Due to the inherent matching between the circuit elements produced by the monolithic integrated circuit process, the circuit has a good performance as it stands with regard to intermodulation products and feedthrough of input signals. Good thermal matching is also achieved because the elements result from the same diffusion processes and are in close physical proximity to one another. However, the performance can be improved by the introduction of a small d.c. differential off-set current to the upper long tailed pairs (VT1 to VT4). The current required is small, being typically of the order of a microamp. The effect of this off-set current which is applied to the RF input, can be seen in Figures 2, 3 and 4. The input-output characteristics of the device when used as

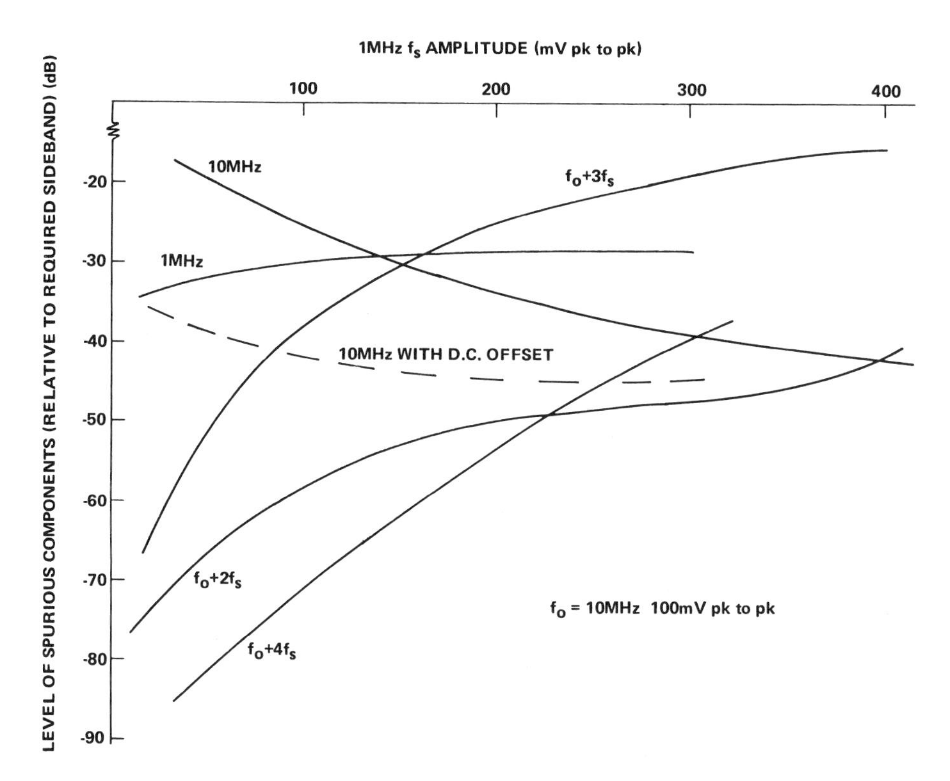

FIGURE 2. Performance as a Frequency Converter (f_s Amplitude Varied)

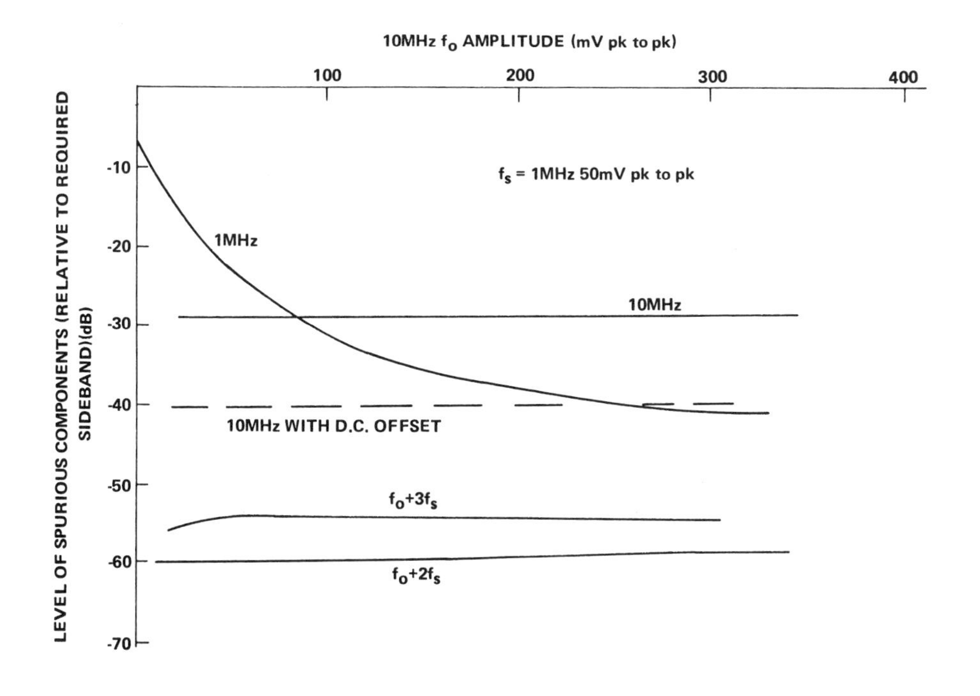

FIGURE 3. Performance as a Frequency Converter (f_o Amplitude Varied)

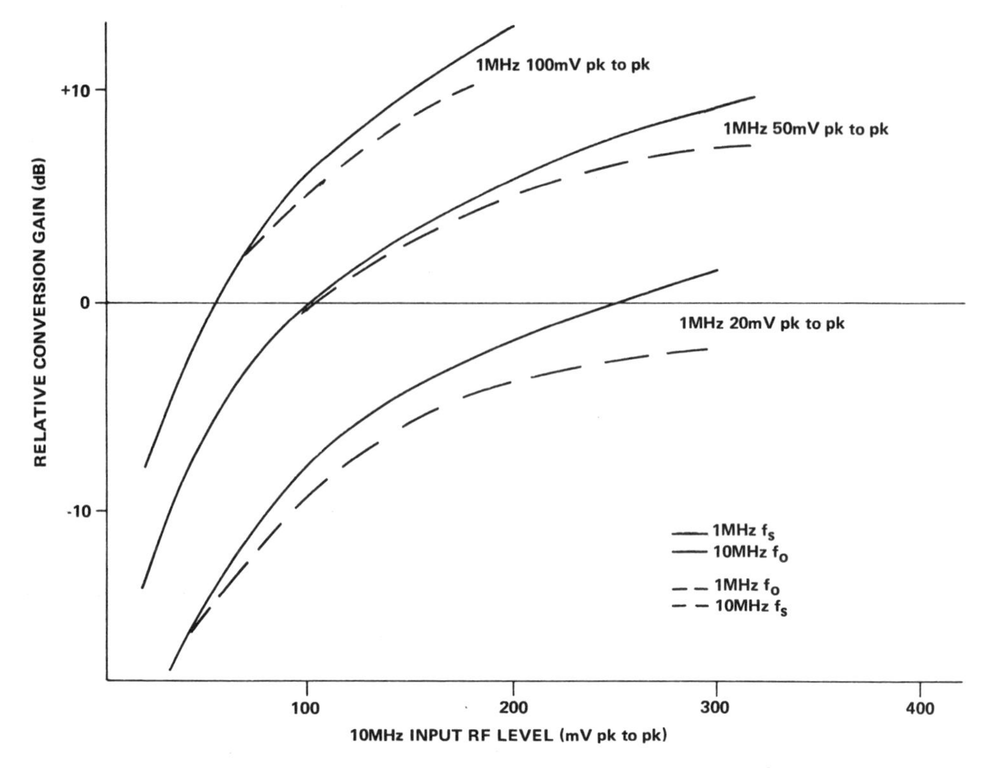

FIGURE 4. Performance as a Frequency Converter (Conversion Gain)

a mixer show that good linearity is preserved up to about 100 mV peak to peak. A typical spectrum analysis of the output of the device when used as a frequency converter is shown in Figure 5. 50 mV peak to peak at 10 MHz is applied to the RF input and 250 mV peak to peak at 1 MHz applied at the oscillator input. The vertical scale is logarithmic (in dBs).

Figure 6 shows the well-known bow-tie linearity display, showing how the output voltage amplitude varies linearly into input voltage. The modulating voltage is the horizontal axis and the output of the device, push-pull across 600 Ω, is the vertical axis. Input voltages are 100 mV peak to peak in both cases.

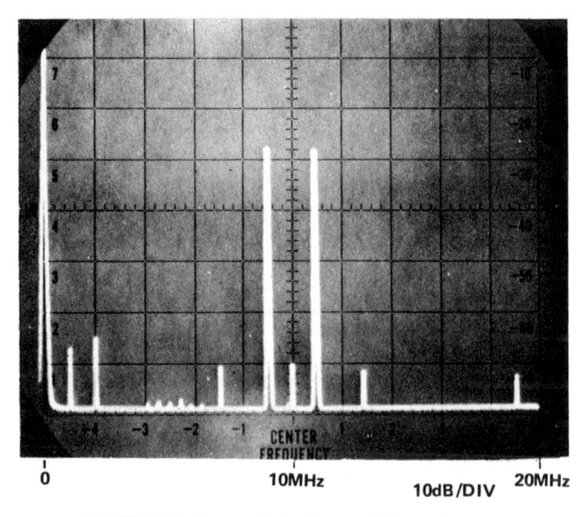

FIGURE 5. Spectral Analysis of Mixer Output

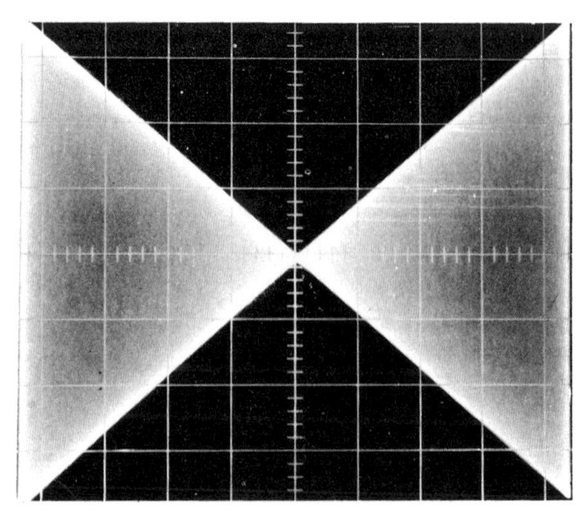

FIGURE 6. "Bow-tie" Display Showing Device Linearity

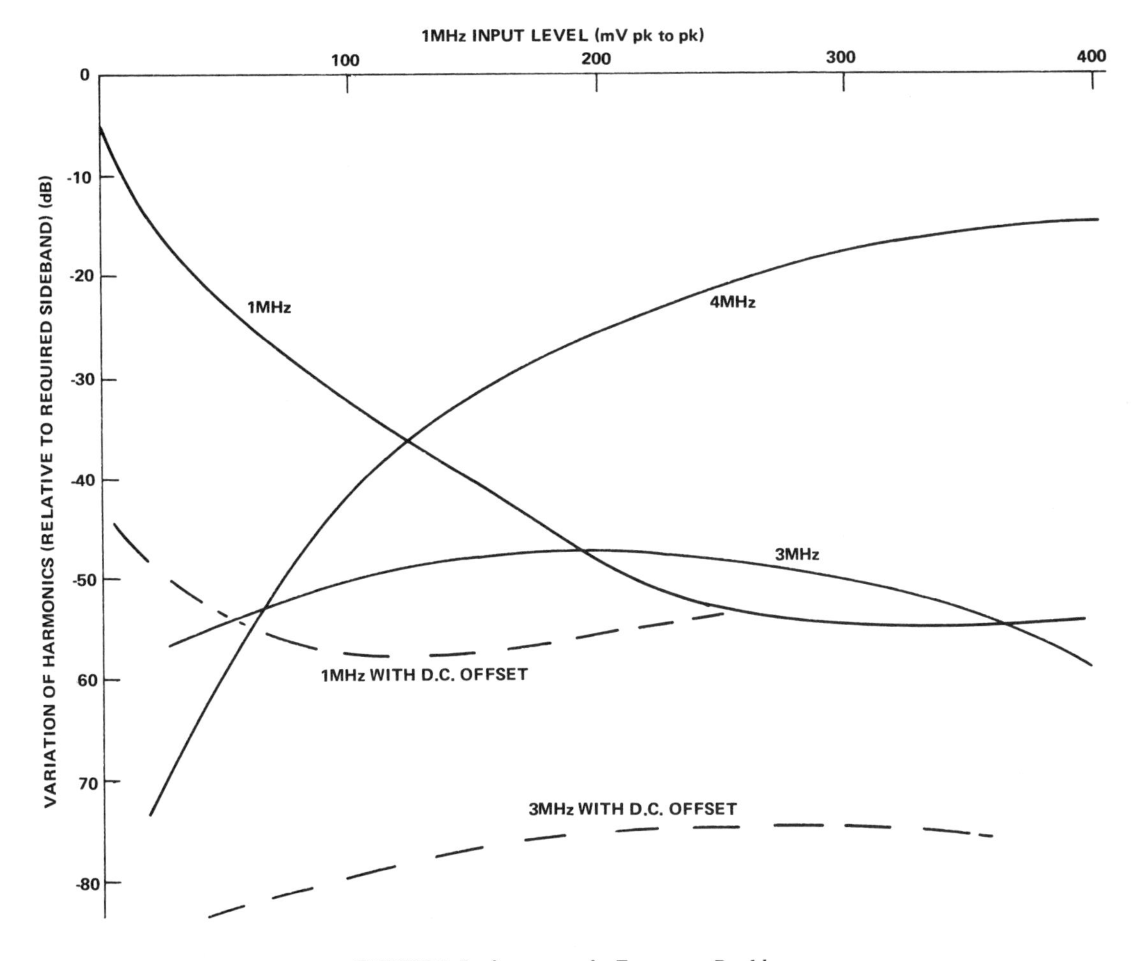

FIGURE 7. Performance of a Frequency Doubler

Frequency Doubler

When the SN56/76514 is used as a frequency doubler the principle employed is that of a multiplier where the same frequency is applied to both input terminals. No tuned circuits are employed and Figure 7 shows the variation of harmonic content in the output waveform with input voltage level relative to twice the input frequency. The user must make the compromise between the tolerable level of 1 MHz component and, in this case particularly, the 4 MHz component. Alternatively, whilst applying the same frequency, different levels can be applied to the input terminals. It has been found that an attenuator placed between the RF and local oscillator inputs, the signal input being applied to the oscillator input, has an effect on the higher harmonics. Figures 8 and 9 show the effect of this attenuator. In the first case (Figure 8) the 1 MHz component is 40dB down on the wanted 2 MHz component; in the second (Figure 9) with the attenuator, this has been reduced to 30dB down, but it will be noticed that the third and fourth harmonics are down on their former

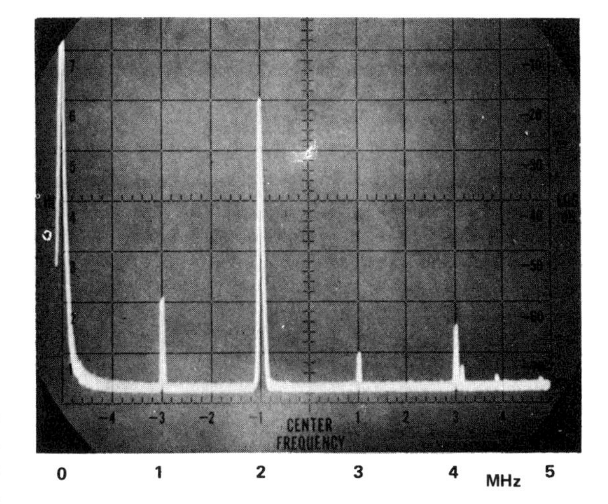

FIGURE 8. Spectral Analysis of Frequency Doubler Operation Without Attenuator

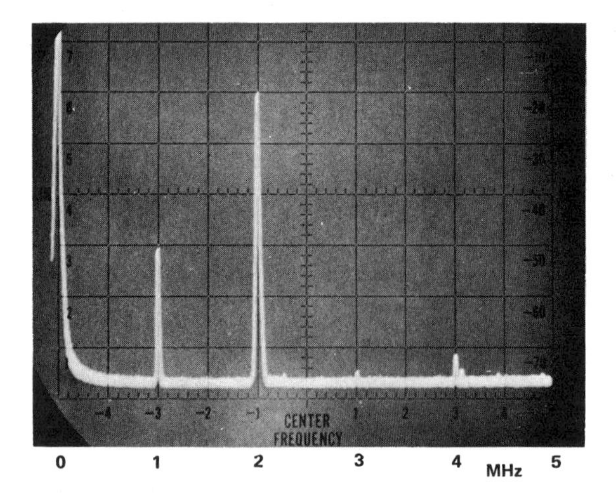

FIGURE 9. Spectral Analysis of Frequency Doubler Operation With Attenuator

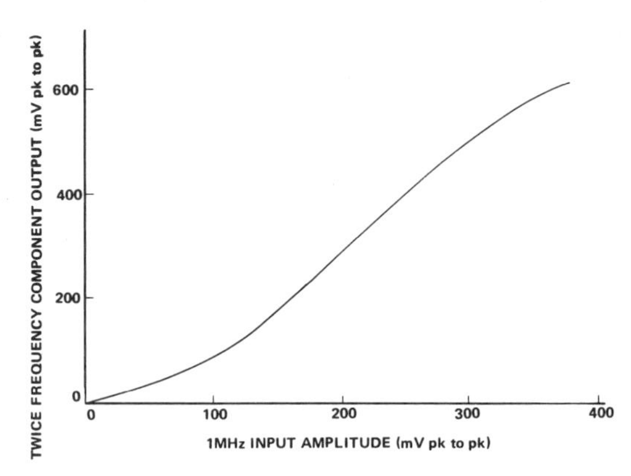

FIGURE 11. Variation of Twice Frequency Component in Frequency Doubler

values. The value of the attenuation required is roughly 10dB but this has to be the subject of the individual application if the optimum performance is to be obtained. The attenuator is required because the RF input will tolerate a lower level of input signal than the oscillator input because of the presence of the emitter resistors in the lower long tailed pair VT5 and VT6. Figure 10 shows the input (bottom trace) and output (top trace) waveforms. Because the device is of monolithic integrated construction, there is no reason why the phase balance should not be good and therefore the phase relationship between input and output waveforms preserved over a wide frequency range. It should be noted that when using a device in a doubler application the use of the balance control to apply a small d.c. differential offset between the bases of transistors VT1 and VT3 improves the performance considerably, particularly with regard to fundamental feed-through. Differential d.c. current into these bases is typically in the microamp region. The effect of this current is shown in Figure 7. Figure 11 shows the variation of the twice frequency component.

Analogue Multiplier

The frequency doubling technique described previously is a particular case of the use of the double balanced mixer operating as a linear multiplier. The equation of the transfer characteristic of the device may be expressed in the form:

$E_{out} = K_1 . e_2 . \tanh K_2 . e_1$

where K_1 and K_2 are constants and e_1 and e_2 represent the input at the signal and oscillator ports respectively.

If the input signal is applied to the oscillator and the bases of transitors VT2 and VT3 with the RF input grounded to a.c. then the phase of the output signal is reversed. For small values of u, tanh u = u, and the device will act as an analogue multiplier. Thus in the previous case of the frequency doubler:

$E_{out} = a^2 \sin^2 \omega t$

$= a^2 (1 - \cos 2\omega t)/2$

Thus in the output there exists a d.c. term and a term at twice the input frequency. In Figure 12 the input waveform

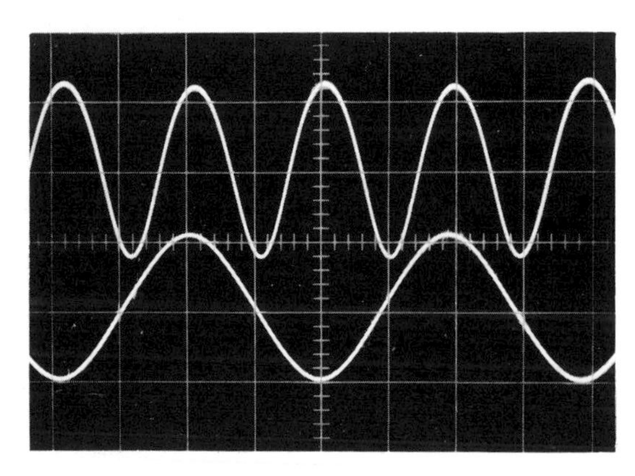

FIGURE 10. Input and Output Waveforms of Frequency Doubler

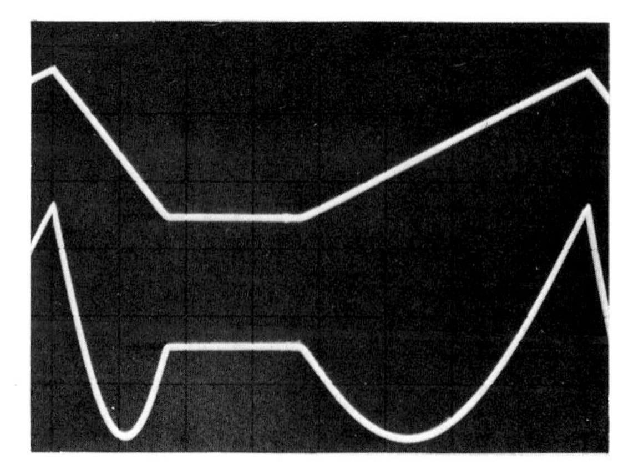

2µs/DIV

FIGURE 12. Analogue Multiplier Waveforms

to both inputs is of ramp form of two different slopes, that is of the form:–

y = a.t where a has two different values of opposite sign dependent upon t.

The output waveform will be:–

$E_{out} = K.a^2.t^2$ which is of parabolic form.

Figure 12 shows the input ramp (top trace at 50 mV/division) and resultant single ended output waveform (bottom trace at 100 mV/division). Note the two parabolic sections and the d.c. section of the output waveform. The measurements were taken with a.c. coupling to the inputs. This means that the mean level will depend upon the input waveform. This level may be modified by applying a d.c. offset voltage to the RF input when the mixer is operating as a frequency doubler. Note that this parabolic waveform generator has no frequency conscious network as in conventional systems and therefore will operate over a wide frequency range without adjustment.

Figure 13 shows a symmetrical input waveform applied to the RF input (top trace at 50 mV/division) and the resultant output (bottom trace at 100 mv/division). It is possible to use the device with d.c. input signals but care must be taken as the input terminals are at different d.c. levels and neither is close to earth potential. If the device is operated with split supplies, the problem is eased as the RF input is now near ground potential, but allowance must be made for the base input current drop across the 600 Ω resistors (typically about 100 mV) and the temperature coefficient of the same. Variation of driving source impedance will also affect the d.c. conditions. The balanced mode of operation is advantageous when the device is driven from an operational amplifier of the '709, '741, etc. type.

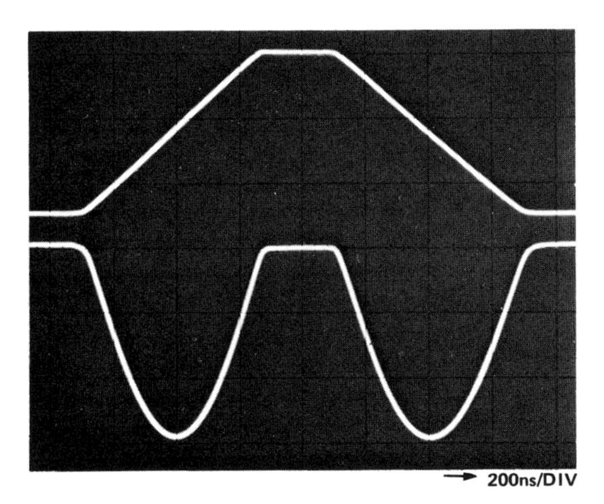

FIGURE 13. Analogue Multiplier Waveforms With Symmetrical Input

Variable Gain Amplifier

There is often a requirement in communication and radar systems for an amplifier, the gain of which can be controlled over a wide range by means of a control voltage. It is possible to use the double balanced mixer as such as a variable gain amplifier as shown in Figure 14. Potentiometer RV1 is used to set the mean level of the input voltage to the oscillator input. If there were no d.c. component present, the integrated circuit would give zero output at a point corresponding to balance. Either side of that point an output is produced but there will be a phase shift of π radians phase change as balance is passed through zero. Figure 15 shows (top trace) a 15 MHz carrier, gain controlled by a ramp waveform, applied to the oscillator input (bottom trace), but with no d.c. applied from RV1. The point of balance is readily seen as well as the π radians phase change as balance is passed through. Note that with no d.c. input the crossover point corresponds to the mean level of the input waveform.

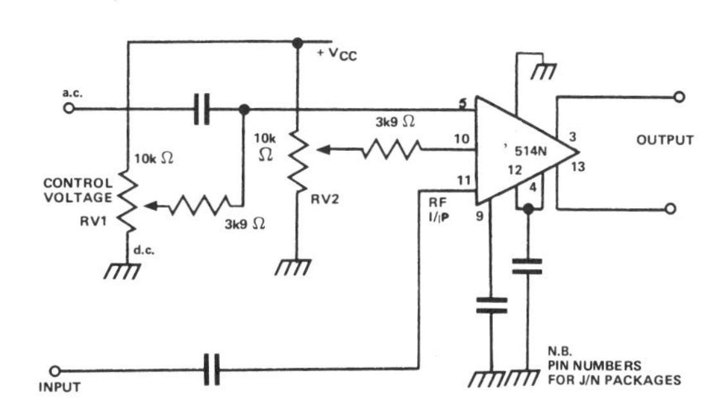

FIGURE 14. Voltage Controlled Attenuator

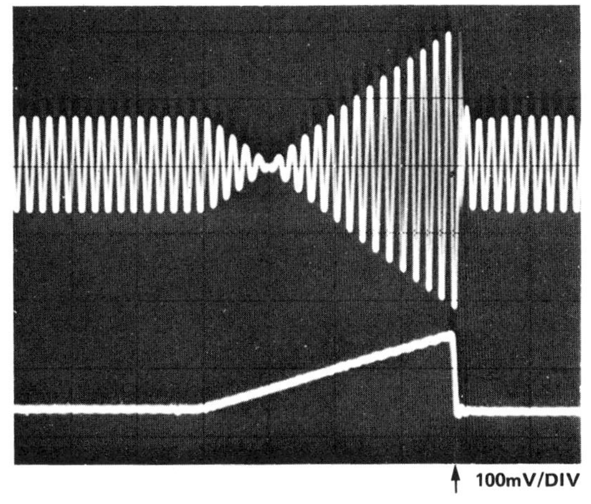

FIGURE 15. Variable Gain Amplifier Waveforms

Figure 16 shows the device used as a swept gain amplifier operating at a signal frequency of 50 MHz. The input controlling waveform (top trace at 100 mV pk to pk) is superimposed to give some idea of control linearity. (Note that this waveform has been displaced on the oscilloscope to display it more clearly.) The single ended output is shown on the bottom trace (50 mV/division). The addition of potentiometer RV2 is a refinement and serves as a trim control to set the positive and negative portions of the modulation envelope to equal amplitudes. In the majority of applications it is not required. The setting of potentiometer RV1 required depends upon the amplitude of the controlling waveforms and, if it is capacitively coupled, its duty ratio. The aim is to arrange that the mixer is just balanced on one peak of the controlling waveform, corresponding to theoretically zero output. In practice the null level will depend upon the carrier frequency. The output waveform of Figure 16 shows the low level of feed-through even at 50 MHz. Care must be taken with the lay-out keeping the input and output separate. A screen between them may be required when operating at high frequencies.

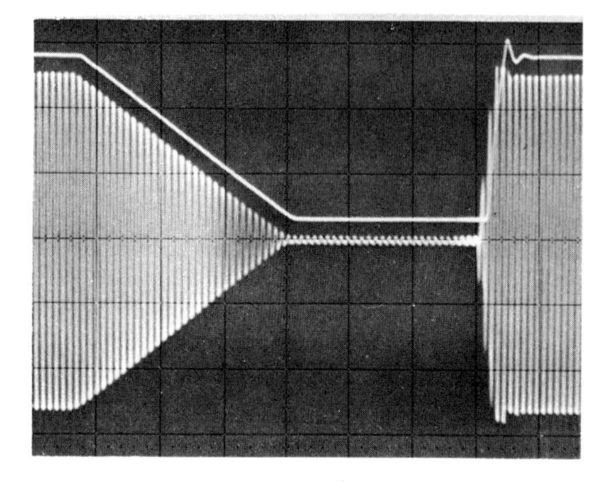

FIGURE 16. Swept Gain Amplifier Waveforms

Amplitude Modulator

The SN56/76514 double balanced mixer can be used as an amplitude modulator in communication systems. Here the modulation can be applied at low level, the output being increased in power level by succeeding linear power amplifiers. Operation is similar to the application as a variable gain amplifier described previously and shown in Figure 14. The RF input is used as the carrier input because it was found that there was less carrier feed-through than when the oscillator input was used. Potentiometer RV2 is not normally required but allows the amplitude of the positive and negative halves of the modulation envelope to be equalised. (Conversely, if some asymmetry is required due perhaps to the characteristic of a later stage, this is readily achieved.) Potentiometer RV1 is used to unbalance the device so that it just gives theoretically zero output on the negative modulation peaks. If over modulation is attempted, instead of the carrier cutting off, it passes through zero before the modulation peak is reached, reverses in phase and then increases again up to the peak of the modulating waveform. The values of capacitors required depend upon the frequencies used, as mentioned at the beginning of the chapter. Figure 17 shows the result of a 150 mV peak to peak 50 MHz carrier, applied at the RF input, amplitude modulated by a 150 mV 1 MHz wave-form, applied at the oscillator input. (The modulation depth is about 98%.)

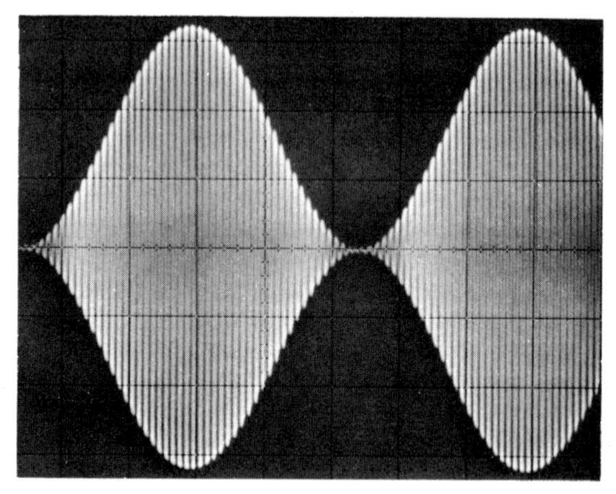

FIGURE 17. Output Waveform of Amplitude Modulator

Chopper

The double balanced mixer may be used as a chopper, a device required frequently in the instrumentation and control fields. Here, as shown in Figure 18, unlike the appli-

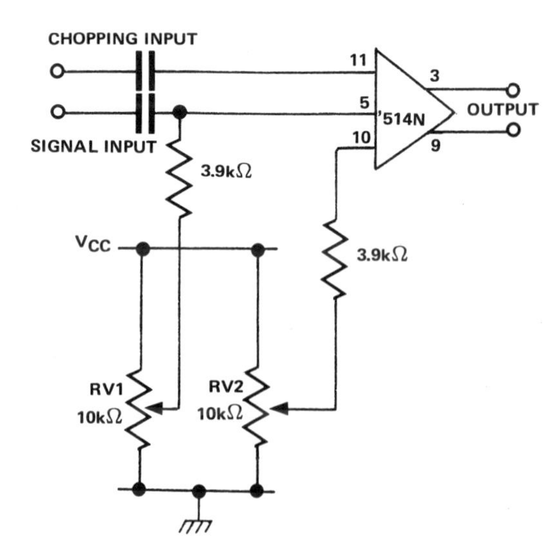

FIGURE 18. Mixer used as a Chopper

cation as an amplitude modulator, the unbalanced d.c. signal is fed to the input with the high frequency carrier. The carrier can be either sinusoidal or rectangular in form. The majority of the d.c. offset is applied to the upper decoupling point, i.e. the bases of VT2 and VT3 by means of potentiometer RV2. The setting required will depend upon the level of carrier input. If control is required over the symmetry of the positive and negative halves of the resultant envelope, the control RV1 potentiometer is used to apply a small d.c. offset to the oscillator input. Figure 19 shows the result of a 10 MHz carrier, applied to the RF input, chopping a 100 kHz sine wave, applied to the oscillator input. Correct adjustment is shown in (a), (b) shows too much carrier amplitude, and (c) too little carrier amplitude.

Balanced Modulator

Double balanced mixers are widely used for the generation of single sideband suppressed carrier signals. There are three basic methods for the production of such signals:–

(i) Filter method, using a balanced modulator to mix audio and a frequency of several hundred kilohertz. The resultant double sideband suppressed carrier signal is passed through a fixed frequency filter to remove one sideband. The remaining single sideband suppressed carrier signal is mixed and amplified to the transmitter frequency and power level.

(ii) Phasing method, using two audio signals from a coherent source but with 90° phase shift between them over the audio range. A similar two-phase carrier source is also required. By mixing all four signals in two double balanced modulators, the two resulting sidebands from each modulator can be added, when it is found that there is cancellation of one, and reinforcement of the other, due to their phase relationships.

(iii) A combination of (i) and (ii) designed by D. K. Weaver. Here the majority of the circuitry is at audio frequency and the filters are easily constructed. The method makes use of the fact that when a lower sideband would theoretically be at a frequency less than zero, it appears at the frequency, but changed in phase by 180°.

The device behaves as a linear mixer as in the section on frequency converters. Use may be made of the characteristic curves given in that section for determining the performance of the device in a particular application. It should be noted that when used as a single sideband suppressed carrier generator, the carrier is required to be suppressed as far as possible. Therefore it should be applied to the oscillator input and the audio to the RF input. A small d.c. offset current applied to the RF input will, if required, enable maximum carrier suppression to be obtained. Many balanced modulators in use today are versions of a two or four diode design which offer no conversion gain. The circuit of Figure 1 gives conversion gain, which is desirable when a filter is used to eliminate one sideband.

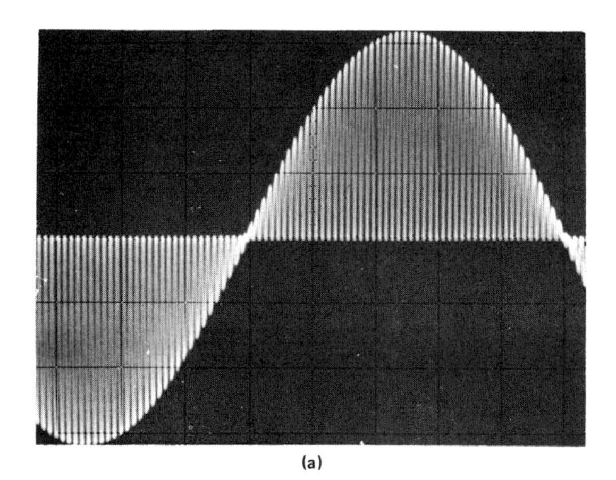

(a)

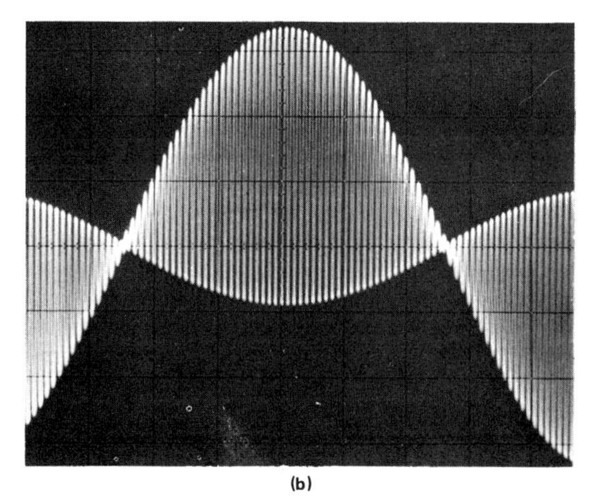

(b)

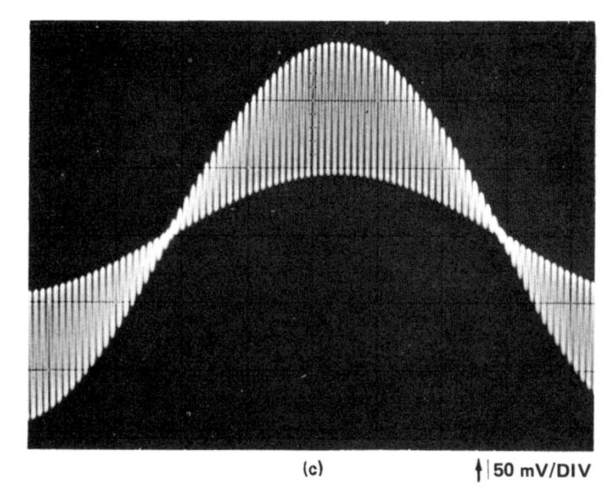

(c)

FIGURE 19. Chopper Waveforms

Phase Detectors

In the applications previously discussed, circuit operation has been with the input signals very much less in amplitude than that which would cause symmetrical limiting by the base-emitter diodes of the long tailed pairs. It is infor-

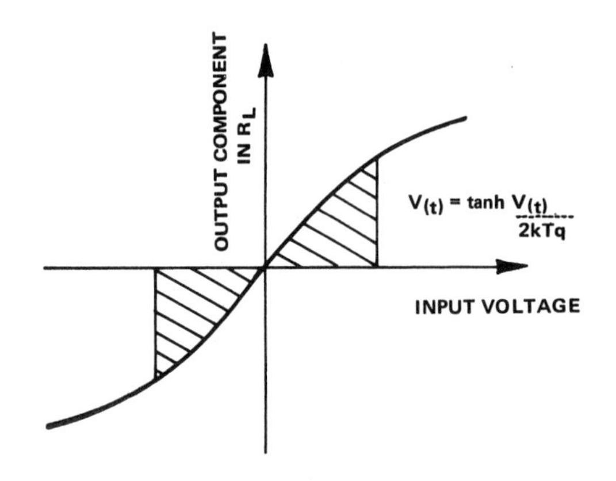

FIGURE 20. Transfer Characteristic

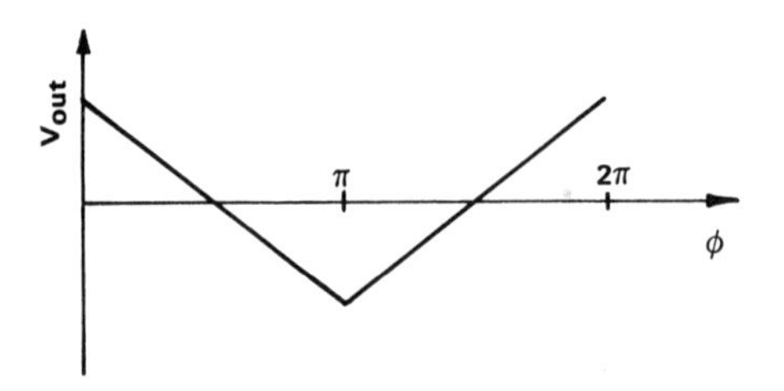

FIGURE 21. Normalised Phase Characteristic

mative to consider what happens when the device is over-driven so that limiting occurs. Figure 20 shows a transfer characteristic for the upper long tailed pairs. The transfer characteristic of a long tailed pair is only hyperbolic at low signal currents. As the current is increased, the curve 'flattens' and the circuit limits. The presence of the emitter resistors in the circuit of the lower long tailed pair produces a linearising effect making the transfer characteristic linear at low and medium signal levels. However non-linearity will still set in at high input levels. Consider the case when both inputs, signal and oscillator, are overdriven, giving effectively square wave input waveforms. If they are at the same frequency with a phase difference then the two square waves can be represented by:–

$$V1 = K1 \cdot \frac{4}{\pi} \Sigma_1^{\infty} (\cos n\pi\omega t)/n$$

as $f(\omega + \pi) = -f(\omega)$, n is odd only

$$V2 = K2 \cdot \frac{4}{\pi} \Sigma_1^{\infty} [\cos n\pi(\omega t + \phi)]/n$$

as $f(\omega + \pi + \phi) = -f(\omega + \phi)$, n is odd only

Where V1 and V2 represent the phase shifted input signals K_1 and K_2 are constants representing amplitude.
Therefore the average value of the product V1.V2:–

$$= (K/\pi^2)\ \Sigma_1^{\infty} (\cos n\phi)/n^2$$

which for $0 < \phi < \pi$ is $1 - (2\phi/\pi)$

and for $\pi < \phi < 2\pi$ is $-3 + (2\phi/\pi)$

This represents the characteristic shown in Figure 21 which is a plot of output voltage against phase shift.

If the input signals are phase shifted by $\pm\pi/2$ radians, the net output is zero. That the relationship is linear over 180° and will give ambiguous outputs if the device is used in a 360° system. Because the mixer is doubly balanced, it operates in a full wave rather than a half wave mode, producing output frequency components twice that of the input. This is useful as it eases smoothing problems. The device may be used in a digital system over the range 0 – 2π radians by means of the circuit shown in Figure 22. Here the input frequencies are divided by two by the dual J.K. master slave flip-flop. The connection between the output of one flip-flop and the Preset or Clear of the other ensures that upon switching on the correct phase relationship between the outputs of the flip-flops is obtained i.e. 0 to π or π to 2π. Because of the low impedance of the RF and oscillator inputs, the values of capacitors C must be chosen such that at the operating frequency their reactances are low compared with 50 Ω. The output ripple frequency will of course in this case be the same as that of V1 and V2. The value of smoothing capacitance required on the output will depend upon the application. Choice of the flip-flops will depend upon operating frequency, the SN74S112 will toggle at 80 MHz but operation will be below this. Operation from ECL logic is also possible.

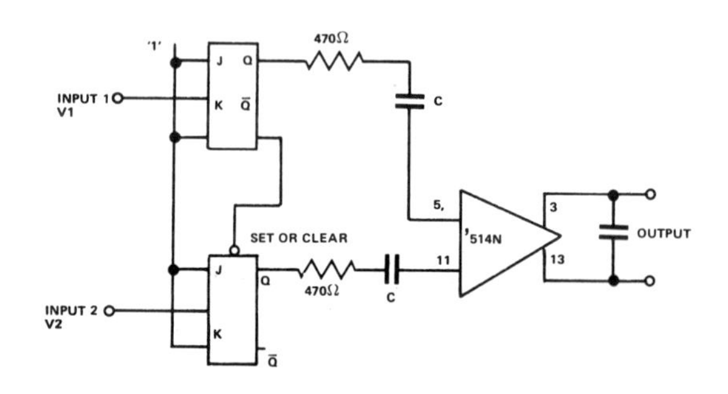

FIGURE 22. Digital Phase Detector Circuit

So far, operation with switching signals on both inputs has been considered. Consider the case of one input acting as a switch, the other being below limiting. Performing the same mathematical operations as before with a sinusoidal input to one terminal and assuming linear transfer characteristic, yields the average output as:–
$V_0 = K.V1.\cos\phi$ where V1 is the low level input.
Thus the average output this time is proportional not only to the phase difference but to the amplitude of the signal as well: precisely what is required for a synchronous detector.

A.C. Sensor Amplifier

The double balanced mixer can be used as a synchronous demodulator for a high frequency capacitance or inductor differential transducer. The ability of the device to operate at frequencies of tens of megahertz makes it useful in this application. Figure 23 shows such a system. Here the different inputs from the sensor are applied to the RF inputs, whilst the reference carrier is fed to the sensor and the oscillator inputs. The carrier should be of high level (limiting) to provide the best system gain as well as stabilising the output level. The mixer feeds a low pass filter and a SN72741N operational amplifier which operates as an output buffer. Resistors R1, R3 and R5 should have the same values as R2, R4 and R6 respectively. Capacitor C1 is a low impedance compared with 50 Ω at the carrier frequency. Capacitor C2 in conjunction with the output impedance and resistors R1 and R2 provide high frequency roll-off to integrate the pulsed output of the detector.

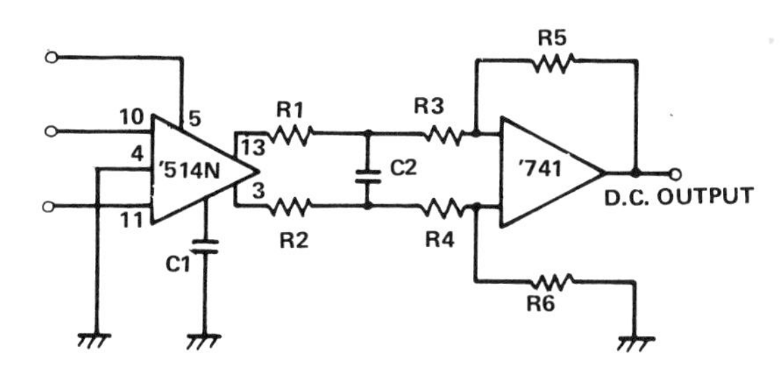

FIGURE 23. A.C. Sensor Amplifier

Frequency Modulation Discriminators

The circuit shown in Figure 24 shows how the double balanced mixer may be used as a frequency discriminator.

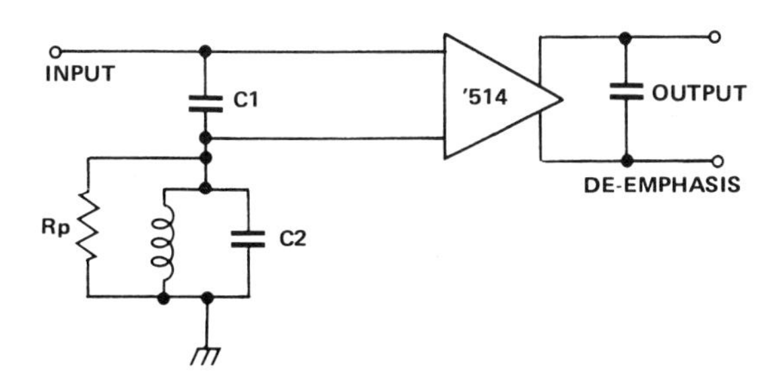

FIGURE 24. Frequency Discriminator

The action of the tuned circuit and C1 is to produce a 90° phase shift between the inputs at the centre frequency. Under these conditions the net output from the device is zero. A change of input frequency will result in a change of phase from the 90°. Thus the device will give an output with variation of input frequency. The signal level at both inputs must be of sufficient amplitude to ensure that limiting occurs. The design of the external coupling network must take into account the input impedance of the oscillator and RF input. The A. M. rejection properties of the device are inherently good at the centre of the characteristic even if the inputs are not limiting, but unless limiting occurs the rejection properties fall off away from centre as in the Travis and Foster-Seeley discriminators. Indeed, the output voltage developed is zero under quadrature input conditions. The advantages of the double balanced configuration are that any low frequency components at the limited output due say to asymmetry in the limiter circuits is cancelled at the output – also the output pulses occur at twice the input frequency and this eases smoothing requirements and reduces possible feedback.

Figure 25 shows an experimental discriminator operating in the 38 MHz region. The oscillator input is tapped down the tuned circuit by a capacitive divider, reflecting roughly 1kΩ across the circuit. Figure 26 shows the response of the circuit with an input voltage level of 100mV r.m.s.

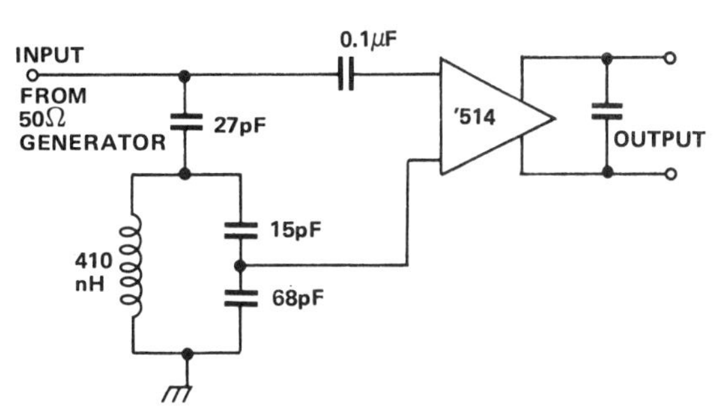

FIGURE 25. Frequency Discriminator Operating at 38 MHz

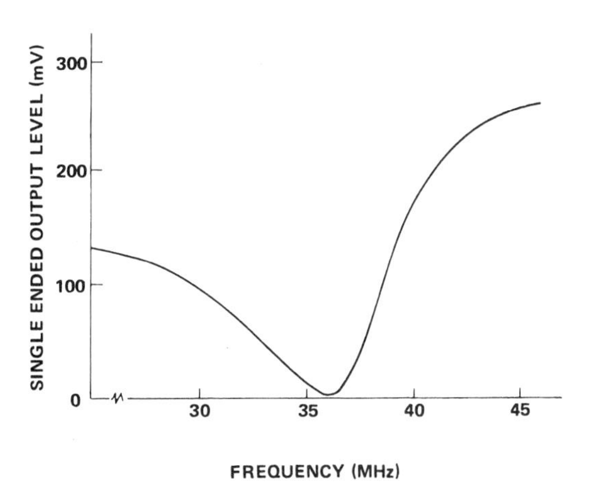

FIGURE 26. Frequency Discriminator Characteristic

Product Detectors

Because the double balanced mixer operates in a linear mode as a voltage multiplier it may be used as a product detector for the reception of single sideband signals. Consider the input signal from the intermediate frequency stages in the receiver to be:–

$e_1 = E_1 \cos(\omega_1 + \omega_2)t$

and the local oscillator to be:

$e_2 = E_2 \cos(\omega_1)t$

if the device acts as a multiplier the output voltage will be:–

$e_0 = KE_1 . E_2 . [\cos(\omega_1)t] . [\cos(\omega_1 + \omega_2)t]$

where K is a constant gain. Now:–

$\cos(\omega_1 + \omega_2)t = \cos\omega_1 t . \cos\omega_2 t - \sin\omega_1 t . \sin\omega_2 t$

and

$e_0 = K' [\cos^2\omega_1 t . \cos\omega_2 t - \cos\omega_1 t . \sin\omega_1 t . \sin\omega_2 t]$

now:

$$\cos^2\omega_1 t = \frac{\cos 2\omega_1 t + 1}{2}$$

and

$$\cos\omega_1 t . \sin\omega_1 t = \frac{\sin 2\omega_1 t}{2}$$

$$e_0 = K' \left[\left(\frac{\cos 2\omega_1 t + 1}{2}\right) . (\cos\omega_2 t) - \frac{\sin 2\omega_1 t . \sin\omega_2 t}{2} \right]$$

$$e_0' = \frac{K'}{2} (\cos 2\omega_1 t . \cos\omega_2 t - \sin 2\omega_1 t \sin\omega_2 t + \cos\omega_2 t)$$

now

$\cos 2\omega_1 t . \cos\omega_2 t - \sin 2\omega_1 t . \sin\omega_2 t = \cos(2\omega_1 + \omega_2)t$

$$\therefore e_0 = \frac{K'}{2} . [\cos(2\omega_1 + \omega_2)t + \cos\omega_2 t]$$

i.e. the sum of a high frequency and a low frequency component. With the appropriate filters the high frequency component can be removed leaving

$$e_0 = \frac{K'}{2} . \cos\omega_2 t$$

The SN56/76514 can also be used for reception of double sideband suppressed carrier signals. Here the phase tolerance is far smaller than in the single sideband case, but if the injected carrier phase is correct, detection will be achieved with low distortion. The device is useful as a product detector as it gives good isolation between ports which results in a minimal amount of injected carrier – affecting the A.G.C. line.

Synchronous Detector

In the case of the synchrodyne detector, where the signal received is a normal amplitude modulated one (full carrier and two sidebands), the injected carrier must be exactly in phase with the carrier. Great interest has recently been shown in this method of detection, a revival of the method proposed by D. G. Tucker in 1947. The requirements for such a system involve a zero-crossing detector to achieve the correct carrier phase relationship. Figure 27 shows the system in principle, with the reference derived from the input signal. This method of detection is widely used in integrated circuits intended for consumer applications, e.g. television video detectors.

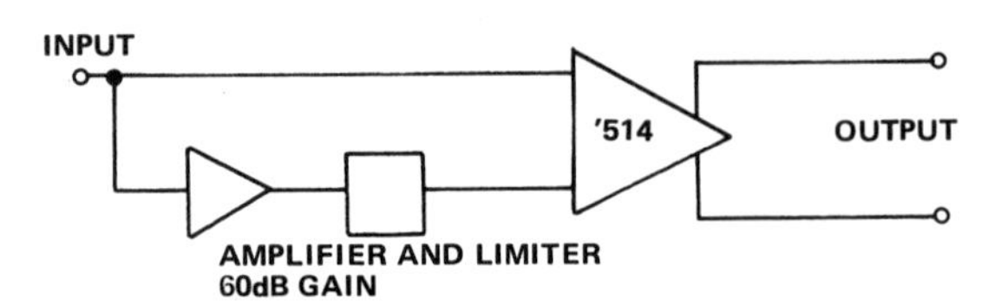

FIGURE 27 Synchronous Detector

The amplifier/limiter combination acts as a zero-crossing detector for the carrier, and gives a square wave output to act as a reference for the double balanced mixer, which operates as a synchronous demodulator. The limiter clips the signal symmetrically to about 1% of the carrier peak level or less. The system will operate with good linearity up to 95% modulation depth or higher.

Pulse Width Modulator

The double balanced mixer may be used as a pulse width modulator. This is shown in Figure 28 The modulation and carrier are applied to the decouple 2 and RF inputs respectively. The mixer operates as a zero-crossing detector. Potentiometer RV2 operates with a large offset which controls the amplitude of the output pulse width modulated envelope. Potentiometer RV1 has a far smaller offset and controls the symmetry of the width modulation. Figure 29 shows the unmodulated output pulse (top trace @ 0·5V/division), the pulse width modulated at 1 kHz (centre trace @ 0·5V/division) and the ramp carrier waveform (bottom trace @ 1V/division). Ideally the carrier would be a sawtooth waveform with very short flyback and rest times. Use of an ideal waveform would result in a symmetrical output pulse duty cycle and the ability to

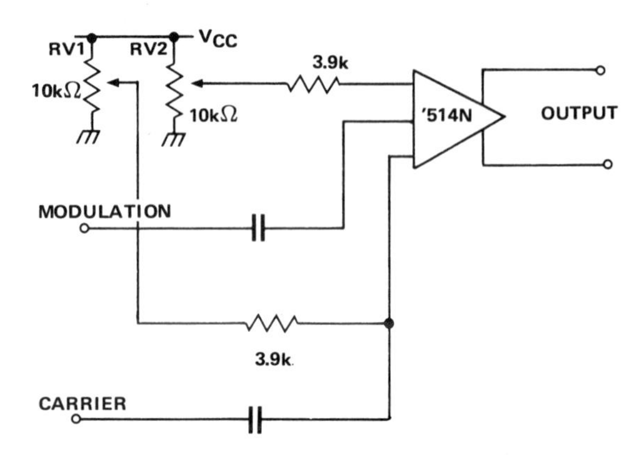

FIGURE 28. Pulse Width Modulator

modulate to a larger depth. Figure 30 shows the output waveform when integrated by a 0·1 μF capacitor superimposed on the input waveform. The slope of the pulse waveform will depend upon the degree to which the device is overdriven.

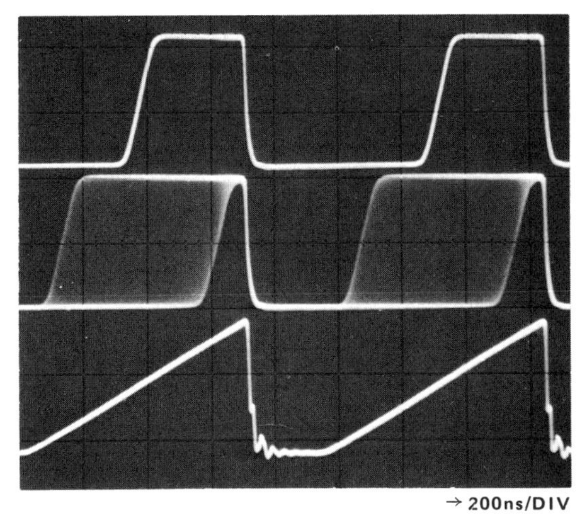

→ 200ns/DIV

FIGURE 29. Operating Waveforms of Pulse Width Modulator

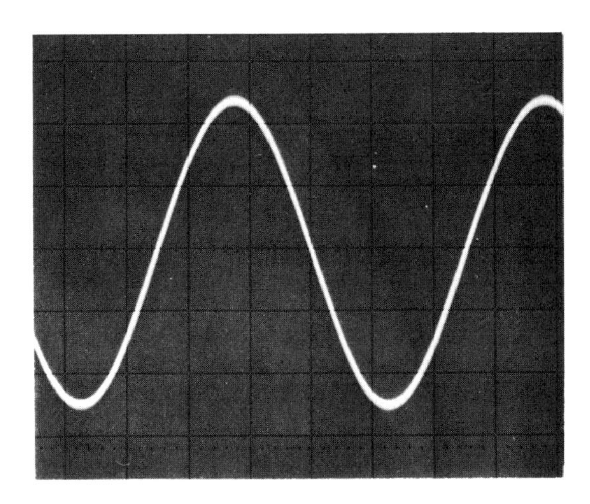

FIGURE 30. Input and Integrated Output of P.W.M. Superimposed

X AN AUDIO POWER AMPLIFIER

by Jonathan Dell

The last special purpose bipolar integrated circuit to be described in this section is an audio power amplifier. Solid state audio amplifiers have evolved from completely discrete designs[1], to designs where integrated, linear, operational amplifiers are used as drivers for the power stages[2]. However, it is now possible to integrate the complete audio power stage and this technique is described in this chapter with reference to the SN76006, 6W power amplifier.

CIRCUIT DESCRIPTION

Figure 1 shows a simplified schematic of the SN76006 integrated audio power amplifier which follows closely typical low frequency amplifier techniques. Transistors VT1 and VT2 form a differential amplifier, the emitters of which are fed by a current source transistor VT3. The differential current in the collectors of VT1 and 2 are combined into a single ended signal in the network comprising the diode D1 and transistor VT4. The current sink, transistor VT4, is modulated by the current in the collector of transistor VT1 – the current change in the collector of transistor VT2 is the sum of current changes in the two arms of the differential stage. This signal is fed into the base of a Darlington stage VT5 and 6. The main reason for using a Darlington connection at this point is to ensure a high impedance at the base of transistor VT5 so that the open loop frequency response of the amplifier can be controlled by the Miller capacitor C1. This Darlington stage runs in class A with a dynamic load, the current source transistor VT7, and develops the drive for the output stage.

A quasi-complementary output stage is used, the pnp device being formed by the connection of transistors VT8, 9 and 10, and the npn by the Darlington connection of transistors VT11 and 12. The quiescent bias current in the output stage is set up by the voltage developed across the diodes D2, 3 and 4. Extra circuits within the IC ensure that this bias current is maintained over a wide range of supply voltage. The two main current source transistors, VT3 and VT7 are set up by the voltage developed across diode D5 by the current flowing in resistor R2.

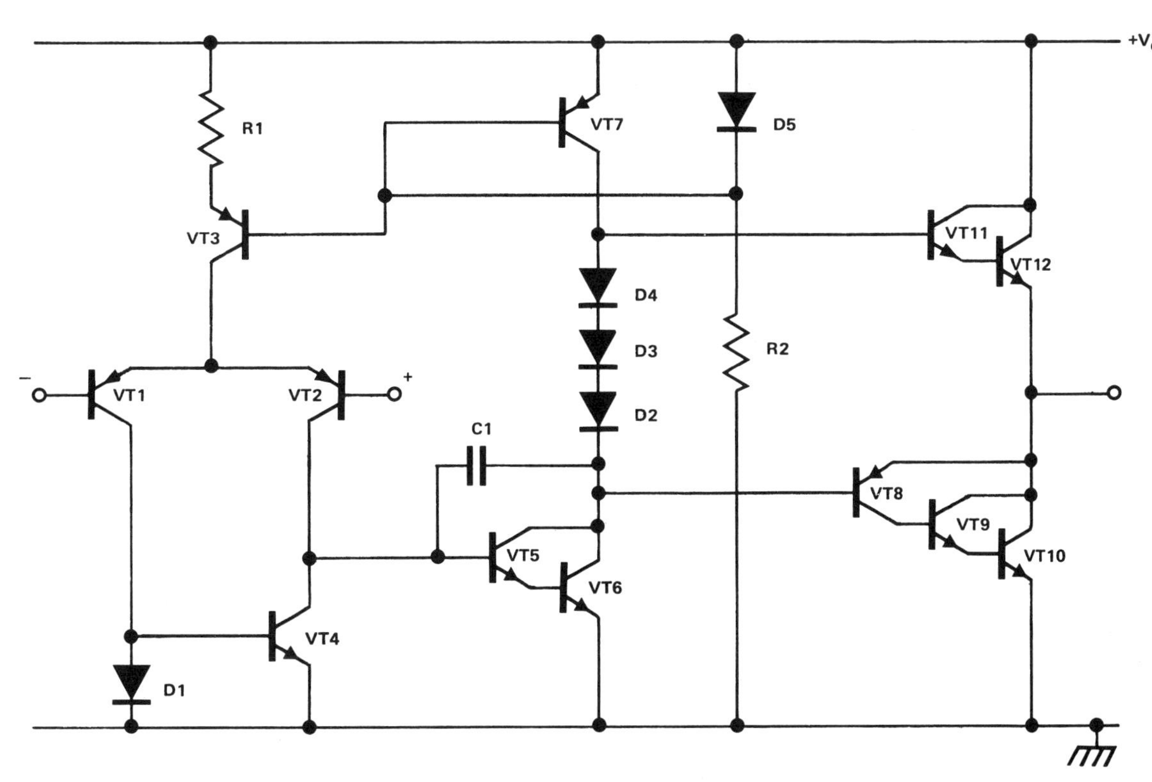

FIGURE 1. Simplified Circuit of '006 Audio Amplifier I.C.

FABRICATION

The first significant difference between audio devices and the familiar operational amplifier appears in their fabrication – the output devices (VT10 and 12) of the audio amplifier have to handle high current, e.g. for an amplifier delivering 6W into an 8Ω load, the peak current is 1.25A; whereas most common operational amplifiers will deliver only 25mA into the load. These high currents call for large devices and a special construction technique to ensure reliable operation.

Figure 2 shows a diagram which represents the relative sizes of an integrated transistor for 5mA and the output transistor for the '006. The diagram represents the metalization pattern on the surface of the IC and the connections to emitter base and collector are indicated. The collector metal connects to the n-type material which passes underneath the whole device area; this is shown by the x-section in Figure 2. The high current transistor is really a large number of the small transistors connected in parallel, this is done so that the high currents are shared evenly over the surface of the device.

A problem arises with large devices of simple construction in that because the device exhibits slightly different characteristics at different points on its surface; current tends to flow preferentially through some areas. These places start to warm up and the characteristics of these areas are further modified to attract more current into them. Catastrophic failure can result if this current build up is not prevented. The parallel connection of a large number of devices is one way to reduce this problem.

Figure 3 shows a general view of a complete audio device and illustrates the size relation between the output device and the rest of the circuit.

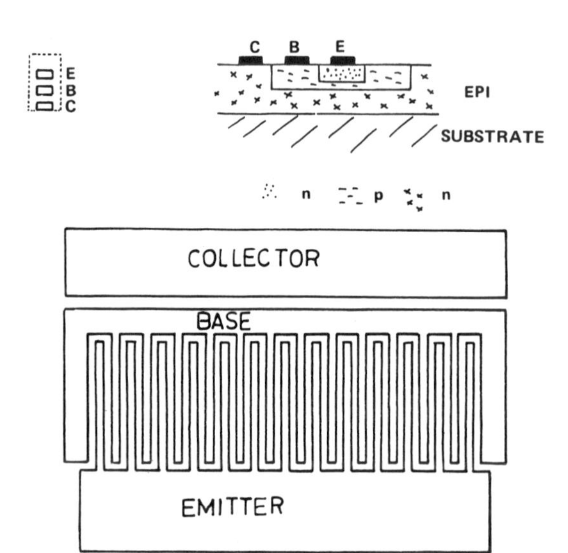

FIGURE 2. Relative Sizes and Construction of Devices in Audio IC.

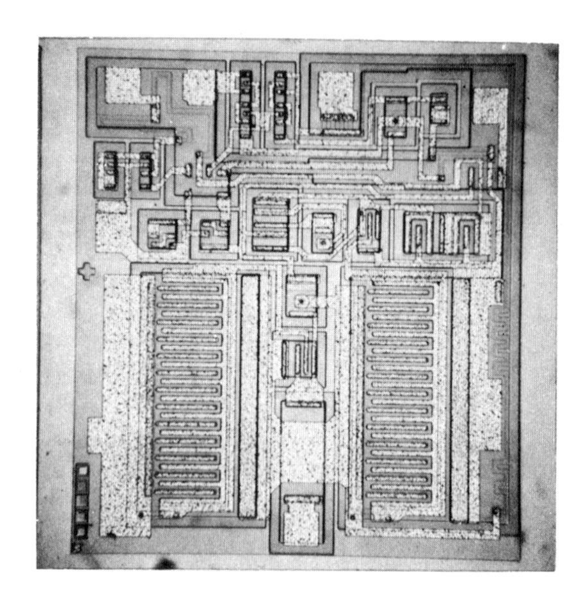

FIGURE 3. General Picture of an Audio Amplifier IC

MOUNTING

The audio amplifier under consideration will generate an appreciable amount of heat internally; for a sinewave output from an amplifier running on 24V and driving an 8Ω load, the maximum internal dissipation is 3·65W. It is clear that some method of removing the heat from the audio IC must be provided. The '006 is mounted in a package similar in design to the common 16 pin, N-pack, but the two centre pins are replaced by a broad lead which runs right across the device, as shown at Figure 4(a). The device is bonded directly onto this lead which is coupled to a heat sink outside the case. When the device heats up, the silicon expands and if the lead material does not expand at the same rate a shear stress will be created in the bond and the device will crack. To avoid this problem a special sandwich material, made of copper and Kovar, is used for the lead. This has good thermal conductivity and a thermal expansion coefficient closely matched to that of silicon. When the leads are cut and formed the wide leads are bent upwards, as shown in Figure 4(b), and in a subsequent stage they are crimped into an extruded aluminium fin which provides a large surface area to radiate the heat away. Figure 4(c) shows the fully assembled device with its heat sink.

POWER DISSIPATION

For a sinusoidal signal an amplifier with a supply voltage of V_{CC}, an output signal of V (volts r.m.s.) and load resistance of R (ohms), the internal power dissipation can be calculated from the equation:-

$$P_D = \frac{V_{CC}.V}{\sqrt{2}.R_L\pi} - \frac{V^2}{2R_L}$$

FIGURE 4. Assembly Steps for I.C.

For a fixed supply, by differentiating, the maximum internal dissipation is found to occur when

$$V = \frac{V_{CC}}{\sqrt{2}\cdot\pi}$$

and the internal dissipation under these conditions is then

$$P_D\,(max) = \frac{V_{CC}^2}{2\cdot\pi^2\cdot R_L}$$

Figure 5 shows the derating of the maximum internal dissipation with increasing ambient temperature. This applies when the device is mounted in an exposed situation. When in an enclosed situation the device should be set up with a known internal dissipation and the case temperature measured when equilibrium is reached. From the fact that the thermal resistance between junction and case is about 12°C/W, the chip temperature can be calculated. The device should not be operated with a junction temperature higher than 150°C – if this temperature is exceeded failure will eventually result.

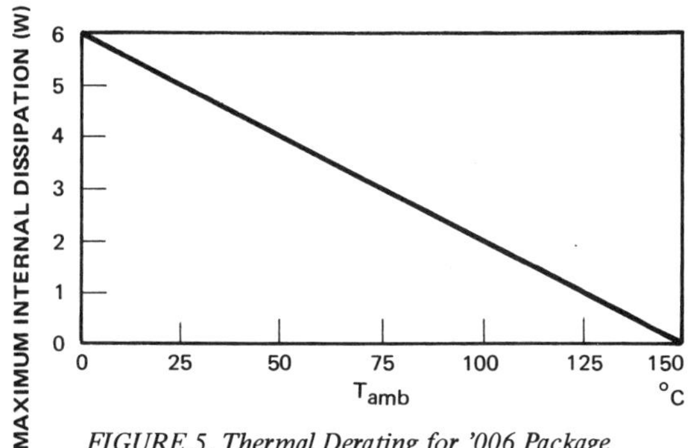

FIGURE 5. Thermal Derating for '006 Package

APPLICATIONS

General Arrangement

Figure 6 shows a diagram of the simplest connection of the '006 for an audio amplifier application. The gain of the amplifier is determined, as long as the reactance of capacitor C1 is very small compared with resistor R2, by the ratio of resistors R1 and R2 according to the equation below:-

$$G = \frac{R1 + R2}{R2} \text{ or } = 20 \log_{10} \frac{R1 + R2}{R2} \text{ dB}$$

The low frequency roll-off is determined by the capacitor C1; the 6dB point being the frequency at which the reactance of capacitor C1 is equal to the resistance of resistor R2.

$$f = \frac{1}{2.\pi.C1.R1}$$

The high frequency roll off is determined by the high frequency roll off incorporated within the IC.

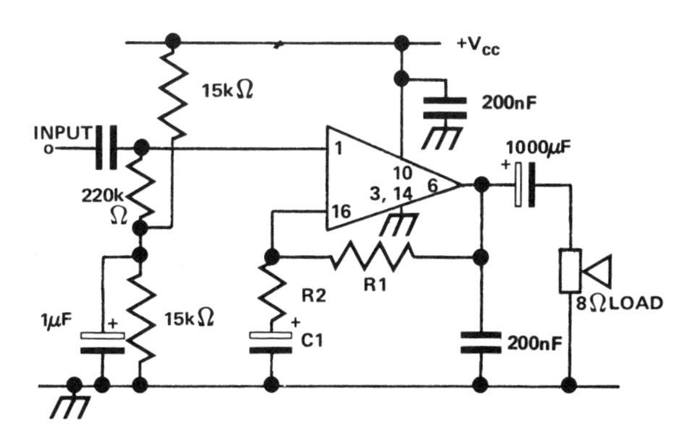

FIGURE 6. Simple Application of '006

Figure 7 shows the open loop frequency response of the unloaded amplifier and the actual frequency response of the loaded amplifier at various settings of the closed loop gain. In all cases the supply was 24V and the load resistance 8Ω.

In order to ensure stability in the audio amplifier connection it is recommended that a 0.2μF is connected directly from the output pin (6) to ground, and between the supply pin (10) and ground, both components being positioned as close as possible to the I.C.

Alternative Supply Configurations

The '006 can be operated satisfactorily with negative or split supply lines. Figure 8 shows the circuit of an amplifier with negative supply. Care must be taken to ensure good decoupling between the negative supply line and the common rail.

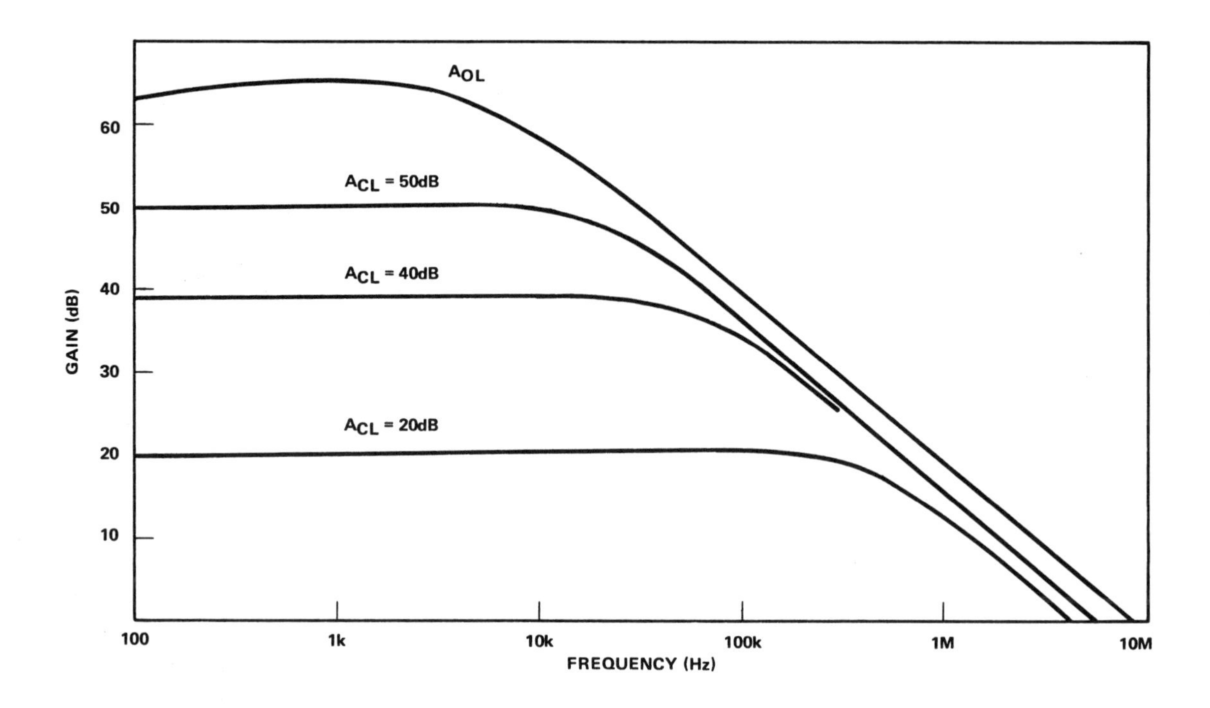

FIGURE 7. Frequency Response of the '006

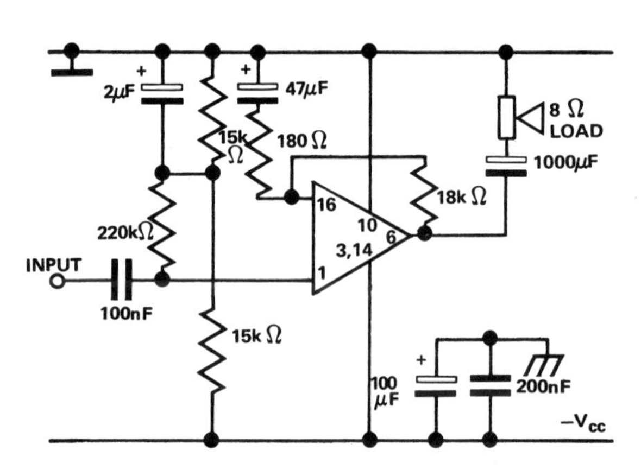

FIGURE 8. Amplifier with Negative Supply

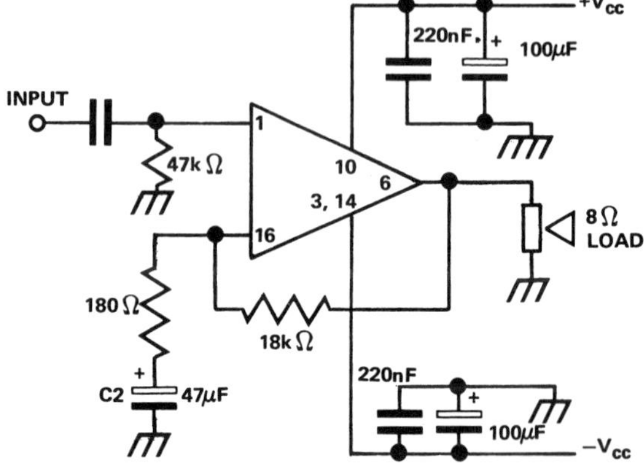

FIGURE 9. Amplifier with Split Supply Lines

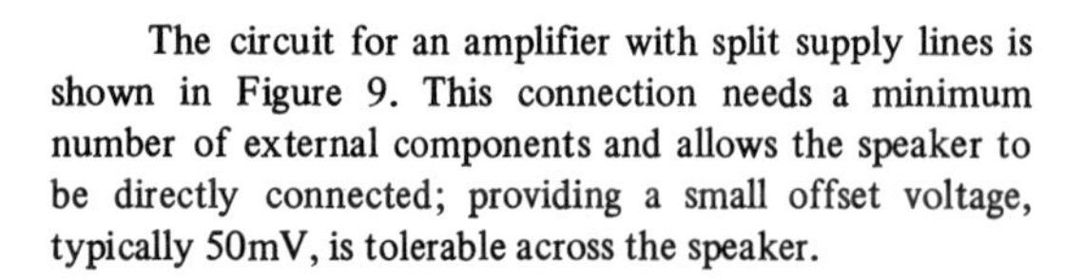

The circuit for an amplifier with split supply lines is shown in Figure 9. This connection needs a minimum number of external components and allows the speaker to be directly connected; providing a small offset voltage, typically 50mV, is tolerable across the speaker.

Capacitor C2 is included so that the offset is not amplified by a high gain at d.c. Again in this configuration it is important to ensure good decoupling between the supply lines and ground.

Addition of Filters

Figures 10 and 11 show how high and low pass filters can be incorporated into the amplifier circuit. The values used here were calculated from the equations:-

Damping factor $\zeta = \sqrt{\frac{R1}{R2}}$ and cut off frequency

$f_o = \frac{1}{2\pi C\sqrt{R1.R2}}$ for a high pass filter [3] and

$\zeta = \sqrt{\frac{C1}{C2}}$ and $f_o = \frac{1}{2\pi R\sqrt{C1.C2}}$ for a low pass filter [4].

These responses are suitable for, respectively, rumble and scratch filtering in an audio system as shown in Figures 12 and 13.

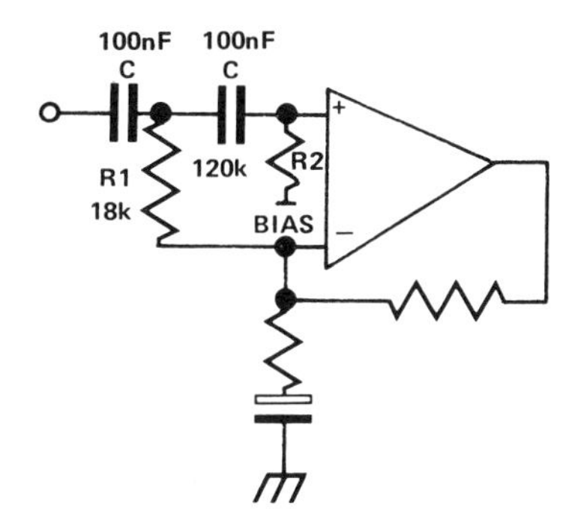

FIGURE 10. High Pass Filter

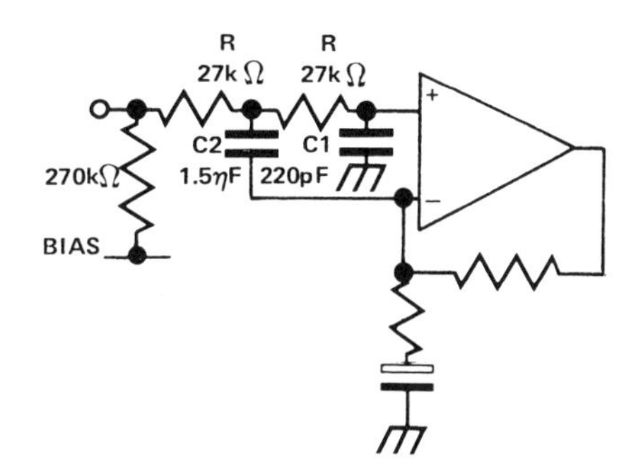

FIGURE 11. Low Pass Filter

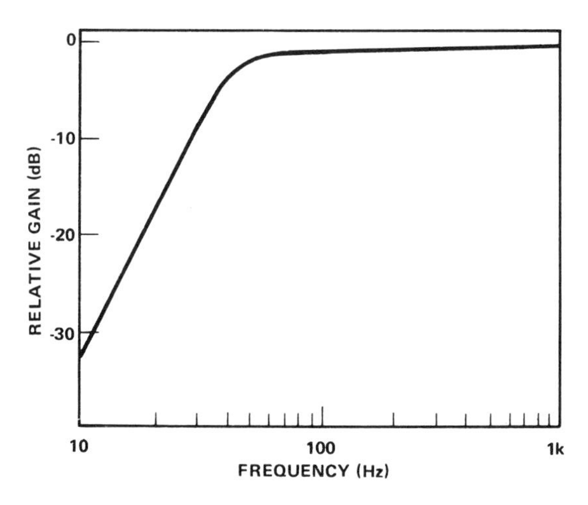

FIGURE 12. Rumble Filter Response

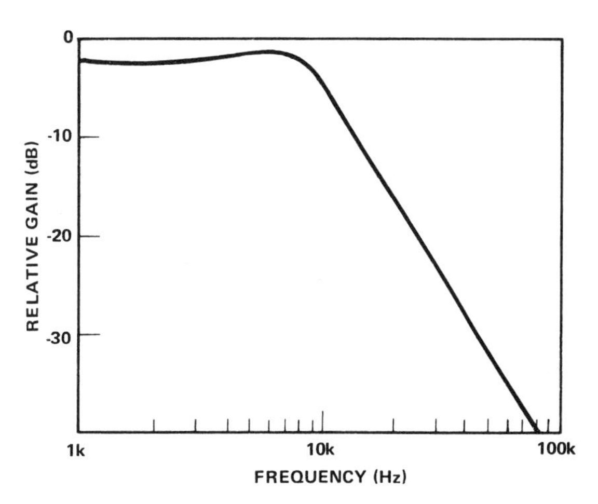

FIGURE 13. Scratch Filter Response

The actual responses deviate slightly from their theoretical shape because of the modifying effect of the feedback path impedance. By incorporating a rumble filter in the early stages of an amplifier system large amplitude, low frequency signals which give rise to transient distortions, are avoided. Therefore, such a filter will not normally be associated with the output stage as shown here.

CHARACTERISATION

The parameters governing the limiting performance of the '006 amplifier are shown in Table 1.

Table 1

ABSOLUTE MAXIMUM RATINGS	
SUPPLY VOLTAGE	28V
REPETITIVE PEAK OUTPUT CURRENT	1.5A
INTERNAL POWER DISSIPATION	5W (For $T_A = 25^\circ C$)

Output Power

For an 8Ω load the maximum output power is limited to 9W, and the maximum internal dissipation, with a 28V supply, is just under 5W. Figure 14 shows the typical

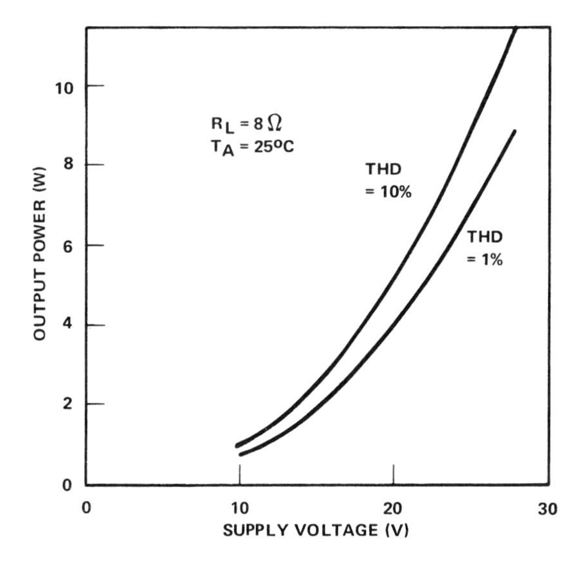

FIGURE 14. Typical Power Output Variation with Supply Voltage

variation of output power with supply voltage. A total harmonic distortion, THD, of 1% represents the situation just before 'clipping' sets in. For a 4Ω load resistance the maximum repetitive output current sets a limit of 4·5W on the maximum output power. The graph of typical output power variation with supply voltage for a 4Ω load, Figure 15, shows that the supply must be limited to about 17V. Under these conditions the maximum internal dissipation will be 3·7W. Optimum performance on low supplies depends on the correct biasing at the output of the I.C., so the effect of input bias currents (typically 1μA) on the bias network must be taken into account.

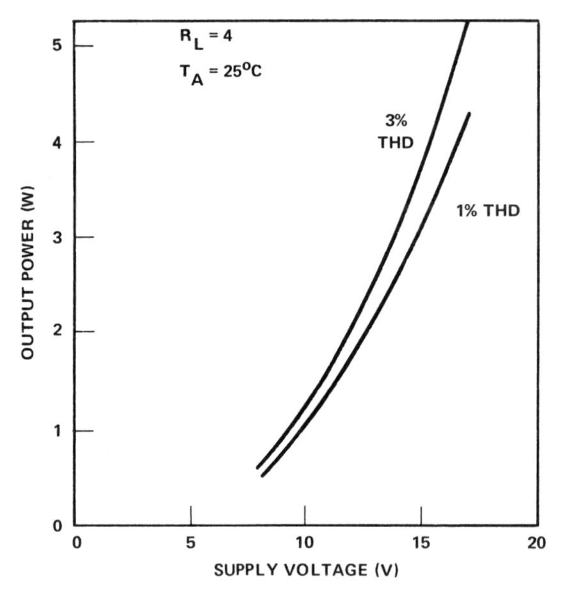

FIGURE 15. Typical Power Input Variation with Supply Voltage

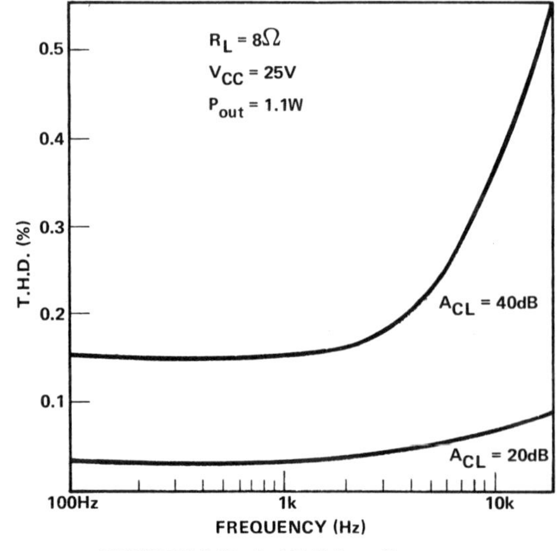

FIGURE 16. Typical T.H.D. vs Frequency

Figure 16 shows a graph of T.H.D. against frequency for two different settings of the closed loop gain (A_{CL}). In the case of an A_{CL} = 40dB, the distortion figure is degraded as soon as the open loop gain (see Figure 7) starts to fall off. If the amount of feedback round the amplifier is increased this effect is greatly reduced and, for a closed loop gain of 20dB, the T.H.D. can be held below 0.1%.

Output Noise

The noise output voltage on the '006 is guaranteed not to exceed 2mV rms when the measurement bandwidth is 40Hz to 15kHz and the source resistance is 10kΩ. Figure 17 shows that the noise voltage is typically much less than this value and that it rises steeply once the source resistance is increased above about 50kΩ.

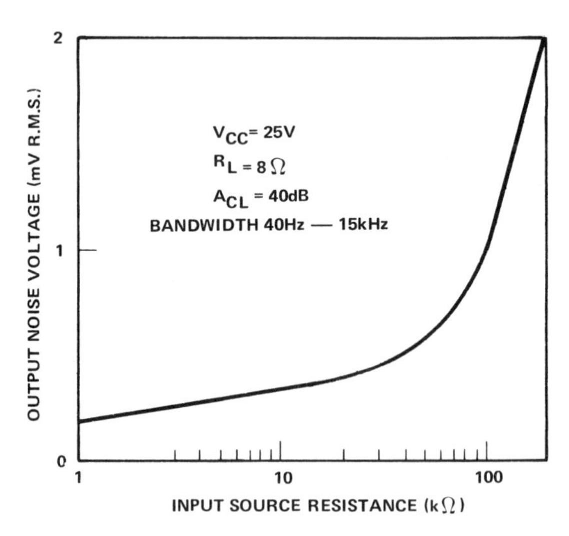

FIGURE 17. Typical Output Noise Voltage vs Input Source Resistance

REFERENCES

1. B. L. Norris, Editor, *Semiconductor Circuit Design*, Vol. I, Texas Instruments Ltd., pp. 161 – 214, April 1972.
2. B. L. Norris, Editor, *Semiconductor Circuit Design*, Vol. II, Texas Instruments Ltd., Chapter XVI, pp. 159 – 172, April 1973.
3. B. L. Norris, Editor, *Semiconductor Circuit Design*, Vol. II, Texas Instruments Ltd., pp. 138 and 160, April 1973.
4. B. L. Norris, Editor, *Semiconductor Circuit Design*, Vol. II, Texas Instruments Ltd., pp. 138 – 9, 163, April 1973.

SECTION 3.

FIELD EFFECT TRANSISTORS

XI THEORY AND OPERATION

by
Alan Chappell

The concept of a field-effect transistor (FET) pre-dates the bi-polar transistor. Just after the Second World War, researchers in semiconductors at Bell Laboratories were trying to develop a semiconductor analog of the vacuum tube. Their first attempts produced a device that is known today as the 'induced channel' or 'insulated gate' field-effect transistor. In this device a thin film of germanium and a metal plate form the two plates of a capacitor, and a channel of conduction is induced along the surface of the germanium by the application of a voltage to the plates of the capacitor. The prototype device failed to yield predicted results because of surface problems. It was their research into these surface problems that led Bardeen and Brattain to the discovery of transistor action. In 1952, Shockley described two field-effect devices in which the conducting channel was inside the semiconductor, removed from the surface. These two devices were the so-called analogue transistor, and, the subject of this section, the field-effect transistor, (initially the unipolar FET).

Unipolar field-effect transistors were first produced commercially in the United States in 1960. Since their introduction, development has been rapid and a large number of companies are producing versions of this device and its modern derivatives such as the MOSFET and MOS integrated circuits (as described in Section 1).

Initially the FET proved most useful in two areas – low-noise applications, and high input impedance applications (because the input terminal is a back-biased diode). However nowadays it is also widely used in RF applications, switching or 'chopping' circuits, and sample and hold techniques.

THEORY

As the MOSFET was described in Chapter I, the narrative in this chapter, although often applicable to the MOSFET, is particular to the junction field effect transistor (JFET) unless otherwise stated. A FET is essentially a semiconductor current path whose resistance is controlled by applying an electric field perpendicular to the current. The electric field results from reverse biasing a pn junction. When a pn junction is reverse biased a 'depletion' or space-charge layer develops on both sides of the junction. That is, the current carriers on either side of the junction are swept across and away from the junction, leaving regions that contain a net charge but no free current carriers except those generated by heat. The current carrier density determines how well a semiconductor will conduct current; therefore, the space charge region on either side of a pn junction will be very low in conductivity.

Resistance of a Semiconductor Bar

Consider a bar of semiconductor silicon crystal having the dimensions shown in Figure 1, excess impurity concentration N, and ohmic (non-rectifying) contacts at each end. The approximate resistance R_0 between terminals S and D is:

$$R_O = \frac{L}{(q\mu)NWT}$$

Where: μ = majority carrier mobility
q = electron charge

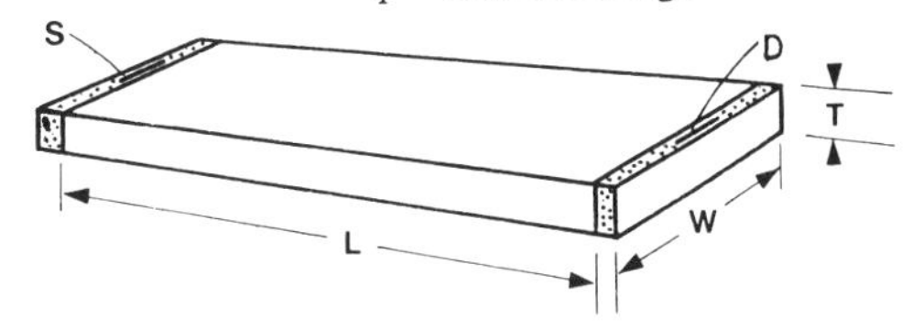

FIGURE 1. Diagrammatic Representation of Semiconductor Bar.

The factor $q\mu N$ in the denominator is a good approximation for the conductivity σ of the semiconductor material if the doping level is such that the minority carrier density is negligible. Since the dimensions of the bar are fixed, the resistance of the bar must be controlled by controlling the conductivity.

Silicon Bar with PN Junctions

Figure 2 shows a n-type bar of silicon which has had p-type impurities introduced into opposite sides, forming pn junctions. The two p regions are usually electrically connected and a bias voltage (V_{GS}) is normally applied to the two junctions. The p regions are called *gates* and the space between the gates is called the *channel.* The resistance R_0 is modulated by depleting carriers from parts of the channel.

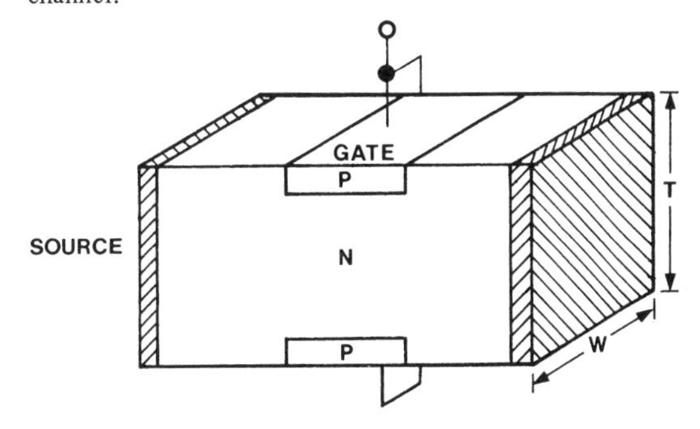

FIGURE 2. Diagrammatic Representation of a JFET (n Channel)

Another view is that the effective thickness of the bar in Figure 1 can be changed by a transverse electric field produced by the bias voltage V_{GS}. If the doping level in the gates is purposely very large compared to that in the channel, the carrier-depleted or 'space-charge' zone will extend principally into the channel. Figure 3 is a graph of the net charge density, electric field and potential through a cross-section of the channel for a given V_{GS}. Uniform charge density and ideal step junctions are assumed. The shaded areas above and below the zero concentration axis are equal, because the depleted regions on either side of the junction must contain equal net charge. The electric field and potential plots of Figure 3(b) and 3(c) are obtained by performing successive integrations.

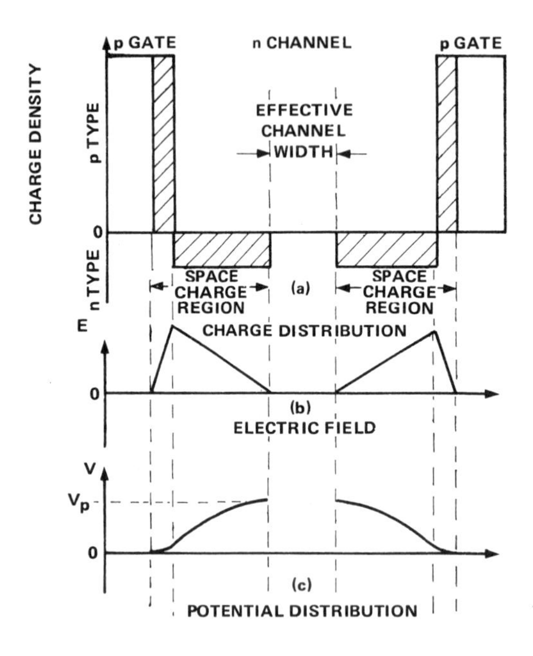

FIGURE 3. Cross Section of Channel for Given V_{GS}.

Behaviour of Space Charge Layer with Channel Current

The simple FET structure of Figure 2 is reproduced in Figures 4 and 6 to describe the behaviour of the space charge layer with an applied drain-to-source voltage. In Figure 4 as the voltage V_{DS} is increased from zero to small values, the current rises linearly. At small currents, the channel between the drain and source behaves as a linear resistor, but as current increases the parts of the channel near the junctions become significantly negative with respect to the source terminal. Since the p-type gates are connected externally to the source, the junctions are reverse biased and the space-charge layers are extended into the n-type channel, lowering the channel conductance. The electrical behaviour of the structure shown in Figure 4 is plotted in Figure 5. Note that the relatively constant slope at low voltages becomes less linear with increasing applied voltage. At some value of V_{DS} the space charge layers,

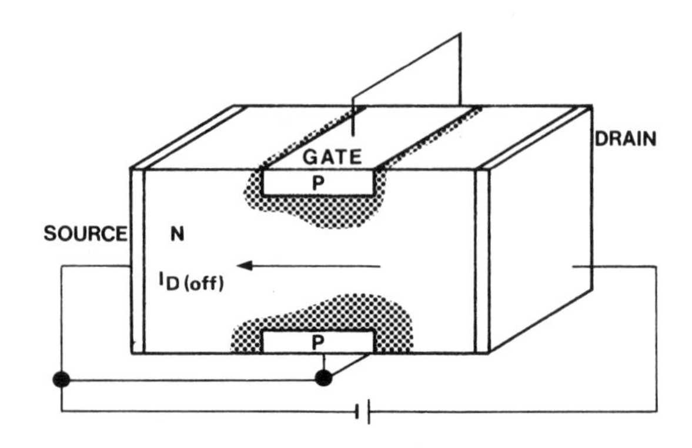

FIGURE 4. Application of Drain-to-Source Voltage

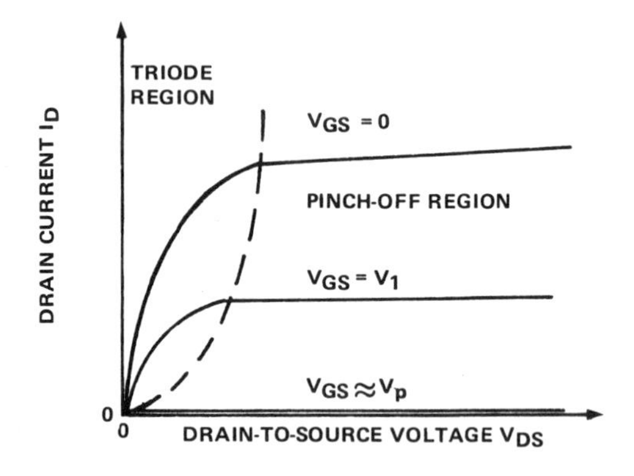

FIGURE 5. Electrical Behaviour

shown by the shaded areas in Figure 4, extend into the channel until they almost meet, this corresponds approximately to the voltage at the 'knee' of the $V_{GS} = 0$ curve in Figure 5. Shockley[1]. called this voltage the *pinch-off* voltage. Above the pinch-off voltage the drain current saturates; i.e., it increases very little for further increases in drain-to-source voltage. The fact that reverse bias on the pn junction is greatest at the drain end gives the space-charge layers their characteristic wedge shape. Most of the potential drop in the channel is confined to the short span where the space-charge layers nearly meet; this is the active or control part of the device. The remainder of the drain-to-source voltage is dropped across the bulk channel resistance between the two terminals and this active part.

In Figure 6 a fixed reverse bias, $V_{GS} = V1$, is applied to the gates. With no channel current, there is no electric field component tangent to the junction and the space-charge layer extends uniformly part of the way into the channel, region A say. When a drain current flows, both tangential and normal components of electric field are present, causing the wedge-shaped space-charge region B. The ratio of the thickness of regions depends on the magnitude of the external reverse bias; higher values of V_{GS} increase the thickness of A relative to B. Obviously, less channel current is required to produce pinch-off as V_{GS}

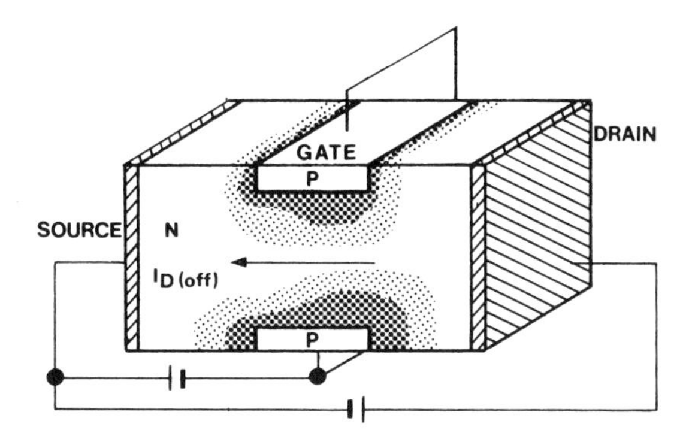

FIGURE 6. Reversed Biased Channel

increases. In Figure 5, the V_{GS} = V1 curve has the same shape as the zero bias curve except that pinch-off occurs at a lower drain-to-source voltage and a lower drain current. The reverse bias on the junction required to bring the two space-charge layers together is the sum of the externally applied bias V_{GS} and the internal self bias due to current flow through the channel resistance. From this it seems that the external bias required to bring the two space-charge layers together should be capable of reducing the drain current to the reverse saturation current of the pn junction. However, this pinch-off condition never occurs. In practice, the drain current approaches some irreducible minimum greater than the diode reverse saturation current.

Figure 5 is part of a set of curves that look remarkably like the output characteristics of a pentode valve, the drain, source, and gate terminals being analogous to the plate, cathode, and grid terminals respectively. Thus although the FET has only three terminals, its electrical behaviour is closer to the pentode valve than to the triode valve.

Operation in the Pinch-Off Region

The operation of the device in the mode or pre-pinch-off region e.g. as a switch (or 'chopper') is described in chapter XIV. Use of the FET as an active element operating in the pinch-off region for linear applications has been extensive. Therefore it is necessary to arrive at equations which define the operation of the device in this region reasonably accurately to allow them to be used to design circuits. At this point it is convenient to re-define the pinch-off voltage V_p as that gate-to-source voltage which should reduce the drain current to the reverse saturation current of the gate-channel diode. In practice, this voltage must be extrapolated from the behavior of drain current with gate-to-source voltage at drain currents significantly greater than zero.

The expression for the saturation drain current as a function of gate-to-source voltage derived by Shockley[1] is:-

$$I_D = I_{DSS}\left[1 - 3\frac{V_{GS}}{V_p} + 2\left(\frac{V_{GS}}{V_p}\right)^{3/2}\right] \quad . \quad . \quad (1)$$

The term I_{DSS} is the saturation drain current with zero gate-to-source bias voltage at any drain-to-source voltage in the pinch-off region below breakdown. Equation (1) was derived assuming a step junction, and is correct for both p-channel and n-channel devices since V_{GS} and V_p carry the same sign. The plot of Equation (1) in Figure 7 is the common-source forward transfer characteristic of the FET analogous to the common-cathode transconductance curve of a vacuum tube. This curve was in good agreement (except at low I_D) with transfer curves of practical FETs made by the old alloy process; alloy junctions closely approximate step junctions. Equation (1) could be modified to take into account the diode reverse saturation and leakage current, I_{GSS}:

$$I_D = (I_{DSS} - I_{GSS})\left[1 - 3\frac{V_{GS}}{V_p} + 2\left(\frac{V_{GS}}{V_p}\right)^{3/2}\right] + I_{GSS} \quad (2)$$

The disagreement between this expression and the behaviour of practical devices was most marked at very low values of I_D. In practice, I_D cannot be reduced to I_{GSS} by the reverse bias on the gate-to-channel diode; as a result, V_p must be inferred rather than measured directly. V_p can be extrapolated from the measurement of V_{GS} at two or more values of I_D, or by measurement of the slope dI_D/dV_{GS} (forward transconductance), of the transfer curve at some value of V_{GS} (preferably $V_{GS} = 0$).
From Equation (2):

$$\left.\frac{dI_D}{dV_{GS}}\right|_{V_{GS}=0} = -\frac{3}{V_p}(I_{DSS} - I_{GSS}) \quad . \quad . \quad . \quad . \quad . \quad (3)$$

I_{GSS} can usually be neglected when compared to I_{DSS}. Equation (3) implies that a tangent drawn to a transfer curve at $V_{GS} = 0$ as in Figure 7 will intersect the $I_D = 0$ axis at $1/3\ V_p$.

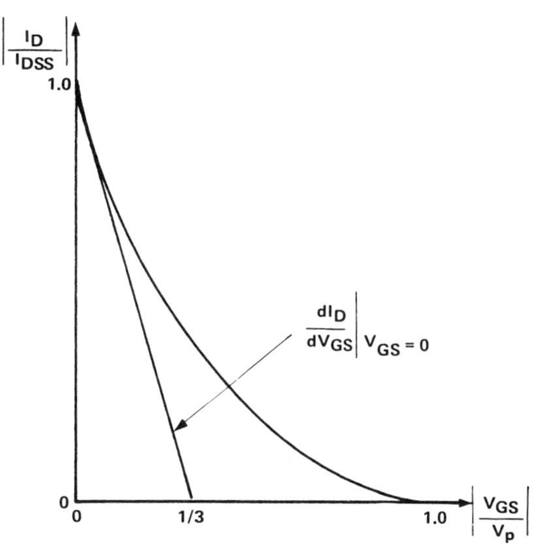

FIGURE 7. Common Source Forward Transfer Characteristic

The derivation of Equation (1) was done with the assumption that carrier mobility remains constant with reverse gate bias, i.e. the longitudinal electric field in the channel does not exceed a critical value (around 600V/cm) above which Ohm's law no longer holds[2]. This assumption was apparently valid for alloy FETs but is not for FETs made by a diffusion process. The longitudinal electric field in the channel of diffused types can exceed 600V/cm, and the carrier mobility then becomes proportional to the square root of the electric field. Dacey and Ross[3] derived an expression for the drain current behaviour with gate-to-source voltage in the pinch-off region for the 'square-root' mobility case:

$$I_D = I_{DSS}\left\{4\left[1-\left(\frac{V_{GS}}{V_p}\right)^{1/2}\right]^3 - 3\left[1-\left(\frac{V_{GS}}{V_p}\right)^{1/2}\right]^4\right\}^{1/2} \quad \ldots\ldots\ldots\ (4)$$

This is a more complicated expression than Equation (1), but it agrees very well with the transfer characteristics of practical diffused type FETs. As in the case of Equation (1), it fails at very low drain currents. An even better approximation to measured transfer curves is given by a simple parabola, properly 'force-fitted' to Equation (4). Figure 8 shows a plot of Equation (4) with the points describing a force-fitted parabola superimposed. The force-fitting technique consists of selecting two points at which the parabola and Equation (4) are forced to coincide. The

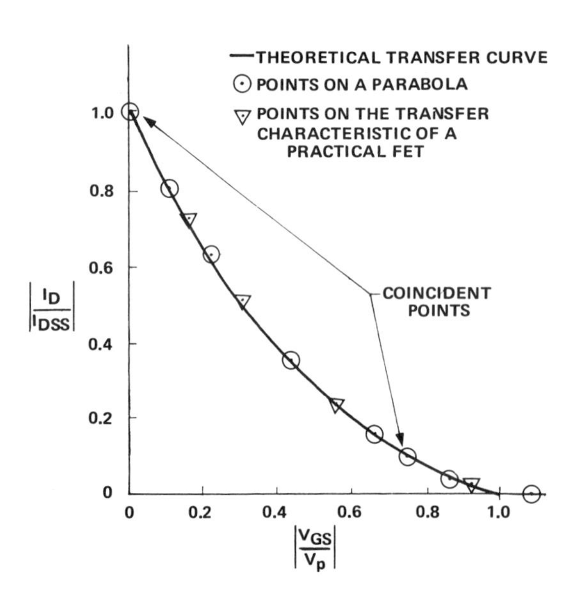

FIGURE 8. Approximating the Transfer Curve With a Parabola

particular points selected, $I_D = I_{DSS}$ and $I_D = 0.1\ I_{DSS}$, give excellent results and are convenient for measurement. The parabola yields a slightly higher V_p than Equation (4), i.e. 1·06/1, but the normalized transfer curve of a typical planar (diffused) FET plotted in Figure 8 shows that the parabola is a better approximation at low currents. The equation of the parabola is:-

$$I_D = I_{DSS}\left(1-\frac{V_{GS}}{V_p}\right)^2 \quad \ldots\ldots\ldots\ (5)$$

Taking into account the effect of I_{GSS}:

$$I_D = (I_{DSS} - I_{GSS})\left(1-\frac{V_{GS}}{V_p}\right)^2 + I_{GSS} \quad \ldots\ (6)$$

Because virtually all FETs are currently made by some type of diffusion, this simple approximation can be a very powerful engineering tool for circuit design.

Low Noise Devices

For low noise high input impedance applications both the bipolar transistor and the MOSFET have severe circuit limitations and generally the most suitable component is the JFET. The bipolar transistor has a very high noise current associated with its base current which is several orders of magnitude worse than that of both the MOSFET and the JFET. The usefulness of the MOSFET for low noise applications is limited by a '1/f' noise voltage below a few MHz. Again, a comparison with the JFET shows the latter to be orders of magnitude better at these frequencies. There are three chief noise mechanisms associated with the JFET: noise current, thermal noise, and '1/f' noise. Depending upon the impedance of the source and the frequency of operation any one or a combination of these noise sources will limit the signal resolution. The noise current of the JFET is determined by the shot noise of the gate leakage current. This is frequency independent and determined by the well known shot noise relationship.:

$$i_n = (2qI_{GS})^{1/2} \quad \ldots\ldots\ldots\ (7)$$

where q is the electronic charge.

A good low leakage JFET, e.g. a BF800, will have a typical noise current of 2.5×10^{-16} A. $Hz^{-1/2}$, compared to a typical bipolar transistor (e.g. 2N3904) of 6×10^{-13} A. $Hz^{-1/2}$, and devices are being developed with noise currents as low as 1×10^{-16} A. $Hz^{-1/2}$

The noise voltage frequency spectrum of the JFET falls into three sections. At low frequencies, the '1/f' or excess noise predominates up to a few kHz where the Johnson or thermal noise in the channel becomes dominant. Above about 200 MHz the gain of the JFET starts to fall due to capacitive coupling and as a consequence the noise voltage increases once again.[4] The generally accepted physical mechanism for the '1/f' or excess noise voltage is generation – recombination centres within the gate depletion region.[5] In the practical case the magnitude of the excess noise component is minimised by careful processing. At frequencies between, say 10kHz and 200 MHz thermal noise is the most significant noise source. The Johnson or thermal noise of the JFET is determined by the noise resistance of the channel[6] and this can be shown to be given by:–

$$R_n \propto \frac{0.65}{y_{fs}} \quad \ldots\ldots\ldots\ (8)$$

where y_{fs} is the gain of the FET. This channel resistance has a noise voltage associated with it which is frequency independent and is given by:-

$$e_n{}^2 = 4.k.T.R.\Delta f \quad \ldots\ldots\ldots\ldots \quad (9)$$

K = Boltzmann's constant
T = absolute temperature
Δf = bandwidth of measurement
Thus from equations (8) and (9),

$$e_n \propto \frac{1}{(y_{fo})^{1/2}} \quad \ldots\ldots\ldots\ldots \quad (10)$$

Hence JFETs designed to have a low thermal noise will also have a high gain. For a FET with gate length of 'L' and width 'W' then it can be shown that:-

$y_{fs} \propto {}^1/_L$
and $y_{fo} \propto W$

In practice the minimum gate length which can be achieved with present production optical alignment techniques is about 2·0 microns. The maximum value of gate width is generally limited by the associated increase in input capacitance. Thus to fit the maximum width gate into the minimum silicon area to get a low noise voltage wafer, e.g. of BF817/8s, an inter-digital structure, as described later, is used. The improvement in thermal noise to be gained from a specific low noise design can be seen by comparing figures for a standard 2N4416 RF FET and a very low noise device such as a BF818, i.e.

	y_{fs}(mS)	e_n – 100kHz (nV.Hz$^{-1/2}$)
2N4416	4·5	1·8
BF818	20	0·85

Devices in development will have noise voltages as low as 0·2nV.Hz$^{-1/2}$.

CONSTRUCTION OF PRACTICAL FETS

JFETs

Virtually all JFETs are fabricated using silicon epitaxial planar technology. A thin epitaxial layer is grown on a low resistivity silicon slice. An isolation diffusion then defines the active device area. The gate diffusion and source/drain diffusions complete the processing apart from the deposition of the contact metallisation pattern.

The most commonly used form of FET is the triode construction shown in Figure 9. Here the top gate diffusion is internally connected to the bottom gate contact via the isolation diffusion. Thus when bias is applied to the gate the channel is pinched from the top and the bottom.

The other method of construction which has more specialised applications is the tetrode form shown in Figure 10. This differs from the triode in that the top and bottom gates are brought out of the device can separately. This structure enables devices to be operated as mixers and can also give improved y_{fs}/C_{iss} ratios.

Low Noise Devices

The design of low noise JFETs provides an insight into the various parameters which influence device performance. As mentioned previously a low gate leakage current is essential for the production of a low noise current FET. In general the gate leakage current is proportional to the periphery of the gate diffusion. In other words the leakage current is a surface rather than a bulk phenomenon. An examination of low noise current JFETs, such as the BF800 in Figure 11, shows them to have very short gates. This will give the minimum gate periphery consistent with certain minimum y_{fs}/e_n requirements. Although a small gate periphery is the major requirement for a low noise current device this is not enough on its own. It is also necessary to ensure that the process conditions are optimised. The critical parameters here being the crystal orientation of the substrate material, doping levels and source, anneal temperatures and the aluminium purity. (It is also worth noting from Figure 11 the small active area necessary for this type of device).

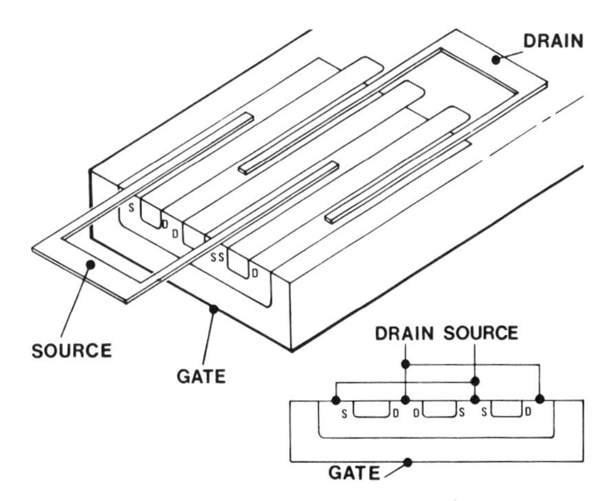

FIGURE 9. JFET With Metallized Contacts

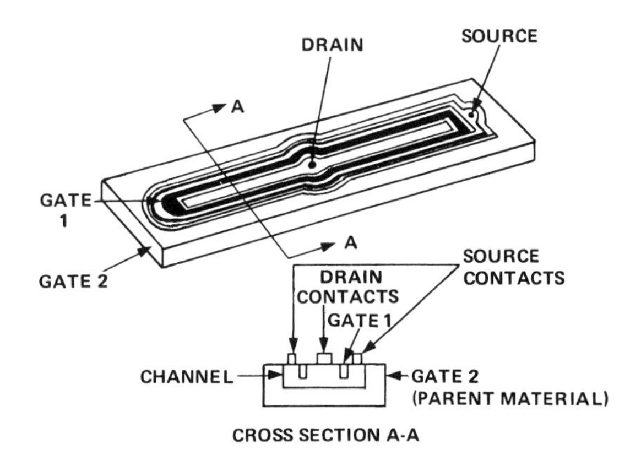

FIGURE 10. Tetrode Form of Construction

FIGURE 11. Photograph of Low Noise Current FET Wafer

The low thermal noise voltage FET is designed to have a high value of y_{fs} as outlined previously. A wide, although of very short length (2 microns), gate is used as can be seen for the BF817/8 shown in Figure 12. The interdigitated structure has been used whereby the gate is split into a series of strips flanked by source and drain contacts. Although it has been stated that a very short gate is necessary to achieve good thermal noise a lengthening of the gate will reduce the '1/f' component. This is at the expense of a reduction in gain and an increase in thermal noise and capacitance.

FIGURE 12. Photograph of Low Noise Voltage FET Wafer

Figure 13 shows an example of how the characteristics of low noise FETs are being improved. This is an experimental device, and has a tetrode structure with a continuous top gate diffusion, metal covered to reduce series resistance. This device has a gain of 120mS and, apart from previously mentioned characteristics, the tetrode can be biased to give up to 20% improvement in thermal noise over a triode FET with the same input capacity.

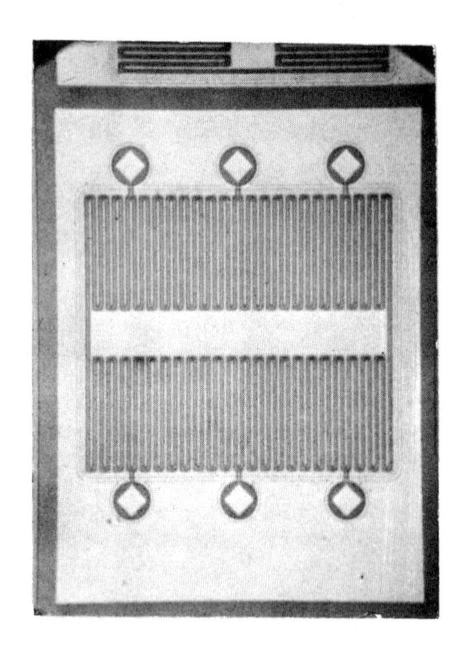

FIGURE 13. Photograph of Very Low Noise Tetrode FET Wafer

MOSFETs

The structure and operation of a MOSFET was described in Chapter I, this being necessary in order to introduce MOS integrated circuits. Figure 14 illustrates again the basic structure of a MOSFET and shows correct biasing in order to induce the p channel.

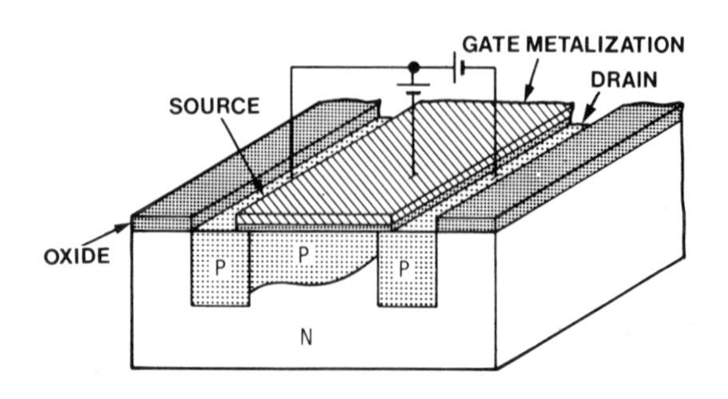

FIGURE 14. Elementary MOSFET with Biasing

When used as RF amplifiers a troublesome FET parameter is the magnitude of the feedback capacitance (or common source reverse transfer capacitance C_{RSS}). This limits the gain and causes instability. The dual gate MOSFET, whose basic structure is shown in Figure 15, has

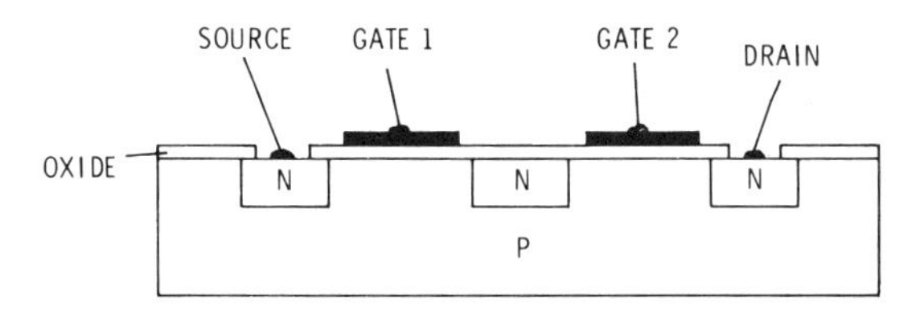

FIGURE 15. Dual Gate MOSFET Structure

an equivalent circuit given in Figure 16. The second FET acts as a shield, and, in a mode analogous to the screen grid in a valve, reduces the C_{rss} by a factor of about 100. This, and for other reasons as mentioned in the next chapter, makes the dual gate MOSFET ideal, therefore, for RF applications. A photograph of a dual gate MOSFET wafer can be seen in Figure 17. The diodes protecting both gates can easily be distinguished.

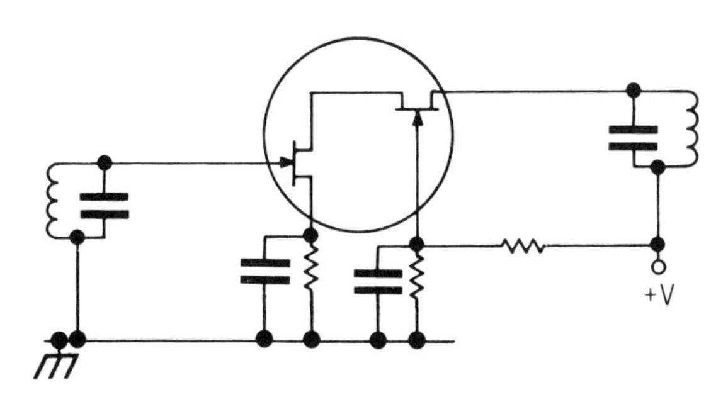

FIGURE 16. Dual Gate MOSFET Equivalent Circuit

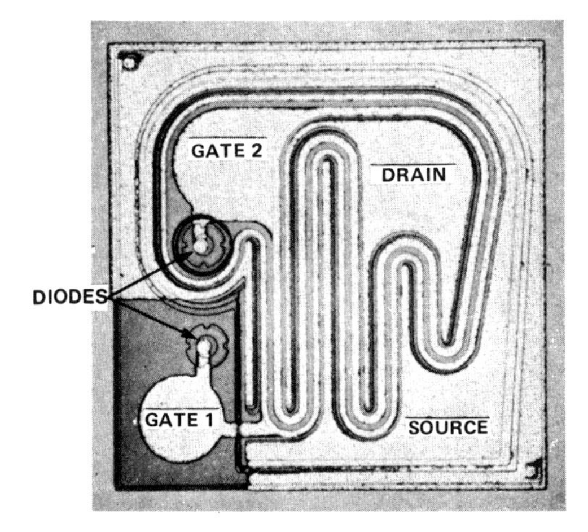

FIGURE 17. Photograph of Dual Gate MOSFET Wafer

STATIC CHARACTERISTICS

Gate Cutoff Current

By connecting the drain to the source and reverse biasing, the gate-channel diode, a measure of the direct-current input impedance and an induction of the quality of the diode can be obtained. A circuit for the measurement of this gate cutoff current I_{GSS} is shown in Figure 18. The voltage used in this measurement is 10 V, the gate being negative with respect to the channel for a n channel device. If this voltage were increased in magnitude, a point would be reached at which the gate-channel diode would break down. Figure 19 shows the typical exponential variation of I_{GSS} with temperature. Static values of short-circuit input impedance are in the thousands of megohms near zero degrees centigrade.

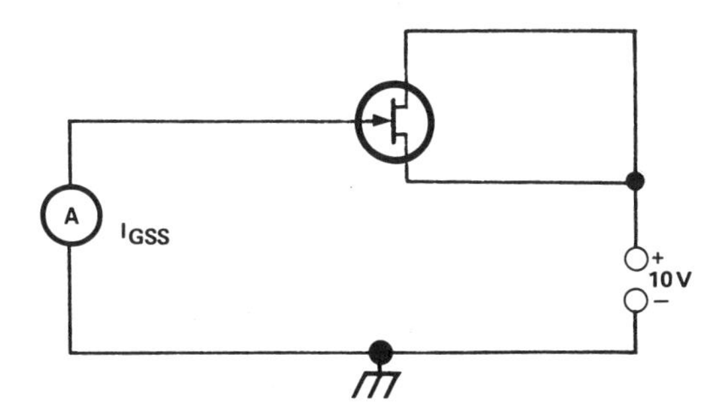

FIGURE 18. Gate Cutoff Current Test Circuit

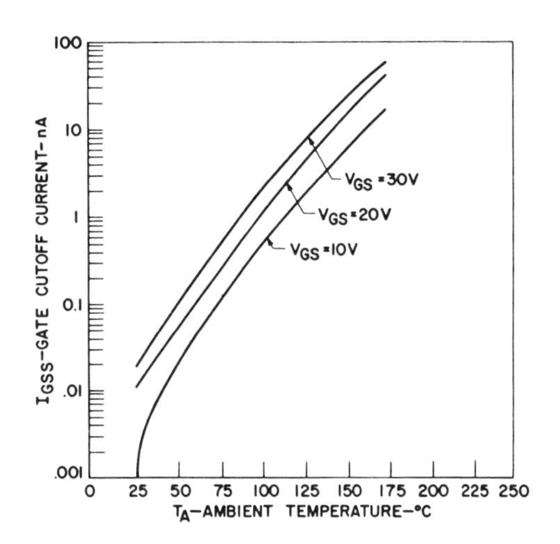

FIGURE 19 Gate Cutoff Current v. Ambient Temperature

Drain Characteristics

A set of typical FET drain characteristics are given in Figure 20. These are curves of drain current I_D as a function of drain-source voltage V_{DS} for the common-source configuration with gate-to-source voltage V_{GS} as a varying parameter. (It will be noted that the gate bias voltage is of opposite polarity to that of the drain supply voltage; hence, for ordinary bias conditions, a greater potential difference exists across the gate-drain diode than exists across the gate-source diode.)

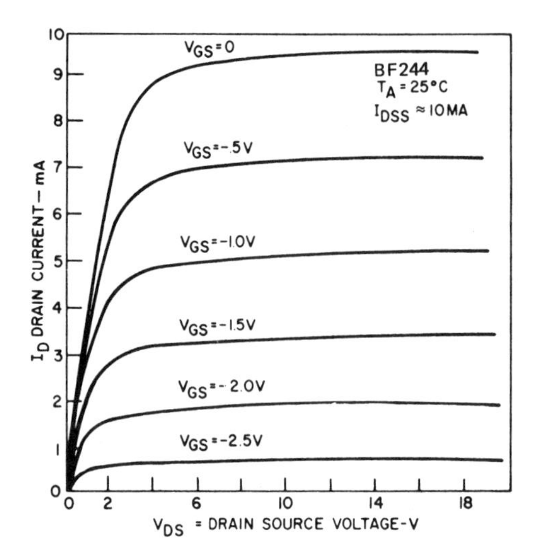

FIGURE 20. Typical FET Drain Characteristics

Saturation Drain Current ($I_{D(on)}$)

I_{DSS} is the standard symbol for the drain current at zero gate-to-source bias at any drain voltage (see the V_{GS} = 0 curve in Figure 20). I_{DSS}, when measured at a specified drain voltage in the pinch-off or current saturation region, is called $I_{D(on)}$. If the output characteristics are relatively flat in the pinch-off region (ie. the output impedance is very high), I_{DSS} can be approximated by $I_{D(on)}$. $I_{D(on)}$ is strongly temperature dependent. The silicon channel has a positive temperature coefficient of resistance due to decreased carrier mobility as temperature rises, but the carrier concentration at the doping levels involved remains fairly constant with temperature.[8] The total charge removed from the depletion regions depends only on the transverse electric field. Therefore, as temperature rises, it takes less current to cause sufficient voltage drop in the channel to produce pinch-off.

Pinch-Off Voltage (V_p)

The data sheet gives a parameter $I_{D(off)}$, called the 'pinch-off current', which is a measure of how much gate bias is required to reduce the drain current below a specified value. While the values of $I_{D(on)}$ and $I_{D(off)}$ give information about the transfer curve near its end points, they do not necessarily convey any useful information about the region between. As, after all, this is the region in which the FET is usually operated, it is essential to be able to describe the behaviour of the FET, particularly its forward transfer characteristic in the pinch-off region. To use a parabola for the transfer curve as described earlier in the chapter, one must know the limits of extrapolated pinch-off voltage for each device number. Some data sheets do not specifically state extrapolated pinch-off voltages, but the means for extracting this information are provided.

Consider the transfer curves in Figure 21 which show parts of parabolas having end points of the maximum and minimum I_{DSS} given by the data sheet, and the maximum and minimum extrapolated pinch-off voltages, as yet undetermined. The curves are correct for n-channel devices at room temperature. The data sheet also guarantees maximum and minimum values of $|y_{fs}|$, the small-signal forward transconductance (measured at 1 kHz), which is simply dI_D/dV_{GS} when $\Delta V_{DS} = 0$.

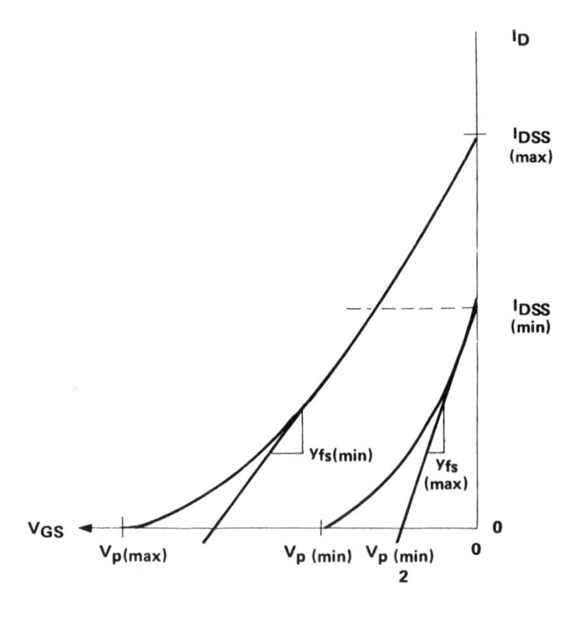

FIGURE 21. Transfer Curves

The test conditions given for $|y_{fs}|$ show that the measurement is made at a drain current corresponding to the minimum I_{DSS} for each type, these points being intersected by the dotted line drawn from I_{DSS} minimum in Figure 21. From Equation 5;

$$\frac{dI_D}{dV_{GS}} = \frac{2I_{DSS}}{V_p}\left(1-\frac{V_{GS}}{V_p}\right) = y_{fs} \quad . \; . \; . \; . \; . \quad (11)$$

Evaluated at $I_D = I_{DSS}$:

$$\left.\frac{dI_D}{dV_{GS}}\right|_{I_D = I_{DSS}} = \left|\frac{2I_{DSS}}{V_D}\right| \quad . \; . \; . \; . \; . \; . \; . \quad (12)$$

Equation (12) implies that the tangent drawn to the transfer curve at $I_D = I_{DSS}$ intersects the $I_D = 0$ axis at ½ V_p. Equation (12) can be used to determine the minimum pinch-off voltage:

$$|V_{p(min)}| = \frac{2\,|I_{DSS(min)}|}{|\,y_{fs(max)}\,|} \quad . \; . \; . \; . \; . \; . \; . \quad (13)$$

It is one of the features of the parabolic square law that it is ideally suited to mixer applications. As will be shown in the next chapter in order to fully utilize the law for a mixer it is necessary to have the oscillator swing as large as possible. Therefore it is necessary to finish these equation derivations by ascertaining formulae for the maximum value of pinch-off voltage.

In Figure 21, the maximum $|y_{fs}|$ tangent to the right-hand characteristic curve at $I_D = I_{DSS(min)}$ is shown intersecting the abscissa at $V_{GS} = ½ V_{p(min)}$. To determine $V_{p(max)}$, Equation (11) must be evaluated for the left-hand curve at $I_D = I_{DSS(min)}$. To do this, V_{GS} at this current must be found from Equation (5).

$$V_{GS}\Big|_{I_D = I_{DSS(min)}} = V_{p(max)}\left(1 - \sqrt{\frac{I_{DSS(min)}}{I_{DSS(max)}}}\right) \quad (14)$$

Substituting into Equation (11) and solving for $|V_{p(max)}|$:

$$|V_{p(max)}| = \frac{2\,|I_{DSS(max)}|}{|y_{fs(min)}|}\sqrt{\frac{I_{DSS\,(min)}}{I_{DSS(max)}}} \quad . \; . \; . \quad (15)$$

When these pinch-off voltages are to be evaluated from the data sheet parameters at data sheet test conditions, $I_{D(on)}$ is substituted everywhere for I_{DSS} in Equations (14) and (15). Experimental evidence available shows that pinch-off voltage varies little with temperature.

BIASING THE FET

In linear circuit applications of the FET, the device is biased by an external supply voltage ('fixed' bias), by self-bias, or by a combination of these two techniques. These methods may be used by the designer to set the bias point for several objectives. Two common objectives and how to achieve them are discussed: the desired voltage gain and temperature stability (of drain current and voltage gain).

Fixed Bias

Figure 22(a) shows the FET biased by an external voltage source – a fixed bias. The input portion of this circuit is redrawn in Figure 22(b) so that a graphical analysis may be used to determine quiescent drain current. The graphical analysis consists of plotting the V–I characteristic looking into the source terminal, and the V–I characteristic looking into the supply-voltage terminal. When the source terminal is connected to V_O, currents I_1 and I_2 are equal. Consequently, the quiescent level source (and drain) current is determined by the point of intersection of the V–I plots. Figure 22(b) shows this graphical analysis; the two I_2 curves illustrate a typical spread of transfer characteristics among devices of the same type (such as a BF244). Quiescent drain current is at the I_{D1} or I_{D2} level, depending upon which FET is used in the circuit.

Self-Bias

Self-bias of the FET circuit will reduce the above variation in quiescent levels of I_D. Figure 23(a) shows the use of a source resistor R_S to develop a gate-source reverse bias voltage. As I_D increases, V_{GS} becomes more negative, thus tending to prevent an increase in I_D. The input portion of the above circuit is redrawn and analyzed graphically in Figure 23(b). The V–I characteristic for the resistor is a straight line, having a slope equal to $1/R_S$. This line intersects the two I_2 plots to produce quiescent drain currents less widely separated than in Figure 22.

Combination Bias

Suppose that it is desired to limit I_D to the range of values between points A and B in Figure 23(b). This feat cannot be accomplished with either fixed bias or self-bias but is possible with a combination of the two as shown in Figure 24. The graphical analysis of the equivalent circuit in Figure 24(b) shows that, by proper selection of power supply and resistance values, I_D can be bounded by points A and B.

An application of combination bias is shown in Figure 25. Here, FET Q1 is biased as a constant-current generator for a differential amplifier to improve the common-mode rejection ratio of the amplifier. The equivalent circuit and graphical analysis for the bias of Q1 are identical to that in Figure 24(b).

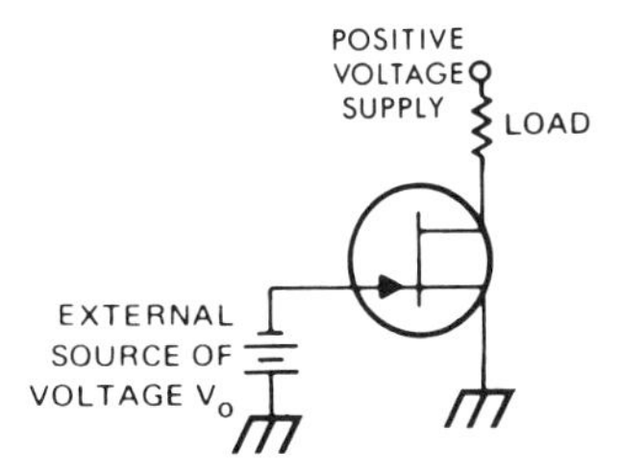

(a) BASIC CIRCUIT CONFIGURATION

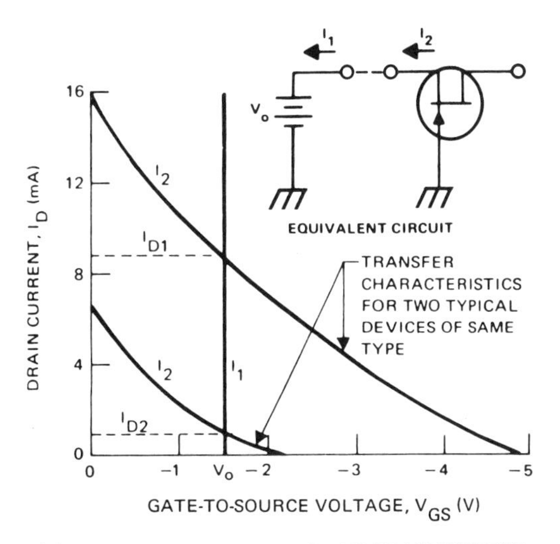

(b) DETERMINATION OF QUIESCENT DRAIN CURRENT USING EQUIVALENT CIRCUIT

FIGURE 22. Biasing with an External Voltage Source

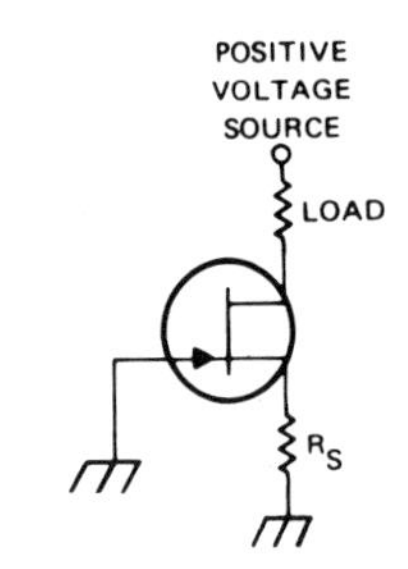

(a) BASIC CIRCUIT CONFIGURATION

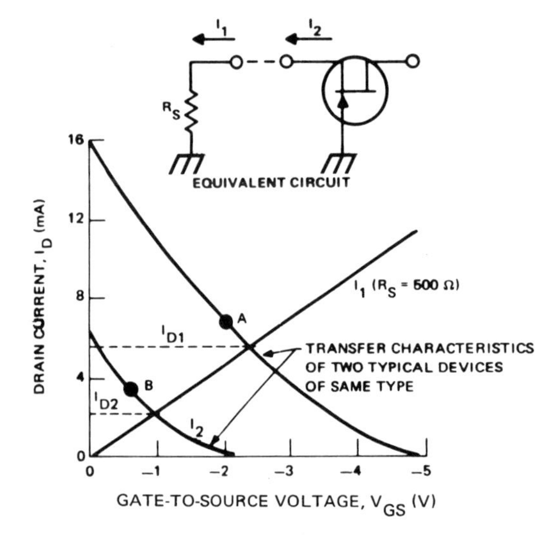

(b) DETERMINATION OF QUIESCENT DRAIN CURRENT USING EQUIVALENT CIRCUIT

FIGURE 23. Biasing with Self-Bias

Biasing for Voltage Gain

Voltage gain A_V of a grounded-source amplifier such as that in Figure 22 is the product of forward transfer admittance and drain load resistance: $A_V = y_{fs} R_L$. If a source resistor is used to establish the bias point as in Figure 23, the resistor is generally bypassed by a capacitor of negligible reactance at the frequency to be amplified; the equation is valid when this bypass capacitor is used.

The term y_{fs} is dependent upon the gate-to-source reverse voltage of the FET as shown in Figure 26. Maximum y_{fs} is obtained at a zero-voltage level for V_{GS} corresponding to a maximum value of I_D. Consequently, the gain of a circuit is increased when I_D and R_L are both made large; this requires a relatively large drain-supply voltage.

Biasing For Temperature Stability

Stability of Drain Current: Figure 27 shows plots of I_D versus V_{GS} for a single FET, measured at various temperatures. The curves pass through a common point

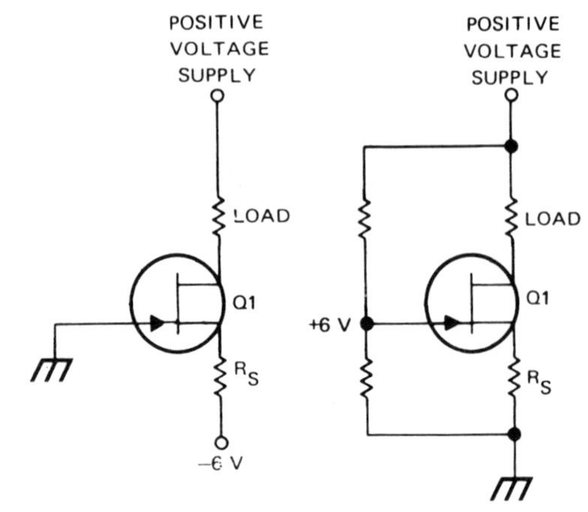

(a) TWO POSSIBLE BASIC CIRCUIT CONFIGURATIONS

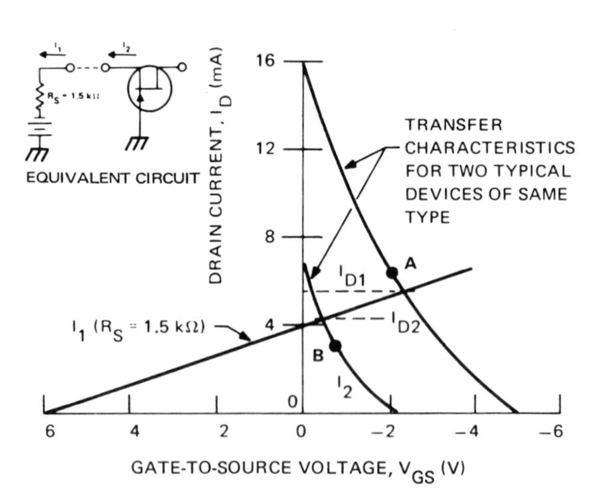

(b) DETERMINATION OF QUIESCENT DRAIN CURRENT USING EQUIVALENT CIRCUIT

FIGURE 24. Biasing with Combination of Fixed Bias and Self-Bias

which is referred to as a zero-temperature-coefficient (zero-TC) point. If the transistor is biased to operate at this point, there will be no change in drain current as ambient temperature of the circuit is varied.

The zero-TC point for drain current of a device is dependent upon its zero-gate-voltage drain current as indicated in Figure 28 for a family of FETs. The I_{D0} curve shows the drain current at which one of these devices should be biassed in order to obtain not greater than approximately ±5% change in I_D over a temperature range of −40°C to +100°C. The other curve shows the value of y_{fs} at the zero-TC point.

Stability of Voltage Gain: A zero-TC point also exists for y_{fs} of the FET and therefore for A_V. This is illustrated in Figure 29 for two devices having considerably different values of I_{DSS}. The I_D plot in Figure 30 shows the drain

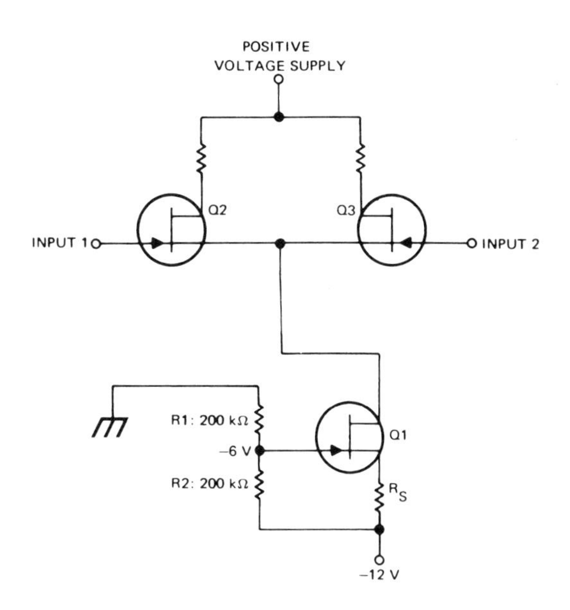

FIGURE 25. Typical Application of FET (Q1) Using Combination of Fixed Bias and Self-Bias: A Differential Amplifier

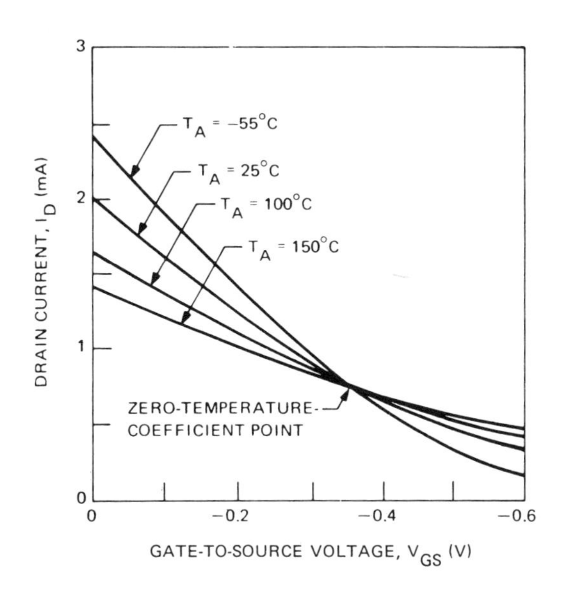

FIGURE 27. Variation of Transfer Characteristic with Ambient Temperature for a Typical 2N3821 N-Channel Junction-Gate FET V_{DS} = 10 V

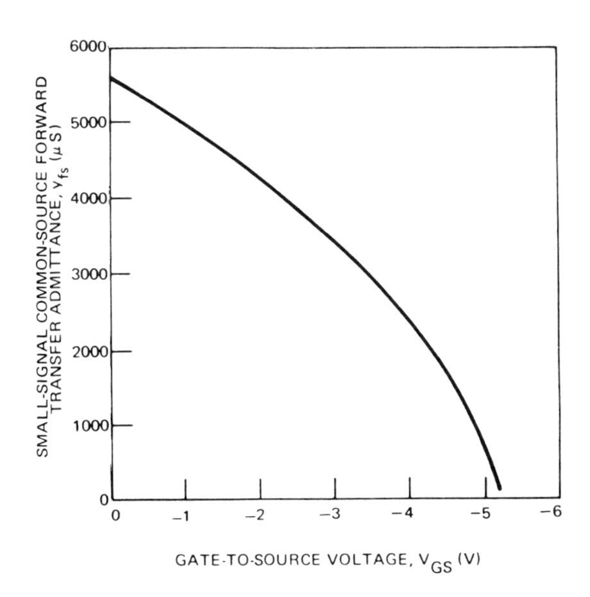

FIGURE 26. Dependence of y_{fs} on V_{GS} for a Typical 2N3823 N-Channel Junction-Gate FET at 1 kHz and V_{DS} = 15 V

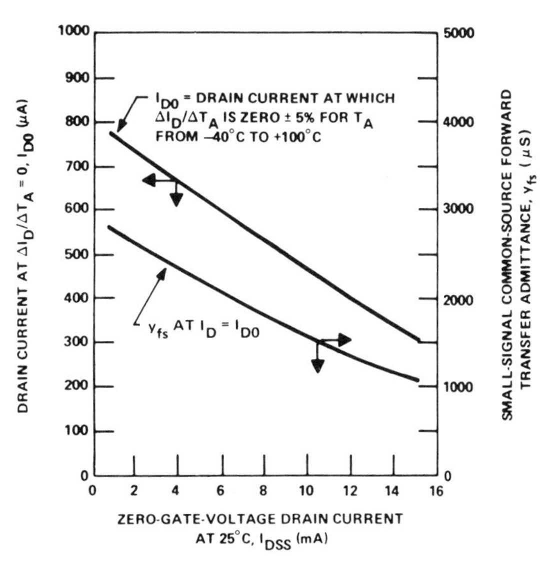

FIGURE 28. Plots for Predicting Temperature-Stable Quiescent Drain Current (And Resultant y_{fs}) from I_{DSS}, for BF244, 2N3821, 2N3822, and 2N3824 FETs

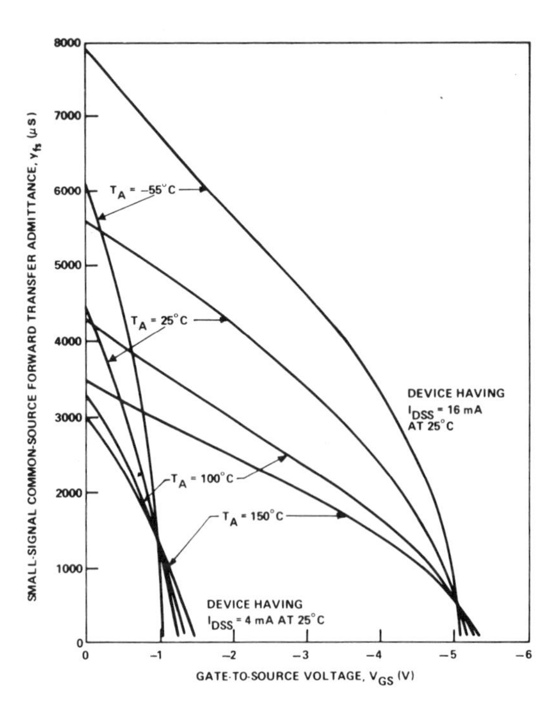

FIGURE 29. Illustration of Zero-Temperature-Coefficient Points of y_{fs} for two 2N3821 FETs (1 kHz; V_{DS} = 15 V)

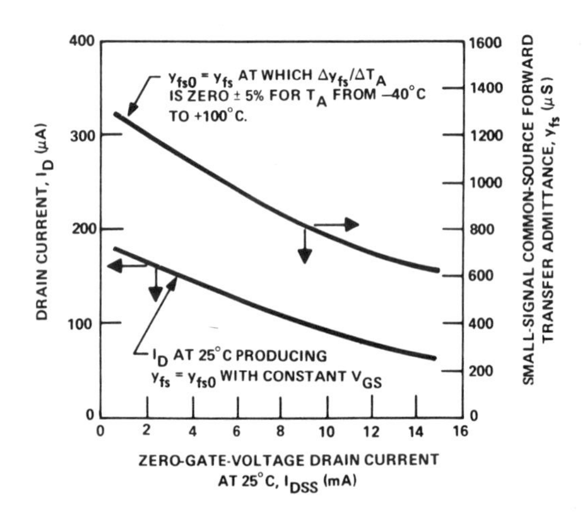

FIGURE 30. Plots for Predicting Temperature-Stable y_{fs} (and Resultant I_D) from I_{DSS}, for BF244, 2N3821, 2N3822, and 2N3824 FETs with VDS = 10 V

current to which a FET from one particular family must be biased, at + 25°C, in order to obtain not greater than approximately ±5% change in y_{fs} over a temperature range of – 40°C to + 100°C. The device must be biased in this case with a voltage source and not by any form of self-bias.

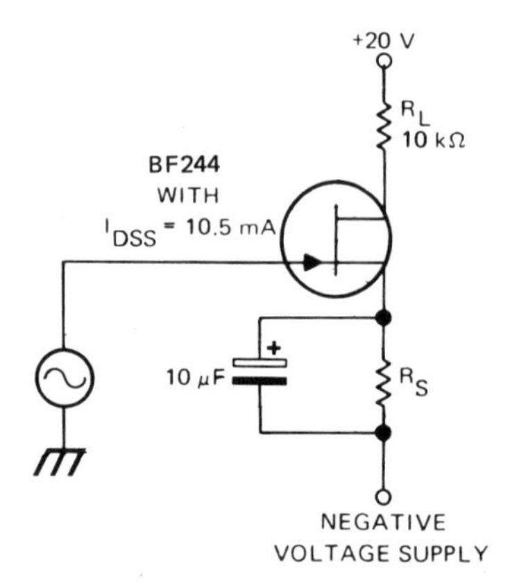

1. I_{DSS} = 10.5 mA
2. FROM FIGURE 28, SELECT I_D = 450μA AT 25°C
3. RESULTING y_{fs} IS 1500 μS, PREDICTING $A_V = y_{fs} R_L$ = 15 AT 25°C
4. MEASURED RESULT: I_D VARIED FROM 444 μA to 453 μA AS T_A VARIED FROM –40°C TO +100°C

FIGURE 31. Biasing for Approximately Constant Quiescent Drain Current Over Ambient Temperature Range from –40°C to +100°C, Using Figure 28

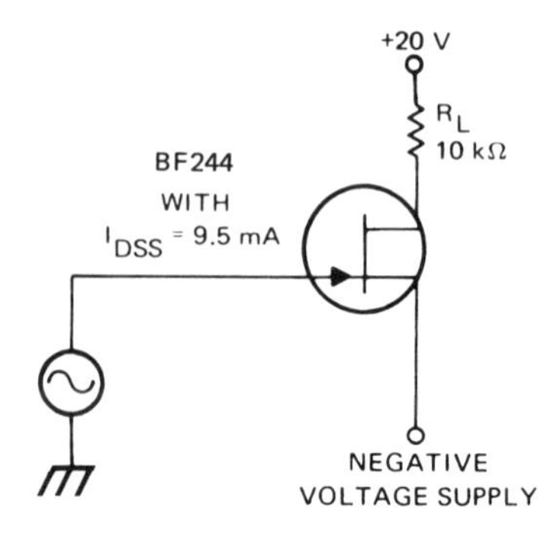

1. I_{DSS} = 9.5 mA
2. FROM FIGURE 30, SELECT I_D = 100 μA AT 25°C
3. RESULTING y_{fs} IS 800 μS, PREDICTING $A_V = y_{fs} R_L$ = 8 AT 25°C

FIGURE 32. Biasing for Approximately Constant y_{fs} Over Ambient Temperature Range from –40°C to +100°C Using Figure 30

Examples: Figures 31 and 32 show two examples of the use of Figures 28 and 30 to select the bias point for temperature stability of drain current and voltage gain respectively.

These examples are typical of how FET performance can be optimized with simple analysis techniques.

REFERENCES

1. Shockley, 'A Unipolar Field-Effect Transistor' *Proc. IRE Vol. 40,* pp. 1365-1376. Nov. 1952.

2. E. J. Ryder and W. Shockley, 'Mobilities of Electrons in High Electric Fields, *Physical Revue,* Vol. 81, No. 1, Jan, 1951.

3. G. C. Dacey and I. M. Ross, 'The Field-Effect Transistor', *B.S.T.J.,* Vol. 34, Nov. 1955.

4. F. M. Klaasen and J. Prins, 'Noise of Field-Effect Transistors at Very High Frequencies', *IEEE Trans. in Electron Devices,* Nov. 1969.

5. C. T. Sah; 'Theory of Low Frequency Generation Noise in Junction-Gate Field-Effect Transistors', *Proc. I.E.E.E.,* July 1964.

6. A. Van Der Ziel, 'Thermal Noise in Field-Effect Transistors', *Proc. IRE,* Vol., pp. 1808-1812, August 1962.

7. R. S. C. Cobbald, *Theory and Application of Field-Effect Transistors',* Wiley Interscience, Chapter 3, 1970.

8. Shockley, *Electrons and Holes in Semiconductors,* D. Van Nostrand Co., Inc., Princeton, N. J., 1950, pp. 18-19.

XII R.F. APPLICATIONS

by Mike Stevens
and Bob Parsons

The characteristics of FETs make them particularly suitable for RF applications, notably mixers and amplifiers. In general the design of a mixer is similar to that of an RF amplifier. The theoretical reason for the superior performance of the FET when compared with, for instance, a bipolar device, is given in this chapter with particular reference to mixers. The important considerations when designing mixer circuits are:–

(i) cross modulation and intermodulation distortion
(ii) the conversion gain
(iii) bandwidth
and (iv) stability.

The first of these, cross modulation and intermodulation distortion, is the most important consideration, because when they take place in any stage of a receiver, it is difficult and often impossible to remove the unwanted signals. They arise from third and higher order terms in the transfer characteristic of the active device. Thus, it is from here that the FET, with its near square-law characteristic, gets its major advantages. Dual-gate MOSFETs, with their more ideal characteristic, have a further advantage over junction FETs. (The MOSFETs' low feedback capacitance, low noise figure, large dynamic range, and second gate available for either AGC or local oscillator injection, adds to their suitability for use in both the RF amplifier and mixer sections of a tuner.)

The intermediate frequency gain is given by the product of the conversion transconductance, g_c, and the impedance presented to the output circuit at the intermediate frequency, Z_{IF}.

The mixer bandwidth is determined by the selectivity of the output tuned circuit, usually a double tuned transformer.

Stability is a problem encountered in the design of most RF circuits. In the case of a mixer, instability is unlikely to occur at either the signal or local oscillator frequencies since there is no appreciable gain at these frequencies. However, there exists the possibility of instability at the IF frequency, particularly if the reverse feedback within the active device is appreciable. IF instability is best avoided by adequate screening of the output circuit and by ensuring that all other terminals of the active device are presented with a low impedance at the IF frequency, if necessary by the use of an IF trap.

This chapter considers the theoretical cross modulation and gain performance of a FET, compares this with the results obtained from practical circuits using junction FETs and describes the use of dual-gate MOSFETs in the 'front end' of a tuner.

NON-LINEAR DEVICES

In the following analysis of mixer operation, it is assumed that the local oscillator voltage is large compared with the signal voltage and hence the transconductance of the active device is determined only by the instantaneous amplitude of the local oscillator voltage. This assumption is valid for most practical circuits. Mixing can only occur in a device which is essentially non-linear. If the output current is considered as a function of the input voltage, i.e.

$I_o = F.(V_{in})$

then the transconductance, g_m, is defined as:–

$g_m = dI_o/dV_{in} = F'.(V_{in})$

If mixing is to occur, then the transconductance must be a function of the input voltage and not a constant. Therefore, the output current must be a non-linear function of the input voltage, i.e.

$I_o = F.(V_{in})^n$

Most active devices fulfil this condition, i.e. for the triode:-

$I_a = F.(V_g)^{3/2}$

and the transistor

$I_c = F.(e^{k.V_{BE}})$

The field effect transistor, however, has a near square-law characteristic of the form:–

$I_D = I_{DSS}.(1 - V_{GS}/V_P)^2$. . . . (Equation 5 of Chapter XI)

and it is therefore this characteristic which is assumed when applying the theoretical results to the FET.

CROSS-MODULATION AND INTERMODULATION DISTORTION

General

Cross-modulation is the transfer of modulation on one carrier to the carrier of another signal. When the active device is used as a linear amplifier, the cross-modulation performance can be analysed by assuming that the input signal is comprised of two sinusoidal voltages, one amplitude modulated and the other an unmodulated carrier. The cross-modulation performance of the device can then be determined from the amount of modulation on the previously unmodulated carrier at the output of the amplifier. When the device is used as a mixer, however, the situation is more complex. In this case, the output circuit is usually tuned to the intermediate frequency – the difference between two input signals and hence the interest lies in any unwanted modulation transferred to the intermediate frequency. The cross-modulation performance of the device as a mixer is, therefore, analysed by assuming that the input signal consists of three sinusoidal voltages, one modulated carrier and two unmodulated carriers. The output circuit is tuned to the difference frequency of the two unmodulated carriers and the amount of unwanted modulation transferred from the modulated carrier to the intermediate frequency determined. It will be shown later that cross-modulation in an active device used as an amplifier and as a mixer is caused by different orders of non-linearity in the transfer characteristic of the device.

Theoretical Detail

If it is assumed that the output current of the device is related to the input voltage by a continuous curve then the output current can be represented by a Taylor's series of the form:–

$$I = I_o + a_1 . V_{in} + a_2 . V_{in}^2 + a_3 . V_{in}^3 + a_4 . V_{in}^4 + \ldots \quad (1)$$

where the coefficients a_1, a_2, a_3, etc. are given by:–

$$a_n = \frac{1}{\underline{n}} \cdot \left(\frac{d^n I}{dV_{in}^n}\right) \quad (2)$$

When the amplitude of the input signals is low or the curvature of the characteristic is of such a value that terms higher than the second degree may be neglected, then the device is essentially square law. On the other hand, if the amplitude of the input signals is large (as in the case of most practical circuits), the first three terms of equation (1) are not always a sufficiently good approximation and it is necessary to include third and fourth order terms in the analysis. For the general case, therefore, it is assumed here that:–

$V_{in} = E_1 + E_2 + E_3$

where $E_1 = E_1 . \sin \omega_1 t$

$E_2 = E_2 . \sin \omega_2 t$

$E_3 = E_3 . (1 + m.\sin pt).\sin \omega_3 t$

The various components of the output current can be examined by substituting for V_{in} in equation (1) and considering the terms of the series one by one.

The first two terms represent the d.c. term I_o and the original signals multiplied by the coefficient, a_1.

The third term:–

$a_2 .(E_1 + E_2 + E_3)^2$

when expanded yields:–

$a_2 (E_1^2 + 2E_1 E_2 + 2E_1 E_3 + 2E_2 E_3 + E_2^2 + E_3^2)$

The squared terms will produce components of twice the frequency of the applied signals and when one of the signals is modulated with a frequency $p/2\pi$, additional components at frequencies of $p/2\pi$, $2p/2\pi$, $(\omega \pm p)/2\pi$ and $(2\omega \pm 2p)/2\pi$ will occur. Terms of the form $E_1 E_2$ will produce components at frequencies equal to the sum and difference of the original signals, i.e.

$(\omega_1 \pm \omega_2)/2\pi$ and $(\omega_2 \pm \omega_3/2\pi$ etc.

If one of the signals is amplitude modulated, the sum and difference components will also be amplitude modulated.

When the device is considered as an amplifier, the components of the output current produced by the second order term in the characteristic are of some importance. In the case of a linear wideband amplifier, the spurious signals generated by the second order term may well be within the passband of the amplifier. If the second order term is large, the d.c. component of the output current can cause a shift in the operating point of the amplifier. If, on the other hand, the amplifier is tuned and narrow band, the majority of spurious components of the output current will lie outside the passband, but if one of the input signals is modulated at an audio frequency $p/2\pi$, the components of the form $(\omega \pm p)/2\pi$ and $(2\omega \pm 2p)/2\pi$ often fall within the amplifier passband.

For mixer applications, the sum and difference terms represent the desired output current components and since the output circuit is tuned to one or other of these components, other spurious components generated by the second order term are usually of no importance. From this, it can be seen that the second order term in the characteristic does not contribute to cross-modulation when the device is used as an amplifier or mixer.

Considering the fourth term in the series of (1) $a_3.(E_1 + E_2 + E_3)^3$, when expanded, this yields:–

$a_3.(E_1^3 + E_2^3 + E_3^3 + 3E_1^2 E_2 + 3E_1^2 E_3 + 3E_1 E_2^2$
$+ 3E_1 E_3^2 + 3E_2^2 E_3 + 3E_2 E_3^2 + 6E_1 E_2 E_3)$

By application of further trigonometry, it can be shown that the following components of current are produced:–

(i) Components at three times the frequency of the input signals, i.e. $3\,\omega_1/2\pi$, $3\,\omega_2/2\pi$ and $3\,\omega_3/2\pi$ and with amplitudes proportional to the cube of the amplitude of the respective input signals.

(ii) Components having all combinations of frequencies of the form $(2\,\omega_1 \pm \omega_2)/2\pi$ and $(2\,\omega_2 \pm \omega_3)/2\pi$ etc. and amplitudes proportional to $E_1^2 E_2$ and $E_2^2 E_3$, etc.

(iii) Components at all the possible combinations of the form $(\omega_1 \pm \omega_2 \pm \omega_3)/2\pi$ and having amplitudes proportional to the products of the amplitudes of the input signals, i.e. $E_1 E_2 E_3$.

and

(iv) Components at frequencies equal to the input signal frequencies and with amplitudes proportional to the cube of the amplitude of the respective input signals.

It is easy to show that the third order term in the characteristic also produces many additional unwanted sidebands. When one of the input signals is an audio frequency $p/2\pi$, then sidebands such as $(\omega_1 \pm 2p)/2\,\pi$ $(\omega_2 \pm 2p)/2\pi$, etc. will be in the same general band as the second order terms $(\omega_1 \pm p)/2\pi$, $(\omega_2 \pm p)/2\pi$, etc. thus producing non-linear distortion within the system. Third order terms of the type $3E_1^2 E_2$ are of particular interest when the device is used as a linear amplifier. If two input signals of the form below are considered,

$E_1 = \bar{E}_1.(1 + m.\sin pt).\sin \omega_1 t$ – modulated carrier

$E_2 = \bar{E}_2.\sin \omega_2 t$ – modulated carrier

then, substituting these in the above third order term:–

$a_3.3E_1^2.E_2 = 3a_3 \bar{E}_1^2 \bar{E}_2.(1 + m.\sin pt)^2.\sin^2 \omega_1 t.\sin \omega_2 t$

$= a_3.\bar{E}_1^2 \bar{E}_2.(1 + 2m.\sin pt + m^2.\sin^2 pt).\sin \omega_2 t.$

$(1 - \cos 2\,\omega_1 t)/2$

This expression contains the term:–

$\frac{1}{2}.a_3.E_1^2.E_2.(1 + 2m.\sin pt).\sin \omega_2 t$

Thus, the modulation in the signal E_1 has been transferred to the previously unmodulated signal E_2. It can, therefore, be concluded that the third order term in the characteristic produces unwanted third order sidebands and cross-modulation between two signals appearing at the input. These are important considerations when the device is used as an amplifier. On the other hand, they are of little consideration when the device is used as a mixer unless the third order sidebands lie in the desired intermediate frequency band.

The fifth term of the Taylor's series is of the form $a_4(E_1 + E_2 + E_3)^4$. A complete expansion of this term is too lengthy to present in full, and so the discussion will be confined to terms of particular interest. Probably the most significant term is that of the form $E_3^2.E_1 E_2$. If E_3 is an undesired modulated carrier and E_1 and E_2 two signals, the sum or difference frequency of which is the desired mixer output frequency, then substitution of these three signals in the above fourth order term yields:–

$$E_3^2.E_1.E_2 = E_3^2.(1 + m.\sin pt)^2.\sin^2 \omega_3 t.E_2 \sin \omega_2 t.\; E_1.\sin \omega_1 t$$

$$= \frac{E_3^2.E_1.E_2}{4}.(1 + 2m.\sin pt + m^2.\sin^2 pt)\,(1 - \cos 2\omega_3 t).\; (\cos(\omega_1 - \omega_2)t - \cos(\omega_1 + \omega_2)t)$$

In this expression $(\omega_1 \pm \omega_2)/2$ are the desired sideband frequencies. From this, it can be seen that the above expression contains the terms:–

$$\frac{E_3^2.E_1.E_2}{4}.(1 + 2m.\sin pt).\cos(\omega_1 \pm \omega_2)t$$

Thus, the modulation on the signal E_3 has been transferred to the desired sidebands. From this, it can be seen that the fourth order term contributes directly to cross-modulation and the production of sum and difference frequencies when the device is used as a mixer. In fact, it can be shown that all even order terms of the series contribute to the production of sum and difference frequencies. Higher order modulation terms can be evaluated from the following expression:–

$$i_n = \frac{a_n}{2^{n-1}} \sum_{i=1\ldots n=1}^{i=m\ldots n=m} E_i.E_j.E_k \ldots E_n \begin{matrix}\sin\\ \cos\end{matrix}.(\omega_i \pm \omega_j \pm \ldots \omega_n t)t$$

Using this expression, it is possible to evaluate the nth order modulation term due to a signal with m frequencies.

Having established the effect of the various non-linear components of output current on the performance of the device both as an amplifier and mixer, it is necessary to examine the transfer characteristic of the FET in more detail.

Application to the FET

As stated, for an ideal FET, the drain current as a function of gate source voltage is given by:–

$I_D = I_{DSS}.(1 - V_{GS}/V_p)^2$

If this expression is differentiated with respect to V_{GS}, it gives:–

$d I_D/dV_{GS} = (V_{GS}/V_p - 1).2.I_{DSS}/V_p$

From this, it can be seen that, ideally, the transconductance is a linear function of the gate source voltage. In a mixer device, mixing action occurs when the device transconductance is varied by the local oscillator voltage. Therefore, the greater the slope of the g_m versus V_{GS} curve, the greater the conversion gain. In the ideal case, the slope is:–

$2\, I_{DSS}/V_p$ .... (Equation 13 of Chapter XI)

and for a square law device, this term is the second order coefficient a_2. There are, of course, no third or higher order terms.

In most practical FETs however, the exponent in the drain current is less than two, due to bulk resistance and finite channel dimensions. Bulk resistance in the source has the effect of linearising the characteristic due to negative feedback. In most current FETs, the actual bulk resistance is usually less than 100 Ω and in some cases, at least an order lower. When the device is used as a mixer, one signal is applied to the gate and the other to the source. In this case, the output impedance of the generator supplying the source signal appears in series with the bulk resistance and is very often appreciable in value.

The effect of various values of both bypassed and unbypassed source resistance on the g_m versus V_{GS} curve for an FET of the BF244 family at 10 MHz is shown in Figure 1. From this, it can be seen that as the source resistance is increased, the slope of the curve is reduced over most of the dynamic range but exhibits an increasingly large change of slope near pinch-off. This series feedback will have considerable effect on the performance of the device as a mixer. With zero external impedance in the source, it is possible to swing the g_m from its zero bias value of approximately $2\, I_{DSS}/V_p$ to zero with a gate-source voltage swing of $0 - V_p$. Under these conditions, the device is working under as near square law condition as possible. As the source impedance is increased, the zero bias g_m falls and the variation of g_m with gate-source voltage decreases over a large portion of the characteristic. In this region, the conversion gain will be reduced. In the portion of the characteristic near pinch-off the g_m falls rapidly to zero, and in this region, the conversion gain will be relatively high due to the increase in second and higher orders of non-linearity. Unfortunately, the increase in the fourth order terms also causes a reduction in the cross-modulation performance.

The effect of source impedance can be determined theoretically by including the feedback voltage in the drain current equation thus:–

$I_D = I_{DSS}.\{1 - (V_{GS} - I_D Z_s)/V_p\}^2$

From this equation the derivatives $d^n I_D/dv^n_{GS}$ (n = 1, 2, 3, etc.) can be evaluated. Although this equation is valid at d.c. and low frequencies, at high frequencies, the effects of the device conductances g_{DS}, g_{GS} and g_{GD} and generator and local oscillator impedances also have an effect on the characteristic. Thus, the situation becomes considerably more complex. It is, therefore, difficult to evaluate the coefficients of the series with reasonable accuracy at very high frequencies. However, it is possible to obtain a fairly good idea of the effect of source resistance on the first four

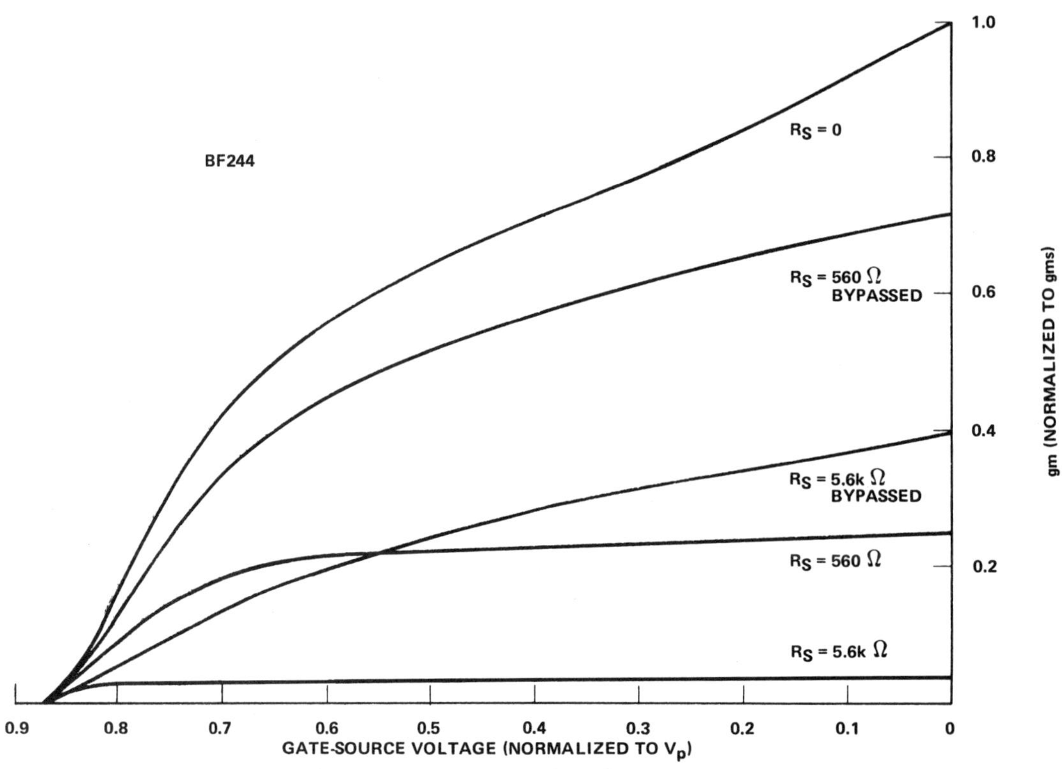

FIGURE 1. Variation of g_m with V_{GS}, Various Values of Bypassed and Unbypassed Source Resistance

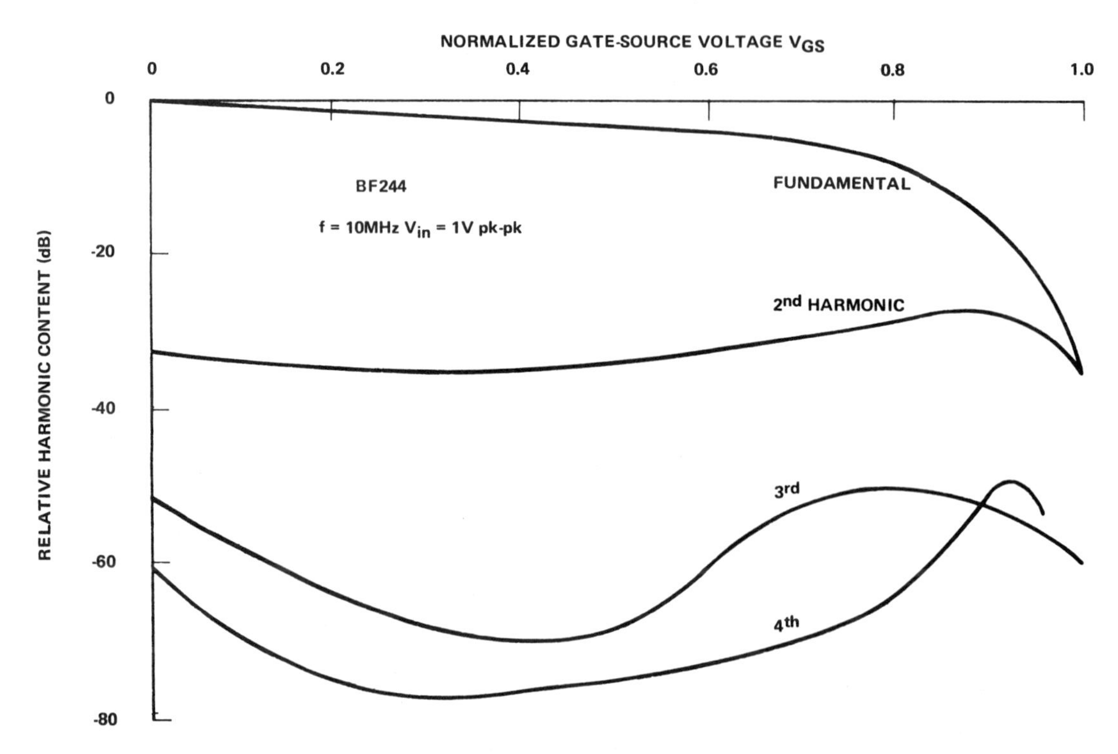

FIGURE 2. Variation of Harmonic Content with V_{GS}, $R_S = 0$

coefficients of the series by using the device as a large signal amplifier with a sinusoidal input signal and measuring the fundamental, second, third and fourth harmonic components of the output current. The variation of these harmonic components with gate-source bias for two values of source impedance for a BF244 at 10 MHz is shown in Figures 2 and 3. From these curves, it can be seen that with zero source impedance, the second harmonic is fairly constant over the majority of the characteristic and the fourth harmonic has a minimum at a bias of approximately $V_p/2$. A useful figure of merit for a mixer based on the Taylor coefficients is the ratio a_2/a_4, which is virtually the ratio of conversion gain to cross-modulation. Thus, with zero source impedance, the figure of merit is a maximum at a bias of $V_p/2$. As the source impedance is increased, the second, third and fourth order components fall in the region near zero bias but rise in the region near pinch-off. Thus, it is apparent that if the gate source voltage swing and bias is such that the dynamic swing is confined to the region of the characteristic near zero bias, then the figure of merit will be improved, but this imposes restrictions on the maximum gate-source voltage swing which are difficult to define. With this mode of operation, the conversion gain will be considerably reduced if the source impedance is at all excessive. The same figure of merit can be obtained over the majority of the characteristic with zero source impedance by reduction of the input voltage swing.

In the preceding discussion, it has been assumed that all the input signals to the device are pure sinusoids. In a mixer, the largest signal is normally the local oscillator voltage which swings the gate-source voltage about the d.c. bias point. The usable range of gate-source voltage for an FET is $V_p < V_{GS} < 0$. The gate-source voltage should never be allowed to exceed zero or the gate-source diode will become forward biased and the input impedance of the device will fall, reducing the selectivity of the input tuned circuit. However, under some conditions of bias, the local oscillator voltage will drive the device into the cut-off region. This condition arises when bias is set at pinch-off and the device is driven on during alternate half cycles of the local oscillator voltage. In this case, the drive voltage is clipped at the point where it exceeds V_p. It is, therefore, necessary to consider also harmonics in the local oscillator voltage when calculating the components of the output current. It can easily be shown that when the input voltage is clipped, the harmonics generated contribute to the conversion gain. If, for instance, the second harmonic of local oscillator voltage is appreciable, then this, in conjunction with the third order term in the characteristic, will contribute to the difference frequency current component. In order to evaluate the effects of the harmonic content of the local oscillator waveform, it is necessary to determine the harmonic amplitudes by a Fourier Analysis.

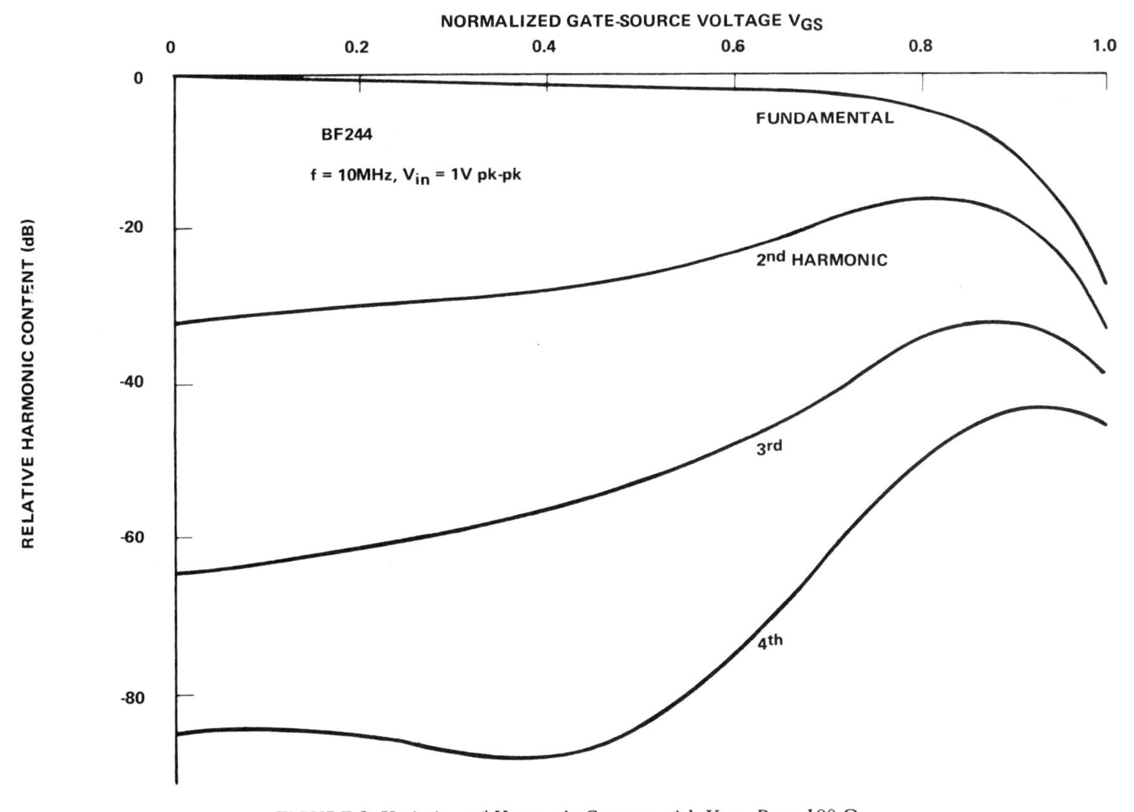

FIGURE 3. Variation of Harmonic Content with V_{GS}, $R_S = 180\ \Omega$

CONVERSION GAIN

If it is assumed that the FET is a perfect square law device and working under conditions of zero source impedance, then the conversion conductance at any bias level and local oscillator injection can be determined by Fourier analysis. The operation of the device biassed at V_p and $V_p/2$ is shown in Figure 4. This shows that the device transconductance varies with time according to the instantaneous value of local oscillator voltage. The output voltage is the product of the instantaneous transconductance and the signal voltage. The instantaneous transconductance as a function of time can be represented by the Fourier series:–

$$g_m = b_o + \sum_{n=1}^{n=\infty} (b_n . \cos n\,\omega t + a_n . \sin . n\omega t)$$

where g_m = instantaneous transconductance

$\omega/2$ = local oscillator frequency

a_n and b_n = coefficients determined by g_m as a function of time.

The coefficients b_o, b_n and a_n can be determined, according to Fourier theory from:–

$$b_o = \frac{1}{2\pi}\int_0^{2\pi} g_m . d(\omega t)$$

$$b_n = \frac{1}{2\pi}\int_0^{2\pi} g_m \cos n\omega t . d(\omega t)$$

$$a_n = \frac{1}{2\pi}\int_0^{2\pi} g_m \sin n\omega t . d(\omega t)$$

The instantaneous drain current is the product of the instantaneous transconductance and the signal voltage, $E_s . \sin\omega_s t$, i.e.

$i_d = g_m . E_s . \sin\omega_s t$

Therefore, using the above series for g_m

$$i_d = {}^{\bullet}b_o + \sum_{n=1}^{n=\infty} (a_n \sin\omega_n t + b_n \cos\omega_n t)\, E_s . \sin\omega_s t$$

If this expression is expanded, it can be seen that the two components of drain current at the difference frequency $(\omega_s - \omega)/2\pi$ are $b_1/2$ and $a_1/2$. These terms represent the conversion transconductance, g_c, which when multiplied by the amplitude of the applied signal, will give the amplitude of the difference frequency component of the drain current. Thus, in order to determine the conversion transconductance, g_c, for the active device, it is necessary to evaluate the coefficients a_1 and b_1.

Assuming an ideal FET, then:–

$$g_m = g_{mo}\left(\frac{V_{GS}}{V_p} - 1\right)$$

i.e. $g_m + g_{mo} = g_{mo} . V_{GS}/V_p$

Therefore, the variation of g_m as a function of time is:–

$g_m . F.(t) = V_{GS} . F.(t) . g_{mo}/V_p$

Using this method, it is possible to evaluate the conversion conductance for the ideal FET under any conditions of bias and local oscillator injection. In this chapter, two conditions of bias only will be considered. Pinch-off bias and half pinch-off bias. From Figure 4, it can be seen that with half pinch-off bias and a peak local oscillator voltage less than $V_p/2$, i.e. $0 < E_{osc} < V_p/2$, both the variation of g_m and local oscillator voltage with time is sinusoidal. Thus:–

$$V_{GS} = E_o [\cos\omega_o t]_0^{2\pi}$$

Since g_m is an even function defined in the range $0 - 2\pi$, the Fourier series will contain cosine terms only, hence:–

$$g_c = b_1/2 = \frac{1}{2\pi}\int_0^{2\pi} g_{mo} . \frac{E_o . \cos\omega_o t}{V_p} . \cos\omega_o t . d(\omega_o t)$$

$$= \frac{g_{mo} . E_o}{2\pi V_p}\int_0^{2\pi} \cos^2\omega_o t . d(\omega_o t)$$

$$= \underline{g_{mo} . E_o/2V_p}$$

From this, it follows that at half pinch-off bias, the conversion transconductance is proportional to the peak amplitude of the local oscillator voltage and the zero bias transconductance and inversely proportional to the pinch-off voltage V_p. Since g_{mo} is given approximately by:–

$g_{mo} = 2 . I_{DSS}/V_p$

then it can be seen that the conversion bias conductance is proportional to:–

$2 I_{DSS}/V_p^2$

which was previously shown to be the second order coefficient of the Taylor's series. If the maximum peak local oscillator swing $E_o = V_p/2$ is substituted in the expression for g_c, the maximum convérsion transconductance is given by:–

$\bar{g}_c = g_{mo}/4$

This expression is dependent only on the zero bias transconductance g_{mo}. The expression obtained for g_c is fairly accurate in practice providing the source impedance at the local oscillator frequency is kept to a minimum and the local oscillator injection is limited to a peak value of $V_p/2$.

When the device is biassed at cut-off and driven on on alternate half cycles of local oscillator voltage as shown in Figure 4, the conversion transconductance is given by:–

$$g_c = \frac{1}{2\pi} \int_{-\pi/2}^{\pi/2} g_{mo}.E_o.\cos\omega_o t.d(\omega_o t) + \int_{\pi/2}^{3\pi/2} 0 \cos_o t.d(\omega_o t)$$

$$= \frac{g_{mo}E_o}{2\ V_p} \int_{-\pi/2}^{\pi/2} \cos^2 \omega_o t.d(\omega_o t)$$

$$= \underline{\underline{g_{mo}.E_o/4.V_p}}$$

In this case, the maximum peak local oscillator voltage is $E_o = V_p$. The maximum conversion conductance is then:– $g_c = g_{mo}/4$

This is the same value as that obtained for $V_p/2$ bias except that in this case, the local oscillator voltage required is twice the previous value. Unfortunately, this expression is not very accurate in practice. Even under conditions of zero source impedance, there is still considerable curvature of the characteristic near pinch-off and this, together with the high harmonic content of the unidirectional pulses of gate voltage, results in much higher mixer gain than predicted and worse cross-modulation performance than in the circuit biassed at $V_p/2$.

PRACTICAL JUNCTION FET MIXER CIRCUITS

General

In the preceding discussion, it was established that distortion and cross-modulation in FET mixer stages is caused, at least in part, by bulk resistance and series impedance in the source of the device. It was also established that the conversion transconductance is proportional to the ratio $2I_{DSS}/V_p^2$. It is, therefore, apparent that the most suitable device for mixer applications is a device with

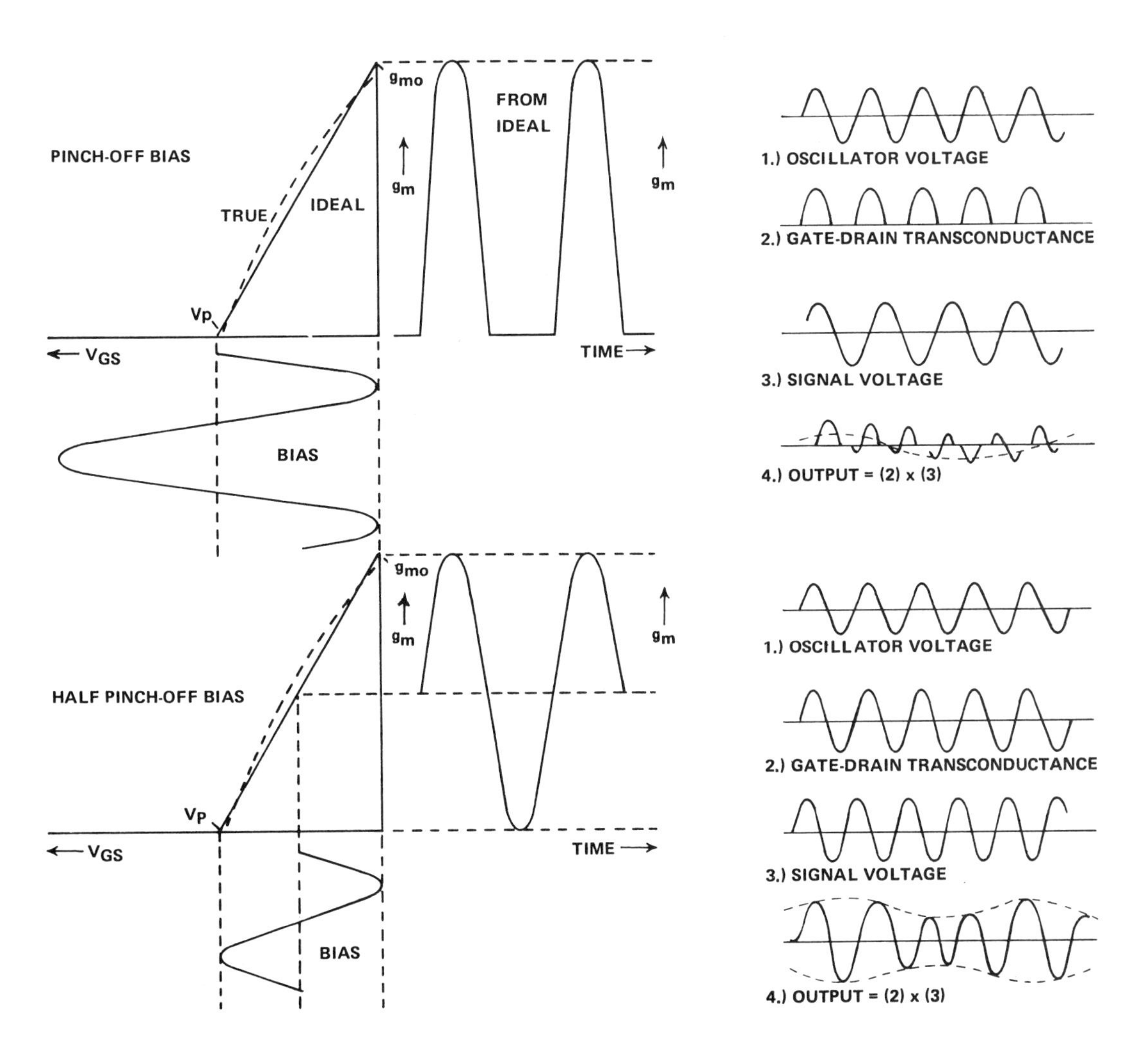

FIGURE 4. Waveforms Illustrating Mixer Action

a high zero bias drain current I_{DSS} and a low pinch-off voltage. The circuit should be designed so that the impedance in the source circuit is as low as possible at the local oscillator frequency. It is, of course, necessary to choose a device with low bulk resistance, but since the FET on resistance is given approximately by r_{DS} (on) $= V_p/2I_{DSS}$, it follows that a high I_{DSS}, low V_p device will also have low bulk resistance and hence a near square-law characteristic. In general, high I_{DSS} FETs have large interelectrode capacities and this often limits their use at high frequencies. At very high frequencies, where stray capacity has to be kept to a minimum a lower I_{DSS} device must be used.

The following examples deal with practical mixer circuits using the BF246 rather than the BF244 FET. The BF246 has a very high ratio $2I_{DSS}/V_p^2$ of approximately 3 mA/V² and relatively large interelectrode capacities. The BF244, on the other hand, has a low ratio $2I_{DSS}/V_p^2$ of approximately 0.6 mA/V² and low interelectrode capacity, and will therefore not perform as well as the BF246 in a mixer circuit.

Cross-Modulation

The cross-modulation performance of an FET used as a mixer can be measured using the circuit of Figure 5. In order to obtain a fair assessment of the performance of the device, the input circuit is untuned. The curves in Figure 6 show the cross-modulation performance obtained from high and low pinch-off samples of a BF246 in the circuit of Figure 5. From these curves, it can be seen that, at half pinch-off bias, the amplitude of the undesired signal producing 1% cross-modulation was approximately equal to $0.12\ V_p$ for the total spread in V_p of device pinch-off voltage. On the other hand, under pinch-off bias, the undesired signal amplitude lies within the shaded area of the graph, high pinch-off samples requiring a higher level of undesired signal. These curves show quite clearly that the best cross-modulation performance is obtained when the device is biassed at half pinch-off.

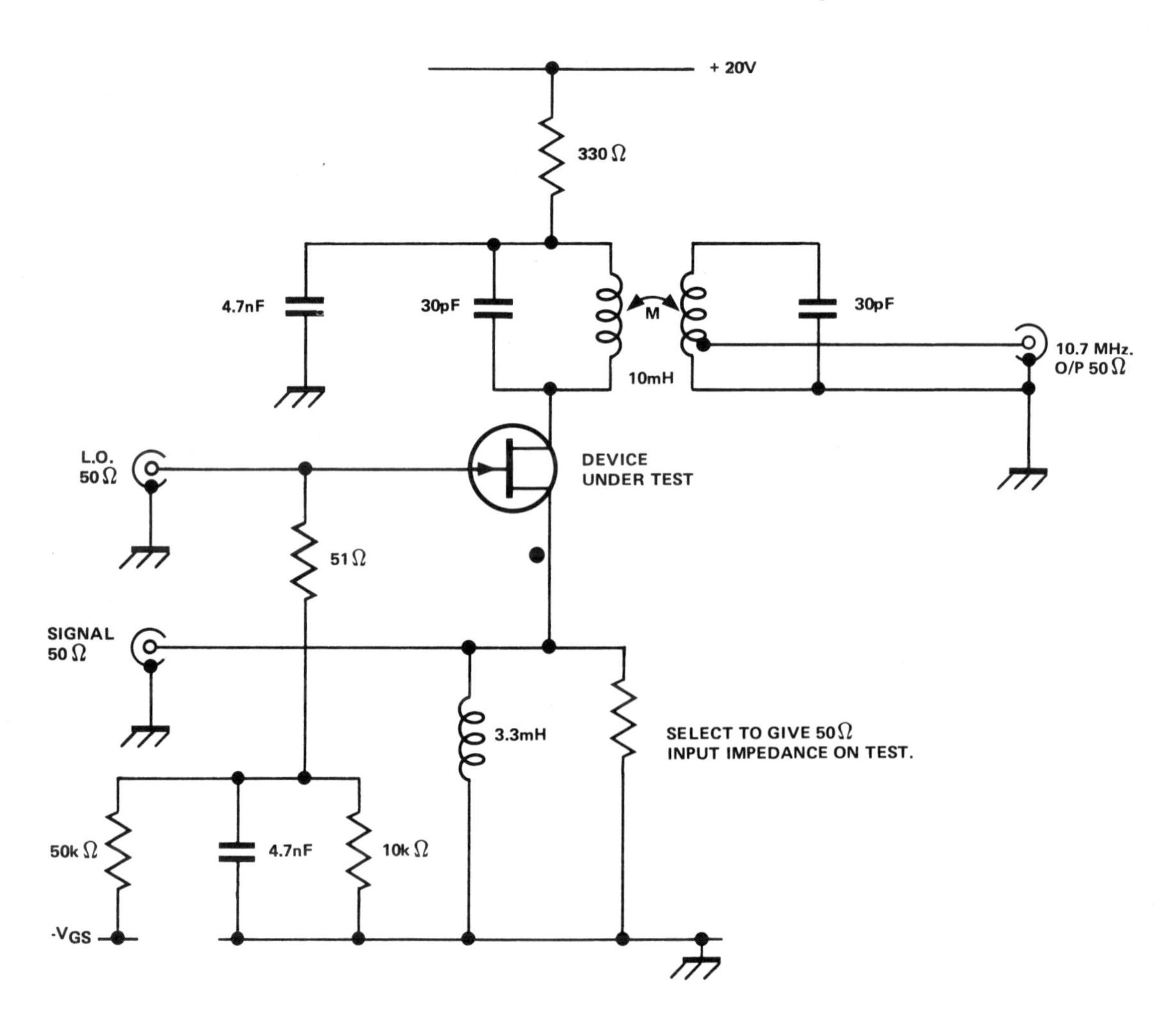

FIGURE 5. Cross-Modulation Test Circuit

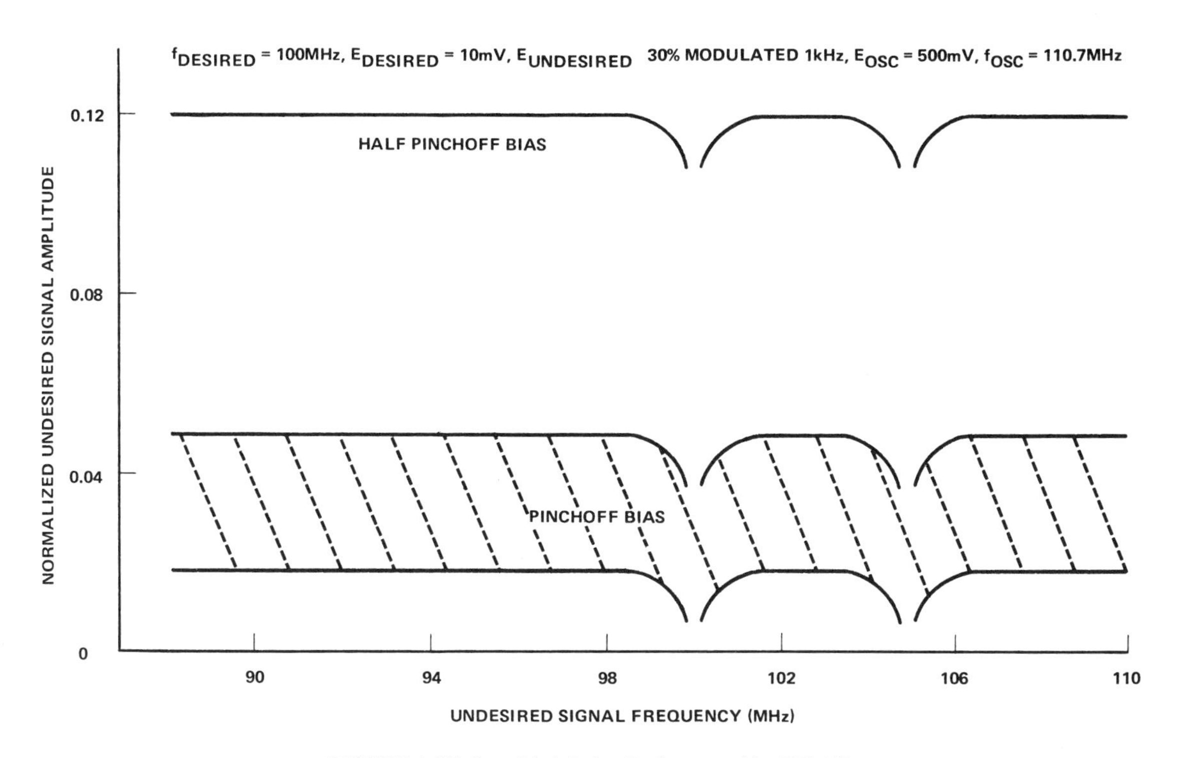

FIGURE 6. 1% Cross-Modulation Performance (for BF246)

Conversion Gain

An assessment of the conversion gain of an FET used as a mixer can be evaluated using the circuit of Figure 7. The signal is applied to the source via a tuned matching transformer and the local oscillator voltage applied to the gate, together with the d.c. gate bias voltage. The output circuit consists of a double tuned 10.7 MHz IF transformer with the 50 Ω load tapped in the secondary to give a loaded Q of approximately 20. The conversion voltage gain, A_c, of the mixer is given by:—

$$A_c = g_c \cdot Z_{IF}$$

where g_c = conversion transconductance

Z_{IF} = impedance presented to the output terminals of the device at the intermediate frequency.

Thus, the Z_{IF} should be as high as possible. The theoretical maximum for a power match is Z_{IF} equal to the output conductance of the FET. Due to the high output conductance of the FET and overload considerations, a power match is rarely practically possible. In view of relatively high values of Z_{IF} necessary to give high gain in FET mixer circuits, shunt losses in the IF transformer should be minimised by designing the transformer to have a high unloaded Q. The transformer in Figure 7 consisted of two equal coils of 10 mH each on a single former tuned with a total capacity of 30 pF.

It was shown in the preceding discussion that the conversion gain is proportional to the ratio $2I_{DSS}/V_p{}^2$, and that for the BF246 and BF244 this ratio is 3 mA/V² and 0.6 mA/V² respectively. It is, therefore, reasonable to assume that under similar conditions a mixer using the BF246 will give about 7 dB more power gain than a BF244 mixer. The conversion gain of several samples of each device was measured using the circuit of Figure 7, under both cut-off and half pinch-off bias conditions, and with the maximum allowable local oscillator injection. Figure 8 shows the variation of conversion gain with peak local oscillator injection (normalised to V_p) for a BF246 mixer under both conditions of bias. From this, it can be seen that, for a given local oscillator injection, maximum conversion gain occurs when the device is biassed near pinch-off. It can also be seen that in this case, the conversion gain tends to flatten off at a local oscillator injection of approximately 0.4 V_p. This is mainly due to two reasons. Examination of a typical curve of g_m versus V_{GS} of Figure 1 shows that the curvature is most pronounced near pinch-off and in this region, third and higher order non-linearities contribute considerably to the gain. It must also be remembered that with the bias set near V_p, the gate voltage is, in effect, a half-wave rectified sine wave and contains a considerable second harmonic content. This, together with the increased third order non-linearity in the characteristic, significantly increases the conversion gain. The second reason is that the source is tapped into the signal tuned circuit, thus there is an impedance in the source circuit at the local oscillator frequency and it has been shown that this tends to linearise the characteristic in the region near V_{GS} = 0, and increases the curvature near pinch-off. The curve of conversion gain against local oscillator voltage for the half pinch-off bias

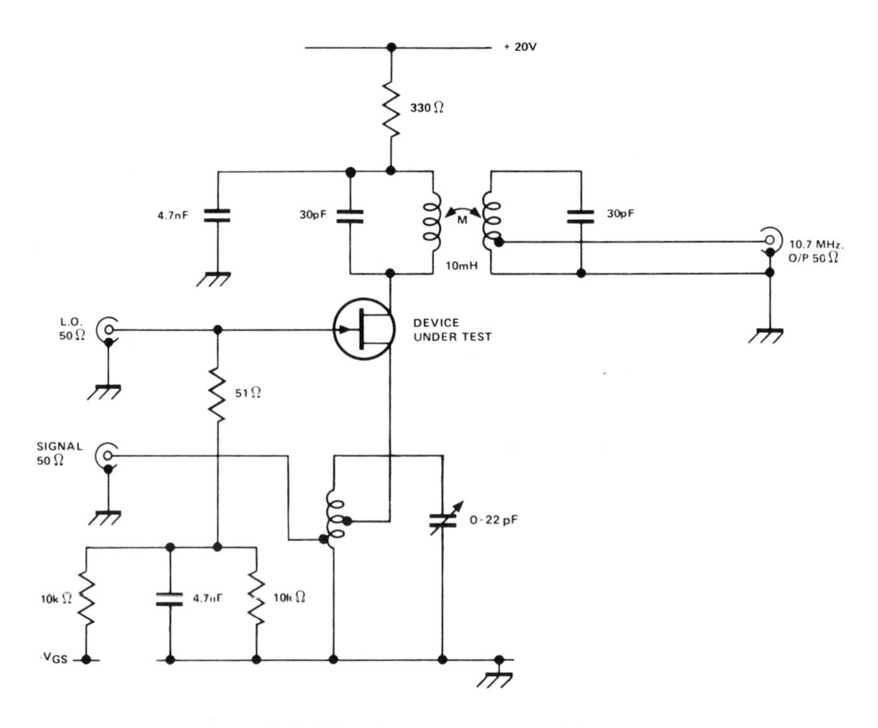

FIGURE 7. Conversion Gain Test Circuit

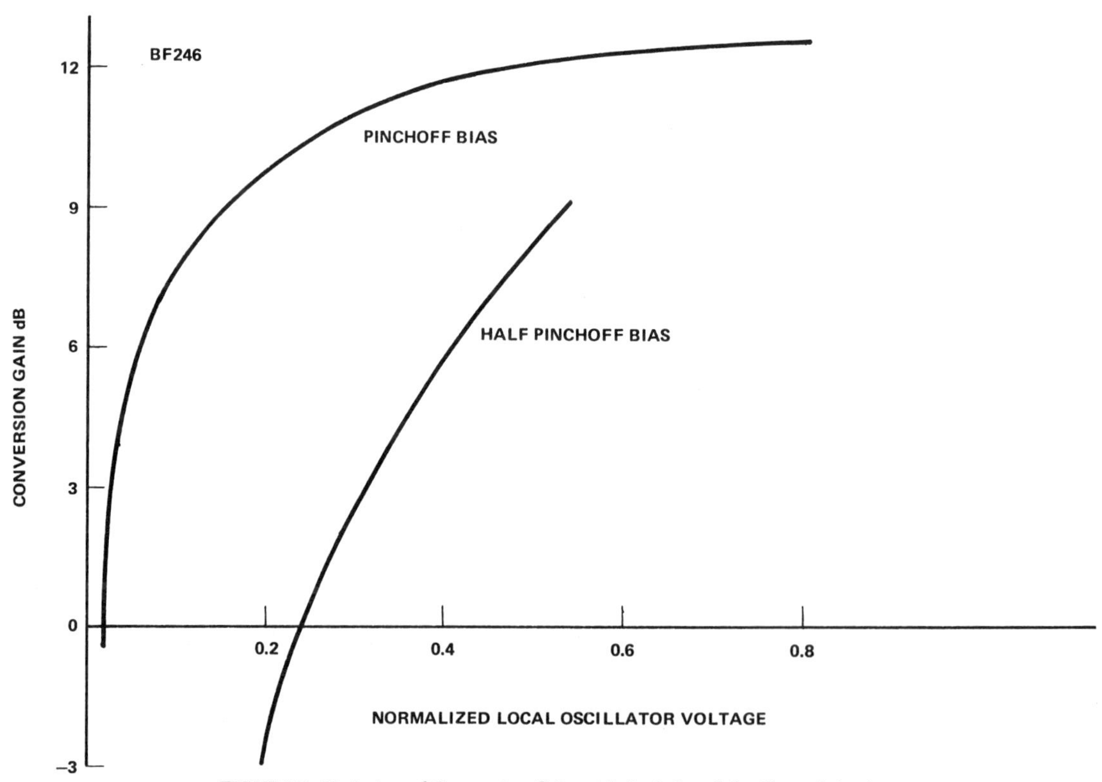

FIGURE 8. Variation of Conversion Gain with Peak Local Oscillator Injection

condition showed that the gain is 4 – 5 dB lower than with the device biassed at pinch-off. The conversion gain also exhibited are almost linear dependent on the local oscillator injection thus indicating that the device was operating under near square law conditions. On comparing with the BF244 device results it was found that the variation of conversion gain is very similar for both devices but that under both conditions of bias, the BF246 gives about 8 dB more gain than the BF244 mixer, i.e. the gain difference is almost identical to the difference between the figures of merit of the devices of 3 and 0.6 mA/V^2.

Circuits With Automatic Bias

In most practical cases, a separate negative supply for the gate bias is not readily available. In this case, the correct bias voltage can be obtained by connecting a resistor between the source of the FET and ground. The device is self-biassed by the voltage drop across this resistor, in the same way as a valve derives automatic bias from a cathode resistor. The resistor should be bypassed to signal frequencies by a suitable capacitor. The correct values of source resistor for automatic bias at $V_p/2$ can be determined by a graphical analysis of the drain current versus gate source voltage curves. For the BF246, the value is 220 Ω. It is obviously impossible to bias the device at cut-off by this method since infinite source resistance would be required to obtain zero drain current. However, cut-off bias can be approximated by the use of a sufficiently large source resistor. A resistor of approximately ten times the value for $V_p/2$ bias will usually reduce the drain current to 1 mA or less. Therefore, for the BF246, a source resistor of 2.7 kΩ will bias the device near cut-off.

The FET mixer circuit with automatic source bias is shown in Figure 9. The variation of conversion gain with normalised local oscillator voltage under the two conditions of bias is shown in Figure 10. From a comparison of Figures 8 and 10 it can be seen that when the device is automatically biassed at $V_p/2$, by a source resistor, the variation of conversion gain with local oscillator is very similar to that with the device biassed with a separate power supply. However, with automatic bias, the conversion gain is slightly higher. This is due to the small d.c. component of the drain current shifting the bias towards pinch-off under large signal conditions. When the device is

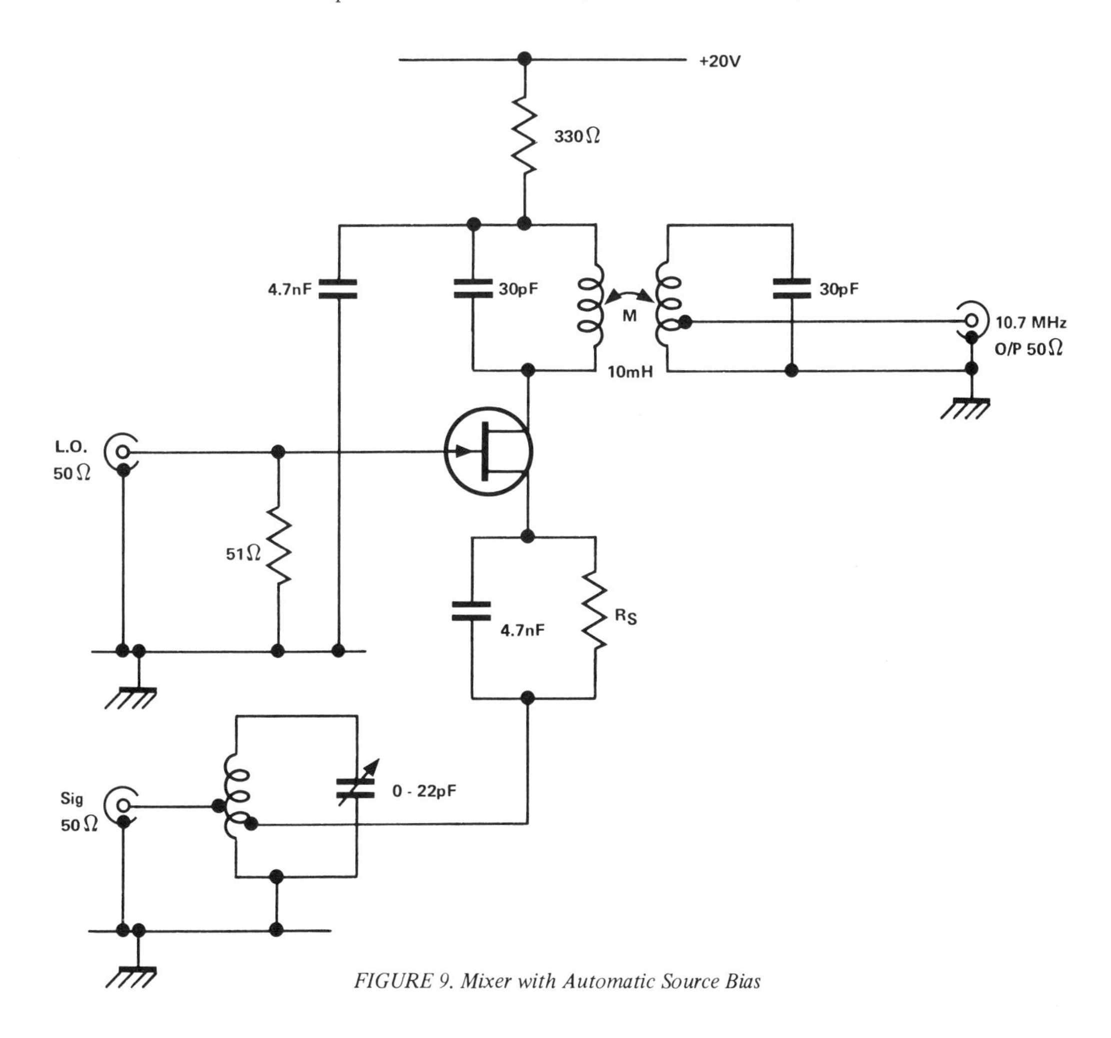

FIGURE 9. Mixer with Automatic Source Bias

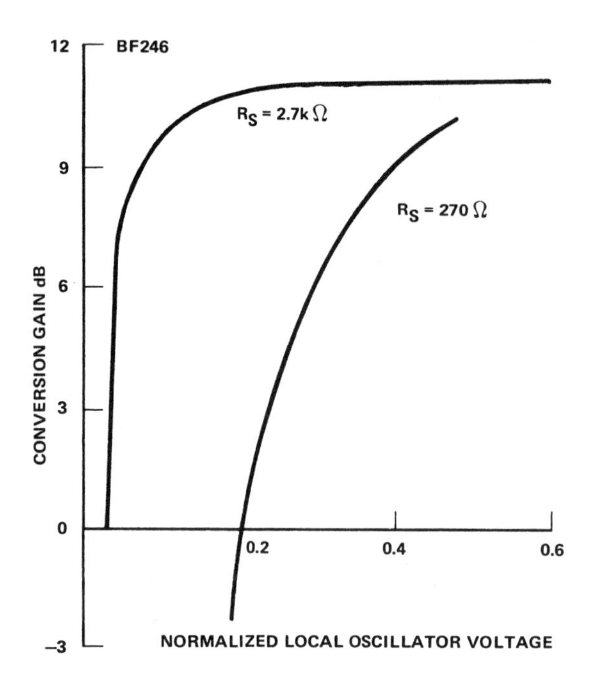

FIGURE 10. Variation of Conversion Gain with Peak Local Oscillator Injection for Automatic Bias Circuit

biassed near cut-off with a large source resistor, the conversion gain curve tends to flatten off far more rapidly than with external gate bias. Examination of the curves of Figure 1 show that the inclusion of a large bypassed source resistor tends to reduce the zero bias transconductance and flatten the g_m versus V_{GS} curve. Since the gate source is effectively a half wave rectified sine wave, it contains a large harmonic content and d.c. component. The d.c. component of the drain current flows through the source resistance and biases the device well into the cut-off region. Thus, as the local oscillator voltage on the gate is increased, the d.c. component tends to keep the device biassed in the cut-off region. The gain, therefore, tends to saturate rapidly as the local oscillator injection is increased. Under these conditions, the cross-modulation performance is worse than when the device is biassed at cut-off by external gate bias.

Conclusions

It has been shown that for the FET, conversion gain is proportional to the ratio $2I_{DSS}/V_p^2$ and that in general, cross-modulation occurs when there is appreciable fourth order non-linearity in the device characteristic. (Since a BF246 is a physically larger device than a BF244, the ratio $2I_{DSS}/V_p^2$ is higher and the device approximates more nearly the ideal square law). It has also been established that impedance in the source circuit at the local oscillator frequency reduces the transconductance, linearises the characteristic in the region near zero bias and increases the slope in the pinch-off region. This has the effect of reducing the conversion gain near zero bias and increasing gain and cross-modulation near pinch-off.

A quantitive analysis of the FET characteristic to determine the extent of the fourth order non-linearity is extremely difficult at high frequencies. However, the effect of source impedance on the linearity of the device was illustrated by harmonic measurements on a large signal FET amplifier. The results indicated that as the source impedance was increased, the harmonic content in the output current increased in the region near pinch-off. Thus, if high source impedance is unavoidable, the dynamic operating range should be confined to the region near zero bias if linear operation is desired.

The curves showing the cross-modulation performance indicate that the best results are obtained from a high pinch-off device under half pinch-off bias. If some relaxation in cross-modulation performance is possible, then high gain is available with the device biassed at pinch-off. Under conditions of pinch-off bias, the conversion gain is relatively independent of the device pinch-off voltage.

In many practical circuits, particularly if the local oscillator and signal frequencies are close to each other, impedance in the source at the local oscillator frequency is unavoidable. In this case, a great improvement in cross-modulation performance can be obtained by the use of a tetrode FET. The signal and local oscillator voltage are applied to the two gates and the source grounded via a suitable bias resistor.

In order to obtain the maximum possible conversion gain from FET mixers, the impedance in the drain circuit at the intermediate frequency (Z_{IF}) should be as high as possible. However, consideration should be given to possible drain overload under large signal conditions. If the instantaneous drain voltage falls below the value required to keep the device in the pinch-off region, the output impedance of the FET will fall and load the output tuned circuit.

A TUNER USING MOSFETs

General

A typical basic tuner block diagram, together with operating levels, is shown in Figure 11. The tuner 'front end', i.e. RF amplifier, mixer and oscillator, is shown in Figure 12. The design philosophy was to provide a tuner that is only limited by the performance of this section. The 'front end' has an overall conversion gain of 22 to 24dB and a noise figure of 2·8dB. Typical gain figures are 8dB for the RF amplifier and 14dB for the mixer. The output of the mixer is capacitively matched into the IF amplifier. This amplifier provides > 70dB of limiting gain at 10·7 MHz. If required, an RF AGC voltage proportional to input level can be obtained from the IF amplifier. This is then detected and the resulting signal used to control the gain of the first RF amplifier preceding the mixer. The amplitude limited output from the IF amplifier would then feed the FM detector. This would provide a demodulated signal and a d.c. level which, with suitable temperature compensation, could be used for AFC. The demodulated output from the detector would then feed into a multiplex decoder that separates the

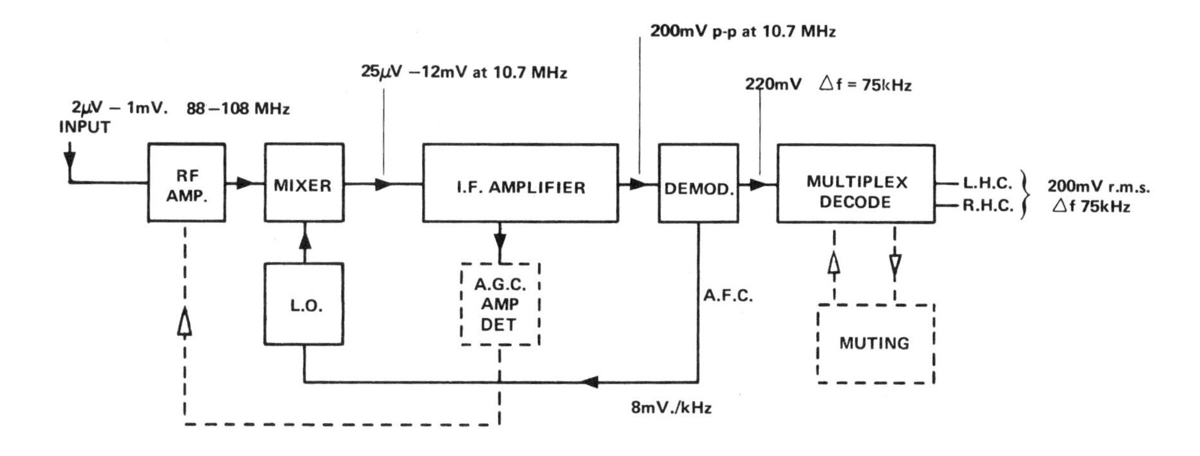

FIGURE 11. Basic Tuner Block Diagram

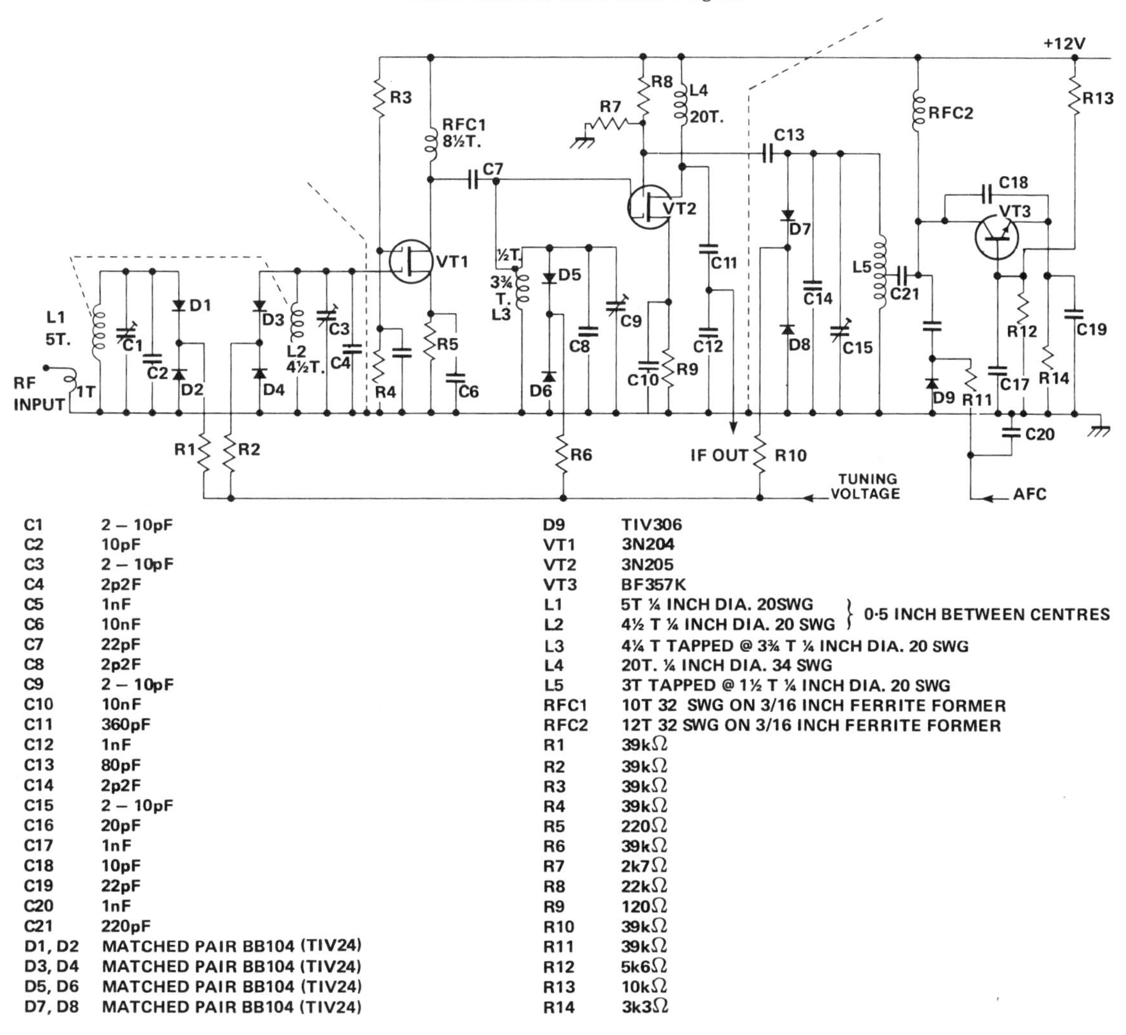

C1	2 – 10pF	D9	TIV306
C2	10pF	VT1	3N204
C3	2 – 10pF	VT2	3N205
C4	2p2F	VT3	BF357K
C5	1nF	L1	5T ¼ INCH DIA. 20SWG } 0·5 INCH BETWEEN CENTRES
C6	10nF	L2	4½ T ¼ INCH DIA. 20 SWG } 0·5 INCH BETWEEN CENTRES
C7	22pF	L3	4¼ T TAPPED @ 3¾ T ¼ INCH DIA. 20 SWG
C8	2p2F	L4	20T. ¼ INCH DIA. 34 SWG
C9	2 – 10pF	L5	3T TAPPED @ 1½ T ¼ INCH DIA. 20 SWG
C10	10nF	RFC1	10T 32 SWG ON 3/16 INCH FERRITE FORMER
C11	360pF	RFC2	12T 32 SWG ON 3/16 INCH FERRITE FORMER
C12	1nF	R1	39kΩ
C13	80pF	R2	39kΩ
C14	2p2F	R3	39kΩ
C15	2 – 10pF	R4	39kΩ
C16	20pF	R5	220Ω
C17	1nF	R6	39kΩ
C18	10pF	R7	2k7Ω
C19	22pF	R8	22kΩ
C20	1nF	R9	120Ω
C21	220pF	R10	39kΩ
D1, D2	MATCHED PAIR BB104 (TIV24)	R11	39kΩ
D3, D4	MATCHED PAIR BB104 (TIV24)	R12	5k6Ω
D5, D6	MATCHED PAIR BB104 (TIV24)	R13	10kΩ
D7, D8	MATCHED PAIR BB104 (TIV24)	R14	3k3Ω

FIGURE 12. RF Amplifier, Oscillator and Mixer

composite input signal into two separate channels required for stereo reception.[1]

As stated in the introduction to the chapter dual gate MOSFETs are ideal for use as the RF amplifier and mixer due to their square low characteristic, low feedback capacitance, low noise figure and large dynamic range. Besides using the second gate for AGC or local oscillator injection, it can provide isolation between input and output ports. This enables high RF and conversion gains to be achieved without the need for neutralisation. The 3N204/5 used in this tuner are n channel depletion mode dual gate FETs with integral back to back zener diodes between both gates and the source. These eliminate the requirement for special handling procedures that are associated with unprotected MOSFETs. At the operating frequency of 100 MHz the reverse transfer admittance (y_{rs}) and input and output conductances of these devices are very small and are not easily measured with any degree of accuracy. This means that the dominant feedback elements are circuit strays, which makes the design dependent on circuit layout and a mathematical analysis difficult.

RF Amplifier

The double tuned bandpass input transformer matches the aerial impedance to the MOSFET VT1's input resistance giving maximum power gain. In order to minimise the tuner noise figure the insertion loss of the input matching network must be low, i.e. the ratio of loaded to unloaded Q small. It is necessary that the insertion loss should be small because the tuner noise figure is degraded in proportion to the losses in the circuits preceding the MOSFET. However, to minimise cross-modulation and increase image rejection, the input tuned circuit should have a high Q. A compromise is provided by the double tuned transformer formed by inductors L1 and L2. Since this RF stage provides a gain in excess of 10dB, the NF of the receiver is, to a first order, determined by this stage. The output tuned circuit is formed by inductor L3, capacitors C8, C9 and varactor diodes D5 and D6. With most bipolar RF amplifiers operating at 100 MHz it is necessary to remove the effects of the reverse transfer admittance with a neutralization circuit. Because the grounded source dual gate MOSFET is very similar to a pair of cascode FETs with the second gate acting as a screen between input and output, its y_{rs} is so small that neutralisation is not required.[2]

Mixer

The mixer stage should have high gain at the IF frequency and a square law transfer function. To obtain good mixing the MOSFET VT2 requires to be biassed near the 'pinch-off' region. This, however, gives low gain which can only be increased by increasing the drain current. In practice, the mixer bias is optimised experimentally to give the greatest conversion gain with a minimum of spurious products. In both the RF amplifier and mixer stages biassing is stabilised by source resistors which give degenerative feedback. Local oscillator injection is achieved by means of the second gate of the mixer MOSFET. This mode of operation is preferred to that of applying the local oscillator and signal to the first gate of VT2. Interaction (e.g. pulling) between oscillator and signal tuned circuits is minimised, easing alignment. Also, improved cross-modulation performance is obtained, together with reduced oscillator feedthrough to the RF stage. This method does, however, require a larger oscillator voltage and gives approximately 4 to 5dB less conversion gain than the single gate mixer.[3,4] The output of the mixer is capacitively matched into the IF amplifier by L4, C11 and C12. The bandwidth of this tuned circuit being determined by the input impedance of the following IF amplifier.

Oscillator

Common base bipolar transistor amplifiers are generally regenerative at VHF frequencies, making them suitable for use as oscillators. Since a MOSFET is used as the mixer, the oscillator must be designed to produce the large injection voltage required to obtain conversion gain. Capacitors C18 and C19 provide positive feedback between the collector and emitter of transistor VT3. Components L5, C14, C15 and C16, varactor diodes D7, D8 and D9 and the transistor collector base capacity form the frequency-determining parallel resonant circuit. Capacitor C13 provides the required injection level to the mixer. AFC is provided by a varactor D9. This is independent of the main tuning varactors. The series drive resistors to the oscillator varactors should not be of so high a value that noise, i.e. change of capacitance, due to diode leakage, occurs.

REFERENCES

1. N. van Hurk, F.L.H.M. Stumpers and M. Weeda, Stereophonic Radio Broadcasting, 1 Systems and Circuits, *Philips Technical Review,* Vol. 26, No. 11/12, 1965.
2. S. Weaver, Selecting FETs for RF Amplifiers, *Electronic Design,* Vol. 17, No. 6, March 15, 1969.

3 & 4. R. Klein, MOSFET FM Tuner Design, and S. Weaver, Dual-Gate MOSFETs in TV IF Amplifiers, both in *IEEE Transactions on Broadcast and Television Receivers,* Vol. BTR16, No. 2, May 1970.

XIII HIGH INPUT IMPEDANCE CIRCUITS

by
Mike Stevens

Amplifiers which will operate satisfactorily from generator impedances of the order of megohms, are substantially independent of environmental changes and have a reliability far in excess of valve amplifiers, are often a requirement of analogue computers, industrial control equipment, measuring instruments and medical electronics. Conventional bipolar transistor amplifiers give excellent performance when generator impedances are below about 1MΩ. Pairs of devices can be matched to extremely low equivalent input voltage drift specifications and exhibit a very small 1/f noise component. However, the bipolar transistor is a current operated device and even when operated with very low collector currents, requires substantial base current drive. When the source impedance is high, variations of base current due to variations in current gain, h_{FE}, can cause considerable drift in the amplifier. The '1/f' component of the equivalent input noise voltage also increases with source impedance. Thus, when the source impedance is high, it is often necessary to employ the vacuum tube or its solid state equivalent, the FET, which, with its pentode-like characteristics, is essentially voltage operated and has a high input impedance. Leakage currents are generally orders of magnitude lower than normal operating base currents of bipolar transistors and the equivalent input noise voltage is extremely low when the device is driven from a high impedance source. FETs are superior to bipolar transistors in d.c. or direct coupled amplifiers when driven from generator resistances of about one megohm or greater.

BASIC DESIGN CONSIDERATIONS

One of the main limitations on the accuracy of an electronic measuring system is the noise generated within the system itself. In a.c. systems, the noise is generally expressed as an equivalent input noise voltage generator. In a d.c. system, however, a further limitation on the accuracy is imposed by drift in the system. Drift usually occurs with a change in environment, in particular with change in temperature. In most instances, drift as a function of temperature is a prime consideration and, again, this is usually referred to the input as an effective drift in input signal.

Drift in direct coupled amplifiers can be attributed to two main causes:–

(i) Gain Drift: This is the drift in the current or voltage gain of the amplifier, and is usually specified as an effective change in input signal. Gain drift is usually reduced to an acceptable level by designing the amplifier with high open loop gain and applying sufficient negative feedback to reduce both gain and drift to the desired level.

(ii) Zero Drift: This is the drift in output with constant or zero input signal and is specified as the input signal required to restore the output to its original level. Zero drift can only be improved by some form of compensation.

There are several methods of reducing zero drift, among the most frequently used are:–

(i) The use of temperature sensitive components such as diodes and silicon resistors for compensation.

(ii) The balanced amplifier, in which the variations in one device are balanced by similar variations in another matched device.

(iii) The use of 'chopper' techniques in which the input signal is chopped and amplified with a gain stable a.c. amplifier. (As described in the following chapter).

The primary causes of gain and zero drift are variations of device parameters with temperature. In the case of the bipolar transistor, the prime temperature sensitive parameters are the base-emitter voltage, V_{BE}; the current gain, h_{FE}, and the leakage current, I_{CBO}. Whereas, in the case of the FET, the sensitive parameters are the drain current, I_D; mutual conductance, g_m; and gate leakage current, I_{GSS}. The factors which affect these changes and how they vary with temperature are now considered.

THEORETICAL TEMPERATURE CONSIDERATIONS

Drain Current Variation

There are two main independent temperature varying parameters which determine the variation of drain current with temperature in a silicon diffused FET. These are:–

(i) The resistivity of the channel, which increases with temperature and decreases the drain current.

(ii) The pinch-off voltage, which increases with temperature and thus increases the drain current.

Since these two parameters have opposing effects on the drain current, it might be expected that they will cancel each other under certain operating conditions. In order to examine the temperature effects in more detail, it can be assumed that the FET is a perfect square law device. Therefore, ignoring for the moment the gate leakage current, I_{GSS}, from equation (5) of chapter XI the drain current is related to the gate-source voltage by the equation:–

$$I_D = I_{DSS}\,(1 - V_{GS}/V_p)^2 \quad . . . . (1)$$

If it is assumed that the temperature dependent variables are the pinch-off voltage, V_p, and the zero bias drain current, I_{DSS}, (I_{DSS} is, in fact, determined by the channel resistivity and the space charge width) then differentiating equation (1) with respect to temperature gives:–

$$\frac{dI_D}{dT} = \left(1 - \frac{V_{GS}}{V_p}\right) . \left\{ \frac{dI_{DSS}}{dT} . \left(1 - \frac{V_{GS}}{V_p}\right) + \frac{dV_p}{dT} . \frac{2I_{DSS}V_{GS}}{V_p{}^2} \right\} \quad . . . . (2)$$

Equation (2) can be written in terms of the device constants:–

$$\frac{dI_D}{dT} = \frac{dI_{DSS}}{dT} . \frac{I_D}{I_{DSS}} - \frac{dV_p}{dT} . g_m . \frac{V_{GS}}{V_p} \quad . . . . (3)$$

Returning to equation (2) and by accepting the existence of a zero temperature coefficient point.

For zero change in drain current then:–

$$\frac{dI_{DSS}}{dT} . \left(1 - \frac{V_{GS}}{V_p}\right) = - \frac{dV_p}{dT} . \frac{2I_{DSS}V_{GS}}{V_p{}^2} \quad . . . . (4)$$

From (4), the gate bias for zero temperature coefficient, V_{GSQ}, is given by:–

$$\frac{V_{GSQ}}{V_p} = \frac{dI_{DSS}/dT}{\dfrac{dI_{DSS}}{dT} - \dfrac{2I_{DSS}}{V_p} . \dfrac{dV_p}{dT}} \quad . . . . (5)$$

The zero temperature coefficient bias current I_{DQ} can be determined by substituting for $\frac{V_{GSQ}}{V_p}$ in equation (1) and solving for $\frac{I_{DQ}}{I_{DSS}}$. Then,

$$\frac{I_{DQ}}{I_{DSS}} = - \frac{2I_{DSS}/V_p \; \dfrac{dV_p}{dT}}{\dfrac{dI_{DSS}}{dT} - \dfrac{2I_{DSS}}{V_p} . \dfrac{dV_p}{dT}} \quad . . . . (6)$$

At this point, it is convenient to deal with the variations of I_{DSS} and V_p separately.

Variation of I_{DSS}: The zero bias drain current, I_{DSS}, which is a function of both the channel resistivity and pinch-off voltage, can be expressed thus:–

$I_{DSS} = a.\mu_n. V_p{}^2$ . . . . (7)

where a is a constant. From this equation, it is apparent that the temperature dependence of I_{DSS} lies in the carrier mobility and pinch-off voltage. From Gartner[1], the lattice mobility of electrons in silicon (n-channel) is given by:–

$\mu_n = 2{\cdot}1 \pm 0{\cdot}2 \times 10^9 \times T^{-2{\cdot}5 \pm 0{\cdot}1}$ $cm^2\ V^{-1}\ sec^{-1}$

$= c\ T^{-2{\cdot}5}$ say . . . . (8)

With normally used impurity levels, the lattice mobility is approximately equal to the carrier mobility. Hence, equation (8) represents the carrier mobility. Substitution of equation (8) into (7) yields:–

$I_{DSS} = c.T^{-2{\cdot}5}V_p{}^2$ . . . . (9)

Differentiating (9) with respect to temperature,

$$\frac{dI_{DSS}}{dT} = 2cT^{-2.5}V_p . \frac{dV_p}{dT} - 2.5cT^{-3.5}V_p{}^2$$

$$= cV_pT^{-2.5} . \left(2\frac{dV_p}{dT} - \frac{2.5V_p}{T}\right) \quad . . . . . (10)$$

Equation (10) shows that the variation of I_{DSS} with temperature is a function of temperature itself and of the temperature variation of the pinch-off voltage. Substituting equations (9) and (10) in equation (7) yields:–

$$\sqrt{\frac{I_{DQ}}{I_{DSS}}} = \frac{2}{2.5} . \frac{T}{V_p} . \frac{dV_p}{dT}$$

or . . . . . (11)

$$\frac{I_{DQ}}{I_{DSS}} = \frac{4}{2.5^2} \frac{T^2}{V_p{}^2} \left\{\frac{dV_p}{dT}\right\}^2$$

Variation of V_p: Under normal operating conditions, the junction voltage is the algebraic sum of the applied voltage and the contact potential. Assuming a constant applied voltage, the temperature dependence of pinch-off voltage is that due to the contact potential ϕ.

$$\phi = \frac{kT}{q} . \log_e \frac{N_aN_d}{n_i{}^2} \quad . . . . (12)$$

where k = Boltzmans constant

T = absolute temperature °K

q = electronic charge

N_a = acceptor impurity density

N_d = donor impurity density

n_i = intrinsic free carrier density

Ignoring for the moment practical values for N_a and N_d, from Gartner[1], the value of $n_i{}^2$ for silicon is:–

$n_i{}^2 = 1{\cdot}5 \times 10^{45} \times T^3 \times \exp(-14028/T)\ m^{-6}$

∴ from (12)

$$\phi = \frac{kT}{q} . \log_e \left(\frac{N_aN_d}{1 . 5 \times 10^{45}}\right) - 3 \log_e T + \frac{14028}{T} \quad (13)$$

Differentiating with respect to temperature

$$\frac{d\phi}{dT} = \frac{k}{q} \log_e \left(\frac{N_aN_d}{1 . 5 \times 10^{45}}\right) - 3(1 + \log_e T) . \quad . \quad . (14)$$

Equation (14) shows that the variation of contact potential with temperature is a function of the temperature itself and of the impurity levels in the channel and gate. Typical values of N_a and N_d for n-channel silicon FETs are now necessary. A representation of a cross section through an FET showing a typical diffusion profile is shown in Figure 1. Since the junction is not abrupt, the gate impurity density, N_a, will vary with applied voltage as the depletion region extends into the gate. For 1 ohm cm channel resistivity, the impurity density, N_d, will be approximately:–

$N_d = 1 \times 10^{21}$ atoms m^{-3}
and under normal operating conditions, a typical value for the gate impurity density, N_a would be:–
$N_a = 1 \times 10^{25}$ atoms m^{-3}
Substituting these values of N_a and N_d in equation (14) yields:–

$$\frac{d\phi}{dT} = \frac{k}{q} \log_e (1 \times 10^{-2}) - 3(1 + \log_e T) \quad . . . . . (15)$$

At room temperature, 300°K, the rate of change is:–

$$\frac{d\phi}{dT} \simeq -0.86 \times 10^{-4} (4.6 + 20.07)$$

$$\simeq 2.1 \text{ mV/°K}$$

It must be appreciated that $d\phi/dT$ is quite strongly dependent on the impurity densities operating voltage and temperature. Values usually lie between 1·8 and 2·7 mV/°K for silicon.

Substituting for $\frac{d\phi}{dT}$ $(= \frac{dV_p}{dT})$ in equation (11) yields:–

$$\frac{I_{DQ}}{I_{DSS}} = \frac{T^2 4}{2.5^2} \left\{\frac{dV_p}{dT}\right\}^2 \quad \text{at } T = 300°K$$

$$\frac{I_{DQ}}{I_{DSS}} = \frac{0.26}{V_p^2} \quad . . . . (16)$$

From equation (8), it can be seen that there is some spread in the value of the lattice mobility and its temperature dependence. Using extreme values, the value of $\frac{I_{DQ}}{I_{DSS}}$ will usually be found to vary between

$$\frac{0.25}{V_p^2} \text{ and } \frac{0.39}{V_p^2}$$

Mutual Conductance Variation:

The mutual conductance, g_m, is given by:–

$$g_m = \frac{dI_D}{dV_{GS}} = \frac{2I_{DSS}}{V_p} \cdot \left\{\frac{V_{GS}}{V_p} - 1\right\}$$

$$\therefore \frac{dg_m}{dT} = \frac{dI_{DSS}}{dT} \cdot \frac{2}{V_p} \cdot \left\{\frac{V_{GS}}{V_p} - 1\right\} - \frac{dV_p}{dT} \cdot \frac{2I_{DSS}}{V_p^2} \left\{\frac{2V_{GS}}{V_p} - 1\right\}$$

By performing the necessary algebraic manipulations, it is possible to show that the bias current for zero temperature coefficient of g_m, I_{DGQ}, is equal to $I_{DQ}/4$, i.e.

$I_{DGQ} = I_{DQ}/4$

It is apparent that I_{DGQ} is a relatively low value of current, usually about 200μA. This is quite useful because it is usual to bias the device at a low value of drain current to achieve high gain.

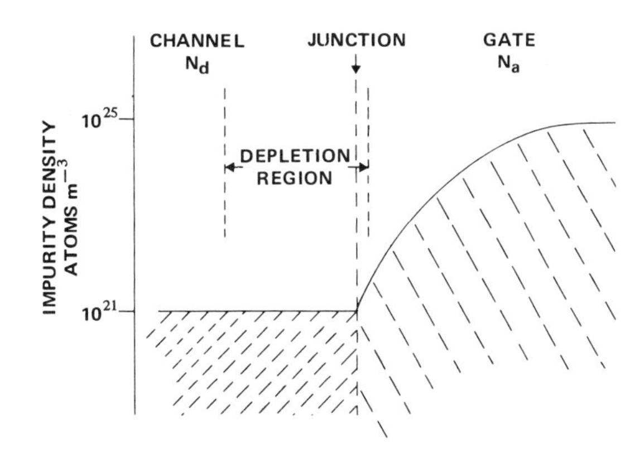

FIGURE 1. Graphical Representation of FET Diffusion Profile

Leakage Current

The remaining temperature dependent parameter to be considered is the gate leakage current. The effect of the leakage current on the performance of the amplifier will depend on the generator resistance and the operating temperature. With normal circuit values, the effect of leakage current is usually negligible except at elevated temperatures. The data sheet parameter is the gate reverse current, I_{GSS}. This is the reverse leakage current between the gate and the source and drain strapped together. This is usually of the order of a few pico-amps at 0°C and increases by a factor of approximately 1·7 for every 10°C rise in temperature. This current is dependent on the gate to channel voltage and to minimise leakage, the drain to gate voltage should be as low as possible. With exceptionally high drain-gate voltage (usually $>$ 30V), large increases in leakage current can occur due to the depletion region extending almost to the drain and carriers entering the drain terminal being swept towards the gate.

PRACTICAL TEMPERATURE CONSIDERATIONS

Gain Drift

In the theoretical discussion, it was predicted that there is a value of bias current at which the temperature coefficient of the mutual conductance, g_m, is zero. Furthermore, it was shown that this bias current is one fourth of the current at which the temperature coefficient of drain current is zero. The variation of mutual conductance with temperature of some sample dual devices was determined using the test circuit of Figure 2, and typical results are shown in Figure 3. (The curves for the second half of the device matched those for the first half shown and graphically no difference could be seen). The curves show that for this particular device the bias current for zero temperature coefficient of g_m, at 300°K is approximately 230μA. From the 'Variation of Drain Current Temperature' curves, Figure 4, the bias current for zero temperature coefficient of drain current at 300°K is approximately 940μA. Thus, the practical results are in good agreement with theory.

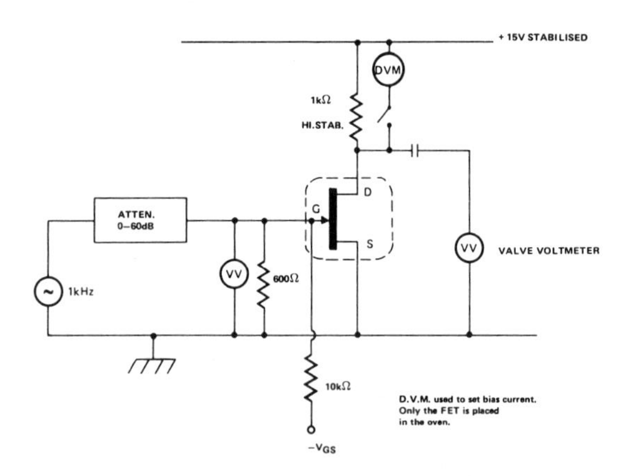

FIGURE 2. Gain Drift Test Circuit

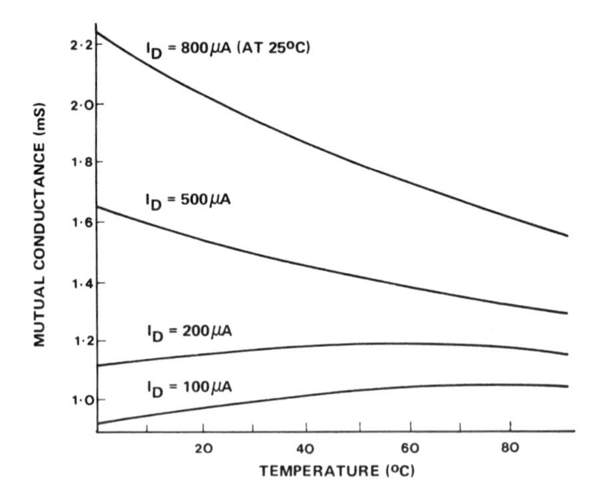

FIGURE 3. Variation of Mutual Conductance with Temperature

Drain Current Drift

In the theoretical treatment of temperature effects, it was shown that the variation of drain current is dependent upon factors which vary from device to device. The existance of a zero temperature coefficient bias current was proposed and the value of this current was found to be, to some extent, dependent on temperature. In order to clarify the situation, the variation of drain current with temperature, several samples of 2N5045 dual FET were measured at various values of bias current using the circuit of Figure 5. Measurements were made on each half of each device separately, and typical results are shown in Figure 4 for the same device and same half as used for Figure 3. From these curves, it can be seen that for each value of bias current chosen, there is a particular temperature at which the slope

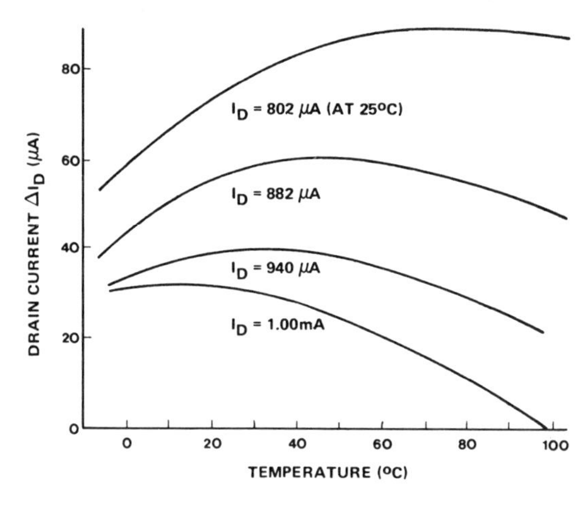

FIGURE 4. Variation of Drain Current with Temperature

or change of drain current is zero. For temperatures below this value, the temperature dependence of pinch-off voltage predominates and above this value, the variation of I_{DSS} predominates. At the point at which the slope of the curve is zero, the two mechanisms cancel.

If, for example, requirements called for a device with minimum drift over the range 10 – 50°C, the bias current would be set at 940μA (Figure 4), where, over this range, the drift would be approximately 2μA. To refer this drift to the input, it is necessary to divide the current drift by the mutual conductance, i.e.

$$\Delta V_{in} = \frac{\Delta I_D}{g_m}$$

At 940μA, the g_m for this particular device is approximately 2·3 mA/V.

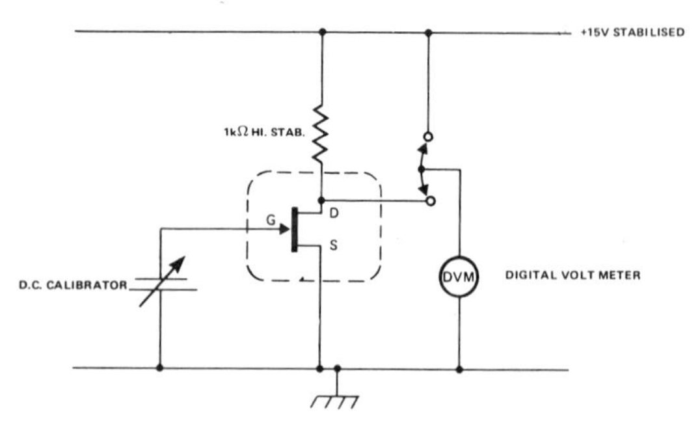

FIGURE 5. Drain Current Drift Test Circuit

$$\therefore \Delta V_{in} = \frac{2 \times 10^{-6}}{2.3 \times 10^{-3}}$$

$$= 0.87 \times 10^{-3} \text{ V}$$

or

$$\frac{0.87 \times 10^{-3}}{40} \quad \text{mV/°C}$$

$$\underline{\underline{22 \mu \text{ V/°C}}}$$

On the other hand, if the bias current had been set at 800μA, the total drift would be about 18μA and the g_m, 1·7 – 1·8 mA/V. Therefore, in this case, the input drift would be approximately 260μV/°C. Figure 4 shows that the zero temperature coefficient bias current at 25°C (or 300°K) is approximately 940μA. For this particular device, the zero bias drain current, I_{DSS}, and pinch-off voltage, V_p, are 3·4mA and 1·25V respectively. With this information it is possible to check the expression previously obtained for I_{DQ}, i.e.

$$\frac{I_{DQ}}{I_{DSS}} = \frac{0.27}{V_p^2} \text{ to } \frac{0.39}{V_p^2} \text{ or } \frac{c'}{V_p^2}$$

Substituting the values for I_{DQ}, I_{DSS} and V_p yields:–

$$\frac{0.94}{3.4} = \frac{c'}{1.25^2}$$

c′ is approximately 0·43. This is in reasonable agreement with the theoretical value of 0·27 to 0·39, especially considering the number of variable factors involved.

The measurements made on drain current drift (Figure 4) clearly show the dependence of drift on bias current and temperature. In order to minimise drift over a particular range of temperature, the bias current should be chosen to yield a point of inflexion in the centre of the temperature range. Thus, in order to bias the device correctly, it is necessary to be able to predict its behaviour with temperature accurately. In the earlier discussion, it was shown that this behaviour depends upon a number of factors which vary from device to device, such as pinch-off voltage, V_p, zero drain current, I_{DSS}, and the impurity concentrations N_a and N_d, on each side of the junction. Therefore, in order to obtain optimum conditions, measurements would have to be made on each individual device. In most cases, individual selection is impractical and the only solution is to use some means of compensation or a balanced amplifier.

Compensation

Compensation is usually achieved by the use of temperature sensitive elements such as diodes or silicon resistors. Whatever element is chosen, the drift should be the exact complement of the drift in the device to be compensated. Under most normal operating conditions, the temperature coefficient of drain current of a device such as the 2N5045 Dual FET changes from positive to negative in the temperature range – 10 to 100°C, thus making accurate compensation virtually impossible. In the earlier part of this chapter, it was shown that it is possible to achieve an equivalent input voltage drift as low as 22μV/°C from a single stage FET amplifier. If a significant improvement in this figure is required, then it is necessary to use a balanced amplifier.

THE BALANCED AMPLIFIER

Device Matching

In the balanced amplifier, the drift in one device is balanced by that in the second device. In the preceeding discussion, it was shown that the drift in drain current with temperature is dependent on the zero bias drain current, I_{DSS}, the pinch-off voltage, V_p, the diffusion profile and the impurity concentrations in the gate and channel. It is, therefore, these parameters which should be matched to optimise thermal tracking between the two devices. The best method to ensure matching all these parameters is to select devices which have undergone identical diffusion. Once selected, they should be mounted in such a way as to be in good thermal contact with each other. If the generator resistance is high, it is usually necessary to match the gate leakage currents, I_{GSS}.

Thermal Tracking

The thermal tracking of the two halves of a 2N5045 was checked by measuring the drain current drift with temperature at various bias currents of each half separately and superimposing the curves. These curves show that, within the limits of measuring accuracy, the drain current drift in the two halves of this device is identical. The same technique was followed to compare the tracking of the mutual conductance of the two devices and the curves showed similar results. Comparable results were obtained with several other samples of a 2N5045, showing that this device is admirably suited to balanced amplifier applications.

Practical Design Considerations

The most common balanced amplifier configuration is the long tailed pair. An approximate analysis of this circuit is given in the Appendix. From this analysis, it can be seen that in order to maintain the performance under dynamic (a.c.) conditions, a number of dynamic parameters should be matched. The gains of the two stages should be identical and thus, matching on the forward transfer admittance, y_{fs}, is essential. If the static bias current is low, and the drain load high, as is usually the case, then it is necessary to match the output admittances, y_{os}. These parameters should be matched under the expected static operation conditions.

The results show that the two halves of a 2N5045 track extremely well at all values of bias current. There is therefore, no apparent reason why the devices should not be biased with low values of drain current and high drain resistors to improve the dynamic gain. In most practical circuits, bias currents usually lie between 50 and 500μA.

The previous experimental data indicates that thermal

tracking is extremely good when both halves of the devices have identical bias current. From the curves obtained previously, it is shown that if the amplifier stage was unbalanced by a differential input signal, then the two devices will have different drain currents and if the unbalance is sufficient to bias one device into a region of positive and the other in a region of negative temperature coefficient, the results could be disastrous. It is quite obvious that unbalance in the amplifier should be minimised and this is usually the case when the FET stage is followed by a high gain integrated circuit amplifier with overall feedback. If the amplifier is required to handle large input voltages, it may be necessary to resort to using two source followers, each with its own constant current generator. Figure 6 shows a practical FET differential amplifier. The values shown are for the devices biased at 940μA, while the values given in brackets are for the devices biased at 230μA. The FETs are biased from a common current source to ensure stable bias conditions and improve the common mode rejection. A brief summary of the performance for each set of circuit values is given on the diagram. The most important feature of these amplifiers is the exceptionally low equivalent input voltage drift, i.e. 2 and 3μV/°C. This drift was measured with no circuit unbalance, i.e. with both devices biased with identical drain currents. Although this type of circuit is capable of providing considerable gain, it has the disadvantage in that when an input signal is applied, the drain currents in the two FETs become unbalanced, the degree of unbalance being proportional to the amplitude of the difference signal on the gates. Thus, under normal operating conditions, it is to be expected that the drain currents in the two devices will not be identical and that drift will be considerably worse than that measured under balanced conditions.

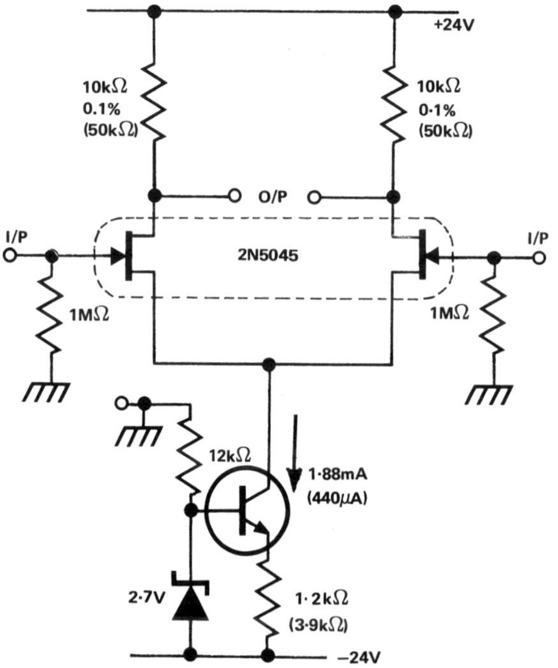

VOLTAGE GAIN ≏23 (56)
COMMON MODE REJECTION ≏96 db (100 dB)
EQUIVALENT INPUT DRIFT AT BALANCE =3μV/°C (<2μV/°C)

FIGURE 6. D.C. Balanced Amplifier Circuit

Drift Under Balanced Conditions

In order to assess the effect of unbalance on the drift performance of the amplifier, the equivalent input voltage drift with temperature was measured for various values of unbalance from 0 – 25%. The measurements were taken at two values of static bias current, i.e. 940 and 230μA, at 25°C. The results are shown in Figure 7. In these graphs, the effective input drift over a temperature range of 0 – 100°C is plotted against percentage unbalance 0 – 25%. These curves indicate that the drift is proportional to the percentage circuit unbalance. For a given circuit unbalance, the drift is least in the amplifier with the lowest bias current, i.e. 230μA. These results indicate that under conditions where considerable circuit unbalance is expected, it is necessary to bias the devices at a low value of drain current where the temperature coefficient of drain current does not change sign over the desired temperature range. Over the temperature range 0 – 100°C, the best results are obtained at bias currents of between 50 and 200μA.

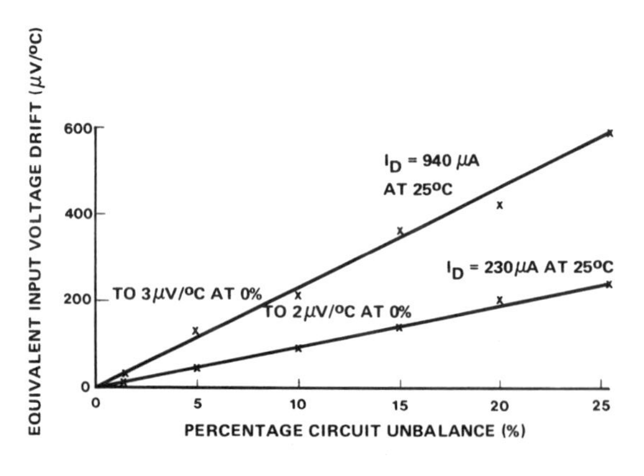

FIGURE 7. Variation of Drift with Circuit Unbalance

In circuits where unbalance cannot be minimised and the input stage is to be used as an impedance transformer rather than as an amplifier, a pair of source followers biased with identical drain currents with separate current sources, as shown in Figure 8, will yield input drifts as low as 2μV/°C and a voltage gain near unity. This type of circuit is suitable for driving most currently available I.C. amplifiers. Dual FETs with tighter matching specifications on V_{GS} temperature drift, y_{fs}, I_{DSS}, reduced leakage and capacitance etc., than the 2N5045 e.g. the 2N5545/6/7, would obviously give a better balanced amplifier.

HIGH INPUT IMPEDANCE AMPLIFIERS

Simple Bootstrapped Configuration

As the input impedances of FETs lie in the gigaohm region an amplifier with an input resistance of 1GΩ can easily be designed using a FET. The circuit diagram (Figure 9) shows an amplifier acting as source follower with a voltage gain close to one. The input resistance may be realised with a gate resistor of a minimum value of 1GΩ. Because such high-ohmic resistors are too big and too expensive, a gate voltage divider is used. This consists of two 10MΩ resistors and a bootstrapping capacitor from the source to the midpoint of this voltage divider. Thus a gate resistor of 22MΩ will, by using the bootstrapping effect, give an input resistance of more than 1GΩ. The output admittance of the FET,

$y_{21S} \triangleq 1\,mS$ at $I_D = 0.2mA$

thus the voltage gain

$$A_V = 100 \times 10^3/(100 \times 10^3 + 1/y_{21S})$$
$$= 10^5/(10^5 + 10^3) = 0.99$$

and the input resistance

$$r_{in} = 22 \times 10^6 \cdot 100 \times 10^3 / (1/y_{21S})$$
$$= 2.2 \times 10^9\,\Omega$$

The measured input resistance was about 1·5GΩ greater than the calculated value. This circuit is especially applicable as an electrostatic microphone preamplifier, a measuring amplifier, a preamplifier for oscilloscopes, etc.

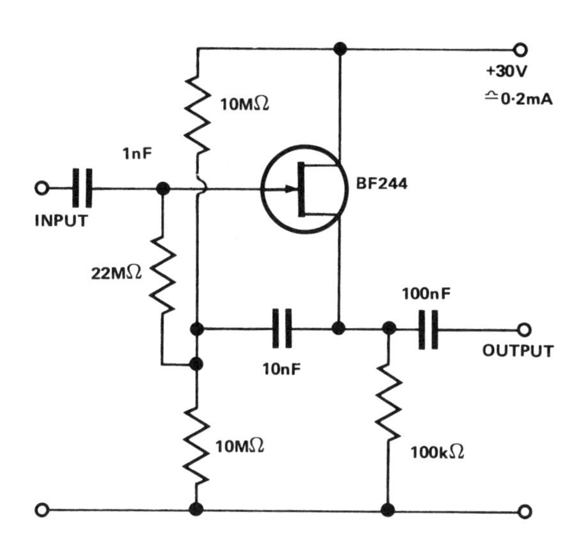

FIGURE 9. High Input Impedance Amplifier

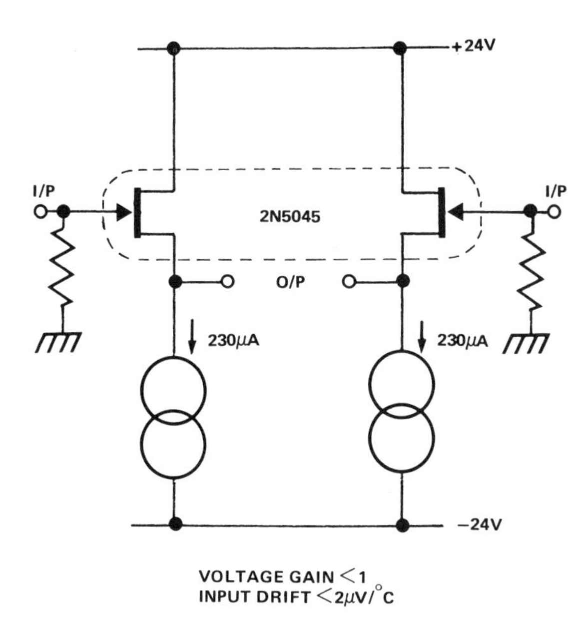

FIGURE 8. Low Input Drift Configuration

Low Noise Current Amplifier

A low frequency high impedance application requiring the use of a low noise current FET is the infra-red pyroelectric detector. The detector element is usually either a ceramic, such as lead zirconate titanate (PZT), or the organic tri-glycine sulphate (TGS). The impedance of the detector crystal is usually of the order of 10^{12} Ω and the FET current noise generator limits the overall noise equivalent power. A circuit similar to that shown in Figure 10 has been used with a TGS detector to give detectivities (D*) of $4{\cdot}5 \times 10^8$ cm. $Hz^2 W^{-1}$. This circuit performance is only made possible by the use of a very low leakage JFET such as BF800. Although the application outlined is particularly useful for specialised applications such as night vision systems, intruder alarms, etc. it also has wider applications. These include a range of high impedance circuits such as electromates, pH meters and smoke/fire detectors.

Low Noise Voltage Amplifier

Circuits for applications such as a large area X-ray spectrometer need to use very low thermal noise devices, e.g. a BF818. Using the circuit shown in Figure 11, resolutions of less than 2keV have been achieved. The same type of FET and circuit can also be used for a range of low noise wide bandwidth applications. Extensions to this type of circuit using an experimental very low noise FET (of typical thermal noise 0.4nV. $Hz^{-1/2}$) are currently being used to evaluate the performance of lead-tin-telluride photovoltaic detectors.

Channel Multiplier Preamplifier

A channel electron multiplier is used with a scanning electron microscope or similar equipment, to detect small currents in the 10^{-14} to 10^{-10} A range. The wall resistance or output impedance of a channel multiplier is 3GΩ so that, running at its nominal output potential of 1.5kV, 500mA

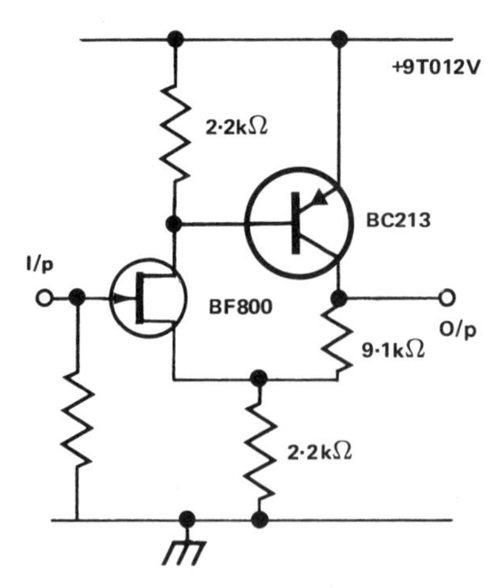

FIGURE 10. Low Noise Current Amplifier

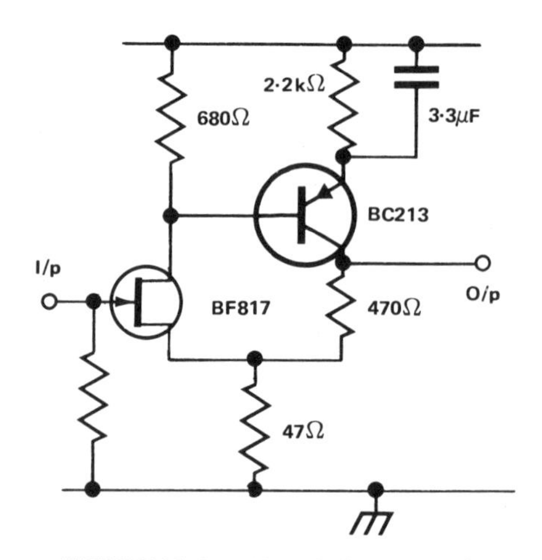

FIGURE 11. Low Noise Voltage Amplifier

flows in the wall. In order for the channel multiplier to operate in a linear amplifying mode the signal output current must not exceed one or two percent of the wall current (5 or 6 nA say). Thus this almost perfect current source will require a low noise wideband preamplifier stage in order to amplify its 5–6 nA output up to the mA region for conventional circuit processing. A first suggestion for a circuit to perform this function might be a high performance operational amplifier with a large feedback resistor from its output to its inverting input. A pole is, however, produced in the response of the feedback loop due to reaction with the input capacitance; which is likely to cause oscillation. Placing a capacitor across the feedback resistor to compensate and remove this pole will reduce the bandwidth.

The FET circuit, shown in Figure 12, however, will amplify 6nA current with 1MHz bandwidth. The 6nA current flowing in the 1MΩ signal resistor produces a voltage signal of 6mV at the input of the preamplifier. The open circuit input noise of the preamplifier is less than 400μV peak to peak so that the signal to noise ratio at the preamplifier is better than 35dB. The input device in the preamplifier is a 2N4416 n-channel FET operating as a

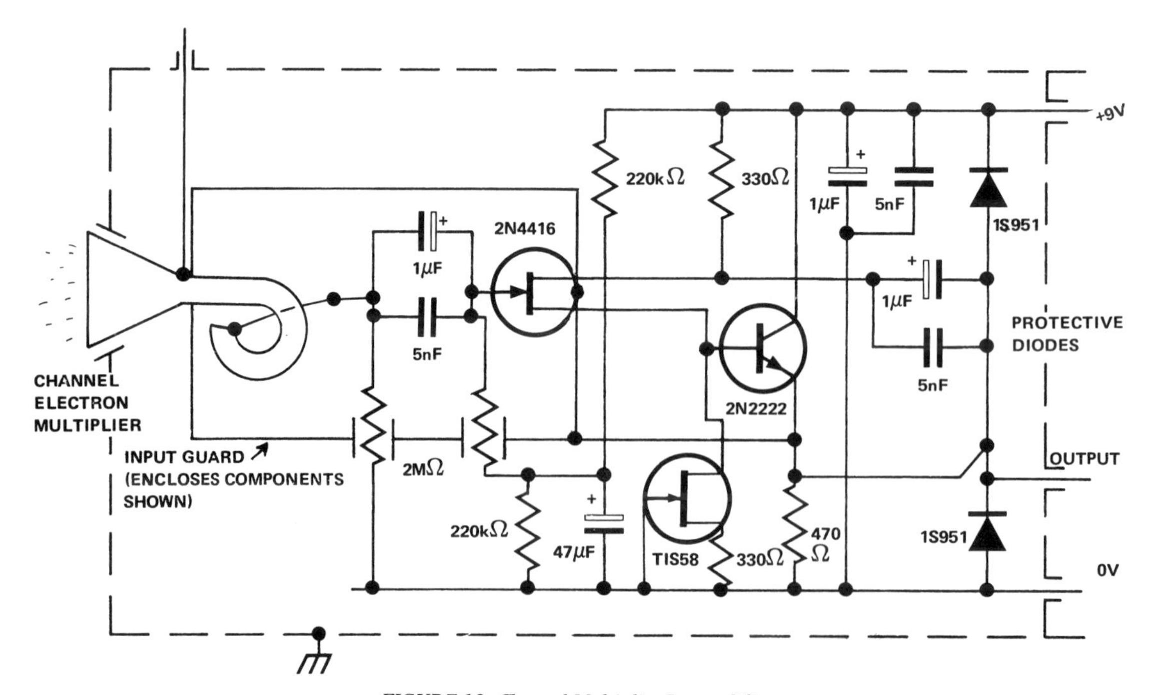

FIGURE 12. Channel Multiplier Preamplifier

source follower. The drain current flowing in the 2N4416 FET is stabilized at 3mA by a TIS58 FET connected as a current source driving into the source of the 2N4416. This ensures that the voltage gain of the 2N4416 is very close to unity and the gate to source capacitance is 'bootstrapped' out. The signal from the 2N4416 source is converted to very low impedance by a transistor operating as an emitter follower. Positive feedback from the emitter of this transistor is applied via a 1μF capacitor to the drain of the 2N4416 to bootstrap out its gate to drain capacitance. A copper guard encloses the output end of the channel multiplier, the 1μF input coupling capacitor and the can of the 2N4416 which is connected to the guard. The guard is connected to the preamplifier output, hence stray capacitance at the input is also 'bootstrapped' out. The 2MΩ signal resistors pass through holes in the guard to remove most of their end to end capacitance. The input capacitance of the prototype preamplifier was measured at 0·15 pF ± ·05 pF at 1MHz.

REFERENCE

1. W. W. Gartner, 'Temperature Dependence of Carrier Densities, Mobilities, Diffusion Constants and Conductivities in Germanium and Silicon' *Semiconductor Products,* July, 1960.

ACKNOWLEDGEMENT

The author would like to express his thanks to C. S. den Brinker for many helpful discussions and ideas.

APPENDIX

A simplified equivalent circuit of a junction FET operating in the pinch-off region is shown in Figure 13a. At d.c. and low frequencies, the input resistance R1 is usually of the order of 100 MΩ and the output resistance R3 in excess of 10 MΩ. The input and output capacities C1 and C3 are strongly voltage dependent but generally only a few picofarads in value. The feedback resistance and capacitance R2 and C2 are of the order of 1 MΩ and 1 – 3 pF respectively, the capacitance being voltage dependent. In most practical circuits, the effects of the input and reverse transfer admittances y_i and y_r can be ignored, and providing the load admittance is very much greater than the output admittance, y_{os}, this too can be ignored. The gate leakage current is generally less than 0·25nA at 25°C and 250nA at 150°C and since the effect of leakage current is dealt with in the preceeding text, it will be ignored for the purposes of this analysis.

The equivalent circuit then reduces to that shown in Figure 13b, enabling a very simple analysis to be performed. Assuming that g_{DS}, g_{SG} and $g_{DG} \triangleq 0$:–

$$i_{D1} = g_{m1} V_{GS1} \qquad i_{D2} = g_{m2} V_{GS2} \quad \ldots (1)$$

$$V_{GS1} = V_{G1} - R_s i_s \qquad V_{GS2} = V_{G2} - R_s i_s \quad \ldots (2)$$

$$i_s = i_{D1} + i_{D2} \quad \ldots (3)$$

From (1) and (2)

$$i_{D1} = g_{m1}(V_{G1} - R_s i_s)$$

From (3)

$$i_{D1} = g_{m1}(V_{G1} - R_s(i_{D1} + i_{D2}))$$

i.e.

$$i_{D1}(1 + g_{m1}R_s) + i_{D2}\, g_{m1}R_s = g_{m1} V_{G1} \quad \ldots (4)$$

By symmetry

$$i_{D2}(1 + g_{m2}R_s) + i_{D1}\, g_{m2}R_s = g_{m2} V_{G2}$$

i.e.

$$i_{D1}(g_{m2}R_s) + i_{D2}(1 + g_{m2}R_s) = g_{m2} V_{G2} \quad \ldots (5)$$

Solving (4) and (5) for i_{D1} yields

$$i_{D1} = \frac{\begin{vmatrix} g_{m1} V_{G1} & g_{m1}R_s \\ g_{m2} V_{G2} & (1 + g_{m2}R_s) \end{vmatrix}}{\begin{vmatrix} (1 + g_{m1}R_s) & g_{m1}R_s \\ g_{m2}R_s & (1 + g_{m2}R_s) \end{vmatrix}}$$

i.e.

$$i_{D1} = \frac{g_{m1} V_{G1}(1 + g_{m2}R_s) - g_{m2}g_{m1}R_s V_{G2}}{(1 + g_{m1}R_s).(1 + g_{m2}R_s) - g_{m1}g_{m2}R_s^2} \quad .(6)$$

and by symmetry

$$i_{D2} = \frac{g_{m2}V_{G2}(1 + g_{m1}R_s) - g_{m1}g_{m2}R_s V_{G1}}{1 + R_s(g_{m1} + g_{m2})} \quad \ldots (7)$$

Single Ended Gain, i.e. $V_{G2} = 0$

then

$$i_{D1} = \frac{g_{m1} V_{G1}(1 + g_{m2}R_s)}{1 + R_s(g_{m1} + g_{m2})}$$

i.e.

$$\frac{V_{D1}}{V_{G1}} = \frac{g_{m1}(1 + g_{m2}R_s)R_{D1}}{1 + R_s(g_{m1} + g_{m2})} \quad \ldots (8)$$

Assuming matched transistors, i.e. $g_{m1} = g_{m2}$

$$\frac{V_{D1}}{V_{G1}} = \frac{(g_m + g_m^2 R_s) R_{D1}}{1 + 2g_mR_s}$$

$$= \frac{(\frac{1}{R_s} + g_m)R_{D1}}{\frac{1}{g_mR_s} + 2}$$

If R_s is very large

$$\frac{V_{D1}}{V_{G1}} \triangleq \frac{g_m R_{D1}}{2}$$

For the output at D_2

$$i_{D2} = \frac{-g_{m1}\, g_{m2}R_s V_{G1}}{1 + R_s(g_{m1} + g_{m2})}$$

If $g_{m1} = g_{m2}$

$$i_{D2} = \frac{g_m^2 R_s V_{G1}}{1 + 2R_s g_m}$$

$$\frac{V_{D2}}{V_{G1}} = -\frac{g_m R_{D2}}{2} \quad \text{for } R_s \text{ very large}$$

Differential Gain

$$i_{D1} - i_{D2} = \frac{V_{G1}(g_m + g_m^2 R_s) - g_m^2 V_{G2} R_s - V_{G2}(g_m + g_m^2 R_s) - g_m^2 V_{G1} R_s}{1 + g_m R_s^2}$$

If $R_{D1} = R_{D2}$ then

$$V_{D1} - V_{D2} = V_{G1} - V_{G2} \frac{(g_m + g_m^2\, 2R_s)R_D}{1 + g_m R_s^2}$$

for large R_s

$$\frac{\Delta V_D}{\Delta V_G} = g_m R_D$$

Single Ended Common Mode Gain

i.e. $V_{G1} = V_{G2} = V_G$

$$i_{D1} = \frac{V_G \cdot g_m + g_m^2 R_s - g_m^2 R_s}{1 + 2g_m R_s}$$

$$\frac{V_{D1}}{V_G} = \frac{g_m R_{D1}}{1 + 2g_m R_s}$$

$$\frac{R_{D1}}{2R_s}$$

Conditions for No C.M. Gain

$$V_{D1} = R_{D1} \frac{g_{m1} V_{G1}(1 + g_{m2} R_s) - g_{m2} V_{G2} g_{m1} R_s}{1 + R_S(g_{m1} + g_{m2})}$$

$$V_{D2} = R_{D2} \frac{g_{m2} V_{G2}(1 + g_{m1} R_s) - g_{m1} V_{G1} g_{m1} R_s}{1 + R_s(g_{m1} + g_{m2})}$$

$V_{D1} - V_{D2} = \Delta V$

$$= \frac{\left[R_{D1}\left\{g_{m1} V_{G1}(1 + g_{m2} R_s) - g_{m2} V_{G2} g_{m1} R_s\right\} - R_{D2}\left\{g_{m2} V_{G2}(1 + g_{m1} R_s) - g_{m1} V_{G1} g_{m1} R_s\right\}\right]}{\left\{1 + R_s(g_{m1} + g_{m2})\right\}}$$

For no C.M. gain coefficient of V_{G1} = coefficient of V_{G2}, i.e.

$$R_{D1} g_{m1}(1 + g_{m2} R_s) - g_{m2} g_{m1} R_s R_{D2} = g_{m2}(1 + g_{m1} R_s) R_{D2} - g_{m1} g_{m2} R_s R_{D1}$$

or

$$\frac{R_{D2}}{R_{D1}} = \frac{g_{m1}}{g_{m2}}$$

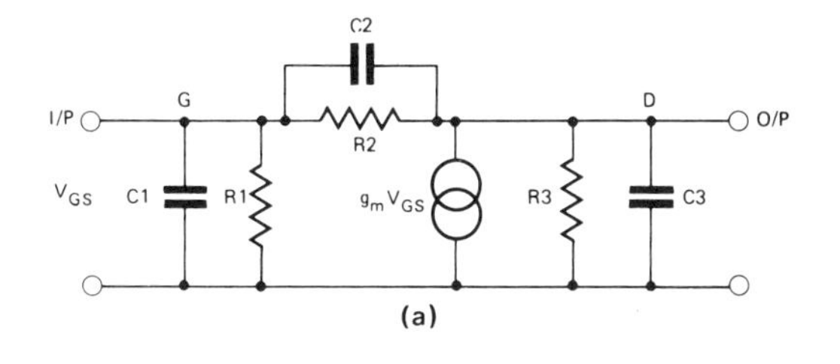

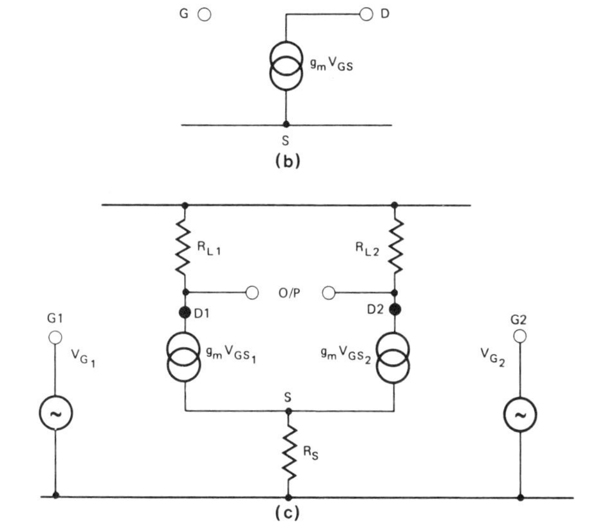

FIGURE 13. Approximate Small Signal Equivalent of Long Tailed Pair Circuit

XIV SWITCHING OR 'CHOPPER' CIRCUITS

by
Mike Stevens

When very low frequency or d.c. signals are amplified by conventional direct coupled amplifiers, zero drift in the amplifier caused by ageing or ambient temperature changes, (discussed in the preceding chapter), sets a lower limit to the amplitude of the input signal that can be measured to a given accuracy. In order to eliminate errors due to zero drift, it is necessary to modify the input signal before it is applied to the amplifier. (Errors due to zero drift are absolute and not a percentage of the input signal as are errors due to gain drift). The most common system is to chop the input signal and then amplify with a gain stable a.c. amplifier. The input signal can be chopped by placing a fast acting switch in series, shunt or series and shunt with the amplifier and alternately connecting and disconnecting the signal. The signal appearing at the amplifier input appears to be chopped when viewed on a time scale. The switching system is thus referred to as a 'chopper'.

The basic requirement of this type of chopper system is a fast acting switch which passes and blocks the signal perfectly. The characteristics of the ideal switch are zero resistance and zero voltage sources in the 'on' condition, infinite resistance and zero current sources in the 'off' condition and zero switching time. The control terminal should be completely isolated from the input and output terminals and there should be no limit to the current through the switch in the 'on' condition or voltage across it in the 'off' condition. Other practical considerations are drive power requirements, size and reliability. The characteristics of some chopper FETs, e.g. the 2N4856A series, closely approach those of the ideal switch. The 'off' resistance is very high, of the order of 10^{10} Ω, and the leakage current very low, less than 0.25nA, at 25°C. The offset voltage is zero and the 'on' resistance 25 Ω maximum for the 2N4856A. The effect of the other parameters, such as the interelectrode capacities, on the performance of the device as a switch is discussed in detail in this chapter.

RELEVANT CHARACTERISTICS

General

Figure 1 shows a typical FET output characteristic with two distinct regions marked. To the right of the

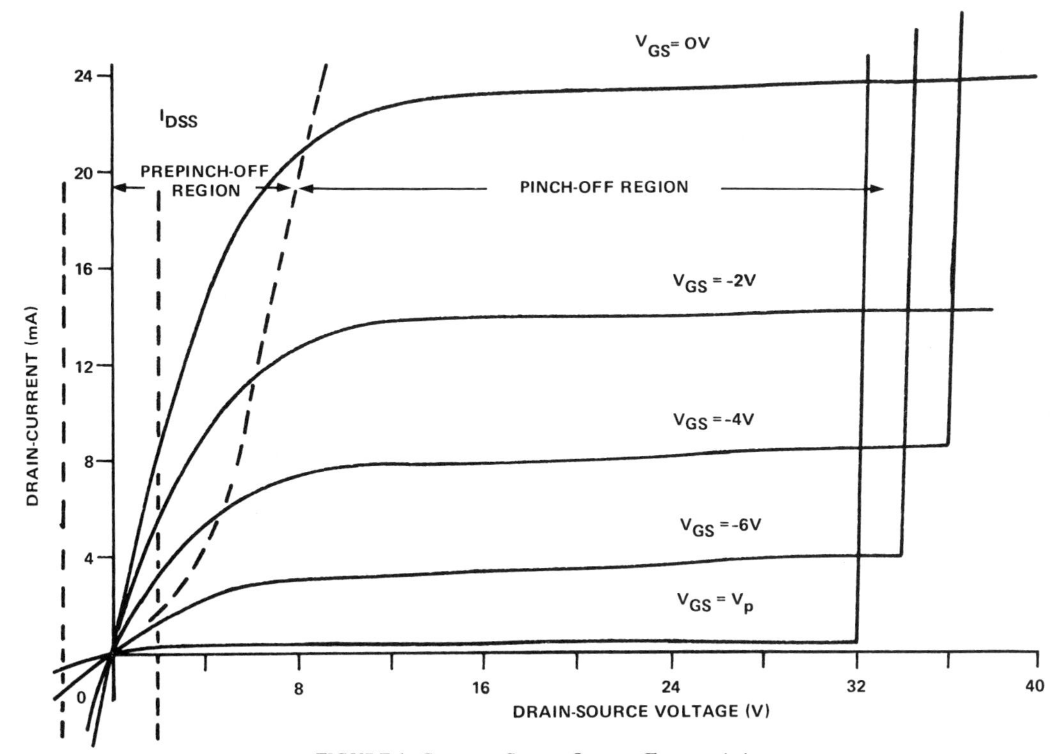

FIGURE 1. Common Source Output Characteristics

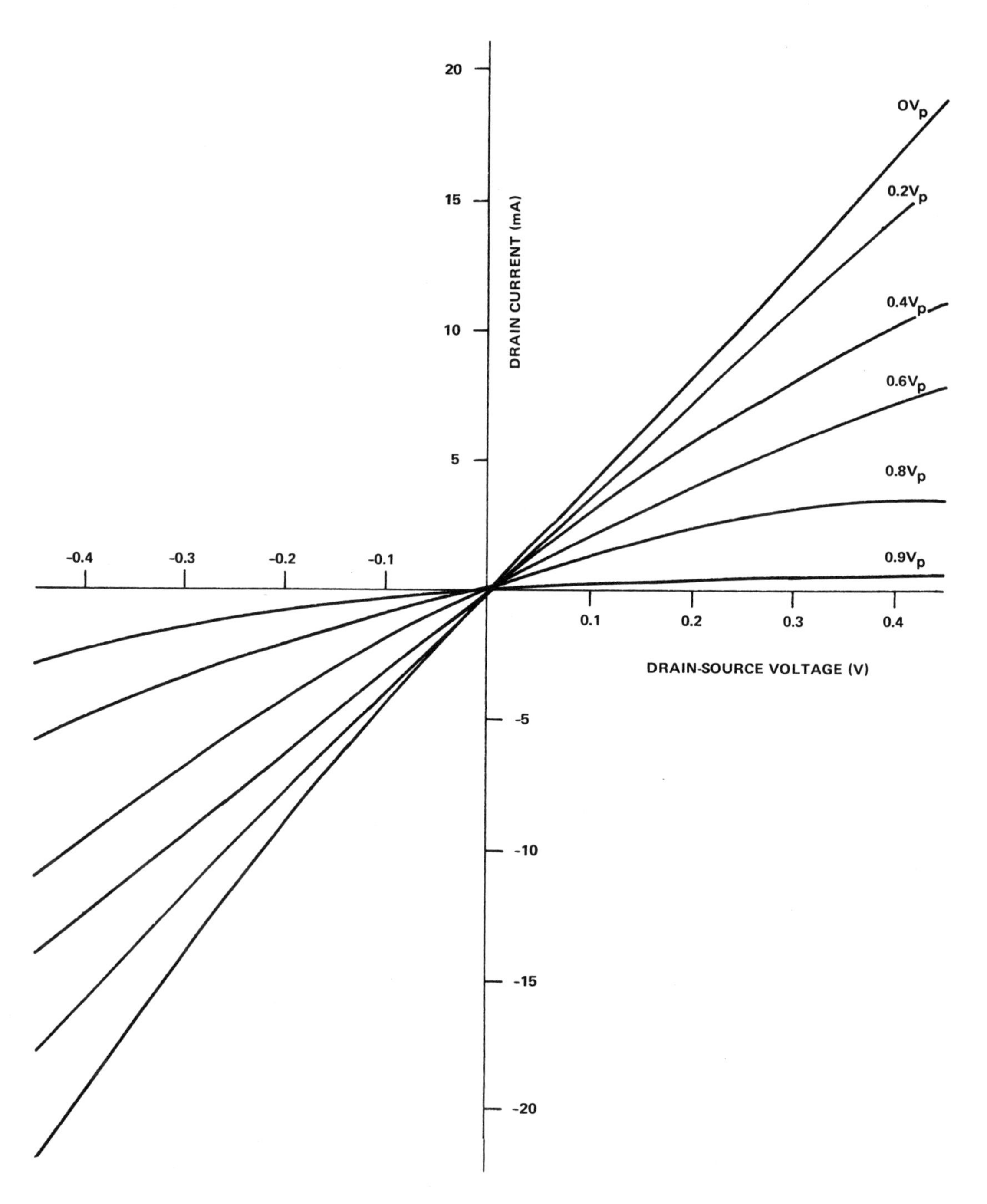

FIGURE 2. Output Characteristics Near the Origin

dotted line is the pinch-off region. In this region, the characteristics are near horizontal and hence the dynamic output impedance is high. To the left of the dotted line is the prepinch-off region. It is this region that is of particular interest when the device is used in small signal switching circuits. In order to examine the characteristics near the origin, the portion within the dotted area has been enlarged as shown in Figure 2. These curves show that, with low drain-source voltages, the device behaves as a bilateral linear resistor, the value of which depends upon the gate-source voltage. An important feature of the FET is that all the output characteristics pass through the origin. This clearly shows the absence of any inherent off-set voltage. A gate voltage step of 0 to V_p will switch the device from a low impedance ($V_{GS} = 0$) to a high impedance ($V_{GS} > V_p$).

Since the FET is a majority carrier device, the main limitation on the switching speed is the ability of the circuit to charge and discharge the parasitic capacitance. Under certain conditions, the turn 'on' and turn 'off' times are as low as 5ns.

Equivalent Circuits

Simplified equivalent circuits of the FET in both the 'on' and 'off' conditions are shown in Figure 3 (a) and (b). The leakage currents are represented by the current generators I_{GDO}, I_{GSO} and $I_{DS\ (off)}$. The diodes are included to show that, in the case of an n-channel device, gate current will flow if the gate potential is made positive to either drain or source. Both the 'on' and 'off' equivalent circuits will be discussed in detail.

'On' Equivalent Circuit: The simplified 'on' equivalent circuit is shown in Figure 3 (a). In most practical circuits, the effect of leakage current when the device is in the 'on' state can be neglected and hence the leakage current generators may be omitted. Since the device is in the 'on' condition the resistance between drain and source is extremely low, e.g. a maximum of 25 Ω for the 2N4856A, and there is no offset voltage. The interelectrode capacities associated with the FET, C_{GS}, C_{GD} and C_{DS}, are a combination of the header capacity and the depletion layer of the reverse biased junctions. In general, the smaller the device geometry, the lower the interelectrode capacities. However, large geometry devices have low 'on' resistance and a compromise has to be made between 'on' resistance and capacitance when selecting a device for a particular switching application. The gate-to-channel capacities are responsible for the feed-through of the high frequency components of the gate signal to the drain and source. In particular, these capacities cause transient spikes to appear at the drain and source when the gate is driven by a square wave with fast rising edges. Since the bulk of the device capacities are due to the depletion layer capacitance of the reverse biased junction, they are voltage dependent. Thus, when the device is in the 'on' condition and all three terminals are virtually at the same potential, the capacities are a maximum.

'Off' Equivalvent Circuit: This simplified 'off' equivalent circuit is shown in Figure 3 (b). The leakage current generators are included since these can be a source of error in the 'off' state at elevated temperatures. When the device is turned 'off', the drain-source resistance increases to a value of the order of 10^{10} Ω. ($I_{DS(off)}$ is determined mainly by the drain-source leakage current $I_{DS(off)}$). The gate is usually biased at a fairly large negative potential with respect to the drain and source, and thus the device capacities are lower than in the 'on' state. The drain-source capacitance is of great importance in analogue switching applications as it determines the ability of the device to block high frequency input signals.

THE SERIES CHOPPER

Basic Circuit Description

The basic FET series chopper circuit is shown in Figure 4 (a). In this circuit, the device is connected in series with the signal and switched 'on' and 'off' thereby alternately connecting and disconnecting the load R_L to the generator. Such a circuit is suitable for chopping small positive and negative input signals of amplitude less than about 500mV. The gate drive voltage should switch the gate from ground to a negative potential equal to or greater than the pinch-off voltage, V_p.

Feedthrough Spikes: Internal capacities associated with the FET are responsible for the generation of both positive and negative transient spikes at the output of all FET chopper circuits with square wave gate drive. Although the duration of the spikes is usually very short, their amplitude can easily exceed a few tenths of a volt, producing undesirable off-set voltages at the output and in some cases overloading succeeding stages. The amplitude and duration of the feedthrough spikes depends upon the capacitance between the gate and the output, the load and generator resistances and the amplitude and rise time of the gate drive

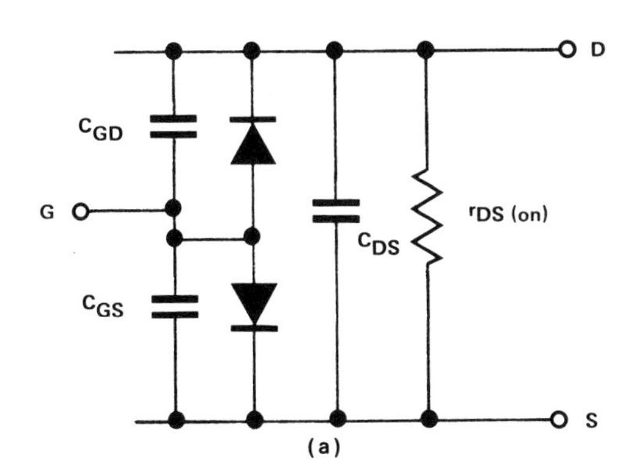

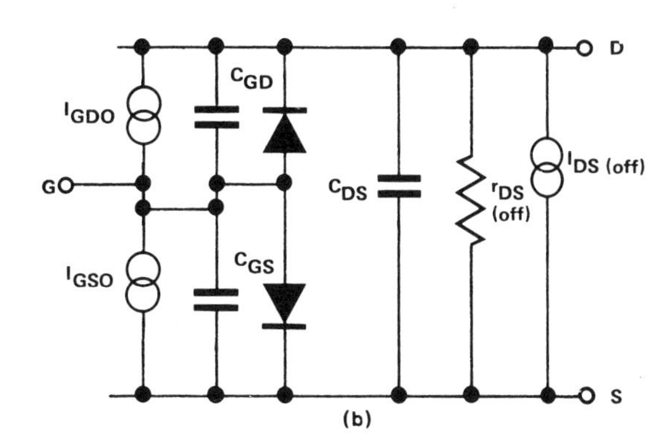

FIGURE 3. Simplified Switch Equivalent Circuits

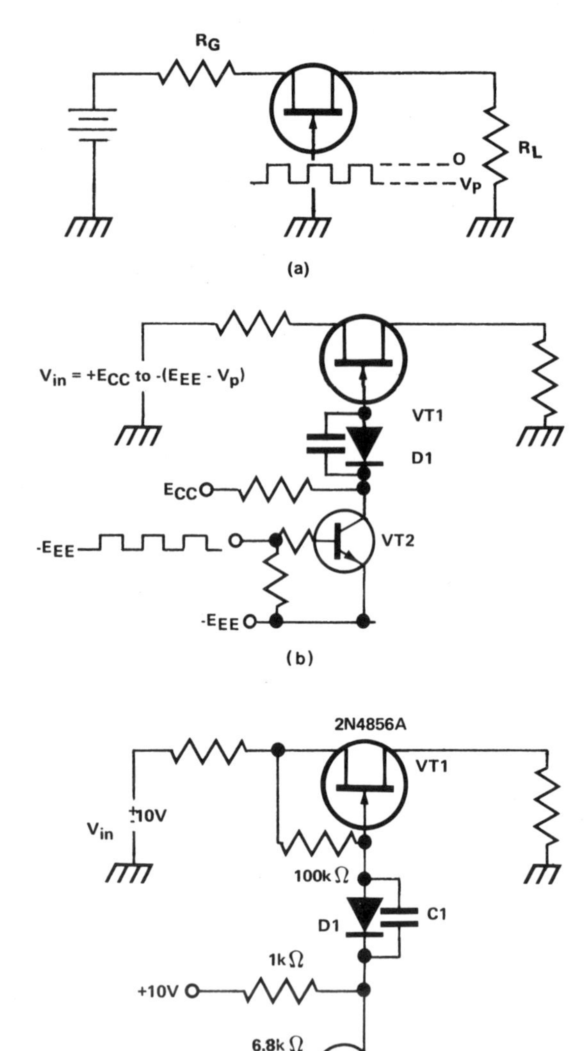

FIGURE 4. Series Chopper Circuits

signal. When the device is used as a series chopper, the amplitude of the feedthrough spikes is very much dependent on the generator resistance. Consider the basic circuit of Figure 4 (a). When the device is in the 'on' condition and a fast rising negative going edge applied to the gate to turn it 'off', a negative transient spike is transmitted to the output through the drain-gate and gate-source capacities. If the generator impedance is very low, the transient spike at first sees a very low resistance, i.e. R_G and $I_{DS(on)}$. As the amplitude of the gate drive voltage increases, the device begins to turn 'off'. The output spike is then due solely to the drain-gate capacitance and, as the device turns off, the load resistance R_L. Since the time constant C_{DG}. R_L is usually fairly long, the result is a large negative transient spike at the output. When the device is in the 'off' state and turned 'on' by the positive going edge of the drive voltage, a positive transient spike is transmitted to the output. The FET is initially in a high impedance state and thus the gate to drain capacity has to charge through the load resistance. As the drive voltage increases positively, the device turns 'on' thus providing a low resistance path to charge C_{DS} via the generator and the device on resistance. In circuits where the generator resistance is significantly lower than that of the load, the positive transient spike is of shorter duration than the negative spike.

As previously stated, undesirable off-set voltages at the output and possible overload of succeeding amplifier stages can be produced by spike feedthrough. Since the latter is independent of input signal amplitude, the problem is most acute with very small input signals. Careful design of chopper circuitry can reduce transient spikes to very low levels enabling very small input voltages to be chopped without serious error being introduced. Decreasing the load resistance will produce a correspondingly shorter time constant especially if a low capacitance device is used. This, however, results in an increase in error because of the device 'on' resistance mentioned earlier. An additional decrease in transient error voltage results when the drive pulse frequency is reduced and the amplitude arranged so that it does not greatly exceed the pinch-off voltage. The increasing of the rise and fall times of the drive waveform, reducing the high frequency content of the pulse, improves the error considerably and for best results, a waveform approaching a sine wave should be used if possible. Because the rise and fall times of the drive waveform must in some cases be very fast, $<1\ \mu s$, care must be taken to ensure that additional capacitance is not introduced by the construction, and shielding may be needed between the drive and output circuitry of the switch.

'Off' State Error: When the device is in the 'off' state, the output voltage should ideally fall to zero. The actual value of the output voltage will depend on the values of the load resistance, the device 'off' resistance and the generator resistance. The error voltage in the 'off' state is given by:–

$$\Delta V = \frac{V_{in} \cdot R_L}{R_L + R_G + r_{DS(off)}} \qquad \text{.............. (2)}$$

Since $r_{DS(off)}$ is very large at low frequencies (of the order of $10^{10}\ \Omega$) this error only becomes important when the load resistance is very large, for instance when the chopper is feeding into a source follower. Since the device is an extremely high series impedance in the 'off' state, the series chopper is not suitable for driving capacitively coupled loads.

'On' State Error: The main source of error in the 'on' state is the device on resistance, $r_{DS(on)}$ In the 'on' state, the output voltage is given by:–

$$V_o = \frac{V_{in} \cdot R_L}{r_{DS(on)} + R_G + R_L}$$

The error voltage, ΔV, is therefore:–

$$\Delta V = V_{in} - V_o$$

$$\Delta V = \frac{V_{in} r_{DS(on)} + R_G)}{r_{DS(on)} + R_G + R_L} \quad \ldots\ldots\ldots\ldots\ldots (3)$$

This error is a minimum when $r_{DS(on)}$ is very small and R_L is very large. The requirement for large R_L is not compatible with the condition for minimum error in the 'off' condition.

Leakage Current Error: Leakage currents are also a source of error at elevated temperatures. Gate leakage current in the 'on' state causes an increase in the voltage drop across the generator resistance. This error is given by:–

$$\Delta V = I_{GSS} \frac{R_G}{R_G + R_L}$$

$$= I_{GSS} \frac{R_G}{R_L} \text{ if } R_G << R_L \quad \ldots\ldots\ldots\ldots (4)$$

When the device is in the 'off' state, leakage current between drain and source, $I_{DS(off)}$, and leakage current between gate and drain, I_{DGO}, produce an error voltage equal to:–

$$\Delta V = (I_{DGO} + I_{DS(off)}) R_L \quad \ldots\ldots\ldots\ldots\ldots\ldots (5)$$

Provided that the load and source resistances are not exceptionally high, errors produced by the leakage currents are negligible except at elevated temperatures.

Practical Circuits

Feedthrough Spikes: In order to illustrate the effect of component values and gate drive voltage amplitude and rise time on the feedthrough spikes, the output transients of the circuit of Figure 4 (a) were examined with zero input signal and two values of load resistance and gate signal rise time.

The oscillographs of Figure 5 clearly show the effect of decreasing gate voltage rise time. Figure 5 (a) and 5 (b) show the positive and negative output transients with a 2kΩ load resistance and gate drive voltage of 500ns rise time and just sufficient amplitude to switch the device under test. With these circuit parameters the amplitude of the positive transient is about 110mV and its half amplitude duration about 50ns. The amplitude and half amplitude duration of the negative, or turn-off, transient are 95mV and about 80ns respectively. Thus, it can be seen that although the amplitude of the transients is very similar, the duration of the turn 'off' transient is much greater due to the increasing circuit resistance.

Figures 5 (c) and (d) show the output transients under similar conditions but with the gate voltage rise time reduced to 200ns. The amplitude of both transients has increased to about 160mV each with a half amplitude duration of about 30ns and 65ns for the positive and negative transients respectively. These oscillographs clearly show the increase in spike amplitude with decreasing gate voltage rise time. Although the amplitudes of the turn 'on' and turn 'off' transients is very similar, the energy contained within the turn 'off' transient is considerably greater and this produces greater contribution to offset voltages at the output.

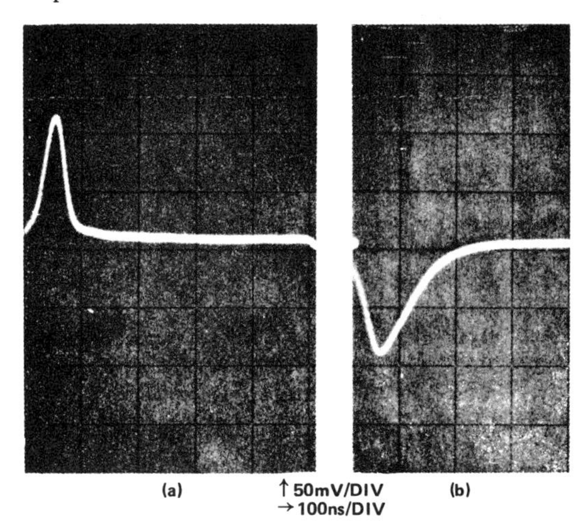

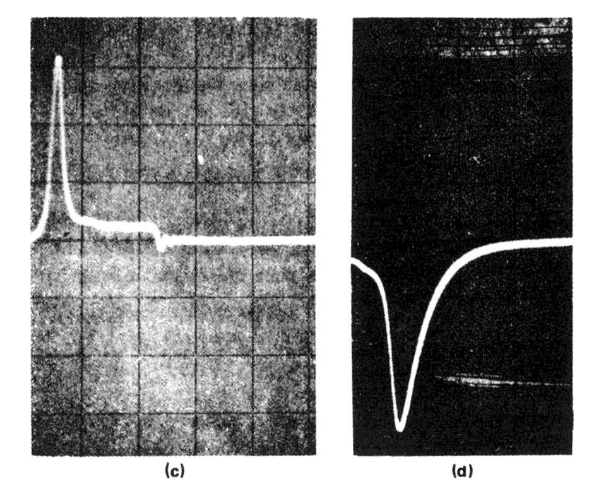

FIGURE 5. Oscillographs of Output Transients with $R_L = 2k\Omega$

The oscillographs of Figure 6 (a) and (b) show the output transients with a load resistance of 1kΩ and a gate rise time of 200ns. Comparing these oscillographs with those of Figure 5 (c) and (d), it can be seen that reducing the load resistance has reduced the amplitude of the turn 'on' transient and both the amplitude and duration of the turn 'off' transient.

The oscillographs of Figure 6 (c) and (d) show the effect of increasing the gate drive amplitude to -10V, the value required to ensure switching of the whole spread of a 2N4846A. (The pinch-off voltage of the test device was about 5V.) The amplitude and duration of both transients has considerably increased. (Note that in these two oscillographs, the vertical sensitivity has been increased to 100mV/division).

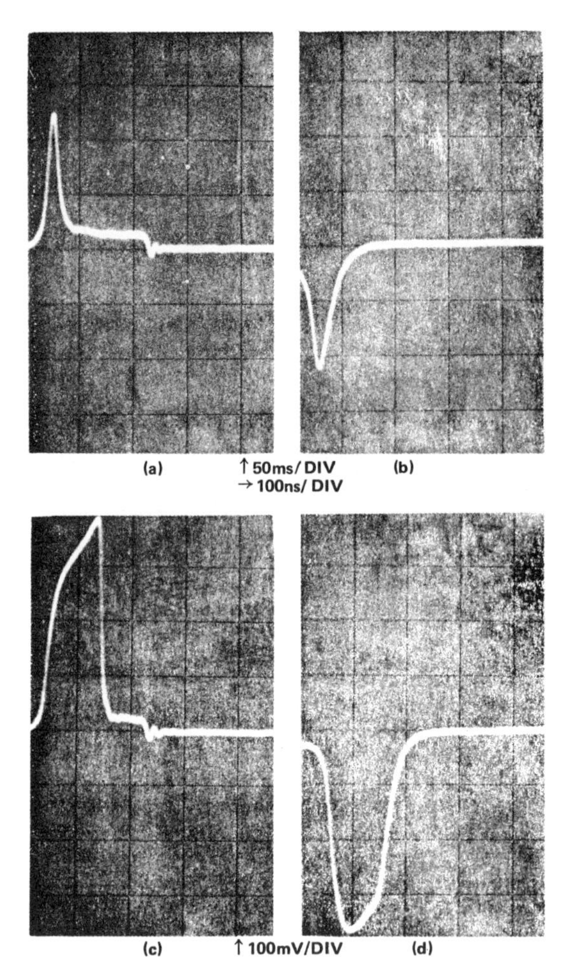

FIGURE 6. Oscillographs of Output Transients with $R_L = 1k\Omega$

Practical Errors: The 'on' and 'off' state errors of the series chopper circuit can be calculated from equations (2) and (3). With a 2kΩ load resistance and negligible generator resistance, the 'on' state error is:–

$$\Delta V = \frac{V_{in}\, r_{DS(on)}}{r_{DS(on)} + R_L}$$

The maximum 'on' resistance of a 2N4856A is 25 Ω.
Therefore:–
ΔV max. = 1.23% V_{in}
The 'off' state error is of the order of 25 x 10^{-8}% of V_{in} and is virtually immeasurable. The 'on' state error can be reduced by increasing the load resistance. For example, with R_L = 20kΩ, the error is:–
ΔV max. = 0.125% V_{in}
The 'off' state error is increased to approximately 20 x 10^{-7}%. The 'off' state errors calculated are only valid for d.c. or very low frequency input signals where the effect of the drain-source capacity on the 'off' resistance of the device may be neglected.

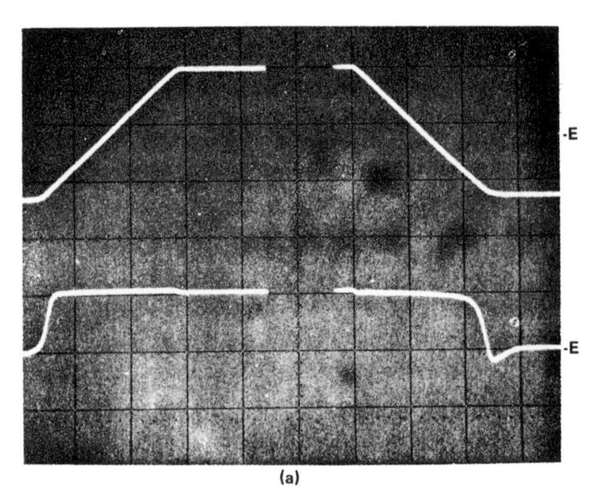

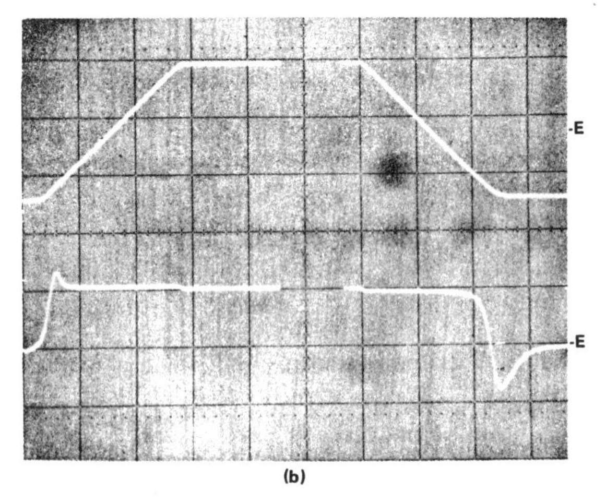

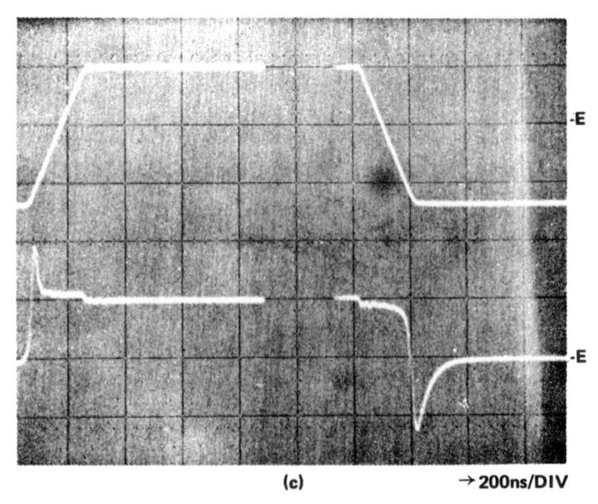

FIGURE 7. Typical Output Transients

The oscillographs of Figure 7 show typical output transients (bottom traces ↑ 100mV/division) from the circuit of Figure 4 (a) with a + 100mV input signal applied to the source and the gate drive (top traces ↑ 2V/division) operating at a repetition rate of 400 Hz. In Figure 7 (a) the load resistor R_L is 1kΩ and the gate drive rise time 500ns; in Figure 7 (b) R_L is 2kΩ and the rise time 500ns; and in Figure 7 (c) R_L is maintained at 2kΩ but the rise time reduced to 200ns. In each oscillograph expanded views of input and output edges together with the gate drive voltage are shown. Although the series chopper is not suitable for feeding capacity coupled loads, small values of shunt load capacity reduced the amplitude of the output transients due to the potential divider effect of C_{DG} and C_L. The basic circuit of Figure 4 (a) is not suitable for input signals in excess of a few hundred millivolts. With large positive input signals, the gate source voltage is not zero with zero gate voltage and the device does not turn 'on' properly. With large negative input signals, the gate-drain diode becomes forward biased with zero gate voltage.

A modified circuit which overcomes this difficulty is shown in Figure 4 (b) in which a diode has been included in series with the gate to prevent gate-channel conduction. So that the circuit can chop large input signals, it is necessary to modify the gate drive voltage. If, for example, the maximum expected input signal is ± 10V, the gate must be switched from 10V to -(10V + V_p) i.e. for a 2N4856A, V_{GS} = + 10V to −20V. The pulse amplifier, transistor VT2, is used to obtain the correct gate voltage levels. The inclusion of the series diode presents certain difficulties. When the device is being turned 'on', a fast positive going edge is applied to the gate. If the diode is of the fast recovery type, it cuts off before the device capacities are charged to the new gate potential. These capacitances therefore have to charge through the extremely high impedance of the reverse biased diode, resulting in an extremely long turn 'on'' time on the output voltage. The oscillographs of

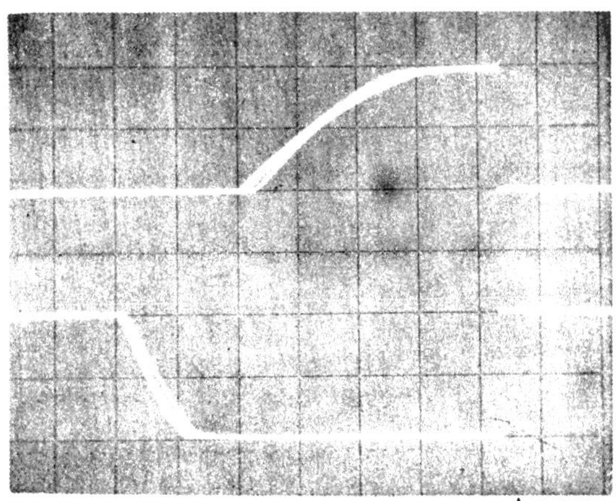

FIGURE 8. Oscillographs of Output Voltages of Figure 4 (b).

Figure 8 show the output voltage with a positive (top trace) and negative (bottom trace) 10V input signal and a fast silicon diode (1S44) in series with the gate. From these oscillographs, it can be seen that the rise time of output voltage is 15ms with the positive and 5ms with the negative input. The difference is due to the fact that the device capacities do not have to charge to as high a voltage with negative input signals.

This problem can be overcome in one of three ways.

(i) A slow recovery diode such as a zener diode should be used in series with the gate.

(ii) A fairly large capacitor (≈100pF) can be placed in shunt with the diode to enable the device capacities to charge. (The diode can be a fast recovery silicon diode). This method improves the output rise time but the circuit is relatively slow to react to changes in input signal and on initial switch 'on'.

(iii) The final and most frequently used method is to use a fast diode D1 with a small capacitor C1 in parallel (2 – 5pF) and connect a fairly large resistor between gate and source (≈100kΩ). This is shown in Figure 4 (c). This method usually results in a fast rising output which reacts very quickly to changes in input level. The only disadvantage of this method is that the gate signal is fed through into the generator via the gate-source resistor.

The output voltage rise and fall times of the circuit of Figure 4 (c) is shown in the oscillograph of 9. The top trace is the output voltage and the bottom trace the gate drive voltage; (V_{in} = -10V and C1 = 4pF).

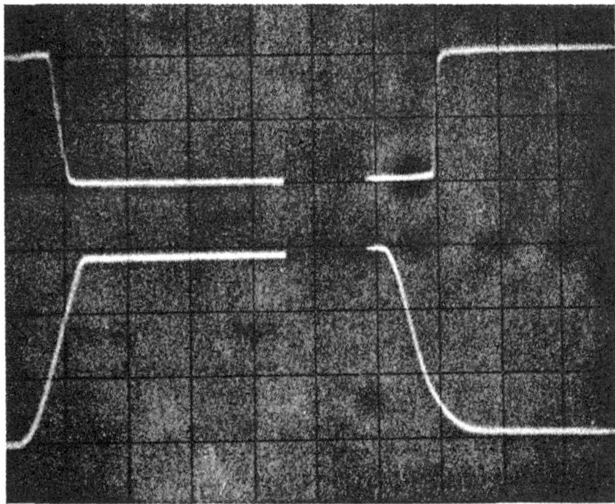

FIGURE 9. Oscillographs of Voltages of Figure 4 (c).

Series Chopper with High Frequency Input Signal: The junction FET can be used to chop high frequency signals. The main limitation on the ability of the device to effectively block very high frequency input signals is the drain-source capacity. The effect of device capacity depends very much on the impedance from gate to ground.

If the impedance is very high, the drain gate capacity in series with the gate-source capacity also appear across the device in the 'off' condition. If the gate-ground impedance is very low, these two capacities appear in shunt with input signal and the load. The oscillographs in Figure 10 show the output signal (lower traces -500mV/division) of the circuit of Figure 4 (b) with a 10 MHz input signal, V_{in}, of amplitude 1V pk-pk and 'on' and 'off' times, t_{on} and t_{off} equal to 500ns. The gate, (top traces -2V/division) is driven from a 50 Ω pulse generator and the load resistance R_L is 1kΩ. The output signal has an 'on' to 'off' ratio at the output of 100:1. This shows that an FET such as the 2N4856A can be usefully employed to chop high frequency signals.

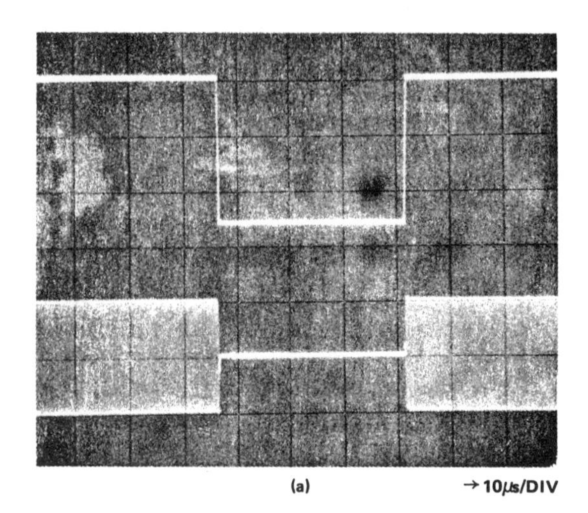

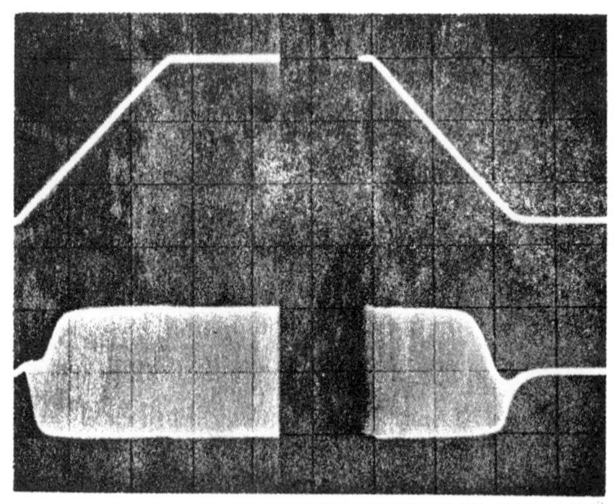

FIGURE 10. Oscillographs of High Frequency Signal Operation

THE SHUNT CHOPPER

Basic Circuit Description

The basic FET shunt chopper circuit is shown in Figure 11 (a). The device is in parallel with the load resistance and alternately switched 'on' and 'off' by the gate drive voltage. When the device is in the 'off' state, the generator voltage is applied to the potential divider R1 in series with R_L and $r_{DS(off)}$ in parallel. When the device is in the 'on' state, the load R_L is shorted to ground and the output voltage should ideally fall to zero. The series resistor R1 is necessary when chopping signals from a low impedance source to limit the current through the device in the 'on' state and enable the output voltage to fall to near zero. This resistance, however, introduces some error by preventing the full generator voltage from appearing across the load when the device is in the 'off' state. The source terminal of the device is grounded and thus large positive or small negative signals can be chopped by simply switching the gate from ground to a negative potential equal to or greater than the pinch-off voltage, V_p. Large negative input signals cannot be accommodated in the basic circuit since, with the gate at zero voltage and a negative potential on the drain, the drain gate junction is forward biased.

Feedthrough Spikes: When the device is in the 'on' state, a fast rising negative going pulse is applied to the gate to turn it 'off', the transient spike conducted by the drain gate capacity, C_{DS}, sees a very low impedance r_{on} which

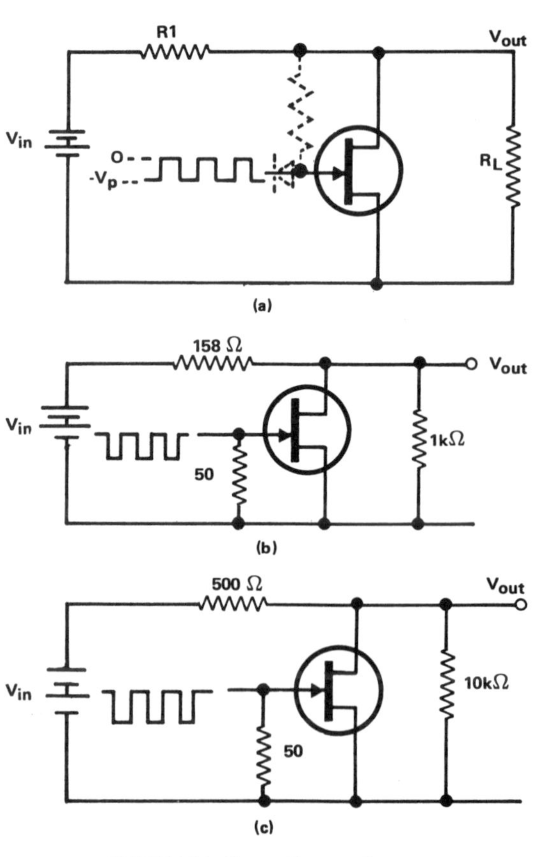

FIGURE 11. Shunt Chopper Circuits

increases as the device turns 'off'. Thus a negative transient spike will appear at the output. When the device is in the 'off' state and turned 'on' by the positive going edge of the gate voltage, the charge on C_{DS} is initially dissipated into the load and then into the decreasing 'on' resistance of the FET. The positive spike is usually much smaller than the negative spike. The amplitude of the transient spikes, as in the series chopper, depends upon the capacity (C_{DG}), the load and generator resistances. The techniques for reducing transient spikes in the shunt chopper are basically the same as those for the series chopper. The chopping frequency should be low, the amplitude of the gate drive signal should be adjusted to just equal the pinch-off voltage of each individual device, the rise time of the gate signal should be as long as possible and the load resistance as low as possible.

'Off' State Error: When the device is in the 'off state, the output voltage should equal the generator voltage, V_{in}. However, series resistor R1 prevents the full input voltage from appearing across the load. The input voltage is applied to a potential divider consisting of R_G, R1 and R_L in series (assuming the shunting effect of $R_{DS(off)}$ on R_L is negligible). The output voltage is given by:–

$$V_{out} = \frac{V_{in} R_L}{R_G + R1 + R_L}$$

The error voltage is given by:–

$$\Delta V = V_{out} - V_{in}$$

$$= \frac{-(R1 + R_G) V_{in}}{R1 + R_L + R_G} \qquad \text{.......... (6)}$$

This error tends to be a minimum as R1 approaches zero and R_L approaches infinity. The generator resistance R_L plays an important part in the total circuit error and if this is reduced to a minimum, then a larger value of R1 can be used for a given error.

'On' State Errors: With the device in the 'on' state, the output voltage should ideally fall to zero. However, because of the finite 'on' resistance of the FET, the output voltages does not fall to zero and is given by:–

$$\Delta V = \frac{r_{DS(on)} \cdot V_{in}}{R1 + R_G + r_{DS(on)}} \qquad \text{.......... (7)}$$

Assuming that $r_{DS(on)} << R_L$.

For a given value of $r_{DS(on)}$, the error in the 'on' state is minimised by having large values of R1 and R_G. This requirement is incompatible with the conditions for minimum error in the 'off' state.

A compromise which will yield the optimum value of R1 to produce minimum error in the output in both the 'on' and 'off' state is the geometric mean of $r_{DS(on)}$ and R_L, i.e.

Optimum $R1 = \sqrt{r_{DS(on)} R_L}$ ... . (8)

By making R_L very large, high values of R1 can be tolerated. This can be achieved by feeding the signal into a high impedance buffer stage such as an emitter follower or preferably a source follower. The error in the 'off' state, equation (6), can be eliminated by following the chopper by an amplifier having a gain equal to the attenuation produced by the voltage divider.

Leakage Current Error: At elevated temperatures, the drain gate leakage current may cause errors, particularly in the 'off' state. Thus, leakage current flows through the resistors R1 and R_G in parallel with R_L. If R1 and R_G is very much smaller than R_L, then the error voltage is I_{DG}. ($R1 + R_L$). If this error is unacceptable, it can be reduced by some form of compensation.

Practical Circuits

Feedthrough Spikes: Figures 11 (b) and (c) show two practical shunt chopper circuits with load resistances of 1kΩ and 10kΩ and the corresponding values of series resistance obtained from equation 8. The oscillographs of Figure 12 show the spike output obtained from the circuit of 11 (c) on an expanded time scale and with zero input signal. (In all cases load resistance R_L is 10kΩ).

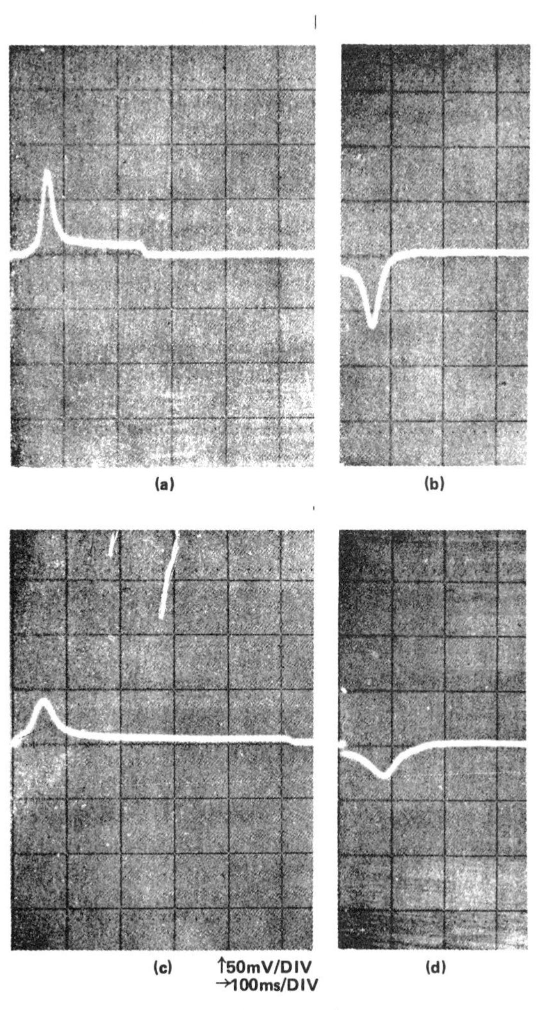

FIGURE 12. Oscillographs of Spike Output Obtained from Figure 11 (c)

Figures 12 (a) and (b) show the positive and negative output transient spikes with gate drive amplitude adjusted to just equal the pinch-off voltage of the test device and a 200ns rise and fall time. These oscillographs clearly show that when driven from a low resistance generator, the spike output from the shunt chopper is very much less than that from the series chopper. This is due to the fact that the drain terminal is common to both input and output and there is a relatively low resistance path to ground via R1 and the generator in both the 'on' and 'off' conditions.

The oscillographs of Figure 12 (c) and (d) show a further reduction in spike feedthrough by increasing the gate voltage rise-time to 500ns.

Practical Errors: From equations (6) and (7), the errors in the circuit of Figure 11 (b) are:–
'off' state error assuming zero generator resistance

$$\Delta V = \frac{158}{158 + 1000} V_{in}$$

$$= \underline{13{\cdot}6\%\ V_{in}}$$

'on' state error for a 2N4856A

$$\Delta V = \frac{25}{158 + 25} V_{in}$$

$$= \underline{13{\cdot}6\%\ V_{in}}$$

The corresponding errors for the circuit of Figure 11(c) are 4.5% and 5% respectively. From these results, it can be seen that the errors in the shunt chopper circuit, when driven from a low impedance generator, are much larger than those of the series chopper. Comparison of the errors in the circuits of (b) and (c) show that errors are reduced as the load resistance is increased.

The output voltage of the chopper circuit of Figure 11 (b) with a + 100mV input signal are shown in the oscillographs of Figure 13 (a) and (b), with a 200ns gate voltage turn 'on' and 'off' time. (V_{in} = + 100mV and R_L = 10kΩ). If the gate drive voltage amplitude is increased to -10V to ensure correct switching of the whole spread of a 2N4856A, the spike amplitude and duration will be considerably increased as in the case of the series chopper. When the shunt chopper is driven from a low impedance source, care must be taken in the selection of the value of the series resistor R1 to ensure that, when the device is in the 'on' condition, the current taken is less than the zero bias drive current of the particular device, i.e.

$$\frac{V_{in}}{R_G + R1 + r_{DS(on)}} \lhd I_{DSS}$$

I_{DSS} is a minimum of 50mA for a 2N4856A. The basic circuits shown in Figure 11 are only suitable for positive or small negative input signals. If the device is required to chop negative input signals in excess of about 500mV, it is necessary to modify the basic circuit as shown in Figure 14. In this circuit, a diode has been added in series with the gate and the gate voltage is now switched from zero to a negative potential equal to the sum of the maximum negative input signal and the pinch-off voltage, i.e. V_{GS} = 0 to $-(V_p + V_{in})$. In order to improve the switching speed, it is necessary to use a very slow recovery diode for D1 or if a fast silicon diode is used, such as the 1S44, it should be bypassed with a fairly large capacitor, as in the case of the series chopper. Although this circuit switches extremely fast, it is often slow to respond to changes in input level. The response of the circuit can be improved by connecting a small capacitor across the diode and adding a resistor between gate and drain. However, since the drain is common to both input and output, a portion of the gate drive voltage will be fed through to the output. When the device is in the 'off' condition, the gate signal is applied to a

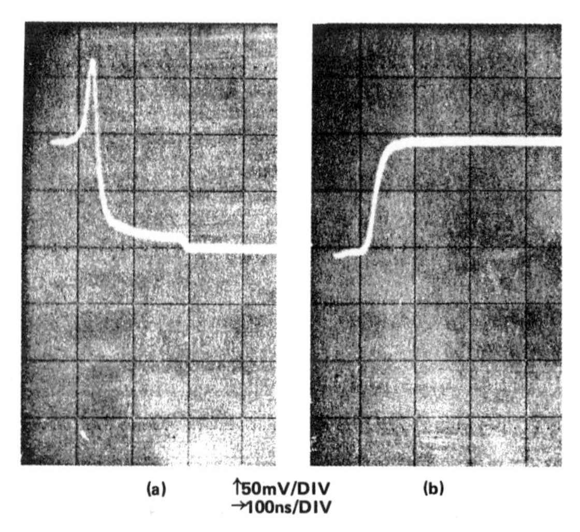

FIGURE 13. Oscillographs of Output Voltage of Figure 11(b) with V_{in} = + 100mV.

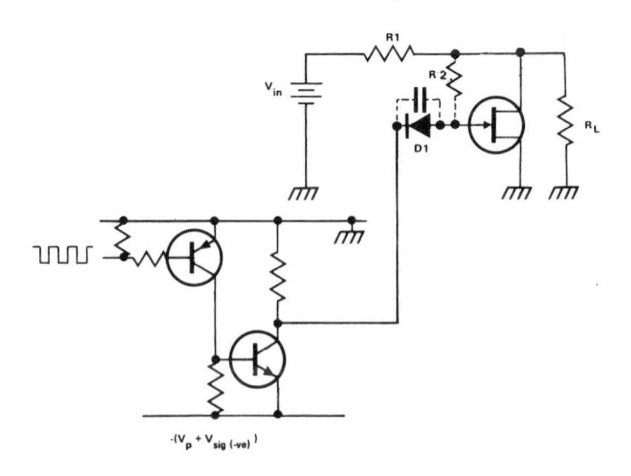

FIGURE 14. Modified Shunt Chopper for Negative Input Signals

potential divider consisting of R2 in series with R1 and R_L in parallel. Considering the circuit of Figure 11 (b). If the maximum expected input signal is ± 10V, then the gate must be switched from 0 to -20V (V_p maximum for a 2N4856A is -10V). Neglecting the shunting effect of $r_{DS(off)}$ and assuming zero generator resistance, the feed-through gate signal appearing at the output is given by:–

$$\Delta V = \frac{V_{GS} \times \frac{R1 R_L}{R1 + R_L}}{R2 + \frac{R1 R_L}{R1 + R_L}}$$

$$= \frac{20 \times 470}{100 \times 10^3 + 470} = \underline{94mV}$$

This feedthrough signal imposes a limitation on the accuracy of the circuit and hence the small signal performance. Thus, this circuit is not suitable for chopping small signals.

In both the series and shunt chopper circuits, a compromise has to be made on the circuit values in order to minimise errors in both 'on' and 'off' states. In the case of the shunt chopper, the series resistance should be high when the device is in the 'on' state and low when the device is in the 'off' state. For the series chopper, the load resistance should be low when the device is in the 'off' state and high when the device is in the 'on' state. The simplest way in which these conditions can be fulfilled is the series-shunt chopper. This circuit also reduces the spike feedthrough.

THE SERIES-SHUNT CHOPPER

Basic Circuit Description

The basic series-shunt chopper circuit is shown in Figure 15. Two FETs are used, one in series with the signal, the other in shunt with the load and alternately switched with antiphase gate signals. When the series device and the shunt device are 'off' the load is connected to the generator. When the series device is 'off' and the shunt device 'on', the load is shorted to ground. Such a circuit is suitable for chopping small positive and negative signals of less than about 500mV amplitude. The gate drive voltages must be in antiphase and switch the gates between zero and a negative potential equal to or greater than the pinch-off voltage. The most common form of drive circuit is a multi-vibrator running from a negative supply of sufficient amplitude to switch the particular type of device used. The gates can be connected directly to the antiphase outputs.

Feedthrough Spikes: The mechanism of spike feed-through in the series-shunt chopper is basically the same as that of the series and shunt choppers, i.e. the device and stray circuit capacity from the gates to the output. However, since the devices are switched in antiphase, one device feeds through a negative gain spike whilst the other device feeds through a positive going spike. If these spikes occur simultaneously and are of the same amplitude and duration they will cancel, thus eliminating any feedthrough.

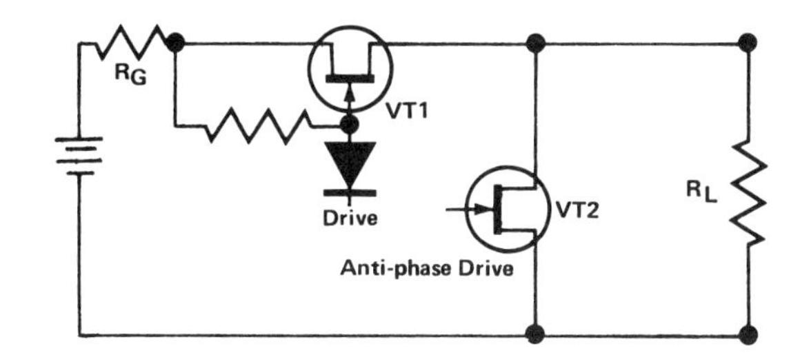

FIGURE 15. Basic Series-Shunt Chopper

It is instructive to examine the generation of both spikes in detail. If the shunt device is in the 'on' state and the series device in the 'off' state, a fast rising negative edge is applied to the gate of the shunt device to turn it 'off'. The transient spike first sees a fairly high resistance consisting of the 'off' resistance of FET VT1 in parallel with R_L. At the same time, a fast rising positive edge is applied to the gate of FET VT1 to turn it 'on'. Thus, the resistance seen by the negative spike falls rapidly to the 'on' resistance of FET VT1 in series with R_G. The positive edge applied to the gate of FET VT1 first sees a low resistance of the order of $r_{DS(on)}$ of FET VT2 which increases to R_L as FET VT2 turns 'off'. When the shunt device is in the 'off' state, and the series device is in the 'on' state, a fast rising positive edge is applied to the gate of the shunt device, VT2, to turn it 'on'. The transient spike at first sees a low resistance consisting of the 'on' resistance of VT1 in series with R_G. At the same time, a fast rising negative edge is applied to the gate of FET VT1 to turn it 'off'. Thus, the resistance seen by the positive spike rises rapidly to R_L. The negative going edge applied to the gate of VT1 first sees a fairly high resistance R_L which drops rapidly to $r_{DS(on)}$ as FET VT2 turns 'on'.

From the preceding discussion, it is apparent that during the transient period, the resistances seen by the positive and negative edges differ considerably. The gate-drain capacities of the devices are very dependent on the gate-drain voltage. Since the devices are being switched in antiphase, the gate-drive capacities will differ considerably. Perfect cancellation of the spikes is therefore virtually impossible. However, in most practical circuits, spike feed-through from the series-shunt chopper is at least an order lower than that from either the shunt or series chopper.

Sources of Error: In this type of circuit, the errors introduced by the device 'on' resistance, generator and load resistances are considerably reduced. When the series device is 'on' and the shunt device 'off', the output voltage is given by:–

$$V_o = \frac{V_{in} \cdot \frac{R_L r_{DS(off)}}{R_L + r_{DS(off)}}}{R_G + r_{DS(on)} + \frac{r_{DS(off)} R_L}{R_L + r_{DS(off)}}}$$

The error voltage $\Delta V = V_o - V_{in}$.

$$= \frac{-V_{in}(R_G + r_{DS(on)})}{R_G + r_{DS(on)} + \dfrac{r_{DS(off)} R_L}{R_L + r_{DS(off)}}}$$

This error is a minimum when $r_{DS(on)}$ and the generator resistance R_L are small and the parallel combination of $r_{DS(off)}$ and R_L is large, i.e. large R_L. When the series device is 'off' and the shunt device 'on', the output voltage should ideally fall to zero. The actual value of output voltage is given by:–

$$V_o = V_{in} \cdot \frac{\dfrac{r_{DS(on)} R_L}{R_L + r_{DS(on)}}}{r_{DS(off)} + R_G + \dfrac{r_{DS(on)} R_L}{R_L + r_{DS(on)}}} \qquad (10)$$

This is a minimum when the parallel combination of $r_{DS(on)}$ and R_L is low and the value of $r_{DS(off)}$ is high. If the value of $r_{DS(on)}$ is extremely low (as in the case of a 2N4856A), large values of R_L do not contribute significantly to the error in the 'off' state. Thus, it is apparent that there is virtually no incompatibility in the requirements for minimum error in 'on' and 'off' conditions. The value of $r_{DS(on)}$ should be as small as possible and the value of R_L large. With fairly low values of load resistance, of the order of 1kΩ the errors in the series-shunt chopper are similar to those of the series chopper. However, with low values of generator resistance, R_G, there is always a low resistance path to ground enabling the device capacities to be charged rapidly thus reducing switching times. When the chopper is driving a high impedance load in excess of about 100kΩ, such as an SN72709 integrated circuit amplifier or an amplifier with an FET input stage, the series-shunt chopper shows considerable improvement in both errors and switching speed over the series chopper. In many cases, when the chopper is driving an exceptionally high load resistance, a device with a higher 'on' resistance such as a 2N5549 ($r_{DS(on)}$ = 100 Ω maximum) may be used without introducing appreciable errors.

Practical Circuits

Using N-channel Devices: Figure 16 is the test circuit used to assess the performance of the series-shunt chopper. The gate drive signals were derived from a single source via a phase splitter to enable the rise times to be varied simultaneously and to ensure minimum delay between the two gate signals. With gate signal rise and fall times of 200ns and amplitude just sufficient to ensure correct switching of the

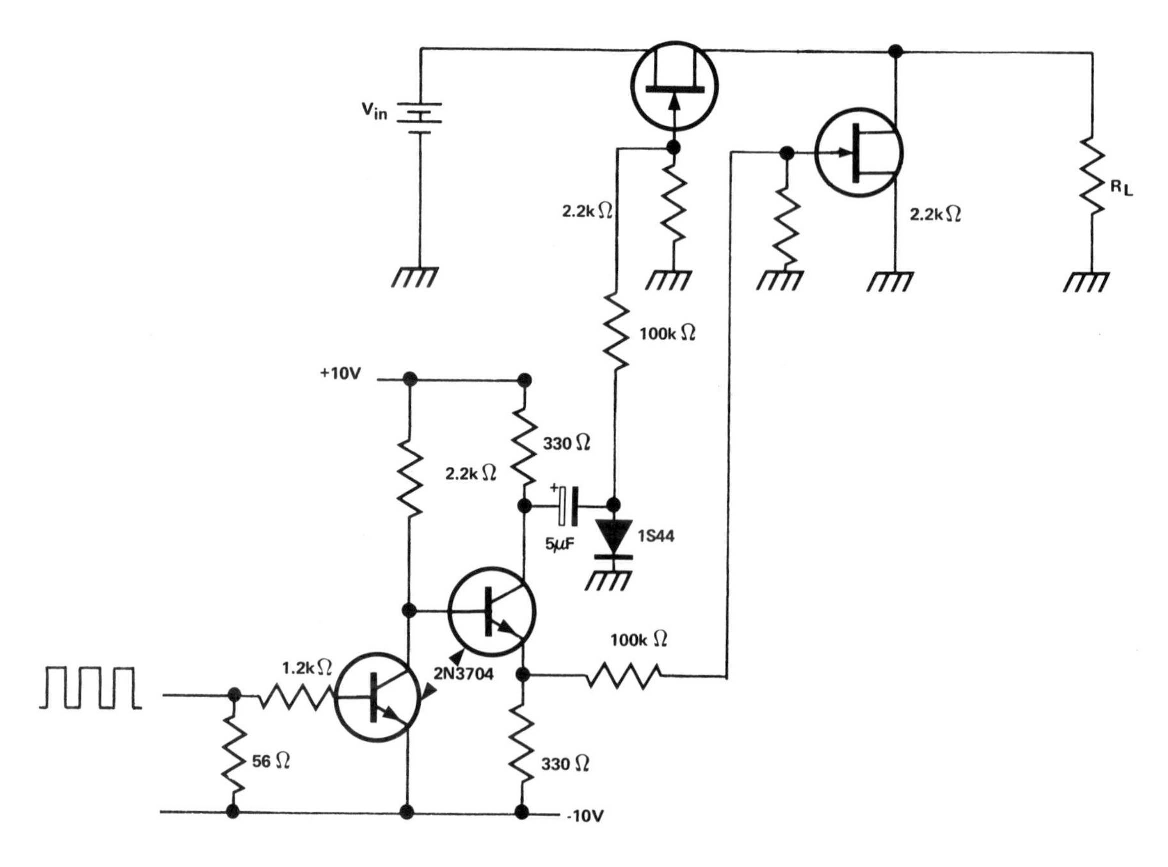

FIGURE 16. Practical Series-Shunt Chopper

devices under test, the spike feedthrough was virtually zero. The oscillographs of Figure 17 show an expanded portion of the output voltage across a 2.2kΩ load from a 50mV input signal. (The drive waveform is at 400 Hz). Apart from what appears to be some slight ringing in the circuit, there is virtually no spike feedthrough.

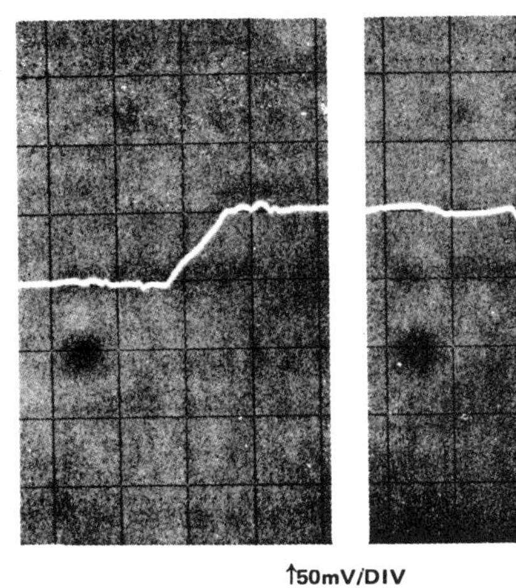

FIGURE 17. Oscillographs of Expanded Portion of Output Voltage

Figure 18 shows the series-shunt chopper driving an SN72709 integrated circuit amplifier. Feedback is applied to set the voltage gain to 60dB (1000) and the bandwidth to about 500kHz. The potentiometer R1 was included to correct the output offset voltage. The oscillographs of Figure 19 show a portion of the output voltage on an expanded time scale. The relatively slow rise time is due to the limited bandwidth of the amplifier and the complete absence of spike feedthrough is due to the combined effects of cancellation and limited bandwidth. The input voltage was -5mV, the chopping frequency 400Hz and the gate voltage rise and fall times 200ns. The output voltage is a -5V square wave and can be restored to either a positive or negative d.c. signal by a suitable FET synchronous switch.

The Complementary Series-Shunt Chopper

In many practical applications the antiphase drive voltages required for the series-shunt chopper using two n-channel devices are not readily available. In these cases it is more convenient to use a complementary chopper circuit of the type shown in Figure 20. In this circuit the series device is an n-channel 2N4856A and the shunt device a p-channel 2N3993. Since the devices are switched alternately and require gate voltages of opposite polarity to turn

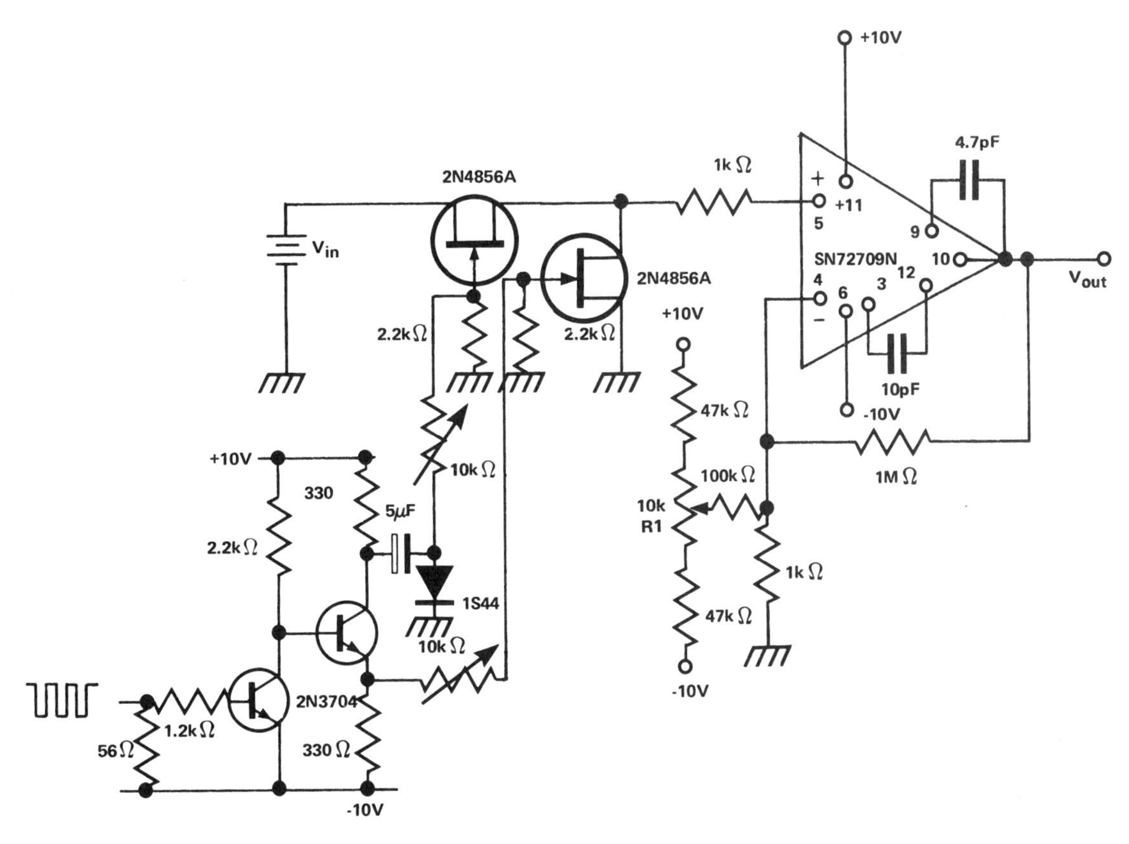

FIGURE 18. Series-Shunt Chopper Amplifier Using Integrated Circuit

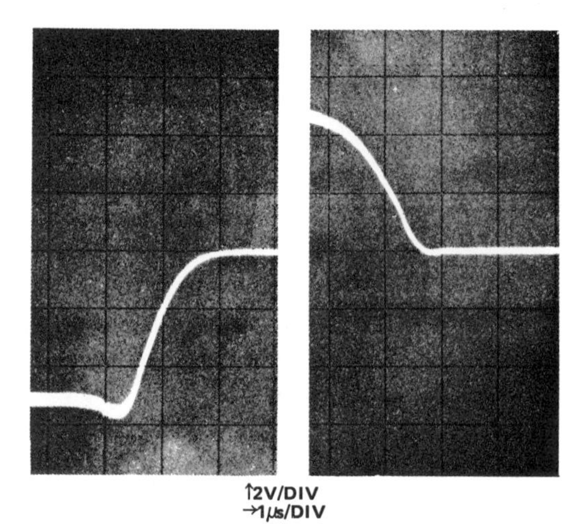

FIGURE 19. Oscillographs of Output Voltage of Figure 18

them 'off' the gates may be strapped together and connected to a common point. This point must be switched positive and negative such that when positive, the voltage is sufficient to pinch-off the p-channel device and when negative, sufficient to pinch-off the n-channel device. In this circuit, diodes in series with the gates are essential because of the large forward bias on them in the 'on' condition. The diodes should be of the slow recovery type or if fast diodes are used, small capacitors should be connected in parallel with them.

In general, p-channel FETs do not have such low 'on' resistances as n-channel devices, e.g. the maximum 'on' resistance of a 2N3993 is 150 Ω. This is of little consequence in most series shunt chopper circuits but if the load resistance is very low, the p-channel device should be placed where it produces least error.

CONCLUSIONS

The main advantages of using the FET as an analogue switch are the absence of offset voltage, low 'on' resistance,

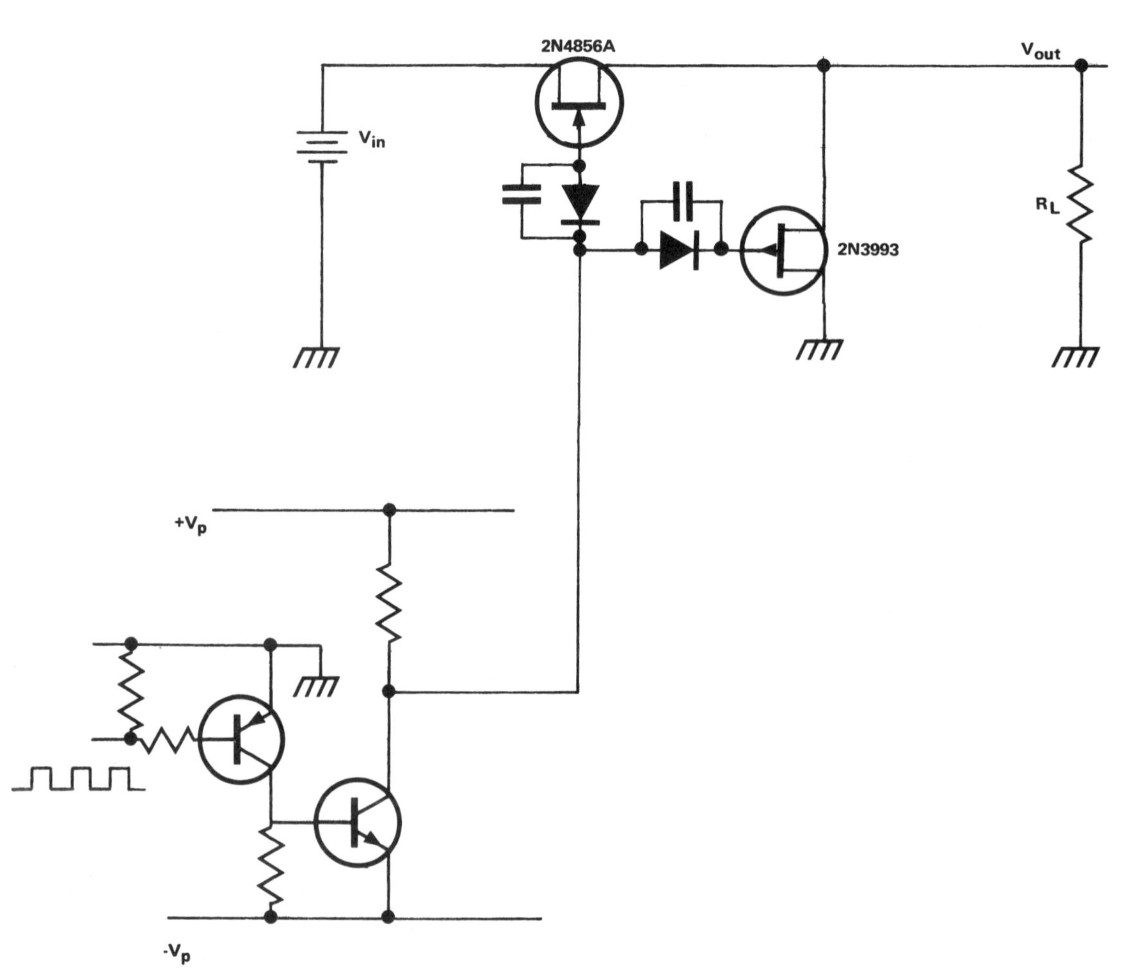

FIGURE 20. Complementary Series-Shunt Chopper Circuit

low drive power requirements and simplicity of drive circuitry. The main disadvantage is the relatively high inter-electrode capacitance and the resulting transient spike feed-through from gate to drain and source. Under adverse conditions the spike feedthrough can impose serious limitations on the performance of FET choppers. However, with careful circuit design, layout and adjustment of the drive voltage, the spike feedthrough, although not completely eliminated, can be reduced to acceptable levels.

Three basic chopper configurations were considered and the results showed that when the load resistance is low and switching speed not important, the most convenient configuration is the series chopper. The errors are low, the circuit is capable of chopping large input signals, drive circuitry is extremely simple and spike feedthrough is moderate.

When the load resistance is high and switching speed and spike feedthrough are prime considerations (as in the case with low input signals), the series shunt chopper offers superior performance.

The shunt chopper produces relatively large errors although spike feedthrough is lower and switching speed higher when compared with series chopper. The shunt chopper does not appear to have any great advantage over the series chopper except where large signals are involved and spike feedthrough and switching time has to be minimised.

SECTION 4.

RADIO FREQUENCY POWER APPLICATIONS

XV RF POWER TRANSISTORS

by Garry Garrard

Bipolar transistors delivering powers of up to 100W are available over much of the RF spectrum, and the power level at which valves can economically be replaced by transistors is now at least 1kW, not only in the H.F. band, but even at L band for pulsed radar applications. In high power transmitters the methods used to combine the outputs of a number of transistors result in not just improved reliability, but what is effectively a new concept in reliability. Hybrid couplers isolating individual output transistors ensure that the failure of one transistor has only a minor effect on the total output power. Under these circumstances, mean time before failure (MTBF) is meaningless, since a catastrophic device failure does not result in transmitter failure, and the transmitter operates on a principle of reliability through redundancy.

The successful use of RF power transistors at any power level and frequency requires careful selection of the most suitable devices and a skillful blend of theory and techniques in their application. Frequently, limitations on performance will be imposed by the practical realisation of the components theoretically required.

CLASS OF OPERATION

The class of operation for VHF power transistors is determined by the circuit performance required in the particular application.

Class A

Class A amplifiers are used where extremely high linearity is required – for example CATV amplifiers and drive stages for S.S.B. transmitters. Due to the high dissipation of Class A stages – efficiency rarely exceeds 25% – they are never used unless absolutely necessary, in spite of the fact that power gain is considerably higher than that of Class B or C stages.

Class B

When linearity is still important, but heat dissipation limitations preclude the use of Class A, then Class B is used. In the output stage of S.S.B. transmitters, delivering maybe 125W from a push-pull pair of devices, Class B is essential. Class B operation has a collector conduction angle of 180°. This requires sufficient base bias to overcome the transistor base-emitter voltage of about 0·7V. It is usual to operate with a small amount of quiescent current under no-signal conditions.

Class C

The majority of RF power transistors are used in the Class C mode. Under this condition gain is not as high as Class B but efficiency is considerably increased. Usually the base of the transistor is held at the same d.c. potential as the emitter, using an RF choke, as in Figure 1a. The 0·7V V_{BE} is sufficient to ensure Class C operation. Further bias may be applied by use of a resistor as in Figure 1b.

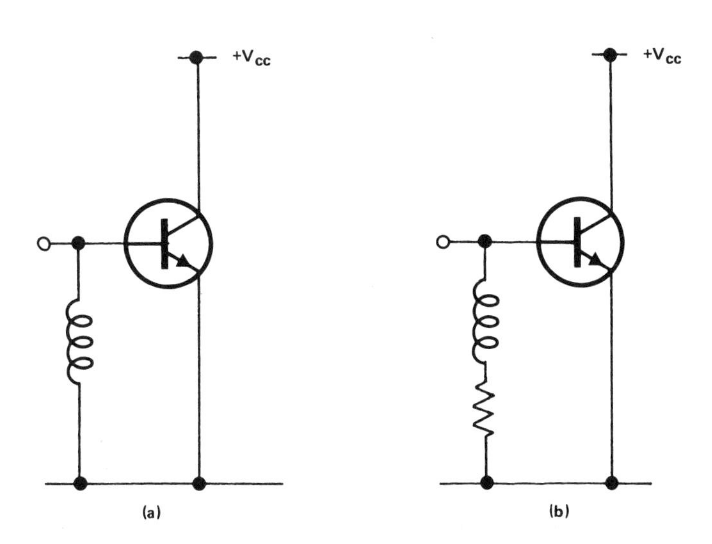

FIGURE 1. Class C Bias Configurations.

MODULATION AND TRANSISTOR REQUIREMENTS

The RF signals generated by high frequency, high power transistors will usually be required to carry information (speech, data, music etc.) by means of some form of modulation. The type of modulation used and the method of generation are important factors in the choice of suitable transistors.

Frequency Modulation (FM)

This has the least effect on the transistor requirements. Transistors may be selected simply at carrier power level and the appropriate supply voltage.

Amplitude Modulation (AM)

In this type of modulation the instantaneous amplitude is proportional to the modulating signal. The peak power requirement will be four times the carrier power if the circuit is designed for 100% modulation depth.

The choice of transistors for AM requirements requires care and will be decided by the system used for applying the modulation to the signal. Three common amplitude modulation methods are described below, and in each case the output transistor requirements are given for a 10W carrier power with 100% AM applied. In high-level AM systems it is usual to modulate the drive stage also, but the principles involved are identical with those described below.

A mixture of high and low level modulation may be used in some equipments, often with envelope feedback to improve modulation distortion.

High Level Transformer Modulation: This is the best known method of amplitude modulation. As shown in Figure 3 audio power is supplied to a transformer in series with the d.c. supply. Transistor supply voltage in the illustrated example is 13V unmodulated and 0–26V under 100% modulation. The RF output transistor must be capable of delivering 40W at 26V and 10W at 13V.

High Level Series Regulator Method: The principle here is similar to transformer modulation inasmuch as output power is varied by altering the supply voltage on the RF output transistor collector. In this method shown in Figure 4, the supply voltage is halved to 6·5V without modulation and 13V peak to peak with 100% modulation applied. The d.c. supply is connected via a power transistor used as a series regulator. This has the audio signal superimposed on its reference voltage. It is now often more economic to use power semiconductors in place of transformers. An added bonus is the resulting saving in weight. In the example shown, the transistor must be capable of delivering 40W at 13V and 10W at 6·5V. Power gain must obviously be good at 6·5V.

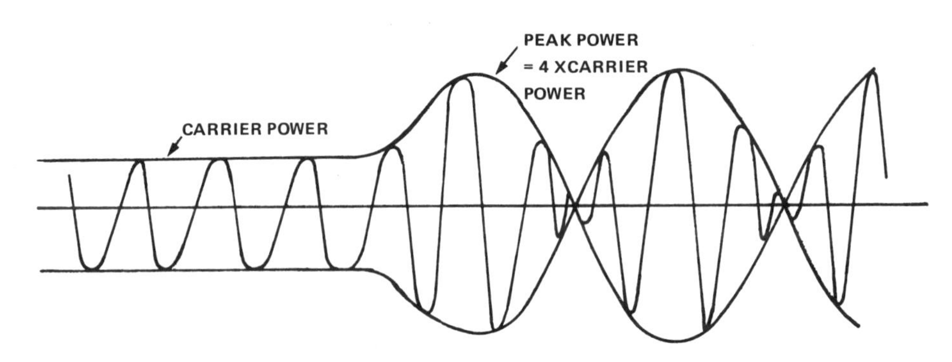

FIGURE 2. A.M. Envelope

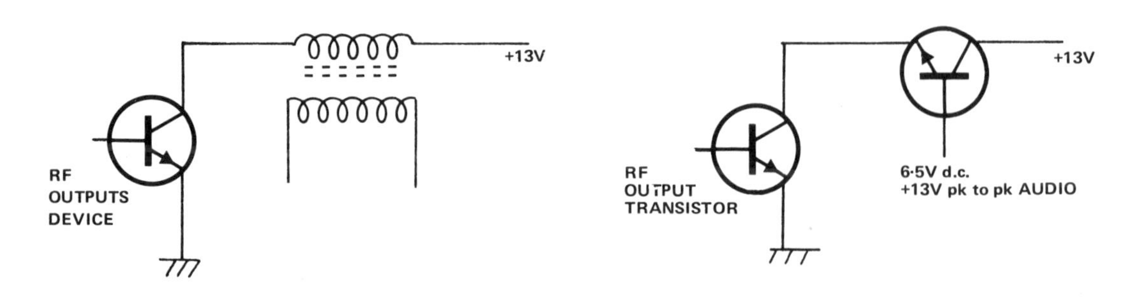

FIGURE 3. Transformer Modulation.

FIGURE 4. Series Regulator Method.

Low Level Modulation: In this method, as shown in Figure 5, the collector supply voltage is kept constant and the RF signal is modulated in an earlier low-level stage. The advantage of this is that it is not necessary to generate any audio power. However, the output transistor must be very linear and it is possible that Class B may be required. Problems associated with the use of RF power transistors at very low voltages are however avoided.

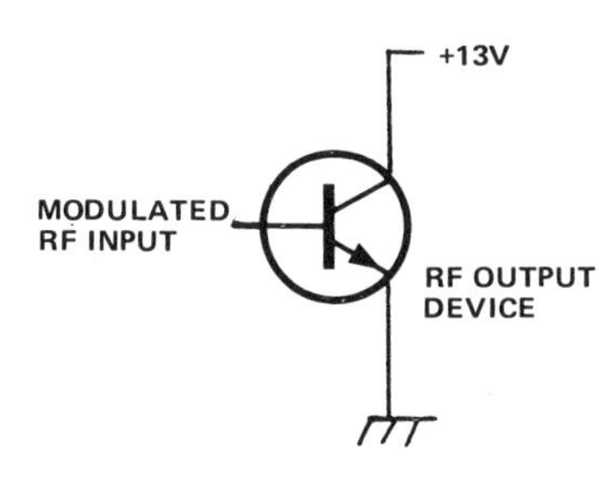

FIGURE 5. Low Level Modulation

Single Sideband (SSB)

Single sideband modulation is a sophisticated form of AM giving greatly improved transmitter efficiency. It is commonly used in the 1·5 – 30MHz frequency band in professional equipments, although amateur radio enthusiasts use this form of modulation at 144MHz and even 432MHz.

SSB signals can only be generated at low power levels however and require very linear power amplifiers. These are usually run in Class B, with the exception of some drive stages operating in Class A. Because of the large bandwidths involved, SSB amplifiers are nearly always push-pull to reduce the level of even harmonies so devices are used in pairs. Transistors intended for SSB use are always specified for linearity in addition to power gain. Due to the practical difficulties involved in making push-pull circuits operate at high frequencies and over broad bandwidths, transistors are often used apparently below their normal rating in order to achieve adequate linearity. For example, two 80W transistors may be used to obtain 125W of output power.

BROADBAND AMPLIFIER TECHNIQUES

The majority of requirements for RF power amplifiers may be satisfied by tuned amplifiers, which are covered in detail in Chapter XVII. There is, however, an increasing need for amplifiers covering complete communication bands – for example 66 – 88 MHz, 145 – 175 MHz and 225 – 400MHz. In general it is necessary to have a better knowledge of impedance levels when designing broadband circuits than is necessary when designing tuned amplifiers. Some aspects of this are discussed later in the chapter. The subject of broadband impedance matching networks is complex and only a brief description of available methods is possible here.

Broadband Transformers

The performance of transformers at high frequencies is limited by leakage inductance and self-capacity. If these are combined in the correct ratio a transmission line results and good impedance transformations are possible at frequencies up to 200MHz. The principle disadvantage of this method is the mechanical problem of making low impedance transmission lines in a small space. It is possible to compensate for lines higher in impedance than theoretically required. The use of this technique is illustrated in Chapter XVII.

The circuit configuration shown in Figure 6 is one of the most versatile broadband circuits. The optimum method of obtaining the ladder network values will depend on the fractional bandwidth and centre frequency of the amplifier. As the centre frequency increases, any given fractional bandwidth becomes more difficult to achieve.

Lumped Element Ladder Networks

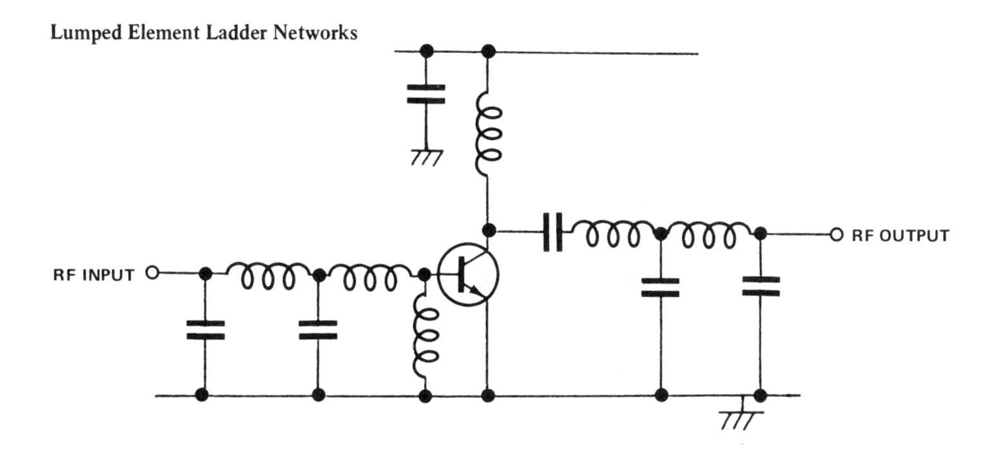

FIGURE 6. Typical Ladder Network Broadband Circuit

For extremely broadband circuits (e.g. 225–400 MHz) a computerised optimisation procedure used in conjunction with precise impedance measurements will be almost indispensible. Since the transistor impedances are frequency dependent, published tables of impedance transformation networks are not adequate: in nearly all cases they are suitable only for use with a constant resistive load. A technique is described in section 11.09 of reference[1] which provides a possible solution to the design of broadband matching networks with a frequency dependent load. This method however is best avoided unless the use of a computer is not available.

For applications such as the VHF mobile communications bands (66 – 88 MHz and 144 – 175 MHz) involving a fractional bandwidth of less than 30%, circuit values may be taken directly out of Matthieu's tables[2], for a first estimation. Providing impedances are known approximately final optimisation of circuit values should not be too difficult. It is important to reproduce the calculated values as accurately as possible when constructing the circuit. In particular any inductance in series with the shunt capacitors will alter the frequency characteristics of the network. Over a bandwidth of 30% it may be possible to compensate for some parastic inductance but the optimisation procedure will be made more difficult. The use of this method is illustrated by the following example. If the required bandwidth is 66 – 88 MHz,

$$w(\text{fractional bandwidth}) = \frac{(88 - 66) \times 2}{88 + 66} = 0{\cdot}29$$

The required impedance transformation is 50Ω to the 1Ω base input impedance; ∴ r = 50.
From reference[2],
With 2 elements, ripple $A_L = 3{\cdot}08$ dB (w = 0·3)
With 4 elements, ripple $A_L = 0{\cdot}1$ dB (w = 0·3)
Four elements will be required.

$g1 = 2{\cdot}75$ — L1
$g2 = {\cdot}359$ — C2
$g3 = {\cdot}359 \times 50 = 17{\cdot}95$ — L3
$g4 = \frac{2{\cdot}75}{50} = {\cdot}055$ — C4

$$L1 = \frac{2{\cdot}75 \,.\, 10^9}{2.\pi \,.\, 77 \,.\, 10^6} \text{ nH} = 5{\cdot}6\text{nH}$$

$L3 = 36{\cdot}7$nH

$$C2 = \frac{{\cdot}359 \times 10^{12}}{2\,.\,\pi\,.\,77 \times 10^6} \text{ pF} = 739\text{pF}$$

$C4 = 113$pF.

Therefore the completed ladder network is as shown in Figure 7.

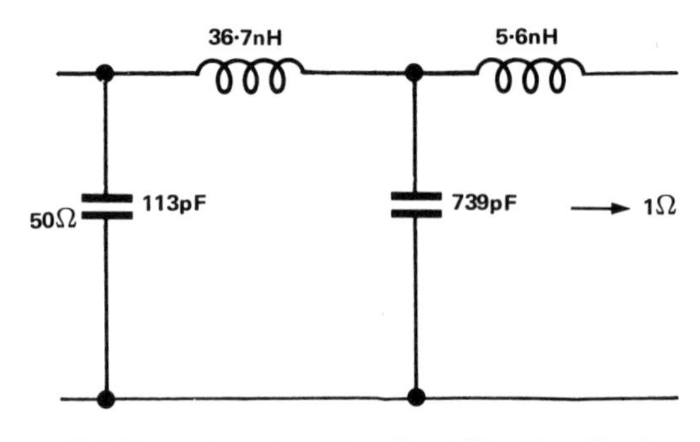

FIGURE 7. Completed Broadband Matching Circuit.

Distributed Transformers

At higher frequencies – usually not below 150MHz – the use of distributed transformers in stripline construction is often an elegant solution to broadband matching problems. The resulting circuit is highly reproducible when properly designed, and very simple in mechanical construction. Design is quite straightforward with sufficient information. Full details of the design of this type of circuit may be found in reference[1], which contains a considerable amount of information on stripline design and other distributed techniques.

IMPEDANCES

All the circuits and techniques involved with high frequency power transistors are completely dependent on an adequate knowledge of the transistor impedances. In small signal design, input and output matching circuits can be adjusted to give suitable stability and performance, using impedance measurements that are extremely accurate. Under the large signal conditions of Class C amplifiers accurate values of the base input impedance and the collector load impedance are extremely difficult to obtain.

Collector Load Impedance

Collector load impedance is usually calculated from the well-known formula:

$$P_{out} = \frac{(V_{CE} - V_{sat})^2}{2R_L}$$

This is quite adequate for tuned amplifiers in the VHF region, but is at best a considerable approximation. It assumes a sinusoidal collector voltage with peak to peak amplitude equal to twice the supply voltage. In tuned amplifiers in particular this is rarely true. The collector current is approximately sinusoidal but due to the non-linear nature of the output capacity, the collector voltage is extremely 'spiky' and will have an amplitude considerably greater than twice the supply voltage. Many engineers have been alarmed to find maybe 60V peak-to-peak of RF on a transistor with a d.c. breakdown voltage of 18V. This is quite normal and has been investigated by at least two authorities[3,4,5]. The output matching network becomes more critical in broadband circuits and the collector load impedance must satisfy requirements for gain, efficiency and saturated power output. These requirements are usually in conflict and it may be necessary to sacrifice some power gain in order to obtain sufficient saturated output power. As the frequency increases, the expression given above for collector load impedance becomes completely unusable, due to changes in waveforms, phasing, conduction angle and collector RF saturation voltage. It is impracticable to analyse these effects and extensive measurements may be necessary for extremely critical applications. 'Load pulling' measurements can interrelate the required performance parameters and details of this method are given in reference 6. Load pulling measurement facilities may not be available to some engineers and some alternative approaches are also described.

Input Impedance

Base input impedance is a critical factor in determining the network used to transfer RF power into the transistor. The input Q is usually the limiting factor on available bandwidth and the low value of input resistance requires care in the design of the input matching network if serious losses are to be avoided.

The dynamic input impedance of any RF power transistor is very different under large signal conditions to the more usual small signal measurements. It is dependent on almost every other operating parameter – input level, supply voltage, frequency, and, in particular, mounting arrangements. Input impedance can be expressed approximately as:

$$Z_{in} = (r_b + \omega_T \cdot L_e) + j\,(\omega L_e - \frac{(\omega_T)}{(\omega\ )}\, r_e)$$

where $\omega_T = 2.\pi.f_T$

and L_e = emitter parasitic inductance.

From this expression it is apparent that the resistive part of the input impedance is dependent on the emitter inductance. Increasing emitter inductance will reduce the input Q but, at the same time, will reduce power gain and emitter inductance must normally be minimised, unless power gain can be sacrificed. As in the case of collector load impedance, the accuracy with which the base input impedance must be determined is dependent on the type of application.

For non-critical, tuned amplifiers, similar to those described in the next chapter, only an approximate value of input impedance is necessary, even small signal measurements are sufficient in many instances if available. It is usual in this type of circuit to use adjustable capacitors and these can compensate for any errors in calculation. Some improvement in accuracy may be obtained by reducing the real part of the small signal input impedance by 50%. If h_{ie} has a value of 7 + j5, then the large signal value may be estimated at 3·5 + j5. Obviously this is completely empirical but experience shows it to be reliable.

For broadband circuits a better indication of input impedance will be necessary. As a minimum requirement, a large signal measurement is necessary: this information may be found on some data sheets. However, this is often of limited value. As mentioned earlier input impedance is very dependent on mounting arrangements and the actual arrangement being used will probably differ from that used by the transistor manufacturer. Changes in reference points on the leads will alter both real and imaginary parts of the input impedance. Also, the transistor may be operating at a different supply voltage, power level or frequency and all of these will affect the input impedance. For bandwidths of up to 30% at VHF, published data may be sufficient but anything in excess of this will require measurements to be done in situ. The transistor should be working into its intended collector matching circuit for any base impedance measurements, since changes in loading will be reflected in the input.

Measuring Techniques

When measuring low or high impedances at VHF, UHF and microwave frequencies, the slotted line is the most accurate instrument available. In the slotted line, a probe is inserted into a coaxial line and the standing wave pattern observed with a detector, see Figure 8. The

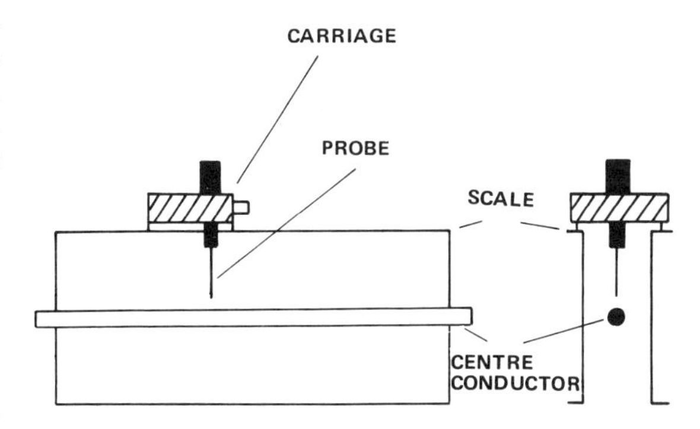

FIGURE 8. Slotted Line

apparatus required for small signal slotted line measurements is shown in Figure 9. A 1000Hz modulation signal is applied to the signal generator and a 1000Hz tuned amplifier is used after the detector. This system is very sensitive and limited by detector noise at low amplitudes and by the detector deviating from the square law characteristic with high level signals. For large voltage standing wave ratio, (VSWR), the limitations are the dynamic range available from the detector and the effect of the probe at voltage maxima.

This system, however, is not applicable to large signal measurements on active devices for the following reason. An active device is always non-linear and will generate harmonics from a sinewave. These harmonics will be present in the wave reflected from the device. The standing wave pattern will be not only the sum of two single

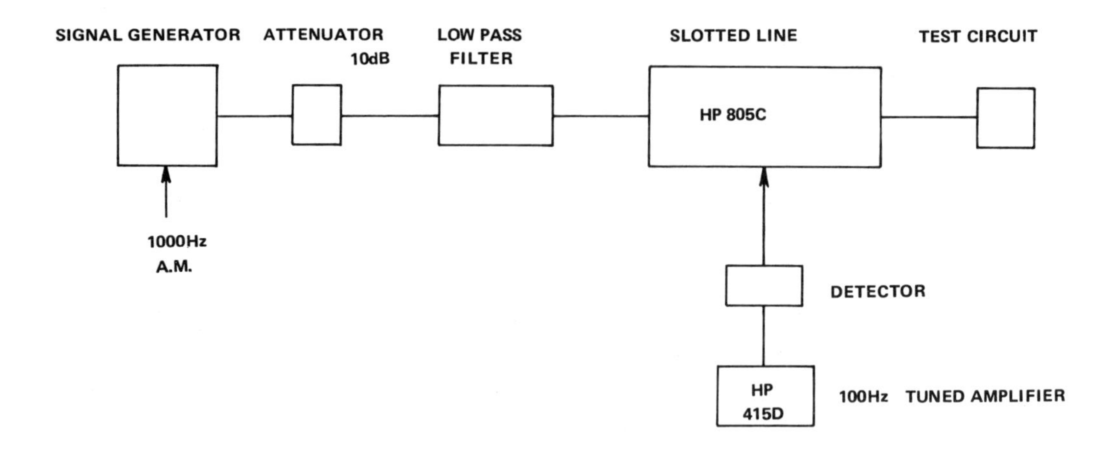

FIGURE 9. Small Signal Impedance Measurement

frequency components, but also some higher frequencies. These will confuse the standing wave pattern and make simple interpretation impossible. The way in which this problem is overcome is not to use a broadband detector but one tuned to the measurement frequency. It is possible with such a detection system to measure just the standing wave pattern produced by the fundamental frequency. Two detectors that could be used are a vector voltmeter and a spectrum analyser. The vector voltmeter is, however, very difficult to use. It has high impedance sampling probes which can be fitted into a BNC adaptor. The carriage on the slotted line could be modified to eliminate the detector diode and the vector voltmeter probe connected in place of this. With a 20W UHF amplifier near the probe, there is a large amount of radiation present and even with careful screening of the amplifier, the high impedance probes and the leads into the vector voltmeter would pick up large amounts of radiation. A sensitivity of 0·1mV is necessary, but it would be difficult to reduce the pick-up below 0·3mV. In some applications it could be used and then it would offer a simplified system.

The apparatus used for large signals is shown in Figure 10. This differs from the small signal apparatus in the inclusion of double stub tuners to achieve a power match on input and output, and the different detector. This adaptation of the slotted line technique to measure large signals gives an accuracy of a few per cent over a wide frequency range. It is important to realise in these measurements that the generator impedance seen by the slotted line is much different from 50Ω. It would appear

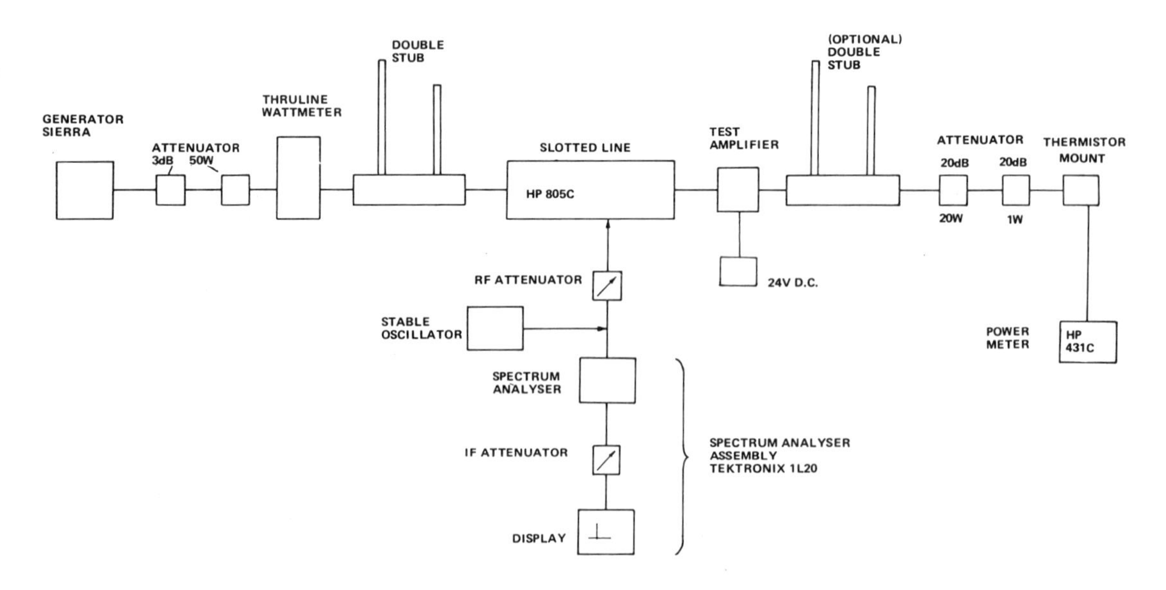

FIGURE 10. Large Signal Input Impedance

that this mismatch on the generator side of the slotted line would affect the VSWR measured on the line. However, if the reflection coefficient at the load is ρ (where ρ = reflected voltage)/ incident voltage), it can be shown that $\rho = (Z_L - Z_0)/(Z_L + Z_0)$ where Z_0 = characteristic impedance of the line and Z_L = impedance of the load. Since the VSWR = $(1+ |\rho|)/(1 - |\rho|)$, it is a function of the load impedance Z_L and the characteristic impedance of the line Z_0 only. Thus, although the double stub tuner produces a large mismatch at the input to the slotted line, the standing wave pattern is determined only by the load impedance. Two methods can be used to obtain the VSWR from the measurements. The simple method is to measure peak voltage, V_p, minimum voltage, V_M and then VSWR = V_p/V_M (see Figure 11). The

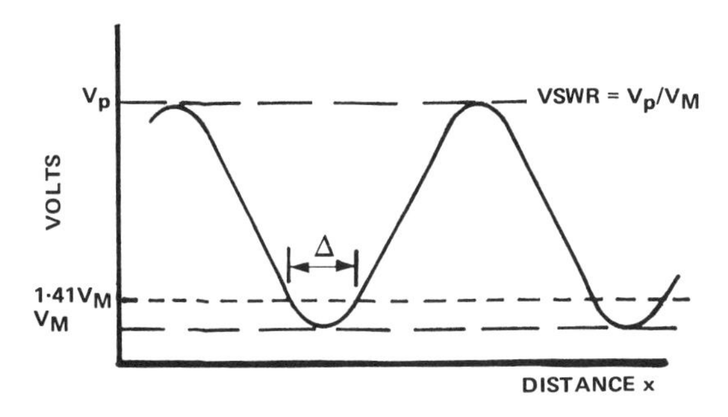

FIGURE 11. Voltage Standing Wave

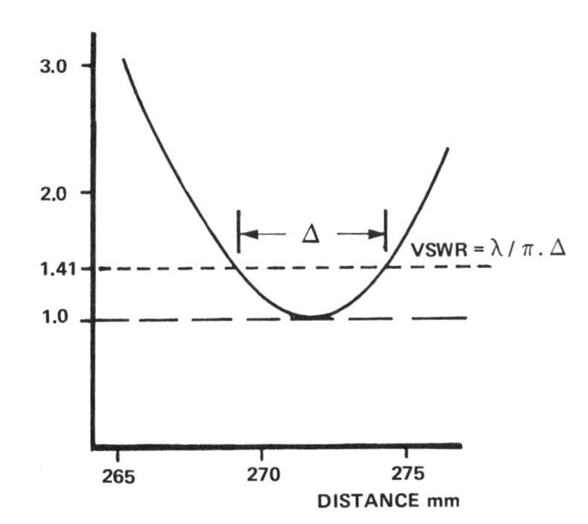

FIGURE 12. Voltage Near a Minimum

VSWR produced by the transistor is at least 50 and for a VSWR this high, the simple method has two disadvantages:–

(i) The probe on the slotted line is adjustable for penetration and in order to get a signal well above noise at the minimum of the standing wave pattern, the penetration must be large. This means that at the voltage maximum, the interaction of the probe with the standing wave pattern can be significant.

(ii) The large ratio of V_P to V_M requires a large dynamic range for the detector, 30 – 40dB. This dynamic range requirement can be eliminated by the use of either RF attenuators before the spectrum analyser, or IF attenuator provided on the spectrum analyser. The IF attenuator is convenient for use, but still requires a linear mixer (in the spectrum analyser). The RF attenuator method is less convenient but makes no demand on the dynamic range of the detector.

The second method of obtaining VSWR from the standing wave pattern is to plot the shape of the pattern near a minimum, see Figure 12. For this method, the distance between the points on the standing wave pattern, where the power is twice that at the minimum, is Δ; then VSWR = $\lambda/\pi\,\Delta$ (λ = wavelength on line) for VSWR > 10. This technique has several advantages which overcome the disadvantage of the tedious nature of the measurements.

(i) Since the probe is at all times near a voltage minimum, interaction between the probe and the pattern is a minimum.

(ii) The dynamic range needed from the detector is small (less than 10dB).

(iii) If the short slotted line (50cms) is used at low frequencies, a minimum and maximum do not both exist on the line, and extension lines would be needed to measure both V_p and V_M

(iv) In order to find the imaginary part of the device impedance, the position of the minimum must be determined precisely and this measurement is more accurate if the field around the minimum is plotted.

The problem of pick up, which occurs with a vector voltmeter, is eliminated by the use of a spectrum analyser, which has 50Ω coaxial inputs and double screened 50Ω coaxial cable can be used for connection. This reduces the pick-up to below the noise level of the spectrum analyser (–110dBm). The Sierra Generator gives 80W output and this is isolated by a pair of 3dB 50W attenuators, see Figure 10. The frequency of this generator can shift by several MHz when either the coupling or output control is varied or when the double stub tuner is adjusted. A frequency stability of 0·05% is required over the period of several minutes while the pattern is being plotted to avoid a shift greater than 0·1mm. A stable reference signal with a stability better than 0·0025% is introduced to the spectrum analyser and the frequency of the Sierra generator is adjusted to coincide with this before each measurement.

The double stub tuner matches the 50Ω source impedance into the device. This is a 50:1 transformation, representing a high Q matching circuit with high losses which, in fact, were as large as 6dB. Thus, only 5W of drive power is available into the device and for higher power testing a lower loss matching component would have to be used. No simple circuit, tunable over an octave, is easily devised to give a lower loss match, so the loss is tolerated.

The test amplifier is shown in Figure 13. A 50Ω transmission line is maintained up to the base of the device

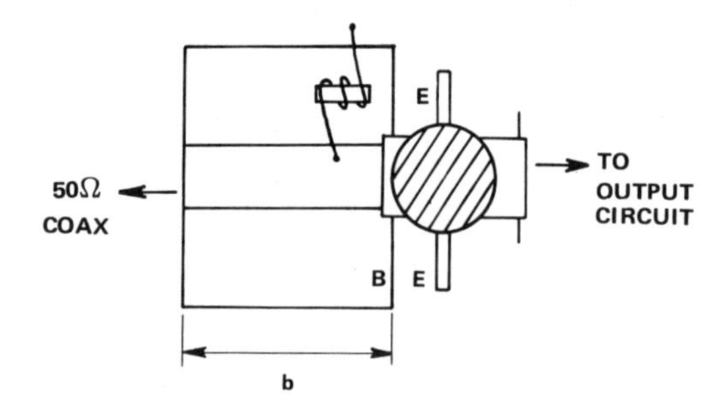

FIGURE 13. Test Amplifier

which is grounded with a high impedance base choke. This is wound on a ferrite toroid and its impedance is greater than 1kΩ from 10MHz to above 400MHz. The whole amplifier is enclosed in a copper screen which should be well earthed at input and output. The H.T. lead is screened cable and passed through the copper by means of a feed through capacitor. These precautions are essential to reduce the pick-up from the d.c. supply lead to below −110dBm.

Obtaining Results: With the probe at a minimum of the standing wave pattern, the gain of the spectrum analyser is adjusted to give full scale deflection. The 3dB of I.F. attenuation is switched in and the probe positions for equal deflections noted. This is repeated for different attentuations so that a complete graph of the minima can be drawn (see Figure 12). The probe is then moved to a voltage maximum and the I.F. attenuation needed to give full scale deflection noted. Then the amplifier is replaced by a short circuit with a length equal to the length of the line to the transistor. The new position of the minimum is then determined. The impedance is given by:–

$$\frac{Z}{50} = \frac{1 - j(SWR)\tan L}{(SWR) - j\tan L}$$

where $L = 2\pi d/\lambda$
d = shift of minimum when the short circuit is applied,
and λ = wavelength on the line
When $SWR >> 1$ and $d << \lambda$ i.e. $\tan L << 1$ or $\tan L \simeq L$, then $Re(Z) = 50/(SWR)\,\Omega$ and $Im(Z) = 100\,\pi d/\lambda.\Omega$. These relations are used to find the real and imaginary parts of the input impedance.

HEATSINK DESIGN

Care must be taken to provide adequate heatsinking for VHF power transistors. The design of heat dissipators is outside the scope of this book, but some aspects of this specific application need special attention. Two points in particular make the requirements greater than may initially seem necessary.

Due to the relatively low power gain of most output devices, the contribution to total power dissipation of the drive power and the driver stage can become significant. For example, consider a 10W output stage with a gain of 6dB, and a collector efficiency of 65%.

$$P_C = 10 \cdot \frac{35}{65}\ W = 5{\cdot}4\ W$$

To this must be added the input power of 2·5W, so that the dissipation in the output stage is (5·4 + 2·5)W = 7·9W. If the driver stage has 65% efficiency and 10dB gain,

$$P_D = (0{\cdot}25 + 2{\cdot}5 \times \frac{35}{65}) = 1{\cdot}6W$$

So total dissipation in both stages is (1·6 + 7·9) = 9·5W; nearly double the output stage collector dissipation.

The other major factor contributing to dissipation is operation under mismatched load conditions. Modern high frequency power transistors will usually withstand any phase of infinite VSWR, but the heatsink must be able to handle the resulting power dissipation. Under short circuit conditions, not only is all the output power dissipated within the output transistor, but the collector current will actually increase by a factor of up to 1·5. Thus for the transistor considered above:–
Output stage efficiency = 65%
Collector current (V_{CC} = 13V)

$$= 10 \times \frac{100}{65} \times \frac{1}{13} = 1{\cdot}19A$$

If this increased by 1·5 under short circuit conditions,

I_{SC} = 1·78
and collector or dissipation is increased to
P_C = 1·78 x 13 = 23W.

Adding on the driver dissipation, the heatsink must now dissipate approximately 27W instead of 9·5W under matched conditions.

REFERENCES

1. George L. Matthieu, Leo. Young and E.M.T. Jones, *Microwave Filters, Impedance Matching Networks and Coupling Structures'*, McGraw Hill.
2. George L. Matthieu, 'Tables of Chebyshev Impedance Transforming Networks of Low Pass Filter Form, *Proc. IEEE,* pp. 939-963, Aug. 1964.
3. B. Reich, E. B. Hakin and G. J. Malinowski, 'Maximum RF Power Transistor Collector Voltage', *Proc. IEEE (Letters),* Vol. 57, pp. 1789-1791, October 1969.
4. John Chroma, Jr., 'Comments on Maximum RF Power Transistor Collector Voltage', *Proc. IEEE (Letters),* Vol. 58, pp. 918-919, June 1970.
5. John Chroma Jr., 'High Frequency Breakdown in Diffused Transistors', *IEEE Transactions on Electron Devices',* Vol. Ed. 18 No. 6, pp. 347-349, June 1971.
6. Octavius Pitzalis Jr., and Russell A. Gibson, 'Broadband Microwave Class-C Transistor Amplifiers', *IEEE Transactions on Microwave Theory and Techniques',* Vol. MTT-21 No. 11, pp. 660-668, November 1973.

XVI TUNED AMPLIFIER DESIGN

by

Garry Garrard

The majority of VHF/UHF transmitter applications require the use of tuned Class C amplifiers. The design of these is principally an exercise in designing reactive filter networks. These perform two functions – the transformation of impedance levels and the rejection of harmonics of the signal. There are two approaches to the design of these networks – graphical and mathematical. Both methods are equally valid and will give identical results – the choice depends purely on personal preference.

GRAPHICAL APPROACH TO FILTER DESIGN

Impedance-Admittance (z – y) Chart

The use of this chart for the analysis of filters which combine series and parallel reactances is described in the literature[1, 2] The advantage of the method is that a plot on the chart is obtained which shows the part played by each component in the impedance transformation and the effect of changing the value of a component can be easily assessed. The z – y chart is made up by laying a transparent Smith chart over a second chart with the zero point of the upper chart over the infinity point on the lower one. For series elements in a network the upper (z) chart is used and for parallel elements the plot is continued on the lower (y) chart. The component values used have to be normalised to some arbitrary resistance value. The best method of demonstrating the application of the chart is to take an example of an actual amplifier design. Although the calculations are made at 175MHz, the circuit configurations and the methods of calculation are valid at any frequency.

The design presented is a 15W VHF amplifier suitable for mobile transmitters operating in the 145 – 176MHz band. The transistors used are the BLY61, BLY62 and BLY63, which are specially designed for optimum gain at low supply voltages, and to withstand any phase of infinite VSWR at the full rated 15W output power.

Output Matching Network

To calculate the load resistance required at the collector for a particular value of output power, P_{out}, a peak RF voltage at the collector equal to the rail voltage is assumed. This makes no allowance for the saturation voltage, but has been found to yield a result sufficiently accurate for most design purposes. In this case:

Peak voltage $V_p = V_{rail} = 13.5V$

Load resistance $R_L = (V_p)^2/2P_{out} = 6\ \Omega$

The problem now is to determine a filter which will transform the 50 Ω load to 6 Ω at the collector and which will attenuate the harmonics to an acceptable level for normal VHF communications purposes. A single tuned series resonant circuit is suitable for this and its component values may be determined by the use of the impedance-admittance chart. In the present case, a single tuned circuit filter is required which will convert the nominal 50 Ω output load resistance to present 6 Ω to the transistor collector. In practice the working Q is chosen as a compromise between good harmonic rejection and low losses in the filter. A value of 5 is chosen in this case.

The type of filter shown in Figure 1 has the advantage of simplicity and also it puts no large parallel capacity between the transistor collector and ground. Non-linear capacities in the transistor contribute to high collector efficiency and large circuit capacities swamp these internal capacities.

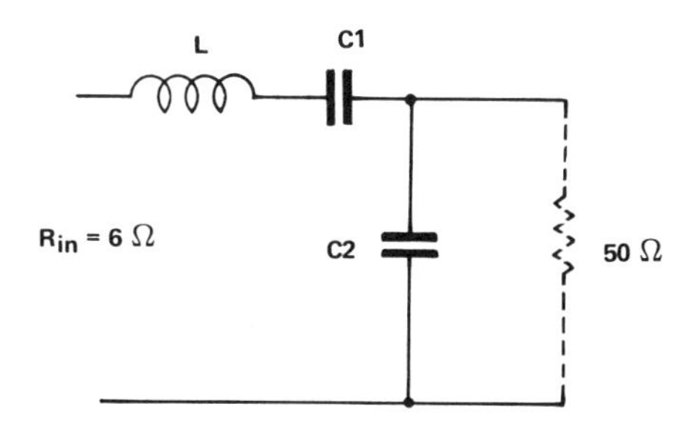

FIGURE 1. Output Matching Network

The matching action is that capacitor C2 effectively reduces the 50 Ω load to a series 6 Ω and a series tuned circuit is formed by inductor L, capacitor C1 and the series equivalent to capacitor C2 and the 50 Ω

The plot of this circuit is shown on the z – y chart in Figure 2. An explanation of the steps in the plot now follows. The chart has a normalising impedance and admittance. In this case we chose $Z_o = 50\ \Omega$ and hence $Y_o = 0.02S$.

(i) Load into which power is delivered = $R_l = 50 + j0\ \Omega$
Normalised $r_l = 1 + j0$

This is plotted at centre of chart (point B)

(ii) Resistance to be presented at collector $R_{in} = 6 + j0\ \Omega$
Normalised $r_{in} = 0.12 + j0$

This is plotted at point A.

(iii) Trace an arc AC anticlockwise along a constant R circle (r = 0.12) of the upper Z chart to point C. Point C is determined by the required loaded Q of the circuit. The Q is defined by the ratio series reactance to series resistance of any point on the chart and it is possible to draw a series of curved lines from L to M which are lines of constant Q. The lines can be drawn in the upper or lower half of the chart.

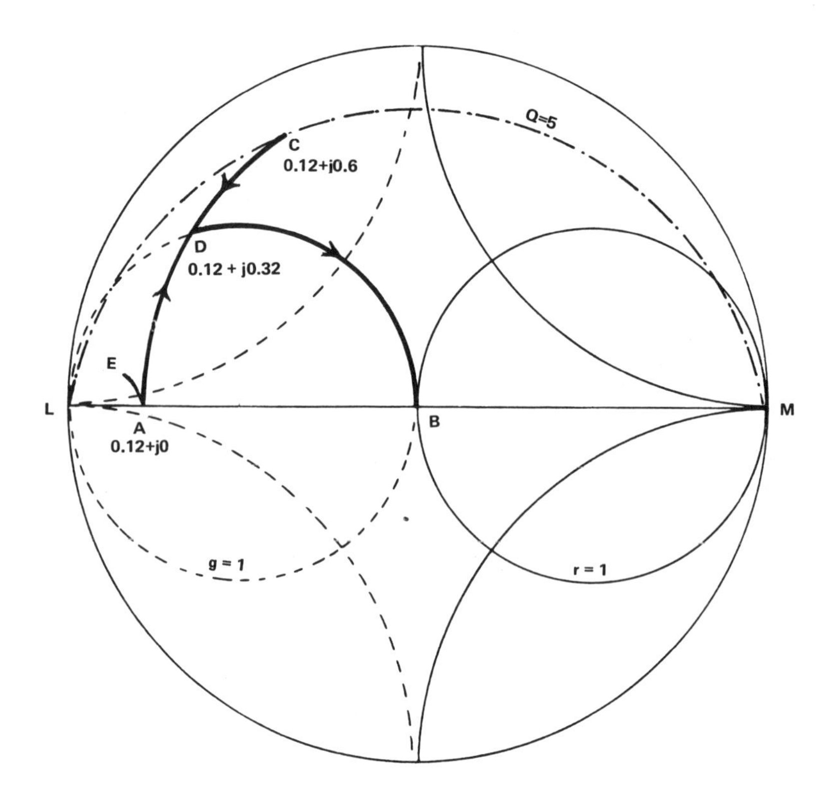

FIGURE 2. Impedance-Admittance Chart for Output Matching Network

The Q = 5 line is drawn in Figure 2 and contains point C. The plot of a filter section may cross several lines of constant Q. When this happens the operating Q may be taken as that of the highest value of Q touched by the plot. The assumption is that all other values are overridden by the high Q section of the circuit. Point C represents the highest Q point in the circuit under discussion. In Figure 2 the series inductance L is represented by the total positive reactance change from A to C.

i.e. from 0 to + j0.6

$\therefore X_L = + j0.6$

De-normalising $Z_L = + j\,\omega\, L = + j0.6 \times 50$

$\therefore L = (0.6 \times 50 \times 10^9)/(2\,\pi \times 175 \times 10^6)$ nH

$= 27$nH

(iv) The next element, working towards the 50 Ω load, is the series capacitor C1. As shown when adding a series inductance to the circuit an arc is traced on the chart clockwise along a constant resistance circle. To add series capacity therefore a trace is made along the same arc in an anti-clockwise direction to point D; Point D is located by the fact that it lies on the constant g = 1 circle on the y chart (see later). Capacitor C1 is represented by arc C to D.

i.e. + j0.6 to + j0.32

$\therefore X_{C1} = - j\,(0.6 - 0.32) = - j0.28$

Denormalising $X_{C1} = 0.28 \times 50$

$\therefore C1 = 10^{12}/\ (11 \times 10 \times 0.28 \times 50)$

$= 64$pF

(v) The final element is a parallel capacitor C2 across the 50 Ω load. Parallel susceptance is added by tracing round constant conductance circles on the Y chart. This means tracing clockwise to add parallel capacity and anti-clockwise to add parallel inductance. In the present case the final goal is the centre of the chart point B which represents 1 + j0 or 50 Ω. Hence, we move on the g = 1 circle on the y chart to point B and the amount of parallel capacity needed to do this is proportional to length of arc DB.

i.e. from D to B

from + 2.68 to 0

Susceptance $b_{C2} = + 2.68$

Denormalising $B_{C2} = + j2.68 \times .02 = + j\omega C2$

$\therefore C2 = 2.68 \times .02 \times 10^{12}/\ 11 \times 10^8$

$= 49$pF

Hence the value of capacitor C2 is fixed.

(vi) There are two other elements to be considered in the circuit of Figure 2. These are the transistor output capacity. C_{oep} for BLY63 devices is 45pF. The radio frequency choke cannot be a self resonant choke at 175MHz for reasons explained later and the value is chosen so that it resonates with C_{oep} at 175MHz. This value is 18nH. The effect of these two components on the filter z – y plot is quite small, but for the sake of completeness, these elements are represented by the arc AE in Figure 2. The capacity contributes a susceptance B_C given by

$B_C = j\,\omega\, C = 2\,\pi\ 1.75\ 10^8.45.10^{-12}$ S

$= 0.0495$S

Normalising, $b_C = 0.0495/0.02 = j\ 2.43$

The choke contributes an equal negative susceptance.

Interstage Transformer Between Driver and Output Stages

The minimum gain figure for the BLY63 transistor shows that for 15W of output power, a drive power of 5W is required. The load resistance to be presented to the collector of the BLY62 transistor equals

$13.5^2/2 \times 5 = 18.2\ \Omega$

There are two or more networks which will do this job equally well. The arrangements shown in Figure 3 was chosen. The large signal input impedance of the device is at A (1.6 – j1 ohms) on the z – y chart in Figure 4, and the R_L (= 18.2 ohms) is at D. The plot is formed by tracing backwards along a series reactance from A to the Q = 7 line at point B.

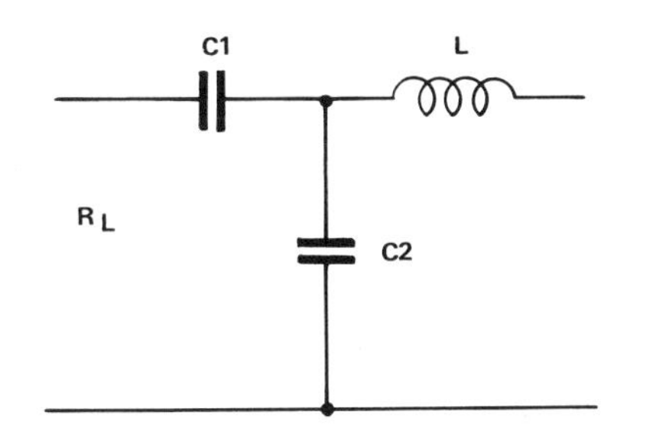

FIGURE 3. Interstage Network

The other two components are given by a parallel susceptance CB and a series reactance D.C. The direction of plot is arranged as shown as that:

DC is the series capacitance C1

CB is the parallel capacitance C2

BA is the series inductance L

From the z – y chart

Reactance X_{C1} = j0.65, or – j(0.65 x 50)

$\therefore$ C1 = 28pF

Susceptance b_{C2} = + j (4.25 – 1.2) = + j3.05

$\therefore$ + j ω C2 = + j (3.05 x .02)

$\therefore$ C2 = 55pF

Inductive reactance X_L = + j (0.23 – 0.02) = + j0.21

$\therefore$ + j ω L = + j (0.21 x 50)

$\therefore$ L = 9nH

Interstage Transformer Between Input and Driver Stages

The large signal input impedance of the BLY62 transistor at 175MHz is 3.4 + j2. The gain of the transistor is such that a maximum of 1.0W input is required for 5W output power.

$\therefore$ Collector the load required by a BLY61 transistor is:

$13.5^2/2 \times 1 = 91\ \Omega$

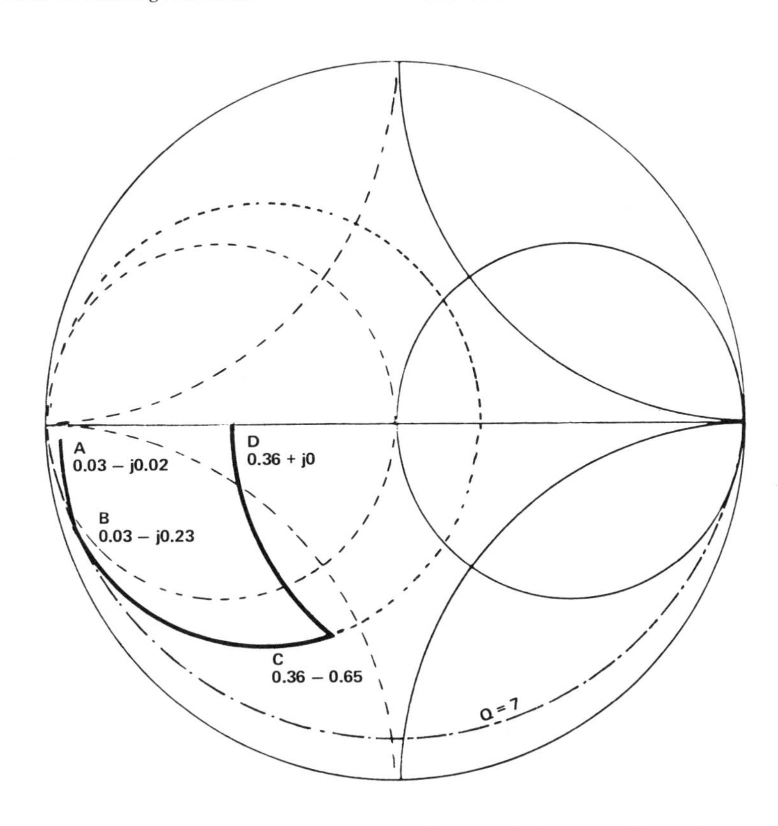

FIGURE 4. Impendance-Admittance Chart for the Interstage Networks

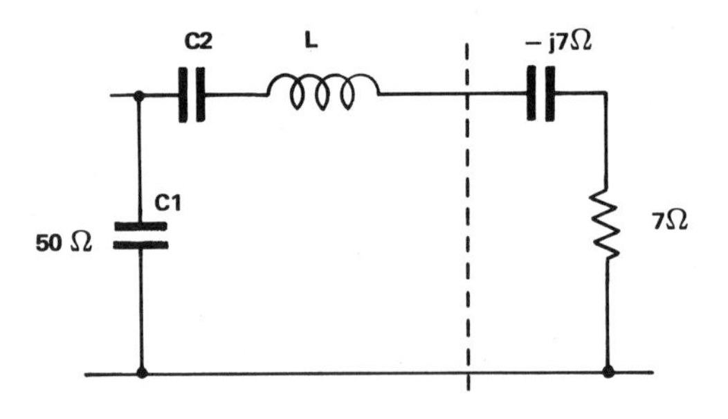

FIGURE 5. Input Matching Network

An identical configuration to that used for the other inter-stage network is employed. The procedure is exactly the same, and the element values for a Q of 7 are:–

L = 19nH
C1 = 10.7pF
C2 = 32.4pF

Input Matching Network

The large signal input impedance of the BLY61 transistor is 7 – j7 at 175MHz. The circuit in Figure 5 is used to match this impedance to 50 Ω. A z – y plot is shown in Figure 6.

From the chart:–
L (represented by arc AC) = 38nH
C2 (represented by arc CD) = 51pF
C1 (represented by arc CB) = 45pF

Practical Amplifier

The complete circuit is shown in Figure 7. The capacitors in all the matching circuits are variable. This is to enable the circuit to tune over the 146 to 175MHz frequency band, and in addition to allow for approximations in the matching circuit calculations.

A frequent problem in VHF power amplifiers is that of low frequency oscillation. The principal precaution that must be taken is good decoupling of the supply line at low frequencies as well as at VHF. If this is combined with the use of lossy ferrite chokes for the base d.c. returns and a careful layout, few problems arise. Spurious oscillations are usually under load mismatch conditions, and mismatch tests should include examination for spurious, which may cause damage or complete failure of VHF power transistors.

The most convenient way to construct a practical amplifier is to use double sided printed circuit board. One side is used as an earth plane and connections are made by normal printed circuit track on the opposite side. Clearance holes are used for the stud mounting transistors, allowing

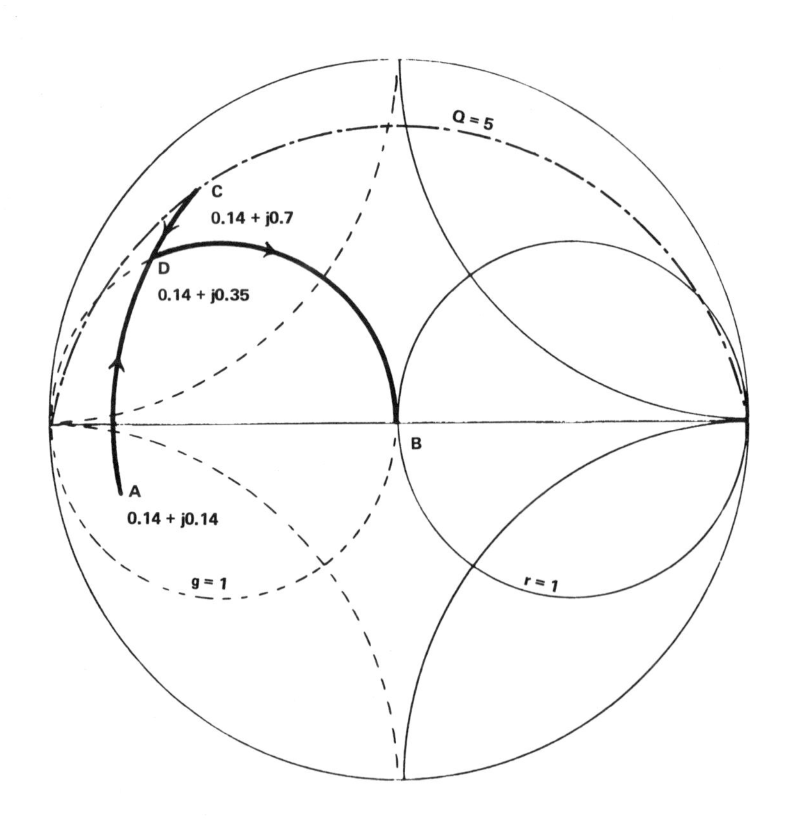

FIGURE 6. Impedance-Admittance Chart for Input Matching Network

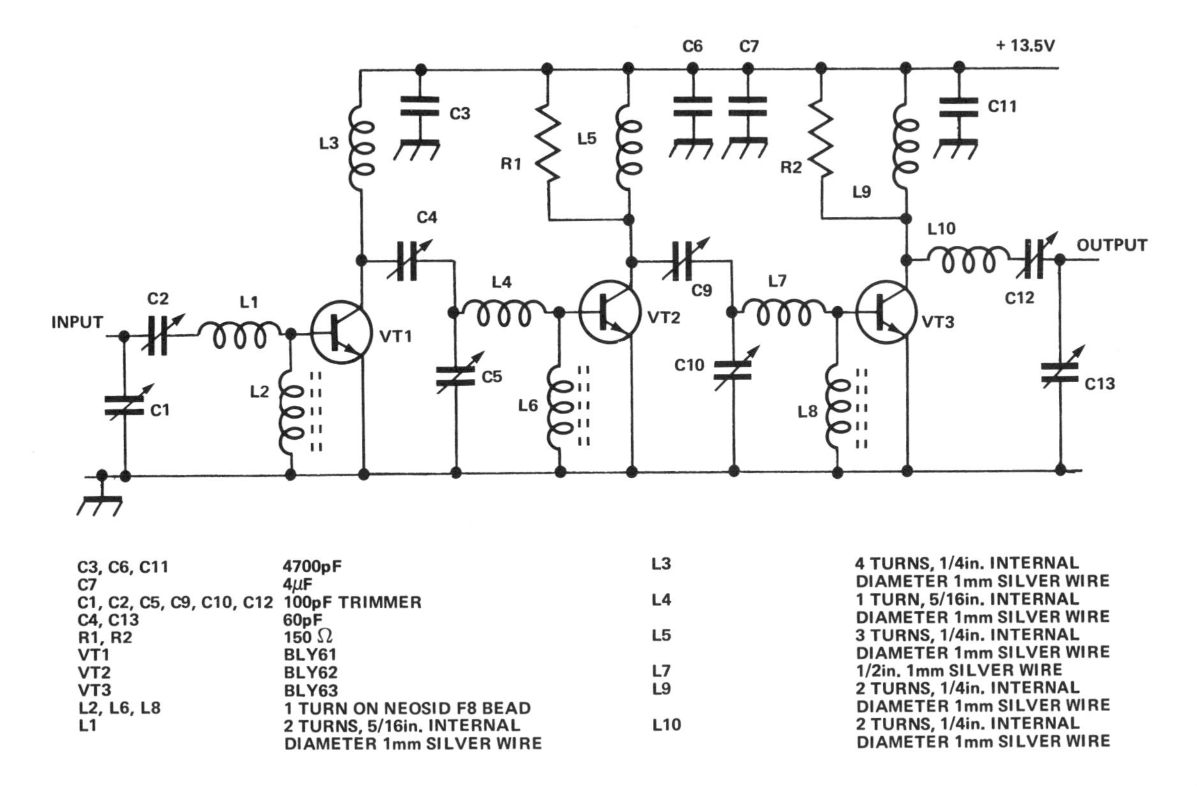

FIGURE 7. 15W 146-175MHz Power Amplifier Circuit

FIGURE 8. Photograph of Completed Power Amplifier

the circuit to be fitted to any suitable heatsink. Layout is not critical, the use of a solid copper earth plane on one side of the board eases this problem considerably. Components are mounted on the earth side of the board, all holes in the earth plane have the copper cleared from around them. A photograph of such a construction is shown in Figure 8.

The overall performance of the amplifier is summarized by the following results which were made at 175MHz using transistors with typical gains:

Output power = 15W
Input power = 45mW
D.C. current = 2.05A
Supply voltage = 13.5V
Overall Efficiency = 54%
Harmonic output > 30dB down on fundamental

SIMPLE MATHEMATICAL APPROACH TO FILTER DESIGN

Equivalent Circuits

Any series combination of resistance and reactance may be converted at a given frequency to an equivalent parallel combination of similar elements-resistance and capacitance or resistance and inductance.

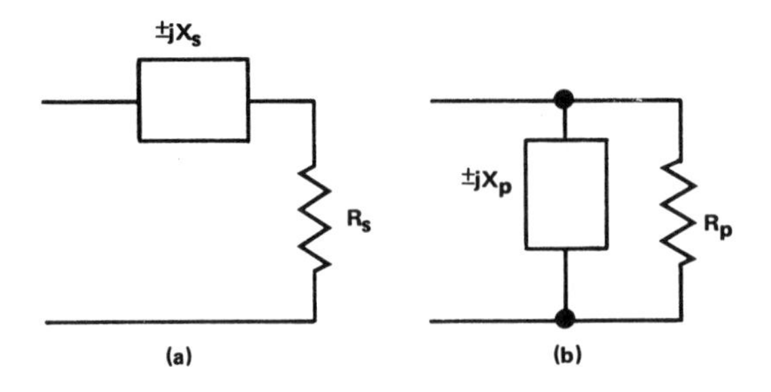

FIGURE 9. Series/Parallel Equivalent Circuits

In Figure 9, X_S and X_P are reactances, and may be capacitors or inductors, but must be the same in each circuit. For Figure 9 (a):–

$$y_{in} = \frac{1}{\pm jX_S + R_S} = \frac{R_S \pm jX_S}{R_S^2 + X_S^2}$$

for Figure 1(b):–

$$y_{in} = \frac{1}{\pm jX_P} + \frac{1}{R_P}$$

If the real and imaginary parts of the two circuits are equated:–

$$\frac{1}{R_P} = \frac{R_S}{R_S^2 + X_S^2}$$

$$\therefore R_P = \frac{R_S^2 + X_S^2}{R_S} \quad \text{.... Equation 1}$$

$$\pm\frac{1}{jX_P} = \pm\frac{jX_S}{R_S^2 + X_S^2}$$

$$\therefore X_P = \frac{R_S^2 + X_S^2}{X_S} \quad \text{.... Equation 2}$$

A similar procedure may be adopted for a parallel to series conversion. In this case,

$$R_S = R_P \cdot \frac{X_P^2}{R_P^2 + X_P^2} \quad \text{.... Equation 3}$$

$$X_S = X_P \cdot \frac{R_P^2}{R_P^2 + X_P^2} \quad \text{.... Equation 4}$$

If the equivalent reactance in equations (2) or (4) is tuned out by a complementary reactance, then the equivalent resistance in equations (1) or (3) remains. A series to parallel conversion always increases resistance and a parallel to series conversion reduces it. More complicated matching networks may be calculated using this method, by breaking the circuit into L sections, and making the conversion in several steps. Examples of this are given in Figure 10.

It should be noted that the reactances calculated are the net reactance values in any branch of the circuit. Where bandwidth is not a critical factor, additional reactances may be added providing the sum in any branch remains the same at the required frequency. This is particularly important at UHF since it is difficult to obtain trimmer capacitors which have not got significant inductance at this frequency. As an example, if a reactance of – j30 is required in one branch, this may be made up of – j65 and + j35 in series. The total

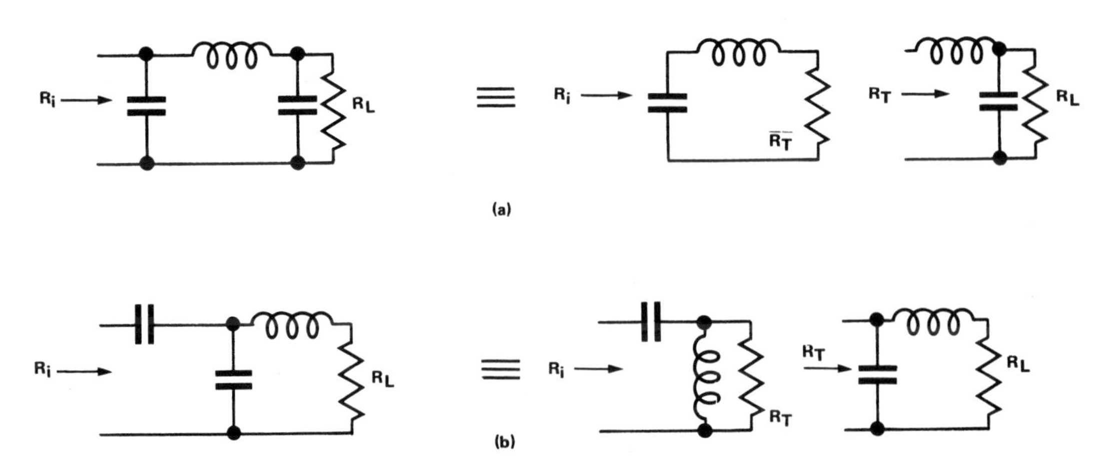

FIGURE 10. Build Up of Matching Circuits

circuit Q will, of course, be changed. In many instances, this will be both necessary and desirable. As with the graphical approach the application of this method is best illustrated by a design example.

The design chosen in this instance is a 470MHz amplifier, using the BLW12/13/14 series of transistors.

Output Matching Network

For an output power, P_{out}, of 7W from a 13V supply voltage, the load resistance, R_L

$$= \frac{13^2}{2.7} = 12\Omega.$$

Therefore it is necessary to transform from the 50 Ω load to the 12 Ω at the collector. A parallel to series conversion will ensure a good collector efficiency. As a low pass filter is desirable, a shunt capacitor is used, as shown in Figure 11.

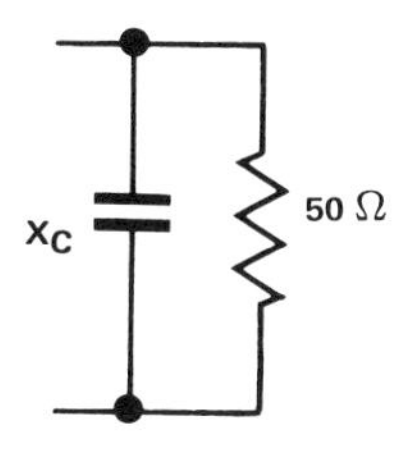

FIGURE 11. Shunt Capacitor across Output Load

Using equation (3):–

$$12 = 50.\frac{X_C^2}{X_C^2 + 2500}$$

i.e. $X_C = 28.1\ \Omega$

Using equation (4), the equivalent series reactance will be:–

$$28.1\frac{50^2}{50^2 + 28.1^2} = -j21.4\,\Omega$$

This is capacitive, and may be tuned out with a similar valued inductor. However, this value of inductance is very small, and in addition, it is desirable to have reasonable Q in the output, to maintain efficiency and reject harmonics. If a Q of 4 is used then $X_L = +j\,(5 \times 12) = +j60$.

To keep the total branch reactance the same, a capacitor of reactance $-j(60 - 21.4) = 38.6$ must be added in series.

The matching circuit is then as in Figure 12.

The above reactances may be converted into circuit values.

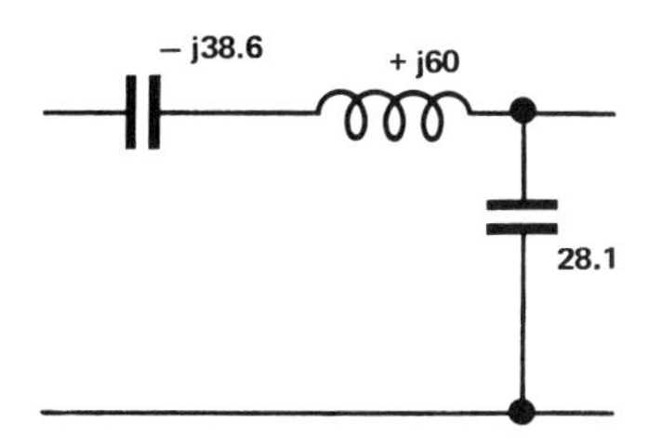

FIGURE 12. Output Matching Circuit

$$-j38.6 = \frac{1}{2.\pi\,.4.7.10^8.38.6} = 8.7\text{pF}$$

$$-j28.1 = \frac{1}{2.\pi\,.4.7.10^8.28.1} = 12\text{pF}$$

$$+j60 = \frac{6}{2.\pi\,.4.7.\,10^8} = 20\text{nH}$$

The only remaining element in the output circuit is the collector choke. This should resonate with the output capacity at 470MHz. From data sheet, C_{OBO} = 12·5 pF, therefore, C_{out} = 25pF. To resonate this at 470MHz required 5nH.

Interstage Transformer Between Driver and Output Stages

From the data sheet, a BLW14 transistor requires 2W in for 7W out. Therefore the required collector load for the BLW13 transistor is:–

$$\frac{13^2}{2{\cdot}2} = 42\Omega$$

The input impedance Ri of the BLW14 transistor at 470MHz is 4·5 + j7 and therefore 4·5 Ω must be transformed into 42 Ω. The simplest transformation is an ordinary series to parallel conversion, but this would result in a shunt capacity across the collector of the BLW13 transistor, and loading at harmonic frequencies. The circuit in Figure 10(b) is more suitable. This gives a series tuned circuit at the collector. The intermediate transformation resistance (R_T) is arbitrary, but must be greater than R_i. As there is a single inductor in the circuit in series with the load resistance, the Q may be easily calculated from

$$Q = \frac{X_L}{R_L}$$

To make R_T greater than R_i, it is necessary that:–

$$\frac{R_i}{R_L} < (1 + Q^2)$$

$$\therefore \frac{42}{4{\cdot}5} < (1 + Q^2) \qquad\qquad \therefore Q > 2{\cdot}89$$

To keep a practical value of inductance, it is necessary to have a moderately high Q. If a Q of 8 is used then $X_L = +j8 \times 4.5 = +j36\ \Omega$. The transistor input impedance will contribute + j7, so the required inductor will be $+ j(36 - 7) = +j29\ \Omega$. The above values are now converted into the parallel equivalent using equations (1) and (2).

$$\text{i.e. } R_p = \frac{4{\cdot}5^2 + 36^2}{4{\cdot}5} = 286$$

$$X_p = +j\frac{4{\cdot}5^2 + 36^2}{36} = +j36{\cdot}4$$

The resistive part of this must now be converted to 42 Ω. Since it will be necessary to provide adjustment in the circuit, it is convenient in this case to use a high-pass filter element, shunting the intermediate value of resistance with an inductance, and tuning out with a series capacitor.

To transform 286 Ω to 42 Ω, use equation (3). Then:–

$$42 = 286 \cdot \frac{X_p^2}{286^2 + X_p^2}$$

$\therefore X_p = 119$ (In this case, an inductance).
The equivalent series reactance will be:-

$$X_s = +j119 \cdot \frac{286^2}{286^2 + 119^2} = j102\Omega$$

This must be tuned out with an equivalent capacity. The two transformations are shown in Figure 13.

To combine the two circuits, it is necessary only to add a shunt capacity to change the inductance in Figure 13a of +j36.4 to the required value of +j119.

$$\frac{-36{\cdot}4\ X_C}{36{\cdot}4 - X_C} = 119$$

$\therefore X_C = -j51{\cdot}6$

The completed matching circuit then becomes as shown in Figure 14a, which, when converted to circuit values is as shown in Figure 14b.

The only remaining element for this network is the collector choke. From data sheet, C_{OBO} = 6.8pF. Therefore, the output capacity ≃ 10pF. This requires 11 nH to resonate it at 470MHz.

Interstage Transformer Between Input and Driver Stages

An identical procedure is used for calculating this network as employed for the preceding network. The BLW13 transistor requires 0.5W in for 2W out. Therefore, the collector load for a BLW72 transistor is 169 Ω. The input impedance of the BLW13 transistor is 6 + j9. Using a Q of 8 again, gives the circuit shown in Figure 15.

The collector choke must be 14 nH.

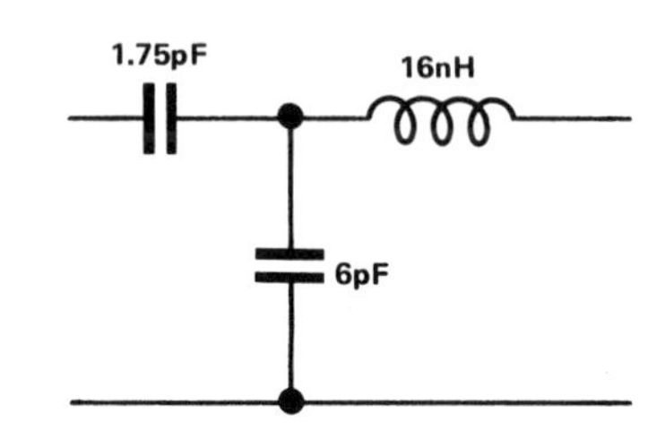

FIGURE 15. Interstage Matching Network

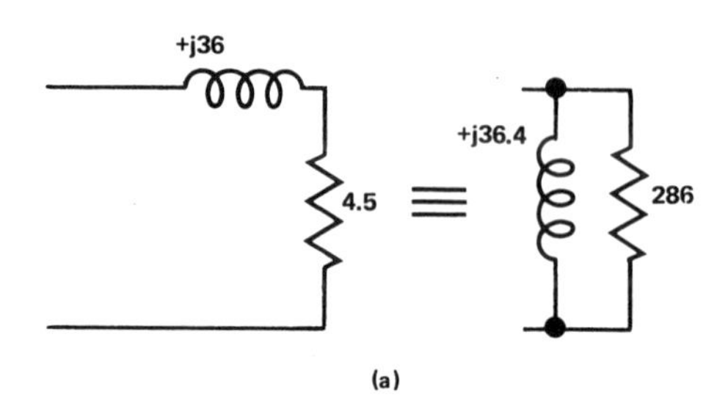

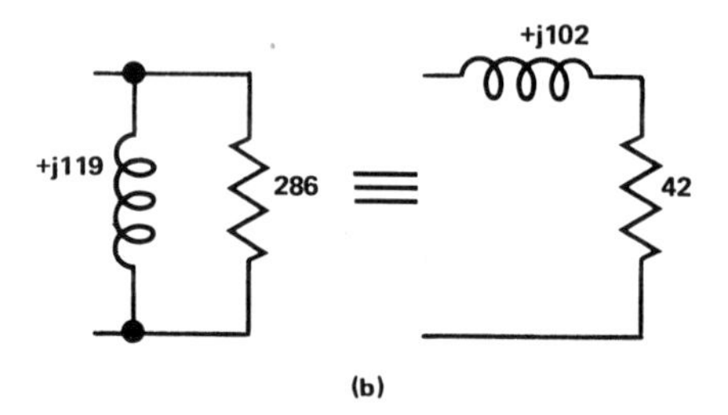

FIGURE 13. Interstage Matching Transformations

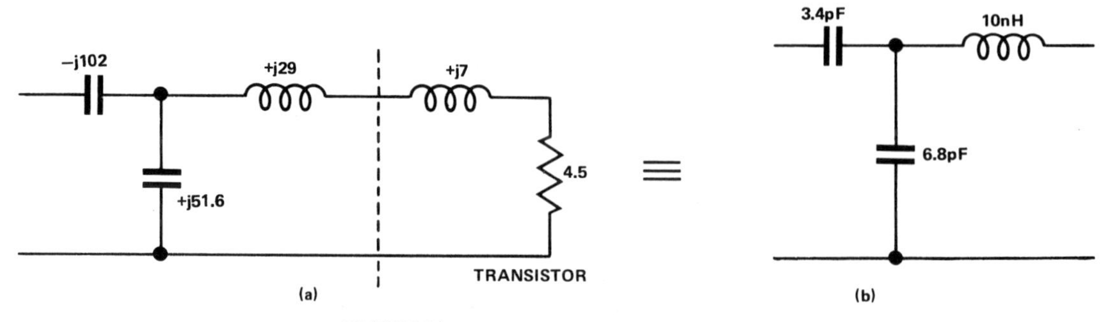

FIGURE 14. Completed Interstage Matching Circuit

Input Matching Network

The input impedance of the BLW12 transistor is 8 + j7. To transform 8 Ω into 50 Ω a series to parallel conversion is employed.

By equation (1), $50 = \dfrac{8^2 + X_S^2}{8}$

$\therefore X_S = +j18.35$

This represents, however, an impracticably small inductor. If a Q of 6 is used, then $X_L = +j(6 \times 8) = +j48$. To restore the branch reactance to +j18.35, a capacitor of reactance $-j(48-18.35) = -j29.65$ is added. The equivalent parallel reactance is $\dfrac{8^2 + 18.35^2}{18{\cdot}35} = +j21.8$. This is tuned out with −j21.8. The resulting input network is shown in Figure 16.

A complete circuit is shown in Figure 17. Trimmers are used for all matching circuit capacitors; to allow adjustment for all approximations made in the calculations and also any parasitic reactances that may be present.

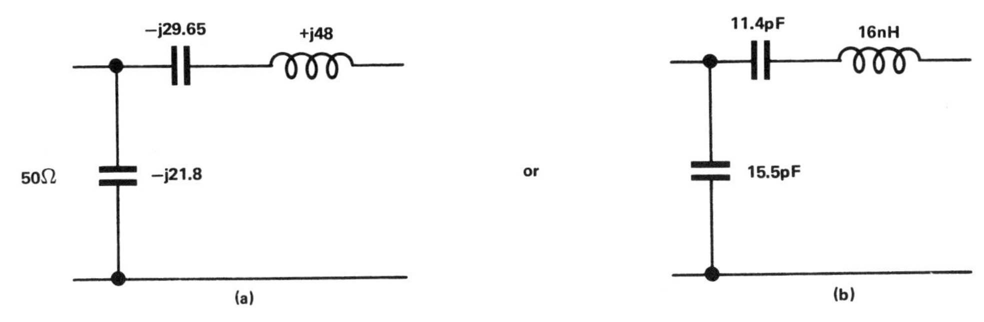

FIGURE 16. Input Matching Network

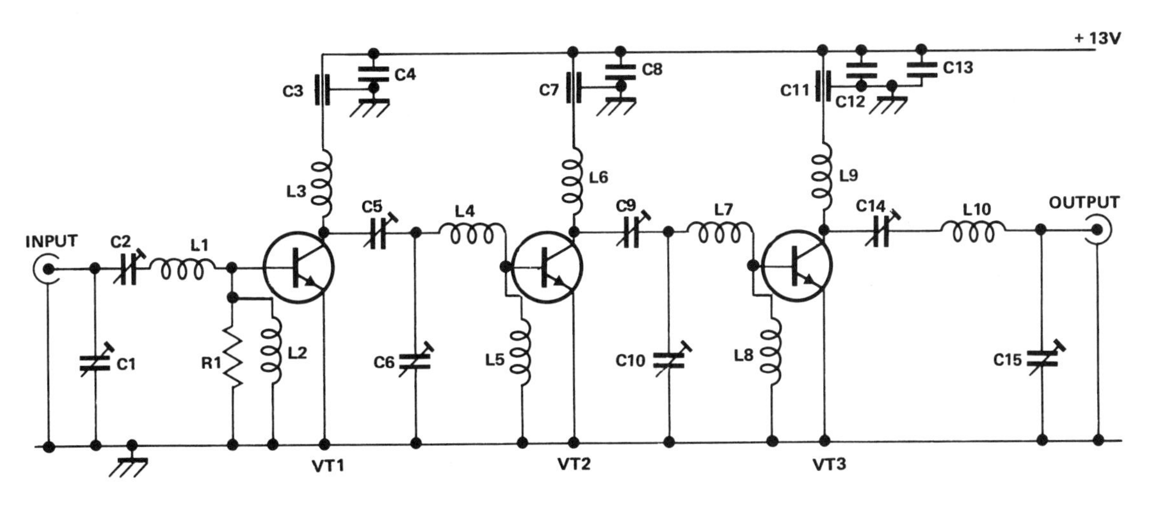

C1, C2, C5, C6, C9, C10, C14, C15	1 – 14pF OXLEY MINIATURE AIRSPACED TRIMMER
C3, C7, C11	1000pF CERAMIC FEEDTHROUGH
C4, C8, C12	10nF CERAMIC
C13	4μF 40V ELECTROLYTIC
L2, L5, L8	3 TURNS 20 SWG ENAMELLED WIRE, 0·125" INTERNAL DIAMETER. TURNS SPACED 1 WIRE DIAMETER.
L1	1" 2mm SILVERED COPPER WIRE BENT TO 'U' SHAPE.
L3	1·5 TURNS 1mm SILVERED COPPER WIRE, 0·0125" INTERNAL DIAMETER.
L4	0·75" 2mm SILVERED COPPER WIRE BENT TO 'U' SHAPE.
L6	1 TURN 1mm SILVERED COPPER WIRE, 0·125" INTERNAL DIAMETER.
L7	0·5" 2mm SILVERED COPPER WIRE, BENT TO 'U' SHAPE.
L9	1" 2mm SILVERED COPPER WIRE.
L10	1·5 TURNS 2mm COPPER WIRE, SPACED 1 WIRE DIAMETER, INTERNAL DIAMETER 0·25"
R1	100Ω ERIE TYPE 16
VT1	BLW12
VT2	BLW13
VT3	BLW14

FIGURE 17. 7W 470MHz Tuned Amplifier Circuit

A picture of the completed amplifier may be seen in Figure 18. A piece of $\frac{1}{32}$" brass, bent as shown, serves as both a heatsink and ground plane. Earthing is extremely important, and all R.F. earth connections are made directly to the brass. The emitter leads are soldered to islands of $\frac{1}{10}$" brass, either brazed or soldered to the main heat sink. This avoids about $\frac{1}{10}$"of emitter lead that would be involved if connection were made directly to the earth-plane. The amplifier would work with connections this long, but the gain would be reduced by about 2dB. All other circuit connections are made on a piece of fibreglass printed circuit board, copper side up, which covers two-thirds of the width of the heat sink. Layout is not critical with the exception of the above points. Other circuit·precautions were as discussed in the preceding chapter.

FIGURE 18. Photograph of the Completed 470MHz Amplifier

66-88MHz AMPLIFIER

The techniques described in the first two sections of this chapter are valid at all frequencies where quasi-lumped circuit design is possible. A VHF low-band (66-88MHz) amplifier is shown in Figure 19 and the similarity in configuration to those already described is obvious when the circuit diagrams are compared.

The overall performance of this amplifier may be summarised as follows:

P_{out}	15W
P_{in}	70mW
V_{CC}	13V
Overall efficiency	60%
Harmonics	– 30dB maximum

The overall Q is relatively low, giving a 1dB bandwidth of about 2.5MHz.

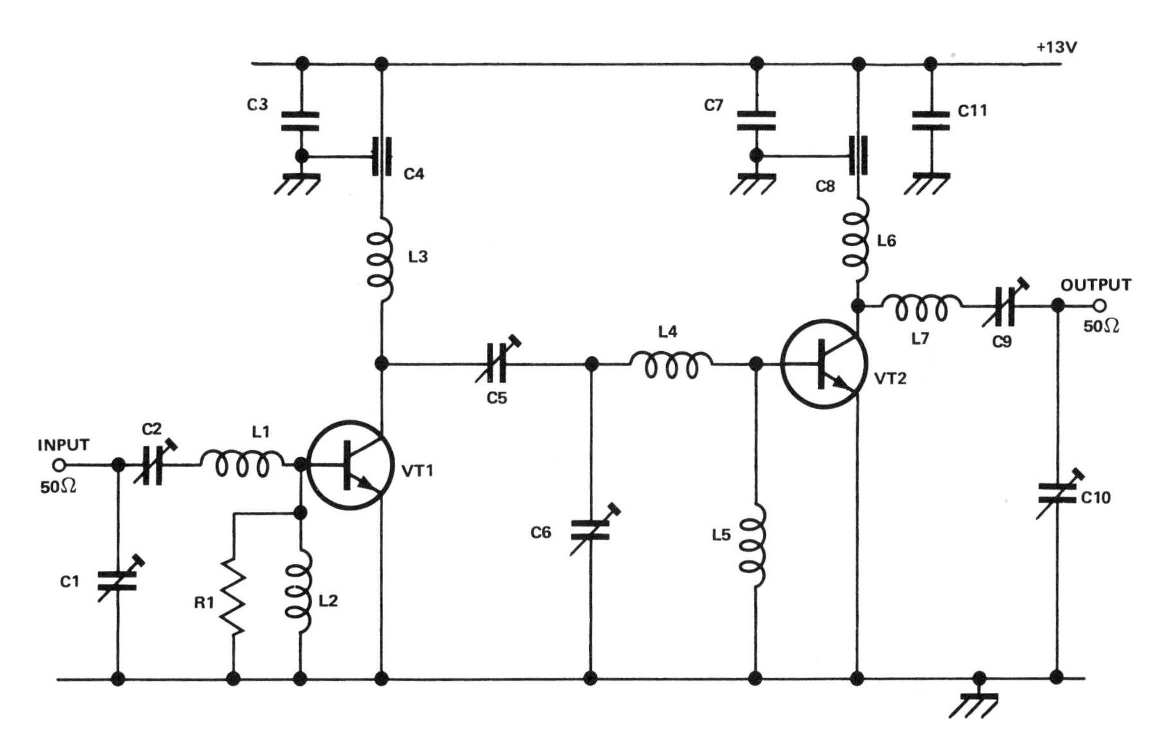

C1, C2, C3, C6, C9	4 - 100pF P.T.F.E. DIELECTRIC TRIMMERS
C5	4 - 60 pF P.T.F.E. DIELECTRIC TRIMMER
C4, C8	1000pF CERAMIC FEEDTHROUGH
C3, C7	0·01 μF CERAMIC
C11	4 μF ELECTROLYTIC
R1	100Ω
VT1	BLY62
VT2	BLY63
L1	5 TURNS: 040" SILVERED COPPER WIRE, 0·25" INTERNAL DIAMETER. TURNS SPACED 1 WIRE DIAMETER
L3	4 TURNS: 040" SILVERED COPPER WIRE, 0·375" INTERNAL DIAMETER. TURNS SPACED 1 WIRE DIAMETER
L4	2 TURNS: 040" SILVERED COPPER WIRE. 0·25" INTERNAL DIAMETER. TURNS SPACED 1 WIRE DIAMETER
L6	5 TURNS: 040" SILVERED COPPER WIRE, 0·25" INTERNAL DIAMETER. TURNS SPACED 1 WIRE DIAMETER
L7	5 TURNS 040" SILVERED COPPER WIRE, 0.25" INTERNAL DIAMETER. TURNS SPACED 1 WIRE DIAMETER.
L2, L5	0.47 PAINTON SUB-MINIATURE R.F.C.

FIGURE 19. Circuit of 88MHz Tuned Amplifier

REFERENCES

1. Linvill and Gibbons, *Active Circuits,* McGraw-Hill

2. "RF Large Signal Transistor Power Amplifiers *Electronic Design News,* Part III July 1965.

XVII LOW VOLTAGE SINGLE SIDEBAND AMPLIFIERS

by
Garry Garrard

If single sideband amplifiers operate from low voltage power supplies (for example, in mobile applications) rather than the more usual 28 volt supply, the design requirements are much more difficult to meet. Not only does the transistor current handling capability need to be much greater, but also the collector impedance matching becomes more difficult because of the lower impedances involved. This makes the wideband transformer design more critical.

The principal cause of nonlinearity in transistors used for SSB amplifiers is change in internal cutoff frequency, f_T, with collector current. The transistors used should have an f_T that is nearly constant over the working current range. The BLY 63 transistors used in the circuit in this chapter were originally intended as VHF mobile devices, but due to their high robustness, and constant f_T characteristics, they are very suitable for SSB applications.

CIRCUIT DESCRIPTION

A circuit diagram of the push-pull amplifier, capable of delivering 20 W of linear power over the full 1.6 to 30 MHz H.F. Band is shown in Figure 1. It is intended for operation from a 13.5 V supply, but is suitable for operation with voltages of 10 V to 16 V.

Input Circuit

Transformers T1 and T2 form a 180° power-splitting hybrid. Transformer T1 provides two outputs nominally of equal amplitude and 180° phase difference. Any imbalance is corrected by transformer T2. Errors in phase and power are dissipated in resistor R1.

This circuit also gives sufficient impedance matching to provide a reasonable input Voltage Standing Wave Ratio (VSWR).

Output Circuit

The collector load (R_L) required may be calculated from the well known expression:

$$P_{out} = \frac{(V_{CC} - V_{CE(sat)})^2}{2\ R_L} \qquad (1)$$

If

$$P_{out} = 10 \text{ W for each device}$$

$$V_{CC} = 13.5 \text{ V}$$

$$V_{CE(sat)} = 2 \text{ V}$$

Then

$$R_L = 6.6\ \Omega \text{ theoretically}$$

Thus the required impedance transformation is

$$\frac{50}{6.6} = 7.6$$

However, using distributed transformers, only certain integer values of impedance transformation are possible. The nearest of these values to 7.6 is 8, given by a 4:1 impedance transformer and an additional impedance ratio of 2.1 in the unbalance-to-balance transformation.

There are several ways of combining 4:1 transformers and balance-to-unbalance transformers to achieve the required push-pull output. The configuration used was chosen because it was possible to achieve the required performance with relatively simple transformer windings. Even though the number of ferrite cores required is not the minimum possible, the overall mechanical complexity is less than that required if more complex winding techniques are used.

T3 and T4 are 4:1 distributed transformers, transforming the 6.25 Ω collector load to 25 Ω. The two anti-phase 25 Ω outputs are combined and transformed to 50 Ω in transformers T5 and T6, which forms a similar hybrid to transformers T1 and T2 on the input.

If some relaxation in performance is permissible, transformer T5 may be omitted. This will worsen the intermodulation distortion by 2 or 3 dB at rated output, and also give higher harmonic output.

Transformer Design

All the transformers are of distributed construction and are designed using the principles described in references 1 and 2. Optimum winding impedances for each transformer are given in Table 1. Constructing windings to the impedances in Table 1 will result in very large transformers, in spite of the fact that only very small ferrite cores are necessary to handle the power.

Table 1

Transformer	Optimum Characteristic Impedance (Ω)
T1	50
T2	25
T3	12.5
T4	12.5
T5	25
T6	50

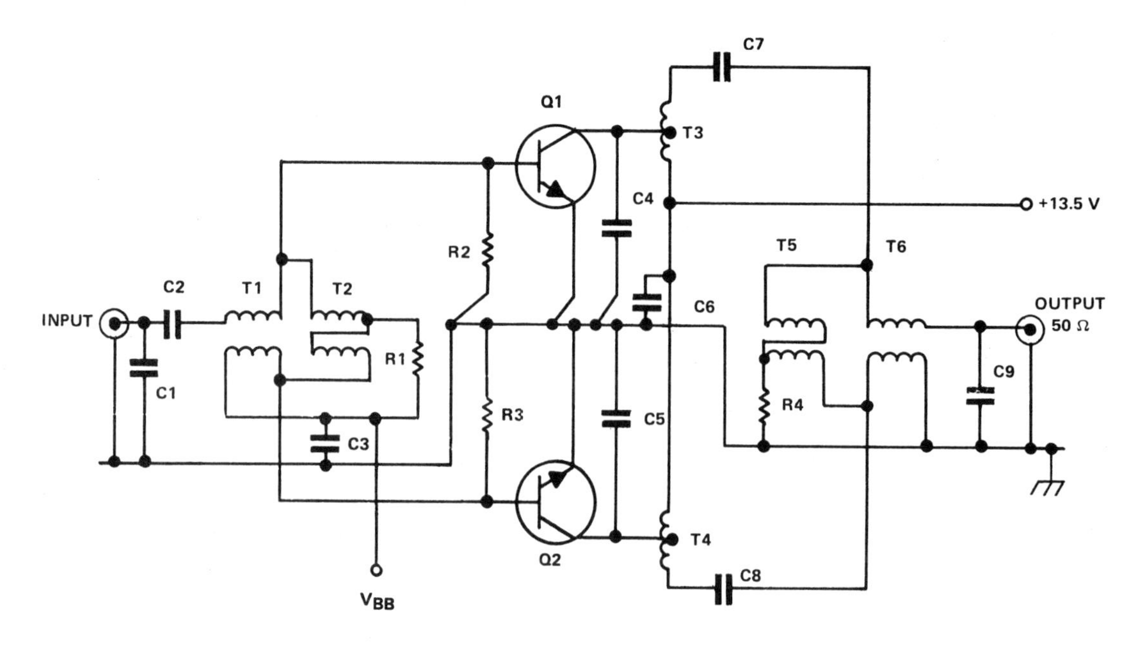

CAPACITORS

C1	200 pF CERAMIC
C2, C3, C6, C7, C8	0.1 μF CERAMIC
C4, C5	270 pF CERAMIC
C9	39 pF CERAMIC

RESISTORS

R1	12.5 Ω NON-INDUCTIVE
R2, R3	22 Ω
R4	6 Ω NON-INDUCTIVE

TRANSFORMERS

T1, T2, T3, T4, T6	18 TURNS OF TWISTED PAIR 30 SWG (28 AWG) ON INDIANA GENERAL CF 106 TORROID OR ≡.
T5	18 TURNS OF 2 TWISTED PAIRS (4 STRANDS TWISTED TOGETHER) 34 SWG (31 AWG) ON INDIANA GENERAL CF 106 TORROID OR ≡.

TRANSISTORS

Q1, Q2	BLY 63

FIGURE 1. 20 Watt, 1.6 to 30 MHz Push-Pull Amplifier

In this design, all transformer windings, except T5, are wound with a single pair of twisted wires giving a characteristic impedance of approximately 70 Ω. In order to achieve satisfactory low frequency performance, 18 turns are necessary for transformers T3 and T4 on the ferrite cores used. This gives a winding length of 18 cm, or an equivalent electrical length ($\beta\ell$) at 30 MHz of 6.5°.

From information in Reference 1:

$$Z_{in} = Z_o \left\{ \frac{Z_L \cos\beta\ell + j\, Z_o \sin\beta\ell}{2Z_o(1 + \cos\beta\ell) + j\, Z_L \sin\beta\ell} \right\} \quad (2)$$

Where

Z_{in} = low impedance input (collector load)

Z_o = winding impedance

Z_L = load impedance

With a 25 Ω load, and a winding as above,

$$Z_{in} = (5.88 + j\,2.2)\,\Omega$$

Thus there is an inductive element in the collector load when using a high line impedance, together with a lower resistive part than required.

Experience shows that a complex collector load impedance with an inductive element giving a phase angle of even 10° can give serious degradation of intermodulation distortion even though the change in modulus is quite small. A collector load of the same complex value and phase angle but with capacitive reactance will have little effect on linearity, however. This makes it necessary to compensate for the above inductive element in the collector load.

The transformer input impedance above may be considered as an equivalent parallel circuit as shown in Figure 2. The addition of a shunt capacitor of reactance $-j\,18$ will result in a resistive load of 6.7 Ω at 30 MHz: C = 300 pF.

Capacitors C4 and C5 on the circuit diagram, together with the output capacity of the transistors make up this compensating reactance. Capacitor C9 performs the same function for the output hybrid. As the frequency is reduced the line impedance becomes less critical and the capacitors have less effect on the circuit.

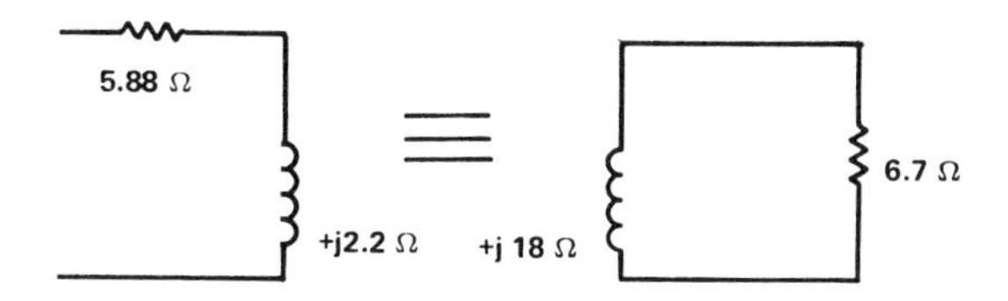

FIGURE 2. Transformer Input Impedance Considered as an Equivalent Parallel Circuit

Bias Supply

The bias circuitry is not critical providing it has a reasonably low output impedance, and may be adjusted to give about 10 mA of quiescent current in the BLY 63 transistors.

Fairly simple temperature compensation may be used. Ballasting built into the transistors will prevent thermal runaway. The bias circuit used for making measurements is shown in Figure 3.

It is advisable to use a pair of BLY 63 transistors with dc gain matched to within approximately 10% for optimum performance, unless separate bias supplies are used for the two devices.

Performance

Detailed information on performance is given in Figures 4, 5, 6, 7, and 8. It may be summarized briefly as follows:

Frequency Range	1.5 to 30 MHz
P_{out}	20 W
Supply Voltage	13.5 V nominal
Gain	16 dB minimum
Intermodulation Distortion	−30 dB relative to either signal of two tone output.

The amplifier will withstand any mismatch at full output power.

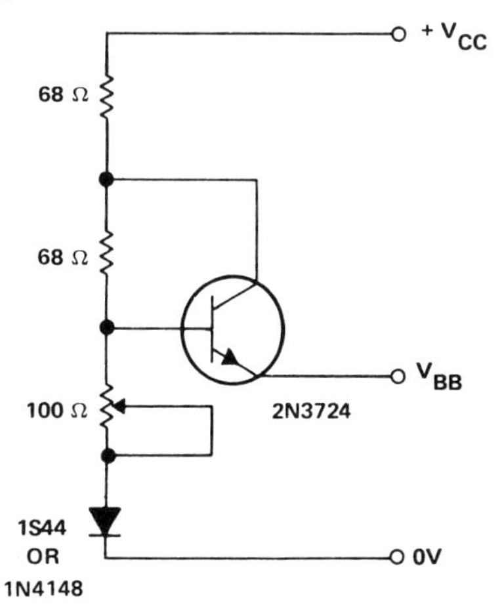

FIGURE 3. Bias Circuit Used for Measurements

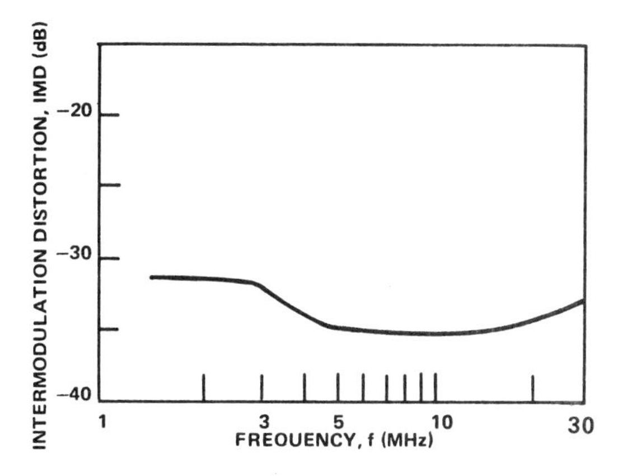

FIGURE 4. Intermodulation Distortion versus Frequency. (V_{CC} = 13.5 V. P_{out} = 20 W PEP, 10 W Average.)

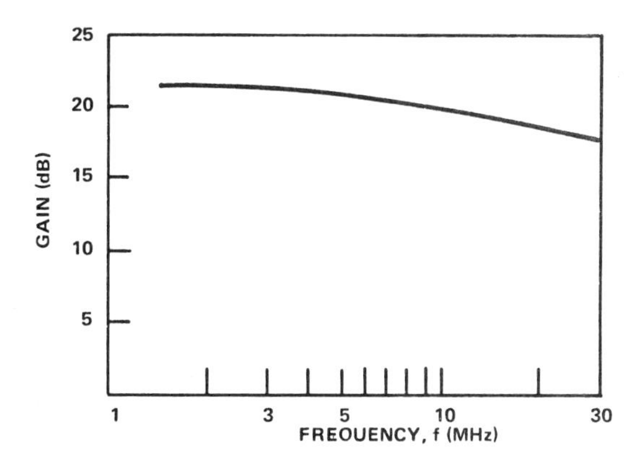

FIGURE 5. Gain versus Frequency. (V_{CC} = 13.5 V. P_{out} = 20 W PEP, 10 W Average.)

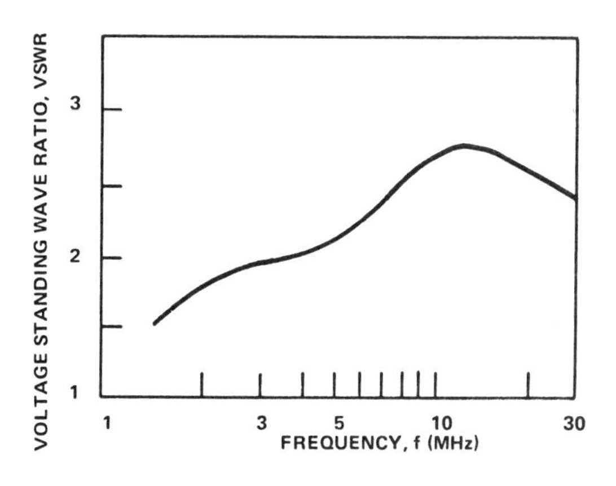

FIGURE 6. VSWR versus Frequency. (V_{CC} = 13.5 V. P_{out} = 20 W PEP, 10 W Average.)

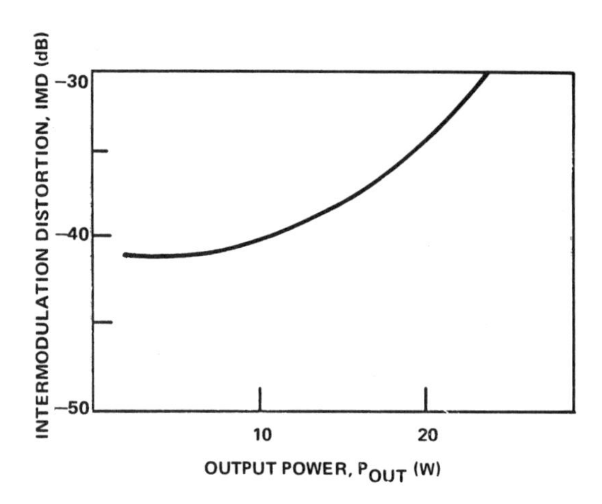

FIGURE 7. Intermodulation Distortion versus Output Power (V_{CC} = 13.5 V. Frequency = 30 MHz.)

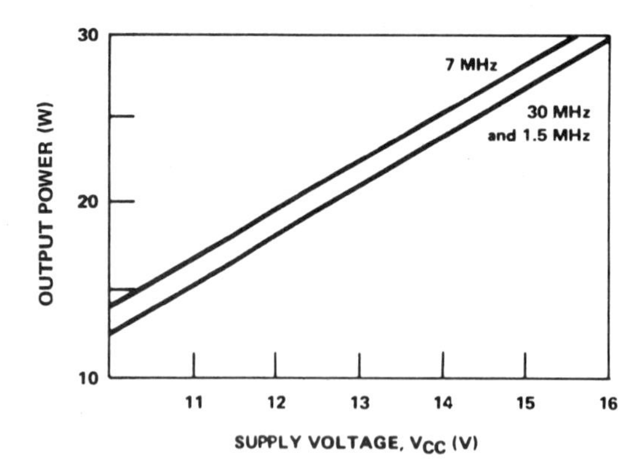

FIGURE 8. Linear Output Capability versus Supply Voltage. (IMD = –30 dB.)

DRIVER STAGE

With 16 dB gain, the maximum drive level required is 0.5 W. This may be simple obtained from a single BLY 62 transistor in class A operation.

A suitable circuit is shown in Figure 9. Overall gain of the driver and push-pull output stage is 33 dB minimum. With the drive level required, the addition of the extra stage results in very little degradation of linearity from that resulting from the output stage. The maximum input power then required is 10 mW at the top of the band, and considerably less at the center of the band.

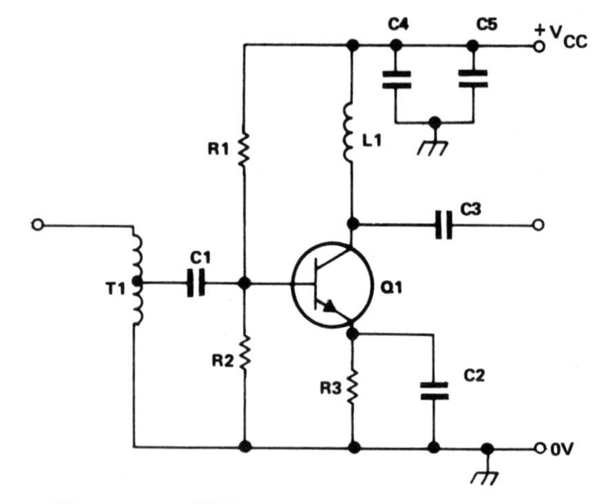

R1		150 Ω
R2		22 Ω
R3		2.7 Ω
C1, C2, C3, C4,		0.1 μF CERAMIC
C5		4 μF ELECTROLYTIC
L1	24T	30 SWG ENAMELLED WIRE (28AWG) ON INDIANA GENERAL CF102 TORROID OR ≡.
T1	16T	OF TWISTED PAIR 30 SWG (28AWG) ENAMELLED WIRE ON INDIANA GENERAL CF102 TORROID OR ≡.
Q1	BLY62	

FIGURE 9. Driver Stage

REFERENCES

1. Ruthroff, C. L., Some Broadband Transformers, Proc. IRE, August 1959, pp. 1337-1342.

2. Couse, T. and Pitzalis, O., Broadband Transformer Design for RF Transistor Power Amplifiers, Proc. 1968 Electronics Components Conference, pp. 207-216.

XVIII FREQUENCY MULTIPLIERS

by
Garry Garrard

The requirements of any frequency multiplier must be compatible with the overall system it is used in, and the characteristics of multipliers should be considered at an early stage in the system design.

The majority of transmitters must maintain frequency stabilities that can be obtained only from crystal oscillators. Although it is possible to make crystal oscillators at frequencies up to at least 150MHz, for many equipments the practical limit will be considerably lower than this. VHF or UHF signals must be derived either directly by frequency multiplication or indirectly by phase-lock methods.

The frequency of the crystal oscillator should be as high as possible to reduce the number of multiplier stages. This will simplify the rejection of unwanted harmonics. If frequency modulation is required it is possible to obtain excellent linearity by direct modulation of the crystal oscillator, using a varactor as the modulating element. This avoids the high order of multiplication necessary if phase modulation is used.

The crystal oscillator should use an FET as the active element, to improve stability. The power output will typically be about 5mW, limited by the necessity to keep the crystal dissipation down to a small fraction of a milliwatt. As frequency multipliers are less efficient than amplifiers, optimum system efficiency will be obtained if multiplication is made at as low a power level as possible – that is, directly after the oscillator, or after a buffer stage, if required. Power amplification is now quite straightforward with transistors at VHF and UHF. An added advantage is that any succeeding tuned stages will contribute to spurious rejection.

TUNED FREQUENCY MULTIPLIERS

General

Tuned transistor multipliers are sometimes considered as falling into two distinct types – parametric multipliers and class-C multipliers. Parametric transistor multipliers, which use the nonlinear collector-base capacity as a varactor, may be used to obtain outputs from a transistor at frequencies in excess of its f_T. To make full use of this effect relatively complicated circuits are required.

Class-C multipliers operate theoretically by using the harmonic content of a pulse train. However, the parametric action of the collector to base capacity is still present, and all efficient multipliers depend to a certain extent on this property.

The order of multiplication is quite important. Most multipliers are either doublers or triplers. The second harmonic is predominant in the output of a high-frequency power transistor; this contributes to making doublers much easier to design than triplers.

To obtain good efficiency it is essential that no power is taken from the collector at any unwanted harmonic. At all frequencies other than the required output the collector should see an open circuit. In theory a series tuned output circuit would be suitable, but in practice it is often not possible to obtain sufficient loaded Q. In this case, a parallel resonant 'stop' may be required.

When properly tuned under these conditions, the transistor is terminated in an open circuit at the input frequency. Very high r.f. voltages will be developed at the collector. High-frequency power transistors will withstand r.f. voltages considerably in excess of the d.c. ratings, due to the finite time interval before voltage breakdown occurs. This time interval reduces as the voltage peak is increased, and is inversely proportional to the f_T of the device. If a device is used with an input frequency substantially lower than that intended for it, the effect may cause voltage breakdown in some circuits. Either the supply rail must be reduced, or a transistor with higher breakdown voltages must be used.

The choice of circuit configuration should be carefully considered. Either common base or common emitter operation is possible. In theory common base circuits will give the best gain and efficiency, particularly at low levels. However, problems with instability are so serious that it is advisable to use common emitter circuits in most cases.

The circuit techniques that may be used are best illustrated by examples. The circuits following are chosen to have a variety of tuning arrangements. Any of these may be used at other frequencies, using appropriate transistors.

43.5 to 174MHz Quadrupler and Amplifier

A circuit which acts as both a quadrupler and amplifier is shown in Figure 1. Here transistors VT1 and VT2 act as doubler stages, and transistor VT3 is a 174MHz amplifier. The circuit is intended for use immediately after a crystal oscillator, and requires an input level of 3mW. Inductor L1 provides an approximate input impedance match to 50Ω. Since the input level is too low to turn on transistor VT1 at any point in the r.f. cycle, slight forward bias is applied by resistors R1 and R2; operation is approximately class-B. The output capacity of transistor VT1 is resonated at 43·5MHz by the combination of inductors L2 and L3. This ensures a high circulating current in the output capacity of transistor VT1; this is required for good efficiency. The base of transistor VT2 is connected through a series tuned circuit (L4, C4) at 87MHz to the junction of inductors L2

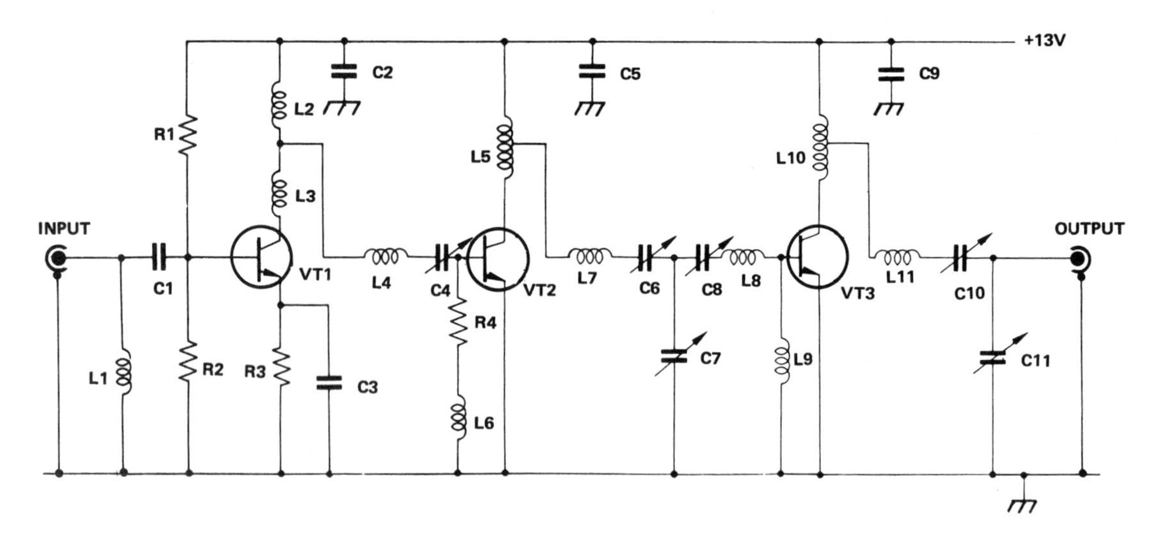

C1, C2, C3, C5, C9	5nF CERAMIC
C4, C6, C8, C10	STEATITE 2·5 to 6pF 7-S-TRIKO
C7, C11	STEATITE 4 TO 20pF 10-S-TRIKO–06
R1	4·7kΩ
R2	220 Ω
R3	33 Ω
R4	47 Ω
L1, L4, L8, L11	PAINTON CHOKE, TYPE-C10, 0·22μH
L2	PAINTON CHOKE, TYPE-C10, 0·33μH
L3	PAINTON CHOKE, TYPE-C10, 1·0μH

L5	10 TURNS, 26 SWG WIRE ¼ in DIA. TAPPED AT 5 TURNS
L6, L9	RFC 6 TURNS WOUND ON SIEMENS HALSKE 4mm TORROID, N22 MATERIAL.
L7	5 TURNS, 26 SWG WIRE, ¼ in. DIA.
L10	5 TURNS, 26 SWG WIRE, ¼ in. DIA. TAPPED AT 2·5 TURNS.
VT1	TIS49
VT2	2N3866
VT3	BLY61

FIGURE 1. 43.5 to 174MHz Quadrupler and Amplifier Circuit

and L3 providing impedance transformation. Operation of transistor VT2 is similar in principle to that of transistor VT1. No forward bias is necessary; in fact, the stage works well in Class-C; a small reverse bias is provided by resistor R4. The output capacity is tuned at 87MHz by inductor L5, and once again, impedance transformation is made by tapping into this coil. To reduce spurious levels, a more complicated network is used to transfer power to the base of transistor VT3. This final stage operates as an orthodox tuned amplifier.

Transistor VT1 has extremely low dissipation and may be a silect device. This is chosen to have a high output capacity and cut-off frequency. Although the TIS49 is characterised as a switching device, it performs very well as a frequency doubler. Transistor VT2 has rather higher dissipation, and requires a TO39 device. A BLY61 gives very good gain, but the high r.f. voltages developed at the collector may cause voltage break-down. For this reason a 2N3866 was selected. The increase in maximum voltage rating more than compensates for the fact that the transistor is used at a much lower frequency than that intended for it. The choice of transistor VT3 is quite straightforward. The BLY61 is designed specifically as a 175MHz amplifier, with a 13V supply and an output power of about 1W.

The circuit was built on a normal printed circuit board, using a good quality dielectric. Layout is not critical providing the following points are noted:

(i) The earth path should be as broad and direct as possible and earth loops avoided.

(ii) The capacitors decoupling the collector coils should be earthed as near to the respective emitters as possible.

(iii) All connections should be reasonably short.

The overall performance of the circuit is summarized by the following figures:-

Input	3mW at 43.5MHz
Output	0.9W at 174MHz
Overall Efficiency	45%
Spurious Rejection	Better than –50dB for all spurious not harmonically related to 174MHz.

235 to 470MHz Doubler

This example shows how a simple circuit can operate very effectively. The circuit diagram may be seen in Figure 2. Components C1, C2 and L2 match the base of transistor VT1 to 50Ω, at 235MHz. The Q of this circuit is about 6. The output capacity of transistor VT1 is resonated at

235MHz by inductor L3, and impedance transformation to the output made by tapping into this coil. The circuit relies on the fact that the second harmonic predominates in the output from a VHF power transistor. Because of this, it is necessary only to prevent the fundamental from reaching the output. Components L3 and C3 provide a very high impedance at 235MHz.

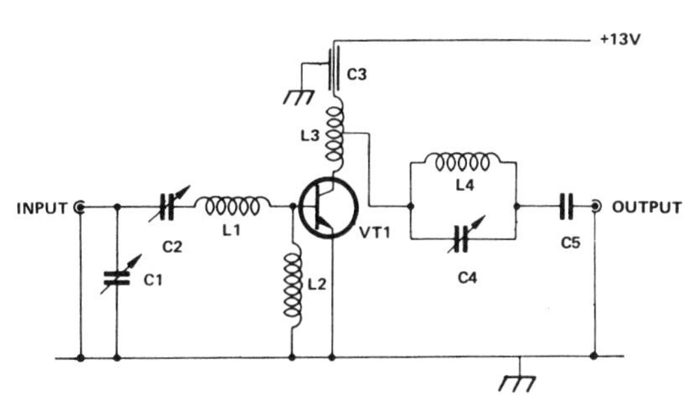

C1	10 TO 6-pF STEATITE 10-S-TRIKO-06	L1	3T ¼ in. DIAMETER 1mm WIRE
C2	4 TO 20pF STEATITE 10-S-TRIKO-06	L2	10T 30 SWG WOUND ON SIEMENS HALSKE N22 TORROID 4mm DIA.
C3	1000pF LEADLESS DISC		
C4	3 TO 14pF WINGROVE AND ROGERS MINI-TRIMMER	L3	4T, ¼ in. DIAMETER, TAPPED AT 1·75 TURNS
		L4	3T, ¼ in. DIAMETER
C5	1000pF CERAMIC	VT1	BLW12

FIGURE 2. 235 to 470MHz Doubler Circuit

Layout is quite important, and a sketch of the suggested layout is shown in Figure 3. A piece of printed-circuit board is used, copper side up. This is mounted on a piece of brass, which is used only as a heat sink.

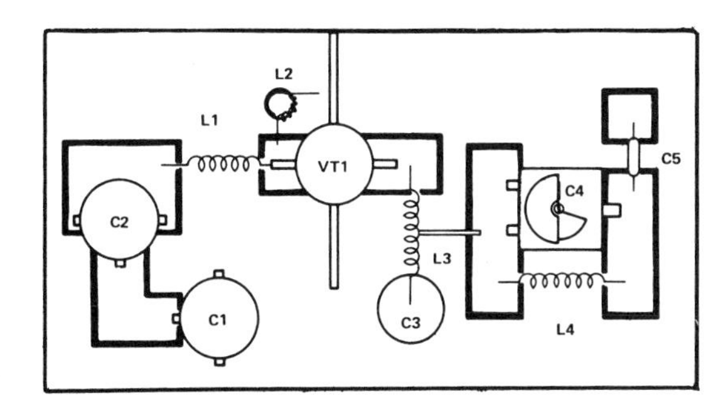

FIGURE 3. Suggested Layout of 235 to 470MHz Doubler Circuit

The overall performance of this circuit is summarized by the following figures.

Input	50mW at 235MHz
Output	250mW at 470MHz
Efficiency	50%
Spurious levels	235MHz–45dB
	705MHz–20dB
	940MHz–30dB

The circuit will function satisfactorily over a range of input levels from 20 – 80mW, but for optimum efficiency at any level, the tap position in inductor L3 should be adjusted.

156.7 to 470MHz Tripler

This is much more complicated than the previous circuits, as may be seen in Figure 4.

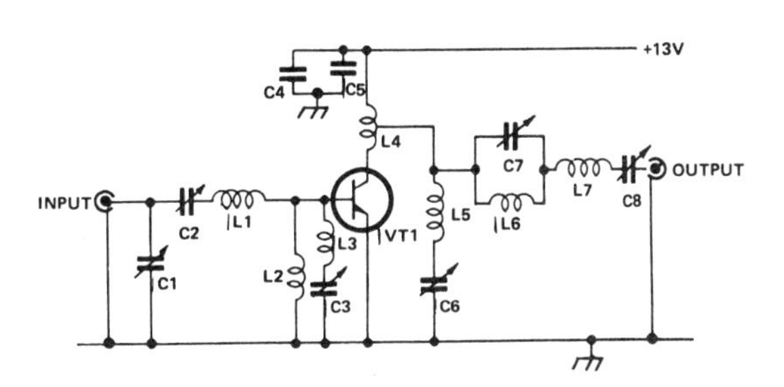

C1, C2, C3	40pF MICA COMPRESSION TRIMMER
C4	1000pF CERAMIC
C5	0·01μF CERAMIC
C6, C7, C8	3 TO 14pF WINGROVE AND ROGERS MINITRIMMER
L1, L6, L7	4 TURNS 1 mm SILVER WIRE: ¼ in. DIAMETER
L2	1μH CHOKE, PAINTON TYPE C10
L3	SELF-INDUCTANCE OF C3
L4	4 TURNS 1 mm SILVER WIRE, ¼ in. DIAMETER, TAPPED AT 2 TURNS
L5	2 TURNS 1 mm SILVER WIRE, ¼ in. DIAMETER
VT1	BLW12

FIGURE 4. 156.7 to 470MHz Tripler Circuit

The base input impedance of transistor VT1 is matched to 50Ω by components C1, C2, L1 at 156·7MHz. Components L3 and C3 form a series-tuned circuit at the output frequency, and provide a low impedance return for the collector-base capacity. These two components may be omitted with a loss in gain of 1dB and a similar loss of efficiency. Inductor L4 resonates the output capacity (in fact collector to base capacity) at 156·7MHz, ensuring high circulating current at the fundamental frequency. Inductors L5, L6 provide a low-impedance path for 313·4MHz. This recirculates the second harmonic component through the collector-base capacity improving the efficiency. Components C7, L7 prevent any output at 156·7MHz, and L7, C8 form a series tuned circuit at 470MHz, to reduce the level of all unwanted harmonics.

Although layout is not critical, care should be taken, particularly with earth connections. In the prototype, all r.f. earths were made to a 1/32in brass earth-plane, and components mounted on printed-circuit board, copper side up. A sketch is shown in Figure 5 of a suggested layout for the tripler.

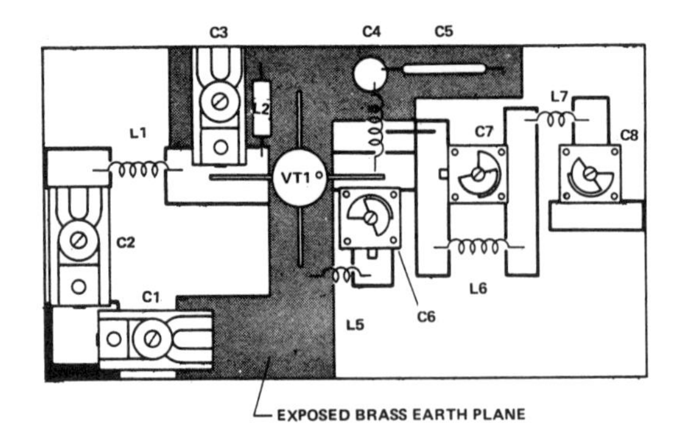

FIGURE 5. Suggested Layout of Tripler Circuit

The performance of the circuit is shown in the graphs in Figure 6.

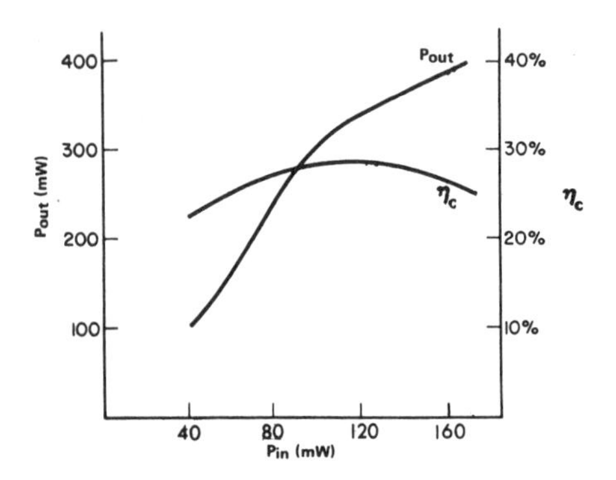

FIGURE 6. Performance Graphs of Tripler Circuit

At the optimum level:–

P_{in}	= 100mW	
P_{out}	= 300mW	
Efficiency	= 28%	
Spurious	Fundamental	–50dB
	2nd Harmonic	–42dB
	4th Harmonic	–28dB
	5th Harmonic	–60dB

The gain and efficiency may be seen to be much lower than that for the doubler even though a much more complicated circuit is used.

500MHz to 1GHz Doubler

At 1GHz, the wavelength is comparable with the size of components used, and distributed techniques must be used. Even using Rexolite, which has a relatively low dielectric constant, a quarter-wavelength is only about 2in; so even a very short connection may have significant effects on the circuit. The circuit diagram is shown in Figure 7. Operation is similar in principle to previous doublers. Components C1, C2 and L1 provide an impedance match at 500MHz. Components L3 and C4 provide a low impedance path for 1GHz, which is developed in the collector to base capacity. The collector to base capacity is resonated at 500MHz by line 1 and capacitor C3. Line 2 tunes with capacitor C5 at 1GHz, rejecting unwanted harmonics.

Layout, particularly in the collector circuit, is critical. Construction is in stripline form, using 1/16" double sided copper clad rexolite. A sketch is shown in Figure 8.

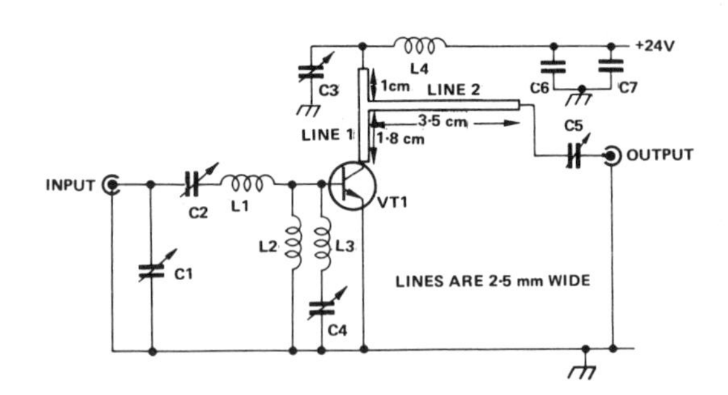

C1, C2	3 TO 14pF WINGROVE AND ROGERS MINI-TRIMMER
C3	1000pF CERAMIC DISC
C4	30pF AIRTRONIC
C5	10pF AIRTRONIC
C6	1000pF CERAMIC
C7	0.01μF CERAMIC
L1	1 TURN 1 mm SILVER WIRE, ¼ in. DIA.
L2	3 TURN, 24 SWG, ⅛ in. DIAMETER
L3	SELF-INDUCTANCE OF C4
L4	3 TURNS, 24 SWG, ⅛ in. DIAMETER
VT1	2N4429

FIGURE 7. 500MHz to 1GHz Doubler Circuit

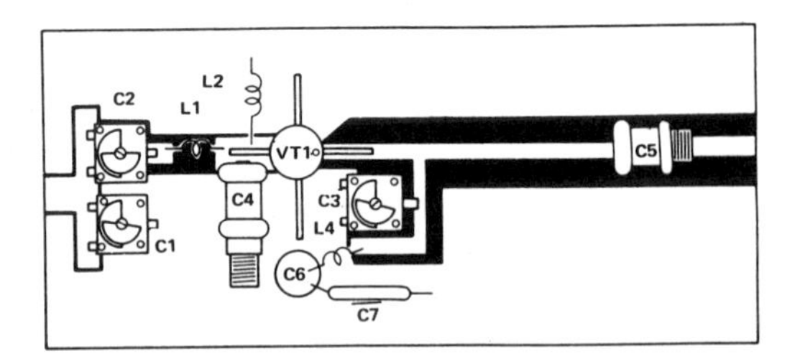

FIGURE 8. Suggested Layout of 500MHz to 1GHz Doubler Circuit

The overall performance of this circuit is summarized by the following figures:-

Input	100mW at 500MHz
Output	300mW at 1GHz
Efficiency	25%
Harmonic	Fundamental –30dB
Rejection	3rd Harmonic –20dB

PUSH-PUSH FREQUENCY DOUBLERS

General

The balanced doubler, or push-push doubler, is an extremely versatile circuit with many possible transmitter applications, at frequencies up to about 200MHz.

The principle of operation is similar to a full wave rectifier. The base-emitter junctions of two transistors are used as diodes, and the two half-wave signals combined at the collectors, after amplification. In a full wave rectifier the output ripple is at twice the input frequency. Instead of rejecting the fundamental with tuned circuits, theoretically there is no fundamental component in the output. In fact, any unbalance between the two halves of the circuit, and internal transistor capacities will give some fundamental output, but the level will be considerably lower than the second harmonic even without any tuned circuits.

One advantage of the circuit is that satisfactory operation is possible over a significant bandwidth, without any retuning. As the frequency of operation is increased, the output capacity of the transistors has more effect, and must be resonated for optimum performance. If no additional capacity is used, the Q of the output circuit will increase with frequency, but the absolute bandwidth will remain approximately constant.

Output circuit $Q=\frac{R_L}{X_C}=R_L\omega C$

where R_L=collector load

ω=output frequency (angular)

C=transistor output capacitance (sum of two devices)

Also $Q=\frac{\omega}{\Delta\omega}$

where $\Delta\omega$=3dB bandwidth

Therefore $\frac{\omega}{\Delta\omega}=R_L\omega C$

Thus $\Delta\omega=\frac{1}{RC}$ or $\Delta f=\frac{1}{2\pi RC}$

So $\Delta\omega$ is constant.

For example, using TIS18 transistors, $C=2\times1{\cdot}7\text{pF}=3{\cdot}4\text{pF}$. If $R_L=400\Omega$, then $\Delta f=37{\cdot}5\text{MHz}$.

It may be necessary to compromise between gain and bandwidth. If a larger bandwidth is required, resistor R_L must be reduced, but loss in gain and efficiency may result.

The following examples show some of the possibilities of this type of circuit.

88.5 to 175MHz Doubler

As shown in Figure 9, the transistors used in this 88·5 to 175MHz doubler are the Silect TIS18 type, which have low C_{OBO} and good high-frequency gain. The input signal feeds the primary of a wideband transformer. The two secondary windings are connected to give outputs in opposite phases; these are used to drive the transistor bases. The collector circuit is designed to resonate the output

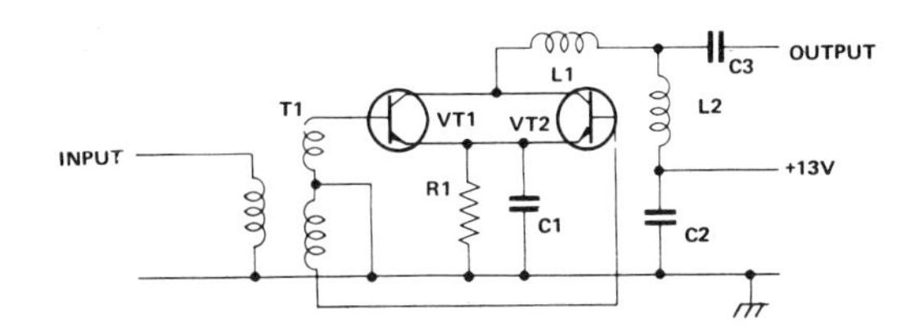

T1	3 STRANDS 30 SWG WIRE TWISTED TOGETHER; 3 TURNS OF THIS WOUND ON SIEMENS HALSKE U-60 TWIN HOLE BEAD.
VT1, VT2	TIS18
R1	100Ω
C1, C2, C3	0·047μF CERAMIC
L1	7 TURNS, 24 SWG, ¼ in. DIA., 0·4 in. LONG
L2	2·2μH PAINTON CHOKE TYPE C10

FIGURE 9. 88·5 to 175MHz Push-Pull Doubler Circuit

capacity at 175MHz, and also match the 50Ω load to a suitable value at the collector. Inductor L2 is merely an r.f. choke. The remainder of the collector circuit may be simply redrawn as in Figure 10.

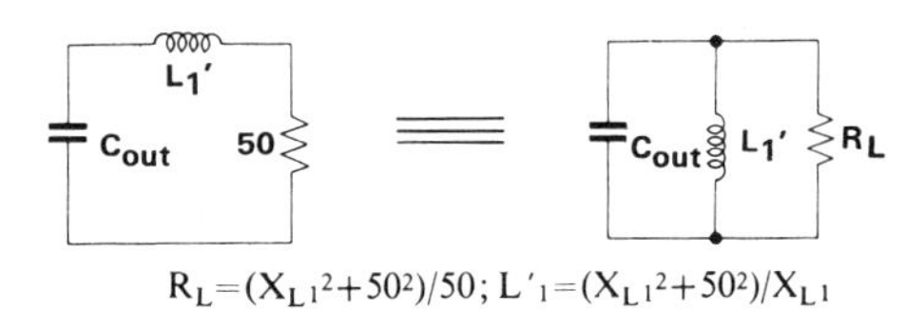

$R_L=(X_{L1}^2+50^2)/50$; $L'_1=(X_{L1}^2+50^2)/X_{L1}$

FIGURE 10. Colllector Circuit and Its Equivalent Circuit

Matching is achieved in the normal manner by series-to-parallel conversion. The predicted 3dB bandwidth is given by

$$\frac{2\times1{\cdot}75\times10^8\times0{\cdot}12\times10^{-6}}{50}=\frac{f}{\Delta f}$$

$$\Delta f=\frac{50}{2\times0{\cdot}12}=67\text{MHz}$$

The performance of the circuit may be seen in Figure 11. The 3dB bandwidth is about 75MHz; very close to that predicted. Efficiency varies from 34% at the centre frequency to 20% at the 3dB points.

47·5 to 95MHz Doubler

The circuit diagram of a 47·5 to 95MHz push-pull doubler is shown in Figure 12.

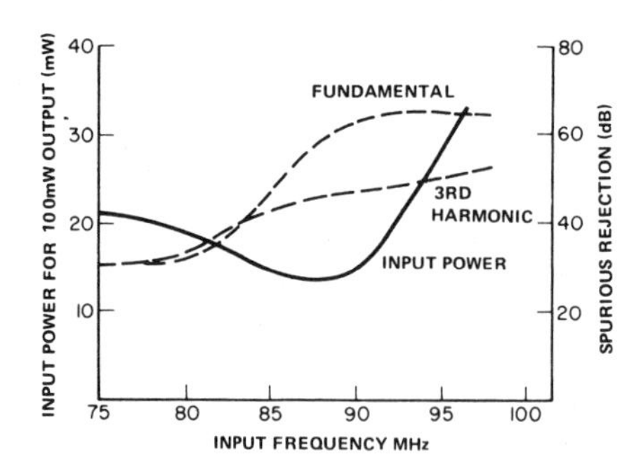

FIGURE 11. Performance Graphs of 88·5 to 175MHz Doubler Circuit

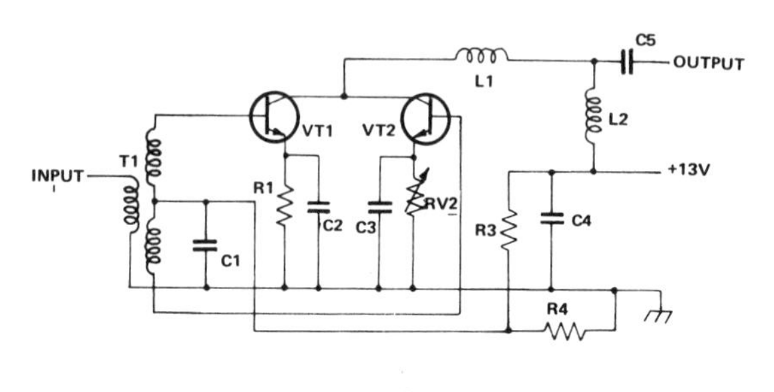

R1	56Ω
RV2	200Ω PRESET
R3	47k Ω
R4	470Ω
C1, C2, C3, C4, C5	0·047μF CERAMIC
L1	0·47μH PAINTON CHOKE TYPE C10
L2	2·2μH PAINTON CHOKE TYPE C10
T1	AS IN FIGURE 9
VT1, VT2	TIS18

FIGURE 12. 47·5 to 95MHz Push-Pull Doubler Circuit

Operation of this circuit is similar to the 175MHz example. The main difference is that the input level is much lower and it is necessary to forward bias the transistors. Operation in this case is very roughly Class B. The emitters in this example have separate bias resistors. One of these is variable, making it possible to optimise the fundamental rejection.

The performance of the circuit is shown in Figure 13.

Wideband Doubler

By using a wideband transformer to couple the output, satisfactory operation is achieved in this circuit over an output frequency range from 15 to 90MHz. The low-frequency response is limited only by the transformer inductance, and could easily be extended. The circuit may be seen in Figure 14. The base circuit is identical to the last example. The collector circuit consists of a broadband 4:1 impedance transformer. (As described in reference 1 of the preceding chapter).

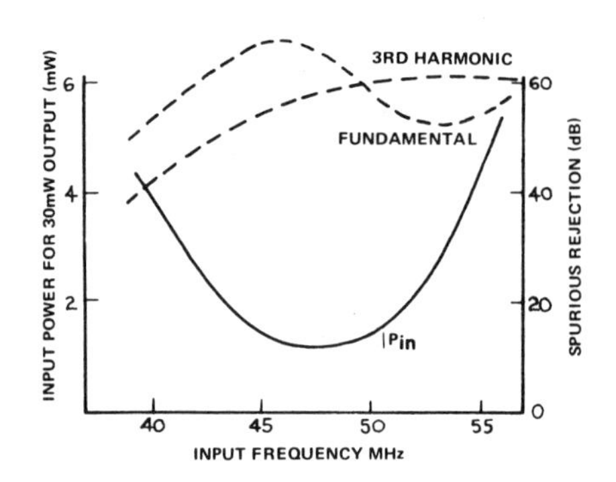

FIGURE 13. Performance Graphs of 47·5 to 95MHz Doubler Circuit

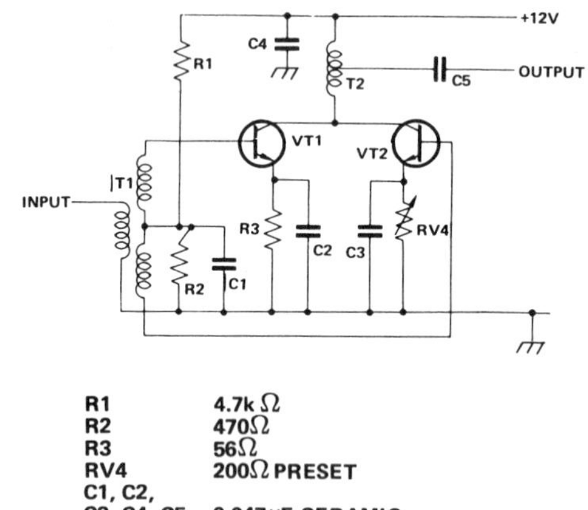

R1	4.7k Ω
R2	470Ω
R3	56Ω
RV4	200Ω PRESET
C1, C2, C3, C4, C5	0·047μF CERAMIC
T1	AS IN FIGURE 9
T2	2 STRANDS 30 SWG WIRE TWISTED TOGETHER. THREE TURNS ON SIEMENS HALSKE U-60 TWIN HOLE BEAD.
VT1, VT2	TIS18

FIGURE 14. Wideband Doubler Circuit

The performance of the wideband circuit is shown in Figure 15.

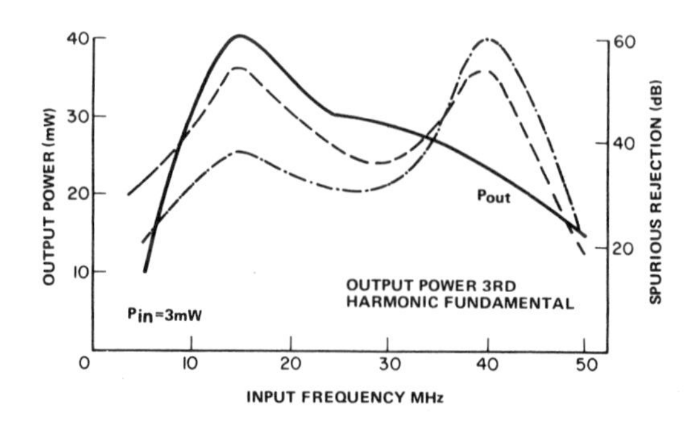

FIGURE 15. Performance Graphs of Wideband Doubler Circuit.

Index